Understanding ArubaOS

Version 6.X

David A. Westcott

WESTCOTT CONSULTING, INC.

Copy Editors: Elizabeth Campbell, Elizabeth Welch, Happenstance Type-O-Rama
Design and Production: Maureen Forys, Happenstance Type-O-Rama
Proofreader: Elizabeth Welch, Happenstance Type-O-Rama
Indexer: Valerie Perry, Happenstance Type-O-Rama
Cover image © TaLaNoVa/Shuttertock

Copyright © 2017 by David A. Westcott/Westcott Consulting, Inc.

ISBN: 978-0-998-47040-5
ISBN: 978-0-9984704-1-2 (ebook)

No part of this publication may be reproduced, stored in a retrieval system or transmitted in any form or by any means, electronic, mechanical, photocopying, recording, scanning or otherwise, except as permitted under Sections 107 or 108 of the 1976 United States Copyright Act, without either the prior written permission of the Publisher, or authorization through payment of the appropriate per-copy fee to the Copyright Clearance Center, 222 Rosewood Drive, Danvers, MA 01923, (978) 750-8400, fax (978) 646-8600.

10 9 8 7 6 5 4 3 2 1

I dedicate this book to my family.

To my wife Janie, for your support and patience during the hundreds of hours that I spent writing, editing, or proofreading. I know you will not miss hearing me say, "I have to work on the book."

To Savannah, for always telling me how much you miss me when I am on the road teaching, and for all of your hugs and kisses. There are not many things better in life than hugs and kisses from a four-year-old.

To Jennifer and Samantha, may you always have health and happiness as you find your paths in life.

To my parents, Kathy and George, for all that you have done for me, and for your excitement and enthusiasm for this book.

To Ann and John, for all of your support and thoughtfulness.

Contents at a Glance

Acknowledgments xiv
About the Author. xvi
Foreword xvii
Introduction xix

Chapter 1: Wireless Overview. 1

Chapter 2: Understanding the ArubaOS Environment 17

Chapter 3: Aruba Controller and Software Overview 39

Chapter 4: Getting Started 61

Chapter 5: Profiles. 107

Chapter 6: Authentication and Encryption 143

Chapter 7: Role Derivation. 193

Chapter 8: Policy Enforcement Firewall 219

Chapter 9: Captive Portal. 259

Chapter 10: Network Expansion. 281

Chapter 11: Access Points 333

Chapter 12: Adaptive Radio Management 373

Chapter 13: Network Monitoring. 399

Chapter 14: Wireless Mesh 459

Chapter 15: Wireless Intrusion Prevention 483

Index. 509

Contents

Acknowledgments xiv
About the Author xvi
Foreword xvii
Introduction xix

Chapter 1: Wireless Overview 1
    Institute of Electrical and Electronics Engineers 2
    Evolution of 802.11 2
    Evolution of Wireless LAN 3
    Wi-Fi Alliance 4
    Certified Wireless Network Professional 6
    Regulatory Domain 7
    IEEE 802.11 Basics 9
        Basic Service Set 10
        Extended Service Set 10
        Basic Service Set Identifier 11
    Radio Terminology 12
    Thin Access Points 14

Chapter 2: Understanding the ArubaOS Environment 17
    The ArubaOS Architecture 17
        The Initial (Master) Controller 18
        AP Boot Process 20
            Static 21
            DHCP Options 43 and 60 22
            Aruba Discovery Protocol 22
            DNS Lookup 23
            OS Update 23
            Configuration Download 23
            Establishing the GRE Tunnel 24
            Layer 2 Addressing 24
        GRE Tunnel Explanation 25
        Adding a Local Controller 27
        Multi-Controller AP Boot Process 29
    AP Forwarding Modes 32
        GRE/Tunnel 33
        Bridge 34
        Decrypt-Tunnel 35
        Split-Tunnel 37

Chapter 3: Aruba Controller and Software Overview 39
    User Interface 39
        Terminal Access 39

CONTENTS

    Console Port..40
    SSH and Telnet...42
    CLI Command Environment..42
    Pipe Operator..42
  Web User Interface...45
  Wizards..47
 Controllers..48
  Firewall...49
  Virtual Private Network Server...49
  RFProtect..50
  Operating Hardware...50
    Partition Structure..50
    CPBoot...55
    Saving Changes...56
    View Commands/Hide Commands...57
 Resetting Controller to Factory Defaults...................................58

Chapter 4: Getting Started 61
 Initial Setup Menu..62
  Initial Setup Objectives...62
  CLI Setup Wizard...63
  WebUI Setup Wizard...68
 Licensing..74
  Adding Licenses..75
 Networking Basics...77
  CLI Configuration..77
    CPsec..77
    Creating and Configuring VLANs...78
    Configuring a Trunk Port...79
    Configuring Access Ports...79
    Default Gateway..80
    DHCP Server..81
    Controller IP..82
    Disable Spanning-Tree..82
    Enable Bypass..83
    Time Zone and Network Time Protocol (NTP).............................83
    SNMP...83
    Syslog...84
    Disable VLAN 1...84
    Install Licenses, Save, and Reboot.....................................84
  WebUI Configuration..84
    CPsec..85
    Creating VLANs...85
    Assigning IP Addresses...86
    Configuring a DHCP Server..86
    Default Gateway..87
    Controller IP..87
    Disable VLAN 1...87
    Time Zone and Network Time Protocol (NTP).............................87
    SNMP...88

Syslog	88
Install Licenses, Save, and Reboot	89
Access Point Configuration	89
AP Console CLI	90
~#	90
apboot>	91
Controller WebUI—AP Installation	96
Controller WebUI—AP Wizard	98
Provision-AP Controller CLI Command	102

Chapter 5: Profiles 107

David's Bicycle Store	108
Basic Customer	108
Intermediate Customer	108
Advanced Customer	108
Configuring ArubaOS	109
Wizards	109
Web User Interface	109
Command Line Interface	109
Profile Hierarchy	110
Understanding Virtual APs	111
Authentication Server and Server Group	115
Access Control	119
Authentication Profile	120
AAA Profile	122
SSID Profile	124
VLAN	127
Virtual AP Profile	127
AP System Profile	130
AP Group	132
WebUI Configuration Menus	133
All Profiles	134
Authentication	135
AP Configuration	136
Managing Profiles	136
Show References	137
Cloning Profiles	138
Show Profile-hierarchy	140

Chapter 6: Authentication and Encryption 143

Security Basics	144
Authentication, Authorization, and Accounting	145
Layer 2 vs. Layer 3 Authentication	148
Authentication Methods	149
802.1X/EAP Authentication	150
Authentication Server (802.1X/EAP Authentication)	151
Internal Database (802.1X/EAP Authentication)	151
RADIUS Server (802.1X/EAP Authentication)	152

CONTENTS

LDAP Server (802.1X/EAP Authentication) 153
Server Group (802.1X/EAP Authentication). 154
802.1X Authentication Profile (802.1X/EAP Authentication). 161
Firewall Policy (802.1X/EAP Authentication) 161
Firewall Role (802.1X/EAP Authentication) 162
AAA Profile (802.1X/EAP Authentication). 162
SSID Profile (802.1X/EAP Authentication). 163
VLAN(s) (802.1X/EAP Authentication). 164
Virtual AP Profile (802.1X/EAP Authentication) 166
MAC Authentication 167
Internal Database (MAC Authentication) 168
Internal Server Group (MAC Authentication) 170
MAC Authentication Profile (MAC Authentication) 170
Firewall Policy (MAC Authentication) 171
Firewall Role (MAC Authentication) 171
AAA Profile (MAC Authentication) 171
SSID Profile (MAC Authentication) 172
VLAN(s) (MAC Authentication) 172
Virtual AP Profile (MAC Authentication). 174
Captive Portal Authentication. 174
SSID Authentication 174
Firewall Policy (SSID Authentication) 175
Firewall Role (SSID Authentication). 175
AAA Profile (SSID Authentication) 176
SSID Profile (SSID Authentication). 176
VLAN(s) (SSID Authentication). 176
Virtual AP Profile (SSID Authentication) 176
Preshared Key Authentication. 177
802.1X Authentication Profile (Preshared Key Authentication). 178
Firewall Policy (Preshared Key Authentication). 178
Firewall Role (Preshared Key Authentication) 178
AAA Profile (Preshared Key Authentication) 179
SSID Profile (Preshared Key Authentication) 179
VLAN(s) (Preshared Key Authentication) 179
Virtual AP Profile (Preshared Key Authentication). 179
Encryption Techniques 180
Wired Equivalent Privacy. 180
WPA/TKIP 180
WPA2/AES. 181
Digital Certificates 181
Obtaining a Certificate 182
Certificate Signing Request. 183
Self-Signed Certificate 186
WebUI Management Certificate 188
Captive Portal Certificate 189
802.1X/EAP Certificate. 190

Chapter 7: Role Derivation. 193
Role Assignment 194
Physical Connection. 196

Layer 2 Authentication	198
Logon Role	198
Initial Role	199
User Rules	201
Role Conditions	202
User Rule Derivation	204
Role Derivation with Server Authentication	204
Vendor-Specific Attribute–Assigned Role	205
Server-Assigned Role	205
Default Role	207
MAC Authentication	207
802.1X/EAP Authentication	208
Machine Authentication	209
Server Authentication	209
Layer 2 Authentication Synopsis	210
Layer 3 Authentication	210
External Services Interface	211
Role Derivation Review	212
802.1X/EAP Authentication	212
WPA2 Passphrase Role/VLAN Derivation	214
Captive Portal Authentication	216

Chapter 8: Policy Enforcement Firewall — 219

Access Control Lists	220
Firewall Policy Structure	221
Source, Destination, and Aliases	222
any	222
user	222
controller and *mswitch*	223
controller6	223
ipv6-reserved-range	223
localip	224
vrrp_ip	224
Creating a Destination Alias	224
Invert Option	227
Firewall Service	228
Services	233
Creating a Service Alias	235
Actions	236
deny	237
dst-nat	237
src-nat	237
dual-nat	238
permit	238
redirect	238
route	238
Extended Actions	239
blacklist	239
classify media	239
disable-scanning	240

   dot1p-priority..240
   log..240
   mirror...240
   position...241
   queue..241
   send-deny-response..241
   time-range..241
   tos..242
  Implicit Deny All 242
 AppRF 243
  AppRF Deep Packet Inspection...244
  Web Content Classification 246
 User Roles..251
  Global Session ACL 255
  Role Default Session ACL 256

Chapter 9: Captive Portal 259
 Captive Portal Process 260
 Captive Portal Overview 264
  Authentication Server and Server Group 264
  Post Logon Role...267
  Captive Portal Profile..267
  Initial Role 269
  AAA Profile 270
  SSID Profile 270
  VLAN and DHCP Server 271
  Virtual AP Profile..273
  AP Group 274
  Captive Portal Page 274
 Guest-Provisioning Account..274
  Guest-Provisioning Page...275
 Connecting to ClearPass Guest 276
  Guest User Database 277
  Captive Portal Profile..277
  Initial Role 278

Chapter 10: Network Expansion 281
 Master/Local Communications...282
  IKE Preshared Keys 283
  IKE Certificates..285
  Local Controller Settings 288
 Fault Tolerance 289
  Virtual Router Redundancy Protocol..289
   Configuring VRRP Using the WebUI..290
   Configuring VRRP Using the CLI..293
  Redundancy Design 295
   Active/Standby 295
   N:1 Active/Standby 296
   Active/Active 296
  AP Redundancy Using VRRP...297

Backup LMS-IP...298
AP Fast Failover..299
        Client State Synchronization...302
        Oversubscription...303
Master Controller Redundancy...304
        Master Redundancy Configuration......................................305
        Master Redundancy Verification...309
Redundancy Comparison...312
Centralized Licensing...314
Centralized Upgrade...316
AP Image Preload..324
AP Image Preload with Centralized Upgrade.................................326

Chapter 11: Access Points ... 333

AP Types...334
    Campus AP..334
    Remote AP...334
    Instant AP..334
    Unified AP...336
Aruba Activate...336
    Activate Folders...339
    Adding an AP to Activate..340
    Individually Assigning an AP to a Folder...............................341
    Assigning APs to Folders Using Rules.....................................342
Campus AP...343
    Control Plane Security...344
    Converting IAPs to Campus APs...347
        Converting Using Virtual Controller....................................347
        Converting Using Activate...348
Remote AP..348
    VPN Server Configuration..349
    Creating an AP Group..350
    Configuring a RAP..350
        Manual Provisioning..351
        Aruba Activate...356
    VAP Data Forwarding Modes..356
        Tunnel...357
        Bridge..359
        Split-Tunnel..361
        Decrypt-Tunnel..364
    VAP Remote-AP Operation Modes..364
        Standard..365
        Always...365
        Backup..365
        Persistent...366
    Forwarding Modes with Operation Modes............................366
Air Monitor..367
Spectrum Monitor..369
Mesh AP..370
Secure Jack...370

Chapter 12: Adaptive Radio Management 373
ARM History 373
ARM Radio Configuration 376
    ARM Scanning 376
    AP Channel and Power Selection 379
    Dynamic Frequency Selection Channels 380
Client Match 380
    Client Match Data Collection 382
    Sticky Clients 385
    Band Steering/Band Balancing 386
    Load Balancing 387
    Move Client Process 390
    Client Match Process Review 393
ARM Profile Settings 394

Chapter 13: Network Monitoring 399
Logging 399
    Logging Configuration 401
    Configuring the Syslog Server 407
Packet Analysis 411
    Port Monitoring 411
    packet-capture Command 413
        controlpath 414
        datapath 415
        Destination 416
        packet-capture-defaults 420
    Firewall Mirroring 421
    AP/AM Capture 423
        Capture Procedures 423
    Packet Capture Synopsis 431
Spectrum Analysis 432
    Configuring a Spectrum Monitor 433
        Spectrum Monitor Group 433
        Spectrum Local Override 434
        Hybrid Mode 436
    Spectrum Monitoring Using the WebUI 437
        RF Options 439
        Types of Detected Devices 440
    Chart Types 441
        Real-Time FFT 444
        FFT Duty Cycle 445
        Swept Spectrogram 446
        Quality Spectrogram 447
        Active Devices 448
        Active Devices Table 449
        Active Devices Trend 450
        Channel Metrics 451
        Channel Metrics Trend 452
        Channel Summary Table 453
        Channel Utilization Trend 453

Device Duty Cycle...454
Devices vs. Channel...455
Interference Power...455
Spectrum Analysis CLI Command...457

Chapter 14: Wireless Mesh...459
Mesh Architecture...460
    Mesh Point Portal...460
    Mesh Point...463
    Mesh Link...464
    Mesh Cluster...465
Configuring a Mesh Network...465
    Mesh Cluster Profile...466
    Mesh Radio Profile...469
    WLAN Profile...469
    802.11 Radio Profile...470
    Mesh High-Throughput SSID Profile...472
    AP Wired Port Profile...472
    Recovery Profile...474
Mesh AP Provisioning...477
Mesh Status...478

Chapter 15: Wireless Intrusion Prevention...483
Channel Scanning...484
WIP Device Classification...486
    AP Classification...486
    Client Classification...487
Using the WIP Wizard...487
    Rogue Classification...487
    WIP Policy...489
    Infrastructure...490
    Intrusion Detection...490
    Protection...494
        Deauth-Only (Wireless)...496
        Tarpitting (Wireless)...497
        ARP Cache Poisoning (Wired)...497
Detection Methods...498
    Ad Hoc and Wireless Bridge Identification...498
    MAC Address Match Methods...499
    AP Traffic Inspection...499
        Layer 2: Transmission from Valid AP...500
        Layer 2: Transmission from Rogue AP...501
        Layer 3: Transmission from Rogue AP...502
Security Summary Dashboard...503
IDS Commands...504

Index...509

Acknowledgments

I would like to thank Devin Akin, Kevin Sandlin, Scott Turner, and Scott Williams for their vision and development of the CWNP certification program. I was a student in one of the first CWNA classes in 2002, barely knowing how to spell wireless. Between Devin's enthusiasm for wireless and the coolness of the technology, I was excited to learn more. I soon became a wireless guy.

I would also like to thank Chris Leach for calling me shortly after I sat in one of his first Aruba classes in 2004 and asking me, "Hey there. I have two Aruba classes running the same week. Do you want to teach one of them for me?" Okay, those may not have been his exact words, but that was probably close. Since that first class in Colorado Springs, and with a little help from Kevin Huey, I have had a long fun ride.

I also need to thank (or curse out) David Coleman for telling Sybex editor Jeff Kellum that he would not write the first CWNA book without me as a coauthor. I don't remember his exact words (okay, I do, but I won't write them here), but he commented about my editing skills and about me being meticulous. With the release of that first book, we became known as "The Davids" and have written seven books together. Unfortunately he could not join me on this latest writing endeavor. It has been strange writing this book without him, but I am sure we will be updating one of the CWNP books again in the near future.

There are so many people who helped to make this book a reality. I want to start off with the editing and production team. Although this is not my first book, it is the first book that I am writing without the assistance of a large publisher. I was fortunate to be introduced to Maureen Forys and Happenstance Type-O-Rama. Maureen was able to help guide me through the process and provide me with a team of people to perform the behind-the-scenes and production services. Thank you to her and her team: Elizabeth Campbell, Elizabeth Welch, and Valerie Perry.

ACKNOWLEDGMENTS

One of the tough parts of writing this book was trying to find technical editors. People who are good at what they do are typically very busy doing it. And understandably, it is tough to find people who are willing to take on additional work and responsibility. After much effort and searching, I wound up with four amazing people who read through every chapter and helped immensely to improve the quality of the product, and I cannot thank these guys enough:

Tim Cappalli	Sunil Nalge
Kelly Kutz	Tim Ritterbush

Throughout the course of the book many other people helped to provide editing, feedback, or review of portions of the book. Thank you to the following:

Simon Forget	Andrew Hejnar	Stewart Trammell
Eddie Forero	Jerrod Howard	Brad Wach
Florent Granier	William Krutke	
Anil Gupta	Michael Landry	

Finally, there are many other people who helped out in assorted ways, providing knowledge or resources, and helping make some aspect of creating this book a little easier for me. I sincerely thank you for your support and assistance:

Kiran Ashokan	Kimberly Graves	Makarios Moussa
Neil Bhave	Kelly Griffin	Albert Pang
Mick Connor	Carlen Hoppe	Ken Peredia
James Copello	Kevin Huey	Sean Rynearson
Satpal Dhillon	Mark Jordan	Brig Stone
Jamie Easley	Colin Joseph	Muthukumar Subramanian
Michael Ellis	De-Lung Lin	
Alan Emory	Scott McGrath	Michael Tennefoss
Tarun George	Sanjay Mistry	Micah Wilson
Joey Gerodias	Cesar Morales	Michael Wong

About the Author

DAVID WESTCOTT is an independent consultant and technical trainer with more than 30 years of experience in information technology, specializing in wireless networking and security. David has been teaching Aruba classes since 2004, and has trained over 5,000 Aruba employees, partners, and customers.

David is the coauthor of seven books about wireless networking, security, and analysis, including the bestselling *CWNA: Certified Wireless Network Administrator Official Study Guide*.

He has earned certifications from Aruba Networks, CWNP, Ekahau, Cisco, Microsoft, EC-Council, CompTIA, and Novell. David is Aruba Certified Mobility Expert (ACMX) #23 and Certified Wireless Network Expert (CWNE) #007.

When he is not travelling around the world, David lives in Concord, Massachusetts. He can be reached via e-mail at david@westcott-consulting.com. You can also follow him on Twitter, @davidwestcott.

Foreword

As one of the founders of Aruba Networks, I have been fortunate to be able to build a company that has helped shape and transform the wireless industry. In the beginning, we recognized the need to provide a wireless infrastructure platform for companies as they transitioned from a desktop-centric environment to a mobile, laptop-enabled workforce.

With the introduction of the iPad and the acceptance of personal handheld devices in the workplace, enterprise wireless LANs became a necessity as manufacturers removed Ethernet from client devices in favor of wireless. Not only has wireless changed the way people use devices and networks, it has also changed the devices they use. Wireless networking and Internet access is now available to any technology that people wear, use, or install in their home or business.

Wireless is now the primary, if not only, connectivity method for most users. Many organizations have replaced traditional phone systems in favor of computer-based communications and collaboration. Hospitals, police, corporations, universities, and so many other industries have deployed wireless to provide networking for mission-critical tasks. Installation and support of an Aruba-based enterprise wireless network requires an understanding of the IEEE 802.11 standard and ArubaOS.

Wireless networks are poised to continue to grow, both in size and importance. With this continued demand for wireless networks, I am very pleased that David Westcott has written this book, which provides another avenue for customers to learn about ArubaOS. This book will complement the technical resources that are available within the Airheads online community. I am certain it will become a go-to resource for Airheads mobility experts globally.

David has provided training to thousands of Aruba customers and has coauthored numerous books about wireless networking. David brings experience and enthusiasm to this book, allowing you to understand and learn about ArubaOS, whether you are a beginner or an expert.

KEERTI MELKOTE
Aruba Founder, Senior VP, and General Manager

Introduction

I HAVE WANTED TO WRITE THIS BOOK since 2007. Shortly after David Coleman and I wrote our first CWNA book, I put together a table of contents for an ArubaOS book. I even met with some of the executive team at Aruba and discussed the book with them. However, at that time I did not move forward with the project, because I was busy working on other writing projects: a CWSP book, a CWAP book, and three more editions of the CWNA book. Another reason I did not pursue the Aruba book was that I did not want to write an "operating system" book. Because of how quickly technology changes, I was concerned about writing a book that would quickly become obsolete with the release of each new version of the OS. I also did not want to write a book that just regurgitated the commands that were in the Aruba manuals.

So the obvious question is, "What changed that made me now want to write this book?"

Having taught highly technical networking classes for the past 30 years, and Aruba classes for the past 13 years, I know that the students who attend these classes are extremely smart and knowledgeable, which is logical due to the technical level of the Aruba products.

When teaching at this level I never consider myself the smartest person in the room, nor do I ever claim to have all of the answers. What I can do better than most people is stand up in the front of a room of students, engage them, and make them understand how the technology works.

Over the past 13 years of Aruba classes, hundreds of weeks of training, and thousands of students, I have learned a great deal about teaching. At the beginning of every class, I have the students introduce themselves and explain why they are attending the class, and what they want to get out of the course. Two common responses from students are, "I want to learn more about the product," and "I want to understand how it works."

The sentence that you just read is the reason I have written this book.

I realized that there needed to be a book that could help someone understand ArubaOS. There are documents and papers that describe how the product functions and how to install, manage, and support ArubaOS. With this book, I want to help the reader understand ArubaOS architecture and profiles, and how the pieces fit together.

This book is not intended to be an A through Z complete reference on how to install and manage an Aruba network. ArubaOS is so broad, complex, and capable that I am not even sure if that would be possible. There will be many topics that have been left out of this book, some intentionally, and some unintentionally.

I hope that this book helps you understand the key concepts of the ArubaOS environment—managing, supporting, and troubleshooting it. If you understand the foundations and fundamentals of ArubaOS and how the pieces relate to each other and work together, then it should become easier for you to learn and understand the details of the product through formal Aruba training classes, hands-on experience, conversations with other support people, and through the many other resources that Aruba provides.

I would love to hear your comments about what you like or do not like about the book, along with suggestions for either a follow-up Aruba book, or for a second edition of this book. Please send any e-mail comments or requests to david@westcott-consulting.com.

CHAPTER 1

Wireless Overview

IN THIS CHAPTER, YOU WILL LEARN ABOUT THE FOLLOWING:

- Institute of Electrical and Electronics Engineers
- Evolution of 802.11
- Evolution of Wireless LAN
- Wi-Fi Alliance
- Certified Wireless Network Professional
- Regulatory Domain
- IEEE 802.11 Basics
    - Basic Service Set
    - Extended Service Set
    - Basic Service Set Identifier
- Radio Terminology
- Thin Access Points

AN IMPORTANT PART OF LEARNING AND UNDERSTANDING ANY new technology is to understand some of the history that has brought us to where we are. This history provides us with a foundation of knowledge to reference and from which we can grow. Understanding the history of wireless networking includes not only the chronological history, but also learning about some of the important industry organizations, technologies, and terminology.

This first chapter will provide a basic overview of wireless networking. It is important for you to understand the topics covered in this chapter, since these terms and concepts will be used and referenced throughout the rest of this book. It is not possible to teach you everything you need to know about wireless networking in one chapter, or even in a single book, nor will I try. The goal of this chapter is to briefly review key wireless terms and concepts that relate to the Aruba operating system (ArubaOS), and make sure that you understand them. Later in this chapter, I will introduce you to Certified Wireless Network Professional (CWNP), an organization that provides vendor-neutral enterprise Wi-Fi certification and training. The CWNP is a great source of books, classes, and knowledge relating to wireless networking. CWNP has numerous levels of certifications. I believe the Certified Wireless Network Administrator (CWNA) is the minimum level of certification required to support an enterprise WLAN, and it is the basis for the information in this chapter. If you would like to learn more about something in this book relating to 802.11, then I recommend researching it on the Internet or in *CWNA Certified Wireless Network Administrator Official Study Guide: Exam CWNA-106* (Sybex, 2014).

Institute of Electrical and Electronics Engineers

The 802.11 standard and amendments are developed by the *Institute of Electrical and Electronics Engineers*, also known as the *IEEE*. The IEEE is a global professional society with over 400,000 members. The IEEE's core purpose is to "foster technological innovation and excellence for the benefit of humanity." Since 1980, the IEEE has been responsible for creating the 802 family of networking standards, which define OSI layer 1 and layer 2 communications technologies. The IEEE is responsible for developing both wired and wireless standards. The 802.11 standard and amendments focus on wireless LAN (WLAN) communications.

Evolution of 802.11

In June of 1997, the IEEE 802.11 standard was published, and wireless networking began as we know it today. Okay, definitely not as we know it today, but that was the year when the original standard was ratified. This standard addresses only the first two layers of the seven-layer OSI model. The two layers referenced in the standard are the physical layer and the lower half of the data-link layer, known as the media access control (MAC) sublayer.

The original standard supported transmission rates of 1 and 2 megabits per second (Mbps), in the 2.4 GHz Industrial Scientific and Medical (ISM) frequency band; using frequency hopping spread spectrum (FHSS) and direct sequence spread spectrum (DSSS). Back then, each access point (AP) could advertise a single network, and each AP was an individually managed, stand-alone device, now commonly referred to as an *autonomous AP*.

In 1999, the 802.11b and 802.11a amendments were ratified, enhancing the original standard. Amendment 802.11b introduced an enhanced DSSS technology called *High-Rate DSSS (HR-DSSS)*, with two new transmission rates of 5.5 and 11 Mbps, while operating in the same 2.4 GHz ISM band, and maintaining backward compatibility with 802.11.

Many changes were introduced with 802.11a over the original standard. It was the first 802.11 technology to operate in the 5 GHz Unlicensed National Information Infrastructure (U-NII) frequency band. It also introduced a new radio frequency (RF) technology called *orthogonal frequency division multiplexing (OFDM)*, with supported transmission rates of 6, 9, 12, 18, 24, 36, 48, and 54 Mbps. Initially, 802.11a was more costly than 802.11b. Vendors were also slow at introducing 802.11a products into the market. Because of these two factors, initially, only a few organizations implemented 802.11a.

In 2003, 802.11g was ratified, and quickly became the most popular technology for wireless networking. It essentially took the technologies from 802.11a, but deployed them in the 2.4 GHz frequency band. More importantly, 802.11g was backward compatible with 802.11b, providing coexistence along with a migration path. It also provided the faster data rates that OFDM offered, which helped start the widespread sales and implementation of wireless networks.

The introduction of 802.11n in 2009 truly changed the way companies looked at wireless networking. It defined a new operating mode know as *high throughput (HT)*, and a new transmission technology known as multiple-input multiple-output (MIMO). Initial products supported transmission rates of up to 300 Mbps, with subsequent products supporting rates of 450 and 600 Mbps. One of the key enhancements that helps achieve these faster speeds is the optional support of channel bonding, which can spread the transmission across a pair of adjacent 20 MHz channels, forming a single 40 MHz wide channel. This is similar to doubling the width of a road to allow more vehicles to travel along the road. An 802.11n radio also operates in either the 2.4 or 5 GHz frequency bands, while providing backward compatibility with the earlier technologies. With the introduction of 802.11n, wireless networking was now fast enough that companies began considering transitioning to WLANs as the primary method of connecting users to the organization's network.

December of 2013 saw the introduction of 802.11ac: the technology that will increase throughput and capabilities for at least the next few years. The 802.11ac standard defines data rates of up to 6.933 gigabits per second (Gbps). It operates only in the 5 GHz U-NII band, and will be implemented in multiple phases. The first phase (known as *Wave 1*) supports data rates up to 1.3 Gbps, with the first chipsets of the second phase (known as *Wave 2*) supporting higher data rates up to 1.73 Gbps. Wave 2 of 802.11ac also introduces a revolutionary technology known as *multi-user MIMO (MU-MIMO).* MU-MIMO allows an AP to transmit to multiple devices simultaneously, whereas previously, an AP could only transmit to one device at a time. It is important to note that the majority of throughput gains with 802.11ac come from the ability to bond channels. Channel widths up to 160 MHz wide are supported, but the usability of wider channels is limited because of restrictions in the 5 GHz frequency band.

Evolution of Wireless LAN

In the late '90s and early 2000s, the installation of wireless networks gradually increased. Since each AP was an individually managed device, companies that installed autonomous APs found that their wireless networks became more difficult and time-consuming to manage. In 2002, Aruba Networks was founded to develop a method for centrally managing wireless networks. Instead of configuring each access point individually, the Aruba Mobility Controller (originally called a *wireless switch*) could be configured to deploy configuration settings to groups of APs. Instead of having to individually manage 30 APs in a warehouse, all 30 of these APs could be treated as a group and managed as one entity. AP groups can scale from a single AP to thousands of APs, providing organizations with much needed flexibility and control.

Wi-Fi Alliance

The *Wi-Fi Alliance*, founded in 1999, is a global, nonprofit industry association with the goal of driving adoption of high-speed wireless local area networking. The Wi-Fi Alliance consists of hundreds of companies devoted to seamless network connectivity.

One of the main efforts of the Wi-Fi Alliance is to provide certification testing of the 802.11 standards that the IEEE develops, in order to maintain compatibility across vendors. Companies such as Aruba Networks send their Wi-Fi equipment to Wi-Fi Alliance certification testing facilities, and if their equipment passes the testing process, the company receives a certification confirming interoperability compliance. The Wi-Fi Alliance website, www.wi-fi.org, provides the ability to look up a device and see the specific certifications that each device has achieved. Figure 1.1 shows a Wi-Fi Interoperability Certificate for an Aruba Mobility Controller with an AP-325 access point.

FIGURE 1.1a
Wi-Fi Interoperability Certificate

FIGURE 1.1b
Wi-Fi Interoperability Certificate (continued)

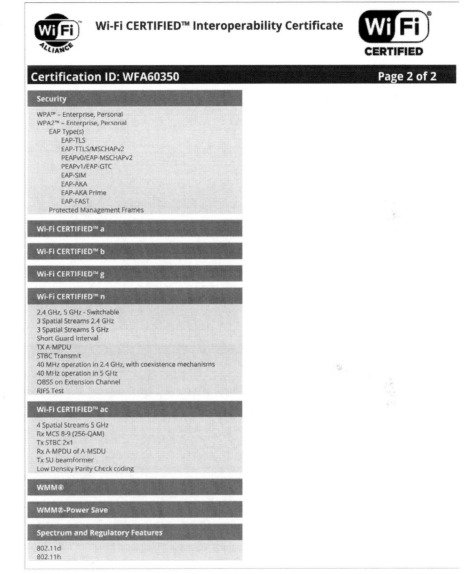

An IEEE standard often includes features or technologies that are optional. Because of this, not all of the specifications in an IEEE standard are actually implemented by manufacturers of WLAN products. The Wi-Fi Alliance certification process performs compatibility tests based upon key components and functions defined in the 802.11 standard and amendments. The Wi-Fi CERTIFIED program includes the following certifications:

- Core Technology & Security
- Wi-Fi Multimedia (WMM)

- WMM PowerSave (WMM-PS)
- Wi-Fi Protected Setup (WPS)
- Wi-Fi Direct
- CWG-RF
- Voice Personal
- Voice Enterprise
- WMM-Admission Control

Certified Wireless Network Professional

In 1999, the Certified Wireless Network Professional (CWNP) organization was founded with the mission to become the "IT industry standard for vendor-neutral enterprise Wi-Fi certification and training." Since then, CWNP has developed multiple levels of vendor-neutral training and certifications. The first Certified Wireless Network Administrator (CWNA) class was held in the fall of 2001. I attended one of the early CWNA classes in 2002 and was hooked.

The CWNP currently offers six unique certifications that progress through four levels. These include:

- Entry Level
  - CWTS: Certified Wireless Technology Specialist
- Administrator Level
  - CWNA: Certified Wireless Network Administrator
- Professional Level
  - CWSP: Certified Wireless Security Professional
  - CWDP: Certified Wireless Design Professional
  - CWAP: Certified Wireless Analysis Professional
- Expert Level
  - CWNE: Certified Wireless Network Expert

CWNP publishes videos, white papers, and blogs, along with other material to help educate networking professionals about WLAN technologies and prepare them to pass the certification tests. Whether you want to earn one of the CWNP certifications or learn more about the wireless technologies that you are installing and supporting, I recommend that you visit their website (www.cwnp.com) to learn more about the organization and to explore the vast number of resources that they have available.

Regulatory Domain

In order to operate a wireless device in a country, the device must be approved for operation in that country. The controlling agency in a country regulates both licensed spectrum and unlicensed spectrum. Licensed spectrum allows the operator or user some level of exclusive use in a geographical region. Unlicensed spectrum is still controlled by the governing agency, but anyone can use that frequency, as long as they meet the regulations defined by the agency for that frequency.

It is common for smaller countries to adopt the wireless regulations of a larger or neighboring country; however, this is not mandatory. Some examples of country regulatory agencies are the Federal Communications Commission (FCC), which is the governing body for the United States, and the Australian Communications and Media Authority (ACMA), which is the regulatory domain for Australia.

The Aruba Mobility Controller and access points operate in unlicensed spectrum, with regulations typically governing the following four areas of operation:

- Bandwidth
- Frequency
- Maximum power radiated from the antenna
- Operational location (indoor or outdoor)

When installing an Aruba Mobility Controller, one of the first steps during the initial configuration is to specify the regulatory domain that the controller will be configured to support. This is done by entering a two-character country code from the command line interface (CLI) or the country name from the web user interface (WebUI). The country codes are based on the ISO 3166 standard, which defines codes for countries and regions.

If a controller is to be deployed in certain countries, such as the United States, Israel, or Japan, those governments require that the controller is specifically purchased for use in that country. These controllers have the country code set in the hardware, preventing the WLAN administrator from changing the controller to a different country code. In the future, it is possible that other countries will require the country code to be permanently set.

Aruba controllers that do not have the country code restricted in the hardware are known as *Rest of World* or *RoW* controllers; sometimes referred to as *WorldWide (WW)* controllers. During initial setup, the country code still needs to be properly configured for the country where it will be operating; however, this setting can be changed if the controller will be redeployed in a different country.

When deploying APs, for example in the United States (US), all APs must be US-labeled APs and must terminate on a mobility controller located in the United States. Due to FCC regulation, these APs cannot connect to a controller located outside of the

US, or to a RoW controller. Only US-designated APs and controllers can be used within the US, and all non-US APs and controllers must remain outside of the United States.

If you would like to see what channels ArubaOS supports for a specific regulatory domain, you can use the following CLI command, replacing the CC with whichever country code you want to check. If you are not familiar with how to access the CLI, this knowledge will be covered in Chapter 3, "Aruba Controller and Software Overview."

```
#show ap allowed-channels country-code CC
```

The command will show the channels that are allowed for the specified country code. The command also shows whether the channel is allowed for indoor or outdoor use, and whether a technology known as Dynamic Frequency Selection (DFS) is supported. Channels labeled as 40 MHz are 802.11n or 802.11ac channel bonding pairs. Channels labeled as 80 MHz are 802.11ac channel bonding groupings.

This command will work whether or not your controller is configured for the specified country code, or whether its hardware is even capable of being configured for that country. Following is a listing of channels that are allowed by ArubaOS for a controller configured with country code for China:

```
#show ap allowed-channels country-code cn


Allowed Channels for Country Code "CN" Country "China"
------------------------------------------------------
PHY Type                   Allowed Channels
--------                   ----------------
802.11g (indoor)           1 2 3 4 5 6 7 8 9 10 11 12 13
802.11a (indoor)           36 40 44 48 52 56 60 64 149 153 157 161 165
802.11g (outdoor)          1 2 3 4 5 6 7 8 9 10 11 12 13
802.11a (outdoor)          149 153 157 161 165
802.11g 40MHz (indoor)     1-5 2-6 3-7 4-8 5-9 6-10 7-11 8-12 9-13
802.11a 40MHz (indoor)     36-40 44-48 52-56 60-64 149-153 157-161
802.11g 40MHz (outdoor)    1-5 2-6 3-7 4-8 5-9 6-10 7-11 8-12 9-13
802.11a 40MHz (outdoor)    149-153 157-161
802.11a 80MHz (indoor)     36-48 52-64 149-161
802.11a 80MHz (outdoor)    149-161
802.11a 160MHz (indoor)    36-64
802.11a 160MHz (outdoor)   None
802.11a (DFS)              52 56 60 64
```

Even though the controller allows a set of channels for a specific regulatory domain, not all APs have the necessary regulatory certifications to operate on these channels. To display the channels supported by a specific AP type in a particular country, you can use the following CLI command using the specific AP model:

```
#show ap allowed-channels country-code US ap-type ap-325
```

IEEE 802.11 Basics

Before you begin learning about the Aruba controller, we need to briefly review the components that make up an 802.11 WLAN, along with some of the basic IEEE 802.11 terms that will be used throughout this book. If you cannot explain the meaning of each of the following terms, then you should take the time to read this section.

- BSA (basic service area)
- BSS (basic service set)
- BSSID (basic service set identifier)
- DS (distribution system)
- ESS (extended service set)
- ESSID (extended service set identifier)
- SSID (service set identifier)
- STA (station)
- WDS (wireless distribution system)

Figure 1.2 is a logical representation of an extended service set (ESS) and will be referenced throughout the following few sections.

FIGURE 1.2 Extended service set

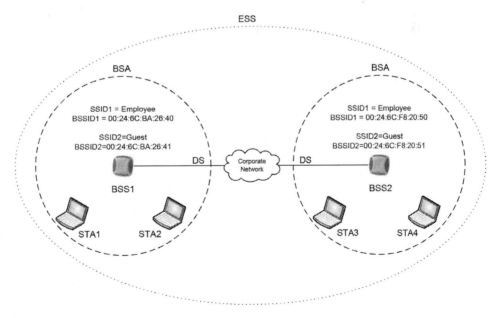

Basic Service Set

In order to distinguish one 802.11 wireless network from another, an AP advertises a logical name known as the service set identifier (SSID). The SSID can be up to 32 characters long and is case sensitive. Figure 1.2 shows two different SSIDs: Employee and Guest.

The most fundamental configuration of a wireless network is known as a basic service set (BSS). A BSS is defined as an AP with one or more client devices, technically known as *stations (STAs)*, connected to it. The term *STA* is an IEEE 802.11 term which refers to any device that has an 802.11 wireless radio in it. Technically this means that both client devices and access points are stations. However, since APs are specialized stations that perform tasks other than just RF communications, the term STA is generally used only when referring to client devices, which is how the term will be used in this book.

Figure 1.2 shows two basic service sets: BSS1 and BSS2. Each BSS is providing wireless service to two stations. BSS1 has STA1 and STA2 connected to it, and BSS2 has STA3 and STA4 connected to it. The area of coverage of a BSS is known as the basic service area (BSA). The dashed circles in the figure are representing the BSAs.

Extended Service Set

APs are typically connected to the rest of the network using a wired network, typically Ethernet. The wired connection is known as the distribution system (DS), also identified in Figure 1.2. When the APs are connected together using wireless connections, such as in a mesh network, it is known as a wireless distribution system (WDS).

When two or more APs are connected together using a DS or a WDS, and they advertise the same SSID with the same security settings, they will appear as if they are one AP to the logical link control layer of the STA. This is known as an *extended service set (ESS)*. Figure 1.2 shows BSS1 and BSS2 advertising the same SSID, creating an ESS. Each AP and SSID will have a different MAC address, known as a *BSSID*. BSSID will be explained in the next section of this chapter. It is not a requirement for the two BSAs to overlap or provide continuous connectivity to a STA moving between the two BSSs; however, should you want your client to maintain a network connection as it roams, overlap is required.

When an ESS is created, the network name is known as an *extended service set identifier (ESSID)*, although it is still very common to refer to it as the *SSID*. Practically speaking, the only real difference between an ESSID and an SSID is the letter "E," since it is essentially an SSID that has been extended across the distribution system. On the Aruba controller, the following CLI command displays the ESSIDs that are configured for the controller. This command includes the number of APs that are configured with each ESSID, the number of clients that are connected to each ESSID, the virtual LAN (VLAN) that is assigned to the ESSID, and the authentication and encryption method that is configured for the ESSID.

```
#show ap essid


ESSID Summary
-------------
ESSID      APs  Clients  VLAN(s)  Encryption
-----      ---  -------  -------  ----------
wps2psk    2    0        93       WPA2 PSK AES
camera     2    0        93       Open
employee   2    0        91       WPA2 8021X AES
guest90    2    0        93       Open
Num ESSID:4
```

Basic Service Set Identifier

When an STA connects to an ESSID, even though multiple APs are advertising the same ESSID, the station connects to an individual AP and needs to differentiate one AP from another. In order for an AP to distinguish itself from another, the AP advertises a unique basic service set identifier (BSSID). The BSSID uniquely identifies a BSS. The BSSID is a 48-bit (6-octet) media access control (MAC) address that is the layer-2 identifier of each BSS. The BSSID is commonly referred to as the APs "wireless MAC address." In Figure 1.2, the BSSID for BSS1 is 00:24:6C:BA:26:40, and the BSSID for BSS2 is 00:24:6C:F8:20:50.

In an enterprise environment, companies typically install dual-radio APs, with one radio broadcasting in the 2.4 GHz band and the other radio broadcasting in the 5 GHz band. If each radio was configured to advertise the same SSID, then the AP would need two BSSIDs; one to uniquely identify the BSS on each radio. To take this logic one step further, it is common for an AP to advertise multiple SSIDs. So if each radio were configured to advertise 3 ESSIDs, an Employee SSID, a Guest SSID, and a Voice SSID, then each radio would need 3 BSSIDs, for a total of 6 BSSIDs for the AP (3 BSSIDs for the 2.4 GHz radio and 3 BSSIDs for the 5 GHz radio). In this example, each AP would need a MAC address for each physical Ethernet port that could be connected to the DS, and 6 additional MAC addresses to support the 6 BSSIDs. Depending on the model, an Aruba AP can typically be configured with up to 8 or 16 BSSIDs per radio. It is recommended that each radio is configured with a maximum of 3 or 4 SSIDs per radio since each additional SSID requires the transmission of additional beacons. At a rate of 10 beacons per second, per SSID, this consumes valuable airtime in the frequency used.

Instead of allocating a group of MAC addresses to each AP, Aruba assigns one MAC address to the Ethernet 0 port of the AP. Using the Ethernet 0 MAC address, Aruba applies an algorithm to generate virtual MAC addresses, depending on how many BSSIDs are needed. You can display all of the BSSID addresses on a controller by issuing the show ap bss-table command, as displayed in the following CLI output. In order to make it easier to read and to focus on BSSID addressing, some columns of information were removed from the following output.

```
#show ap bss-table

fm (forward mode): T-Tunnel, S-Split, D-Decrypt Tunnel, B-Bridge (s-standard,
p-persistent, b-backup, a-always), n-anyspot


Aruba AP BSS Table
------------------
bss                  ess   ip            phy    type  ch/EIRP/max-EIRP   ap name
---                  ---   --            ---    ----  ----------------   -------
18:64:72:c7:87:00    emp   10.1.90.153   g-HT   ap    11/6/25.5          AP115-70-1
18:64:72:c7:87:10    emp   10.1.90.153   a-HT   ap    44+/18/19          AP115-70-1
d8:c7:c8:89:72:80    emp   10.1.90.151   g-HT   ap    6/6/21.5           AP135-80-1
d8:c7:c8:8c:ce:10    emp   10.1.80.150   a-HT   ap    149+/18/22.5       AP135-80-3
d8:c7:c8:89:72:90    emp   10.1.90.151   a-HT   ap    157+/18/22.5       AP135-80-1
d8:c7:c8:8c:ce:00    emp   10.1.80.150   g-HT   ap    1/6/21.5           AP135-80-3
d8:c7:c8:89:82:40    emp   10.1.90.152   g-HT   ap    6/6/21.5           AP135-80-2
d8:c7:c8:89:82:50    emp   10.1.90.152   a-HT   ap    48-/18/22          AP135-80-2

Channel followed by "*" indicates channel selected due to unsupported configured
channel.
"Spectrum" followed by "^" indicates local Spectrum Override in effect.


Num APs:8
Num Associations:0
```

The far-right column of this output shows the ap_name. Each unique name is a different AP. In this example, notice that each AP is listed twice; once for the 2.4 GHz radio and once for the 5 GHz radio. The radio band is displayed in the phy column, with the details displayed in the ch/EIRP/max-EIRP column.

Radio Terminology

When the 802.11 standard was first ratified in 1997, it supported frequency hopping spread spectrum (FHSS) and direct sequence spread spectrum (DSSS). As additional 802.11 amendments were ratified, each of the amendments added new physical (PHY) technology that supported faster wireless transmissions, and thus faster data rates.

- 802.11b introduced high-rate direct sequence spread spectrum (HR-DSSS) with speeds of 5.5 and 11 Mbps in the 2.4 GHz frequency band.
- 802.11a introduced orthogonal frequency division multiplexing (OFDM) with speeds up to 54 Mbps in the 5 GHz frequency band.

- 802.11g introduced OFDM to the 2.4 GHz frequency band, providing speeds up to 54 Mbps.
- 802.11n introduced high throughput (HT) with speeds up to 600 Mbps, and is capable of transmitting in both the 2.4 GHz and the 5 GHz frequency bands.
- 802.11ac introduced very high throughput (VHT) with speeds up to 6.933 Gbps, but it only operates in the 5 GHz frequency band. Although the 802.11ac maximum speed is defined as 6.933 Gbps, the maximum speeds currently implemented by the industry are much slower.

As each of these technologies was introduced, the industry commonly referred to the technologies by their amendment names. The industry also used the amendments to reference the frequency bands. The 5 GHz frequency band commonly became known as the *802.11a band* (or *channels*), or simply the *a band*; and the 2.4 GHz frequency band became known as the *802.11g band* (or channels), simply referred to as the *b/g band*. Although the intentions were good, there was an underlying flaw with these references. To use an analogy to illustrate the flaw, all iPads are tablets, but not all tablets are iPads. Similarly, 802.11a is a 5 GHz technology, and at the time when 802.11a was introduced, it was the only Wi-Fi technology using the 5 GHz frequency band. Then, 802.11n was introduced and supported both 2.4 GHz and 5 GHz frequencies; thus a reference to 802.11n could mean either of the frequency bands, potentially causing more confusion.

When 802.11n was ratified, it introduced a new technology known as *high throughput (HT)*. Some references to 802.11n devices use *n* or *11n* to identify support of the amendment; however, it has become more common to use the technology reference of *HT* to identify support for 802.11n (a-HT or g-HT).

Table 1.1 shows some common references used when referring to 2.4 GHz or 5 GHz wireless networks, both supporting and not supporting the higher data rates of 802.11n.

TABLE 1.1: 802.11 Common References

COMMON REFERENCE	AMENDMENTS SUPPORTED
802.11g	2.4 GHz with support for 802.11b or 802.11g only
802.11g/n	2.4 GHz with support for 802.11b, 802.11g, and 802.11n
802.11g-HT	Same as 802.11g/n
802.11a	5 GHz with support for only 802.11a
802.11a/n	5 GHz with support for 802.11a and 802.11n
802.11a-HT	Same as 802.11a/n
802.11a-VHT	5 GHz with support for 802.11a, 802.11n, and 802.11ac

The phy column in the following CLI output shows some examples of radio references. In order to make it easier to read, some columns of information were removed from the following output.

```
#show ap bss-table


fm (forward mode): T-Tunnel, S-Split, D-Decrypt Tunnel, B-Bridge (s-standard,
p-persistent, b-backup, a-always), n-anyspot


Aruba AP BSS Table
------------------
bss                  ess        ip            phy      ap name
---                  ---        --            ---      -------
9c:1c:12:88:57:a3    guest90    10.1.90.150   g-HT     AP225-90-1
9c:1c:12:88:57:a0    employee   10.1.90.150   g-HT     AP225-90-1
9c:1c:12:88:57:b2    wps2psk    10.1.90.150   a-VHT    AP225-90-1
9c:1c:12:88:57:b1    camera     10.1.90.150   a-VHT    AP225-90-1
9c:1c:12:88:57:b3    guest90    10.1.90.150   a-VHT    AP225-90-1
9c:1c:12:88:57:a2    wps2psk    10.1.90.150   g-HT     AP225-90-1
9c:1c:12:88:57:a1    camera     10.1.90.150   g-HT     AP225-90-1
9c:1c:12:88:57:b0    employee   10.1.90.150   a-VHT    AP225-90-1


Channel followed by "*" indicates channel selected due to unsupported configured
channel.
"Spectrum" followed by "^" indicates local Spectrum Override in effect.


Num APs:16
Num Associations:0
```

Thin Access Points

With the introduction of the wireless controller and its ability to manage many APs from a central system, Aruba needed to create a new, scalable AP management framework. In this framework, the AP configuration could be created and changed centrally and distributed to the APs, thus the birth of the *thin AP*. These days the term *thin AP* has been replaced by the term *controller-based AP*.

With the introduction of the term *thin AP*, the traditional stand-alone AP was often referred to as a *fat AP*; however, *autonomous AP* is the generally accepted term these days.

At times people have referred to controller-based APs as *dumb APs* or *stupid APs*; however, they are far from that. Thin APs have operating system software on them that typically exceeds the capabilities found in the operating system software of autonomous APs. The piece that is missing on the controller-based AP is the ability to configure the AP itself. That must be done from the controller. Upon startup, the thin AP boots its operating system, enables its network interface, obtains an IP address using DHCP, discovers a controller, and communicates with the Aruba controller. The AP then downloads any new operating system updates and its configuration from the controller, and applies the downloaded configuration, as necessary. In Chapter 2, "Understanding the ArubaOS Environment," you will learn the detailed steps that the AP goes through when it is powered on and connected to the network.

CHAPTER 2

Understanding the ArubaOS Environment

IN THIS CHAPTER, YOU WILL LEARN ABOUT THE FOLLOWING:

- **The ArubaOS Architecture**
    - The Initial (Master) Controller
    - AP Boot Process
    - GRE Tunnel Explanation
    - Adding a local controller
    - Multi-Controller AP Boot Process
- **AP Forwarding Modes**
    - GRE/Tunnel
    - Bridge
    - Decrypt-Tunnel
    - Split-Tunnel

THIS CHAPTER WILL INTRODUCE YOU TO THE architecture of the Aruba Operating System (ArubaOS). This chapter will not teach you how to configure your network step by step, but will explain how it functions conceptually. With each new release of code, the details might change, but the concepts will likely stay the same. In other chapters in this book you will learn how to configure the different components.

A typical ArubaOS network consists of one or more controllers and a collection of APs. In most instances, when client data is transmitted to the AP, the AP forwards the data to a controller, which in turn processes the data and forwards it on to the network. The goal of this chapter is to explain the details of how controllers and APs work together, and to describe how the client traffic is forwarded. For now, sit back, relax, and try to understand the processes, concepts, and components that are being explained.

The ArubaOS Architecture

Let us begin by making believe that you work for a privately owned company. Your boss, the owner of the company, has decided that she wants to install a wireless network. She has heard about Aruba from a friend who works at another company that already has an Aruba network installed. He has told your boss about how his company was able to start with a small group of APs and a single central controller managing the APs. As his company grew, they were able to add additional APs, along with additional controllers to support the increased requirements of the APs and users. One of the features that he was really impressed with was the ability to manage all of the controllers and APs from one central controller. He explained that this main controller was known as the *master controller*. After hearing about the capabilities of the Aruba system and seeing a demo of it, your boss has told you to go and purchase Aruba wireless network equipment that is capable of initially providing wireless coverage for the administrative and sales offices, which are located in a multi-floor office building.

After speaking with an Aruba salesperson and systems engineer, it is determined that you will need 32 APs to provide the necessary RF coverage for the administrative and sales offices. You decide to purchase a single controller that supports a maximum of 32 APs. You realize that this particular model controller will be at its maximum number of APs and that any growth in the future will require you to purchase another controller. Ideally you would have purchased a larger controller with more growth potential; however, this is purely a make-believe story and this configuration was chosen to help explain the architecture and how the Aruba equipment works.

The Initial (Master) Controller

You spoke with the salesperson and systems engineer and placed your order, and you have received a phone call from the receptionist that the Aruba equipment has just been delivered. You have received the controller, the 32 APs, and the necessary AP licenses. You have also received the Policy Enforcement Firewall (PEF) license and the RFProtect wireless intrusion prevention system (WIPS) license for the controller.

Figure 2.1 illustrates the controller and two of the 32 APs. Since this is the first controller, it is therefore configured as the master controller. There is only one master or master/standby controller on a typical Aruba network, and any additional controllers that you add in the future will all be known as *local controllers*. The illustration shows that the license for the Policy Enforcement Firewall (indicated on the illustration as FW) is installed and integrated within the ArubaOS software on the controller, and that this controller supports 32 APs. The Aruba APs can be connected to the same VLAN as the controller, or they can be in different subnets, routing communications back to the controller.

The first step in deploying any controller is to configure the controller-specific settings. If you have ever configured an Ethernet switch, you know that there is an assortment of localized settings that need to be configured. Step 1 in Figure 2.1 shows that you need to give the controller a hostname and set IP and VLAN information. You may also need to configure some settings on the Ethernet ports, such as full or half duplex, VLAN assignments, or Power over Ethernet (PoE) settings. Another setting that needs to be made is specifying the regulatory domain where the controller is installed. You will also be required to set the admin and enable passwords, and there are additional local settings that you may need to set, again depending upon your environment. Configuration of all of these settings is covered in Chapter 4, "Getting Started."

FIGURE 2.1
Initial controller configuration

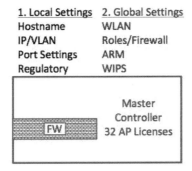

After configuring the local settings (the settings that are specific to each individual controller), the next thing you need to do is to configure the settings that relate to the Aruba environment and the wireless LAN, commonly known as the *global settings*. Figure 2.1 shows Step 2 as the configuration of the global settings. This includes, but is not limited to, the following tasks:

- Creating WLANs
- Setting up firewall roles and policies
- Configuring Adaptive Radio Management (ARM) settings
- Defining wireless intrusion prevention system (WIPS)

In Chapter 1, "Wireless Overview," you learned that the early wireless controllers were originally referred to as wireless switches. This is because they also functioned as Ethernet switches. The controller is typically configured as a layer 2 switch, but can be configured as a layer 3 switch. When functioning as a layer 3 switch, the controller can support static routes or can act as an area border router with one instance of open shortest path first (OSPF).

So the controller is now configured with the wireless LANs, roles, firewall settings, ARM, and WIPS. The next step is to configure your APs to connect to the controller and advertise the wireless network (SSID) so that they can provide connectivity to your wireless users.

AP Boot Process

The Aruba AP is a controller-based AP, meaning that it needs to communicate with a controller to download its running AP image and configuration. In order for an AP to boot and connect to the controller, it needs six pieces of information, as seen in Figure 2.2, Step 3. Any or all of this information can be configured statically or dynamically. A new AP or an AP that has been purged (reset to factory default settings) will have none of these settings configured and will obtain all of them dynamically.

The first three items that the AP needs to boot are its IP settings: IP address, subnet mask, and default gateway. A factory default AP will always obtain the IP settings via DHCP. Once the AP has been configured, the IP settings can continue to use DHCP, or they can be set statically.

FIGURE 2.2
Access point updates

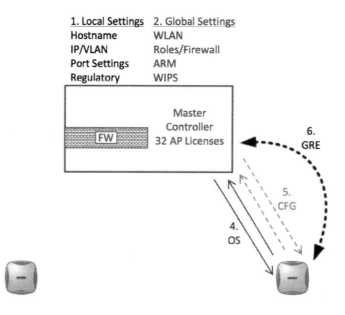

Each AP needs a unique name. There cannot be any duplicate AP names on the network. To ensure that there are no duplicate names when connecting a new AP, a factory default AP uses the MAC address of its Ethernet 0 interface as its name. Figure 2.2 shows an example MAC address of 01:23:45:67:89:AB. The AP name should be changed during AP configuration, and the name must continue to be unique.

Instead of you having to individually program each AP, ArubaOS is designed to allow settings to be applied to groups of APs. An AP is assigned to, and is a member of, a single AP group. Configuration settings that will be assigned to the AP are contained in a configuration holder called an *AP group profile*. The AP group name is used by the AP to notify the controller which group profile should be downloaded to the AP when it boots. A factory default AP is always assigned the `default` AP group. In Chapter 4, "Getting Started," you will learn how to assign a name and group to an AP.

The final piece of information that an AP needs when it boots is the IP address of the controller that the AP will initially communicate with. During these initial communications, the AP will download its OS (if it does not match the OS version of the controller) and its configuration. The AP will use the following four methods to discover the controller that it will initially communicate with:

- Static IP address
- DHCP options 43 and 60
- Aruba Discovery Protocol (ADP)
- DNS lookup

These four methods provide a form of redundancy for the APs to discover a controller. If the controller does not respond, then the AP will not come up.

Most Aruba installations use either DHCP options 43 and 60 or DNS to discover the controller. Aruba recommends the use of DNS because of its flexibility, along with the fact that it requires the fewest changes to the network. Additionally, as you will see, the DNS server can resolve multiple IP addresses to the domain, essentially providing its own form of discovery redundancy.

Static

The first method that the AP can use to discover the controller is to have the controller IP or DNS name statically set in a provisioning parameter known as *master*. Since this example is referencing a new AP, this parameter would not be set already. If you wanted to set this parameter or any other AP parameter, best practice is to set it using the controller's web user interface (WebUI). Alternatively, you could set or change an AP parameter from the controller's command line interface (CLI) using the `provision-ap` command, or by directly connecting to the AP using a console connection and using the setenv command. You will learn about the different user interfaces in Chapter 3, "Aruba Controller and Software Overview."

DHCP Options 43 and 60

If the controller's IP address was not set statically on the AP, then the next method that the AP would use to try to discover the controller is DHCP options 43 and 60. Most people just refer to this as option 43, but I like to reference both of the options since they work together and both have to be configured. Option 43 contains the controller IP address, which is given to the DHCP client and is useless without option 60. Option 60 is the vendor class identifier code, which identifies the client. I have seen people just set option 43 without setting option 60, and then wonder why it did not work. In fact, the first time I set it, I did not realize that both options needed to be configured. We will look at the process in more detail.

In addition to serving up the IP address, subnet mask, and default gateway, you may already know that a DHCP server can serve up other information such as DNS server IP addresses, the DNS domain name, and WINS server IP addresses. DHCP can also be configured to listen for certain information in the DHCP request. When an Aruba AP sends a DHCP request, it identifies itself to the DHCP server by setting the vendor class identifier in its request to ArubaAP. If DHCP option 60 is set to listen for this value and receives a request with this vendor class identifier, the DHCP reply will include the value that you set for DHCP option 43. In this example, it would be the IP address of the Aruba controller that the AP will initially communicate with. Essentially, if the DHCP server hears an Aruba AP, it will tell it the IP address of the initial controller. The ArubaOS Users Guide includes additional information on how to configure these options for various DHCP environments, so this topic will not be explained further in this book.

Aruba Discovery Protocol

The next method of discovery is Aruba Discovery Protocol (ADP). With ADP, the AP will send out multicast and broadcast requests attempting to discover a controller. In order for an AP to discover a controller using ADP, both of the devices need to be on the same layer 2 network. If ADP will be used to discover a controller that is on a different network or VLAN, Internet Group Management Protocol (IGMP) needs to be configured on the routers so that they are able to route the multicast packets to the other network.

When an AP and a controller communicate control traffic between themselves, they use an Aruba protocol known as *Proprietary Access Protocol Interface (PAPI)*. PAPI uses UDP port 8211 to perform these communications. Notice that port 8211 was derived from shortening 802.11, the IEEE standard for wireless networking. When the engineers were defining ADP, they were also very creative in assigning the IP multicast group address of 239.0.82.11, incorporating a derivative of 802.11 into the IGMP address. This makes it a little easier to remember both the UDP and multicast values.

DNS Lookup

The final method that the AP can use to discover the controller is to perform a DNS lookup. Every AP is factory configured to use the domain name of `aruba-master` when using DNS to try to discover the controller. This is done by prepending `aruba-master` to the domain name provided by the DHCP server; thus the domain name would look like `aruba-master.westcott-consulting.com`. One of the benefits of using DNS is that the DNS server can resolve the `aruba-master` domain name to multiple IP addresses. If multiple IP addresses are returned, the AP will try one after another, up to a maximum of four IPs. If the AP is unsuccessful communicating with a controller, it will reboot and try again.

OS Update

Once the AP has successfully contacted the initial controller, it then performs a check to see if the version of the operating system (ArubaOS) on the controller matches the version of the operating system on the AP. If it is different, the AP begins to download the OS from the controller using file transfer protocol (FTP), as illustrated in Step 4 of Figure 2.2. This FTP transfer will take about four minutes to complete; however, it may take longer if many APs are performing simultaneous downloads. The AP will upgrade or downgrade its OS to match the OS that is on the controller. If there are multiple controllers in the environment, it is important that all of the controllers have the same version of ArubaOS installed. If the ArubaOS version does not match on all of the controllers, the AP may wind up in a situation where it ping-pongs between different controllers; upgrading its OS from one controller, rebooting, and then downgrading its OS from another controller, possibly never completing the boot cycle. After the OS is downloaded, the AP will reboot and go through the initialization process again. This time, when it performs the operating system check, the OS on the AP will match the OS on the controller, so the AP will skip the download process and continue booting. Once the OS on the AP matches the OS on the controller, the FTP download of the OS does not happen again until the OS on the controller changes.

Configuration Download

Now that the AP has the same OS as the controller, it is able to download its configuration from the controller. The configuration that it downloads is based upon the group that the AP belongs to. In our example, since this is a new, unconfigured AP, the group that the AP belongs to is `default`, so it is the configuration for the `default` group that will be downloaded from the controller to the AP. The configuration download is illustrated in Step 5 of Figure 2.2.

Establishing the GRE Tunnel

The final step in the AP boot process is the establishment of a data-forwarding method to move the user data from the AP to the controller. Establishing a Generic Routing Encapsulation (GRE) tunnel between the AP and the controller is the most commonly used method of the available options. At this point in the explanation, you only have one controller, so the AP will obviously be establishing the GRE to this controller. If two controllers are involved, the AP will perform two sets of communications with them. First, it will communicate with the initial controller to download its OS, and then obtain the IP address of the second controller. The AP will then communicate with the second controller to download its configuration and to establish the GRE tunnel to transport the user traffic.

These two sets of controller communications can be with the same controller, or with two different controllers. I will explain this in more detail later in this chapter, but at this moment I just wanted to plant that idea in your head.

When a user connects to an AP and transmits data, the AP needs to "forward" the data so that it can traverse the network. Besides GRE tunneling, three other methods can be used. Later in this chapter, in the "AP Forwarding Modes" section, you will learn about the other methods. GRE is the original method and still the most common.

Layer 2 Addressing

An 802.3 Ethernet frame is a layer 2 frame that requires MAC addresses to transmit the frame from the source device to the destination device. So, an 802.3 frame contains two MAC address fields: a source MAC address field and a destination MAC address field.

An 802.11 frame is very different from an 802.3 frame. Like the 802.3 frame, the 802.11 frame is also a layer 2 frame, requiring MAC addresses to communicate between 802.11 devices. However, an 802.11 frame contains either three or four MAC address fields in order to communicate. The details of why and when an 802.11 frame uses three or four MAC address fields is a topic more geared for a book on 802.11 technology, such as the *CWNA: Certified Wireless Network Administrator Official Study Guide: Exam CWNA-106, 4th Edition* (Sybex, 2014). Whether an 802.11 frame uses three or four MAC address fields, these fields represent a total of five pieces of layer 2 MAC address information:

- Source: MAC address where the frame is coming from
- Destination: MAC address where the frame is being sent
- Transmitter: MAC address of the device that is transmitting the frame into the air as an RF signal
- Receiver: MAC address of the device that is supposed to receive the transmitted RF signal
- BSSID: MAC address of the basic service set (BSS) involved in this communication

GRE Tunnel Explanation

In the section "Establishing the GRE Tunnel," you learned that after the AP checks its OS and then downloads its configuration, its next step is to establish a GRE tunnel. So at this point, you may be asking, "What exactly is a GRE tunnel?" Do not worry. You are not the first to ask this question. In my experience, there are many networking people with years of experience who do not know the answer to that question, so let me explain it to you. Before I do, you should know that GRE is an IP protocol, with the protocol number of 47.

When a client, such as a laptop, wants to transmit data, that data is passed along to the laptop's wireless adapter to be transmitted. Assuming encryption is enabled, the wireless adapter will first take the data and encrypt it. After the data is encrypted, the wireless adapter puts the encrypted data into an 802.11 frame, then adds the 802.11 layer 2 addressing information, representing the following five addresses described in the previous section: source, destination, transmitter, receiver, and BSSID. The wireless adapter then transmits the frame to the AP. This process is illustrated in Step 7 in Figure 2.3.

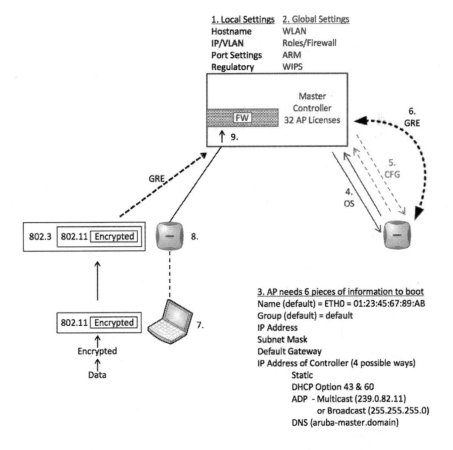

FIGURE 2.3
GRE tunnel

I have friends who are retired and own a condo in Florida. Every winter they go to Florida for a few months to escape the cold Massachusetts weather. They drive their car to Washington, D.C., and then take the Auto Train to Florida. Their car is loaded inside the train and transported to Florida. So take a moment and think about this; why is it that they do not drive their car to Florida on the train tracks? The answer should be fairly obvious. The train tracks were designed to transport trains, not cars. So in order to transport their car to Florida along the train tracks, they have to load the car in a train. The car is enclosed (or *encapsulated*) inside a train. When the train arrives in Florida, the car is then removed from inside the train and placed back on the road, where it can then be driven to its next destination.

The 802.3 GRE tunnel does a similar thing with an 802.11 frame. An 802.11 frame is not designed to travel on an 802.3 Ethernet network. So in order to transport the 802.11 frame from the AP to the controller, the 802.11 frame is encapsulated inside an 802.3 frame. The 802.3 frame is then transported from the AP to the controller, where the 802.11 frame is extracted from the 802.3 frame. At that point, the controller can then forward that frame to its next destination.

When the AP receives the 802.11 frame from the client, the AP creates an 802.3 frame and treats the entire 802.11 frame as data, encapsulating it in the 802.3 frame. An 802.3 header, trailer, and addressing information is added to the frame, and then the 802.3 frame is transmitted across the Ethernet network to its destination, the controller. This is illustrated in Step 8 in Figure 2.3.

In this example, let us assume that the laptop is transmitting a DHCP renew request to a DHCP server connected to an Ethernet port on the Aruba controller. When the controller receives the 802.3 GRE frame from the AP, the first thing that the controller does is to remove the 802.3 header and extract the 802.11 frame. The only purpose for the 802.3 GRE frame is to transport the 802.11 contents, much in the same way that you would use a FedEx, UPS, or DHL envelope to transport a letter. The envelope has no meaning to the person sending or receiving the letter. It is the conduit that is used to transport the contents. Once the envelope has performed its task, it can be thrown away.

The controller will now strip off the 802.11 headers and decrypt the data frame, assuming that the frame was encrypted. Since the frame is going to the DHCP server connected to another Ethernet port, the frame will need to be bridged to that segment and reconstructed as an 802.3 frame. However, it is not immediately bridged and transmitted, because the Aruba controller has a built-in firewall. Since any wireless traffic received is from the untrusted side of the firewall, this traffic must be evaluated by the firewall to determine if the firewall rules will allow it to be forwarded. This is illustrated in Step 9 of Figure 2.3. If the frame passes the firewall rules, it will then be reconstructed as an 802.3 frame and bridged to the Ethernet segment where the DHCP server is located. If the frame does not pass the firewall rules, then the frame will be dropped and will not be forwarded to the DHCP server.

Up to this point, any reference to *GRE tunnel* has been singular, implying that there is only one. This has been intentional to simplify the concept. The reality is that an AP will have multiple GRE tunnels. A GRE tunnel is established per SSID, per radio. Therefore, if an AP has two radios, and each radio is advertising three SSIDs (employee, voice, and guest), then there will be six GRE tunnels. There is also one additional GRE established between the AP and the controller that is used for communicating control traffic between them.

Adding a Local Controller

Your boss just came to you and told you that the company will be expanding and leasing the building next door. She needs you to expand the wireless network to the new space prior to moving in.

When you purchased the original controller, it was configured with the maximum number of access points; therefore, it will be necessary for you to purchase not only additional APs and licenses, but also a second controller. The first controller installed on the network is operating as the master controller, and any additional controllers will operate as local controllers. Any local controllers will pull their WLAN and security configurations from the master controller. You still need to configure the basic controller-specific network settings on every controller (such as IP address, VLANs, and port settings), regardless of whether it is a master or local controller.

So, in order to expand the network, you order the new controller, along with 24 additional APs and licenses. You have determined that these 24 APs will provide the necessary RF coverage in the new building. While waiting for the equipment to arrive, you have fiber network cables installed between the computer room of the existing building and the computer room of the new building.

A week passes, and you receive the equipment. After unboxing the equipment, you connect the new controller to the network, and you establish a console or WebUI connection to the local controller and begin its configuration. Just like with the master controller, you first need to configure the local controller with some of its own personal information, as illustrated in Step 10 of Figure 2.4.

FIGURE 2.4
Local controller installation

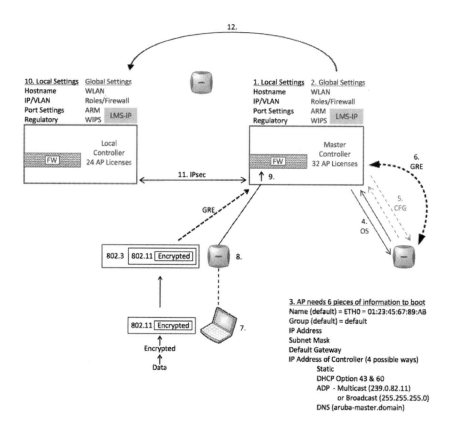

So through whichever interface, either the console connection or the WebUI, you provide the controller with its host name, IP parameters, VLAN settings, regulatory domain information, admin and enable passwords, and any port or PoE settings for the Ethernet ports. Earlier, at this point during the installation when you configured the master controller, the next step was to configure the global settings, such as WLAN, roles/firewall settings, ARM, and WIPS. One of the fundamentals of the design of a controller-based network is that there is a central point of administration, not only for APs, but also for controllers. These global network settings are set in one location, on the master controller, and then the master controller will transfer these settings to each of the local controllers.

In order to make this happen, when the local controller is initially configured, one of the mandatory settings is the IP address of the master controller, along with the IPsec key that the local controller will use to securely communicate with the master, as illustrated in Step 11 in Figure 2.4. The master also needs to have the same IPsec key defined, which you may have already entered when you created the master controller. If not, it is very easy to enter one now. The following command will set a global IPsec key of aruba123 for the master controller to communicate with any local controller.

    (config) #localip 0.0.0.0 ipsec aruba123

For security reasons, you may want to have a unique key for each local controller. You can use the same command to define the specific local controller and the key the master will use to communicate to that local controller.. The following command will set an IPsec key of local123 for the master controller to use to communicate with the local controller with the IP address of 10.1.2.3.

    (config) #localip 10.1.2.3 ipsec local123

Previously, I stated that when initially configuring a local controller, the IP address of the master controller and the IPsec key are mandatory. After installing the local controller, it is possible to change the IPsec key. This may be necessary if you incorrectly entered the key, or if you want to change the key for security reasons. The following command will set an IPsec key of local123 for the local controller to use to communicate with the master controller with the IP address of 10.1.1.1.

    (config) #masterip 10.1.1.1 ipsec local123

After the local controller has been configured, and it is able to communicate with the master controller, all of the global settings that are configured in the startup configuration file of the master controller will automatically be downloaded from the master to the local controller, as illustrated in Step 12 in Figure 2.4.

Multi-Controller AP Boot Process

So you now have two configured controllers, a master and a local, and they are successfully communicating with each other. Any administration of the Aruba network will be performed on the master controller, and the configuration changes will be securely pushed from the master controller to the local controller using IPsec. This is great, but you still need to install and configure the new APs that you purchased. So now you unbox the APs and connect them to the network. Remember, you can connect an AP anywhere on the network as long as the AP can bridge or route back to the controller.

As with any AP, this AP needs its six pieces of information to boot: IP address, subnet mask, default gateway, AP name, AP group, and the IP address of the controller that the AP will initially connect to, as noted in Step 3 in Figure 2.5. Since this is a brand new unconfigured AP, it will receive its IP information from the DHCP server. The name of the AP will be its Ethernet0 MAC address, and its group will be default. Lastly, it needs to discover the controller that it will initially communicate with. Just like the original APs that you installed, the new AP will use the four discovery methods to do this.

FIGURE 2.5
Multi-controller AP boot process

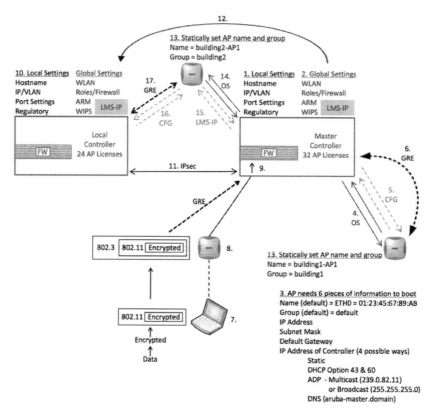

After you built your original master controller, you figured out how to set up DHCP options 43 and 60, and you have been counting on that to provide your APs with the IP address of the master controller. Since these new APs are on the same network as the original APs, when they perform the controller discovery, they will also receive the IP address of the master controller using DHCP.

Once an AP has all six pieces of boot information, it begins to communicate with the controller and checks to see if the OS version on the AP matches the version on the controller. If the OS is different, the AP will upgrade or downgrade itself automatically by downloading the OS that is on the controller using FTP, as illustrated in Step 14 in Figure 2.5. This FTP transfer is established solely and exclusively between the AP and the controller. After the AP has the same OS as the controller, it will then communicate with the controller to download its configuration. When I described this process to you earlier in the chapter, the initial AP then built a GRE tunnel to the master controller, as shown in Step 6 in Figure 2.5. If this new AP attempted to build its GRE tunnel to the master controller, it would not be able to; the master controller only has 32 AP licenses and it is out of capacity, because it already has the original 32 APs connected to it. Remember that the AP capacity is based on the controller model, and ranges from 16 APs to 2,048 APs per controller. In this scenario, a controller with a maximum support for 32 APs was chosen.

So, how can you tell these new APs to build their GRE tunnels to the local controller instead of the master controller? Some of the details were omitted earlier in this chapter when there was only one controller in the story. Now that there are multiple controllers, the complete process will be explained.

To begin with, there is a setting in the configuration file known as the *Local Management Switch IP (LMS-IP) address.* Of the initial six pieces of information that the AP needs to boot, the last piece is the address of the controller that the AP initially communicates with. The first communication between the AP and the controller is to verify and possibly update the OS on the AP (if necessary), as illustrated in Figure 2.5, Step 14. After the OS has been verified or updated, the AP then communicates with the initial controller to download the LMS-IP address, as illustrated in Step 15. The LMS-IP is part of the global settings and is specifically set for each AP group. The LMS-IP address tells the AP which controller to communicate with to download its configuration, as illustrated in Step 16, and to establish its GRE tunnel, as illustrated in Step 17. The AP will always download its configuration from the controller that its GRE tunnels will be terminating to. Although LMS-IP stands for "Local Management Switch IP," this could be the IP address of any controller—a local controller or the master controller. So in this example, you would program the original 32 APs with an LMS-IP of the master controller to terminate their GRE tunnels to the original controller, and you would configure the 24 new APs with an LMS-IP of the local controller to terminate their GRE tunnels to the new controller.

Okay, that sounds great, but how do you distinguish the old APs from the new APs? You do this by naming the APs and creating AP groups. Remember, each AP has six pieces of information that it needs in order to boot. Two of those pieces are the AP name and the group that the AP belongs to. Now is a good time to configure each AP with a unique name other than its MAC address. A proper name can help identify and locate the installed AP. Finally, you need to assign a group to each of the APs. In this example you could assign the AP group name of building1 to the 32 APs in the first building, and an AP group name of building2 to the 24 APs in the second building. Each AP needs a unique AP name, such as building1-AP1 or building2-AP1, as illustrated in both instances of Step 13 in Figure 2.5.

On the master controller, you would create the two AP groups and configure the building1 AP group with the LMS-IP address of the master controller, and then configure the building2 AP group with the LMS-IP address of the local controller.

From then on when the `building2` APs boot, they will be directed to terminate their GRE tunnels to the local controller, as illustrated in Step 17 of Figure 2.5, and the `building1` APs will be directed to terminate their GRE tunnels to the master controller, as illustrated in Step 6 of Figure 2.5.

So now that I have walked you through the boot process of the AP, let us review the process with less explanation—a little more conceptually.

- An AP boots and gets its six pieces of information: IP address, subnet mask, default gateway (all three probably through DHCP), an AP name, a group, and the IP address of the controller it will initially communicate with.
- The AP will discover the address of the initial controller using one of the four methods: statically configured, DHCP options 43 and 60, ADP, or DNS lookup.
- The AP will then communicate with this initial controller to download its OS (if necessary). The OS only needs to be downloaded if the OS of the AP is different from the OS on the controller.
- The initial controller will then look at the config details of the group that the AP belongs to and find the value of the LMS-IP. If the LMS-IP value is blank (not configured), then the initial controller will proceed to provide the full configuration to the AP, and the AP will establish its GRE tunnel to the controller that it initially discovered.
- If the LMS-IP address is set and is the same as the initial controller, then the initial controller will proceed to provide the full configuration to the AP, and the AP will establish its GRE tunnel to this controller.
- If the LMS-IP address is set to an address other than the initial controller, the AP will be given the LMS-IP address of the other controller. The AP will then contact the other controller to download its full configuration and establish its GRE tunnel.

It is important to note that the AP must download the full configuration from the controller that it will establish its GRE tunnel with. The controller where the AP is terminating its GRE tunnels may be in a different geographic location, with a different country code, than the controller that the AP initially discovered. The AP is required to download its configuration from the same controller where it will be terminating its GRE tunnels to make sure that the proper RF regulatory rules are received by the AP. These rules specify the radio power limits and channel availability of the controller that the AP is connecting to.

AP Forwarding Modes

When a station sends data frames to an AP, there are multiple ways that the AP can handle or process the data, depending upon how the *virtual AP* is configured (at this point in the book you have not learned about the term *virtual AP* yet, so for now, think of a virtual AP as the SSID and all of the security and authentication parameters that make that SSID work). Virtual APs will be covered extensively in Chapter 5, "Profiles."

An AP can advertise multiple wireless networks (virtual APs), and each wireless network can have its own settings and configuration. For example, you could have an employee SSID configured with 802.1X/EAP, while also having a guest SSID configured to redirect a wireless user to a captive portal login. Along with the SSID and authentication and encryption settings, the forwarding mode defines how the user data is handled or forwarded on the network. There are four *forwarding modes* that can be used to handle the user data. They are:

- GRE/tunnel (default method)
- Bridge
- Decrypt-tunnel
- Split-tunnel (remote AP only)

All of these AP forwarding modes are described in the following sections, along with how they function and why you may want to use them.

GRE/Tunnel

As the name implies, this mode uses a GRE tunnel to move the user data from the AP to the controller. This process was explained in the section "GRE Tunnel Explanation" earlier in this chapter. When a client station sends data to an SSID (virtual AP) that is configured to forward the data using tunnel mode, the AP encapsulates the 802.11 data frame inside an 802.3 frame and forwards it to the Aruba controller.

Even though all of the user *data* frames are tunneled to the controller, not all of the user *frames* are forwarded to the controller. The 802.11 authentication and association requests are handled directly by the AP, with the authentication and association responses being generated directly by the AP. All other frames, including the data frames, 802.11e or 802.11k action frames, and EAP frames, are sent to the controller inside 802.3 GRE frames. The Aruba controller will then decapsulate the 802.3 frame, decrypt the 802.11 frame if necessary, apply any firewall rules to the user traffic, and forward the traffic as necessary. GRE/tunnel mode is individually configured for each SSID (virtual AP) operating on any Aruba campus or remote AP.

At this point, before I explain the other forwarding methods, I need to briefly explain the difference between a *campus AP (CAP)* and a *remote AP (RAP)*. Some Aruba APs are specially designed to be used as RAPs. Without getting into the details of why some APs are called RAPs and others are not, it is important to know that any Aruba AP can function as a RAP.

So what is the difference between a remote AP (RAP) and a campus AP (CAP)? APs not only communicate client traffic between themselves and the controller, but they also need to communicate administrative traffic, or what we refer to as *control traffic*. This control traffic is essentially the AP and the controller taking care of business; transferring things such as the AP configuration. When a campus AP communicates AP control traffic between itself and the controller, it uses the PAPI protocol to do so. PAPI is not an encrypted communication, and typically does not need to be encrypted on the corporate network. When there is a need or desire to secure this communication, a secure form of PAPI known as *control plane security (CPsec)* can be enabled on the controller and AP, which encrypts the PAPI communications using IPsec. CPsec is enabled by default and is recommended for use in all environments.

CPsec is designed to operate across a corporate or campus network. Sometimes, however, you want to connect an AP at a remote location where the only way of communicating back to the corporate controller is through the Internet or some other potentially unsecured link. In order to provide secure communications between an AP at a remote location and the corporate network, Aruba provides a special AP operating mode, Remote AP (RAP), which allows the AP and controller to communicate using an L2TP/IPsec VPN tunnel. A RAP will communicate all of its control traffic using the secure VPN tunnel. The user data will be tunneled; however, by default it will not be encrypted again as it travels within the L2TP/IPsec VPN tunnel, since the user traffic is typically encrypted at the client station and decrypted at the controller, as described in depth in the "GRE Tunnel Explanation" section earlier in this chapter.

With tunnel mode, since all of the user traffic is being sent to the controller, the controller is able to provide a more centralized visibility of the users and their traffic. This also provides a simpler configuration of the network edge, since all the user VLAN traffic is forwarded through the controller.

Bridge

The next forwarding mode that will be explained is *bridge mode*. When a client station sends a frame to an SSID (virtual AP) that has been configured in bridge mode, the physical AP (not the controller) processes the frame, similar to the way that an autonomous or standalone AP would process the frame. The AP will respond to any of the 802.11 authentication and association requests directly with authentication and association responses. The AP will decrypt any inbound frames from the station, and it will encrypt any outbound frames going to the station. The AP will also perform any firewall enforcement. Any 802.11e or 802.11k action frames will also be processed directly by the AP, which will send out any needed responses to the client.

Bridge mode can be specified for SSIDs (virtual APs) that are configured on any CAP or RAP. When bridge mode is enabled, as stated previously, the AP processes the client frames directly, encrypting and decrypting frames locally. In order to be able to process the encryption and decryption of the frames locally, the encryption keys will be downloaded to the AP from the controller. Even though the AP is processing the frames locally, the AP still needs to communicate with the controller initially to download its configuration. To ensure that the downloading of any encryption keys (along with other AP management traffic) is performed securely, bridge mode is only supported when the AP is communicating the control traffic between itself and the controller using secure communications. This means that bridge mode can be configured on any RAP, since a RAP uses an L2TP/IPsec tunnel to communicate with the controller. Bridge mode can also be configured on any CAP, providing that the AP is configured to use CPsec to communicate with the controller. CPsec provides IPsec secure communications of control traffic between the CAP and the controller. In Chapter 11, "Access Points," you will learn more about CPsec.

One of the reasons for configuring a virtual AP to operate in bridge mode is to cut down on network traffic. As an example, a company may have a small satellite office that is connected to the corporate offices through a secured WAN link. The remote location has an AP, a network printer, and half a dozen wireless users. If the virtual AP was operating in tunnel mode, any time a satellite user prints, the print job would be tunneled across the WAN link to the controller and then routed back across the WAN link to the printer. If the virtual AP was configured for bridge mode, the print job would be sent from the satellite user's computer to the AP, and then forwarded directly to the printer.

Although a virtual AP using bridge mode will forward data directly to the local network without involving the controller, the AP does perform firewall enforcement. When the virtual AP configuration is downloaded from the controller, it also downloads the firewall rules from the controller and applies them locally on any of the user traffic that is being bridged.

Because of its distributed design, bridge mode does not allow support for captive portal authentication. It also requires more configuration of the edge network at each of the APs, and there is a maximum limit of 32 bridge mode APs per subnet.

Decrypt-Tunnel

Another forwarding mode for handling station frames that are transmitted between a client and an AP is known as *decrypt-tunnel*. This method of handling the client traffic is very similar to the GRE/tunnel method; however, the client frames are decrypted at the AP prior to being tunneled to the controller.

As described earlier in the "GRE Tunnel Explanation" section, the client station initially takes the data that is to be transmitted, encrypts it, creates an 802.11 frame, and then transmits the frame to the AP, as illustrated in Step 1 of Figure 2.6. With *decrypt-tunnel mode*, when the Aruba AP receives the 802.11 frames from the station, it first decrypts the frame, and then it encapsulates the 802.11 frame inside an 802.3 frame, as illustrated in Step 2 of Figure 2.6. The AP then forwards the frame to the controller. At this point, the controller will take the 802.11 data, along with the source and destination addresses, process it through the firewall, and forward it as directed by the addressing and as allowed by the firewall, as illustrated in Step 3 of Figure 2.6.

FIGURE 2.6
Decrypt-tunnel

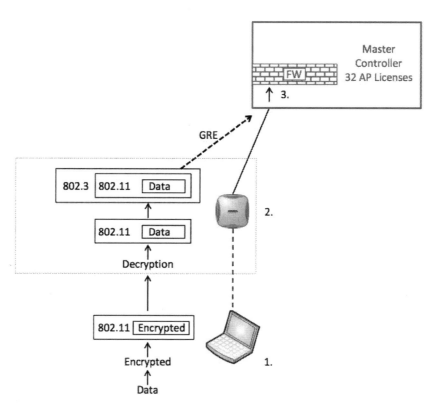

Now that I have explained to you the decrypt-tunnel process, you may be asking, "Why would I want to do this?" Many organizations need to monitor or analyze the traffic that is traveling across the network. Some need to do it for security purposes: monitoring for viruses and spyware, or to prevent users from visiting undesirable websites or downloading content that is not allowed. Other organizations need to record, monitor, or capture data that is traversing their network, or possibly optimize the data or perform load-balancing on the data. If the data is encrypted between the AP and the controller, it would not be able to be read and analyzed. Therefore, the data must be decrypted prior to it being transmitted to the controller. For security purposes, we want the wireless transmissions to be encrypted, which is provided using this process.

As with bridge mode, encryption and decryption of the frames is being performed locally on the AP, which means that the encryption keys need to be downloaded to the AP. Hopefully, at this point you understand that this is done when the AP receives its configuration from the controller. Again, to ensure that the downloading of any encryption keys (along with other AP management traffic) is performed securely, decrypt-tunnel mode is only supported when the AP and controller are using secure communications to exchange the control traffic. So this means that decrypt-tunnel is only supported with RAPs, or CAPs that are configured to use CPsec to communicate with the controller.

Although I just mentioned that decrypt-tunnel is supported with RAPs, it is typically not recommended for deployment with RAPs, unless the RAP connection back to the corporate network is across a secured connection. Although a RAP builds an L2TP/IPsec tunnel back to the controller, the user traffic is not encrypted by the RAP since the user traffic is typically encrypted by the client station all the way back to the controller. If decrypt-tunnel is implemented on an SSID (virtual AP) that is assigned to a RAP, the traffic between the client and the controller is now transmitted as clear text, which can provide a security risk if the RAP is deployed across a public network. You will learn more about how RAPs function in Chapter 11, "Access Points."

Split-Tunnel

Split-tunnel is the fourth and final forwarding mode, and is available only when assigning an SSID (virtual AP) to a RAP. Split-tunnel is not supported on campus APs. If you are already familiar with the term *split-tunnel*, prepare yourself, because this is not your typical split-tunnel technology. The Aruba split-tunnel forwarding mode is also known as *policy-based forwarding*. When a RAP builds its L2TP/IPsec tunnel back to the corporate controller, it is usually not prudent to require *all* of the user traffic to have to travel through the VPN, across the Internet, and back to the corporate network—especially any traffic that is destined for the Internet. Therefore, using the stateful firewall software and intelligence that is incorporated into the Aruba controllers, you can create firewall forwarding rules to process the wireless traffic directly on the RAPs. These rules can allow certain traffic to be forwarded to the controller through the L2TP/IPsec tunnel, such as traffic going to the corporate data center, while traffic that is destined for somewhere else can be bridged onto the local network that the RAP is connected to. This will allow the traffic to be sent directly to the Internet from the local connection. Using policy-based forwarding you could allow only certain traffic onto the local network, such as printing or scanning, while tunneling all other traffic back to the controller. Another configuration could allow all Internet-destined HTTP and HTTPS traffic to be forwarded directly to the Internet, while all other traffic would be tunneled back to the controller. Split-tunnel will be explained in more detail in Chapter 11, "Access Points."

Table 2.1 provides a summary of the four forwarding modes supported by an SSID (virtual AP), along with the three methods an AP can use to communicate with the controller.

TABLE 2.1: AP Forwarding Modes

	CAMPUS AP WITHOUT CPSEC	CAMPUS AP WITH CPSEC	REMOTE AP
GRE/Tunnel	Yes	Yes	Yes
Bridge	No	Yes	Yes
Decrypt-Tunnel	No	Yes	Yes, but only recommended if another form of security or tunneling will provide a secure path for the user data
Split-Tunnel	No	No	Yes

CHAPTER 3

Aruba Controller and Software Overview

IN THIS CHAPTER, YOU WILL LEARN ABOUT THE FOLLOWING:

- **User Interface**
    - Terminal Access
    - Web User Interface
    - Wizards
- **Controllers**
    - Firewall
    - Virtual Private Network Server
    - RFProtect
    - Operating Hardware
- **Resetting Controller to Factory Default**

IN THIS CHAPTER YOU WILL LEARN ABOUT the different user interfaces that can be used to manage and administer the Aruba controller. You will also learn about the controller and some of the software modules that provide additional capability and functionality to the wireless network. This chapter will also explain the memory and partition structure of the controller, along with resetting the controller to factory default configuration.

User Interface

There are essentially two interfaces that can be used to manage or configure an Aruba controller: a command line interface (CLI) or a web user interface (WebUI). Although the wizards are technically part of the WebUI, there is enough uniqueness with the wizards that they will be discussed separately in this section.

Terminal Access

There are two ways to establish terminal access to a controller: first by connecting directly to the console port, and second by establishing an SSH or telnet connection to the controller's IP address.

In order to make a console connection between a computer and an Aruba controller, you need two things: a physical connection between the two devices, and a terminal emulation program. There are two ways of establishing the physical connection. The first method is to physically connect a serial port from the computer to the console port on the controller. The second method is to establish an SSH or telnet session using a TCP/IP connection between the computer and controller. Telnet is disabled by default, but TCP port 23 is still open.

The advantage of having a physical connection to the console port is that unless you have a hardware failure on your controller or computer, the console port will always provide a connection, although it is limited by distance since the console cable does need to be physically plugged into the controller from your computer.

Once the physical connection is established to the port, then the terminal software can use this connection to provide the CLI from the controller to the client. Two Apple OS X–based programs that I have had success with are Zterm (when using a USB-to-serial connection) and iTerm2 (for SSH connections). For Microsoft Windows computers I have had success with PuTTY. Feel free to use any program you like; however, make sure that you have a program that is capable of supporting a serial or USB-to-serial connection.

An SSH connection can be established from anywhere on the network as long as SSH data can be routed to the controller. However, it goes without saying that for an SSH connection to work, basic IP settings need to be configured on the controller. Since IP communications is needed for SSH, that is why a console cable is initially used for configuration.

Console Port

Every Aruba controller is configured with an eight-position, eight-contact (8P8C) modular console port, which allows the administrator to connect directly to the controller and run CLI commands. Throughout the industry, the jack and connector are wrongly known as an RJ-45 jack and RJ-45 connector. Since Aruba documentation (along with most of the networking industry) refers to this port and jack by the term RJ-45, for consistency's sake and to prevent confusion, this book will, too. The newer controllers are equipped with a mini USB port (mini type B) designed to also be a console connection. A console connection is especially useful when the controller has not been configured, or when networking problems are preventing access to the controller through TCP/IP.

In order to connect to the controller using the RJ-45 console port, you need what is commonly referred to as a "console cable." A console cable has a DB-9 female serial connector on one end that is used to connect to the serial port on the computer. On the other end is an RJ-45 plug that is used to connect to the controller's console port. This cable could be assembled out of multiple components or it could be an integrated cable. A console cable does require a "rollover" configuration, where the wires connected to pins 1 through 8 on the RJ-45 connector are rolled over and the connection is reversed to pins 8 through 1.

Please do not refer to this cable as a *crossover cable*. A crossover cable is typically wired so that the transmitting wires on one end of the cable connect to the receiving wires on the other end of the cable. Crossover cables vary greatly and are specific to the communications technology and equipment they are used on.

A rollover cable is a very common cable in the networking world, and many network administrators carry these cables with them in their computer bags. One of the problems I have experienced over the years is that these cables are usually not very long, typically less than six feet in length. This may sound like a long enough cable, but when you have to perform maintenance on a piece of equipment that is in a data rack, the six-foot cable can drastically restrict your movement, often forcing you to stand, holding the laptop in one hand while programming the controller using the terminal emulation software with the other hand.

Most of the older Aruba controllers shipped with a DB-9 to RJ-45 adapter, along with a network cable. The Aruba DB-9 to RJ-45 adapters were wired to provide the rollover in the adapter itself. This means that you can use any straight-through network cable to connect the adapter and the console port on the controller. If the light bulb has not gone off in your head yet, let me help you; this means that with the rollover adapter, any twisted-pair network cable (which is a straight-through cable, often referred to as an *Ethernet cable*) can be used to connect your laptop serial port to the console port on the controller. So if all you have available is the Aruba straight-through cable, then by all means use it. However, if you happen to have a 20-foot Ethernet cable available, by connecting it to the Aruba DB-9 to RJ-45 adapter, you now have a 20-foot console cable, providing you with more flexibility and movement. If you do not have one of these adapters, the controller user guides document the pin-out settings that can be used to build your own adapter.

If you decide to connect your computer to the mini USB console connection, you will need to download a USB console driver for your computer. This driver will allow your computer to recognize the USB connection as a serial connection, allowing your terminal emulation software to perform a console connection through the USB port. The driver can be downloaded from the Tools and Resources section at support.arubanetworks.com.

Once you have a physical console connection between your computer and the controller, you will need to configure your terminal emulation program to communicate with the controller using the serial port, USB-to-serial adapter, or USB port. In addition to knowing which port you are using, you will need to configure your terminal software for the following communications settings, which are fairly common for networking devices:

    Baud rate = 9600

    Data bits = 8

    Parity = none

    Stop bits = 1

    Flow control = none

SSH and Telnet

After the Aruba controller has a basic configuration and is able to communicate on the network using TCP/IP, it is no longer necessary to physically connect to the console port in order to interface with the controller using a CLI. By default, the Aruba controllers support SSH using TCP/IP communications. Telnet is disabled by default and should remain disabled, since it does not provide for secure communications between the client and the controller. Simply open your favorite terminal emulator, select SSH, and connect to the controller's IP address.

CLI Command Environment

I do not think it is necessary to review the details of the CLI command environment because it is similar to many switching or routing products you may already be familiar with, and Aruba has already done of good job of explaining this in their documentation. If you are not familiar with the basic CLI, the *ArubaOS CLI Reference Guide* has a section titled "CLI Access" that does a good job of explaining the interface. As with other networking products, the Aruba CLI provides command help in the terminal as you type. You can get hints by using the question mark "?," along with autocompletion of commands, which helps with syntax and spelling.

Pipe Operator

One command feature that I want to highlight is the pipe function. The pipe is actually a character, the up and down, or vertical line (|). This command can be added to the end of just about any command that generates screen output. As with any command or parameter, the pipe function must have a space before and after it, such as " | ". The pipe function filters or further refines the output that is displayed. The pipe function can be used to refine the output in four ways:

- *command* | include *keyword*
- *command* | exclude *keyword*
- *command* | begin *keyword*
- *command* | redirect-output

When a command is executed, if the pipe is used with:

- include *keyword*, only the lines of output of the command that contain the keyword will be displayed.
- exclude *keyword*, only the lines of output of the command that do not contain the keyword will be displayed.

- begin *keyword*, the first line of output that contains the keyword, and all lines afterward, will be displayed.
- redirect-output instead of displaying the output of the command to the screen, the output will be written to a file called redirect-output.log in the controller's flash partition.

To illustrate this, the following is the output of the command show ap database. In order to make the screen output easier to read in the following examples, I removed three columns of information that were not necessary: Flags, Switch IP, and Standby IP.

```
#show ap database

AP Database
-----------
Name          Group            AP Type   IP Address    Status
----          -----            -------   ----------    ------
AP115-70-1    controller70     115       10.1.90.150   Up 1d:8h:23m:11s
AP135-80-1    controller80     135       10.1.90.151   Up 1d:8h:25m:39s
AP135-80-2    controller80     135       10.1.90.153   Up 1d:8h:25m:32s
AP225-90-1    Roletest-group   225       10.1.90.152   Up 1d:8h:20m:30s


Flags: U = Unprovisioned; N = Duplicate name; G = No such group; L = Unlicensed
       I = Inactive; D = Dirty or no config; E = Regulatory Domain Mismatch
       X = Maintenance Mode; P = PPPoE AP; B = Built-in AP; s = LACP striping
       R = Remote AP; R- = Remote AP requires Auth; C = Cellular RAP;
       c = CERT-based RAP; 1 = 802.1x authenticated AP; 2 = Using IKE version 2
       u = Custom-Cert RAP; S = Standby-mode AP; J = USB cert at AP
       i = Indoor; o = Outdoor
       M = Mesh node; Y = Mesh Recovery

Total APs:4
```

If you were to issue the show ap database command with | include 135, the output only displays the lines that contain the string 135, as illustrated in the following output. Notice in the previous example there are column headers; however, in this example, since the column header line does not contain the string 135, the header is not included in the output.

```
#show ap database | include 135
AP135-80-1    controller80     135       10.1.90.151   Up 1d:8h:26m:48s
AP135-80-2    controller80     135       10.1.90.153   Up 1d:8h:26m:41s
```

If you were to issue the show ap database command with | begin 135, the output would begin displaying from the line with the first instance of 135, as illustrated in the following output:

```
#show ap database | begin 135

AP135-80-1   controller80    135    10.1.90.151   Up 1d:8h:30m:8s
AP135-80-2   controller80    135    10.1.90.153   Up 1d:8h:30m:1s
AP225-90-1   Roletest-group  225    10.1.90.152   Up 1d:8h:24m:59s

Flags: U = Unprovisioned; N = Duplicate name; G = No such group; L = Unlicensed
       I = Inactive; D = Dirty or no config; E = Regulatory Domain Mismatch
       X = Maintenance Mode; P = PPPoE AP; B = Built-in AP; s = LACP striping
       R = Remote AP; R- = Remote AP requires Auth; C = Cellular RAP;
       c = CERT-based RAP; 1 = 802.1x authenticated AP; 2 = Using IKE version 2
       u = Custom-Cert RAP; S = Standby-mode AP; J = USB cert at AP
       i = Indoor; o = Outdoor
       M = Mesh node; Y = Mesh Recovery

Total APs:4
```

If you issue the show ap database command with | exclude 135, the output would display all lines except those containing the text 135, as illustrated in the following output.

```
#show ap database | exclude 135

AP Database
-----------
Name         Group          AP Type  IP Address   Status
----         -----          -------  ----------   ------
AP115-70-1   controller70    115    10.1.90.150   Up 1d:8h:33m:10s
AP225-90-1   Roletest-group  225    10.1.90.152   Up 1d:8h:30m:29s

Flags: U = Unprovisioned; N = Duplicate name; G = No such group; L = Unlicensed
       I = Inactive; D = Dirty or no config; E = Regulatory Domain Mismatch
       X = Maintenance Mode; P = PPPoE AP; B = Built-in AP; s = LACP striping
       R = Remote AP; R- = Remote AP requires Auth; C = Cellular RAP;
       c = CERT-based RAP; 1 = 802.1x authenticated AP; 2 = Using IKE version 2
       u = Custom-Cert RAP; S = Standby-mode AP; J = USB cert at AP
       i = Indoor; o = Outdoor
       M = Mesh node; Y = Mesh Recovery

Total APs:4
```

Each of the previous examples used the pipe operator with a single variable. The pipe can also be used with multiple variables, separating each variable by a comma. The comma cannot have any spaces before or after it. As an example, the following output displays all lines except for those containing the text 115 or 135.

```
#show ap database | exclude 115,135


AP Database
-----------
Name         Group            AP Type   IP Address    Status
----         -----            -------   ----------    ------
AP225-90-1   Roletest-group   225       10.1.90.152   Up 1d:8h:20m:30s


Flags: U = Unprovisioned; N = Duplicate name; G = No such group; L = Unlicensed
       I = Inactive; D = Dirty or no config; E = Regulatory Domain Mismatch
       X = Maintenance Mode; P = PPPoE AP; B = Built-in AP; s = LACP striping
       R = Remote AP; R- = Remote AP requires Auth; C = Cellular RAP;
       c = CERT-based RAP; 1 = 802.1x authenticated AP; 2 = Using IKE version 2
       u = Custom-Cert RAP; S = Standby-mode AP; J = USB cert at AP
       i = Indoor; o = Outdoor
       M = Mesh node; Y = Mesh Recovery


Total APs:4
```

Finally, if you issue the `show ap database` command with `| redirect-output`, the only text that is displayed on the screen is a notification message that the output was written to the file `redirect-output.log` as illustrated in the following output:

```
#show ap database | redirect-output
 'show ap database ' is written into redirect-output.log ...
```

The `redirect-output.log` file is stored in the controller's flash partition, and can be seen by executing the `dir` command from the CLI prompt. You can use FTP, TFTP, or SCP to copy the file from the controller to an external server. The following CLI output shows the command needed to copy the file to a TFTP server:

```
#copy flash: redirect-output.log tftp: 192.168.240.31 redirect-output.log
```

Web User Interface

The web user interface (WebUI) of the controller typically has a three-tier, four-tier, or five-tier menu hierarchy. This references the number of selection points you need to navigate in order to make an addition or change to the configuration of the controller.

Figure 3.1 illustrates a three-tier menu screen. In this instance, a menu selection along the top (tier 1) is selected first. When the menu along the top is selected, the menu to the left (tier 2) will change, appropriate to the selection along the top. Then in the middle of the window is the area (tier 3) where you can add or change the controller's settings.

FIGURE 3.1 Three-tier WebUI layout

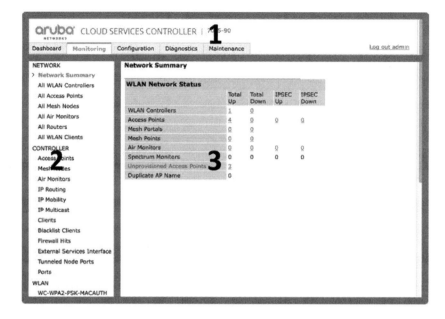

In Figure 3.2, a four-tier menu screen is illustrated. As with the three-tier menu, you would make a menu selection from along the top of the screen (tier 1) followed by a menu selection along the left side of the screen (tier 2). After choosing the menu along the left side of the screen, another submenu (tier 3) will appear just below the top menu, and then in the middle of the window is the area where you can add or change the controller's settings (tier 4).

FIGURE 3.2 Four-tier WebUI layout

Figure 3.3 illustrates a five-tier menu screen. After making a menu choice at the top (tier 1), left side (tier 2), and then the submenu along the top (tier 3), another submenu will appear to the left (tier 4). After a selection from this submenu, you will then be able to make additions or changes in the middle of the screen (tier 5).

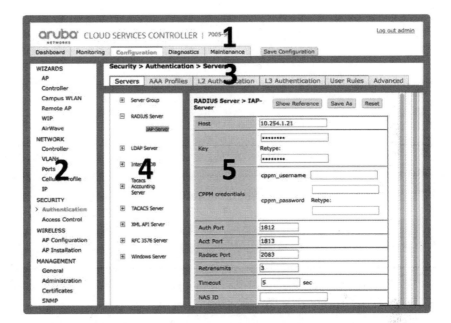

FIGURE 3.3
Five-tier WebUI layout

Wizards

To make configuration easier and more consistent, the WebUI has multiple configuration wizards. The wizards can be found at the top of the Configuration menu. While many hardcore admins frown at the use of wizards, the configuration wizards in the Aruba WebUI are highly functional and quite complete.

They were designed to simplify and automate the configuration of the controller. The wizards prompt you for key information, and then they use that information, along with default parameters, to make configuration changes. You simply invoke the appropriate wizard, and then make the changes you require. As the wizard runs, it will pull in any settings that are in the current configuration. The wizards can be very useful for organizations with basic configuration needs. More advanced organizations use the CLI or WebUI to configure their controllers, since there are many more options and settings available for customizing the controller configuration.

If you are new to ArubaOS, the wizards can also be a great learning tool. If you have a controller that you can use to practice with, it can be very helpful to use the wizards to configure your controller, and then use the CLI or WebUI to look at the details of the configuration. The wizards allow you to easily build a working environment that you can analyze and learn from. The wizards can also save quite a bit of configuration time.

One of the wizards that can be useful to any organization is the AP wizard. As explained in a previous chapter, an AP is typically configured with an AP name and a group name, which it will use during the boot process. The AP will use its Ethernet 0 MAC address initially for its AP name and default for its group name. These should be changed to better identify and configure your APs. The AP wizard allows you to easily provision multiple APs at a time. You can create a filter to display a group of APs and then selectively choose one or more APs from the filtered list. From there, you can configure the AP settings individually or globally for the group. Prior to pushing the configuration to the APs and rebooting the APs with their new settings, you should make sure that you click on the link to print the table of the APs and their settings. This will allow you to review all of the settings before the APs are configured, or if an AP does not reboot properly, the table will allow you to review the configuration to see if you made any mistakes.

Controllers

Aruba is currently in its third generation of controllers. Each generation has introduced higher levels of performance, functionality, and support for newer code. The Aruba controller configuration and management provides for all aspects of support for the wireless users and the APs. As customer requirements expand, the Aruba controller portfolio offers a scalable architecture that provides robust features and high capacity capabilities.

The different Aruba controllers typically support the same features across all models, although there are a few exceptions to this. First, there are some obvious hardware differences between some of the controller models, such as PoE, redundant power, and Fast/Gigabit/10-Gigabit Ethernet. Also, at times, as Aruba has upgraded from older classes of controllers to newer controllers, some features are not supported in the older controllers due to the hardware or memory requirements of the new features. In these instances, the older controllers may operate using the newer version of ArubaOS; however, the newer features may not be supported on the older platform.

If you have multiple controllers on your network, you want to make sure that they are running the same software version (and subversion) of ArubaOS. Even though you will be installing the same software version on all of the controllers, because of some of the hardware differences between the equipment, you may need to download different OS files from the Aruba support site if the controllers are different models. ArubaOS software files are compiled and built for the specific controller models or families.

The key differences between the Aruba controllers are speed, performance, and number of APs and client devices supported. The models of controllers are designed to support different sized networks, from small networks of just a few APs to large networks of thousands of APs.

In a master/local environment, all of the management is performed on the master controller and then the configuration from the master is distributed out to the local controllers (except for the controller-specific settings). Any model of controller can be a master and any model of controller can be a local. However, there are master/local configurations that Aruba will not support. You will need to check with your sales or support person for the exact details; however, the smaller controllers are not designed to support multiple local controllers or support a bigger controller as its local controller.

This section will describe some of the key licensed features that are commonly installed on Aruba controllers. The hardware and memory structure of the controller will also be explained, along with a brief description of the boot process.

Firewall

The ArubaOS Policy Enforcement Firewall Next Generation (PEF-NG) is an add-on module/license that provides identity-based access control of user devices on the network. The PEF-NG license is one of the most purchased licenses, and in my experience, is installed on most Aruba networks. When a client device connects to an Aruba network, it is assigned a user role. A *user role* is a set of rules and settings that control many aspects of the user's connection to the network. Roles may allow or deny the user access to resources on the local network or out to the Internet. The firewall can implement both IP-based and application-based controls and restrictions. Every frame that the user transmits is inspected by the firewall, and the firewall will determine whether the frame is allowed to continue across the network.

When a user connects to an Aruba network, the controller uses a series of derivation rules to identify which role should be assigned to the user. In Chapter 7, "Role Derivation," you will learn the logic that is used to assign a role to a user. In Chapter 8, "Policy Enforcement Firewall," you will learn that a role is constructed of one or more policies, and that a policy is constructed of one or more rules. In the networking world, a group of firewall rules is referred to as an access control list (ACL). A PEF ACL is specifically referred to as a *session ACL*.

Virtual Private Network Server

A virtual private network (VPN) allows secure connections between devices that are communicating across an unsecured or untrusted network. An Aruba controller can be configured to operate as a VPN server, also referred to as a VPN concentrator. An Aruba controller can provide VPN termination for two types of VPN connections: site-to-site VPNs, and remote access clients or devices.

A site-to-site VPN allows a controller at one location, such as a branch or satellite office, to build a permanent secure network connection between it and another location, such as the corporate headquarters. These VPN servers function as network gateways, encapsulating, encrypting, and routing network traffic from one location to the other. Network traffic is dynamically forwarded from one site to the other as needed. A site-to-site VPN provides end users with access to network resources, oblivious to whether the resources are on the local network or the remote network.

Secure communications is also a common requirement for providing access for an individual user or a group of users. In this situation, a VPN client can dynamically initiate and establish a secure connection with a VPN server on an as-needed basis. The VPN client can be standard VPN software built into many operating systems, specialty VPN software such as Aruba's Virtual Internet Access (VIA) client, or VPN client software configured on an access point, referred to as a Remote AP (RAP). In Chapter 11, "Access Points," you will learn about how RAPs operate and how to configure a RAP.

RFProtect

RFProtect is the product name of Aruba's Wireless Intrusion Protection (WIP) software. RFProtect is an add-on module/license that provides intrusion detection and protection. The Aruba controller is capable of identifying and protecting the network from many different security risks and attacks, including rogue devices, attacks against APs, attacks against clients, and attacks against the network.

The RFProtect license adds advanced WIP functionality and features to the controller. Without the RFProtect license, an Aruba controller provides basic WIP capabilities. However, for more advanced WIP capabilities you will need the RFProtect license and you may want to purchase AirWave, which provides extensive, customizable, rogue detection capabilities. AirWave integrates well with the controller platform to provide intrusion remediation and containment. In Chapter 15 you will learn more about RFProtect.

Operating Hardware

The underlying operating system of the Aruba controller is a custom OS based on Linux. As with most operating systems, the Aruba controller has permanent storage and RAM. ArubaOS uses flash non-volatile (NV) RAM for permanent storage, which is divided into multiple partitions to organize the files. Some of the partitions and files are visible to the network administrator, and others are hidden and inaccessible.

Partition Structure

The flash NVRAM is the permanent storage for the ArubaOS. As illustrated in Figure 3.4, the flash NVRAM memory is divided into three partitions: system partition 0, system partition 1, and the remaining memory makes up what is known as the *flash partition*. All controllers are shipped with these partitions already configured and formatted, and it is extremely rare that these partitions would need to be re-created. If you did need to repartition or reformat the flash NVRAM, this task needs to be done from a special system bootstrap command environment known as CPBoot. If you think you need to reformat or repartition your flash NVRAM, you should first discuss this with Aruba technical support. The procedures vary between different models.

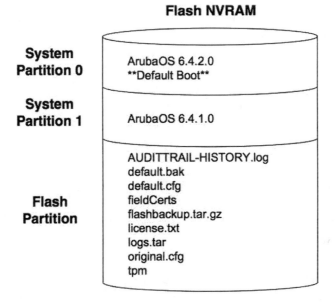

FIGURE 3.4
Flash NVRAM

System Partitions

Each of the system partitions contains a copy of the operating system. The command show image version, as shown next, displays the contents of both system partitions. The system partitions are referred to as 0 and 1, although the command output displays them as 0:0 and 0:1.

```
#show image version
---------------------------------
Partition            : 0:0 (/dev/usb/flash1) **Default boot**
Software Version     : ArubaOS 6.4.1.0 (Digitally Signed - Production Build)
Build number         : 43932
Label                : 43932
Built on             : Mon May 26 12:57:29 PDT 2014
---------------------------------
Partition            : 0:1 (/dev/usb/flash2)
Software Version     : ArubaOS 6.4.1.0 (Digitally Signed - Production Build)
Build number         : 43932
Label                : 43932
Built on             : Mon May 26 12:57:29 PDT 2014
```

One of the two partitions is enabled as the boot partition. This is identified by **Default boot** next to the partition. This does not identify the partition that the controller booted from, but rather the partition that it is programmed to boot from the next time it is rebooted. If you would like to see which partition the controller has booted from, the command show switchinfo displays this information as part of its output. The following is a portion of the output of the show switchinfo command, showing that this controller booted from partition 0.

```
Boot Partition: PARTITION 0
```

Having two system partitions is useful for numerous reasons. They allow you to pre-install a new version of the operating system on the non-boot partition, without affecting the current operation of the controller. It also allows you to easily revert back to the previous operating system if you have a problem during a system upgrade. If you want to upgrade the controller OS, you would upgrade the partition that is not configured as the **Default Boot**. This can be done through the WebUI or through a CLI. This command uses TFTP to upgrade partition 1 with a new copy of the OS:

```
#copy tftp: 192.168.240.150 ArubaOS_70xx_6.4.2.0_45199 system: partition 1
Copying file:................
File copied successfully.
Saving file to flash:
............................
The system will boot from partition 1 during the next reboot.
```

Notice that after the partition is upgraded, it is automatically configured as the boot partition. This means that the next time the controller is booted, the OS in partition 1 will be used. If you do not want to use partition 1 as the boot partition just yet, the following command will allow you to specify the boot partition. In this example, the boot partition is being set back to partition 0.

```
#boot system partition 0
```

You can also upgrade the controller OS from the WebUI interface, as shown in Figure 3.5. As you can see, the OS file can be copied from one of numerous locations: TFTP server, FTP server, SCP server, local file on the computer that you are using to access the WebUI, or USB flash drive plugged into the controller. To upgrade the system partition with a newer version of the OS, go to **Maintenance ➢ CONTROLLER ➢ Image Management ➢ Master Configuration**.

To upgrade the OS using a USB flash drive, refer to the "Using LCD Screen" section of the ArubaOS User Guide or the product documentation that you received with the controller hardware.

FIGURE 3.5
OS Image Management menu

Flash Partition

The flash partition is essentially where all of your configuration and working files are stored, as illustrated previously in Figure 3.4. Although it is called the flash partition, you can think of it as the user partition. Some of the files can be viewed through the WebUI or the CLI, while other files are hidden from the administrator. The `dir` command will display the visible contents of the flash partition, as shown here.

```
#dir

-rw-r--r--    1 root     root        4528 Feb  8 05:11 AUDITTRAIL-HISTORY.log
-rw-r--r--    1 root     root       23907 Feb 11 03:44 default.bak
-rw-r--r--    1 root     root       23907 Feb 10 03:36 default.cfg
drwxr-xr-x    3 root     root        4096 Jul 30  2014 fieldCerts
-rw-r--r--    1 root     root       23656 Feb 11 03:44 flashbackup.tar.gz
-rw-r--r--    1 root     root        1796 Feb  8 02:44 license.txt
-rw-r--r--    1 root     root     2733056 Feb 12 02:50 logs.tar
-rw-r--r--    1 root     root       12788 Jan 24 12:55 original.cfg
drwx------    2 root     root        4096 Jul 30  2014 tpm
```

Let us take a quick look at the contents of this particular controller that are displayed in the directory listing.

AUDITTRAIL-HISTORY.log Created by the operating system, the log contains the last 50 commands that were executed prior to the reboot of the controller. This file is updated when the controller is rebooted.

default.cfg   This is the startup-config file, unless the controller has been programmed to use a different file as the startup-config, which is rarely done.

default.bak and original.cfg   These are backup copies of the startup-config file. I created these using the following command:

```
#copy startup-config flash: default.bak
#copy startup-config flash: original.cfg
```

fieldCerts and tpm   These are two directories created by the operating system that you do not have access to.

flashbackup.tar.gz   This is a backup of the directories and the files in the flash directories. This is a compressed tar file and is created using the following command. This file can be used to recover the controller if a disaster occurs or when migrating to new controllers.

```
#backup flash
```

license.txt   This is a text file that I generate on all controllers that I work on. It is an SQL dump of the licensedb database. When this file is generated, it contains all of the licenses that are installed on the controller at the time that the command is executed. If the controller needs to be rebuilt, all of the licenses can be easily imported back into the controller from this file. You can give the file any name; however, I think the word *license* should be part of the name. Although this file does not display the licenses, it is a text file created from the licenses database, and can be copied from the flash partition to a computer and then opened with a text editor, displaying the license keys. In the first command that follows, I exported the licenses to the file, and in the second command I imported the licenses from the file back into the controller:

```
#license export license.txt
Successfully exported 4 licenses from the license database to license.txt

#license import license.txt
Successfully imported 4 licenses to the license database from license.txt;
please reload to make licenses take effect
```

logs.tar   This is an archive of all of the logs. If you are experiencing a problem with the controller and decide to reboot the controller to see if it will fix the problem, *please* tar the logs prior to rebooting the controller. While the controller is running, the log files are created and stored in RAM. When a controller is rebooted, the log files are deleted, removing the ability to review any of the logs relating to the problem. This file is often requested by technical support. The file is created using either of the following commands. The second version will include additional technical support information.

When working with Aruba's Technical Assistance Center (TAC) team, it is common for them to ask you to provide the tech-support logs to assist in troubleshooting.

```
#tar logs
#tar logs tech-support
```

As with most file systems, you can manipulate or delete files. The following are some of the commands that can be used. It is good to be familiar with these commands, since it is necessary to copy files, such as logs, off the controller to analyze them. Please use these carefully, as you can get yourself into trouble.

- dir
- copy
- rename
- delete

The following CLI output shows examples using these commands. The first command copies the `logs.tar` file from the flash partition to an FTP server at IP address 192.168.240.31. The FTP username is `david`, `ftp-files` is the subdirectory on the FTP server where the file will be copied, and `logs-10-5.tar` will be the new name of the file when it is saved on the FTP server. The next command renames the `logs.tar` file, which resides on the flash/user partition. The new filename is `logs-2016-10-5.tar`. The final command deletes the `logs-2016-10-5.tar` file from the flash/user partition.

```
# copy flash: logs.tar ftp: 192.168.240.31 david ftp-files logs-10-5.tar
Password:********

# rename logs.tar logs-2016-10-5.tar

# delete filename logs-2016-10-5.tar
```

CPBoot

The only reason why I am explaining CPBoot is because I have had many students who entered into the cpboot prompt without knowing how it happened. CPBoot is a core operating environment and set of commands that can be loaded from the hardware ROM. Think of this as similar to the BIOS or UEFI shell of your computer. This provides the controller with a set of initialization commands in the event that system partitions 0 and 1 (which contains the OS) becomes corrupted. During the initial booting of the controller, there is a five-second window, during which you can hit the Enter/Return key and interrupt the controller boot process, placing the controller at the cpboot prompt, as show here:

```
Hit any key to stop autoboot:   0
cpboot>
```

At the cpboot prompt there are many system commands and tests that can get you into trouble if you do not use them properly. If you ever wind up at the cpboot prompt, simply type boot. This will continue the boot process from the point where the boot process was interrupted, and it will use the default settings. Your system will complete its boot process as if nothing happened.

Saving Changes

I want to further dissect the process of making changes to the controller, so that you fully understand what is happening. Please take the time to read this section, because I think it gives a simple and complete overview of making changes on the controller. Figure 3.6 shows the flow of how changes are saved to the controller. As mentioned previously, the startup-config file is stored within the user partition on the NVRAM flash, and is typically the default.cfg file. When the controller boots, the startup-config is copied to the RAM creating the running-config, as illustrated in Step 1. In order for a CLI command to modify the running-config, two things must happen. First, the command must be syntactically correct. If it is not a valid command, it will not work. The second thing that must happen is that you must hit the Enter/Return key on the keyboard. This is illustrated in Step 2. I know this is rudimentary for me to be describing, but as I stated, I am dissecting the process, so go with me on this for a moment. It is the action of hitting of the Enter/Return key that lets the system know to process the command that you just typed.

FIGURE 3.6 Saving changes

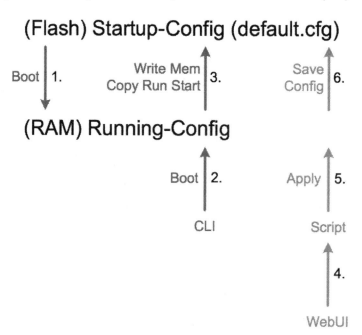

At this point, the command becomes part of the running-config. As shown, the running-config is stored in RAM. Therefore, if you were to lose power at this time, your changes would not be saved. To make sure that you do not lose your changes, you can copy the running-config file and overwrite the startup-config with it, by using either of the following commands, illustrated in Figure 3.6, Step 3. Note that when you issue either command, you are not just saving the "changes" that were made; you are copying the running-config and overwriting the startup-config.

```
#copy running-config startup-config
Saving Configuration...
Configuration Saved.

#write memory
Saving Configuration...
Configuration Saved.
```

Now let us take a look at what happens when you make changes using the WebUI. As you click on buttons or enter information on one of the WebUI screens, the controller builds a CLI script of the changes that you are making, as illustrated in Step 4. If you like the changes that you have made, you can click the Apply button at the bottom-right corner of the screen to execute the script, as illustrated in Step 5. If you do not like what you have done, you can simply choose another menu at the top of the screen or along the side of the screen, and the controller will erase the current script.

At this point, if you have clicked the Apply button, the script has been executed and the changes have become part of the running-config. As noted earlier, the running-config is stored in RAM. If you want to make these changes permanent, you need to click on the Save Configuration button at the top middle of the screen. This is equivalent to a `write memory`, as illustrated in Step 6. You could also issue the `copy running-config startup-config` or `write memory` command from the CLI.

If you are operating an Aruba network that includes a master controller and one or more local controllers, saving changes is slightly more complex. Global configuration settings are made on the master controller. These changes are saved to the RAM of the master controller when the CLI command is executed or you click the Apply button in the WebUI. These changes are not pushed to any of the local controllers until the configuration is saved to the startup-config, by clicking on the Save Configuration button in the WebUI of the master controller, or by issuing the `copy running-config startup-config` or `write memory` command from the CLI or the master controller.

View Commands/Hide Commands

A really cool feature of ArubaOS is that you can view the script of commands that has been created from the configuration changes made with the WebUI. As I explained in the previous section, when you make changes in the WebUI, the controller builds a CLI script of the changes that you are making. At the bottom of the screen is a Commands header, and at the right side of this header, just below the Apply button is a text link: View Commands. When you click on this text, in the Commands section, ArubaOS will display the current CLI script that the system has generated, and the View Commands link will change to Hide Commands, as shown in Figure 3.7. I need to point out that the script that is displayed shows the commands at the time that you clicked on the View Commands link. I mention this because if you make additional changes in the WebUI, these changes are updated in the script; however, what is displayed at the bottom of the screen is not updated. If you want to see the updated script, you will need to click the Hide Commands link to erase what is displayed, and then click the View Commands link to display the current iteration of the script.

FIGURE 3.7
View commands

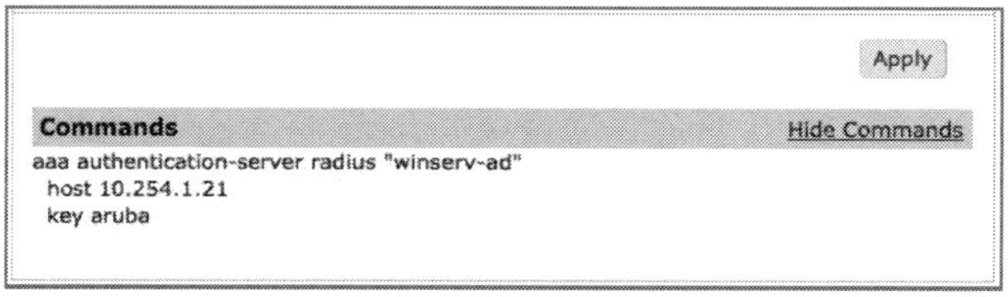

```
Commands                                          Hide Commands
aaa authentication-server radius "winserv-ad"
    host 10.254.1.21
    key aruba
```

When the script is displayed, you can highlight the commands and copy them. You can then paste them into a CLI or into a document. I find the View Commands link very useful for learning and understanding the function of some of the buttons and fields in the WebUI. I often will make changes in the WebUI and then click the View Commands link just to see what changes would be made. As long as you do not click the Apply button, the script is not executed. Simply click another menu on the top or left of the screen and the script will be erased.

Resetting Controller to Factory Defaults

At times, it is necessary to reset a controller to factory defaults. Unfortunately, performing this task is often misunderstood, and even the documentation can be misleading. Rather than saying I am resetting the controller to factory defaults, I say it is "functionally equivalent" to a factory default controller. To do this, you need to issue the command write erase all, as shown in the following CLI output:

```
# write erase all
Switch will be factory defaulted. All the configuration and databases will be
deleted. Press 'y' to proceed :
Write Erase successful
```

The write erase all command (do not forget the all) performs three key tasks. The first task this command performs is to reset the startup-config file to factory default configuration. The second task this command performs is to delete the license key management database. The final task that this command performs is to delete all of the operating databases on the controller, including the wireless management system (WMS) database along with the AP and user databases. When you reboot the controller, it will be functionally equivalent to a factory default controller.

You may wonder why I phrase it the way I do: functionally equivalent to a factory default controller. It is because any files that you created in the flash partition do not get deleted. So the files illustrated previously in Figure 3.4 (`default.bak`, `flashbackup.tar.gz`, `license.txt`, `logs.tar`, and `original.cfg`) would not be deleted. This is important, because these files on the flash partition can be used to rebuild or restore your controller.

So what happens if you just entered the `write erase` command? Well, the only file that would be erased is the startup-config file. I have seen many people use the `write erase` command because the license database does not get erased, and therefore when they have to rebuild the controller, they do not have to reenter the licenses. This is true; however, none of the other databases are deleted either, which can cause problems later.

My recommendation is to always use the `write erase all` command when resetting the controller. Make sure that you have created a `license.txt` file by using the `license export license.txt` command that was described earlier in this chapter. The `licenses.txt` file will provide an easy way to reinstall the licenses.

CHAPTER 4

Getting Started

IN THIS CHAPTER, YOU WILL LEARN ABOUT THE FOLLOWING:

- Initial Setup Menu
  - Initial Setup Objectives
  - CLI Setup Wizard
  - WebUI Setup Wizard
- Licensing
  - Adding Licenses
- Networking Basics
  - CLI Configuration
  - WebUI Configuration
- Access Point Configuration
  - AP Console CLI
  - Controller WebUI-AP Installation
  - Controller WebUI-AP Wizard
  - Provision-AP Controller CLI Command

THE FIRST STEP IN CONFIGURING ANY NEW ARUBA controller is to perform a basic initial setup. When discussing the initial setup of the controller, it is important to define boundaries of what *initial setup* means. This chapter will focus on the steps needed to make the controller a communicative device on the network, along with the installation of licenses. This section will not address centralized licensing, which will be covered in Chapter 10, "Network Expansion."

The first three chapters provided an overview of 802.11 wireless networking followed by a review of the Aruba architecture, hardware, and software products. In this chapter you will learn how to perform the initial setup of the controller and access points, along with some of the fundamental TCP/IP configuration that is typically needed. Since this is a book about ArubaOS and not about network configuration, it will be assumed that you have TCP/IP, VLAN, and networking knowledge and experience.

Remember that the goal of this book is to help you understand ArubaOS. As you are reading this chapter, and especially if you are using it to help you configure a controller, think about what you are trying to accomplish. Aruba often changes and enhances the OS. By the time you read this chapter, the menus, fields, or CLI commands on the controller may be different from what is in this book. Welcome to the world of networking.

Initial Setup Menu

Initial configuration of an Aruba controller can be performed using either a CLI or a WebUI wizard. The CLI initial setup process requires a CLI terminal connection, discussed in the previous chapter. The WebUI initial setup requires an Ethernet connection configured for DHCP, and of course a web browser. In both instances, the controller needs to either be a brand-new controller or a controller that has been returned to factory defaults by issuing the `write erase all` CLI command, as explained in Chapter 3, "Aruba Controller and Software Overview."

I highly recommend using the console connection and the CLI initial setup to configure your controller. The CLI provides much more control and flexibility compared to the WebUI Setup Wizard, due to the simplicity of the CLI and the fact that the controller does not have to be on the network to configure it. Although I prefer to use the CLI interface to initially set up the controller, the procedure for configuring the controller using the WebUI Setup Wizard is also discussed since it is part of the OS and a valid method to configure the controller.

Although this chapter is not intended to be a step-by-step setup guide, I hope to provide with you with an understanding of the process and the tools necessary to perform the initial configuration of your controller. The "Networking Basics" section will provide you with many IP and port configuration commands; however, the command descriptions and explanations will be kept to a minimum since you should already have TCP/IP and networking skills.

Initial Setup Objectives

Before configuring any controller, you need to have a plan. You need to know how the controller will fit into the overall network and how the wireless user's data will be processed. This will allow you to document some key pieces of information: the name of the controller, the IP address and gateway, individual port settings, licenses, and other parameters. In order to walk you through the steps in this book, we also need a plan and an objective, so listed next is the summary of the goals for this chapter. Note that only a small part of this configuration will be performed using either of the initial setup wizards. I find it is better to use the wizards for just the basics, and then do the rest from the controller's primary configuration interfaces: either the CLI or the WebUI.

After the CLI Setup Wizard is explained, the "CLI Configuration" section of the "Networking Basics" portion of this chapter will explain the rest of the necessary commands. Also, after the WebUI Setup Wizard is explained, the "WebUI Configuration" section of the "Networking Basics" portion of this chapter will explain the rest of the procedure necessary to complete the configuration (yes, there are quite a few things that need to be configured—and this is a simple network design). Here are the setup components for this chapter.

Controller:
   Aruba 7010

Hostname:
   7010-50

Licenses needed:
   16 AP licenses
   16 PEF-NG licenses
   16 RFProtect licenses

IP address and VLANs:
   VLAN 50 IP: 10.1.50.101/24 (management VLAN)
   VLAN 51 IP: 10.1.51.2/24 (employee VLAN)
   VLAN 53 IP: 192.168.5.1/24 (guest VLAN)

DHCP helper address:
   VLANs 50 and 51: 10.254.1.21

Enable controller as DHCP server for VLAN 53

Port configuration:
   Port 0/0/0
      Mode: trunk
      Native VLAN 50
      Allowed VLANs 50, 51
   Ports 0/0/1–0/17
      Mode: access ports, VLAN 50

Default gateway: 10.1.50.1

Controller-IP: IP of VLAN 50

NTP server: 10.254.1.21

CLI Setup Wizard

The best way to start the CLI setup process is to enable your console connection on your computer (as explained in Chapter 3, "Aruba Controller and Software Overview") prior to powering on your controller. This allows you to watch the screen output as the controller starts up. If you are configuring a cloud services (branch office) controller, then you will be prompted with the auto-provisioning menu, as displayed in the following CLI output.

```
Starting auto provisioning
Using port gigabitethernet 0/0/15 for auto provisioning
Initiated DHCP, awaiting DHCP response

Auto-provisioning is in progress. Choose one of the following options to
override or debug...
    'enable-debug'  : Enable auto-provisioning debug logs
    'disable-debug' : Disable auto-provisioning debug logs
    'mini-setup'    : Stop auto-provisioning and start mini setup dialog for
branch role
    'full-setup'    : Stop auto-provisioning and start full setup dialog for
any role

Enter Option (partial string is acceptable):
```

For now, we will focus on the configuration of a master controller. You can begin this process by typing **full-setup** or by just typing **f**, since a partial string is acceptable. After typing **full-setup**, or if the controller is an earlier model and is not a branch office controller, then you will be prompted to enter the system name, as displayed in the CLI output that follows:

```
***************** Welcome to the Aruba7010 setup dialog *****************
This dialog will help you to set the basic configuration for the switch.
These settings, except for the Country Code, can later be changed from the
Command Line Interface or Graphical User Interface.


Commands: <Enter> Submit input or use [default value], <ctrl-I> Help
<ctrl-B> Back, <ctrl-F> Forward, <ctrl-A> Line begin, <ctrl-E> Line end
<ctrl-D> Delete, <BackSpace> Delete back, <ctrl-K> Delete to end of line
<ctrl-P> Previous question <ctrl-X> Restart beginning

Enter System name [Aruba7010]:
```

If you boot the controller before enabling your console software, the beginning of the setup may not be as smooth. After the console software starts up on your computer, it is a common practice to hit the Return/Enter key on the keyboard to see if you have connectivity with the controller. If you do this, you will inadvertently respond to the first question and accept the default system name, and move to the next question. If this occurs, do not worry; you can either press Ctrl+X to return to the beginning of the setup dialog, or press Ctrl+P to move back to the previous question. If you have responded to multiple questions, you can move back through the questions by pressing Ctrl+P multiple times. Each successive Ctrl+P will move to the previous question, until ultimately you will be back at the initial system name prompt. All of the Ctrl command options are displayed at the beginning of the setup dialog, as shown in the previous CLI output.

The CLI setup dialog prompts you to enter over a dozen settings, as shown in the following CLI output. If a line has text enclosed in square brackets, such as `[Aruba7010]`, that is the current default value for the line, and hitting the Return/Enter key will accept that value. If you do not want to accept the default value, enter a new value and hit Return/Enter.

```
Enter System name [Aruba7010]:
Enter Switch Role (master|local|standalone|branch) [master]:
Enter VLAN 1 interface IP address [172.16.0.254]:
Enter VLAN 1 interface subnet mask [255.255.255.0]:
Enter IP Default gateway [none]:
Do you wish to configure IPV6 address on vlan 1 (yes|no) [yes]:
Enter VLAN 1 interface IPV6 address [2001::1]:
Enter VLAN 1 interface IPV6 prefix length [64]:
Enter IPV6 default gateway [none]:
This controller is restricted, please enter country code
(US|PR|GU|VI|MP|AS|FM|MH) [US]:You have chosen Country code US for United States (yes|no)?:
Enter Time Zone [PST-8:0]:
Enter Time in UTC [12:09:43]:
Enter Date (MM/DD/YYYY) [5/18/2015]:
Enter Password for admin login (up to 32 chars): ******
Re-type Password for admin login: ******
Enter Password for enable mode (up to 15 chars): ******
Re-type Password for enable mode: ******
Do you wish to shutdown all the ports (yes|no)? [no]:
```

We will walk through each of the configuration steps below.

`Enter System name [Aruba7010]:`

This is where you set the hostname of the controller. It is simply a logical name to distinguish one controller from another. After the controller has been configured and rebooted, you can change the system name by simply typing `hostname 7010-50` at the CLI prompt. So do not worry if you change your mind later.

`Enter Switch Role (master|local|standalone|branch) [master]:`

This is where you set the switch role. Unless you are configuring a branch controller, you should always select master for the switch role, even if this is going to be a local controller connected to a master controller. If the new controller is going to be deployed as a local controller, it is important to make sure that it has the same ArubaOS on it as the master controller before joining them. By configuring the new controller as a master, you can configure it by itself, upgrade it, and then convert it to a local controller, joining it to your corporate master controller.

Before we move on to the next menu selections, I need to explain a term that was just used: *switch role*. In the early days of wireless controllers, many controllers had multiple

Ethernet ports to provide a way for APs to directly connect to the controllers. These controllers were access layer devices, supporting layer 2 and sometimes layer 3 networking. Layer 2 and layer 3 devices are typically known as *switches* in the networking world, and the original wireless controllers were known as *wireless switches*. As time went by, it became apparent that these devices provided many more capabilities than switches, and the industry transitioned to calling them *wireless controllers*. Although *wireless controller* is the better term, it is still common to see the term *wireless switch* used.

```
Enter VLAN 1 interface IP address [172.16.0.254]:
Enter VLAN 1 interface subnet mask [255.255.255.0]:
Enter IP Default gateway [none]:
Do you wish to configure IPV6 address on vlan 1 (yes|no) [yes]:
Enter VLAN 1 interface IPV6 address [2001::1]:
Enter VLAN 1 interface IPV6 prefix length [64]:
Enter IPV6 default gateway [none]:
```

This group of settings is for VLAN 1 IP parameters. VLAN 1 is typically disabled for security reasons, so you should just accept the default values. Later in this chapter in the "Networking Basics" section, you will learn how to create and configure other VLANs. You may want to enter no at the prompt Do you wish to configure IPV6 address on vlan 1 (yes|no). If you do want to configure IPV6, you can do so later. Note that the default value for configuring IPV6 is yes, so you might want to override the default value.

```
This controller is restricted, please enter country code
(US|PR|GU|VI|MP|AS|FM|MH) [US]:
You have chosen Country code US for United States (yes|no)?: yes
```

or

```
Enter Country code (ISO-3166), <ctrl-I> for supported list:
```

You must now specify the country code of your controller. This example is from a US-regulated controller. Earlier versions of the ArubaOS simply asked you to confirm this fact. The list in the previous example defaults to US and allows you to set the controller country code to a US territory (e.g., PR is Puerto Rico). If you are installing the controller in the United States, Israel, or Japan, you must purchase the hardware model specific to that country (these part numbers will end in -US, -IL, and -JP respectively), and you will have no choice but to confirm the country code for one of these countries. This is a restriction/requirement imposed by the regulatory agency of each of these countries.

If you are installing the controller for any other country, referred to as a *Rest of World controller*, then you will need to enter the two-digit ISO-3166 country code. If you do not know the code, you can hit Ctrl+I to display the list of available country codes. After the list is displayed, you will be prompted again to enter the code.

```
Enter Time Zone [PST-8:0]:
```

```
Enter Time in UTC [12:09:43]:
Enter Date (MM/DD/YYYY) [5/18/2015]:
```

At this point, you are prompted for date and time information. Later in this chapter you will learn how to define a Network Time Protocol (NTP) server; however, at this time you should enter the correct time zone, time, and date. The time zone is for the location where the controller is installed, and the time and date is entered for Coordinated Universal Time (UTC), which is also known as Greenwich Mean Time (GMT) or Zulu time.

The easiest way to determine the time zone is to search the Internet for the time for the location of the controller, using keywords such as "Boston time." From there, one of the date and time websites will provide you with the time zone and offset. This needs to be entered in the format displayed in the previous prompt. So, for Boston the time zone would be EST-5:0 or EDT-4:0. When entering the time, be sure to enter the hours, minutes, and seconds. And finally, make sure you enter the date in the format MM/DD/YYYY. As was previously mentioned, later in the chapter you will learn how to override these settings and define an NTP server.

```
Enter Password for admin login (up to 32 chars): ******
Re-type Password for admin login: ******
Enter Password for enable mode (up to 15 chars): ******
Re-type Password for enable mode: ******
```

The next step is to set the admin and enable passwords. This is easily done by entering and then retyping each of the passwords. Both the admin and enable passwords need to be at least six characters long.

```
Do you wish to shutdown all the ports (yes|no)? [no]:
```

The final step before confirming your answers is to specify whether the ports should be initially configured as up (no) or down (yes). Enabling or disabling the ports is a security decision that you need to make. After you choose yes or no and specify the port state, the configuration script will display all of the current settings that you just defined (seen in the following CLI output). The script will then give you the option to accept the settings or not (also seen here). If you do, the settings will be saved and the controller will reboot using the configuration you just specified. If you do not accept the changes, then the script will be restarted from the beginning. Instead of answering yes or no, you can use Ctrl+P to step back through your answers, allowing you to individually change any setting without starting over.

```
Current choices are:

System name: 7010-50
Switch Role: master
VLAN 1 interface IP address: 172.16.0.254
VLAN 1 interface subnet mask: 255.255.255.0
```

```
Option to configure VLAN 1 interface IPV6 address: no
Country code: US
Time Zone: EDT-4:0
Ports shutdown: no

If you accept the changes the switch will restart!
Type <ctrl-P> to go back and change answer for any question
Do you wish to accept the changes (yes|no)
```

WebUI Setup Wizard

In order to use a browser to initially configure a controller, it is necessary for the controller and the client station to be able to communicate with each other using TCP/IP. So how is it that a new unconfigured controller, or one that has been erased and reset to factory defaults, can be configured using TCP/IP and a web browser?

A factory default controller is automatically configured with an IP address of 172.16.0.254 and acts as a DHCP server for the 172.16.0.0/24 network. *Spanning tree*, a network protocol that is used to prevent network bridging loops, is also enabled by default while in this initial state. You should keep this controller isolated by not connecting it to your corporate network until after it is configured. To begin the configuration process, connect a computer to one of the Fast Ethernet or Gigabit Ethernet ports of the controller, and the computer will get a 172.16.0.0/24 IP address from the controller. Since, in this scenario, Gigabit Ethernet port 0/0/0 is going to be configured as a trunk port, we will assume that the computer will be connected to Gigabit Ethernet port 0/0/1.

From the computer, you can browse to the controller address of 172.16.0.254 and use the Mobility Controller Setup Wizard initial setup to configure the controller. Initially, you may be prompted that the web certificate is invalid. Accept this certificate to proceed to the Mobility Controller Setup window, shown in Figure 4.1.

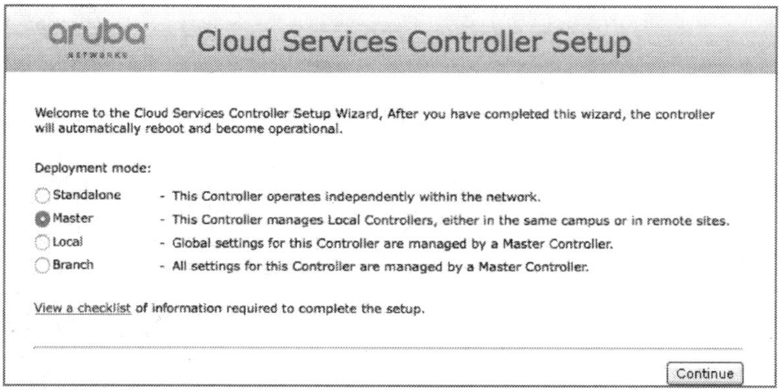

FIGURE 4.1 Mobility Controller Setup window

As stated previously in this chapter, I r
initially as a master controller, even if it i
like the recommendation from the cor
is indeed going to operate as your mas
need to be changed. If the controller
it initially as a master will allow you
important for a local controller to
update the OS first, and then con

From the Mobility Controller
and then click the Continue but
dow, shown in Figure 4.2, prompt
WLANs, and then click the Continue but

FIGURE 4.2
Deployment mode

FIGURE 4.3
Basic information

In this next window, you will start to enter some of the key controller parameters, as shown in Figure 4.3. The basic information window prompts you for the controller name, country code, admin password, and enable password. The time zone is for the location where the controller is installed and the time and date is entered for UTC. You also have the option of entering the IP address of an NTP server instead of entering the date and time. After entering this information, click the Next button to move to the next window.

The Licenses window allows you to add your licenses to the controller, as shown in Figure 4.4. Each license key is entered one at a time. If this is a master controller, you may want to enter your keys at this time. If this is going to be a local controller, you most likely will install the licenses on the master controller and use centralized licensing to distribute the licenses. Therefore, you probably would not install the licenses on this controller. Regardless of whether you are installing licenses, you will click the Next button to move to the next window.

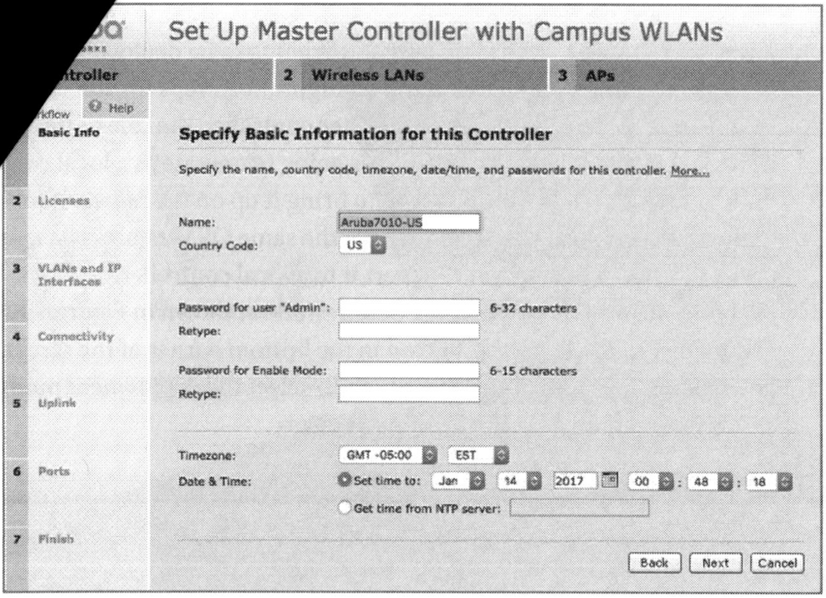

FIGURE 4.4
Licenses menu

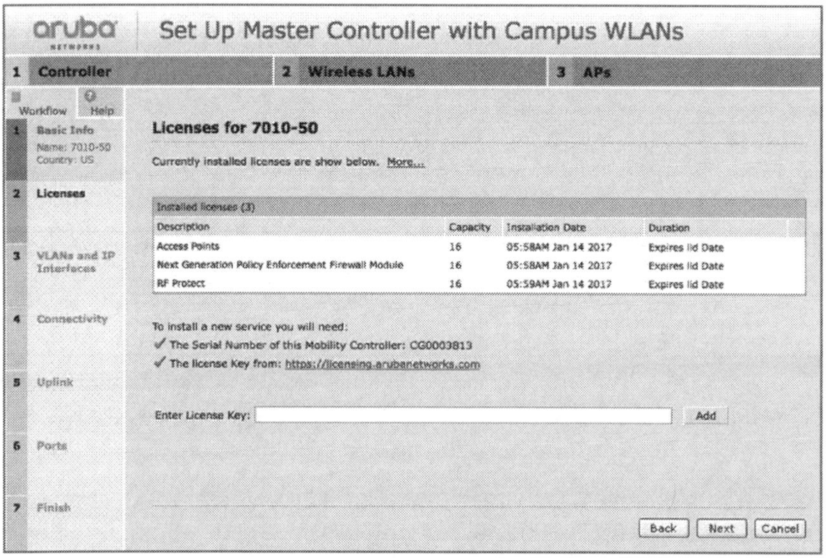

If you are configuring the controller using TCP/IP and an Ethernet connection, you will most likely want to continue interacting with the controller using the network connection after the initial configuration is completed. To do this you will need to configure port and IP settings to ensure that you can communicate with the controller when it reboots.

In this example, the controller will be configured with VLAN 50 as its management VLAN, with an IP address of 10.1.50.101/24. This VLAN will also be assigned to all of the ports.

The first step is to create a named VLAN by clicking the New button and entering the VLAN name, as shown in Figure 4.5. This figure shows the creation of the VLAN named management. The VLAN name is simply a label so you can easily identify the VLAN.

FIGURE 4.5
Configuring VLANs and IP interfaces

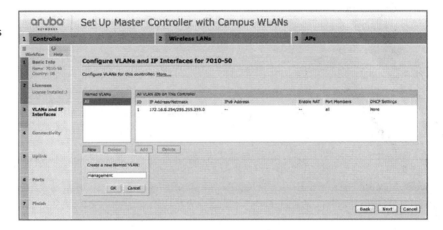

After clicking OK to create the named VLAN, you need to create a new VLAN ID. This ID will then be added to the management VLAN. For this example the VLAN ID will be 50, the IP address will be 10.1.50.101, and the subnet mask will be 255.255.255.0. Then, the VLAN needs to be added to the ports. When adding the VLAN ID to the ports, the Available column shows which ports the VLAN can be assigned to. You can click or Ctrl+click one or more ports and then click > to move them to the Selected column. You can also click >> to move all of the ports to the selected column. The < and << buttons can be used to unselect one or more ports. In this example, the management VLAN will be assigned to all of the ports.

At this point we will not create any other VLANs, although you could. Figure 4.6 shows management VLAN 50 is created and assigned to all of the ports. The Next button will move us to the Connectivity window.

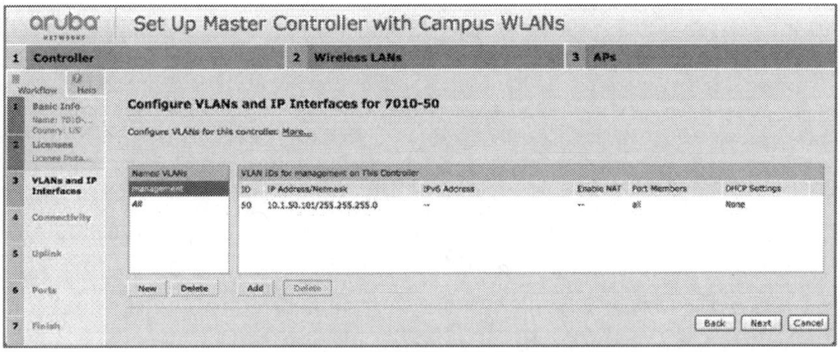

FIGURE 4.6
VLAN and IP configuration

Two very important settings should be made on the Connectivity window: the controller IP address and the default gateway. The default gateway will typically be set as static, and in this example, the gateway address is 10.1.50.1. You should already be familiar with the function of a default gateway.

The next setting, which is very important, is the controller IP address. It is possible and likely that a controller will have multiple IP addresses. When the controller transmits a frame to another network device, it needs to use one of these IP addresses as the source address for the frame. The controller IP address defines the VLAN that the frame will be sourced from. This is especially important with RADIUS authentication, since the RADIUS server is programmed to communicate with the controller using a specific IP address. These settings are shown in Figure 4.7.

Another option on this screen is to set the security parameters for this master controller to communicate with its local controllers. In Chapter 10, "Network Expansion," you will learn more about master-local communications and how they are set up, so for now we will skip this step.

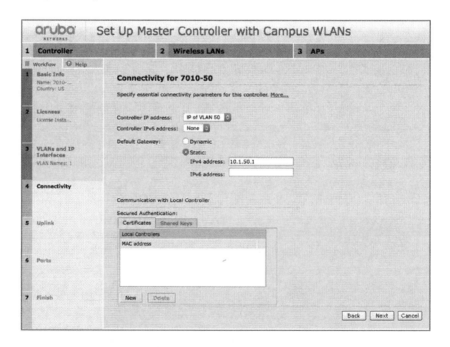

FIGURE 4.7 Connectivity

The next window prompts for uplink information, shown in Figure 4.8. Some Aruba controllers have USB ports that can allow you to use a USB cellular modem as an uplink port. The cellular uplink would typically be used as a backup link for a smaller branch office network. The Uplink menu page allows you to set firewall settings to specify which data you will allow to traverse the uplink connection. You can also specify the primary and secondary links. So if your controller was connected to a cable modem or DSL connection using an Ethernet cable, you would set the wired connection as your primary connection and the cellular as your secondary (backup) link. Figure 4.8 shows the uplink firewall and manager enabled just so that you can see the options. These would typically not be enabled.

FIGURE 4.8
Uplink

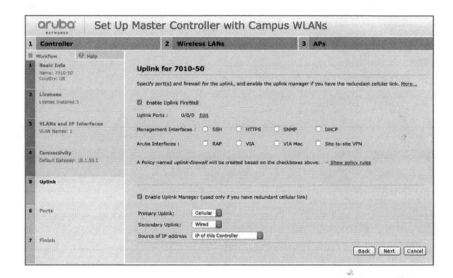

The next menu is the Configure Ports menu, which is shown in Figure 4.9. On this menu you can modify settings individually for each port. The concept of *trusted* and *untrusted* is explained elsewhere in this book. The rest of the settings are network and port settings that you should already be familiar with. These settings include:

- Port enabled/disabled
- PoE enabled/disabled
- Trusted/untrusted
- Port speed 10/100/1000/auto
- Duplex auto/full/half
- Native VLAN
- Trunk mode enable/disabled
- Supported VLANs for trunk mode

In this example, all ports will be kept with the settings of enable, PoE, trusted, and auto/auto for port speed and duplex. Gigabit port 0/0/0 will be configured as trunk mode with the native VLAN and VLANs for trunk mode both being set to 50. Below the ports section, STP should be disabled. Click Next to move to the next window where the configuration will be completed.

FIGURE 4.9
Configure Ports

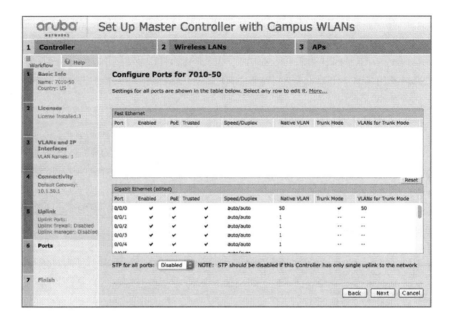

In the middle of the Ready to Push Configuration window, at the end of the paragraph of text is the Finish Now link. After clicking this link, a summary of the configuration will be displayed in a scrollable window. Below this window are two links, one that will allow you to print the configuration summary and another that will allow you to see the commands that will be pushed to the controller. Clicking the Finish button in the bottom-right corner will complete the installation process, push the configuration to the controller, and reboot the controller.

After the controller reboots, if you want to connect to it using the Ethernet connection, you will need to manually configure an IP address on your client computer. Since the IP address of this controller is 10.1.50.101, any address on this subnet, such as 10.1.50.10/24, should work. After the controller reboots and your IP address is configured on your computer, you should be able to SSH or browse into the controller to continue configuring it.

Licensing

At this point in the chapter, you have learned how to perform the initial configuration of an Aruba controller. Let us now look at what is needed to install the licenses. To begin with, when you purchase a license, you will receive a license certificate ID. Using the licensing website, this certificate ID needs to be linked to the serial number of the controller, which will generate an activation key. The activation key will be entered into the controller to enable the license on the controller.

Prior to centralized licensing, each controller would need a set of licenses. With centralized licensing, it is simplest to link all of the licenses to the serial number of your master controller. Centralized licensing will then make these licenses available to all of the participating controllers. You will learn about centralized licensing in Chapter 10, "Network Expansion".

To create the activation key, go to Aruba's licensing website. If you do not have an account, you can create an account using the certificate ID. Using your license login account, you will need to log in to create the activation key. Make sure that you use the same license login account to activate all of the licenses. In the future, if you need to look up any information about the licenses or if you need to transfer the license to a new controller, it is easiest if they are all linked to the same account.

Adding Licenses

Once you have the activation key, adding the license to the controller requires a simple command, `license add` followed by the activation key, as shown in the following CLI command. You do not need to be in configure terminal mode when adding licenses. The command output states that the operating system needs to be reloaded to enable the new functionality. You can install multiple licenses before rebooting the controller.

```
#License add xc1J+7lK-VrUnP+XN-mjIazi9Z-DSoI3+bv-imWTLax
Limits updated.
Please reload the switch to enable the new functionality.
```

You can see the installed licenses by issuing the following CLI command. Note that in order to shorten the amount of output on each line and make the output easier to read, the output of the `show license` command was edited. The license keys were shortened by about 20 characters.

```
#show license

License Table
-------------
Key                         Installed      Expires  Flags  Service Type
---                         ---------      -------  -----  ------------
CP5nfoJb-WybzdupC-YiofD     2015-05-14     Never    ER     Next Generation Policy
Enforcement Firewall Module: 16
                            19:51:19
xc1J+7lK-VrUnP+XN-mjIaz     2015-05-14     Never    ER     Access Points: 16
                            19:50:07
QsenPoda-qKMR+/At-/Kvue     2015-05-14     Never    ER     RF Protect: 16
                            19:53:03

License Entries: 3

Flags: A - auto-generated; E - enabled; R - reboot required to activate
```

When the licenses are installed, the E flag indicates that they are enabled, and the R flag indicates that you need to reboot the controller to activate them. Whenever you add a new feature, such as the firewall license, you will need to reboot the controller. However, if you are just increasing the license count for a feature that is already installed, a reboot is not required. Prior to rebooting the controller, the running configuration should be saved. The following two CLI commands will save the configuration and reboot the controller.

```
#write memory
#reload
```

When you issue the show license command, the keys that are displayed on the screen are the actual keys that were used with the license add command. If for some reason you do not have access to the licensing website, you can copy these keys and save them to a file or e-mail, should you ever need them in the future. Note that since each license is activated to a specific controller's serial number, each key can be used only on the controller to which it was issued.

If you want to see the license limits installed on a controller, the following CLI command will provide you with that information.

```
#show license limits

License Limits
--------------
Limit  Value
-----  -----
16     Access Points
16     RF Protect
0      xSec Module
0      120abg Upgrade
0      121abg Upgrade
0      124abg Upgrade
0      125abg Upgrade
16     Next Generation Policy Enforcement Firewall Module
0      Advanced Cryptography
0      Service provider AP
0      WebCC
0      Beta AP
```

As explained in Chapter 3, "Aruba Controller and Software Overview," the following CLI commands show how to create or export the licenses to a license file, along with how to import the licenses from a license file that you have already created. Note that *Licenses* is simply the name chosen for the output file. This file can be named whatever you like.

```
#license export Licenses
Successfully exported 3 licenses from the license database to Licenses
```

```
#license import Licenses
Successfully imported 3 licenses to the license database from Licenses; please
reload to make licenses take effect
```

Networking Basics

Neither of the initial setup methods are designed to fully configure a controller. They are designed to make the controller operational on your network, allowing you to configure the controller using a terminal session, the WebUI, or the wizards (which are part of the WebUI). You will learn about many of the common tasks that Aruba Systems Engineers, partners, and customers perform when installing and configuring a controller.

This section has been divided into two subsections: CLI and WebUI. Each subsection will explain and describe some of the common tasks and show how to perform them. All of these tasks will be based on the initial setup objectives that were defined previously in the "Initial Setup Objectives" section of this chapter.

The CLI section describes and explains the configuration commands that you need to issue after running the CLI initial setup. The WebUI describes and explains the configuration steps you need to perform after running the WebUI Setup Wizard.

CLI Configuration

As mentioned previously, the CLI provides the most power and flexibility for configuring the controller. This section will show many of the core commands used when configuring a controller, along with brief explanations of the tasks being performed. This section assumes that you have performed the CLI initial setup and are at the point where the controller has rebooted.

After rebooting the controller, you need to log in using the admin account along with the password that you defined during the initial setup.

CPsec

CPsec is used to secure PAPI traffic. It is enabled by default; however, in order for the APs to establish a secure connection with the controller, the APs need to be white listed on the controller. CPsec will be explained in more detail in Chapter 11, "Access Points." For now, you can configure the controller to automatically allow any new APs to connect to the controller by issuing the following CLI command:

```
#configure terminal
(config) #control-plane-security
(Control Plane Security Profile) #auto-cert-prov
```

In the past, many companies disabled CPsec on their networks. However, due to the higher level of security that it provides, it is better to leave it enabled. CPsec is also required when WLANs are operating in bridge or decrypt-tunnel forwarding mode. If you decide that you do not want to use CPsec, it can be disabled using the following CLI commands. You can read an explanation of CPsec, its advantages, and how to configure it in Chapter 11, "Access Points".

```
(config) #control-plane-security
(Control Plane Security Profile) #no cpsec-enable
```

Creating and Configuring VLANs

When considering network design and implementation of the controller-based installation, multiple VLANs need to be configured on the controller to support both the controller traffic and the user traffic. To start off, the controller needs a management VLAN to support communication between the controller and the network it is connected to. The controller should also have at least one VLAN to support users for each planned SSID that will be broadcast as part of a WLAN.

One of the advantages of an Aruba network is that the wireless clients do not have to share the same IP subnets as the wired users. When planning an IP design, it is important to account for the expected number of stations that will be connected, and plan DHCP scope sizes to support that. By having unique VLANs for the wireless users, the IP scopes for the wired network users will not need to be changed. Thus, scalability is not an issue. To support our design scenario, we will create three VLANs:

VLAN 50: used for management traffic

VLAN 51: used for secure employee WLAN traffic

VLAN 53: used for guest WLAN traffic

```
(config) #vlan 50
(config) #interface vlan 50
(config-subif)#ip address 10.1.50.101 255.255.255.0
(config-subif)#ip helper-address 10.254.1.21

(config) #vlan 51
(config) #interface vlan 51
(config-subif)#ip address 10.1.51.2 255.255.255.0
(config-subif)#ip helper-address 10.254.1.21

(config) #vlan 53
(config) #interface vlan 53
(config-subif)#ip address 192.168.5.1 255.255.255.0
```

Configuring a Trunk Port

After the appropriate VLANs are created, a next logical step is to assign the VLANs to physical ports. The following CLI commands will define a trunk port, assign the native VLAN, and specify the allowed VLANs:

```
(config) #interface gigabitethernet 0/0/0
(config-if)#switchport mode trunk
(config-if)#switchport trunk allowed vlan 50,51
(config-if)#switchport trunk native vlan 50
```

The following CLI command will display the configuration of any trunk ports:

```
#show trunk

Trunk Port Table
----------------
Port    Vlans Allowed  Vlans Active  Native Vlan
----    -------------  ------------  -----------
GE0/0/0 50-51          50-51         50
```

Configuring Access Ports

Any ports that are not trunk ports will most likely be configured as access ports. The following CLI commands will specify a range of ports, define them as access ports, and assign a VLAN to them.

```
(config-if)#interface range gigabitethernet 0/0/1-0/17
(config-range) #switchport mode access
(config-range) #switchport access vlan 50
```

The following CLI commands can be used to display VLAN, port, and IP address information. The physical ports of the controller are defined as follows: *PortType slot module port* (e.g., GE0/0/3).

- PortType: this is the physical port type.

    FE: Fast Ethernet

    GE: Gigabit Ethernet

    PC: port channel

- Slot: some controllers have multiple slots. If a controller does not have multiple slots, then the default value is 0.
- Module: this is not currently used and is specified to maintain consistency with other product families. The default value is 0.

▶ Port: the individual physical port. The first port number begins at 0.

```
#show vlan

VLAN CONFIGURATION
------------------
VLAN  Description  Ports         AAA Profile  Option-82
----  -----------  -----         -----------  ---------
1     Default      Pc0-7         N/A          Disabled
50    VLAN0050     GE0/0/0-0/17  N/A          Disabled
51    VLAN0051     GE0/0/0       N/A          Disabled
53    VLAN0053                   N/A          Disabled

#show ip interface brief

Interface   IP Address    / IP Netmask      Admin Protocol VRRP-IP (VRRP-Id)
vlan 1      172.16.0.254  / 255.255.255.0   up    up       none    (none)
vlan 50     10.1.50.101   / 255.255.255.0   up    up       none    (none)
vlan 51     10.1.51.2     / 255.255.255.0   up    up       none    (none)
vlan 53     192.168.5.1   / 255.255.255.0   up    down     none    (none)
loopback    unassigned    / unassigned      up    up
mgmt        unassigned    / unassigned      up    down
```

Default Gateway

In order to communicate across a multi-network environment, a default gateway needs to be defined. The following CLI command will define the default gateway. The default gateway IP address needs to be in the same subnet as the native VLAN on one of the connected Ethernet ports. In our case, we will set a default gateway in the VLAN 50 subnet.

```
(config) #ip default-gateway 10.1.50.1
```

If you want to check the default gateway, the following CLI command will display your IP route table. S* indicates the static route is the default gateway.

```
#show ip route

Codes: C-connected, O-OSPF, R-RIP, S-static
       M-mgmt, U-route usable, *-candidate default, V-RAPNG VPN/Branch

Gateway of last resort is Imported from DHCP to network 0.0.0.0 at cost 10
Gateway of last resort is Imported from CELL to network 0.0.0.0 at cost 10
Gateway of last resort is Imported from PPPOE to network 0.0.0.0 at cost 10
Gateway of last resort is 10.1.50.1 to network 0.0.0.0 at cost 1
S*    0.0.0.0/0  [1/0] via 10.1.50.1*
C     172.16.0.0/24 is directly connected, VLAN1
C     10.1.50.0/24 is directly connected, VLAN50
C     10.1.51.0/24 is directly connected, VLAN51
```

DHCP Server

If you are creating a guest wireless network, it is typical to put the guest traffic on a separate VLAN from any of the wired and secure wireless VLANs. This aids in controlling and isolating the guest user traffic. VLAN 53 was specified as the guest VLAN in the initial setup objective at the beginning of this chapter. Guest users can obtain a DHCP address from the Aruba controller or from an external DHCP server. If the guest network is large and will have more than 512 IP addresses assigned to guest devices, you should consider using an external DHCP server. If the number of assigned addresses is less than 512, then you can configure and use the internal DHCP server on the controller.

The threshold for using the internal DHCP server or an external server varies depending on the model controller you are using, so do some research before configuring a controller as a DHCP server. If you decide to configure the controller as a DHCP server, the following CLI commands will create an address pool for network 192.168.5.0. Make sure that you issue the `service dhcp` command. This command starts the DHCP server process on the controller. It is a recommended best practice to use an external public DNS server. Guest DNS queries should never be answered by an internal DNS server.

```
(config)    #ip dhcp pool guest-pool
(config-dhcp)#network 192.168.5.0 255.255.255.0
(config-dhcp)#default-router 192.168.5.1
(config-dhcp)#dns-server 8.8.8.8
(config-dhcp)#lease 0 2 0 0
(config-dhcp)#exit
(config)    #service dhcp
(config)    #end
```

The configuration line `lease 0 2 0 0` sets a two-hour DHCP lease for the scope. Due to the transient nature of guest networks, it is a good idea to put a short lease time on the IP address to help guard against lease depletion due to IP addresses being tied up too long for users that are no longer on the network.

If you want to check the DHCP pool, the following CLI command will display all of the configuration settings. If you created more than one pool, all of the pools will be displayed along with their respective settings.

```
#show ip dhcp database

DHCP enabled

# guest-pool
subnet 192.168.5.0 netmask 255.255.255.0 {
    default-lease-time 7200;
    max-lease-time 7200;
    option vendor-class-identifier   "ArubaAP";
    option vendor-encapsulated-options   "172.16.0.254";
```

```
    option domain-name-servers 8.8.8.8;
    option routers 192.168.5.1;
    range 192.168.5.2 192.168.5.254;
    authoritative;
}
```

Controller IP

The `controller-ip` address is the management address. It is used as the source address when the controller initiates a network communication. If an AP discovers this controller during the AP boot process, `controller-ip` is the IP address that the AP will be directed to for establishing PAPI and GRE communications. Setting or changing the `controller-ip` requires a reboot of the controller. The following CLI command will set the `controller-ip` address to the interface IP of VLAN 50.

```
(config) #controller-ip vlan 50
Since controller IP address will change, connectivity to this controller might
be affected. Do you want to proceed with this action [y/n]: y

This configuration change requires a reboot.
 PLEASE SAVE THE CONFIGURATION AND REBOOT.
```

The following CLI command will display the current `controller-ip` value. Since the controller has not yet been rebooted, the new `controller-ip` using VLAN 50 has been configured, but the current value is still the VLAN 1 address.

```
#show controller-ip

Switch IP Address: 172.16.0.254

Switch IP is configured to be Vlan Interface: 50

Switch IPv6 address is not configured.
```

Since the `controller-ip` address is being changed to VLAN 50, the IP address assigned to VLAN 1 should be removed. However, since the controller has not been rebooted, the IP for VLAN 1 is still being used as the `controller-ip`. After the controller is rebooted and the VLAN 50 address becomes the `controller-ip` address, the IP address should be removed from VLAN 1. This process is documented later in this chapter and should be performed after the controller configuration is saved and rebooted.

Disable Spanning-Tree

It is typical to connect the controller to the network using a single network connection. If this is the case, then Spanning-Tree Protocol is not needed. The following CLI command will globally disable Rapid Spanning Tree Protocol (RSTP):

```
(config) # no spanning-tree
```

Enable Bypass

When logging into the controller, you are placed in user mode, indicated by the > prompt. Very few commands can be performed in this mode. Therefore, most people go into privileged mode immediately by using the `enable` command. The following CLI command bypasses user mode and places you directly into privileged mode when you log into the controller:.

```
(config) #enable bypass
```

Time Zone and Network Time Protocol (NTP)

Network authentication and management often requires communications between the controller and other servers. Because of this, time synchronization has become much more important, even critical these days, than it was in the past. The following CLI commands perform the noted necessary time-related tasks:

1. Set the time zone and offset from UTC
2. Specify the second Sunday of March as the start of daylight savings time (beginning at 2AM), and the first Sunday of November as the end (ending at 2AM)
3. Direct the controller to the NTP server

```
(config) #clock timezone EST -5
(config) #clock summer-time EDT recurring 2 sunday march 02:00 1 sunday november 02:00 -4
(config) #ntp server 10.254.1.21
```

SNMP

Simple Network Management Protocol (SNMP) allows other servers, such as AirWave, to query the controller. A *community string*, similar to a passphrase or a key, needs to be set on the controller to allow other servers to retrieve statistical data from it. The following CLI command sets the community string to `aruba123`:

```
(config) #snmp-server community aruba123
```

The following CLI command will display the SNMP settings:

```
#show snmp community

SNMP COMMUNITIES
----------------
COMMUNITY   ACCESS      VERSION
---------   ------      -------
 aruba123   READ_ONLY   V1, V2c
```

Syslog

You should also define your syslog server. The following CLI command will configure syslog messages to be sent to a syslog server operating with the IP address of 192.168.240.31:

```
(config) #logging 192.168.240.31
```

Disable VLAN 1

Since VLAN 1 will not be used as the management VLAN, the IP address that was assigned to it by default should be removed. The following CLI commands will remove the IP address 172.16.0.254 from VLAN 1, and then remove the interface:

```
(config) #interface vlan 1
(config-subif)#no ip address
(config-subif) #exit
(config) #no interface vlan 1
```

Install Licenses, Save, and Reboot

At this point, the licenses should be added before the controller is rebooted. For reference, refer to the "Licensing" section earlier in this chapter, which described licenses and how to install them from the command line.

The following CLI commands will install three licenses (AP, PEF, RFP), save the configuration, and reboot the controller. Note that you can install multiple licenses before rebooting the controller.

```
#License add xc1J+7lK-VrUnP+XN-mjIazi9Z-DSoI3+bv-imWTLax
Limits updated.
Please reload the switch to enable the new functionality.

#license add CP5nfoJb-WybzdupC-YiofDTts-dSJvfMDC-kWtW35U
Limits updated.
Please reload the switch to enable the new functionality.

#license add QsenPoda-qKMR+/At-/KvueS78-IG1SYlxn-VfnP1h+
Limits updated.
Please reload the switch to enable the new functionality.
#write mem
#reload
```

WebUI Configuration

Earlier in the chapter, the WebUI Setup Wizard was explained, along with the steps to perform the initial configuration. In this section, you will learn how to use the WebUI to complete the initial configuration. These tasks will mimic what was explained in the "CLI

Configuration" section. After making changes using the WebUI, do not forget to click the Apply button in the bottom-right corner of each menu.

Many of the settings described previously in the "CLI Configuration" section can also be set during the WebUI Setup Wizard, since the wizard has screens and menus for installing the licenses, configuring the VLANs, and defining the port settings. In this section, we will cover setting these options because you should understand how it is done.

CPsec

CPsec is used to secure PAPI traffic between the controllers and APs. It is required if you configure a WLAN for bridge or decrypt-tunnel forwarding mode. It is not configured in the initial wizard, and is enabled by default. Although it is enabled by default, APs will not be able to connect to the controller until they are white listed. You can configure the controller to automatically allow any new APs to connect by enabling a feature known as *Auto Cert Provisioning*. This configuration is shown in Figure 4.10. If you go to **Configuration ➢ NETWORK ➢ Controller ➢ Control Plane Security**, it will bring you to the menu where you can configure this. CPsec will be explained in more detail in Chapter 11, "Access Points".

FIGURE 4.10
Control Plane Security

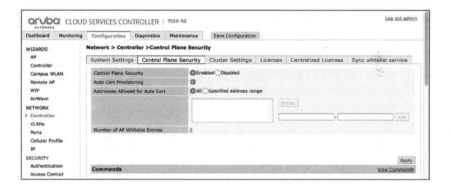

Many companies disabled CPsec in the past; however, it is recommended that you leave it enabled to provide more security. If you decide that you want to disable CPsec, you can do so from the same menu where Auto Cert Provisioning is configured.

Creating VLANs

Most controllers are configured to support multiple VLANs. Common VLANs are used for management traffic, employee data, and guest data. VLAN 50 was created during the initial setup. If you go to **Configuration ➢ NETWORK ➢ VLANs ➢ VLAN ID**, it will bring you to where you can add VLANs, such as 51 and 53, that were specified in the initial setup objective at the beginning of this chapter. When a VLAN is created, although the menu has other options, it is typical to simply enter the VLAN number and click Apply.

Assigning IP Addresses

After the appropriate VLANs are created, the next logical step is to assign IP addresses to them. Going to **Configuration ➢ NETWORK ➢ IP ➢ IP Interfaces** will bring you to where you can edit the VLAN settings and assign IP addresses to them. From the initial setup objectives, the following IP addresses need to be assigned:

- VLAN 51 address: 10.1.51.2/24
- VLAN 53 address: 192.168.5.1/24
- VLAN 53 DHCP helper address: 10.254.1.21

The DHCP helper address can also be defined in the IP settings for the VLAN. The guest network will use the Aruba internal DHCP server, so VLAN 53 does not need a DHCP helper address. These settings are shown in Figure 4.11.

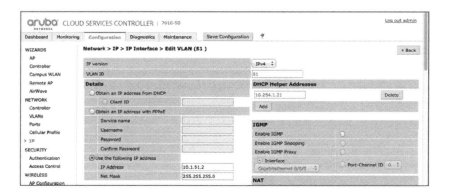

FIGURE 4.11 Assigning IP addresses

Configuring a DHCP Server

VLAN 53 will be configured as a virtual interface on the controller. This means that it is not assigned to any port interface. Virtual interfaces present a challenge, since there is not a trunk to forward DHCP requests to. This means that you need to either forward DHCP discover packets to the DHCP server (using a DHCP helper address) or configure a DHCP server on the controller.

VLAN 50 and 51 devices will be assigned IP addresses from the corporate DHCP server. Devices on VLAN 50 will be assigned IP addresses through the trunk, while VLAN 51 devices will be assigned IP addresses with the assistance of a DHCP helper address. VLAN 53 is the guest VLAN and will use the DHCP server from the controller to assign addresses.

You can access the DHCP server menu by going to **Configuration ➢ NETWORK ➢ IP ➢ DHCP Server**. Here, you can check the box to enable the DHCP server. You would also need to add the pool configuration, as shown in Figure 4.12.

FIGURE 4.12
DHCP server configuration

Default Gateway

The default gateway was defined using the setup wizard and can be found or modified by going to **Configuration ➢ NETWORK ➢ IP ➢ IP Routes & DNS**.

Controller IP

The controller IP address was defined using the setup wizard and can be found by going to **Configuration ➢ NETWORK ➢ Controller ➢ System Settings** in the Controller IP Details section near the bottom of the screen. There is also the option to set a loopback IP address on the controller. The loopback IP address is not used much anymore. It can still be set, but only in the WebUI or CLI, not in the setup wizard.

Any time you change the controller IP address or define the controller loopback IP you are changing the identity of the controller. This will require you to reboot the controller.

Disable VLAN 1

During the initial configuration, the controller IP address should be set to a VLAN that you created. In this example, that was VLAN 50. After you confirm that VLAN 1 is not being used as the controller IP, you can disable it. VLAN 1 can be disabled by selecting the Disable action on the VLAN ID menu. The Disable action can be found here: **Configuration ➢ NETWORK ➢ VLANs ➢ VLAN ID**.

Time Zone and Network Time Protocol (NTP)

In the setup wizard, you have the option to set an NTP server IP and select the time zone, or to simply set a time and date on the system. There is no option in the wizard to adjust for daylight savings time. The three time settings listed can be located and set by selecting **Configuration ➢ MANAGEMENT ➢ Clock** (shown in Figure 4.13).

1. Set the time zone and offset from UTC.

2. Specify the second Sunday of March as the start of daylight savings time, and the first Sunday of November as the end.
3. Direct the controller to the NTP server.

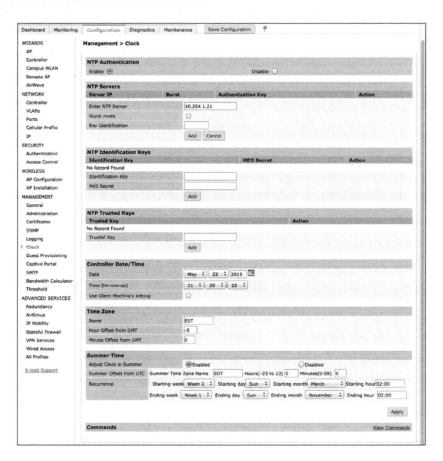

FIGURE 4.13 Clock settings

SNMP

Simple Network Management Protocol (SNMP) is not configured in the setup wizard but may be configured in the AirWave Wizard in the WebUI. You can also set the community string, located in the System Group section of the SNMP menu, and accessed by choosing **Configuration ➢ MANAGEMENT ➢ SNMP**.

Syslog

You should also define your syslog server. Selecting **Configuration ➢ MANAGEMENT ➢ Logging ➢ Servers** will take you to the logging screen where you can define the syslog server and parameters.

Install Licenses, Save, and Reboot

The initial setup wizard has a screen for installing licenses. If you need to add more licenses or manage licenses you can do it here: **Configuration ➢ NETWORK ➢ Controller ➢ Licenses**.

After the licenses are added, the next step is to save the configuration and then reboot the controller to load the new configuration. At the top center of the screen is the Save Configuration button. Clicking this button performs the same task as the `write memory` CLI command. You can reboot the controller by selecting **Maintenance ➢ CONTROLLER ➢ Reboot Controller ➢ Controller Reboot**.

Access Point Configuration

In Chapter 2, "Understanding the Aruba OS Environment," you learned about the boot process of the AP. The AP needs six pieces of information to boot: IP address, subnet mask, default gateway, AP name, AP group, and the IP address of the controller the AP will initially communicate with. All six pieces of information can be configured statically, or can be obtained dynamically. Typically, the AP name and group are statically configured and the rest are obtained dynamically.

The process of assigning the AP its configuration is called *provisioning the AP*. This section will explain how to provision an AP, assigning an AP name and AP group, which in most instances are the only settings you need to assign. Some of the other settings will also be explained, but most will not be covered in detail since they are rarely used. These settings are known as *environment variables*, which are used by the AP to enable or configure boot parameters.

An AP can be provisioned from one of four interfaces from which you can set these variables:

- AP console CLI
- Controller WebUI AP Installation menu
- Controller WebUI AP Wizard
- Controller console CLI using the `provision-ap controller` command.

The AP CLI interface allows you to configure a single AP by physically connecting a console cable to the AP. The WebUI interface allows you to provision multiple APs at the same time; however, all of the APs have to be the same model. The AP Wizard allows you to configure multiple APs at the same time, and the APs can be different models. The `provision-ap` command is capable of configuring multiple APs at the same time, but there are limitations, so it is recommended that you only use this to provision one AP at a time. The following is a list of the four AP configuration interfaces, along with a brief summary of the limitations of each:

- AP console CLI: configure single AP
- WebUI: configure multiple APs of the same model
- AP Wizard: configure multiple APs of the same or different model
- The `provision-ap controller` command: configure multiple APs; however, due to limitations, you should only configure a single AP

AP Console CLI

An AP is essentially a computer running a Linux-based operating system. As with many Linux-based computers, you can connect to it using a console connection. Most Aruba APs have 8P8C modular connectors (also known as *RJ45 console ports*) on them. Some APs can even be connected to using a Bluetooth low energy (BLE) radio. The same RJ45 console cable and configuration that you use to console into the controller can be used to console into an AP.

There are two console prompts that the AP can display. The first prompt, ~#, will appear if the AP is allowed to complete its boot cycle. The second prompt, apboot>, will appear if the AP boot process is interrupted. The functions of both of these and their capabilities will be explained in a moment.

It is important to note that you typically have more capabilities for configuring an AP from the controller's WebUI interface or using CLI commands on the controller. Therefore, it is highly recommended that you manage the APs from the controller and not from the AP console connection. One process that can be easily performed from the AP console is resetting the AP to factory defaults. This process will be explained in the apboot> section.

~#

~# is the tilde-pound prompt. This prompt appears after the AP completes its boot process. However, it does not mean that the AP is properly configured. Configuration of the AP is performed within the apboot> prompt, which will be covered in the next section.

There is not much that can be done from the ~# prompt. Two commands that can be issued from here are `ping` and `ifconfig`. You should be familiar with using `ping` to test communications with another IP device. The command will perform a continuous ping, requiring a Ctrl+C to stop it.

The `ifconfig` command will display the interface configuration of the AP. The following is part of the CLI output generated by the `ifconfig` command. This command is useful to determine the IP address assigned to an AP. There are easier ways of doing this on the controller if the AP is communicating with the controller.

```
br0       Link encap:Ethernet  HWaddr 24:DE:C6:CF:5E:D8
          inet addr:10.1.50.150  Bcast:10.1.50.255  Mask:255.255.255.0
          inet6 addr: fe80::26de:c6ff:fecf:5ed8/64 Scope:Link
          UP BROADCAST RUNNING ALLMULTI MULTICAST  MTU:1500  Metric:1
          RX packets:517 errors:0 dropped:0 overruns:0 frame:0
          TX packets:382 errors:0 dropped:255 overruns:0 carrier:0
          collisions:0 txqueuelen:1000
          RX bytes:0 (0.0 B)  TX bytes:0 (0.0 B)
```

If an AP has successfully booted, but it is not able to contact the controller, it will periodically reboot itself, continuously attempting to establish a connection with the controller. Essentially, the AP is in one of two states: connected to the controller or trying to connect to the controller.

apboot>

As mentioned previously, there are two console prompts that the AP can display. If the AP is allowed to complete its boot cycle, it will display the ~# prompt, from which there are only a couple of commands that can be issued, which you learned about in the previous section. The other console prompt is where you can set the AP's boot configuration parameters. This is the apboot> prompt.

In order to get to the apboot> prompt, you should first have a console connection established to the AP. Then, power on the AP and you should begin to see output from the AP booting up. About 5–10 seconds after the AP begins booting, the prompt Hit <Enter> to stop autoboot: 2 will appear (shown in the following CLI output). The number 2 is the start of a two-second countdown timer. As stated, within this two-second period of time, you must hit the Return/Enter key in order to interrupt the boot and enter the apboot> prompt. If you do not hit the Return/Enter key in time, simply power off the AP, power it back on, and try again.

```
APBoot 1.5.3.9 (build 43867)
Built: 2014-05-21 at 19:31:10

Model: AP-21x
CPU:   P1010E, Version: 1.0, (0x80f90010)
Core:  E500, Version: 5.1, (0x80212151)
Clock:
       CPU0: 800 MHz
       CCB:  400 MHz
       DDR:  400  MHz (800 MT/s data rate) (Asynchronous)
       LBC:   unknown (LCRR[CLKDIV] = 0x00)
L1:    D-cache 32KB enabled
       I-cache 32KB enabled
```

```
I2C:    ready
DRAM:   Configuring DDR for 800 MT/s data rate
DDR:    256 MB (DDR3, 32-bit, CL=6, ECC off)
POST1: memory passed
Flash: 32 MB
L2:     256 KB enabled
Power: 802.3at POE
PCIe1: RC, link up, x1
        dev fn venID devID class  rev    MBAR0    MBAR1    MBAR2    MBAR3
        00  00  14e4  4360 00002  03  80000004 00000000 00000000 00000000
PCIe2: RC, link up, x1
        dev fn venID devID class  rev    MBAR0    MBAR1    MBAR2    MBAR3
        00  00  14e4  4360 00002  03  a0000004 00000000 00000000 00000000
Net:    eth0
Radio: bcm43460#0, bcm43460#1

Hit <Enter> to stop autoboot:  2
apboot>
```

In the previous section, I stated that the AP is always either connected to a controller, or trying to connect to a controller. If that is the case, then how is it that the boot process of the AP can be intercepted and the AP can just sit there at the apboot> prompt? The answer to this question is that the AP will stay at the apboot> for up to two minutes of inactivity, and then it will automatically reboot. As long as you are interacting with the CLI, the AP will not reboot. So, if you do not want it to reboot, simply hit the Return/Enter key and the AP will not consider rebooting for another two minutes.

Now that you are at the apboot> prompt, what can you do? The apboot> prompt is one of the places where you can configure the AP. These configuration settings are environment variables that the AP reads when booting. Chapter 2, "Understanding the Aruba OS Environment," explained that the AP needs six pieces of information to boot: IP address, subnet mask, default gateway, AP name, AP group, and the IP address of the controller that the AP will initially speak to. This information could be obtained dynamically or configured statically, with the AP name and AP group typically being the two settings that are statically set.

The help command displays all of the available apboot> commands, as shown in the following CLI output:

```
apboot> help
?              - alias for 'help'
boot           - boot the OS image
clear          - clear the OS image or other information
dhcp           - invoke DHCP client to obtain IP/boot params
dir            - list files in a directory (default /)
factory_reset  - reset to factory defaults
help           - print online help
mfginfo        - show manufacturing info
```

```
osinfo        - show the OS image version(s)
ping          - send ICMP ECHO_REQUEST to network host
printenv      - print environment variables
purgeenv      - restore default environment variables
reset         - Perform RESET of the CPU
saveenv       - save environment variables to persistent storage
setenv        - set environment variables
tftpboot      - boot image via network using TFTP protocol
upgrade       - upgrade the APBoot or OS image
version       - display version
```

This section will explain how to use the following commands, since these are the key commands that you should be using to configure an AP. The env on the end of some of the commands is optional, and the abbreviated command is shown in parentheses.

- boot
- printenv (print)
- purgeenv (purge)
- reset
- saveenv (save)
- setenv (set)
- dhcp

Typically, the first thing you would want to do at the apboot> prompt is to view the current configuration of the AP. You can do this by entering the printenv command, as displayed in the following CLI output:

```
apboot> printenv
bootdelay=2
baudrate=9600
autoload=n
boardname=Tomatin
servername=aruba-master
bootcmd=boot ap
autostart=yes
bootfile=e500.ari
ethaddr=24:de:c6:cf:5e:d8
stdin=serial
stdout=serial
stderr=serial
ethact=eth0

Environment size: 206/131068 bytes
```

Before configuring any AP, it is a good habit to purge its current configuration. This will reset all of the environment variables on the AP. The AP does not have a running-config and startup-config like some operating systems; however, it does have RAM and flash memory. All configuration changes are made in the RAM. If you want these changes to survive a reset or reboot of the AP, you need to save them to the flash memory by issuing the save command. Remember that the AP will automatically reboot itself if you have not typed anything at the apboot> prompt for two minutes. If the AP reboots and you did not save your changes, they will be lost and you will need to reenter them. Note that the purge command erases the flash memory, so a save is not required after executing this command; however, to instill good habits, it is recommended that you still enter the save command after any apboot> commands, including purge.

The following output shows the CLI commands to purge an AP and save the configuration, along with the output of each command:

```
apboot> purge
Un-Protected 1 sectors
. done
Erased 1 sectors
Writing 9....8....7....6....5....4....3....2....1....
apboot> save
Saving Environment to Flash...
Un-Protected 1 sectors
. done
Erased 1 sectors
Writing 9....8....7....6....5....4....3....2....1....
```

After the AP is purged, the setenv command is used to set the environment variables that the AP will use to boot. Remember the AP needs six pieces of information to boot, obtained statically or dynamically. The following output shows the CLI commands to set the IP address, subnet mask, and default gateway. Remember, these are typically not set, but obtained dynamically using DHCP.

```
apboot> setenv ipaddr 10.1.50.111
apboot> setenv netmask 255.255.255.0
apboot> setenv gatewayip 10.1.50.1
```

If you are planning to let the AP obtain this information using DHCP, you can manually perform a DHCP request using the dhcp command. The following shows the CLI command, along with the output of the command, indicating that the AP has successfully obtained an IP address.

```
apboot> dhcp
eth0: link up, speed 1 Gb/s, full duplex
DHCP broadcast 1
DHCP IP address: 10.1.10.151
DHCP subnet mask: 255.255.255.0
DHCP def gateway: 10.1.10.1
DHCP DNS server: 10.254.1.21
DHCP DNS domain: arubarack.com
```

Two environment variables that need to be configured manually are the AP name and the AP group. The following output shows the CLI commands to set the AP name to AP1 and the AP group to Building1:

```
apboot> setenv name AP1
apboot> setenv group Building1
```

The last environment variable that is also typically obtained dynamically is the IP address of the controller that the AP will initially communicate with to download its OS (if needed) and its configuration. This is usually obtained dynamically using DHCP options 43 and 60, ADP, or DNS. The following CLI command will statically configure the IP address of this initial controller. Even though the environment variable is master, this address does not have to be the IP address of the master controller. The address can be the address of the master controller, or any local controller.

```
apboot> setenv master 10.1.50.101
```

If you need to change the value of an environment variable, such as the AP name, simply enter the setenv command with a new value, as shown in the first line of the following CLI output. If you want to remove or delete an environment variable, such as the AP group, simply enter the setenv command with no value, as shown in the second line of the following CLI output:

```
apboot> setenv name NewName
apboot> setenv group
```

Do not forget to save all of these changes, as shown in the following CLI output:

```
apboot> save
Saving Environment to Flash...
Un-Protected 1 sectors
. done
Erased 1 sectors
Writing 9....8....7....6....5....4....3....2....1....
```

Two commands that are often misunderstood are the reset command and the boot command. The difference between these two commands is minimal. As with the rest of the commands in this section, the boot and reset commands only operate at the apboot> prompt.

The reset command performs a complete reboot of the AP, as if it were starting from initial power-up. During the reboot process, the RAM memory will be reset and the environment variables will be reloaded from the permanent flash memory.

During the startup of the AP, if you hit the Return/Enter key to stop the boot process, you are stopping it prior to the AP loading the environment variables from the permanent flash memory. At the apboot> prompt you can change the environment variables using the setenv command, and then save them to the flash memory. The boot command instructs the AP to load the environment variables from flash memory and then continue the boot process. With either the reset or boot command the environment variables will be loaded from flash.

Controller WebUI—AP Installation

The WebUI is an excellent user interface, and probably the most common interface for provisioning APs. There are two ways that you can reach the AP provisioning menu. The first method is through the Configuration menu by selecting **Configuration ➢ WIRELESS ➢ AP Installation ➢ Provisioning**.

The second method is from the Network Summary screen, which is the default screen that displays when you click the Monitoring menu selection along the top menu bar. This screen displays a quantity summary of the network devices and operational status. One of the lines on this screen lists the number of unprovisioned access points, as shown in Figure 4.14. If there are any unprovisioned APs, click the number next to this line and it will take you directly to the provisioning menu.

FIGURE 4.14
Network Summary

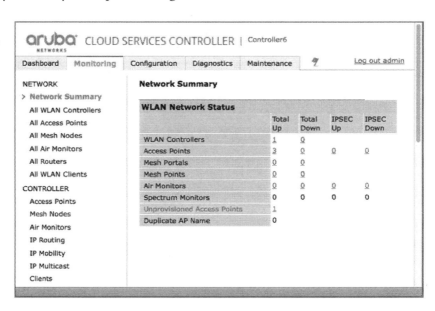

From the provisioning menu you can provision a new AP, or you can reprovision an existing AP. If you need to provision multiple APs with the same settings, you can, if they are the same model AP. If the AP models are different, you will need to configure each AP individually. The AP Wizard, which will be explained later in this chapter, does allow different AP models to be configured at the same time.

The provisioning menu allows you to configure at least two dozen different settings on an AP. As mentioned previously in this chapter, the AP needs six settings to boot. The

AP name and group need to be set statically. The IP address, mask, gateway, and the IP address of the controller the AP will initially communicate with are rarely set manually, and are typically obtained dynamically.

Figure 4.15 displays the upper portion of the AP provisioning menu, and Figure 4.16 displays the lower portion of the AP provisioning menu. Typically, the two items that you want to set for an AP are in the first and last sections on the provisioning menu. The first is choosing the AP group, as shown in the AP Parameters section at the top of Figure 4.15, and the second is naming the AP, as shown in the AP list section at the bottom of Figure 4.16. Choosing the AP group is done by simply selecting the group from the drop-down list. Naming the AP requires you to delete the existing name in the AP name field, and type in the new name.

FIGURE 4.15
AP provisioning menu (upper)

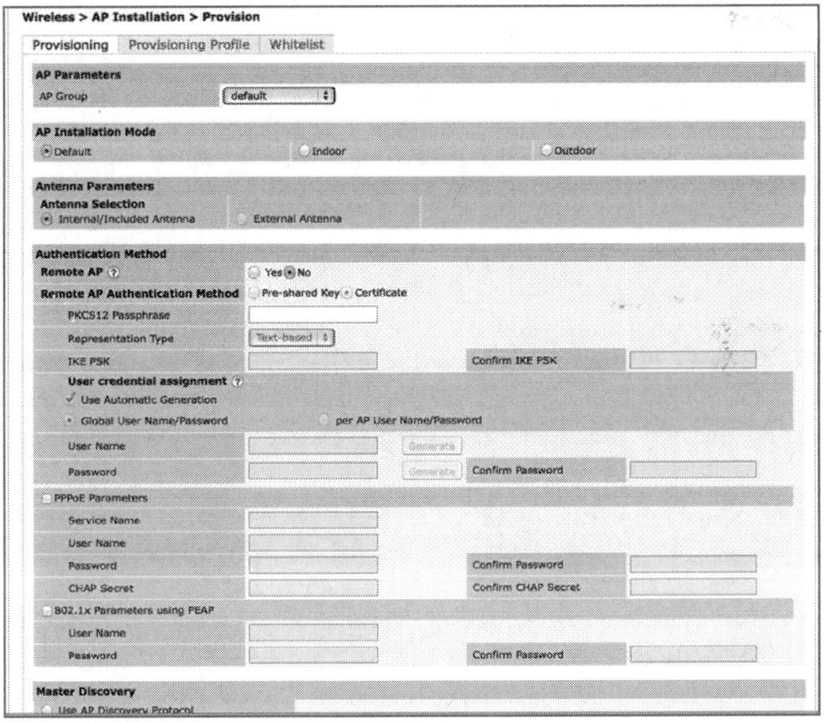

If you want to set the IP address, subnet mask, and default gateway parameters for the AP, you can do so in the IP Settings section, as seen in Figure 4.16. By default, the AP will use DHCP, but this can be manually overridden by selecting Use the Following IP Address and filling in the settings you want.

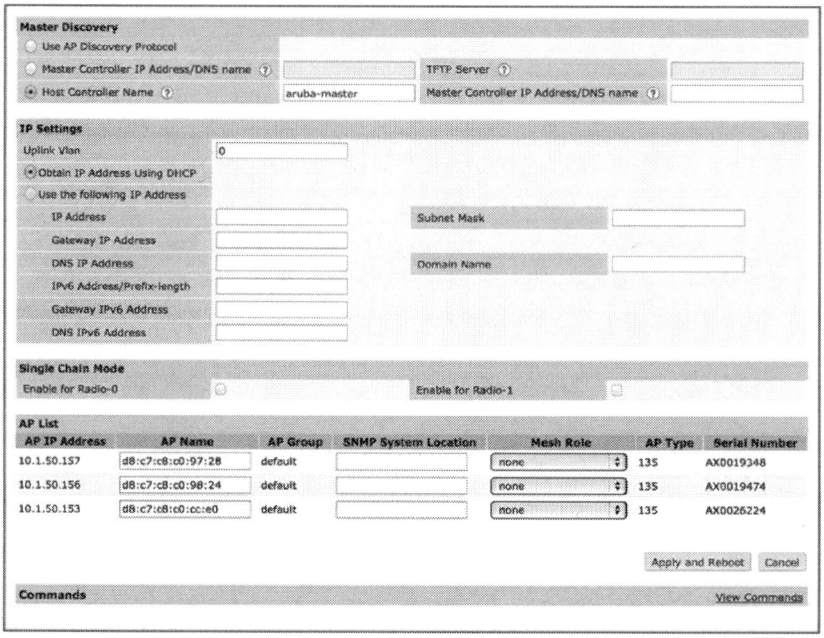

FIGURE 4.16
AP provisioning menu (lower)

The last of the six settings is the IP address of the controller that the AP will initially communicate with. If you want to manually specify this address, in the Master Discovery section, select the second line, and enter the master controller IP address or DNS name. As you fill in this field, the WebUI will also enter this value into the TFTP server field. The TFTP address tells the AP where to go to download its software image if the image is missing or was erased. The TFTP server is rarely ever needed.

Controller WebUI—AP Wizard

The AP Wizard is a very flexible tool that allows you to provision a single AP or multiple APs. It also allows you to provision different AP models at the same time. The AP Wizard can be selected from the Configuration menu, by selecting **Configuration ➢ WIZARDS ➢ AP**.

When entering the AP Wizard, you can choose to configure the AP to operate in one of four deployment scenarios: LAN, remote, LAN mesh, or remote mesh. In this section, we will focus on configuring a campus AP in a LAN environment.

After LAN is selected for the deployment scenario, the next step is to choose the APs that will be configured. The wizard can display a list of APs in four different ways, allowing you to narrow down the number of APs to select from. The four display filters are:

- APs that are new/unprovisioned
- APs in a particular AP group
- APs meeting specified search criteria
- All APs

As shown in Figure 4.17, you can display only APs in a specific AP group by selecting a specific group. This can be useful if you need to reprovision some or all of the APs in a group.

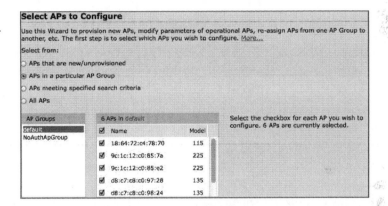

FIGURE 4.17 APs in a particular AP group

Another very nice feature of the AP Wizard is the ability to display the APs using search criteria. Figure 4.18 shows the options for searching and filtering the AP list. You can search any one or multiple columns. The example in Figure 4.18 shows AP-135 model APs of which the MAC address contains the hex characters c0:9. The name or MAC address fields can contain an asterisk * as a wildcard for any match. Note that the search is not case sensitive. The following three examples describe how the * wildcard can be used:

*9A   Any characters ending with 9A

9A*   9A followed by any characters

9A   Starts with, ends with, or contains 9A

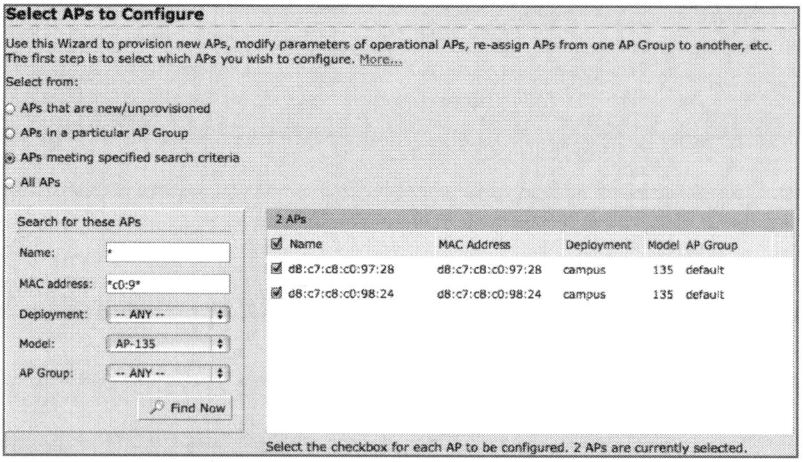

FIGURE 4.18
AP search criteria

The Deployment field allows you to search based on deployment types of campus, remote, local mesh, or remote mesh. The Model field allows you to search based on the AP model, which you can choose from a list of all Aruba AP models. Finally, the AP Group field allows you to search based on a specific AP group, which you can choose from a list of all the AP groups that you have defined.

No matter which method you choose to display the list of APs, you need to click one or more boxes at the left of the APs to select the APs that you are provisioning. After selecting the APs, the next menu allows you to specify how the AP will discover the IP address of the controller it will initially communicate with. Except in rare instances, this type of discovery should be set to Automatic. If you do need to manually specify a controller, you can do so for all of the selected APs, or you can specify it on a per-AP basis, as shown in Figure 4.19.

FIGURE 4.19
Specify Controller

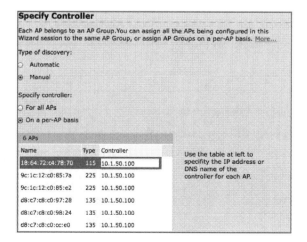

ACCESS POINT CONFIGURATION   101

The next menu has three tabs that allow you to configure network IP settings; antenna type and gain settings; outdoor location, altitude, antenna bearing and tilt settings. You can also change the AP name on any of these tabs by selecting the MAC address and typing in a new AP name. The three menus are shown in Figure 4.20.

FIGURE 4.20
Specify AP Settings

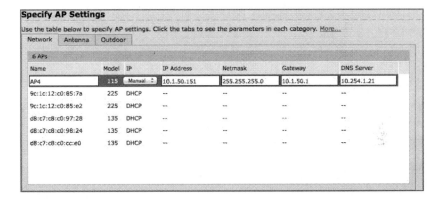

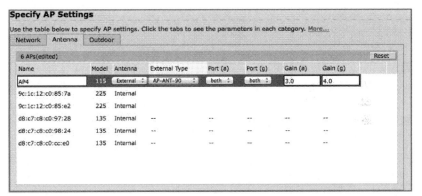

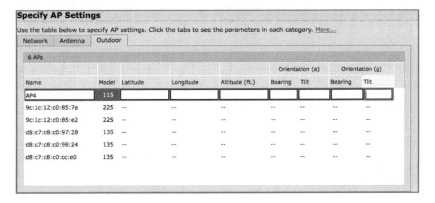

The next menu is the final selection menu and allows you to specify the AP Group that the APs will be a member of. This menu allows you to specify a single group for all of the APs that you are provisioning, or you can specify the group on a per-AP basis, as shown in Figure 4.21.

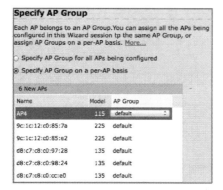

FIGURE 4.21 Specify AP Group

After you have chosen the group or groups that the APs will be members of, the final screen provides a simple summary of the APs and allows you to complete the configuration. Before you do this, you should click the text that reads Click Here, shown in Figure 4.22. This will initiate a printout of the configuration settings that will be pushed to each of the APs. This document is a very helpful troubleshooting tool. If an AP is not configured properly, you may have mistyped a setting, which can be verified using this document.

FIGURE 4.22 Ready to Push Configuration to APs

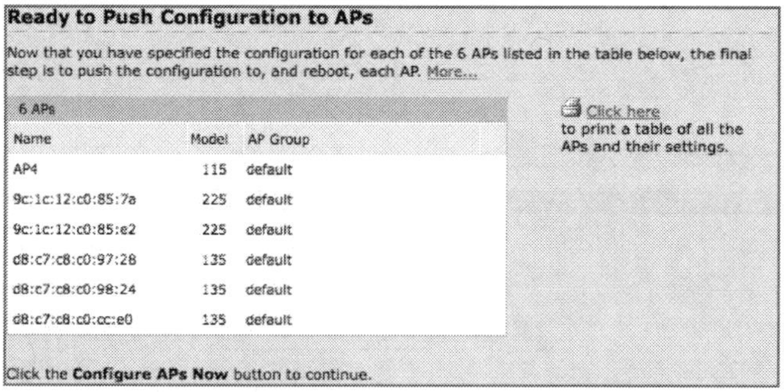

Provision-AP Controller CLI Command

The final way to provision an AP is by using the `provision-ap` command from the CLI prompt of the controller. This command is very powerful, and can be used to provision an AP with a complex configuration. A script can also be created offline and pasted into the controller CLI to configure an AP. The script can be easily modified offline and pasted into the controller CLI to configure additional APs.

The provision-ap command is not a common or well-known command. Additionally, it can be confusing to understand. Hopefully, this section of the book will rectify that. The general process for using the provision-ap command is as follows: read the configuration variables from an AP and copy them into a temporary workspace on the controller, make changes to the settings in the temporary workspace, and then copy the configuration from the temporary workspace back to the AP. When the AP is reprovisioned with the new settings, the AP will automatically reboot using its new configuration.

To begin the process, the first logical step is to display the current settings of the AP that you are planning to provision or reprovision. The following output shows the CLI command to display the current configuration of an AP. Although this step is not necessary, it is useful because it verifies that the controller is able to communicate with the AP, since the provisioning parameters output is pulled from the AP. In this example, the AP is identified by its name; however, you can also use any of the following to identify it: ap-name, bssid, ip-addr, ip6-addr, or wired-mac. To save space, only the first 10 parameters are included in the output displayed. There are over 50 configurable parameters on an AP. This is also illustrated in Step 1 of Figure 4.23.

```
#show ap provisioning ap-name ap1

AP "ap1" Provisioning Parameters
--------------------------------
Item                                            Value
----                                            -----
AP Name                                         ap1
AP Group                                        building1
Location name                                   N/A
SNMP sysLocation                                N/A
Master                                          10.1.50.101
Gateway                                         N/A
IPv6 Gateway                                    N/A
Netmask                                         255.255.255.0
IP Addr                                         10.1.50.151
IPv6 Addr                                       N/A
```

After verifying that the controller can communicate with the AP, Step 2, shown in Figure 4.23, reads the configuration of the AP and copies it to the provisioning params workspace. Before copying the configuration, I like to clear the workspace first. The following CLI output shows the commands to enter the Provision-AP mode, clear the workspace, and read the AP configuration into the workspace.

```
#configure terminal
Enter Configuration commands, one per line. End with CNTL/Z
```

```
(config) #provision-ap
(AP provisioning) #clear provisioning-params
(AP provisioning) #read-bootinfo ap-name ap1
```

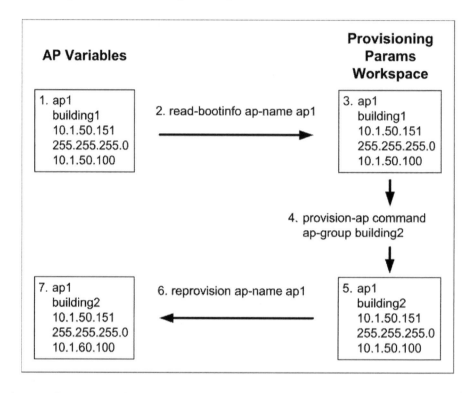

FIGURE 4.23
Provision-AP process flow

Any changes that you need to make to the AP will initially be made to the configuration in the workspace, and then copied to the AP. The example in Figure 4.23 shows the AP group being changed in Step 4. At any time, you can display the configuration that is in the workspace. You may want to do this before and after making changes, as illustrated in Steps 3 and 5 in Figure 4.23. The following CLI output shows the commands to display the configuration in the workspace, change the AP group to building2, and then display the new configuration. The output of the show provisioning-params command was truncated to save space.

```
(AP provisioning) #show provisioning-params

AP provisioning
---------------
Parameter                                               Value
---------                                               -----
AP Name                                                 ap1
AP Group                                                building1
```

ACCESS POINT CONFIGURATION

```
Location name                                       N/A

(AP provisioning) # ap-group building2
NOTE: For cert RAP; ap-group provisioned in RAP whitelist entry would take the
highest preference

(AP provisioning) #show provisioning-params

AP provisioning
---------------
Parameter                                           Value
---------                                           -----
AP Name                                             ap1
AP Group                                            building2
Location name                                       N/A
```

After you have made the necessary changes and verified that the settings in the workspace are correct, the next step is to copy the contents of the workspace to the AP, as illustrated in Step 6 of Figure 4.23. The following CLI command will copy the contents of the provisioning params workspace to the AP. Immediately after this command is executed, the AP is rebooted with its new configuration.

```
(AP provisioning) # reprovision ap-name ap1
```

When the AP reboots, you can use the following CLI command to display its configuration. Again, the output of this command was truncated to save space. Displaying the configuration is illustrated in Step 7 of Figure 4.23.

```
(AP provisioning) # show ap provisioning ap-name ap1

AP "ap1" Provisioning Parameters
--------------------------------
Item                                                Value
----                                                -----
AP Name                                             ap1
AP Group                                            building2
Location name                                       N/A
```

CHAPTER 5

Profiles

IN THIS CHAPTER, YOU WILL LEARN ABOUT THE FOLLOWING:

- **David's Bicycle Store**
  - Basic Customer
  - Intermediate Customer
  - Advanced Customer
- **Configuring ArubaOS**
  - Wizards
  - Web User Interface (WebUI)
  - Command Line Interface (CLI)
- **Profile Hierarchy**
  - Understanding Virtual APs
- **WebUI Configuration Menus**
  - All Profiles
  - Authentication
  - AP Configuration
- **Managing Profiles**
  - Show References
  - Cloning Profiles
  - Show Profile-hierarchy

When Aruba introduced profiles as part of ArubaOS, one of the key components of the architecture was that all of the settings were modular. This provided an incredible level of flexibility and interchangeability for features and functions; however, with it came a higher level of complexity.

If you ask an ArubaOS administrator about their experience learning and becoming familiar with ArubaOS, most administrators will tell you that they had the most difficulty learning and understanding profiles. ArubaOS has many profiles or *pieces* that make up the wireless environment. Individually, most of the profiles are fairly easy to understand and to configure. It is often more difficult to understand and remember how the profiles relate to each other, along with the dependencies between them. When building something, such as a bicycle, attaching the seat to the bicycle is a straightforward and easily understood task. Add this task to all of the other tasks needed to assemble the rest of the components of the bicycle (tires, gears, brakes, pedals, handlebars, and so on), and assembling the bicycle becomes a more complex process, even though each task individually is fairly straightforward.

This chapter will explain many of the profiles that you will use when configuring access points and wireless LANs. It will also explain some of the relationships and dependencies that exist between many of these profiles. As I explain profiles, you will also learn the commands needed to create an 802.1X/EAP wireless network.

David's Bicycle Store

It has been many years since I began working in the computer industry. Let us make believe that I have decided to leave the wireless networking industry and open a bicycle store: David's Bicycle Store. In doing research for my bicycle shop, I have identified that my customer base consists of three different types of customers: basic, intermediate, and advanced. Each type of customer has different requirements, which will be addressed in the following sections.

Basic Customer

The basic customer either does not know much about bicycles or wants the purchase to be quick and easy. To take care of this type of customer, I have a standard set of frames, wheels, and other components preassembled—what I call standard or default components. When working with a basic customer, I have a simple set of questions that I ask him. Based upon his answers to my questions, I offer a limited set of options from which he can select his seat, handlebars, pedals, and gears. The configuration of the bicycle, based on the responses to my questions, will provide basic customers with a functional bicycle that will satisfy their stated needs.

Intermediate Customer

The intermediate customer is more knowledgeable and typically more serious about her bicycle purchase. For my intermediate customers, I have developed an in-depth checklist of standard or default options available, along with a long list of components, options, and features that are available to customize the bicycle. The intermediate customer needs to be knowledgeable about her choices, since some options may not be compatible with other options. If the intermediate customer understands the options that she chooses and plans carefully, she will have a very capable, finely tuned and customized bicycle.

Advanced Customer

The advanced customer wants to be able to completely customize his bicycle. I provide a basic set of components for the customer, who can then build his own optimal bicycle. An advanced customer has the option of using the basic components or replacing them with any custom component that he desires. Unlike the intermediate customer, there is no checklist. I provide assistance to the advanced customer by providing feedback and suggestions, as needed; however, the advanced customer needs to know the components that are required to construct the bicycle along with the steps and process required to build the bicycle.

Configuring ArubaOS

After reading the previous three sections you may be wondering why you are reading about the sale of bicycles in a book that is supposed to be about understanding ArubaOS. Well, the reality is that you really were reading about using ArubaOS to configure a controller. Just as my bicycle store has three types of customers and ways of building their bicycles, there are three methods or interfaces that you can use to configure a controller:

- Wizards
- Web user interface (WebUI)
- Command line interface (CLI)

Wizards

Configuring the controller using the wizards is similar to building a bicycle for the basic customer. A wizard prompts for basic or key information. The wizard takes this information, along with default settings, and uses them to configure the controller. Most of the settings made by the wizard use default values. The user defines key parameters, which are integrated with the default values to configure the controller and access points.

Web User Interface

Using the web user interface (WebUI) to configure the controller is similar to building a bicycle for an intermediate customer. The WebUI displays lists of settings and fields. The user can select individual settings or fill in fields to customize the controller. The WebUI does not prompt the user for input like the wizard does; it merely displays the available options. The user needs to understand the function of the fields and settings that are being changed, along with how they may interact or conflict with other options.

Command Line Interface

Configuring the controller using the command line interface (CLI) is akin to an advanced customer building a bicycle. Each CLI command is entered individually. The person entering the commands must understand what the command does, along with the necessary parameters and options needed with each command. The CLI commands can provide basic prompting for options and parameters, but they do not provide any description or explanation. The CLI provides the highest level of customization, but it also requires the most knowledge and understanding of ArubaOS.

Profile Hierarchy

So now that you have some basic understanding of the user interface options for configuring a controller, let us take a look at some of the Aruba profiles, what they do, and how they relate to each other. Just as a bicycle is constructed of different pieces, the functionality of an Aruba controller is also made up of different pieces known as *profiles*. Each profile has a specific function, and integrates with the other profiles to provide the capabilities that you need for your network. Figure 5.1 illustrates some of the profiles and relationships between these profiles. This list does not attempt to show all of the profiles, as there are too many to list. It does, however, include some of the key profiles, some mandatory and some optional, that you will configure on a controller and when creating wireless LANs.

FIGURE 5.1
Profile hierarchy

Just as when you are building a bicycle, either as a basic, intermediate, or advanced customer, you are concerned with certain details of the bicycle, but other aspects of it you accept as is. For example, you may decide that you want a yellow bicycle frame and so you choose one. However, there are so many other aspects of what went into building that yellow frame that you have accepted without any concern or consideration, such as the type of paint, the type of primer, how and if the frame was welded together, the weight of the frame, and the materials used to build the frame. To someone like an Olympic cyclist, these details would likely be important, but most other people do not care about these details.

As I stated before, building a bicycle is like configuring an Aruba controller. There are many options that can be configured. As the administrator of your network, you modify and configure the settings that are important to your environment, and accept the defaults for the rest. All of the settings in all of the profiles have default values, most of which you will leave alone.

Most categories of profiles include a default profile, which is configured with default settings that provide for a "known good" working environment. By practice, except in a couple of rare situations, you should not modify any default profiles. They should be left untouched, allowing you to reference them in the future. Later in this chapter you will learn how to copy an existing profile. By leaving the default profiles untouched, you can copy them and use them as trustworthy building blocks for your network.

Understanding Virtual APs

Imagine that you work for a small accounting office and the owner of the company asked you to install a wireless network for the employees and a wireless network to provide internet access for clients. For the moment, we will assume that you have very little wireless networking experience. After doing some research, you decide that the best way to provide the wireless access that the owner requested is for you to purchase two autonomous access points. After purchasing the access points, you configure them as illustrated in Figure 5.2.

FIGURE 5.2
Guest and employee APs

- Guest SSID
- Captive Portal Authentication
- Open Encryption
- VLAN 20
- Channel 11
- Power 14 dBm

- Employee SSID
- 802.1X/EAP Authentication
- AES Encryption
- VLAN 30
- Channel 6
- Power 14 dBm

You configure the first AP with a guest SSID, captive portal authentication, and open encryption. You configure the AP to place the guest traffic on VLAN 20, which is routed directly out to the Internet. You set the radio on the AP to channel 11 with a power level of 14 dBm.

You configure the second AP with an employee SSID and enable 802.1X/EAP authentication with AES encryption. Authentication for 802.1X/EAP requires user accounts, which are configured in a user database on the AP. You configure the AP to place the employee traffic on VLAN 30, which is allowed access to the internal network, along with access to the Internet. Finally, you set the radio on the second AP to channel 6, also with a power level of 14 dBm.

For the first six months everything is working wonderfully, and the owner of the firm is happy with the two networks that you provided. Unfortunately, you arrived at work late one Monday morning to discover that the guest AP is not working because it has been damaged due to a water leak in the ceiling. Since installing the network, you have become friends with an IT consultant in the building, and decide to ask him for some help and for a suggestion for replacing the damaged AP. When your friend comes to your office to see the damaged AP, he explains that you do not have to buy a new AP; you can simply configure the one working physical AP with what he calls two virtual APs (VAPs). Many autonomous APs are not capable of supporting virtual APs, but the ones that you purchased fortunately are.

He explains that you can install one physical access point, but make it behave like two different access points, thus the term *virtual access point (VAP)*. As illustrated in Figure 5.3, the radio on the AP is configured to channel 11, with a power level of 14 dBm. There is nothing special about the channel or power level; these are just the values that you had chosen, and since the network was working well, your friend decided to keep these settings.

Your friend then shows you how you can configure two sets of wireless network parameters. Just as before, you configure the guest SSID, captive portal authentication, and open encryption. You configure this VAP to place the guest traffic on VLAN 20, which is still routed directly out to the Internet.

Your friend then shows you how to configure the second set of wireless parameters. Just as before, you configure the employee SSID, enable 802.1X/EAP authentication with AES encryption, and configure the user database on the AP. You also configure this VAP to place the employee traffic on VLAN 30, which is still allowed access to the internal network, as well as the Internet.

Whenever anybody enables a client device to look for a wireless network, they will see two separate, distinct networks. Each network will appear as if it is a separate and unique AP; however, there is only one physical AP advertising the two wireless networks, or two separate virtual APs.

FIGURE 5.3
Guest and employee VAPs

- Guest SSID
- Captive Portal Authentication
- Open Encryption
- VLAN 20

- Employee SSID
- 802.1X/EAP Authentication
- AES Encryption
- VLAN 30

- Channel 11
- Power 14 dBm

Each distinct wireless network is defined by a group of settings that is the virtual AP. The guest network parameters, and the employee network parameters, by themselves are merely configuration settings that define how an AP should perform. When these parameters are applied to a physical AP, it is then that the AP begins to advertise the wireless network. Many APs are capable of supporting multiple VAPs. Many APs can support up to eight or even 16 different VAPs per radio, although you should limit the number of VAPs to three or four; usually one per encryption type and authentication method required. The reason to limit the number of VAPs is to reduce the amount of extra traffic that is transmitted. For every VAP assigned to an AP, the AP must transmit an additional 10 beacon management frames per second (one per VAP every 100 ms), in addition to other transmissions. This additional traffic is overhead and reduces the amount of air-time available for other data transmissions, along with delaying the transmission of other wireless data. Minimizing overhead traffic should increase performance for the rest of the devices on the channel.

When configuring an 802.1X/EAP network, just as there are many parts needed to build a bicycle, there are many settings and profiles needed to configure a wireless network. Wireless networks need SSID settings, authentication and encryption settings, and typically, VLAN settings. Some wireless networks, such as an open (unsecured) or a preshared key network, are simpler to configure, while others such as an 802.1X/EAP or a captive portal network are more complex. In all of these networks, there are core features or functions that need to be configured. In this section you will learn about the settings and components needed to configure an 802.1X/EAP network. This is one of the most secure and most common networks in enterprise environments, because of the high level of security it provides. The knowledge you obtain from learning how to configure this type of VAP will easily transfer over to configuring other types.

Since this is a book about ArubaOS and not a book about wireless networking, at this point in the book I will not be explaining the details of 802.1X/EAP. You need to be familiar with 802.1X/EAP if you plan to continue working in the wireless industry. It will be discussed more in Chapter 6, "Authentication and Encryption," relative to its use and configuration in the Aruba environment. You should become knowledgeable about the 802.1X/EAP framework, how it works, and how to configure it. There are many places where you can learn about 802.1X/EAP. I suggest going to www.cwnp.com to learn about the Certified Wireless Network Administrator (CWNA) certification and the Certified Wireless Security Professional (CWSP) certification. Consider reading *CWNA: Certified Wireless Network Administrator Official Study Guide: Exam CWNA-106* (Sybex, 2014), and *CWSP: Certified Wireless Security Professional Study Guide: Exam CWSP-205* (Sybex, 2016). You may also consider attending a CWNA or CWSP class. Note that the CWNA knowledge is considered a prerequisite to CWSP. The CWNA and CWSP certifications and body of knowledge are vendor-neutral and cover most topics and technologies that you will be involved with in the wireless networking and wireless security industries. I believe that the CWNA certification should be a prerequisite for anyone working in this industry, and both the CWNA and CWSP certifications should be prerequisites for anyone working with wireless security.

To begin learning how to configure a VAP, let us start out by looking at all of the key pieces in one diagram: Figure 5.4.

Each of the pieces in the diagram will be explained in detail in the following sections. Each of the boxes is labeled and has a number at the beginning of the label. The boxes labeled as (1) are integrated with their respective (1A) box. The (1) task should be completed before the partner (1A) task. All of the (1) and (1A) tasks should be completed before creating the (2) AAA Profile. The (3) VAP Profile is composed of the three tasks labeled as (2). And finally the (3) VAP Profile and the (3) AP System Profile are assigned to the (4) AP Group. I do not expect you to fully understand all of this at the moment. Each piece will be examined and explained individually, hopefully giving you a clearer understanding of it.

FIGURE 5.4

802.1X/EAP VAP

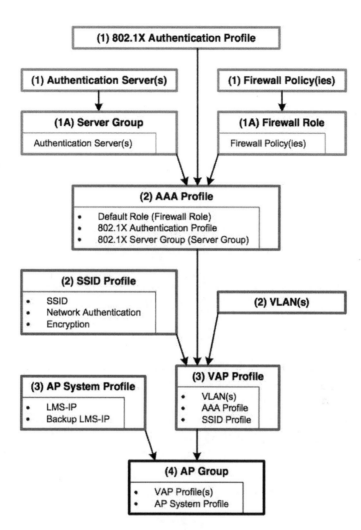

Authentication Server and Server Group

One of the aspects of 802.1X/EAP that makes it such an important and valuable technology is its ability to perform user identification. For example, anyone connecting to an 802.1X/EAP-PEAP network is required to provide some form of credentials (such as a username and password) in order to connect to the wireless network. The credentials need to be validated, but you must also supply a user identity. This makes 802.1X/EAP networks more secure and easier to control.

The user credentials need to be validated by the controller. Most often, the user's credentials are stored externally to the controller, usually on a RADIUS server. Therefore, when creating an 802.1X/EAP VAP, one of the initial tasks is defining the authentication server, as shown in Figure 5.5.

FIGURE 5.5
Authentication server/group

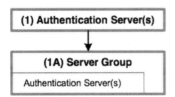

An Aruba controller can be linked to more than one authentication server. There are numerous reasons to have multiple authentication servers. You may have two separate databases of users. You could have a group of Active Directory (AD) users on a Windows server and you could have a group of users on a Linux server. In a multiple database environment, when a user logs into the network, you may want to look up the user account in the Windows AD database, the Linux database, or maybe both databases. Another reason to have multiple authentication servers is to have a primary user database and a backup user database for redundancy.

So the first task is to define each of the authentication servers. The following CLI commands define two RADIUS servers. The first server is named radius01, with an IP address of 10.254.1.21 and a shared secret key of aruba123. The second server is named radius02, with an IP address of 10.254.1.23, and a shared secret key of aruba123.

```
(config) #aaa authentication-server radius radius01
(RADIUS Server "radius01") #host 10.254.1.21
(RADIUS Server "radius01") #key aruba123
(config) #aaa authentication-server radius radius02
(RADIUS Server "radius02") #host 10.254.1.23
(RADIUS Server "radius02") #key aruba123
```

Configuration ➢ SECURITY ➢ Authentication ➢ Servers ➢ RADIUS Server will bring you to the menu where you can create the RADIUS servers using the WebUI.

The following CLI command displays the configuration of the specified authentication server, in this instance, radius01:

```
#show aaa authentication-server radius radius01

RADIUS Server "radius01"
------------------------
Parameter                           Value
---------                           -----
Host                                10.254.1.21
Key                                 ********
```

```
CPPM credentials                        N/A
Auth Port                               1812
Acct Port                               1813
Radsec Port                             2083
Retransmits                             3
Timeout                                 5 sec
NAS ID                                  N/A
NAS IP                                  N/A
Enable IPv6                             Disabled
NAS IPv6                                N/A
Source Interface                        N/A
Use MD5                                 Disabled
Use IP address for calling station ID   Disabled
Mode                                    Enabled
Lowercase MAC addresses                 Disabled
MAC address delimiter                   none
Service-type of FRAMED-USER             Disabled
Radsec                                  Disabled
Radsec Trusted CA Name                  N/A
Radsec Server Cert Name                 N/A
Radsec Client Cert                      N/A
called-station-id                       macaddr colon disable
```

It is going to sound strange, but the 802.1X/EAP network does not get configured to authenticate against an authentication server. As I mentioned earlier, you can have one or more servers or databases. To provide for this, Aruba defines what is known as a *server group*, which is what the 802.1X/EAP network will authenticate against.

A server group may contain one or more servers. Figure 5.5 shows that the authentication server is added to the server group. As shown in Figure 5.6, some RADIUS servers maintain internal user databases that can be used to authenticate user credentials during login. An Aruba ClearPass server is an example of a RADIUS server that maintains an internal database that can be used for authentication.

FIGURE 5.6
RADIUS servers with internal databases

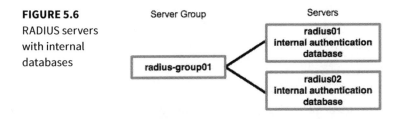

The following CLI commands define a server group named radius-group01. This server group contains two RADIUS servers: radius01 and radius02.

```
(config) #aaa server-group radius-group01
(Server Group "radius-group01") #auth-server radius01 position 1
(Server Group "radius-group01") #auth-server radius02 position 2
```

The controller will process the list of servers from top to bottom. When an 802.1X/EAP client logs in, the Aruba controller will attempt to authenticate the user credentials against `radius01` since it is the first server on the list. If `radius01` is unreachable, the Aruba controller will then attempt to authenticate the user credentials against `radius02`.

The default behavior is for the controller to advance through the list of servers based on timeout. If the first authentication server responds, either successfully or unsuccessfully, the controller will not continue on to the second server. If the first server in the list times out (does not respond), the controller will advance to the second server in the list and attempt to contact it. Again, subsequent servers are only checked if the previous servers are unreachable.

This configuration of two servers would be used when you have two identical databases. The `radius02` server provides redundancy if `radius01` is unreachable. If the Load Balance option is enabled, since the two servers contain identical copies of the same database, requests are balanced across all servers defined in the server group.

To create the server group and assign the RADIUS servers to the server group, go to **Configuration ➢ SECURITY ➢ Authentication ➢ Servers ➢ Server Group** (shown in Figure 5.7).

FIGURE 5.7
Server group

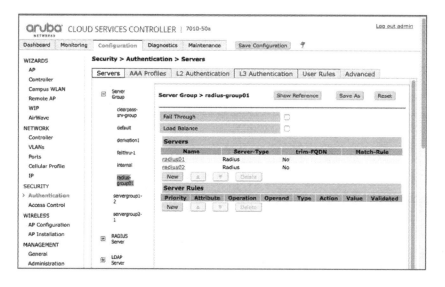

The following CLI command displays the configuration of the specified authentication server group, in this instance `radius-group01`:

```
#show aaa server-group radius-group01

Fail Through:No
Load Balance:No
```

```
Auth Servers
------------
Name        Server-Type   trim-FQDN   Match-Type   Match-Op   Match-Str
----        -----------   ---------   ----------   --------   ---------
radius01    Radius        No
radius02    Radius        No

Role/VLAN derivation rules
--------------------------
Priority   Attribute   Operation   Operand   Type   Action   Value   Validated
--------   ---------   ---------   -------   ----   ------   -----   ---------
```

I explained previously that in a multiple database environment, we may want to look up the user account in one database, such as a Windows AD database, and then if the user was not found in the first database, look up the user in a different database, such as a Linux database. The preferred way of doing this would be to have the RADIUS server point to both databases. However, you could configure the server group to point to two different RADIUS servers, as shown in Figure 5.6. This is known as *fail through*. Fail through would send a request to verify the user credentials to the first server in the list. If the user is not found, or the credentials are invalid, the server would reply in the negative to the controller. Next, the controller would send a request to verify the user credentials to the next server in the list. The controller stops processing the list of authentication servers in the server group if there is a positive response, or when the controller reaches the end of the list.

There are numerous limitations and reasons why you should be cautious when configuring fail through, which are explained in the ArubaOS documentation.

Access Control

A key component of 802.1X/EAP is the ability to provide different levels of access control to the users after successfully logging in. By providing the controller the ability to define different levels of access, each user may be given a different access profile, based upon their unique connection.

In fact, the title of the 802.1X amendment is "Port-Based Network Access Control." So, how is it that we can use a "port-based" technology to identify a connection, when wireless networks do not have ports? As I described in the previous section, 802.1X/EAP performs authentication (confirmation of the user's credentials). Once the user is authenticated, the system then knows the identity of the user. From this identity, the controller can then provide unique access control using the built-in firewall capability of the controller.

After a user successfully logs into an 802.1X/EAP network, the user is assigned a user role. In the controller, a user role is a set of permissions and controls in the form of a firewall role. A firewall role is made up of one or more firewall policies, and a firewall policy is made up of one or more firewall rules. So essentially, the user is assigned a set of firewall rules that governs their access to resources on the network. Figure 5.8 illustrates that after one or more firewall policies are created, the policy or policies are then assigned to a firewall role.

FIGURE 5.8 Firewall policy and role

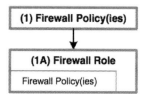

In Chapter 7, "Role Derivation," you will learn that there are numerous ways in which a client can be assigned a role. This process is known as *role derivation* and involves a very extensive set of rules and conditions, processed in a specific order. A default role will be assigned to a user if the user does not receive a role through any of the other role derivation methods. A default role is defined in the authentication profile, which will be explained in the next section.

You will learn more about roles and role derivation in Chapter 7, "Role Derivation." In Chapter 8, "Policy Enforcement Firewall," you will learn about the rules and policies that make up firewall roles. For now, understand that a user role is simply a set of permissions that are assigned to a user when the user successfully authenticates to the network.

Authentication Profile

The authentication profile defines parameters that are used for the authentication process. There are different authentication profiles for different authentication methods, but essentially the profile defines the details for how the authentication will be performed. A couple of basic authentication profile settings include the maximum number of authentication failures allowed and the reauthentication interval. The Advanced tab on the WebUI of the 802.1X authentication profile includes an extensive list of settings that can be used to customize the 802.1X authentication process.

The following CLI command will create an authentication profile named 1x-auth-profile. As I mentioned previously, the 802.1X authentication profile has an extensive list of settings; however, default values will be used for each of the settings, unless otherwise specified.

```
(config) #aaa authentication dot1x 1x-auth-profile
```

Configuration ➢ SECURITY ➢ Authentication ➢ L2 Authentication ➢ 802.1X Authentication will bring you to the menu where you can create the 802.1X authentication profile using the WebUI.

PROFILE HIERARCHY

The following CLI command displays the configuration of the specified 802.1X authentication profile, in this instance 1x-auth-profile. If you want to learn more about any of the parameters, the *Aruba CLI Reference Guide* and *User Guide* contain information about them.

```
#show aaa authentication dot1x 1x-auth-profile

802.1X Authentication Profile "1x-auth-profile"
------------------------------------------------
Parameter                                                   Value
---------                                                   -----
Max authentication failures                                 0
Enforce Machine Authentication                              Disabled
Machine Authentication: Default Machine Role                guest
Machine Authentication Cache Timeout                        24 hr(s)
Blacklist on Machine Authentication Failure                 Disabled
Machine Authentication: Default User Role                   guest
Interval between Identity Requests                          5 sec
Quiet Period after Failed Authentication                    30 sec
Reauthentication Interval                                   86400 sec
Use Server provided Reauthentication Interval               Disabled
Use the termination-action attribute from the Server        Disabled
Multicast Key Rotation Time Interval                        1800 sec
Unicast Key Rotation Time Interval                          900 sec
Authentication Server Retry Interval                        5 sec
Authentication Server Retry Count                           3
Framed MTU                                                  1100 bytes
Max number of requests sent during an Auth attempt          5
Max Number of Reauthentication Attempts                     3
Maximum number of times Held State can be bypassed          0
Dynamic WEP Key Message Retry Count                         1
Dynamic WEP Key Size                                        128 bits
Interval between WPA/WPA2 Key Messages                      1000 msec
Delay between EAP-Success and WPA2 Unicast Key Exchange     0 msec
Delay between WPA/WPA2 Unicast Key and Group Key Exchange   0 msec
Time interval after which the PMKSA will be deleted         8 hr(s)
Delete Keycache upon user deletion                          Disabled
WPA/WPA2 Key Message Retry Count                            3
Multicast Key Rotation                                      Disabled
Unicast Key Rotation                                        Disabled
Reauthentication                                            Disabled
Opportunistic Key Caching                                   Enabled
Validate PMKID                                              Enabled
Use Session Key                                             Disabled
Use Static Key                                              Disabled
xSec MTU                                                    1300 bytes
Termination                                                 Disabled
Termination EAP-Type                                        N/A
Termination Inner EAP-Type                                  N/A
```

```
        Token Caching                                           Disabled
        Token Caching Period                                    24 hr(s)
        CA-Certificate                                          N/A
        Server-Certificate                                      N/A
        TLS Guest Access                                        Disabled
        TLS Guest Role                                          guest
        Ignore EAPOL-START after authentication                 Disabled
        Handle EAPOL-Logoff                                     Disabled
        Ignore EAP ID during negotiation.                       Disabled
        WPA-Fast-Handover                                       Disabled
        Disable rekey and reauthentication for clients on call  Disabled
        Check certificate common name against AAA server        Enabled
```

AAA Profile

AAA is an acronym for *Authentication, Authorization* and *Accounting*. Historically, authentication has been the most visible piece of AAA. *Authentication* is the process of validating the user or device credentials when connecting to the network.

ArubaOS has supported 802.1X/EAP with authentication for many years. Over the past few years, with the surge of the bring your own device (BYOD) workforce, and headless IoT devices (devices without monitors, such as cameras and printers), authorization has become a huge topic, and it is still in its infancy. *Authorization* is typically handled by gathering additional information about the user or device, and adding it to the access control logic. Typically, an external RADIUS or network access control (NAC) server is used for this process. This is sometimes referred to as a policy engine or policy server. With this process, the network access device (such as a controller) sends connectivity and data usage information to the policy server (such as ClearPass). The access server can use this information for monitoring the network connections. This information can also be used to make further decisions about access control for the client.

The last piece of AAA is *accounting*, which provides tracking and monitoring of the client connecting.

The AAA profile incorporates and specifies the key components of authentication, authorization, and accounting. If you have configured an Aruba controller following the order of the previous sections, you would have already defined the following components:

- Authentication server
- Server group
- Firewall policy
- User role
- 802.1X authentication profile

It is now time to group these together to create the AAA profile. The *AAA profile* links together the server or servers that you will authenticate against (authentication server and server group), the method that you will use to perform the authentication (802.1X Authentication Profile), and the default role that will be assigned if you do not receive a server assigned role (firewall policy and user role). Figure 5.9 illustrates how these components are integrated into the AAA profile.

One method of remembering the components that you need for an AAA profile is to ask and answer the following three questions: Where are you authenticating against (authentication server and server group), how are you authenticating (authentication profile), and what permissions will you receive after you authenticate (firewall policy and user role)?

FIGURE 5.9
AAA profile

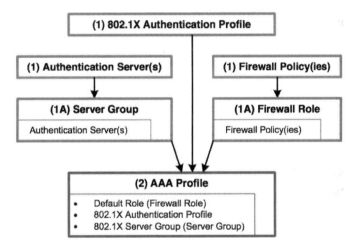

The following CLI commands create the AAA profile and then link the server group, authentication profile, and the default role to the profile:

```
(config) #aaa profile employee-aaa-profile
(AAA Profile "employee-aaa-profile") #dot1x-server-group radius-group01
(AAA Profile "employee-aaa-profile") #authentication-dot1x 1x-auth-profile
(AAA Profile "employee-aaa-profile") #dot1x-default-role authenticated
```

Selecting **Configuration ➢ SECURITY ➢ Authentication ➢ AAA Profiles** will bring you to the menu where you can create the AAA profile using the WebUI.

The following CLI command displays the configuration of the specified AAA profile, in this instance employee-aaa-profile. The authentication profile, default role, and server group are highlighted.

```
#show aaa profile employee-aaa-profile

AAA Profile "employee-aaa-profile"
```

```
Parameter                              Value
---------                              -----
Initial role                           logon
MAC Authentication Profile             N/A
MAC Authentication Default Role        guest
MAC Authentication Server Group        default
802.1X Authentication Profile          1x-auth-profile
802.1X Authentication Default Role     authenticated
802.1X Authentication Server Group     radius-group01
Download Role from CPPM                Disabled
L2 Authentication Fail Through         Disabled
Multiple Server Accounting             Disabled
User idle timeout                      N/A
Max IPv4 for wireless user             2
RADIUS Accounting Server Group         N/A
RADIUS Interim Accounting              Disabled
XML API server                         N/A
RFC 3576 server                        N/A
User derivation rules                  N/A
Wired to Wireless Roaming              Enabled
SIP authentication role                N/A
Device Type Classification             Enabled
Enforce DHCP                           Disabled
PAN Firewall Integration               Disabled
Open SSID radius accounting            Disabled
```

SSID Profile

Configuring the SSID is a fairly simple task. The SSID profile defines the SSID that will be advertised, the authentication method that will be used, and the encryption that will be implemented, as illustrated in Figure 5.10. Realize that the SSID profile specifies the type of authentication and encryption that will be used, but the details of the authentication method are defined in the AAA profile.

FIGURE 5.10 SSID profile

> **(2) SSID Profile**
> - SSID
> - Network Authentication
> - Encryption

The following CLI commands create the SSID profile with an SSID of employee, wpa2 as the authentication protocol, and wpa2-aes as the encryption protocol:

```
(config) #wlan ssid-profile employee-ssid-profile
(SSID Profile "employee-ssid-profile") #essid employee
(SSID Profile "employee-ssid-profile") #opmode wpa2-aes
```

The SSID profile is often created from within the AP Configuration menu when creating the virtual AP profile, as shown in Figure 5.11.

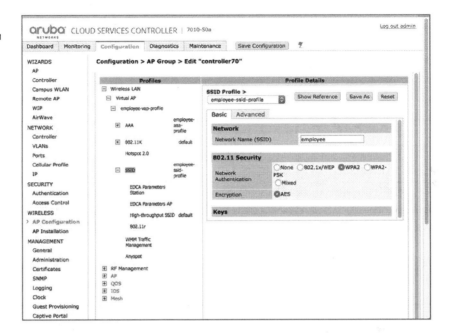

FIGURE 5.11
SSID profile menu

The SSID profile can also be created by itself from the All Profiles menu. In fact, any profile can be created, modified, or deleted from the All Profiles menu. Think of the All Profiles menu as the global repository for all profiles. As you become more familiar with profiles, you will find that it is often simpler and easier to work with profiles from the All Profiles menu, especially when modifying or deleting profiles. Some system configuration profiles can *only* be accessed from the All Profiles menu. Choosing **Configuration** ➢ **ADVANCED SERVICES** ➢ **All Profiles** ➢ **Wireless LAN** ➢ **SSID** in the WebUI All Profiles menu, will bring you to where you can create, modify, or delete an SSID profile.

The following CLI command displays the configuration of the specified SSID profile, in this instance employee-ssid-profile:

```
#show wlan ssid-profile employee-ssid-profile

SSID Profile "employee-ssid-profile"
------------------------------------
Parameter                                           Value
---------                                           -----
SSID enable                                         Enabled
ESSID                                               employee
```

Encryption	wpa2-aes
Enable Management Frame Protection	Disabled
Require Management Frame Protection	Disabled
DTIM Interval	1 beacon periods
802.11a Basic Rates	6 12 24
802.11a Transmit Rates	6 9 12 18 24 36 48 54
802.11g Basic Rates	1 2
802.11g Transmit Rates	1 2 5 6 9 11 12 18 24 36 48 54
Station Ageout Time	1000 sec
Max Transmit Attempts	8
RTS Threshold	2333 bytes
Short Preamble	Enabled
Max Associations	64
Wireless Multimedia (WMM)	Disabled
Wireless Multimedia U-APSD (WMM-UAPSD) Powersave	Enabled
WMM TSPEC Min Inactivity Interval	0 msec
Override DSCP mappings for WMM clients	Disabled
DSCP mapping for WMM voice AC (0-63)	N/A
DSCP mapping for WMM video AC (0-63)	N/A
DSCP mapping for WMM best-effort AC (0-63)	N/A
DSCP mapping for WMM background AC (0-63)	N/A
Multiple Tx Replay Counters	Disabled
Hide SSID	Disabled
Deny_Broadcast Probes	Disabled
Local Probe Request Threshold (dB)	0
Auth Request Threshold (dB)	0
Disable Probe Retry	Enabled
Battery Boost	Disabled
WEP Key 1	N/A
WEP Key 2	N/A
WEP Key 3	N/A
WEP Key 4	N/A
WEP Transmit Key Index	1
WPA Hexkey	N/A
WPA Passphrase	N/A
Maximum Transmit Failures	0
EDCA Parameters Station profile	N/A
EDCA Parameters AP profile	N/A
BC/MC Rate Optimization	Disabled
Rate Optimization for delivering EAPOL frames	Enabled
Strict Spectralink Voice Protocol (SVP)	Disabled
High-throughput SSID Profile	default
802.11g Beacon Rate	default
802.11a Beacon Rate	default

```
Video Multicast Rate Optimization              default
Advertise QBSS Load IE                         Disabled
Advertise Location Info                        Disabled
Advertise AP Name                              Disabled
802.11r Profile                                N/A
Enforce user vlan for open stations            Disabled
Enable OKC                                     Enabled
```

VLAN

There is not much to be said about VLAN. When you create a virtual AP you will assign a VLAN to it. Therefore, the VLAN needs to be created on the controller. The user traffic on the VAP will be placed on this VLAN. The following CLI commands create VLAN 51 and assign it the IP address of 10.1.51.2:

```
(config) #vlan 51
(config) #interface vlan 51
(config-subif) #ip address 10.1.51.2 255.255.255.0
```

To get to the menu where you can create the VLAN using the WebUI, go to **Configuration ➢ NETWORK ➢ VLANs ➢ VLAN ID**.

Select **Configuration ➢ NETWORK ➢ IP ➢ IP Interfaces** to get to the menu where you can assign the IP address to the VLAN using the WebUI.

The following CLI command displays the VLANs that are configured on the controller and the IP addresses that are assigned to them.

```
#show ip interface brief

Interface           IP Address   /   IP Netmask       Admin    Protocol
vlan 50             10.1.50.100  /   255.255.255.0    up       up
vlan 51             10.1.51.2    /   255.255.255.0    up       down
vlan 53             192.168.5.1  /   255.255.255.0    up       down
loopback            unassigned   /   unassigned       up       up
```

Virtual AP Profile

At this point, all of the necessary components have been created to build the VAP profile: AAA profile, SSID profile, and VLAN. Now we simply need to combine these components together to create the VAP profile, as illustrated in Figure 5.12.

FIGURE 5.12
VAP profile

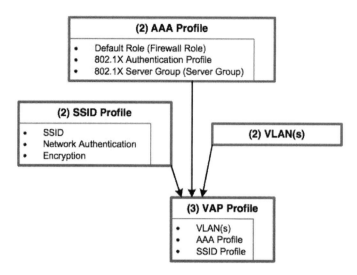

In addition to assigning the AAA profile, SSID profile, and VLAN to the VAP profile, you may also want to specify the forwarding mode for the user data between the AP and the controller. In Chapter 2, "Understanding the ArubaOS Environment," I explained the four forwarding modes: tunnel, bridge, decrypt-tunnel, and split-tunnel. The default and most commonly used forwarding mode is tunnel. The following CLI commands create the VAP profile and assign the VLAN, AAA profile, SSID profile, and forwarding mode to the VAP:

```
(config) #wlan virtual-ap employee-vap-profile
(Virtual AP profile "employee-vap-profile") #vlan 51
(Virtual AP profile "employee-vap-profile") #aaa-profile employee-aaa-profile
(Virtual AP profile "employee-vap-profile") #ssid-profile employee-ssid-profile
(Virtual AP profile "employee-vap-profile") #forward-mode tunnel
```

You can create the VAP profile using the WebUI by going to **Configuration ➢ ADVANCED SERVICES ➢ All Profiles ➢ Wireless LAN ➢ Virtual AP**.

The following CLI command displays the configuration of the specified VAP profile, in this instance, employee-vap-profile:

```
#show wlan virtual-ap employee-vap-profile

Virtual AP profile "employee-vap-profile" (Invalid: Named VLAN "employee" is not mapped)
--------------------------------------------------------------------------------
Parameter                                           Value
---------                                           -----
AAA Profile                                         employee-aaa-profile
802.11K Profile                                     default
Hotspot 2.0 Profile                                 N/A
SSID Profile                                        employee-ssid-profile
Virtual AP enable                                   Enabled
```

```
VLAN                                              51
Forward mode                                      tunnel
Allowed band                                      all
Band Steering                                     Disabled
Steering Mode                                     prefer-5ghz
Dynamic Multicast Optimization (DMO)              Disabled
Dynamic Multicast Optimization (DMO) Threshold    6
Drop Broadcast and Unknown Multicast              Disabled
Convert Broadcast ARP requests to unicast         Enabled
Authentication Failure Blacklist Time             3600 sec
Blacklist Time                                    3600 sec
Deny inter user traffic                           Disabled
Deny time range                                   N/A
DoS Prevention                                    Disabled
HA Discovery on-association                       Enabled
Mobile IP                                         Enabled
Preserve Client VLAN                              Disabled
Remote-AP Operation                               standard
Station Blacklisting                              Enabled
Strict Compliance                                 Disabled
VLAN Mobility                                     Disabled
WAN Operation mode                                always
FDB Update on Assoc                               Disabled
WMM Traffic Management Profile                    N/A
Anyspot profile                                   N/A
```

Earlier in this chapter, you read about how a virtual AP consists of all the configuration settings necessary to advertise a wireless network. In this section, you learned the commands to create the VAP profile, along with the commands to assign the configuration settings to the VAP profile.

Figure 5.4 illustrates all of the pieces necessary to configure and enable an 802.1X/EAP VAP. Figure 5.13 illustrates the last steps necessary to complete the configuration of the 802.1X/EAP wireless network. At this point, an AP system profile needs to be created, and then it and the VAP profile need to be assigned to an AP group. After these steps are completed, the configuration parameters must be pushed out to all of the APs that are members of the AP group, and the wireless network will be up and running.

FIGURE 5.13
AP group

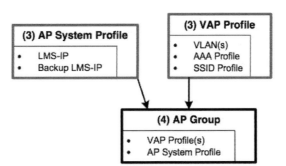

AP System Profile

The AP system profile contains all the settings required by the APs to be able to communicate with the controller. As with the other profiles, the AP system profile has many configuration parameters. Again, most of these parameters can be left at their default settings. Two important parameters that should be configured in this profile are the local management switch IP address (LMS-IP) and the backup local management switch IP address (BKUP-LMS-IP).

In Chapter 2, you learned about the boot process of the AP. As explained there, when the AP initially boots, it needs six pieces of information: IP address, subnet mask, default gateway, AP name, AP group, and the IP address of the controller that the AP will initially communicate with. After the AP has these six pieces of information, the AP communicates with the initial controller and checks its OS version, possibly updating the OS if needed. The AP then communicates with the initial controller again. This time the AP provides the controller with its AP name and AP group. The controller uses the name and group information to identify the AP so that the controller can tell the AP the IP address of the controller that will provide the AP with its configuration, and that the AP will use to terminate its GRE tunnel.

If the LMS-IP address is set, the AP will download its configuration from the specified controller (LMS-IP) and continue to terminate its GRE to that controller. If the LMS-IP controller is unreachable, the AP will attempt to communicate with the BKUP-LMS-IP controller. If the LMS-IP and BKUP-LMS-IP values are not set, or set incorrectly, the AP will download its configuration from the controller that it initially discovered, and also terminate its GRE to that controller. If you only have one controller on your network, it is not necessary to specify an LMS-IP value. However, if you have more than one controller, you should always define the LMS-IP value. The following CLI commands create the AP system profile and define the LMS-IP address:

```
(config) #ap system-profile building1-ap-system-profile
(AP system profile "building1-ap-system-profile") #lms-ip 10.1.50.100
```

The AP system profile is also commonly created from within the AP Configuration menu when creating the virtual AP profile, as shown in Figure 5.14.

Remember: the AP system profile, as with any profile, can also be created, modified, or deleted from the All Profiles menu.

FIGURE 5.14
AP system profile menu

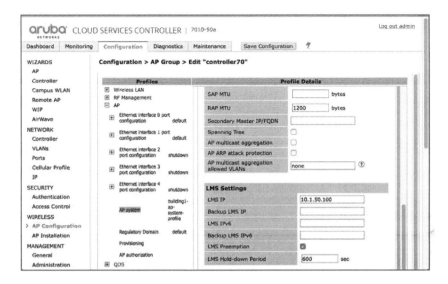

The following CLI command displays the configuration of the specified AP system profile, in this instance, building1-ap-system-profile:

```
#show ap system-profile building1-ap-system-profile

AP system profile "building1-ap-system-profile"
-----------------------------------------------
Parameter                                    Value
---------                                    -----
RF Band                                      g
RF Band for AM mode scanning                 all
Native VLAN ID                               1
Tunnel Heartbeat Interval                    1
Session ACL                                  ap-uplink-acl
Corporate DNS Domain                         N/A
SNMP sysContact                              N/A
LED operating mode (11n/11ac APs only)       normal
LED override                                 Disabled
Driver log level                             emergencies
SAP MTU                                      N/A
RAP MTU                                      1200 bytes
LMS IP                                       10.1.50.100
Backup LMS IP                                N/A
LMS IPv6                                     N/A
Backup LMS IPv6                              N/A
LMS Preemption                               Disabled
LMS Hold-down Period                         600 sec
LMS ping interval                            20
Remote-AP DHCP Server VLAN                   N/A
```

```
Remote-AP DHCP Server Id              192.168.11.1
Remote-AP DHCP Default Router         192.168.11.1
Remote-AP DHCP DNS Server             N/A
Remote-AP DHCP Pool Start             192.168.11.2
Remote-AP DHCP Pool End               192.168.11.254
Remote-AP DHCP Pool Netmask           255.255.255.0
Remote-AP DHCP Lease Time             0 days
Remote-AP uplink total bandwidth      0 kbps
Remote-AP bw reservation 1            N/A
Remote-AP bw reservation 2            N/A
Remote-AP bw reservation 3            N/A
Remote-AP Local Network Access        Disabled
Bootstrap threshold                   8
Double Encrypt                        Disabled
Dump Server                           N/A
Heartbeat DSCP                        0
Maintenance Mode                      Disabled
Maximum Request Retries               10
Request Retry Interval                10 sec
Number of IPSEC retries               85
AeroScout RTLS Server                 N/A
RTLS Server configuration             N/A
RTLS Server Compatibility Mode        Enabled
Telnet                                Disabled
Spanning Tree                         Disabled
AP multicast aggregation              Disabled
AP ARP attack protection              Disabled
AP multicast aggregation allowed VLANs  none
Console enable                        Enabled
Shell Password                        N/A
Password for Backup                   ********
AP USB Power override                 Disabled
RF Band for Backup                    all
Operation for Backup                  off
BLE Endpoint URL                      N/A
BLE Auth Token                        N/A
BLE Operation Mode                    Disabled
```

AP Group

The configuration of the 802.1X/EAP WLAN is just about complete. The final step is to assign the VAP profile and the AP system profile to the AP group, as previously illustrated in Figure 5.13. The following CLI commands create the AP group and assign the AP system profile and VAP profile to the group:

```
(config) #ap-group building1
(AP group "building1") #ap-system-profile building1-ap-system-profile
(AP group "building1") #virtual-ap employee-vap-profile
```

You can also navigate to **Configuration** ≻ **WIRELESS** ≻ **AP Configuration**, where you can create the AP group using the WebUI. After you create the AP group, you select the AP group that you created. From there you select Wireless LAN to add the VAP to the AP group, and you click AP, and then AP System to add the AP system profile to the AP group.

The following CLI command displays the configuration of the specified AP group, in this instance, building1:

```
#show ap-group building1

AP group "building1"
----------------------
Parameter                                    Value
---------                                    -----
Virtual AP                                   employee-vap-profile
802.11a radio profile                        default
802.11g radio profile                        default
Ethernet interface 0 port configuration      default
Ethernet interface 1 port configuration      default
Ethernet interface 2 port configuration      shutdown
Ethernet interface 3 port configuration      shutdown
Ethernet interface 4 port configuration      shutdown
AP system profile                            building1-ap-system-profile
VoIP Call Admission Control profile          default
802.11a Traffic Management profile           N/A
802.11g Traffic Management profile           N/A
Regulatory Domain profile                    default
RF Optimization profile                      default
RF Event Thresholds profile                  default
IDS profile                                  default
Mesh Radio profile                           default
Mesh Cluster profile                         N/A
Provisioning profile                         N/A
AP authorization profile                     N/A
```

WebUI Configuration Menus

One of the good features, and sometimes not-so-good features, of the WebUI is that profiles can be created, edited, or viewed in multiple places. Having different places where you can access the profiles can be very convenient, but can also be confusing for users who are new to ArubaOS. The following sections will describe the three main locations on the WebUI where you can access the profiles: All Profiles, Authentication, and AP Configuration.

All Profiles

As explained earlier in this chapter, if you need to create, modify, or delete a profile, the All Profiles menu is a great place to go, especially if you need to modify or delete a profile. The All Profiles menu has an expanding tree structure that contains every profile created on the controller. It will also contain profiles that may no longer be assigned to an AP group, but are not deleted from the controller.

To get to the All Profiles menu, you need to first select Configuration along the top menu bar. Then, along the left side at the bottom of the Configuration menu, in the ADVANCED SERVICES section, is the All Profiles selection. The All Profiles menu is organized into eight sections, as displayed in Figure 5.15. Within these eight sections you have access to every profile.

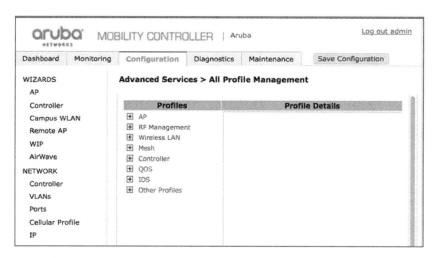

FIGURE 5.15
All Profile Management screen

The All Profiles section is a great resource because it provides a central menu with direct access to every profile. Although the All Profiles menu is organized into eight sections, it is not always easy to find the profile you are looking for, because there are close to a hundred different profiles, and unfortunately, there does not appear to be a logical or alphabetical order for listing the profiles. Figure 5.16 displays all the profiles in the order that they appear, and separated into each of the eight sections.

FIGURE 5.16 All Profiles

AP	Wireless LAN	Mesh
AP system	802.11K	Mesh High-throughput SSID
Regulatory Domain	Handover Trigger	Mesh Radio
Wired AP	RRM IE	Mesh Cluster
AP Ethernet Link	Beacon Report Request	
AP LLDP-MED Network Policy	802.11r	**Controller**
AP LLDP	TSM Report Request	Mgmt Config
AP wired port	SSID	Valid Equipment OUI
AP Authorization	High-throughput SSID	Upgrade
EDCA Parameters Profile (Station)	ANQP Venue Name	
EDCA Parameters profile (AP)	ANQP Network Authentication	**QOS**
Spectrum Local Override	ANQP Roaming Consortium	WMM Traffic management
	ANQP NAI Realm	Traffic management
RF Management	ANQP 3GPP Cellular Network	VoIP Call Admission Control
802.11a radio	H2QP Operator Friendly Name	
802.11g radio	H2Qp WAN Metrics	**IDS**
Adaptive Radio Management (ARM)	H2Qp Connection Capability	IDS General
High-throughput radio	H2Qp Operating Class Indication	IDS Rate Thresholds
RF Optimization	ANQP IP Address Availability	IDS Signature Matching
RF Event Thresholds	ANQP Domain Name	IDS Signature
AM Scanning	Advertisement	IDS Denial Of Service
	Hotspot 2.0	IDS Impersonation
	Virtual AP	IDS Unauthorized Device
	VIA Client WLAN	IDS
	AAA	IDS WMS Management
	XML API Server	IDS WMS General
	RFC 3576 Server	IDS WMS Local System
	MAC Authentication	IDS RAP WML Table
	Captive Portal Authentication	IDS RAP WML Server
	WISPr Authentication	
	802.1X Authentication	**Other Profiles**
	SSO	VIA Authentication
	RADIUS Server	VIA Connection
	LDAP Server	VIA Web Authentication
	TACACS Server	VIA Global Configuration
	Server Group	Mgmt Password Policy
	VPN Authentication	VoIP Logging
	Management Authentication	SIP settings
	Wired Authentication	Dialplan
	Stateful NTLM Authentication	Traffic Control Prioritization
	Stateful Kerberos Authentication	Configure Real-Time Analysis
	Stateful 802.1X Authentication	License provisioning
	Alias Group	File syncing
		Airgroup AAA
		CPPM IF-MAP
		Palo Alto Networks Servers
		Palo Alto Networks Active

Authentication

The second place where you can create or modify profiles is in the authentication menu. After you select Configuration from the menu along the top of the WebUI, the Authentication menu can be found about a third of the way down the left side menu, in the SECURITY section. The Authentication Menu logically groups all of the profiles related to client authentication. The menu consists of six submenus:

- Servers
- AAA Profiles
- L2 Authentication

- L3 Authentication
- User Rules
- Advanced

One of the characteristics of the ArubaOS WebUI is that AAA profiles cannot be edited from the VAP profile or the AP Group screens. The AAA profiles must be configured from within the Authentication menu or the All Profiles menu. Furthermore, all of the key AAA configuration profiles can be found in the submenus, making it easy to navigate between tasks. These sections will be explained in greater detail in later chapters of this book.

AP Configuration

The third location where you will work with profiles is in the AP Configuration menu. Sometimes this menu is referred to as the AP Group menu. This menu is different than the other two in the sense that your focus here is not on the creation of the profiles, but on assigning profiles to an AP group.

Although you can create many of the profiles from within an AP group, it is better to have the profiles already created, and primarily use this menu to assign profiles to the AP group. This is emphasized by the fact that you cannot create or modify the AAA profile from within this menu. This is a precautionary feature. While modifying security settings for a specific AP group, you may not realize that the changes could be affecting many AP groups, since profiles can be applied simultaneously in multiple places on your controller. The AAA profile cannot be created or modified from the AP Configuration menu.

Since the AAA profile is such an important profile, and since it is essentially a mandatory profile assigned to every AP group, hopefully you will train yourself to configure profiles through one of the other menus, and use AP Configuration primarily for assigning profiles to the AP groups.

After selecting Configuration from the menu along the top of the WebUI, the AP Configuration menu can be found about a third of the way down the left side menu in the WIRELESS section. From this menu you have the ability to create your AP group and then assign profiles to it, or you can select an existing AP group and modify it.

Managing Profiles

One of the fundamental concepts of profiles is that they are the configuration building blocks of ArubaOS. Profiles make it easy to apply settings across groups of APs. An example of this would be if you created a VAP profile specifically for warehouse devices, and then applied that one VAP profile to each AP group that is deployed at

30 warehouses around the country. In this example, a change to that single VAP profile would propagate to every warehouse and every AP in each warehouse.

Being able to make a change to one profile and have it applied in many places is a great feature and benefit when managing the wireless network. However, at times you may not want the change made across all of the locations. It may be necessary to make a minor change across a single location or maybe a different grouping of locations. In order to make this happen, there are a few tasks that can help, that will be explained in the following sections: show references, cloning profiles, and show profile-hierarchy.

Show References

Before you make changes to a profile, it is important to know where that profile is applied and which devices will be affected by the change. The show command is used to list a specific type of profile, the list often includes a references column displaying how many times each profile is referenced. An example of this is displayed in the following CLI output that shows all of the server groups defined:

```
#show aaa server-group

Server Group List
-----------------
Name                  References    Profile Status
----                  ----------    --------------
clearpass-srv-group   1
default               23
derivation1           0
failthru-1            0
internal              2             Predefined
radius-group01        1
servergroup1-2        0
servergroup2-1        0

Total:8
```

Displaying the number of times a profile is referenced is useful to understand how much a profile is applied; however, when it comes time to make changes, you need to specifically know where the profile is being used. The show references command provides this information.

The show references command is available from both the CLI and the WebUI, and can be used with most profiles to display the places where the profile is referenced. The following CLI output shows that the internal server group is referenced by seven AAA profiles. Figure 5.17 shows the internal server group references using the WebUI. In this figure, the Hide Reference button, when clicked, will toggle back to being the Show

Reference button. The Instances column shows the different profiles where the internal server group is referenced.

```
#show references aaa server-group internal

References to Server Group "internal"
-------------------------------------
Referrer                                                          Count
--------                                                          -----
aaa profile "r-1x-aaa_prof" mac-server-group                      1
aaa profile "WC-1X-MACAUTH-aaa_prof" mac-server-group             1
aaa profile "WC-Guest-CP4-MACAUTH-aaa_prof" mac-server-group      1
aaa profile "WC-WPA2-1X-aaa_prof" mac-server-group                1
aaa profile "WC-WPA2-PSK-MACAUTH-aaa_prof" mac-server-group       1
aaa authentication captive-portal "Captive-Portal-1" server-group 1
aaa authentication vpn "default-cap" server-group                 1
Total References:7
```

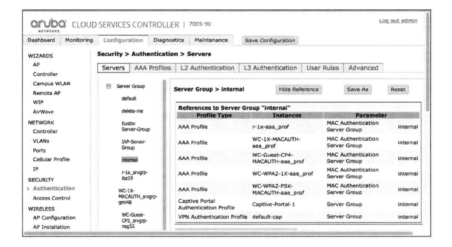

FIGURE 5.17 Showing references using the WebUI

Cloning Profiles

As networks grow and evolve, at times it becomes necessary to consolidate configurations, and at other times it becomes necessary to split configurations or branch off parts of the configuration in new directions. If you are branching off, the current configuration may only need minor changes to achieve the new goal. To make this easier, ArubaOS provides the ability to copy, or *clone*, an existing configuration, creating a duplicate profile with a different name. This new profile can then be modified and applied separately from the original. Profiles can be cloned from either the CLI or WebUI.

Here is an example of how and why you might use cloning. Your company may have a virtual AP profile configured for 802.1X/EAP authentication, advertising a corporate

SSID, and authenticating user accounts against an Active Directory server in North America. Your company decides to expand operations into Europe and install a separate Active Directory server in Europe. To simplify the implementation of the wireless network in Europe, you could clone the corporate virtual AP profile, creating a separate VAP for the corporate network in Europe. From there you could make the necessary modifications, such as VLAN, server group, and regulatory domain.

The cloning process is easy, whether from the CLI or the WebUI. In the described scenario, the first task is to identify the profile that you will be cloning. This is easily done using the show command, as shown in the following CLI output. The output shows all of the VAP profiles, but specifically the na-corporate VAP profile that we want to clone.

```
#show wlan virtual-ap

Virtual AP profile List
-----------------------
Name                             References   Profile Status
----                             ----------   --------------
default                          0
na-corporate                     1
s-1x-vap_prof                    0
WC-1X-MACAUTH-vap_prof           0
WC-Guest-CP2-vap_prof            0
WC-Guest-CP3-Wizard-vap_prof     0
WC-Guest-CP4-MACAUTH-vap_prof    0
WC-MACAUTH-vap_prof              0
WC-WEP-PSK-vap_prof              0
WC-WPA-PSK-vap_prof              1
WC-WPA2-1X-vap_prof              0
WC-WPA2-PSK-MACAUTH-vap_prof     0
WC-WPA2-PSK-vap_prof             0

Total:13
```

The next step is to create the new VAP profile. This profile will be named eu-corporate and the clone command will be used to copy all of the parameters from the existing profile to the new profile. This is shown in the following CLI output:

```
(config) #wlan virtual-ap eu-corporate
(Virtual AP profile "eu-corporate") #clone na-corporate
```

Cloning a profile using the WebUI is performed by using the Save As button in the details window of the profile you are cloning. In Figure 5.18, the na-corporate VAP profile is selected from the All Profiles menu by going to **Configuration ➢ ADVANCED SERVICES ➢ All Profiles ➢ Wireless LAN ➢ Virtual AP ➢ na-corporate**. Cloning the na-corporate VAP profile is as easy as clicking the Save As button and typing in the new name.

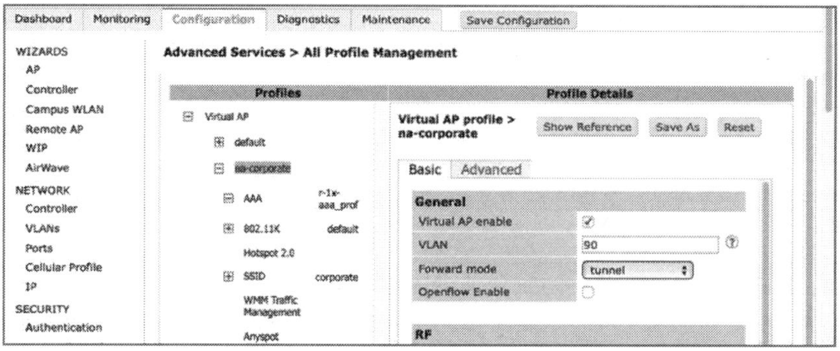

FIGURE 5.18
Cloning using Save As feature

Show Profile-hierarchy

ArubaOS provides a vast group of profiles nested within each other. This architecture provides you with power and flexibility; however, it can be difficult to remember the hierarchy. The show profile-hierarchy command displays the hierarchy of the profiles in an indented format so that it is easier to visualize the dependencies that they have on each other. The following shows the command and the output that it generates:

```
#show profile-hierarchy

ap-group
    wlan virtual-ap
        aaa profile
            aaa authentication mac
            aaa server-group
                aaa authentication-server radius
                    aaa radius modifier
            aaa authentication dot1x
            aaa xml-api server
            aaa rfc-3576-server
        wlan dot11k-profile
            wlan handover-trigger-profile
            wlan rrm-ie-profile
            wlan bcn-rpt-req-profile
            wlan tsm-req-profile
        wlan hotspot hs2-profile
            wlan hotspot advertisement-profile
                wlan hotspot anqp-venue-name-profile
                wlan hotspot anqp-nwk-auth-profile
                wlan hotspot anqp-roam-cons-profile
                wlan hotspot anqp-nai-realm-profile
                wlan hotspot anqp-3gpp-nwk-profile
                wlan hotspot anqp-ip-addr-avail-profile
                wlan hotspot h2qp-wan-metrics-profile
                wlan hotspot h2qp-operator-friendly-name-profile
```

```
            wlan hotspot h2qp-conn-capability-profile
            wlan hotspot h2qp-op-cl-profile
            wlan hotspot h2qp-osu-prov-list-profile
            wlan hotspot anqp-domain-name-profile
      wlan ssid-profile
          wlan edca-parameters-profile station
          wlan edca-parameters-profile ap
          wlan ht-ssid-profile
          wlan dot11r-profile
      wlan wmm-traffic-management-profile
      wlan anyspot-profile
rf dot11a-radio-profile
    rf spectrum-profile
    rf arm-profile
    rf ht-radio-profile
    rf am-scan-profile
rf dot11g-radio-profile
    rf spectrum-profile
    rf arm-profile
    rf ht-radio-profile
    rf am-scan-profile
ap wired-port-profile
    ap wired-ap-profile
    ap enet-link-profile
    ap lldp profile
        ap lldp med-network-policy-profile
    aaa profile
        aaa authentication mac
        aaa server-group
            aaa authentication-server radius
                aaa radius modifier
        aaa authentication dot1x
        aaa xml-api server
        aaa rfc-3576-server
ap system-profile
wlan voip-cac-profile
wlan traffic-management-profile
    wlan virtual-ap
        aaa profile
            aaa authentication mac
            aaa server-group
                aaa authentication-server radius
                    aaa radius modifier
            aaa authentication dot1x
            aaa xml-api server
            aaa rfc-3576-server
        wlan dot11k-profile
            wlan handover-trigger-profile
            wlan rrm-ie-profile
            wlan bcn-rpt-req-profile
```

```
                    wlan tsm-req-profile
                wlan hotspot hs2-profile
                    wlan hotspot advertisement-profile
                        wlan hotspot anqp-venue-name-profile
                        wlan hotspot anqp-nwk-auth-profile
                        wlan hotspot anqp-roam-cons-profile
                        wlan hotspot anqp-nai-realm-profile
                        wlan hotspot anqp-3gpp-nwk-profile
                        wlan hotspot anqp-ip-addr-avail-profile
                        wlan hotspot h2qp-wan-metrics-profile
                        wlan hotspot h2qp-operator-friendly-name-profile
                        wlan hotspot h2qp-conn-capability-profile
                        wlan hotspot h2qp-op-cl-profile
                        wlan hotspot h2qp-osu-prov-list-profile
                        wlan hotspot anqp-domain-name-profile
                wlan ssid-profile
                    wlan edca-parameters-profile station
                    wlan edca-parameters-profile ap
                    wlan ht-ssid-profile
                    wlan dot11r-profile
                wlan wmm-traffic-management-profile
                wlan anyspot-profile
        ap regulatory-domain-profile
        rf optimization-profile
        rf event-thresholds-profile
        ids profile
            ids general-profile
            ids signature-matching-profile
                ids signature-profile
            ids dos-profile
                ids rate-thresholds-profile
            ids impersonation-profile
            ids unauthorized-device-profile
        ap mesh-radio-profile
            ap mesh-ht-ssid-profile
        ap mesh-cluster-profile
        rf arm-rf-domain-profile
        ap provisioning-profile
        ap authorization-profile
```

Chapter 6

Authentication and Encryption

IN THIS CHAPTER, YOU WILL LEARN ABOUT THE FOLLOWING:

- Security Basics
- Authentication, Authorization, and Accounting
- Layer 2 vs. Layer 3 Authentication
  - Authentication Methods
- Encryption Techniques
  - WEP
  - WPA/TKIP
  - WPA2/AES
- Digital Certificates
  - Obtaining a Certificate
  - WebUI Management Certificate
  - Captive Portal Certificate
  - 802.1X/EAP Certificate

IN CHAPTER 5, "PROFILES," YOU LEARNED ABOUT virtual APs (VAPs) and the profiles that are needed to create an 802.1X/EAP VAP. Due to its high level of security, 802.1X/EAP has become the most commonly used authentication method for creating a secure wireless network.

The focus of this chapter is authentication and encryption. In this chapter you will learn about 802.1X/EAP along with other commonly used authentication methods that can be configured on an Aruba controller. In addition to learning about the authentication methods, you will also learn about some of the encryption methods that are supported. Most of the profiles explained in this section have many options. This chapter will focus almost exclusively on the core components and settings needed for authentication and encryption. Ignoring all of the other settings and options is by no means implying that they are not needed or important; however, there are just too many options and variables to address.

Remember, this is a book about ArubaOS and not a book about authentication and encryption. Although this chapter tries to explain many of these concepts, there is an assumption that you are familiar with Microsoft Active Directory, RADIUS servers, and NPS Server. To learn more about authentication and encryption, I suggest researching these topics on the Internet and reading *CWNA: Certified Wireless Network Administrator Official Study Guide: Exam CWNA-106* (Sybex, 2014) and *CWSP: Certified Wireless Security Professional Study Guide: Exam CWSP-205* (Sybex, 2016).

Security Basics

Related to security, more emphasis is being placed on authentication and encryption. Network access control (NAC) is an important topic today when installing most wireless networks. Due to its uncontained nature, wireless networks have been at the forefront of NAC for many years. The Aruba Networks controller with ArubaOS is one of the networking industry's finest solutions for wireless access control. Following is a basic explanation of the main elements that make up access control security.

There are four fundamental security components of wireless connectivity:

- Authentication
- Encryption
- Data integrity
- Access control

Authentication validates the identity of the user or device connecting to the network. More advanced connection methods are also capable of mutual authentication, which validates both the user and the server to which the user is establishing a connection.

Encryption is used to secure the data that is being transmitted from one location to another, making sure that only specified devices are able to read the data. Encryption does not hide the fact that there is data; it simply ensures that the data is only seen by its intended recipient.

Data integrity is the verification that the data received is exactly what was transmitted, making certain that the data was not accidentally or intentionally modified between the transmitter and the receiver. Data integrity is often ignored or forgotten because it is typically part of the encryption suite. Since data integrity is handled by the encryption suite or by other protocols, and is not configurable (except for selecting a robust encryption suite), it will not be addressed again in this book.

Access control refers to the methods used to restrain or restrict free access to network resources after the user has been identified as a valid user on the network. After a user connects, authenticates, and is identified to the wireless network, access control allows or restricts the user from accessing resources on the internal network or connected networks, such as the Internet.

The Aruba Networks solution for access control is one of the most robust solutions available. Access control has been one of the key features of the Aruba OS since the introduction of the product. ArubaOS uses identity-based access control, commonly known as *role-based access control (RBAC)*. RBAC expands the concept of access control by providing different levels of access to users, based upon individual or group identity. RBAC allows multiple users to connect to the same wireless network, using the same authentication method, while assigning each user a different set of rights and restrictions.

RBAC has great implications for design and performance of wireless networks. Most WLAN vendors control access to a given SSID, and then apply the same access rights in the form of access control lists (ACLs) to all users who are granted access. This has led to a proliferation of task-based SSIDs and the undesirable effect of excess overhead. When the number of SSIDs was trimmed, it led to a reduction in security, because more resource access was granted due to the lack of granularity. ArubaOS with RBAC gives an incredibly large number of possible access profiles, based on the identity of the user as they connect to the same SSID.

Authentication, Authorization, and Accounting

Authentication, Authorization, and Accounting (AAA) is a security framework for providing network access control (NAC). AAA is not a specific protocol, but a concept based on a broad group of protocols that work together. These protocols provide user identification, access control, and tracking of user activity.

Historically, AAA was primarily used for authentication and accounting. However, as the name implies, AAA operates in three layers. Authentication is used to verify the user identity. Authorization is used to determine if the user has rights to a given resource, in this case the wireless network. Finally, accounting incorporates methods to track the user's activities, such as connection status and data usage.

With all the different methods of authentication, it ultimately boils down to one question: "Are you who you say you are, and is your account still valid?" Authentication collects identity credentials (which can be in many forms) and validates them against an authoritative source. The most widely deployed authoritative sources, or account repositories, are Remote Authentication Dial-In User Services (RADIUS) and Microsoft Active Directory (AD).

After a user is authenticated, the process of authorizing the user begins. The first layer of authorization starts by querying the authentication source for any information that it may have to describe the user. This information is known as *authorization attributes* and can include things like the department the user works in, the user's job title, and the building location. Even information such as phone number and e-mail address can be returned by the authentication source. These account attributes are configured by the user account administrator and will vary depending on the needs of the company.

A second layer of authorization can also take place. In recent years, with the proliferation of bring your own device (BYOD), in addition to user identity, device identity has become important. Authorization to access resources can be based upon physical attributes, such as what type of device is connecting to the network, the time of day, where the connection is coming from, the connection type (wired, wireless, VPN), or many other parameters or combinations of parameters.

In addition to authentication and authorization, accounting is used to monitor connection status, data usage, resources, and activities. This information can be used for logging or reporting user activity on the network. The accounting record can provide information for enforcement based on user activity, which can then be used to disconnect a user from the network if the user state has changed, such as if the user has exceeded activity thresholds or allowances.

Historically, 802.1X/EAP is affiliated with AAA. However, with advancements over the past few years with RADIUS and network access control products such as Aruba's ClearPass, AAA functionality and capabilities have been extended to other access methods. Figure 6.1 shows the key AAA components, along with the logical exchange that occurs between these devices.

FIGURE 6.1 Authentication process

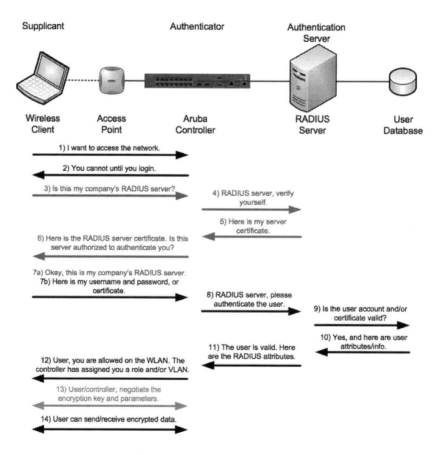

There are three key components in an 802.1X/EAP connection: the supplicant, authenticator, and authentication server. The wireless client or device is known as the *supplicant*. Technically, the supplicant is a software applet that runs as part of the network service on the client. The access control device is known as the *authenticator*. In Figure 6.1, the Aruba controller is the authenticator. The authenticator is also often called a *network access device (NAD)*. The final component is the *authentication server*, which is typically a RADIUS server. The RADIUS server will either utilize its internal database or communicate with an external database or server, such as a Windows Network Policy Server (NPS) connected to an Active Directory database. In Figure 6.1, an external database is illustrated.

When you are trying to understand the authentication process, realize that the supplicant is ultimately communicating with the authentication server. The authenticator acts like a guard, limiting access to the network, while passing messages between the supplicant and the authentication server. To understand this better, Figure 6.1 displays 14 logical exchanges between these devices. The following is a step-by-step description of the process.

1. The client connects to the WLAN and activates the supplicant as part of the network profile.
2. The authenticator blocks access to the network and negotiates access and authentication parameters with the client's supplicant. This requires the supplicant to go through an authentication process.

Before the user provides credentials, the supplicant may want to validate the identity of the authentication server. If so, then steps 3 through 7a will be executed. If not, then these steps are skipped.

3. The supplicant checks to see if the RADIUS sever is a trusted server.
4. The authenticator passes this message to the authentication server.
5. The authentication server responds to the supplicant's request by providing a public server authentication certificate.
6. The authenticator relays the server certificate to the supplicant.
7a. The supplicant verifies the server certificate. The supplicant most likely has a copy of the server certificate previously installed on it. It compares this certificate with the one that was just presented to it, verifying that it is the same authentication server.
7b. The supplicant sends the username and password to the authenticator.
8. The authenticator forwards this to the authentication server.
9. The authentication server verifies the username and password in the user database.

10. In addition to returning the user confirmation from an internal or external database, user attributes can be retrieved. These attributes can be used by the authentication server to determine what actions the user is authorized to perform.

11. The authentication server returns the user validation to the authenticator. Additionally, it may return attributes, which is information about the user that the authenticator may use to assign things such as user role or VLAN assignments.

12. The supplicant is notified that the authentication was successful.

13. Depending upon the authentication method being used, the supplicant and the authenticator may negotiate encryption keys and exchange the necessary parameters.

14. At this point, the authenticator allows traffic to travel between the client and the network. Since this is an Aruba controller, this will be dependent upon the role that has been assigned to the user.

Layer 2 vs. Layer 3 Authentication

Before describing the different authentication methods, it is important to realize that all of these authentication methods fall into one of two categories. Each of these is either a layer 2 authentication method or a layer 3 authentication method. Which category it falls in is determined solely by whether the device obtains its TCP/IP address prior to the authentication process, or after the authentication process.

Layer 3 authentication methods require IP services to transfer credentials. IP addressing occurs at the network layer: layer 3. A layer 3 authentication method requires that the client obtain an IP address prior to authenticating to the network. Two primary layer 3 authentication methods are used in the networking industry:

- Captive portal
- Virtual private network (VPN)

Captive portal is used extensively in wireless networks and will be discussed further in this chapter and in Chapter 9, "Captive Portal." VPN is rarely used anymore for wireless connectivity, but is heavily used as a support technology for site-to-site connections and remote APs (RAPs). When you deploy a layer 3 authentication method, if encryption is being performed, it is applied to the data at higher levels: layer 4 through layer 7.

Layer 2 authentication occurs prior to the client receiving an IP address. With a layer 2 authentication method, the client is blocked from all network access except for sending authentication traffic. If authentication is successful, then the client can attempt to obtain an IP address. If authentication is not successful, the client is not connected to the network, and cannot proceed with any layer 3 through layer 7 communications.

When discussing layer 2 authentication, we are merely analyzing whether the layer 2 connection is established, allowing the client to then obtain an IP address. If the layer 2 connection is successful, an IP address can be obtained. If the layer 2 connection is not successful, an IP address cannot be obtained. It is as simple as that.

If a layer 2 authentication method is also implementing encryption, then the data that will be encrypted is layer 3 through layer 7.

Four primary layer 2 authentication methods will be discussed in this chapter:

- 802.1X/EAP
- MAC
- SSID
- Preshared key

Authentication Methods

As you read the beginning sections of this chapter, you should have gained an understanding of security basics, AAA, and the authentication process. In this section you will learn about five different authentication methods:

- 802.1X/EAP
- MAC
- Captive portal
- SSID
- Preshared key

You may think that SSID and preshared key are questionable as authentication methods since no identity information is being authenticated. However, they are both layer 2 authentication methods. If either method is used and is unsuccessful, the client will be unable to obtain an IP address. Also, since they play a part in role assignment and access control, they need to be included in this discussion.

In the following sections you will learn about these authentication methods, along with the components needed to configure each one as part of a virtual AP. Each authentication method will include a diagram showing all of the profiles needed, along with a step-by-step explanation and instructions to create these profiles.

802.1X/EAP Authentication

One of the most commonly used protocols is 802.1X/EAP because of its extremely secure authentication and encryption. In Chapter 5, "Profiles," setting up an 802.1X/EAP wireless LAN was used to help explain profiles, and was chosen as an example because of its complexity. In this section, we will go over the process and components, adding some additional profiles and parameters. Much of this section will be a review from the profile chapter, but since profiles can be complex, it will be good to take a closer look at the process. Let us begin by looking at Figure 6.2 and the steps to create an 802.1X/EAP-enabled VAP.

FIGURE 6.2
802.1X/EAP VAP

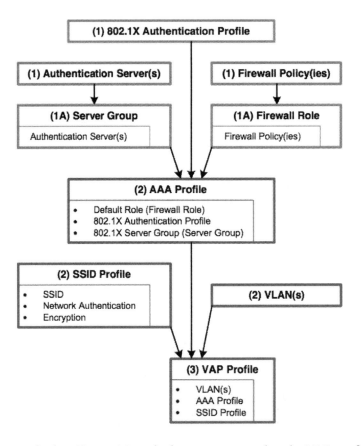

When you look at Figure 6.2, at the bottom you see that the VAP profile is a collection of three sets of information:

▷ SSID profile

▷ AAA profile

▷ VLAN(s)

The AAA profile is made up of three sets of information, but it is ultimately five pieces of information:

- Authentication server(s)
- Server group
- 802.1X authentication profile
- Firewall policy(ies)
- Firewall role

In all, Figure 6.2 displays nine components that need to be configured and linked together to create an 802.1X/EAP wireless LAN. The following subsections will describe each of these components, along with the settings that are needed.

Authentication Server (802.1X/EAP Authentication)

The first step is to define one or more servers (typically RADIUS servers) that users will authenticate against. Remember that 802.1X/EAP requires users to log into the network using some form of credentials, such as a username and password combination or a certificate. These credentials need to be validated. This is usually done by a RADIUS server. While this book will define the process of configuring the VAP to use a RADIUS server for the authentication process, other authentication servers are configured and perform in a similar manner.

The authentication server is typically a separate server on the network that the controller must communicate with. This means that the authentication server must recognize the controller as a valid authenticator. This requires some setup on the authentication server, as well as configuration on the controller, as defined in this chapter.

It is also possible to use the internal user database on the controller. This option does not require any external authentication servers; however, this is not considered a good, scalable solution for large organizations.

Internal Database (802.1X/EAP Authentication)

ArubaOS has an internal database that is stored on the master controller. Typically, this internal database is used for guest accounts, although it can be used for other authentication methods such as 802.1X/EAP or MAC authentication. An 802.1X/EAP authentication is performed against a RADIUS server. However, the internal database is not a RADIUS-compliant server and cannot be used without additional configuration. To enable the internal database to be used with 802.1X/EAP, EAP termination must be enabled on the controller.

EAP termination is also known as *FastConnect* or *EAP offload*. EAP termination allows the 802.1X/EAP authentication to be terminated at the Aruba controller. The controller can then communicate directly with the internal database, using non-802.1X/

EAP communications. EAP termination is enabled in the dot1x profile, as shown in the following CLI output. The output shows the outer and inner EAP types also being configured in this profile. If the outer and inner EAP types are not specified, the default settings are EAP-PEAP with MS-CHAPv2.

```
(config) #aaa authentication dot1x "1x-eap-term"
(802.1X Authentication Profile "1x-eap-term") #termination enable
(802.1X Authentication Profile "1x-eap-term") #termination eap-type eap-peap
(802.1X Authentication Profile "1x-eap-term") #termination inner-eap-type eap-mschapv2
```

RADIUS Server (802.1X/EAP Authentication)

When you define the RADIUS server (Authentication Server) on the Aruba controller, you are simply defining a name, entering a shared key, and pointing the Aruba controller (Authenticator) to the IP address of the RADIUS server. The Aruba controller points to the RADIUS server, and the RADIUS server must be programmed to recognize the Aruba controller. Examples of this information are also listed below.

- Logical name of RADIUS server = radius02
- IP address of RADIUS server = 10.254.1.23
- RADIUS shared secret key (this is a key that you define) = aruba123

The following CLI commands will create and define the RADIUS server:

```
(config) #aaa authentication-server radius radius02
(RADIUS Server "radius02") #host 10.254.1.23
(RADIUS Server "radius02") #key aruba123
```

The following CLI command displays the configuration of the specified authentication server, in this instance radius02:

```
#show aaa authentication-server radius radius02

RADIUS Server "radius02"
------------------------
Parameter                         Value
---------                         -----
Host                              10.254.1.23
Key                               ********
CPPM credentials                  N/A
Auth Port                         1812
Acct Port                         1813
Radsec Port                       2083
Retransmits                       3
Timeout                           5 sec
NAS ID                            N/A
NAS IP                            N/A
```

```
Enable IPv6                             Disabled
NAS IPv6                                N/A
Source Interface                        N/A
Use MD5                                 Disabled
Use IP address for calling station ID   Disabled
Mode                                    Enabled
Lowercase MAC addresses                 Disabled
MAC address delimiter                   none
Service-type of FRAMED-USER             Disabled
Radsec                                  Disabled
Radsec Trusted CA Name                  N/A
Radsec Server Cert Name                 N/A
Radsec Client Cert                      N/A
called-station-id                       macaddr colon disable
```

To get to the menu where you can define the RADIUS server using the WebUI interface, go to **Configuration ➢ SECURITY ➢ Authentication ➢ Servers ➢ RADIUS Server**.

LDAP Server (802.1X/EAP Authentication)

A Lightweight Directory Access Protocol (LDAP) server is typically accessed through a RADIUS server. This is often the case for accessing Active Directory servers, where a NAC solution, such as ClearPass, or a Microsoft NPS are used. However, in some environments you may want to configure the Aruba controller to communicate directly with an LDAP server. An LDAP server is a type of user database server that is based upon a directory structure. If you want to define an LDAP server, the following information is required. Examples of this information are also listed.

- Logical name of LDAP server = `ldap01`
- IP address of LDAP server = `10.254.1.51`
- Distinguished name of an admin user. This user needs read and search privileges for the LDAP database = `cn=Arubacontroller,cn=Users,dc=aruba,dc=com`
- The admin user's password = `password`
- The distinguished name or top level of the node where the entire user database exists = `dc=aruba,dc=com`

The following CLI commands will define the LDAP server on the controller:

```
(config) #aaa authentication-server ldap ldap01
(LDAP Server "ldap01") #host 10.254.1.51
(LDAP Server "ldap01") #base-dn dc=aruba,dc=com
(LDAP Server "ldap01") #admin-dn cn=Arubacontroller,cn=Users,dc=aruba,dc=com
(LDAP Server "ldap01") #admin-passwd password
(LDAP Server "ldap01") #enable
```

The following CLI command displays the configuration of the specified authentication server, in this instance ldap01:

```
#show aaa authentication-server ldap ldap01

LDAP Server "ldap01"
-------------------
Parameter                                    Value
---------                                    -----
Host                                         10.254.1.51
Admin-DN
cn=Arubacontroller,cn=Users,dc=aruba,dc=com
Admin-Passwd                                 ********
Allow Clear-Text                             Disabled
Auth Port                                    389
Base-DN                                      dc=aruba,dc=com
Filter                                       (objectclass=*)
Key Attribute                                sAMAccountName
Timeout                                      20 sec
Mode                                         Enabled
Preferred Connection Type                    ldap-s
maximum number of non-admin connections  4
```

Configuration ➢ SECURITY ➢ Authentication ➢ Servers ➢ LDAP Server will bring you to the menu where you can define the LDAP server using the WebUI interface.

The following CLI command displays a list of all servers defined on the controller:

```
#show aaa authentication-server all

Auth Server Table
-----------------
Name       Type    FQDN   IP addr         AuthPort   AcctPort   Status    Requests
----       ----    ----   -------         --------   --------   ------    --------
Internal   Local   n/a    10.1.50.100     n/a        n/a        Enabled   0
radius01   Radius  none   10.254.1.21     1812       1813       Enabled   0
radius02   Radius  none   10.254.1.23     1812       1813       Enabled   0
ldap01     Ldap    n/a    10.254.1.51     389        n/a        Enabled   0
```

Server Group (802.1X/EAP Authentication)

Aruba AAA profiles do not access or use authentication servers directly. Instead, they are configured to reference the authentication servers as part of a server group. Server groups contain one or more servers. When you configure the AAA profile, you tell it which server group to use for authentication. If a server group contains more than one server, the server group not only defines which servers to authenticate against, but also the order in which to search them.

The following CLI commands would create two server groups, servergroup1-2 and servergroup2-1. Notice that both server groups would contain the same servers, but in different orders.

```
aaa server-group servergroup1-2
  auth-server radius01 position 1
  auth-server radius02 position 2

aaa server-group servergroup2-1
  auth-server radius02 position 1
  auth-server radius01 position 2
```

Server groups are evaluated in a top-down order. If a server group has multiple servers, the first server in the group is used to validate the login request. If the first server is unavailable, then the next server down the list is used. This would continue until the login request is validated against one of the servers, or until all of the servers have been queried and did not respond. If any server responds with an authentication failure, then the login request would be unsuccessful. This process is known as *fall-through authentication*. This is useful if both RADIUS servers contain the same user information and you need redundancy.

A downfall of fall-through authentication is that, by default, all authentications are always validated against the first server in the server group. Any subsequent servers are only checked if the first server is unavailable. To improve performance and to distribute the load among the different servers, a load balancing option was added to the server group profile.

The controller uses a load balancing algorithm to compute the expected authentication time and chooses the server with the faster expected response time. Load balancing can be enabled by issuing the `load-balance` command as part of the AAA server group.

Fail-Through Authentication (802.1X/EAP Authentication)

If the server group contains two servers, and both servers contain different sets of user accounts, you will likely want to search both databases to find a user account. Examples of when you would want to enable fail-through authentication include having a database of employees in Europe and a database of employees in Asia, or two companies are merging and users need to be authenticated using two different directory sources. You can enable fail-through authentication using the following CLI commands:

```
aaa server-group failthrough-1
  auth-server radius01 position 1
  auth-server radius02 position 2
  allow-fail-through
```

There are conditions regarding the use of fail-through authentication, so before attempting to enable it, read the ArubaOS documentation.

Dynamic Server Selection (802.1X/EAP Authentication)

One of the problems with fail-through authentication is that if a user identity exists in the second server, every time that user attempts to log in, the first server is always searched to attempt to validate the user before the second server is searched. This requires extra, unnecessary searching, which takes processing time and power. Assume that we have three unique RADIUS servers (Boston, London, and Dallas) with separate unique databases. The following CLI commands will create a server group dynamic1 containing these three servers:

```
aaa server-group dynamic1
  auth-server boston position 1
  auth-server london position 2
  auth-server dallas position 3
```

If fail-through authentication is enabled, every time a user from Dallas attempts to log in, the network first checks for the user in the Boston server, then the London server, and finally the Dallas server. To prevent these unnecessary database searches, the Aruba controller supports a feature known as *dynamic server selection.*

With dynamic server selection, the administrator creates rules that instruct the controller to dynamically choose which server to use for authentication, based upon information contained in the user's login credentials.

A user authentication often includes username and domain information, such as the following:

user@boston.domain.com

dallas.domain.com\user

host/mypcname.london.domain.com

Dynamic server selection allows you to create a rule to analyze the client and user information to see if it contains, begins with, or exactly matches a specific string. The rule is part of the command that assigns the server to the server group. As an example, you can check to see if the authentication string contains the specific subdomain, and assign the appropriate authentication server accordingly. The following CLI commands will create a server group dynamic2 containing these three servers, along with their server selection rules:

```
aaa server-group dynamic2
  auth-server boston match-authstring contains boston.domain.com position 1
  auth-server london match-authstring contains london.domain.com position 2
  auth-server dallas match-authstring contains dallas.domain.com position 3
```

Server-Derivation Rules (802.1X/EAP Authentication)

A *server-derivation rule* allows an authentication server to dynamically assign the user a role or VLAN as part of the authentication process. This process will be explained in more detail in Chapter 7, "Role Derivation;" however, since it is part of the server group commands, it will be briefly covered in this section.

When the user authentication is successful, in addition to returning the successful authentication message, the RADIUS server can return attributes to the Aruba controller (Figure 6.1, Step 11). The value of the attribute is defined and determined on the authentication server. For this example, we will not concern ourselves with why a specific value was returned. Whatever the logic, the authentication server is typically configured to send a specific attribute, such as an Aruba vendor specific attribute (VSA), or an IETF attribute such as filter-id. Since the controller handles Aruba VSAs differently than IETF attributes, they will be explained separately.

Let us first take a look at how the controller handles a commonly used IETF attribute such as filter-id. When the controller receives the attribute, there needs to be a rule defined in the server group that maps the value returned to an actual firewall role on the controller. The first way to do this is to create a rule that essentially reads "if the value of filter-id is ABC then set the firewall role to XYZ." This can be done using the following set role CLI command, which will set the role of the authenticating user to chem-role if the value of filter-id is chemistry:

```
aaa server-group derivation1
  auth-server radius01 position 1
  auth-server radius02 position 2
  set role condition filter-id equals chemistry set-value chem-role
```

This is an interesting and useful command, but what if you wanted to assign different roles based upon different filter-id values? As an example, what if you were configuring roles for a university that had 30 different departments and you wanted to assign a different role for each department? Using the set role condition command you just learned, you would have to enter 30 different commands, one for each department. This would not be easy to do, and additionally, you would not want each login request having to be processed by up to 30 separate logic statements. There is a much simpler way.

Instead of creating 30 separate lines, you can create one single set role condition command. This command would essentially read "set the role to the value that is returned in the attribute filter-id." This can be done as a server group setting using the following set role CLI command:

```
aaa server-group derivation1
  auth-server radius01 position 1
  auth-server radius02 position 2
  set role condition filter-id value-of position 1
```

Navigating to **Configuration** ➢ **SECURITY** ➢ **Authentication** ➢ **Servers** ➢ **Server Group** will bring you to the server group menu, where you can add the role condition using the WebUI interface. From the server group menu, you would select a group, and then at the bottom of the configuration window is the Server Rules area, where you would click the New button to add a rule.

If you want to see a listing of all the server groups that you have created, the following displays the CLI command and corresponding output:

```
#show aaa server-group summary

Server Groups
-------------
Name              Servers  Rules  hits  Out-of-service
----              -------  -----  ----  --------------
default           1        1      0
derivation1       2        1      0
failthrough-1     2        0      0
internal          1        1      0
radius-group01    2        0      0
servergroup1-2    2        0      0
servergroup2-1    2        0      0
```

After the list of server groups is displayed, you can display detailed information about any of the server groups, as shown in the following CLI output:

```
#show aaa server-group derivation1

Fail Through:No
Load Balance:No

Auth Servers
------------
Name     Server-Type  trim-FQDN  Match-Type  Match-Op  Match-Str
----     -----------  ---------  ----------  --------  ---------
radius01 Radius       No
radius02 Radius       No

Role/VLAN derivation rules
--------------------------
Priority  Attribute  Operation  Operand  Type    Action    Value  Validated
--------  ---------  ---------  -------  ----    ------    -----  ---------
1         filter-id  value-of            String  set role         Yes
```

The IETF attribute `filter-id` has been used for many years because it is a standards-based attribute that is supported by, and provides interoperability between, different vendors. With the proliferation of BYOD devices, the assignment of roles and VLANs has become an integral component of the AAA process. Advancements in AAA and authentication servers, such as ClearPass, have enhanced the attributes that are exchanged between the authenticator and the authentication server. Many vendors, including Aruba, have VSAs to provide a more customizable and more powerful AAA environment.

When you are using an IETF attribute such as `filter-id`, a rule must be created to translate the attribute into a role. A VSA does not require a rule. When the authentication server sends a VSA to the authenticator, it is essentially saying "I am setting the role and here is the value." In this example, the VSA that would be returned is `Aruba-User-Role` and the value of this VSA is the role assignment.

In order for a VSA to be used, the authentication server must support Aruba VSAs. The authentication server must have a RADIUS dictionary file with the vendor name of Aruba or the vendor-specific code of 14823, vendor-assigned attribute number, attribute format, and attribute value. For each VSA, the dictionary must have the vendor-assigned attribute number and the attribute format, such as `String` or `Integer`. The following CLI command will display all the RADIUS attributes that the Aruba controller supports. This list contains the Aruba VSAs, along with other vendor attributes also. The RADIUS attributes list is very long, therefore only a portion of the command output is displayed.

```
#show aaa radius-attributes

Dictionary
----------

Attribute                           Value  Type     Vendor      Id
---------                           -----  ----     ------      --
WISPr-Session-Term-End-Of-Day       10     Integer  WISPr       14122
MS-CHAP-NT-Enc-PW                   6      String   Microsoft   311
essid                               304    String
ARAP-Security                       73     Integer
Tunnel-Client-Endpoint              66     String
Aruba-Mdps-Max-Devices              18     Integer  Aruba       14823
MS-CHAP-Challenge                   11     String   Microsoft   311
AP-Name                             317    String
Tunnel-Server-Auth-Id               91     String
MS-MPPE-Encryption-Policy           7      String   Microsoft   311
Prefix                              1003   String
Prompt                              76     Integer
Password                            2      String
Aruba-CPPM-Role                     23     String   Aruba       14823
MS-BAP-Usage                        13     String   Microsoft   311
macaddr                             306    String
ARAP-Features                       71     String
CHAP-Challenge                      60     String
Aruba-Mdps-Device-Version           21     String   Aruba       14823
--More-- (q) quit (u) pageup (/) search (n) repeat
```

The complete list of Aruba VSAs is displayed in Table 6.1. This list may change with newer versions of the OS. The following CLI command will display the list of all Aruba VSAs that are supported on your controller:

```
show aaa radius-attributes | include 14823
```

TABLE 6.1 Aruba vendor-specific attributes

Aruba-Auth-SurvMethod

Aruba-Admin-Path

Aruba-Admin-Role

Aruba-AirGroup-Device-Type

Aruba-AirGroup-Shared-Group

Aruba-AirGroup-Shared-Role

Aruba-AirGroup-Shared-User

Aruba-AirGroup-User-Name

Aruba-AirGroup-Version

Aruba-AP-Group

Aruba-AP-IP-Address

Aruba-AS-Credential-Has

Aruba-AS-User-Name

Aruba-Auth-Survivability

Aruba-Calea-Server-Ip

Aruba-CPPM-Role

Aruba-Device-Type

Aruba-Essid-Name

Aruba-Framed-IPv6-Address

Aruba-Location-Id

Aruba-Mdps-Device-Iccid

Aruba-Mdps-Device-Imei

Aruba-Mdps-Device-Name

Aruba-Mdps-Device-Product

Aruba-Mdps-Device-Profile

Aruba-Mdps-Device-Serial

Aruba-Mdps-Device-Udid

Aruba-Mdps-Device-Version

Aruba-Mdps-Max-Devices

Aruba-Mdps-Provisioning-Settings

Aruba-Named-User-Vlan

Aruba-Network-SSO-Token

Aruba-No-DHCP-Fingerprint

Aruba-Port-Bounce-Host

Aruba-Port-Id

Aruba-Priv-Admin-User

Aruba-Template-User

Aruba-User-Group

Aruba-User-Role

Aruba-User-Vlan

Aruba-WorkSpace-App-Name

802.1X Authentication Profile (802.1X/EAP Authentication)

While standards are used for most authentication servers, there are communication settings that can differ. The 802.1X authentication profile defines the details of how the controller will communicate with the 802.1X authentication server. The 802.1X authentication profile contains settings for communication ports, timeouts, and other behavior.

In many instances, you can create an 802.1X authentication profile and simply accept the default settings. The menu where you can create or modify the profile using the WebUI interface is at **Configuration ➢ SECURITY ➢ Authentication ➢ L2 Authentication ➢ 802.1X Authentication.**

The following CLI command can also be used to create the 802.1X authentication profile:

```
(config) #aaa authentication dot1x 1x-auth-profile
```

Firewall Policy (802.1X/EAP Authentication)

Firewall policies are sets of firewall rules. Firewall rules typically allow or deny specific protocols or ports to traverse from one network segment to another. Firewall policies let the network administrator group a set of rules together, allowing or denying network access based upon a logical function. Administrators can also assign a functional name to the firewall policy, such as allow-browsing or deny-ftp-tftp.

Just as firewall rules are grouped together to create firewall policies, firewall policies are grouped together to create firewall roles. Chapter 8, "Policy Enforcement Firewall," will explain how this is done in much greater detail. For now, realize that when you create a virtual AP profile, firewall policies need to be defined as part of the process.

Firewall Role (802.1X/EAP Authentication)

A firewall role is a set of firewall policies. Every user who connects to an Aruba wireless network is assigned a role. Different roles allow different levels of access to the network. For example, a guest user may only be allowed to send traffic to and from the Internet, whereas an employee would be allowed access to both the Internet and the corporate network. Ultimately, the AAA profile guides the assignment of roles to the users as they authenticate.

The creation of an AAA profile includes defining default roles for each authentication type. Although a default role is defined, a role can be assigned through multiple methods. This assignment process is known as *role derivation* and will be covered in detail in Chapter 7, "Role Derivation."

In addition to explaining how roles are assigned to users, Chapter 8, "Policy Enforcement Firewall," will explain how roles are created. For now, realize that when you create a virtual AP profile, a default role needs to be defined and then assigned to the AAA profile.

AAA Profile (802.1X/EAP Authentication)

The purpose of the AAA profile is to tie all the resources required for authentication and role assignment together into a logical structure. The AAA profile specifies the server group that the 802.1X user will be authenticating against, how the authentication will be performed (802.1X/EAP authentication profile), and the default permissions the user will be assigned when the authentication is successful (firewall role). The AAA profile is essentially an assembly of the AAA parameters, as illustrated in Figure 6.3, bringing all these individual pieces together into one profile. Remember that the server group is made up of one or more servers, and the firewall role is made up of one or more firewall policies; therefore, the AAA profile is effectively the aggregation of the following five components:

- Authentication server(s)
- Server group
- Firewall policy(ies)
- Firewall role
- 802.1X authentication profile

FIGURE 6.3
AAA profile

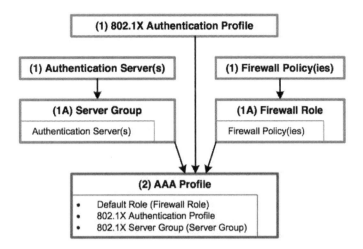

The following CLI commands create the AAA profile and then link the server group, authentication profile, and the default role to the profile:

```
(config) #aaa profile employee-aaa-profile
(AAA Profile "employee-aaa-profile") #dot1x-server-group radius-group01
(AAA Profile "employee-aaa-profile") #authentication-dot1x 1x-auth-profile
(AAA Profile "employee-aaa-profile") #dot1x-default-role authenticated
```

Configuration ➢ SECURITY ➢ Authentication ➢ AAA Profiles will bring you to the menu where you can create the AAA profile using the WebUI interface.

SSID Profile (802.1X/EAP Authentication)

Whereas the AAA profile defines the authentication methods that the client must execute while connecting to the network, the SSID profile defines the connection properties that the client must have in order to connect to the SSID. Thus, the SSID profile exerts its influence on the client before the AAA profile kicks in. The SSID profile defines multiple core components: the WLAN identity that the client will connect to (the SSID), the network authentication method that will be used, the encryption method that will be used, along with other components such as data rates and QoS parameters.

To configure the SSID profile for an 802.1X/EAP authentication, you first define the SSID; you can use up to 32 characters, it is case sensitive, and it should not contain spaces.

Any 802.1X/EAP network should be configured with WPA2 authentication and AES encryption. The authentication method that Aruba refers to as simply *WPA2* is typically known as *WPA2-Enterprise* by many operating systems.

AES encryption is the only encryption method that should be used. The IEEE and the Wi-Fi Alliance have stated that WEP and TKIP are deprecated encryption methods. They are still supported for backward compatibility with older devices; however, if you choose either of them, that VAP will only operate using the older pre-802.11ac and pre-802.11n data rates. As with many vendors, Aruba has implemented this policy.

The following CLI commands can be used to create the SSID profile and assign WPA2 authentication with AES encryption:

```
wlan ssid-profile employee-ssid-profile
  essid employee1
  opmode wpa2-aes
```

To get to the All Profiles menu, where you can create and configure the SSID profile, navigate to **Configuration** ➢ **ADVANCED SERVICES** ➢ **All Profiles** ➢ **Wireless LAN** ➢ **SSID**.

VLAN(s) (802.1X/EAP Authentication)

As mentioned previously, the user will authenticate his credentials and then request an IP address. An important part of configuring the VAP is assigning a default VLAN to the wireless LAN. The default VLAN is assigned as part of the VAP profile. This VLAN can be overridden later in the authentication process.

The following CLI commands will create VLAN 51, which in this example we will be assigning to this wireless LAN. Assuming that the DHCP server for VLAN 51 is on a different subnet, a DHCP helper address also needs to be assigned.

```
(config) #vlan 51
(config) #interface vlan 51
(config-subif)#ip address 10.1.51.2 255.255.255.0
(config-subif)#ip helper-address 10.254.1.21
```

The *VAP profile* is essentially all of the WLAN components brought together. One of the pieces is the VLAN, which is assigned to the VAP profile, as shown in the following CLI commands:

```
(config) #wlan virtual-ap "employee-vap-profile"
(Virtual AP profile "employee-vap-profile") #vlan 50
```

VLAN Pools (802.1X/EAP Authentication)

As wireless LANs have grown across floors, buildings, and campuses, so have the number of users and the need for more IP addresses. One method of increasing the number of available IP addresses is by supernetting the address range. A potential problem with supernetting is the increased number of devices, multicasts, and broadcasts across the supernetted range. As an alternative to supernetting, VLAN pools were introduced.

VLAN pools are bundles of subnets; typically, class C subnets. Instead of assigning a single VLAN to a VAP profile, multiple VLANs or ranges of VLANs can be assigned to the VAP profile, as shown in the following CLI commands. In this example, VLANs 50, 52, 55, 56, 57, and 58 are all being assigned to the VAP profile.

```
(config) #wlan virtual-ap "employee-vap-profile"
(Virtual AP profile "employee-vap-profile") #vlan 50,52,55-58
```

With VLAN pooling, when a wireless client connects to the WLAN, it will be assigned an IP address from one of these six VLANs. The controller will use one of two methods to choose the VLAN that the client will receive its address from; hash or even. The *hash* method uses a hash algorithm on the client's MAC address to choose the VLAN, and the *even* method will attempt to evenly distribute client devices across the VLANs. If you plan to do VLAN pooling, you will need to do a little research in the ArubaOS documentation to determine which method will work better for you.

If the VLAN pools are configured properly on each of the controllers, as a client roams between APs, the client will maintain its IP address, assuming that each of the controllers support the same pool of VLANs.

Named VLANs (802.1X/EAP Authentication)

One of the challenges with multicontroller environments is that the user VLANs may differ between locations, and the controller at each location would be configured to support the local user VLANs. For example, two controllers in the same campus might need to support different user VLANs because one controller operates in building 1 and the other controller operates in building 2, with each building supporting different user VLANs with the same SSID. This creates a challenge when specifying the VLAN in the VAP profile. VAP profiles are global configurations, but they reference VLANs that are local to each controller. Named VLANs can be used to provide more flexibility by linking the local VLANs to a global alias.

The process is simple:

1. Create a VLAN name, essentially an alias, on the master controller. This name is then automatically synchronized to all of the local controllers.
2. On the local controllers, assign the actual VLAN ID to the VLAN name. This maps the locally defined VLAN to the aliased name.
3. Now, when you assign a VLAN to the VAP profile, assign the (aliased) VLAN name instead. This is a global setting; however, when the VAP is distributed to the local controller, the VLAN name will be replaced by the local VLAN.

Figure 6.4 illustrates an Aruba network with controllers in Boston, New York, and London. In each of these locations, two VLANs were created to be used for the employee WLAN.

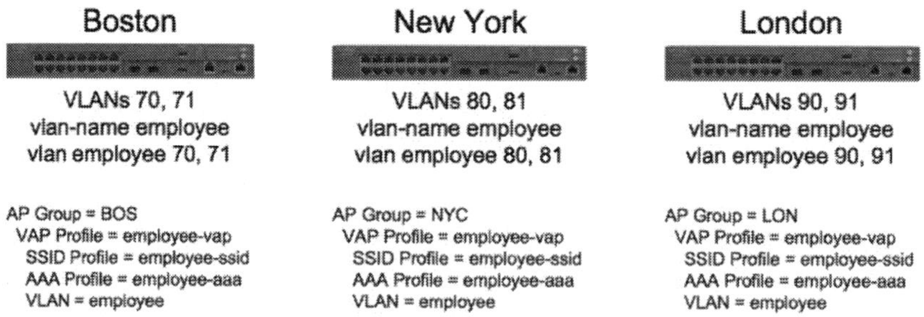

FIGURE 6.4
Multicontroller network

Boston
VLANs 70, 71
vlan-name employee
vlan employee 70, 71

AP Group = BOS
VAP Profile = employee-vap
SSID Profile = employee-ssid
AAA Profile = employee-aaa
VLAN = employee

New York
VLANs 80, 81
vlan-name employee
vlan employee 80, 81

AP Group = NYC
VAP Profile = employee-vap
SSID Profile = employee-ssid
AAA Profile = employee-aaa
VLAN = employee

London
VLANs 90, 91
vlan-name employee
vlan employee 90, 91

AP Group = LON
VAP Profile = employee-vap
SSID Profile = employee-ssid
AAA Profile = employee-aaa
VLAN = employee

Boston: VLANs 70 and 71

New York: VLANs 80 and 81

London: VLANs 90 and 91

When the virtual AP (VAP) profile is created, one or more VLANs are assigned to it. Since each location has different VLANs, a VAP would need to be created for each location. This is not very efficient or flexible. Instead of creating many VAPs, named VLANs can be used.

A *named VLAN* is similar to an alias. To use a named VLAN, the VLAN name would be created on the master controller. This named VLAN is then automatically created on each of the local controllers. In this example, the named VLAN called `employee` was created. After the named VLAN is created, the local VLANs at each location are assigned to the VLAN name. At this point, instead of assigning a VLAN number to the VAP, the `employee` named VLAN will be assigned to the VAP. This allows a single VAP, in this example `employee-vap`, to be assigned to each of the three AP groups; `BOS`, `NYC`, and `LON`, with each location having different VLANs assigned to the WLAN.

Virtual AP Profile (802.1X/EAP Authentication)

The final step in the creation of an 802.1X/EAP wireless LAN is to configure the VAP profile. This is performed by simply assigning the AAA profile, SSID profile, and VLAN to the VAP profile, as shown in the following CLI commands, and illustrated in Figure 6.5.

```
(config) #wlan virtual-ap employee-vap-profile
(Virtual AP profile "employee-vap-profile") #vlan 51
(Virtual AP profile "employee-vap-profile") #aaa-profile employee-aaa-profile
(Virtual AP profile "employee-vap-profile") #ssid-profile employee-ssid-profile
```

FIGURE 6.5
Virtual AP

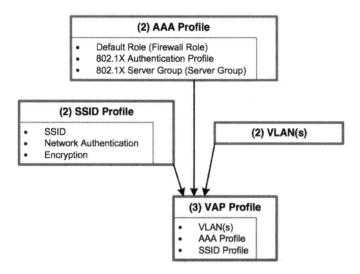

Going to **Configuration ➢ ADVANCED SERVICES ➢ All Profiles ➢ Wireless LAN ➢ Virtual AP** will bring you to the menu where you can create and configure the VAP profile using the WebUI interface.

MAC Authentication

While not considered secure, it is sometimes necessary to use MAC authentication for older devices that do not have a robust user interface for connecting to the SSID. MAC authentication does not require any input or interaction from the user, since it happens automatically when the user connects to the SSID. When a wireless client is configured for MAC authentication, the AAA profile executes the MAC authentication process before any other form of authentication.

MAC authentication is a layer 2 authentication method that authenticates the full MAC address of the client against a database. The database used is typically the internal database on the Aruba controller, but could be an external server such as a RADIUS server or Aruba ClearPass. MAC authentication is not a very secure authentication method, since it is very easy to change the MAC address on some client computers and impersonate another computer. Although it is not considered very secure, there are times when it is still used.

Similar to the creation of an 802.1X/EAP VAP, there are nine components that need to be configured and linked together to create a MAC authenticated wireless LAN, as displayed in Figure 6.6.

FIGURE 6.6
MAC authentication VAP

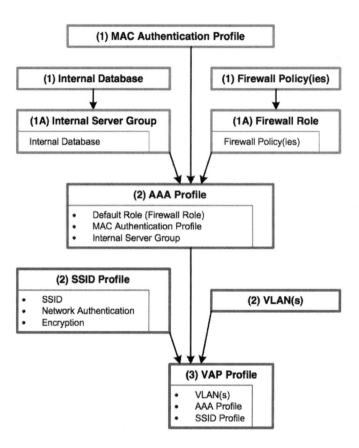

Internal Database (MAC Authentication)

It is common to import lists of device MAC addresses into the controller and then use the internal database as the source for MAC authentication. When doing this, the MAC address must be entered in both the username and password fields of the user account. Then, when the AAA profile formats the MAC authentication request, it will use the MAC address of the authenticating device for both the username and password. It is important to note that the MAC address being sent by the AAA profile must exactly match the MAC address in the internal database.

Remember that the internal database is stored on the master controller, so if the master controller is down and you do not have a backup, MAC authenticating clients will not be able to be verified.

When adding the MAC address to the database, it must be entered as both the username and the password, and it must be entered in one of the following four delimited formats:

None: 00112233aabb

Colon: 00:11:22:33:aa:bb

Dash: 00-11-22-33-aa-bb

OUI-NIC: 001122-33aabb

The following CLI command can be used to create a MAC address user account in the internal database, and assign the camera role to this account:

```
#local-userdb add username 00:24:d7:6a:71:24 password 00:24:d7:6a:71:24 role camera
```

A MAC address user account can also be created from the following WebUI menu: **Configuration ➢ SECURITY ➢ Authentication ➢ Servers ➢ Internal DB**. This menu is displayed in Figure 6.7.

FIGURE 6.7 Adding MAC address to internal DB

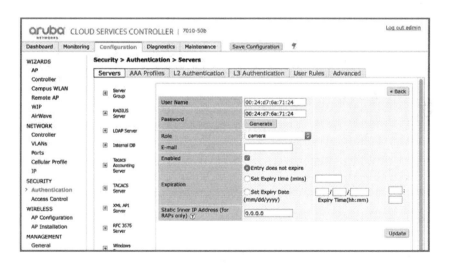

The following CLI command displays a list of the user accounts that are in the internal database:

```
#show local-userdb

User Summary
------------
Name                Password   Role     E-Mail   Enabled   Expiry   Status →
----                --------   ----     ------   -------   ------   ------ →
00:24:d7:6a:71:24   ********   camera            Yes                Active →
00:24:d7:6a:51:f0   ********   camera            Yes                Active →
```

```
→ Sponsor-Name   Remote-IP   Grantor-Name
→ ------------   ---------   ------------
→                0.0.0.0     admin
→                0.0.0.0     admin

User Entries: 2
```

Internal Server Group (MAC Authentication)

ArubaOS has a built-in server group named `internal`, which contains the internal server. If you would like to create your own server group you are welcome to do so; however, the `internal` server group is fine to use for MAC authentication.

MAC Authentication Profile (MAC Authentication)

The MAC authentication profile defines the details of how the MAC authentication will be performed. Mostly, it defines how the controller formats the MAC address before sending it to the authentication server. Many authentication servers are not flexible in how they process a MAC address for credentials, so it is important that the controller format the address properly before sending it.

When the client connects to the WLAN, the controller takes the MAC address and uses it as both the username and password for the client. These need to be an exact match with what was entered in the authentication server. This is definitely true for the internal database.

So, if the MAC address was entered into the database in a colon-delimited format (eg, 00:11:22:33:44:55), the MAC authentication profile must be configured with the same format. There are four possible delimiter formats; none, colon, dash, and OUI-NIC, which were explained earlier in this chapter.

There is also a case-sensitive option to force the MAC address to uppercase or lowercase. Since the MAC address is a hexadecimal number, letters A–F could be entered into the authentication database as upper- or lowercase values. This also needs to be configured in the MAC authentication profile.

The following CLI command defines the MAC authentication profile, delimiter, and case:

```
(config) #aaa authentication mac camera-macauth-profile
(MAC Authentication Profile "camera-macauth-profile") #delimiter colon
(MAC Authentication Profile "camera-macauth-profile") #case lower
```

A MAC authentication profile can also be configured at **Configuration ➢ SECURITY ➢ Authentication ➢ L2 Authentication ➢ MAC Authentication**. This menu is displayed in Figure 6.8.

FIGURE 6.8
MAC authentication profile

Firewall Policy (MAC Authentication)

Firewall policies should be created to define what the MAC authenticated device can do on the network. Since MAC authentication is not very secure, you should be careful to limit the capabilities to only those that are required. Firewall policies are used to construct firewall roles. Firewall policy was described earlier in this chapter in the "802.1X/EAP Authentication" section and will be explained in more detail in Chapter 8, "Policy Enforcement Firewall."

Firewall Role (MAC Authentication)

Because every user that authenticates to the controller is assigned a role, there needs to be a default role assigned to the AAA profile. A user can also obtain a role through other methods, which will be explained in Chapter 7, "Role Derivation." The default role is used as a fallback for users who do not receive a role through one of the other methods.

AAA Profile (MAC Authentication)

The AAA profile specifies where the user's MAC address will be authenticated against (server group), how the authentication will be performed (MAC authentication profile), and the firewall role the user may be assigned when the authentication is successful (default role). The key function of the AAA profile is to tie these pieces together.

The following CLI commands can be used to create the AAA profile, link the server group to it, assign the MAC authentication profile to it, and specify the MAC authentication default role:

```
(config) #aaa profile macauth-aaa
(AAA Profile "macauth-aaa") #mac-server-group "internal"
(AAA Profile "macauth-aaa") #authentication-mac camera-macauth-profile
(AAA Profile "macauth-aaa") #mac-default-role camera
```

You can also create a MAC authentication AAA profile in the WebUI by going to **Configuration ➢ SECURITY ➢ Authentication ➢ AAA Profiles ➢ AAA**. This menu is displayed in Figure 6.9.

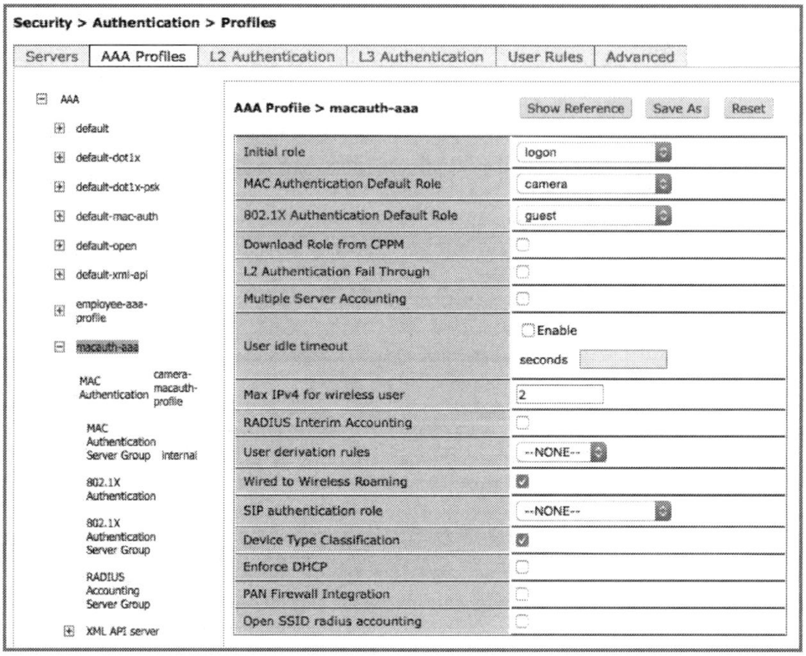

FIGURE 6.9 MAC authentication AAA profile

SSID Profile (MAC Authentication)

The SSID profile defines three core components: the SSID, the network authentication method that will be used, and the encryption method that will be used. A MAC authenticated VAP is typically configured with an open SSID, using no encryption, as shown in the following CLI commands. This is typically done because you do not have control or access to the client devices to be able to configure them with encryption or authentication. Whatever the reason, the following CLI commands can be used to create the SSID profile, assign the SSID, and configure it with no encryption:

```
(config) #wlan ssid-profile camera-ssid-profile
(SSID Profile "camera-ssid-profile") #essid camera
(SSID Profile "camera-ssid-profile") #opmode opensystem
```

VLAN(s) (MAC Authentication)

As with any WLAN, you should create a separate VLAN for the MAC authenticated wireless users. Since MAC authentication is insecure, it is recommended that this VLAN is not shared with other traffic. The following CLI commands will create VLAN 93, assign an IP address, and point the DHCP requests to the DHCP server 10.254.1.21, which is running on a different network. Remember that VLANs need to be created on the controller terminating the user traffic, which may be a local controller.

```
(config) #vlan 93
(config) #interface vlan 93
(config-subif)#ip address 192.168.9.1 255.255.255.0
(config-subif)#ip helper-address 10.254.1.21
```

VLAN pools and named VLANs can also be created, and were described previously in this chapter. The Aruba controller can be a DHCP server if the number of expected DHCP clients is less than the number of supported leases. The total number of supported leases varies depending upon how powerful of a controller you are running, and currently ranges from 256 to 15,000. If the controller is the DHCP server for multiple VLANs, the total number of supported leases is tallied across all VLANs.

The following CLI command will display the number of DHCP leases supported by your controller. This model of controller supports 1024 leases:

```
#show ip dhcp statistics

DHCPv4 disabled; DHCPv6 disabled

DHCP Pools
----------
Network Name  Type  Active  Configured leases  Active leases  Free leases  Expired leases  Abandoned leases
------------  ----  ------  -----------------  -------------  -----------  --------------  ----------------

Current leases         0
Total leases           1024
```

A MAC authenticated WLAN may be a candidate for using the internal DHCP server. The following CLI commands will configure the controller to operate as a DHCP server for VLAN 93. Configuring the controller as a DHCP server was explained in more detail in Chapter 4, "Getting Started."

```
(config) #ip dhcp pool guest-pool

(config-dhcp)#network 192.168.9.0 255.255.255.0
(config-dhcp)#default-router 192.168.9.1
(config-dhcp)#dns-server 10.254.1.21
(config-dhcp)#exit
(config) #service dhcp
(config) #end
```

Virtual AP Profile (MAC Authentication)

The final step in the creation of a MAC authenticated wireless LAN is to configure the VAP profile. This is performed by simply assigning the AAA profile, SSID profile, and VLAN to the VAP profile, as shown in the following CLI commands:

```
(config) #wlan virtual-ap camera-vap
(Virtual AP profile "employee-vap") #vlan 93
(Virtual AP profile "employee-vap") #aaa-profile camera-aaa
(Virtual AP profile "employee-vap") #ssid-profile camera-ssid
```

You can get to the menu where you can create and configure the VAP profile using the WebUI interface by going to **Configuration ➢ ADVANCED SERVICES ➢ All Profiles ➢ Wireless LAN ➢ Virtual AP**.

Captive Portal Authentication

Since this is a chapter about authentication and encryption, there needs to be a section about captive portal, since it is one of the most commonly used authentication methods on wireless networks. *Captive portal* is a layer 3 authentication method, which means that the wireless client must receive an IP address prior to authenticating. Although captive portal can be configured with encryption, it is extremely rare. Captive portal is so popular and important that an entire chapter is devoted to its configuration and deployment. To learn the details of captive portal, go to Chapter 9, "Captive Portal."

SSID Authentication

It may be difficult to think of SSID as an authentication method, and this is understandable since there is no identity component being verified, such as a username or even a MAC address. To understand it as an authentication protocol, look past this missing component for the moment and consider the following: if the SSID is hidden, and you know what the SSID is, you can connect to it. Assuming everything is configured properly, you will receive an IP address. If you do not know the SSID, you would not be able to connect to it. This would be true whether the SSID is hidden or not. If you select the specific SSID, you will connect to it, and if you did not select it, you would not be connected. Since there is both a positive and a negative state to being connected to the network, we will categorize it as an authentication method. Also, getting an IP address is dependent upon the creation of the link; therefore, SSID authentication is a layer 2 authentication method.

Figure 6.10 displays the profiles and components needed to configure a WLAN with SSID authentication. Since SSID authentication is not validating a user identity, a server and server group are not needed. An authentication profile is also not needed.

FIGURE 6.10
SSID authentication components

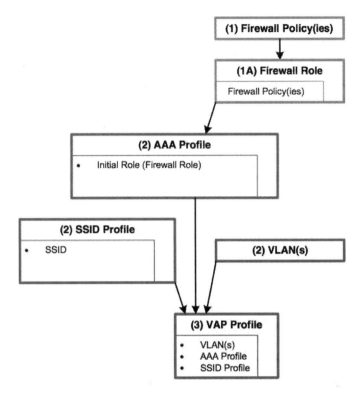

Firewall Policy (SSID Authentication)

As with any of the authentication methods, after the client connects to the WLAN, a role will be assigned to the client. This consists of one or more policies, each consisting of one or more firewall rules. SSID authenticated networks are not secure, so you should be careful to limit the permissions that will be assigned to the users. Firewall policy was described earlier in this chapter in the "802.1X/EAP Authentication" section and will be explained in more detail in Chapter 8, "Policy Enforcement Firewall."

Firewall Role (SSID Authentication)

When a client connects to an SSID authenticated network, the role that will be assigned is the *initial role*. Since this is an open network, the firewall role should provide very limited access or very specific access. Firewall roles were described earlier in this chapter in the "802.1X/EAP Authentication" section and will be explained in more detail in Chapter 8, "Policy Enforcement Firewall." Chapter 7, "Role Derivation," will cover in detail how roles are assigned.

AAA Profile (SSID Authentication)

The AAA profile for SSID authentication is very simple. There is no server group and there is no authentication profile, so the AAA profile is effectively just defining the initial role, as shown in the following CLI output. After the client has completed its connection to the WLAN, it is likely that the initial role will be the final role that is assigned.

```
(config) #aaa profile open-aaa
(AAA Profile "open-aaa") #initial-role authenticated
```

SSID Profile (SSID Authentication)

The SSID profile defines the SSID, the encryption method, and the network authentication method. Since there is no formal authentication or encryption performed with SSID authentication, the SSID profile simply needs to define the SSID, as shown in the following CLI output:

```
(config) #wlan ssid-profile open-ssid
(SSID Profile "open-ssid") #essid open
```

VLAN(s) (SSID Authentication)

A separate VLAN should be created for the WLAN. The following CLI commands will create VLAN 93, assign an IP address, and forward any DHCP requests to DHCP server 10.254.1.21. Remember that the VLAN needs to be created on the controller where the user traffic is terminating.

```
(config) #vlan 93
(config) #interface vlan 93
(config-subif)#ip address 192.168.9.1 255.255.255.0
(config-subif)#ip helper-address 10.254.1.21
```

VLAN pools and named VLANs can also be created, and were described previously in this chapter. The Aruba controller can be a DHCP server if the number of expected DHCP clients is less than the number of supported leases. Configuring the controller as a DHCP server was explained previously in this chapter and in more detail in Chapter 4, "Getting Started."

Virtual AP Profile (SSID Authentication)

The VAP profile is simply a consolidation of the AAA profile, SSID profile, and VLAN, as shown in the following CLI commands:

```
(config) #wlan virtual-ap open-vap
(Virtual AP profile "open-vap") #aaa-profile open-aaa
(Virtual AP profile "open-vap") #ssid-profile open-ssid
(Virtual AP profile "open-vap") #vlan 93
```

Preshared Key Authentication

You walk into a coffee shop for your favorite coffee and you notice that the shop is advertising its recently installed Wi-Fi network. You pick up your phone, identify the SSID, and try to connect to it. After selecting the SSID, you are prompted for a password. This password is formally called a *passphrase* or a *preshared key (PSK)*. To state it simply, a key is a word or phrase that is shared or given to you to allow you to connect to the WLAN. This key is also used to encrypt your wireless communications.

PSK authentication is a layer 2 authentication. It is similar to the SSID authentication, since there is no identity component being verified. If the PSK on the client matches the PSK assigned to the WLAN, then the client can successfully connect to the WLAN and receive an IP address. If the PSK does not match, then the client cannot connect to the WLAN and will not receive an IP address. Although an identity is not authenticated, unlike SSID authentication, an *802.1X Authentication Policy* needs to be defined. Figure 6.11 shows the profiles and components needed to configure a WLAN with PSK authentication.

FIGURE 6.11 Preshared key authentication components

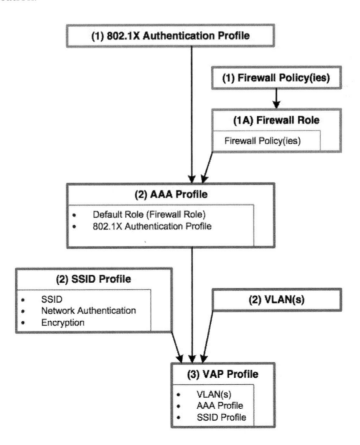

802.1X Authentication Profile (Preshared Key Authentication)

The 802.1X authentication profile defines the details of how the PSK encryption will be performed. Although it is named *802.1X authentication profile*, 802.1X is not implemented. Hopefully, and in many instances, all you need to do is create an 802.1X authentication profile and simply accept the default settings. The ArubaOS default configuration includes a predefined 802.1X authentication profile called default-psk. You can use this profile when creating any number of PSK SSIDs. This section will describe the components necessary to create a PSK-enabled WLAN.

The following menu path will bring you to the menu where you can create or modify the 802.1X authentication profile using the WebUI interface: **Configuration** ➢ **SECURITY** ➢ **Authentication** ➢ **L2 Authentication** ➢ **802.1X Authentication**.

The following CLI command can also be used to create the 802.1X authentication profile. Note that this command is simply creating the profile. Since there are no additional commands, all of the default values are being accepted for this profile.

```
(config) #aaa authentication dot1x wpa2psk-1x-profile
```

Firewall Policy (Preshared Key Authentication)

As with any of the authentication methods, after the client connects to the WLAN, a role will be assigned to the client. This consists of one or more policies, each consisting of one or more firewall rules. If the necessary firewall policy does not exist, it will need to be created. Firewall policy was described earlier in this chapter in the "802.1X/EAP Authentication" section and will be explained in more detail in Chapter 8, "Policy Enforcement Firewall."

Firewall Role (Preshared Key Authentication)

When a client connects to a PSK authenticated network, the role that will be assigned is the initial role. In general, the initial role is often a limited-access role, which is overridden by another role after authentication is performed. This is typically not the case with PSK authentication. Although PSK networks do not provide user authentication, they can offer a moderate level of encryption. Therefore, it is not uncommon for a PSK-authenticated network to have an initial role allowing more than limited access to the network. Firewall roles were described earlier in this chapter in the "802.1X/EAP Authentication" section and will be explained in more detail in Chapter 8, "Policy Enforcement Firewall." Chapter 7, "Role Derivation," will cover how roles are assigned.

AAA Profile (Preshared Key Authentication)

The AAA profile for PSK authentication specifies the initial role and the 802.1X authentication profile that will be used, as shown in the following CLI output:

```
(config) #aaa profile wpa2psk-aaa
(AAA Profile "wpa2psk-aaa") #initial-role authenticated
(AAA Profile "wpa2psk-aaa") #authentication-dot1x "wpa2psk-1x-profile"
```

SSID Profile (Preshared Key Authentication)

The SSID profile defines the SSID, the encryption method, and the network authentication method. WPA2-PSK network authentication is being implemented with AES encryption. The following CLI output shows the SSID profile, which defines the SSID, the WPA2-PSK passphrase, and the encryption method (opmode) being used:

```
(config) #wlan ssid-profile wpa2psk-ssid
(SSID Profile "wpa2psk-ssid") #essid wps2psk
(SSID Profile "wpa2psk-ssid") #wpa-passphrase aruba123
(SSID Profile "wpa2psk-ssid") #opmode wpa2-psk-aes
```

VLAN(s) (Preshared Key Authentication)

As with most WLANs, a separate VLAN should be created. The following CLI commands will create VLAN 93, assign an IP address, and forward any DHCP requests to DHCP server 10.254.1.21. Remember that the VLAN needs to be created on the controller where the user traffic is terminating.

```
(config) #vlan 93
(config) #interface vlan 93
(config-subif)#ip address 192.168.9.1 255.255.255.0
(config-subif)#ip helper-address 10.254.1.21
```

VLAN pools and named VLANs can also be created, and were described previously in this chapter. The Aruba controller can be a DHCP server if the number of expected DHCP clients is less than the number of supported leases. Configuring the controller as a DHCP server was explained previously in this chapter, and in more detail in Chapter 4, "Getting Started."

Virtual AP Profile (Preshared Key Authentication)

The VAP profile consolidates the AAA profile, SSID profile, and VLAN, to create the virtual AP, as shown in the following CLI commands:

```
(config) #wlan virtual-ap wpa2psk-vap
(Virtual AP profile "wpa2psk-vap") #aaa-profile wpa2psk-aaa
(Virtual AP profile "wpa2psk-vap") #ssid-profile wpa2psk-ssid
(Virtual AP profile "wpa2psk-vap") #vlan 93
```

Encryption Techniques

Unless there is a very specific requirement, when configuring any WLAN on an Aruba controller, there is only one encryption method that should be chosen: WPA2/AES. This section will provide a brief description of WEP, WPA/TKIP, and WPA2/AES. WEP and WPA/TKIP will be described mainly for historical purposes, and so that you have some understanding of it in case you are in the unfortunate position of having to implement it to support an environment with old, outdated wireless clients. Most commonly, these environments tend to be industrial networks or networks designed for a specific task.

Remember, when configuring any encryption besides WPA2/AES, the SSID must be considered minimally trusted, and extra measures need to be taken to ensure the clients are contained and isolated from other traffic. You may also be exposing your network to liability under legislative or standard compliance rules such as PCI.

Wired Equivalent Privacy

Wired Equivalent Privacy (WEP) has been a part of the 802.11 standard since it was introduced in 1997. WEP uses a shared key to encrypt data, with either a 40- or 104-bit key having to be entered on the client and on the controller. WEP uses an encryption algorithm known as *ARC4*. In 2001, WEP was cracked. These days, it is possible to crack WEP in minutes.

Previously in this chapter, it was stated that the IEEE and the Wi-Fi Alliance have deprecated WEP, although it is still supported for backward compatibility with older devices. However, if you choose to implement it, the VAP can only operate using the older pre-802.11ac and pre-802.11n data rates. As with many vendors, Aruba has implemented this policy.

WPA/TKIP

After WEP was cracked, WPA2/AES (802.11i) was being developed to replace it. For various reasons, an interim solution was needed, and WPA/TKIP was developed and introduced in 2002. WPA/TKIP implemented some of the new technologies that were being developed for WPA2/AES; however, it needed to use the older ARC4 encryption algorithm used by WEP. Temporal Key Integrity Protocol (TKIP) fixed the problems associated with WEP.

As with WEP, WPA/TKIP has also been deprecated by the IEEE and the Wi-Fi Alliance. WPA/TKIP is still supported for backward compatibility with older devices; however, if you choose to implement it, the VAP can only operate using the older pre-802.11ac and pre-802.11n data rates.

WPA2/AES

With both WEP and WPA/TKIP deprecated by the IEEE and the Wi-Fi Alliance, WPA2/AES is left as the encryption method of choice. Advanced Encryption Standard (AES) is a block cipher and is extremely secure. WPA2/AES, also referred to as *802.11i*, was introduced in 2004. Very few devices do not support WPA2/AES, so there is almost no reason to use any other encryption method.

Digital Certificates

Some of the security provided by the Aruba controller is performed using digital certificates. There are three primary uses of digital certificates with an Aruba controller. Certificates are used for administration of the controller through the WebUI, for client authentication using 802.1X/EAP, and for client redirection and authentication using captive portal. There are other instances where certificates are used with ArubaOS, but these are the three most common.

This book assumes that you have some knowledge of certificates. Certificate configuration can be complex, and varies from network to network. This section of the chapter focuses on configuring and enabling certificates on the Aruba controller, along with how they interact with management and client devices. If you need to learn more about certificates, Aruba's Airheads Community and the documentation area of Aruba's support website have numerous documents regarding certificates. Additionally, you can find many excellent documents explaining certificates by simply searching the Internet.

For many years, Aruba controllers have shipped with a default certificate named `securelogin.arubanetworks.com`. Without a certificate installed on an Aruba controller, some controller configuration tasks cannot be performed. Therefore, this default certificate was provided to make initial configuration of the controller easier for customers.

The default certificate was never intended to be used on production networks. Unfortunately, some customers did not invest the time, effort, or money to replace this certificate, while others did not understand certificates or the importance of installing their own certificates. Since every Aruba controller initially has the same certificate, this puts your network at risk for impersonation attacks; therefore, it is important to replace this certificate. This default, publicly signed certificate has been revoked and is no longer included with ArubaOS.

A certificate is a digital identifier and is also used to facilitate data encryption between devices. Three types of certificates can be generated: public, private, and self-signed.

Public Certificate   A public certificate is created when you generate a certificate signing request (CSR), and the CSR is signed by an organization known as a trusted certificate authority (CA). By default, your computer and browser are configured by the OS vendor to trust a group of certificate authorities. The known public CAs are stored in the *root certificate store*. Each certificate store has extensive requirements in order for a CA to get added to its list of trusted CAs. These requirements are in place to ensure the integrity and security of the certificates.

When a public CA signs the CSR, they are saying that they have verified the identity of the entity that issued the CSR, thus establishing a chain of trust. Your OS trusts the root CA, along with the chain of intermediaries, and ultimately the server that sent you the certificate. The public CAs follow strict processes when issuing certificates to customers, such as your company. This strict process extends the trust from the CA to the OS or browser, and ultimately to the user.

Private Certificate   A private certificate is created when you generate a certificate signing request (CSR), and the CSR is signed by a private CA server, typically within an organization. This private CA server is often a Windows Active Directory server or possibly a ClearPass server. The private certificate that was generated and signed is not listed as part of the root certificate store on your user's computers and mobile devices. Private certificates need to be installed on the user's computers in order for them to be trusted. These certificates can be installed manually or through an automated distribution process.

Self-Signed Certificate   A self-signed certificate is generally created by your local machine or device. Self-signed certificates provide no real security, since the certificate is signed by the device that is generating it. A self-signed certificate is useful as a placeholder or in a lab or demonstration environment.

Obtaining a Certificate

There are two methods of obtaining a certificate. The first is to request a certificate from a certificate authority. This request can be made to one of the public trusted CAs, or to a private CA, such as your corporate Windows server. In either scenario, the process is the same. The difference is that the public trusted CA will provide you with a certificate that is universally accepted, whereas the certificate from your corporate CA is not universally accepted. Obtaining a certificate from a publicly trusted CA typically costs money.

The second method of obtaining a certificate is to generate a self-signed certificate. This certificate is generated and approved by the same computer; therefore, it is not trustworthy. Self-signed certificates are easy to create and should only be used for demonstration or testing environments.

ArubaOS does not have the ability to create a self-signed certificate; however, using OpenSSL on a Macintosh or Windows computer, you can generate a self-signed certificate that you can install on your controller.

The following section will explain the tasks necessary to generate a certificate signing request (CSR), and obtain a certificate signed by a CA. This will be followed by directions on how to create your own self-signed certificate using OpenSSL.

Certificate Signing Request

The mechanics of obtaining a certificate are straightforward. The first step is to generate a CSR. You can consider the CSR as an application that you are submitting to the certificate authority, requesting or asking it to generate a globally valid certificate. This can be performed from the WebUI, as shown in Figure 6.12, or from the CLI, as shown in the following output:

```
#crypto pki csr rsa key_len 2048 common_name wlan.mycompany.com country US
state_or_province MA city Concord organization Mycompany unit IT email it@
mycompany.com

CSR generation starting, please wait a few minutes before issuing the command
'show crypto pki csr' to get the results.
```

The components of the previous command are as follows:

`crypto pki csr`	Command to generate the CSR
`rsa key_len 2048`	Generates the request with a Rivest, Shamir, and Adleman (RSA) key with the length of 2048 bits
`common_name wlan.mycompany.com`	Typically the fully qualified domain name (FQDN) of the system that you are securing
`country US`	The two-letter ISO 3166 standard code for your country
`state_or_province MA`	The state or province location of the controller
`city Concord`	The city location of the controller
`organization Mycompany`	The name of the company or organization
`unit IT`	The department or business unit
`email it@mycompany.com`	An e-mail address, typically the certificate administrator

FIGURE 6.12
Creating a CSR

After the CSR is created, you can view it from the WebUI by clicking the View Current button, shown in Figure 6.12, which will display the CSR as shown in Figure 6.13. You can also view it from the CLI, as shown in the following output (portions of this output have been truncated):

```
#show crypto pki csr

Certificate Request:
    Data:
        Version: 0 (0x0)
        Subject: C=US, ST=MA, L=Concord, O=Mycompany, OU=IT, CN=wlan.mycompany.com/emailAddress=it@mycompany.com
        Subject Public Key Info:
            Public Key Algorithm: rsaEncryption
                Public-Key: (2048 bit)
                Modulus:
                    00:9d:7d:dd:fc:95:07:c8:e4:14:8a:a7:6d:6d:a9:
                    c2:67:5a:68:b6:77:fa:3e:82:03:e4:8d:76:3f:db:
                    be:34:c5:aa:e2:c6:23:f2:bb:61:39:01:c4:60:e6:
                    71:54:ad:ec:0b:e1:b4:9c:89:51:cf:bd:46:88:41:
                    7f:cb:30:22:1b:02:f3:4e:be:e1:08:fc:e2:cc:b8:
                    ec:bb:ef:0b:0e:b7:21:68:ef:8b:cb:38:fc:3b:42:
                    f6:22
                Exponent: 65537 (0x10001)
```

```
        Attributes:
            a0:00
        Signature Algorithm: sha1WithRSAEncryption
            7d:5a:9a:a7:1c:27:33:73:1e:cf:8d:0f:96:32:19:cb:d5:bd:
            1c:0b:e5:1a:ff:5e:3e:ec:96:ec:c3:d1:78:93:30:3a:51:7f:
            07:8c:ae:ac:67:e9:32:80:93:0d:d9:82:30:ce:4b:ae:5d:38:
            8f:d2:e6:c7
-----BEGIN CERTIFICATE REQUEST-----
MIIC0TCCAbkCAQAwgYsxCzAJBgNVBAYTAlVTMQswCQYDVQQIDAJNQTEQMA4GA1UE
yOQUiqdtbanCZ1potnf6PoID5I12P9u+NMWq4sYj8rthOQHEYOZxVK3sC+G0nIlR
z71GiEHh9CFkYJ7zEh65PpbyjSyioF/ddsJW2ONgvNHUUlOcKRXI0jSL0hKPE7gk
NOl/yzAiGwLzTr7hCPzizLjsu+8LDrchaO+Lyzj8OOL2IhfIQyMYzLKekeI8u3zD
olE0TmlW
-----END CERTIFICATE REQUEST-----
```

FIGURE 6.13
Viewing the CSR

When a CSR is created, the controller generates a private key and a public key. To ensure security, the private key needs to always be kept secure. To do this, when the CSR is generated, ArubaOS locks the private key inside the controller. The public key needs to be signed by a CA. In the previous CSR output, the public key is the series of characters between `-----BEGIN CERTIFICATE REQUEST-----` and `-----END CERTIFICATE REQUEST-----`. This text, including the BEGIN and END lines, needs to copied and provided to the CA. Remember, this process is the same whether the CA is a publically trusted CA or an internal CA server in your organization.

After the CA generates your signed certificate, you need to import it. The easiest way to import the certificate is through the WebUI, as shown in Figure 6.14. If you want to import the certificate using the CLI, you will first need to copy the certificate to the flash partition, and then import it. The following CLI output shows the TFTP command to copy the certificate to the controller, followed by the command to import the certificate:

```
#copy tftp: 192.168.240.31 mycompany.pem flash: mycompany.pem
#crypto pki-import pem ServerCert mycompany mycompany.pem passphrase
```

FIGURE 6.14 Importing the signed certificate

It was mentioned previously that when a CSR is generated from the controller, the controller permanently secures the private key within the controller. This makes it impossible to export the key from the controller. This also makes it impossible to install the key on any other devices. Therefore, for convenience and flexibility, it is typically better to generate the CSR and private key on an external server. In any environment, it is of the utmost importance to secure and protect the storage and distribution of the private key.

Self-Signed Certificate

If you are working on a lab or demonstration network and do not have a CA available, you can still generate a certificate. Although the Aruba controller is not capable of generating its own self-signed certificate, you can generate a private key along with the self-signed certificate using OpenSSL on a Windows, Macintosh, or Linux computer. OpenSSL is an open source software project that provides a toolkit for Transport Layer Security (TLS) and Secure Sockets Layer (SSL) protocols.

A Macintosh or Linux computer should have OpenSSL already installed. For a lab environment, the version that is installed by default should be capable of performing the required tasks. If you want to use OpenSSL on a production network for any reason, note that there will likely be an updated version available. If you are using a Windows computer, there is a version of OpenSSL that you can download and install. To learn more about OpenSSL and the available download files, browse to www.openssl.org and also search the Internet using the keyword "OpenSSL."

Generating a private key and the self-signed certificate can be performed using a single OpenSSL command. Along with the command, you will need to answer some questions. These are the same questions from the "Certificate Signing Request" section earlier in this chapter, which makes sense because you are creating a CSR and also signing it. The following table shows the parameters in the command and their descriptions.

req	Creates and processes certificate requests
-x509	Generates the self-signed certificate
-sha256	Use SHA-2 hash algorithm, using a hash length of 256 bits
(-new)	This is not part of the command, but it is implied that a new CSR is being created
-newkey rsa:2048	Generate a 2048-bit key using RSA algorithm
-keyout selfcert.pem	Private key filename of selfcert.pem
-out selfcert.pem	Output filename, which contains both the private and public keys: selfcert.pem
-days 1000	Number of days certificate is valid = 1000

Following is the OpenSSL command and output:

```
$ openssl req -x509 -sha256 -newkey rsa:2048 -keyout selfcert.pem -out selfcert.pem -days 1000
Generating a 2048 bit RSA private key
...+++
............................................................................+
++
writing new private key to 'selfcert.pem'
Enter PEM pass phrase: aruba123
Verifying - Enter PEM pass phrase: aruba123
-----
You are about to be asked to enter information that will be incorporated into your certificate request.
What you are about to enter is what is called a Distinguished Name or a DN.
```

```
There are quite a few fields but you can leave some blank
For some fields there will be a default value,
If you enter '.', the field will be left blank.
-----
Country Name (2 letter code) [AU]:US
State or Province Name (full name) [Some-State]:MA
Locality Name (eg, city) []:Concord
Organization Name (eg, company) [Internet Widgits Pty Ltd]:Ourcompany
Organizational Unit Name (eg, section) []:IT
Common Name (e.g. server FQDN or YOUR name) []:wlan.ourcompany.com
Email Address []:it@ourcompany.com
```

After generating your self-signed certificate, you need to import it. The easiest way to import the certificate is through the WebUI, as shown in Figure 6.15. If you want to import the certificate using the CLI, you will first need to copy the certificate to the flash partition, and then import it. The following CLI output shows the TFTP command to copy the self-signed certificate to the controller, followed by the command to import the certificate:

```
#copy tftp: 192.168.240.31 selfcert.pem flash: selfcert.pem
File copied successfully!!!
#crypto pki-import pem ServerCert Test-Certificate selfcert.pem aruba123
```

FIGURE 6.15
Importing a self-signed certificate

WebUI Management Certificate

Once you have installed the certificate, it is available for use. Figure 6.16 shows where you can select the certificate to be used as part of the WebUI Management Authentication Method. In this example, when an administrator logs into ArubaOS using the WebUI, the controller will validate the username and password of the administrator. To ensure that the administrator is connecting to a trusted Aruba controller, the client computer will validate the Aruba controller using the selected certificate; in this example, the certificate named Test-Certificate.

Since there is a select group of people who will be managing the Aruba controller, it is likely that the WebUI management certificate will be signed by an internal CA. The public certificate will need to be installed on each of the computers that will be used for WebUI management.

Navigating to **Configuration ➢ MANAGEMENT ➢ General** will bring you to the menu where you can choose the certificate that will be used for WebUI management.

FIGURE 6.16 Applying a certificate

Captive Portal Certificate

Just as a certificate can validate the identity of the controller for management, a certificate can be used to validate the controller when users connect to the network using a captive portal. The selection of the captive portal certificate is performed on the same menu used to select the WebUI management certificate, as shown in Figure 6.16.

Unlike WebUI management, which is limited to a select few administrators within the organization, captive portal access is often used by large numbers of guest users. A guest user typically does not have a relationship with your organization. In order for a guest user to trust the captive portal certificate, the certificate will need to be signed by a trusted root CA. If the certificate is not signed by a trusted root CA, the guest user will receive a message that the certificate is not trusted even before the captive portal shows up in the browser window. It is recommended that certificates used with captive portal are signed by a trusted root CA.

A single captive portal certificate can be used across multiple controllers. The common name of the certificate does not have to exist in DNS. It is recommended to use an address that is user friendly, such as `network-login.domain.xyz`.

802.1X/EAP Certificate

When a client authenticates to the wireless network using 802.1X/EAP, the supplicant (client) authenticates with the authentication server (RADIUS server). The supplicant typically authenticates itself to the RADIUS server using a username and password, or possibly a client certificate. The supplicant may verify the identity of the RADIUS server by validating the server's certificate.

Since the client devices connecting to the network should be trusted users within the organization, the certificate is often signed by an internal CA. When the client connects to the network and attempts to authenticate itself with the RADIUS server, the RADIUS server will send the certificate to the client to be verified. In this scenario, no certificate needs to be installed or selected on the Aruba controller, since it is the RADIUS server that is providing the server certificate.

When using 802.1X/EAP, there is one instance when the server certificate would need to be installed on the Aruba controller. It is when EAP termination is enabled for an 802.1X authentication profile on the controller. EAP termination was explained earlier in this chapter in the "Internal Database" section. *EAP termination*, also known as *Fast-Connect* or *EAP offload*, allows the 802.1X authentication to be terminated at the Aruba controller. If EAP termination is enabled, and verification of the server certificate will be performed, then the certificate needs to be imported into the Aruba controller and selected in the 802.1X authentication profile.

In the "Certificate Signing Request" section of this chapter, you learned how to import the certificate. After it is imported into the controller, EAP termination needs to be enabled in the 802.1X authentication profile. Figure 6.17 shows `termination enable`, with `EAP-PEAP` set as the termination EAP-type and `EAP-MSCHAPv2` set as the inner EAP-type.

The following path in the WebUI will bring you to the menu where this can be enabled: **Configuration ➢ SECURITY ➢ Authentication ➢ L2 Authentication ➢ 802.1X Authentication**.

After EAP termination is enabled, the server certificate needs to be selected from the Server Certificate selection dropdown. This can be found near the bottom of the 802.1X authentication profile's Advanced submenu.

FIGURE 6.17
Enabling EAP termination

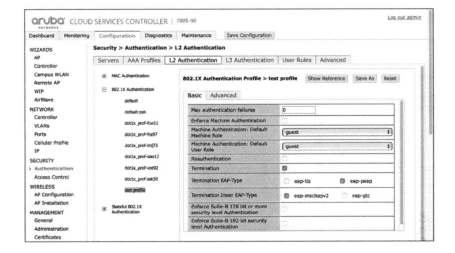

An EAP server certificate can be used across multiple controllers. The common name of the certificate does not have to exist in DNS. It is recommended to use an address that is user friendly, such as network-login.domain.xyz.

CHAPTER 7
Role Derivation

IN THIS CHAPTER, YOU WILL LEARN ABOUT THE FOLLOWING:

- Role Assignment
- Physical Connection
- Layer 2 Authentication
- Logon Role
- Initial Role
- User Rules
  - Role Conditions
  - User Rule Derivation
- Role Derivation with Server Authentication
  - Vendor-Specific Attribute Assigned Role
  - Server-Assigned Role
  - Default Role
- MAC Authentication
- 802.1X/EAP Authentication
  - Machine Authentication
  - Server Authentication
- Layer 2 Authentication Synopsis
- Layer 3 Authentication
- External Services Interface
- Role Derivation Review
  - 802.1X/EAP Authentication
  - WPA2 Passphrase Role/VLAN Derivation
  - Captive Portal Authentication

ARUBA'S POLICY ENFORCEMENT FIREWALL (PEF) IS A key feature of the Aruba operating system. Firewall policies can be applied directly to the physical interfaces or VLANs on the controller, however, they are typically assigned to wireless users in the form of firewall roles, known as *role-based access control (RBAC)*. Identification of individual users through user authentication allows multiple devices to connect to an SSID, while maintaining different levels of access and control for each device.

For example, instead of a school having an SSID for students and a separate SSID for faculty and administrators, everybody could access the same SSID. Students could be assigned a very restrictive user role, faculty could be assigned a less restrictive user role, and administrators could be assigned a non-restrictive user role.

The Policy Enforcement Firewall is an additional licensed component of ArubaOS, and most customers purchase the license because of the additional capabilities that it offers. For this reason, this book only addresses the behavior of the controller with the PEF license installed.

This chapter and the next will explain the many ways that roles affect wireless, and in some cases wired, users. This chapter will focus solely on the role assignment process; a process known as *role derivation*. The next chapter, Chapter 8, "Policy Enforcement Firewall," will focus on the specific rules and policies that are used to build the roles, along with the permissions that user roles provide.

Role Assignment

A distinguishing feature of ArubaOS is the Policy Enforcement Firewall. Any time a client connects to the wireless network, it is assigned a set of permissions: a *role*. A role is also known as a *user role*. The user role governs the characteristics of the client's access to the network. Every wireless user and any wired user on an untrusted port will be assigned a role.

A user role is assigned to all wireless clients because the wireless connection is always an untrusted connection. Any device that connects to an untrusted connection is therefore treated as an untrusted device, and is assigned a role through the role derivation process.

Wired ports on Aruba network devices by default are trusted, functioning as simple switch ports and allowing full access. Wired ports include the physical Ethernet ports on the controller, along with additional Ethernet ports on any Aruba AP or RAP. When a wired port or VLAN is set as untrusted, any device connecting will be assigned a user role.

It is important to determine the need to secure wired ports on the AP and controller. Many Aruba controllers are secured in a datacenter or wiring closet, physically limiting unauthorized access to these physical ports. In this type of environment, allowing full access on these ports is often not a high security risk. However, controllers are not always kept in secure locations, and APs typically are not. In these environments it is important to be able to make sure that unused controller or AP ports cannot allow unauthorized access to the network. Port security can be provided by making these ports untrusted.

This chapter will explain the most common ways in which a client can be assigned a role. A client can only be assigned one role at a time. If a client is assigned a role, but already has a role assigned to it, the new role will supersede the previous role. ArubaOS has many rules, exceptions, and scenarios in which roles can be assigned. However, there often are too many variables or exceptions, such that they should not be implemented. That is why this chapter focuses on the core methods by which roles are assigned.

Bear in mind that the methods described here to assign a role to an untrusted user may also be used to assign a VLAN to the untrusted user as well.

The role derivation process and logic is complex. In order to help you understand this process, an ArubaOS role derivation flowchart has been created, and is shown in Figure 7.1. A PDF version of this flowchart is available to download at: www.westcott-consulting.com.

ROLE ASSIGNMENT

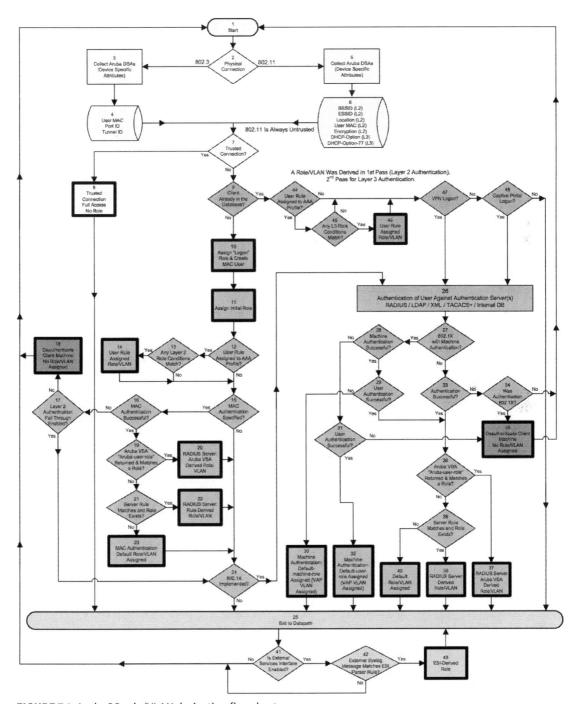

FIGURE 7.1 ArubaOS role/VLAN derivation flowchart

Each task in this flowchart is numbered. The task numbers do not represent any specific order; rather they are simply there to make it easier to identify and reference each task. The bold rectangular tasks are points in the flowchart where a new role is assigned.

If you are looking at a color version of this flowchart, tasks with similar types of logic or function have the same color. Since some versions of the flowchart are black and white, this book will reference the tasks solely by their numbers and not their colors.

This chapter will begin by explaining what occurs in each task on the flowchart. After every task and the entire process are explained, a streamlined overview will be given for each of the following client connections:

- 802.1X/EAP authentication
- WPA2 passphrase/preshared key
- Captive portal authentication

Physical Connection

Figure 7.2 displays eight tasks on the role derivation flowchart. These tasks identify the initial connection of the client device, identifying whether the connection is wired or wireless, and whether the connection is trusted or untrusted.

FIGURE 7.2
Identifying the initial connection

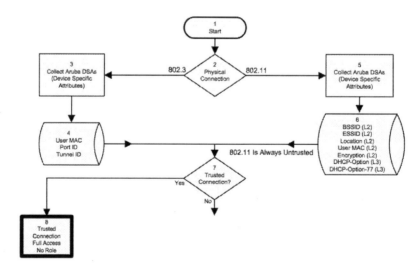

When a device starts to communicate, as illustrated in Task 1 of Figure 7.2, the controller first identifies whether the device is connected using an 802.3 wired physical (PHY) connection or an 802.11 wireless PHY connection, as shown in Task 2. Whether the device is wired or wireless, the controller collects connection information, known as *device-specific attributes (DSAs)*. If the device is a wired device, the following DSAs are collected, shown in Tasks 3 and 4:

- User MAC address
- Port ID
- Tunnel ID

If the device is a wireless device, the following layer 2 DSAs are collected, shown in Tasks 5 and 6:

- BSSID
- ESSID
- Location (AP name)
- User MAC address
- Encryption type

This DSA information can be used to assign a role based upon the value of any of these attributes. This can be performed further on in the derivation process and will be explained later in the "User Rule" section of this chapter.

After the DSAs are collected, the controller must check to see if the client is attached to a trusted or untrusted connection, as illustrated in Task 7. Wireless connections are always untrusted, so this check is only valid for wired connections.

As mentioned earlier, wired ports are trusted by default. If the wired connection is trusted, then the client automatically has full access, no role is assigned, no client authentication occurs, and no further role derivation tasks are performed, as illustrated in Task 8. If the connection is untrusted, then a role will be assigned through the derivation process.

A wired port can be made untrusted by issuing the following CLI commands. In this example, gigabit Ethernet port 0/0/3 is being made untrusted.

```
(config) #interface gigabitethernet 0/0/3
(config-if)#no trusted
```

This task can also be performed from **Configuration > NETWORK > Ports > Port**, as shown in Figure 7.3.

FIGURE 7.3
Setting wired port to untrusted

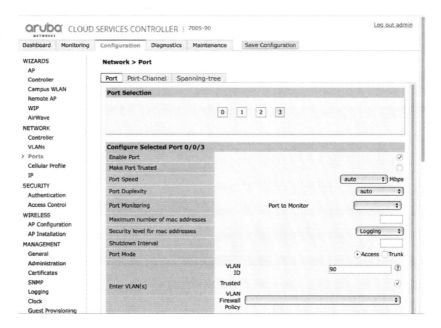

Layer 2 Authentication

After the controller determines that the connection is untrusted, Task 9 in Figure 7.1 determines if the user already exists in the database. By default, the minimum length of time that a user might exist in the database is five minutes; however, this can be changed by adjusting the user idle timeout value. When a client device connects to the network, it must first go through a layer 2 authentication process and then possibly a layer 3 authentication process. Layer 2 authentication occurs prior to receiving an IP address. Think of layer 2 authentication as establishing a connection between the client device and the network. Layer 2 authentication can consist of a full authentication of the client's identity, such as with MAC authentication or 802.1X/EAP, or it can simply consist of the device connecting to the network.

At this time, let us assume that the user is not already connected and not yet in the user database. If the outcome of Task 9 is No (the user does not exist in the database), then the logic path from this point to where the client device exits to the data path (Task 25) is considered layer 2 authentication.

Logon Role

Every untrusted client that is tracked by the controller must have a role assigned to it. This means that as soon as a client device begins communicating with the controller, the controller identifies the device and begins tracking and controlling what the device can do. At this point, Task 10, the controller automatically assigns the logon role to the device. You can think of this initial assignment of the logon role as the starting point or as a placeholder. By default, the logon role provides some basic core network permissions including DHCP, DNS, and ICMP. Even though the logon role provides these capabilities, since the client has not completed its layer 2 connection, these permissions are not yet relevant.

Initial Role

As you just learned, when a client connects to an untrusted network, the client is automatically assigned the logon role. This can be overridden by an initial role, as shown in Task 11 of Figure 7.1. The assignment of the initial role is defined in the AAA profile. When an AAA profile is created, the role logon is always automatically specified as the AAA profile's initial role. The initial role can be set to something other than logon.

The following CLI output shows the creation of an AAA profile WC-Voice-aaa. The show command immediately following the profile creation displays the default values that were assigned to the profile. Notice that the initial role of this profile has been defined as logon.

```
(config) #aaa profile WC-Voice-aaa
(AAA Profile "WC-Voice-aaa") #show aaa profile WC-Voice-aaa

AAA Profile "WC-Voice-aaa"
--------------------------
Parameter                             Value
---------                             -----
Initial role                          logon
MAC Authentication Profile            N/A
MAC Authentication Default Role       guest
MAC Authentication Server Group       default
802.1X Authentication Profile         N/A
802.1X Authentication Default Role    guest
802.1X Authentication Server Group    N/A
Download Role from CPPM               Disabled
Set username from dhcp option 12      Disabled
L2 Authentication Fail Through        Disabled
Multiple Server Accounting            Disabled
User idle timeout                     N/A
Max IPv4 for wireless user            2
RADIUS Accounting Server Group        N/A
RADIUS Interim Accounting             Disabled
XML API server                        N/A
RFC 3576 server                       N/A
User derivation rules                 N/A
```

```
Wired to Wireless Roaming         Enabled
SIP authentication role           N/A
Device Type Classification        Enabled
Enforce DHCP                      Disabled
PAN Firewall Integration          Disabled
Open SSID radius accounting       Disabled
```

There may be a reason to change the initial role to something other than logon. In some cases, the initial role is used to provide registration privileges in the event of a MAC authentication failure on an open or preshared key network. The following CLI output shows the creation of an AAA profile, WC-Guest3-aaa-prof, followed by the assignment of WC3-guest-logon as the initial role. This is verified by the show aaa profile command:

```
(config) #aaa profile WC-Guest3-aaa-prof
(AAA Profile "WC-Guest3-aaa-prof") #initial-role WC3-guest-logon
(AAA Profile "WC-Guest3-aaa-prof") #show aaa profile WC-Guest3-aaa-prof

AAA Profile "WC-Guest3-aaa-prof"
--------------------------------
Parameter                         Value
---------                         -----
Initial role                      WC3-guest-logon
```

The AAA profile, which contains the initial role, is displayed in Figure 7.4. **Configuration > SECURITY > Authentication > AAA Profiles** will take you to the location where you can select the AAA profile and modify the initial role value.

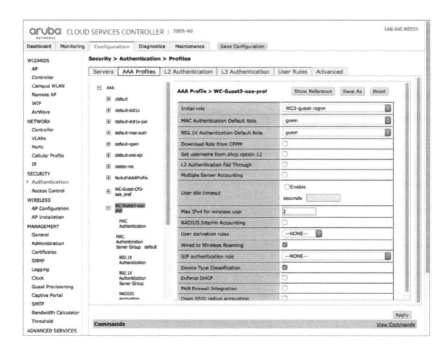

FIGURE 7.4 AAA profile and initial role

When configuring an AAA profile for an 802.1X/EAP authentication, the initial role is irrelevant, although it is highly suggested that you leave it as logon. While a client is authenticating using 802.1X/EAP, the access port is placed in a blocking state until the user has successfully completed the authentication process. Additionally, since 802.1X/EAP is a layer 2 process, an initial role would have no bearing on whether or not the client has access to the network. After the client is authenticated, the controller will proceed to assign a post-authentication role, which will replace any previously assigned role.

User Rules

In Tasks 3 and 5 in Figure 7.1, the controller collects device-specific attributes (DSAs) about the client connection. This information is collected from the connection of the device to the network. The layer 2 attributes are collected at this stage. ArubaOS allows this DSA information to be analyzed to assign a role. This analysis allows certain clients to receive a pre-authenticated role based upon information about their device or connection. An example of when this can be helpful is when non-intelligent devices, such as barcode scanners, need to access, but must be limited by the firewall.

DSA analysis is done through what is known as *user rules*, with each rule consisting of one or more *role conditions*. To use DSAs to assign roles, a user rule must be created and one or more role conditions must be assigned to the rule. The user rule is then applied to the AAA profile. In Figure 7.1, the user rule is processed in Tasks 12, 13, and 14. The following paragraphs will explain how to configure a user rule, followed by an explanation of how these tasks are processed.

The first step is to create a user rule. This is done by simply creating one and giving it a name. **Configuration** ➢ **SECURITY** ➢ **Authentication** ➢ **User Rules** will take you to the menu where you can create a user rule. Figure 7.5 shows the rule Cameras being created.

FIGURE 7.5
User rule creation

Role Conditions

After a user rule is created, it should contain a set of one or more role conditions. To do this, simply select the user rule and then create the desired condition or conditions.

A *role condition* is the actual rule that analyzes the DSA, and if the condition matches, assigns a role or VLAN to the client device. If multiple role conditions are assigned to a user rule, the conditions are processed sequentially, top down, until there is a match or until all conditions are processed. Therefore, the order of the role conditions is important.

The following CLI output shows the creation of a user rule Cameras followed by the creation of two role conditions. Both of these role conditions are checking the OUI value of the MAC address of the client device to see if it matches either of the following strings: 01:23:45 or 12:34:45. The second role condition is being placed in the first position, moving the other role condition down to the second position. Notice that since the description contains a space, it is necessary to enclose it in quotes.

It is recommended that you do not use spaces in any names or descriptions, negating the need to use quotes in CLI commands.

```
(config) #aaa derivation-rules user Cameras
(user-rule) #set role condition macaddr starts-with 01:23:45 set-value Camera-role description "Cameras 01:23:45"
(user-rule) #set role condition macaddr starts-with 12:34:56 set-value Camera-role position 1 description "Cameras 12:34:56"
```

Figure 7.6 shows the form used to create a role condition. This form contains the following fields:

- Set Type: specifies whether the role condition rule will assign a role or a VLAN
- Rule Type: specifies the DSA that will be analyzed. This includes the following:
  - BSSID
  - DHCP-Option-77 (Layer 3)
  - Encryption Type
  - ESSID
  - Location
  - MAC Address
  - DHCP Option (Layer 3)
- Condition: defines the match rule, including:
  - Contains
  - Ends-with
  - Equals

- Not-equals
- Starts-with

▶ Value: the value that is being checked

▶ Roles: the role that will be assigned if the condition matches

▶ Description: text description of the condition

In the Rule Type field, `DHCP-Option-77` and `DHCP Option` are both layer 3 options that would not be analyzed until after the client device requests a DHCP address. This is a form of DHCP fingerprinting. Although the user rules are capable of DHCP fingerprinting, the controller does not maintain a fingerprint database of different device types. Therefore you would need to know the fingerprint you are trying to match, along with creating a role condition for each fingerprint you are trying to identify. If you need to fingerprint many different types of devices, you should consider integrating your controller with an Aruba ClearPass server, which has far more powerful fingerprinting capabilities.

FIGURE 7.6
Role condition

The final step for setting up a user rule is to assign the rule to the AAA profile. This is easily done by going to **Configuration ➢ SECURITY ➢ Authentication ➢ AAA Profiles**. Figure 7.7 shows the `Cameras` User Derivation Rule being assigned to the `Cameras-psk` AAA profile.

The `Cameras` user rule can also be assigned to the `Cameras-psk` AAA profile using the following CLI commands:

```
(config) #aaa profile "Cameras-psk"
(AAA Profile "Cameras-psk") #user-derivation-rules "Cameras"
```

FIGURE 7.7
Assigning User rule to AAA profile

User Rule Derivation

The role derivation flowchart, Figure 7.1, processes user rules in Tasks 12, 13, and 14.

Task 12 identifies if a user rule has been assigned to the AAA profile by the VAP/SSID that the client device is connecting to. If a user rule is assigned, then each role condition is processed and evaluated sequentially.

Task 13 identifies if any layer 2 role condition matches. If not, the client device retains its current user role, and processing continues with Task 15 in the flowchart.

Task 14 assigns a new role to the client if the client's DSA matches one of the role conditions. Remember that role conditions are processed sequentially, and only the first matching role condition will be processed.

Role Derivation with Server Authentication

When a client is authenticated on the network, the client can be assigned a role through one of three methods: RADIUS vendor-specific attribute (VSA)–assigned role, server rule–assigned role, or AAA default role. With both the VSA-assigned role and the server rule–assigned role, the authentication server validates the client's credentials and returns a successful authentication response, but the server also returns additional information, known as *attributes*. ArubaOS can process these attributes, and use the values contained in the attributes to assign a role. This concept of using authentication attributes is being explained now because it is referenced at multiple points in the role derivation flowchart, and used by multiple authentication methods.

Vendor-Specific Attribute–Assigned Role

As part of the authentication response, the RADIUS server can send the controller a vendor-specific attribute (VSA). As the name implies, a VSA is defined by a vendor (Aruba in this case) and has a specific meaning. In a sense, the VSA defines a specific language or command that the authentication server can use to instruct the controller on how to assign the user role.

The VSAs of most significance to this chapter are the Aruba-User-Role and Aruba-User-VLAN. I will not belabor the point, but remember that, in general, what applies to a user role derivation also can also apply to the user VLAN derivation. When the authentication server sends the Aruba-User-Role VSA to the controller, it is essentially saying, "I am setting the role, and here is the value."

The role returned in the VSA must already exist on the controller. If the authentication server returns the attribute Aruba-User-Role, the value of the attribute defines the role that will be assigned to the user. The only way the Aruba-User-Role defined role would not be assigned is if the value of the attribute did not exactly match a defined role on the Aruba controller.

Server-Assigned Role

RADIUS servers are certified and governed by the Internet Engineering Task Force (IETF). IETF defines standards that ensure compliant RADIUS servers are compatible with network access devices, such as wireless controllers and wired switches. The IETF also defines RADIUS attributes.

IETF RADIUS attributes are optional additional information that the RADIUS administrator can configure to describe the user/client being authenticated. The server can send these attributes to the Aruba controller as part of the authentication response.

The controller can read the standard IETF attributes, but they do not have any specific meaning to the controller. This is where the server-defined rule comes into play.

The additional attributes can be processed by the controller to identify characteristics of the user and assign a user role to the client. The assignment of the role can be based upon the contents or value of the attribute that the server returns. The user or client account on the RADIUS authentication server must be specifically configured to return the attribute as part of the authentication process.

There are many defined attributes used by RADIUS servers, but a common attribute that is used to return data to the controller is the IETF attribute Filter-id. If the RADIUS server is configured to return an attribute, such as Filter-id, ArubaOS must be configured with a server rule so that it can process the Filter-id attribute and attempt to assign a user role accordingly. Server-defined rules take an if-then structure; if the condition matches, then the user is assigned a specific role. The server rule is configured as part of the server group in the controller.

From **Configuration ➢ SECURITY ➢ Authentication ➢ Servers ➢ Server Group**, you can choose a server group and create a new server rule.

The server rule consists of the following components:

- Attribute: the attribute that is being inspected; a commonly used IETF attribute is `Filter-id`
- Operation: the method used to compare the value of the attribute to the operand. The methods are:
  - Contains
  - Ends-with
  - Equals
  - Not-equals
  - Starts-with
  - Value-of
- Operand: the string that is being compared to the value of the attribute
- Action: specifies whether a role or VLAN is being assigned
- Value: the actual name of the role or VLAN that is being assigned

A server rule can also be created from the CLI, as shown in the following output. The first command selects or creates the server group and the second command creates the server rule.

```
(config) #aaa server-group IAP-server-group
(Server Group "delete-me") #set role condition Filter-Id equals "surveillance" set-value Camera-role
```

An interesting component of the server rule is the operation value-of. With the value-of operation, you do not need to define a rule that always sets the role to a specific value. If the attribute contains a specific value, the operation value-of can be used to set the role to the value of the attribute. Consider this as a substitution operand, substituting the attribute value for the name of the role. As in the case of VSAs, the attribute must exactly match a role that has already been configured on the controller. If not, the role will not be assigned by the rule.

For example, if the value of the `Filter-id` attribute is marketing, then the controller attempts to set the role to marketing, by looking in its user role table for a role named marketing.

Default Role

What happens when there is not a valid role assigned by one of these previous methods: no VSA returned, no attribute match, or possibly an error in the VSA or server rule? The user will still be assigned a role.

If the user does not receive a role from either of the server-assigned methods, the final method is to assign the default role. The default role is assigned to the authentication method in the AAA profile used by the VAP/SSID.

ArubaOS has numerous default roles depending upon the different authentication methods, such as MAC authentication, 802.1X authentication, and two default roles defined in captive portal authentication. The default roles for the MAC authentication and 802.1X/EAP authentication methods are specified in the AAA profile. For captive portal authentication, the default roles are part of the captive portal profile: one is for user authentication and one for guest authentication.

MAC Authentication

MAC authentication is the process of reading the client MAC address and using that MAC address for authentication. MAC authentication is processed after the user rules are processed but before the other authentication methods.

In the previous section, you learned that user rules can process MAC address information. This could be used to assign a role based upon the MAC address of the client device. User rules are good at performing this task if you are checking part of a MAC address (such as the organizationally unique identifier), analyzing conditions other than equals (such as contains, starts-with, ends-with, or not-equals), or when you are validating the MAC address against a small list of addresses. With user rules, each MAC address would require a separate role condition, which could make for a long and difficult-to-manage list of role conditions. For true MAC authentication, it is better to do so in the AAA profile used by the VAP/SSID. When MAC authentication is performed, the MAC address is authenticated against an authentication server or database. MAC authentication was explained in detail in Chapter 6, "Authentication and Encryption."

The following paragraphs will explain the process and logic used for processing MAC authentication. This will be explained in a step-by-step manner, based on the role derivation flowchart.

Task 15 of Figure 7.1 checks whether MAC authentication is enabled. If it is, then the controller attempts to verify the MAC address with the authentication source listed in the server group that is assigned to MAC authentication. The server group is specified in the AAA profile for the VAP/SSID.

Task 16 of Figure 7.1 checks whether MAC authentication was successful. If the MAC address of the client device does not exist or does not properly match what is in the authentication database, then the user role is not updated. If the result of Task 16 is No, then Task 17 is evaluated to see if layer 2 authentication fail-through is enabled. This is a setting in the AAA profile. When layer 2 fail-through is enabled, if one layer 2 authentication method is unsuccessful, the system will try using other layer 2 authentication methods. The role derivation process will continue evaluation at the next layer 2 authentication method, which is 802.1X/EAP at Task 24. If layer 2 authentication fail-through is not enabled, Task 18 is performed and the client is deauthenticated from the wireless network and removed from the user database. At this point, the user goes back to the starting point at Task 1 where he or she can attempt to reconnect.

If the MAC address does match, then MAC authentication is successful in Task 16 and the server derivation process needs to be evaluated.

Tasks 19 and 20 of Figure 7.1 show the logic for VSA-derived roles. If the authentication server returns a VSA, and the value of the VSA matches a role that exists on the controller, then the client is assigned a new role.

Tasks 21 and 22 of Figure 7.1 show the logic for a server-derived role. If the user authentication was successful and the user did not receive a VSA-derived role, then the user may be assigned a server-derived role. In this scenario, if the server returned an attribute (VSA or IETF) along with the authentication response, the server rule processes the attribute sequentially with each server rule condition. If there is a match and the resulting user role exists on the controller, then the client is assigned a new role: the server-derived role.

Task 23 of Figure 7.1 shows the logic for assigning the MAC authentication default role to a client. If the client device does not receive a VSA or server-derived role, it will be assigned the default role by the AAA profile associated to the VAP/SSID. This default role is specifically defined for the authentication method being used, which in this instance is MAC authentication.

802.1X/EAP Authentication

After MAC authentication, the controller will identify if 802.1X/EAP has been implemented. This is analyzed in Task 24 of Figure 7.1. If 802.1X/EAP has not been implemented, then layer 2 processing is complete and the client proceeds to Task 25 of Figure 7.1, exiting the authentication process and moving on to the datapath. At this stage, the client begins communicating on the network and obtains an IP address (if their role provides them with the necessary permissions to do so).

If Task 24 identifies that 802.1X/EAP is implemented, the client will provide identity information, such as a username and password, or possibly an authentication certificate. Task 26 of Figure 7.1 performs the authentication of the client credentials against one or more authentication servers.

Machine Authentication

When authenticating clients that have been joined to a Microsoft Active Directory domain, you can enable Machine Authentication. With Machine Authentication, not only does the client user account get added to the authentication database, but the machine is also added to the database, so both user and machine authentication are performed. Be aware that if both machine and user authentication are enabled, the machine authentication process only runs on boot, or when no user is logged onto the computer.

Task 27 of Figure 7.1 determines if machine authentication is enabled. If it is, 802.1X/EAP will authenticate both the user account and the machine account. If this is performed, there are four possible authentication outcomes, as shown in Table 17.1.

TABLE 7.1: Machine and User Authentication

MACHINE AUTHENTICATION	USER AUTHENTICATION	ROLE ASSIGNMENT
Failed (Task 28)	Failed (Task 31)	Task 35: Client is deauthenticated and removed from the user database. The client goes back to Task 1 where they can attempt to reconnect.
Failed (Task 28)	Passed (Task 31)	Task 32: Machine authentication; default user role assigned
Passed (Task 28)	Failed (Task 29)	Task 30: Machine authentication; default machine role assigned
Passed (Task 28)	Passed (Task 29)	Tasks 36 and 38: Server derivation process is evaluated. Client can receive a VSA-derived role (Task 37), a server-derived role (Task 39), or the 802.1X default role (Task 40).

Server Authentication

If machine authentication is not enabled, then role derivation with server authentication is performed. In Figure 7.1, Task 33 determines if user authentication was successful. If it was not, Task 34 and 35 verify that the authentication method attempted was 802.1X/EAP and then deauthenticates the client from the network and removes the MAC address from the user database. The client then goes back to the starting point at Task 1 where they can attempt to reconnect.

If the user authentication was successful, Task 36 will verify if VSA role derivation was successful, and if so, then Task 37 will assign the role. If not, then Task 38 will verify if server role derivation was successful, and if so, then Task 39 will assign the role. If neither a VSA- nor a server-derived role was assigned, then Task 40 will assign the default role. This server derivation logic was explained in more detail previously in this chapter in the section "Role Derivation with Server Authentication."

Layer 2 Authentication Synopsis

The layer 2 process was explained previously in this chapter, but because it is complex, it is important to review it once again. With relation to the Figure 7.1 flowchart, layer 2 authentication can be performed with or without 802.1X/EAP. If 802.1X/EAP authentication is not being used, then layer 2 authentication consists of Tasks 10 through 24. At Task 24, the client is passed on to Task 25, which is the datapath where the client will proceed to obtain an IP address and communicate on the network.

If 802.1X/EAP is enabled, then the client is authenticated at Task 26. If the authentication is *not* successful, then Task 35 will deauthenticate the client from the network and remove the client from the user table.

If 802.1X/EAP authentication *is* successful, then the role processing continues and the client is ultimately passed on to Task 25, where the client will proceed to obtain an IP address and communicate on the network.

Layer 3 Authentication

After layer 2 authentication completes, the client will be allowed to obtain an IP address. After the user obtains an IP address and the client begins communicating using TCP/IP, the client may be configured to perform layer 3 authentication. Remember, layer 3 authentication occurs after an IP address has been obtained.

After the client has reached Task 25 of Figure 7.1, the client is passed on to Task 41, where the system checks to see if External Services Interface (ESI) is enabled. ESI will be explained later in this chapter, so for now let us assume that ESI is not enabled and the client is passed back to Task 1 at the top of the flowchart.

At this point the system will identify the physical connection of the device again, Task 2, and then collect the device-specific attributes in Tasks 3 and 4, or in Tasks 5 and 6, depending on whether the client is connected using 802.3 or 802.11. Since the client is now connecting using a layer 3 connection, additional layer 3 attributes will also be collected.

Since the client has already been processed through the flowchart once, we know the connection is untrusted, and Task 7 will pass the client to Task 9. At this point, the client is already in the user database. Therefore, layer 2 authentication has already been performed, which is effectively what Task 9 is asking.

The first layer 3 role evaluation that is performed occurs at Task 44, which identifies if a user rule has been assigned to the AAA profile used by the VAP/SSID that the client device is connecting to. If a user rule is assigned, then each role condition is processed and evaluated sequentially. Task 45 identifies whether any layer 3 role condition matches. If not, the client retains its current user role, and processing continues with Task 47. If a layer 3 role condition does match, then Task 46 assigns a new role to the user.

At this point, the client is passed to Task 47 to see if it is attempting to perform a VPN logon. If so, the user will provide the VPN credentials. The VPN credentials will be passed to Task 26, where they will be authenticated against one or more authentication servers. If the VPN authentication *is not* successful, Task 33 will send the user back to the start. If the VPN authentication *is* successful, then the role processing continues with Task 36 and the client is ultimately passed on to Task 25, communicating on the network with a new post–layer 3 authentication role.

If VPN authentication was not being performed in Task 47, then the client is passed to Task 48 to see if it is attempting to perform a captive portal logon. If so, the user provides the captive portal credentials, and these credentials are processed with the same logic that was used with the VPN credentials.

If VPN authentication or captive portal authentication are successful, the user will end up with a VSA-derived role from Task 37, a server-derived role from Task 39, or a default role from Task 40.

External Services Interface

External Services Interface (ESI) is part of PEF. ESI allows certain types of user traffic to be sent to an external server. This server will then check the user traffic to make sure it matches certain criteria, such as that it is virus-free, worm-free, spyware-free, or that it matches certain corporate compliance settings. The external server can allow or deny the client traffic based upon rules that have been configured on the external server.

If the client traffic is at risk or is not in compliance, not only can the external server restrict the client traffic, it can be configured to return syslog messages to the Aruba controller. On the controller, an ESI syslog parser can be configured to listen for certain syslog messages, and act upon them. When an external server syslog message matches an ESI syslog parser rule, an action can be performed on the Aruba controller. One of the possible actions is to set the user role.

On Task 25 of Figure 7.1, the client device has a role assigned to it through one of the many role derivation methods explained previously in this chapter. At this point, the client is sending data on the network. Task 41 checks to see if the client data is being sent to an external server. If ESI is enabled and an ESI parser rule is enabled, Task 42 monitors syslog messages, comparing each message against the parser rules. If there is an ESI parser rule match, the rule can be configured to assign a new firewall role to the client, as shown in Task 43.

External Services Interface is an older technique for providing this type of service. If you need this capability, Aruba's ClearPass product will provide you with a much more flexible and powerful environment.

Role Derivation Review

The following list shows the three most common connection or authentication methods that are configured on a wireless network:

- 802.1X/EAP authentication
- WPA2 passphrase/preshared key
- Captive portal authentication

The next three sections of this chapter will describe the steps involved with each of these methods when processing role derivation. To simplify the process, three new figures will be introduced. These figures are based on Figure 7.1, which has been referenced throughout this chapter. However, for each of these connection or authentication methods, many of the unused tasks and logic have been removed from the figures. All of the task numbers remain the same. This will allow you to easily follow the logic using these new figures or using Figure 7.1.

802.1X/EAP Authentication

This section will follow the logic and tasks of an 802.1X/EAP client authenticating onto the network. This could be a wired or wireless client. The logic can be followed in either Figure 7.1 or Figure 7.8.

When the client connects, the controller identifies the physical connection and collects the appropriate DSAs, as seen in Tasks 1 through 6.

Since this is an 802.1X/EAP connection it is both untrusted and not already in the user database, so Tasks 7 and 9 responses are both No.

The controller immediately assigns the logon role to the client and adds the MAC address to the user database in Task 10.

If an initial role is assigned in the AAA profile, the value of the initial role will replace the logon role in Task 11.

If a user rule is assigned to the AAA profile (not typically used), it will be processed in Tasks 12 through 14. Each role condition will be checked. The first role condition that matches will assign a new role to the client. If no role conditions match, the client retains its existing role.

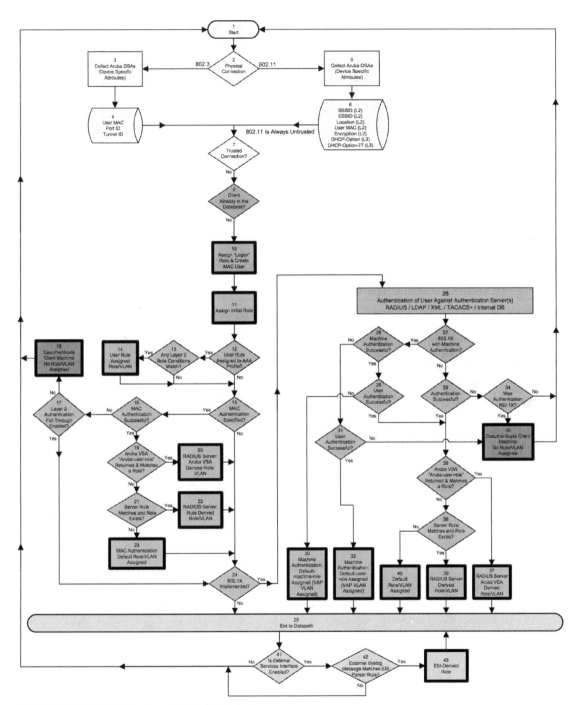

FIGURE 7.8 802.1X/EAP role or VLAN derivation

If MAC authentication is specified (not typically used), then the MAC address is checked against the specified authentication server, and processed in Tasks 15 through 23. If the MAC address is successfully authenticated by the server, then the client will be assigned a VSA-derived role (Tasks 19 and 20), a server-derived role (Tasks 21 and 22), or the MAC authentication default role (Task 23). If MAC authentication has completed successfully, the user will not have any network access unless 802.1X/EAP authentication is also successful.

If MAC authentication is unsuccessful, Task 17 checks if layer 2 authentication fail-through is enabled. If not, the client is disconnected from the network; if so, the client proceeds to Task 24 and continues with 802.1X/EAP authentication.

Since this is an 802.1X/EAP connection, Task 24 is true, and the user will provide authentication credentials. The credentials will be authenticated against one or more authentication servers in Task 26.

If machine authentication is enabled, Tasks 27 through 32 will process the machine and user credentials and assign a role.

If only user authentication is unsuccessful; or machine and user authentication are unsuccessful, the client is deauthenticated from the network and removed from the user database, as shown in Task 35.

If user authentication is successful (Task 33), then the client will be assigned a VSA-derived role (Tasks 36 and 37), a server-derived role (Tasks 38 and 39), or an 802.1X default role defined in the AAA profile (Task 40).

At this stage the user has exited to the datapath (Task 25). If ESI is enabled, the external server can send a syslog message that would trigger an ESI-derived role, as illustrated in Tasks 41 through 43.

WPA2 Passphrase Role/VLAN Derivation

When multiple users connect to a wireless network using a WPA2 passphrase or pre-shared key (PSK), all of the users will generally attach with the same credentials and the same authenticated identity. User rules and MAC authentication can provide the ability to distinguish one client from another. If user rules and MAC authentication are not defined, there is no way to identify each user, and they will all receive the same role. This is sometimes referred to as an *SSID base role*. Because of the limited ability to provide individual identity and controls, WPA2 passphrase should be avoided if possible.

This section will follow the logic and tasks of a client that is connecting to the network using a WPA2 passphrase. This connection would only be a wireless connection, since wired connections do not implement layer 2 encryption. The logic can be followed in either Figure 7.1 or in Figure 7.9.

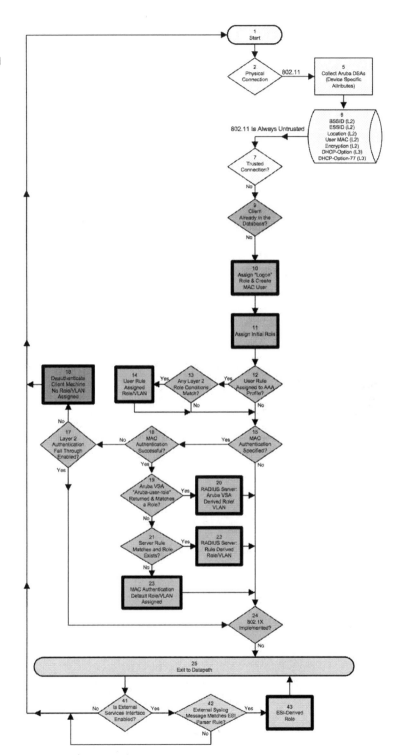

FIGURE 7.9
WPA2 passphrase role/VLAN derivation

When the client connects, the controller identifies that the client is an 802.11 client and collects the appropriate DSAs, as seen in Tasks 1, 2, 5, and 6.

Since this is a wireless connection, it can only be untrusted, and we will assume that it is not already in the user database, so responses to Tasks 7 and 9 are both no.

If the WPA2 passphrase on the client does not match the VAP, and since the encryption keys do not match, communication is never established between the client and the AP. Thus, the user cannot be added to the user database, therefore no initial role is assigned, and no more role derivation is processed.

If the WPA2 passphrase does match, the controller immediately assigns the logon role to the client and adds the MAC address to the user database in Task 10.

If an initial role (other than logon) is assigned in the AAA profile, the value of the initial role will replace the logon role in Task 11. At this point, it is likely that this will be the final role assigned to the client; unless a user rule, MAC authentication, or ESI is implemented (all three are not typically used).

If a user rule is assigned to the AAA profile, it will be processed in Tasks 12 through 14. Each role condition will be checked. The first role condition that matches will assign a new role to the client. If no role conditions match, the client retains its existing role.

If MAC authentication is specified, then the MAC address is checked against the specified authentication server and processed in Tasks 15 through 23. If the MAC address is successfully authenticated by the server, then the client will be assigned a VSA-derived role (Tasks 19 and 20), a server-derived role (Tasks 21 and 22), or the MAC authentication default role (Task 23).

If MAC authentication is unsuccessful, Task 17 checks if layer 2 authentication failthrough is enabled. If not, the client is disconnected from the network; if so, the client proceeds to Task 24.

Since this is not an 802.1X/EAP connection, Task 24 response is no, and the user can begin communicating on the network.

If ESI is enabled, the external server can send a syslog message that would trigger an ESI-derived role, as illustrated in Tasks 41 through 43.

Captive Portal Authentication

This section will follow the logic and tasks of a client that is connecting to the network using an open network connection and then authenticating using captive portal. A complete exploration of captive portal is found in Chapter 9, "Captive Portal," but it is relevant here to explain how a captive portal user obtains a role. This connection can be a wired or wireless connection. The logic can be followed in either Figure 7.1 or in Figure 7.10.

When the client connects, the controller identifies the physical connection and collects the appropriate DSAs, as seen in Tasks 1 through 6.

ROLE DERIVATION REVIEW

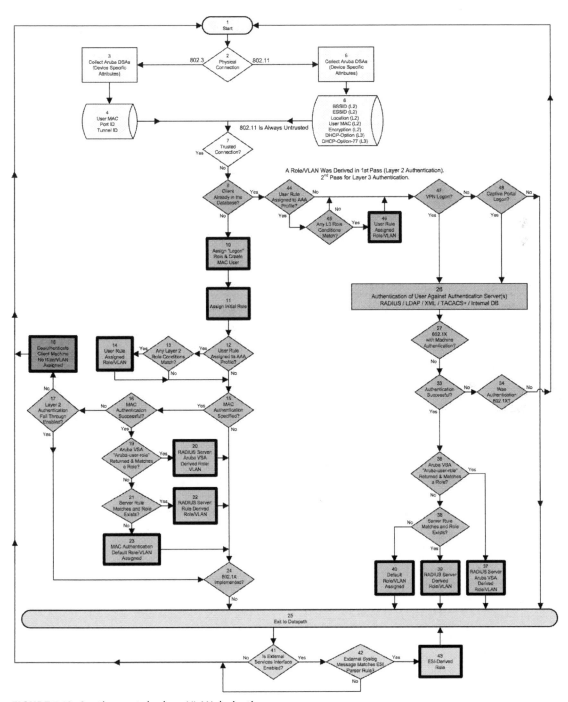

FIGURE 7.10 Captive portal role or VLAN derivation

Since this is going to be a captive portal logon, the client must first go through layer 2 authentication and then layer 3 authentication. Initially, the connection is untrusted and we will assume that it is not already in the user database, so Tasks 7 and 9 responses are both No.

The controller immediately assigns the logon role to the client and adds the MAC address to the user database in Task 10.

If an initial role is assigned in the AAA profile, the value of the initial role will replace the logon role in Task 11. When using a captive portal, it is common to have an initial role other than logon. The role is often named guest-logon, or something similar.

If a user rule is assigned to the AAA profile (not typically used), it will be processed in Tasks 12 through 14. Each role condition will be checked. The first role condition that matches will assign a new role to the client. If no role conditions match, the client retains its existing role.

If MAC authentication is specified (not typically used), then the MAC address is checked against the specified authentication server, and processed in Tasks 15 through 23. If the MAC address is successfully authenticated by the server, then the client will be assigned a VSA-derived role (Tasks 19 and 20), a server-derived role (Tasks 21 and 22), or the MAC authentication default role (Task 23).

If MAC authentication is unsuccessful, Task 17 checks if layer 2 authentication fail-through is enabled. If not, the client is disconnected from the network; if so, the client proceeds to Task 24.

Since this is not an 802.1X/EAP connection, Task 24 response is No, and the layer 2 role derivation process is complete.

At this point the client exits to the datapath in Task 25. As layer 3 captive portal authentication is processed, the client analysis begins again at the top with Task 1.

Tasks 1 through 6 check the physical connection and collect the DSAs. We know this is an untrusted connection, so Task 7 response is No.

At this point, Task 9 is checking to see if this is a layer 2 or a layer 3 authentication. Since the user already exists in the database, it is a layer 3 authentication and the processing continues with Task 44. If a user rule is assigned to the AAA profile (not typically used), it will be processed in Tasks 44 through 46. If either of the layer 3 role conditions match, the client gets the user rule assigned role.

At this point, the two layer 3 authentication methods are evaluated. VPN is rarely used anymore, so we will proceed directly to captive portal and Task 48.

Since this is a captive portal logon, the user credentials are entered and are authenticated against one or more authentication servers in Task 26. Because this is not an 802.1X/EAP authentication, machine authentication is irrelevant in Task 27.

Task 33 checks if the authentication was successful. If it was not, then the layer 3 authentication is unsuccessful for now, and there is no more role derivation.

If user authentication is successful (Task 33), then the client will be assigned a VSA-derived role (Tasks 36 and 37), a server-derived role (Tasks 38 and 39), or an 802.1X default role defined in the AAA profile (Task 40).

CHAPTER 8
Policy Enforcement Firewall

IN THIS CHAPTER, YOU WILL LEARN ABOUT THE FOLLOWING:

- Access Control Lists
- Firewall Policy Structure
    - Source, Destination, and Aliases
    - Firewall Service
    - Actions
    - Extended Actions
    - Implicit Deny All
- AppRF
    - AppRF Deep Packet Inspection
    - Web Content Classification
- User Roles
    - Global Session ACL
    - Role Default Session ACL

ONE OF THE KEY CAPABILITIES OF ArubaOS is the Policy Enforcement Firewall (PEF). The firewall examines all packets sent to the controller through any untrusted connection. The traffic being sent from an AP to the controller through a GRE tunnel is always untrusted. This means that all wireless traffic originating on a virtual AP (VAP) and tunneled or decrypt-tunneled to the controller is processed by the firewall.

When you plug a device into one of the Ethernet ports on an Aruba controller, the Ethernet port is configured as a trusted interface by default. This means that the traffic entering the controller from that interface is bridged or routed as needed; however, the traffic is not processed by the firewall and is not visible in the controller session table. The Ethernet port can be set to be an untrusted port, which means that its traffic will be treated similarly to the wireless traffic where all data will be processed by the firewall prior to being forwarded.

If a user connects to the controller through an untrusted connection, either wireless or wired, the user will be assigned an initial role, and may be required to proceed through an authentication process to gain access to the network. Client authentication was explained in Chapter 6, "Authentication and Encryption," and roles were explained in Chapter 7, "Role Derivation."

A *firewall policy* is a set of rules that examines where the packet is coming from, where it is going, and what type of packet it is. If the packet matches these three conditions, the rule specifies if or how to forward the packet. Since each rule is processed individually, rules are grouped into policies to logically provide a function.

Firewall policies can be created to allow or deny the forwarding of different types of user data. As an example, a firewall policy could be created to allow web browsing, which would allow HTTP and HTTPS traffic. A different firewall policy could be created to allow e-mail, which would allow protocol traffic such as POP and SMTP. After firewall policies are created, user roles can be created. A *user role* is a set of firewall policies, along with other non-firewall-related configurations. As an example, a user role could be created for a temporary employee, consisting of the web browsing policy along with the e-mail policy, as shown in the following CLI commands:

```
ip access-list session allow-web-browsing
  user any svc-http   permit
  user any svc-https  permit

ip access-list session allow-email
  user any svc-pop3  permit
  user any svc-smtp  permit

user-role temp-employee
  access-list session allow-web-browsing
  access-list session allow-email
```

A firewall policy is essentially a building block, consisting of firewall rules, used to construct a user role. It is the user role that is assigned to the wireless user or device, not the policies. A policy can, however, be used by itself if it is being assigned to a physical interface, such as an Ethernet port, or to a logical interface, such as a VLAN. So user roles, which consist of one or more policies, are assigned to users connecting to the network through untrusted connections. Policies, which consist of one or more firewall rules, make up user roles, or can be assigned directly to a physical or logical interface.

Access Control Lists

For as long as I can remember, ArubaOS has supported both access control lists (ACLs) and firewall policies. Although the following six ACL types are supported, their functionality is less than that of a firewall policy, so therefore they should generally not be used.

- Standard ACL
- Extended ACL
- MAC ACL
- Ethertype ACL
- Service ACL
- Routing ACL

The command for creating a firewall policy `ip access-list session` *name* is very similar to creating any of the six ACLs, such as an extended ACL: `ip access-list extended` *name*. This can be confusing. You simply need to remember that when you create a session ACL, you are creating a firewall policy.

Here are some of the differences that make firewall policies better than traditional ACLs:

- ACLs are normally applied to a physical port, whereas firewall policies can be applied to either a physical port or a user.
- ACLs are normally applied individually to the inbound or outbound traffic on a port, whereas firewall policies are bidirectional, keeping track of both the inbound and outbound traffic.
- Firewall policies are stateful, whereas ACLs are not. A stateful firewall tracks the connections initiated by the client devices, and maintains a state table. The client is able to make an outgoing request, and the response is allowed, since the client has established the connection.
- Firewall policies are dynamic. This allows address information to change as it is applied to different users. ACLs, on the other hand, typically have specific IP addresses.

The bottom line is that whatever you can do with an ACL you can do with a firewall policy—and the firewall policy can do it better. Therefore, I recommend you use firewall policies.

Firewall Policy Structure

Now that you have a basic understanding that a user role consists of one or more firewall policies, and that a firewall policy consists of one or more firewall rules, it is time to explain the pieces and the syntax that make up a firewall rule. A firewall rule starts off with the following four mandatory components, and one optional component:

`source destination service action [extended action]`

If the source, destination, and service values match the inbound packet, then the specified action is applied to the packet. In addition to performing the action, an extended action can optionally be applied. In this chapter, most of the examples of firewall policies will be done using CLI commands and syntax because it is easier to explain and describe. Firewall policies can also be created from the WebUI. **Configuration ➢ SECURITY ➢ Access Control ➢ Policies** will bring you to the menu where you can create or modify a firewall policy.

Source, Destination, and Aliases

The source and destination values specify where the packets are coming from and where they are going. They typically relate to TCP/IP addresses; either individual host addresses or IP subnets. If you are using a specific host address for either the source or destination, it can be entered as:

```
host  10.1.90.100
```

If you are specifying a network, it can be entered as:

```
network  10.1.90.0  255.255.255.0
```

In addition to specifying an IP address or network, there is an assortment of pre-defined aliases that can be used. Aliases are used to make writing and reading firewall rules more user-friendly. Instead of having to constantly remember IP addresses or networks, ArubaOS allows logical words to be used instead. Some of these aliases are key words predefined by the system with a specific meaning or reference. System-defined aliases cannot be modified or deleted. Additional aliases can be created and defined by the network administrator. In the following subsections, you will learn about some of the system-defined destination aliases and what they reference. Then you will learn how to create your own aliases. Later in this chapter, you will see example firewall rules using some of these destination aliases, along with explanations of how they are being used.

any

The any alias is a wildcard destination alias and applies to any device whether or not it has an IP address.

user

The user alias is a destination alias that represents the IP address of the user device sending the packet. This alias allows you to refer to the user without having to know the IP address of the user. The user alias can only reference a device that is in the user table of the controller. When used, the IP address of the client device is placed in the firewall rule in place of the word *user*. As an example, the following is a sample firewall rule as it would be entered into a firewall policy:

```
user  host  8.8.8.8  udp  53  permit
```

It is important to realize that *user* has nothing to do with the user's identity or user name. In this environment, *user* is just an alias that represents the source IP address of the inbound packet. In the following CLI output you can see how this rule would be processed against a client packet if the IP address of the user device were 1.2.3.4.

```
1.2.3.4  host  8.8.8.8  udp  53  permit
```

The user alias can also be used as a destination in a firewall policy, and represents the IP address of **any** device that is in the user table. The user alias cannot be used as both the source and destination addresses in a single firewall rule.

controller and *mswitch*

Both the `controller` and `mswitch` destination aliases refer to the primary IPv4 address of the controller, as shown in the following CLI output. These aliases (`controller` and `mswitch`) are dynamically configured automatically by the controller. By using either of these aliases, a firewall rule can allow or deny access to the controller, regardless of the actual IP address.

```
#show netdestination

Name: mswitch

Position  Type  IP addr       Mask-Len/Range
--------  ----  -------       --------------
1         host  10.1.90.100   32

Name: controller

Position  Type  IP addr       Mask-Len/Range
--------  ----  -------       --------------
1         host  10.1.90.100   32
```

controller6

The `controller6` destination alias refers to the primary IPv6 address of the controller. The following CLI output references the address as ::1, which simply represents the actual IPv6 address of the controller.

```
#show netdestination ipv6

Name: controller6

Position  Type  IP addr  Mask-Len/Range
--------  ----  -------  --------------
1         host  ::1      128
```

ipv6-reserved-range

The IPv6 standard has assigned a range of addresses to be used as Global Unicast Address space. This address space is defined as 2000::/3, which translates to all IPv6 addresses from 2000:: through 3FFF::. Any address outside of the range is currently reserved. The `ipv6-reserved-range` destination alias references 2000::/3; however, this destination is inverted, meaning that it is referring to all addresses except these. The following CLI output displays this:

```
#show netdestination ipv6

Name: ipv6-reserved-range (invert)

Position  Type     IP addr  Mask-Len/Range
--------  ----     -------  --------------
1         network  2000::   3
```

localip

The `localip` destination alias is used with remote APs. The alias is mapped to the IP address that is assigned to the Ethernet 0 address of the RAP.

vrrp_ip

The `vrrp_ip` destination alias refers to the VRRP virtual IP (VIP) address. If the controller is configured for VRRP failover, then this refers to any VIP address on the controller (a controller can be configured with multiple VRRPs). If the controller is not configured for VRRP failover, then this simply refers to the primary IPv4 address of the controller. The following CLI output shows a controller with VRRP enabled, with an `mswitch` address of 10.1.50.101 and a `vrrp_ip` address of 10.1.50.100.

```
#show netdestination

Name: mswitch

Position  Type  IP addr      Mask-Len/Range
--------  ----  -------      --------------
1         host  10.1.50.101  32


Name: vrrp_ip

Position  Type  IP addr      Mask-Len/Range
--------  ----  -------      --------------
1         host  10.1.50.100  32
```

Creating a Destination Alias

In addition to the system-defined destination aliases, you can create your own destination aliases. As the network administrator, you may want to create network aliases referencing your internal networks, server groups, DNS servers, or external servers. First we will take a look at creating an alias for your corporate networks.

Let us make believe that your organization has three ranges of addresses that it uses for its internal network: 192.168.1.0/24, 172.16.1.0/24, and 10.100.0.0/16. If you wanted to create firewall rules to allow users full access to these networks, you would need to create three separate rules, one for each network, as illustrated in the following CLI commands. This means that every time you wanted to create a firewall rule referencing the internal network, you would have to create three separate rules.

```
user  network  192.168.1.0  255.255.255.0  any  permit
user  network  172.16.1.0   255.255.255.0  any  permit
user  network  10.100.0.0   255.255.0.0    any  permit
```

To simplify the creation of firewall rules, along with making it easier to review rules that you have already created, aliases are very useful. As you have already seen in this chapter, aliases are easy to understand, and remembering descriptive names is probably easier than addresses, especially down the road. The following CLI output shows the commands used to create an alias `internal-network`.

```
(config) #netdestination internal-network
(config-desk) #network 192.168.1.0 255.255.255.0
(config-desk) #network 172.16.1.0 255.255.255.0
(config-desk) #network 10.100.0.0 255.255.0.0
```

Not only is the alias `internal-network` logical and easy to understand, remembering a single name is easier than multiple networks. It is important to realize that even though a firewall rule may use a single alias, the controller will interpret the single rule as a separate rule for each destination. In this instance, the controller will interpret the rule as three different rules when processing it. The following CLI command shows a single firewall rule allowing users full access to the three internal networks using the `internal-network` alias:

```
user  alias  internal-network  any  permit
```

Even though you typed a single rule, the following illustrates that the controller processes this rule as three separate statements, in the order that you created them:

```
user  network  192.168.1.0  255.255.255.0  permit
user  network  172.16.1.0   255.255.255.0  permit
user  network  10.100.0.0   255.255.0.0    permit
```

Configuration ➢ ADVANCED SERVICES ➢ Stateful Firewall ➢ Destination will bring you to the menu where you can create or modify a destination alias. Figure 8.1 displays the creation of the `internal-network` alias.

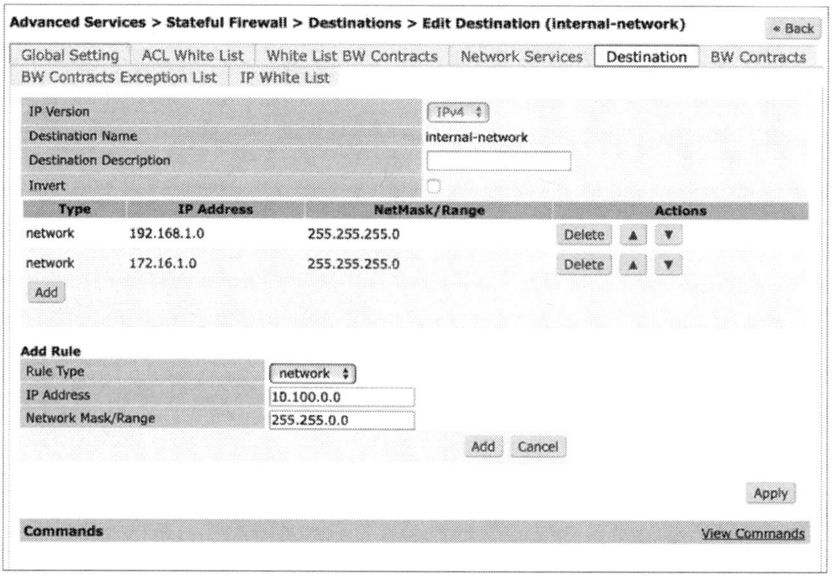

FIGURE 8.1
Destination alias

With the integration of external applications and servers as corporate tools used by many organizations, along with the mass adoption of global content delivery networks, it is becoming commonplace to define destination aliases that point to external URLs or domains instead of IP addresses. The following CLI output shows some examples of this. A few of these examples are cloud authentication providers that may use different IP addresses depending on location, network conditions, or changes in services. In these scenarios, it is important to use domain names in policies. In some instances, it may be necessary to use a wildcard character (*), which would allow any set of characters in place of the wildcard.

```
netdestination msonline-login
    name login.microsoftonline.com
    name *.aadcdn.microsoftonline-p.com

netdestination clearpass-prod
    name clearpass.arubaboston.com
    name clearpass-1.arubaboston.com
    name clearpass-2.arubaboston.com
    name wifi-login.arubaboston.com

netdestination social-twitter
    name api.twitter.com
    name *.twttr.com
    name *.twimg.com

netdestination google-login
    name accounts.google.com
    name *.gstatic.com
```

```
netdestination duo-api
    name api-0c3505b3.duosecurity.com
```

In order to use a URL or domain name as part of a netdestination, the controller will need a DNS server defined and DNS lookup enabled. The following CLI commands will specify the name server, enable DNS lookup (it is enabled by default), and display the status to confirm the settings:

```
(config) #ip name-server 10.254.1.21
Operation may not take effect until a reboot

(config) #ip domain lookup
Operation may not take effect until a reboot

(config) #show ip domain-name
IP domain lookup:    Enabled
IP Host.Domain name: 7005-90.

DNS servers
===========
10.254.1.21

(*) Dynamic DNS entry
```

Invert Option

When creating a destination alias, the invert option can be useful; however, it can also be very dangerous to use. The invert option tells the controller to reference the inverse of what is stated. As an example, the following destination refers to all networks except the defined network of 192.168.1.0.

```
(config) #netdestination not-the-192-network invert
(config-desk) #network 192.168.1.0 255.255.255.0
```

A problem can arise when trying to use invert multiple times in a destination alias. A previous example showed the creation of an alias `internal-network`. This alias referenced the three networks used within the organization. After that destination alias is defined, you may think that you could create a destination alias to define all other networks by using the same logic, except inverting each of the network references, as illustrated in the following CLI command:

```
(config) #netdestination all-other-networks invert
(config-desk) #network 192.168.1.0 255.255.255.0
(config-desk) #network 172.16.1.0 255.255.255.0
(config-desk) #network 10.100.0.0 255.255.0.0
```

Unfortunately, this is not treated as a single set of networks. Remember, the system processes an alias as three separate rules. So, assume you wanted to allow a guest user to communicate with any network, except for the three internal networks. Using the destination alias all-other-networks, you may create a firewall rule, such as the following:

```
user   alias   all-other-networks   any permit
```

The system will translate this single firewall rule to the following three rules:

```
user   network   192.168.1.0   255.255.255.0   invert   permit
user   network   172.16.1.0    255.255.255.0   invert   permit
user   network   10.100.0.0    255.255.0.0     invert   permit
```

If a guest user attempted to communicate with a server with the address 10.100.1.100, the system will compare the packet against the first rule. The first rule would be true, because the user was attempting to communicate with a network other than the 192.168.1.0 network, and the guest would be allowed to successfully communicate with 10.100.1.100, even though this is not what you intended.

Since invert can produce undesired results when used with multiple entries in a destination alias, I suggest that you refrain from using the invert option. If you do decide to use the invert option, only define a single entry in any destination when using it.

Firewall Service

One of the primary differences between a firewall policy and an ACL is that, in addition to filtering traffic based upon the source and destination addresses, a firewall policy can also filter packets based upon the type of packet. The packet type can reference any traffic, a specific IP protocol, a TCP or UDP port or range of ports, an alias (known as a *service*, *service alias*, or *netservice*), or if a feature known as AppRF is enabled, it can be an application, application category, or web category. The AppRF feature will be discussed in more detail later in this chapter.

Following is the list of service values that can be specified, followed by a brief explanation of each:

- Protocol number 0-255
- String
- Any
- App
- Appcategory
- ICMP
- TCP
- UDP

- Web-cc-category
- Web-cc-reputation

Protocol number 0-255 This is the numerical value of a specific protocol. Some common protocol numbers are 6 (Transmission Control Protocol), 17 (User Datagram Protocol), 47 (Generic Routing Encapsulation), and 50 (Encapsulation Security Payload IPsec).

String (listed as Service in the Service/Application column in the WebUI) This is the name of a predefined service alias. Service aliases are explained later in this chapter.

Any This refers to any type of traffic

App (listed as Application in the Service/Application column in the WebUI) This specifies an application name. The parameter app would be followed by an application name. ArubaOS defines over 2,300 applications. If you would like to see the complete list of applications, the following CLI command will display them alphabetically. The following output displays a selection of some of the 2,300 applications that are defined. To make the output easier to read, the last column, Applied, was removed.

```
#show dpi application all

Applications
------------
Name            App ID  App Category        Default Ports
----            ------  ------------        -------------
abc-news        1824    web                 tcp 80,443
adobe-connect   929     streaming           tcp 80,443,1935
bittorrent      15      peer-to-peer        tcp 1024-65535 udp 1024-65535
craigslist      1848    web                 tcp 80,443
dropbox         779     cloud-file-storage  tcp 80,443
google-groups   56      collaboration       tcp 80,443
howstuffworks   1004    social-networking   tcp 80
```

Appcategory (listed as Application Category in the Service/Application column in the WebUI) This specifies an application category. The parameter appcategory would be followed by an application category name. ArubaOS defines over 20 application categories. If you would like to see the list of application categories, the following CLI command will display them alphabetically.

```
#show dpi application category all

Application Categories
----------------------
```

```
Name                      App Category ID  Applied
----                      ---------------  -------
antivirus                 1                0
authentication            2                0
behavioral                3                0
cloud-file-storage        4                0
collaboration             5                0
encrypted                 6                0
enterprise-apps           7                0
gaming                    8                0
im-file-transfer          9                0
instant-messaging         10               0
mail-protocols            11               0
mobile                    23               0
mobile-app-store          12               0
network-service           13               0
peer-to-peer              14               0
social-networking         15               0
standard                  16               0
streaming                 17               0
thin-client               18               0
tunneling                 19               0
unified-communications    20               0
web                       21               0
webmail                   22               0

Total application groups = 23
```

ICMP (option not available in WebUI) This specifies the ICMP protocol.

TCP This specifies the TCP destination port. TCP must be followed by a TCP number in the range of 0–65,535.

UDP This specifies the UDP destination port. UDP must be followed by a UDP number in the range of 0–65,535.

Web-cc-category (listed as Web Category/Reputation in the Service/Application column in the WebUI) This allows you define a web content classification (WebCC) category for traffic matching the specified category. The following CLI command generates a list of all of the web content classification categories. Aruba uses a trusted third party service to classify content categories.

```
#show web-cc categories

Web Content Classification Category Table
-----------------------------------------
Name                          Web Category Id
----                          ---------------
uncategorized                 0
```

real-estate	1
computer/internet-security	2
financial-services	3
business-economy	4
computer/internet-info	5
auctions	6
shopping	7
cult-and-occult	8
travel	9
abused-drugs	10
adult/pornography	11
home/garden	12
military	13
social-networking	14
dead-sites	15
indv-stock-advice-tools	16
training-tools	17
dating	18
sex-education	19
religion	20
entertainment/arts	21
personal-sites/blogs	22
legal	23
local-info	24
streaming-media	25
job-search	26
gambling	27
translation	28
reference/research	29
shareware/freeware	30
peer-to-peer	31
marijuana	32
hacking	33
games	34
philosophy/political-advocacy	35
weapons	36
pay-to-surf	37
hunting/fishing	38
society	39
educational-institutions	40
online-greeting-cards	41
sports	42
swimsuits/intimate-apparels	43
questionable	44
kids	45
hate/racism	46
personal-storage	47
violence	48
keyloggers/monitoring	49
search-engines	50

```
internet-portals                 51
web-advertisements               52
cheating                         53
gross                            54
web-based-email                  55
malware-sites                    56
phishing                         57
proxy-avoidance/anonymizers      58
spyware/adware                   59
music                            60
government                       61
nudity                           62
news/media                       63
illegal                          64
content-delivery-networks        65
internet-communications          66
bot-nets                         67
abortion                         68
health/medicine                  69
spam-urls                        71
dynamically-generated-content    74
parked-domains                   75
alcohol/tobacco                  76
private-ip-addresses             77
image/video-search               78
fashion/beauty                   79
recreation/hobbies               80
motor-vehicles                   81
web-hosting                      82
```

Web-cc-reputation (listed as Web Category/Reputation in the Service/Application column in the WebUI) This allows you define a web content classification (WebCC) reputation for traffic matching the reputation of a website. Aruba uses a trusted third party service that monitors websites and generates Web Reputation Index (WRI) values. These values, between 1 and 100, represent how risky or trustworthy a website is. The following CLI command displays the list of the five risk levels along with the value ranges:

```
#show web-cc reputation

Web Content Classification Reputation Table
-------------------------------------------
RiskLevel          Score
---------          -----
high-risk           1 -  20
suspicious         21 -  40
moderate-risk      41 -  60
low-risk           61 -  80
trustworthy        81 - 100
```

Web-cc-category and web-cc-reputation are part of AppRF, which will be explained in more detail later in this chapter in the AppRF section.

Services

In the same way that you create destination aliases to make it easier to work with firewall rules, you can also create service aliases. A service alias defines a TCP, UDP, or IP protocol, along with one or more ports, and assigns a logical name (you could assign illogical names, but what would be the point of that?). Just as a netdestination is an alias for a host or network, a netservice is simply an alias for a protocol or port.

ArubaOS defines a large list of service aliases, each one representing a commonly used port or protocol. These predefined services include commonly used communications protocols such as DHCP, HTTP, HTTPS, and DNS. The following CLI output shows the command used to display the complete list of services that are configured on your controller. This list includes predefined services along with any services that you may have created. It also specifies which services are system services that are not editable. Realize that netservice definitions may be added by Aruba or by you, so this list may not match the list on your controller.

```
#show netservice

Services
--------
Name                    Protocol   Ports       ALG    Type
----                    --------   -----       ---    ----
svc-ipp-tcp             tcp        631
svc-dhcp                udp        67-68       dhcp
sys-svc-natt            udp        4500                System (not editable)
svc-citrix              tcp        2598
sys-svc-smb-tcp         tcp        445                 System (not editable)
svc-pcoip-udp           udp        50002
svc-netbios-ssn         tcp        139
svc-tftp                udp        69          tftp
svc-papi                udp        8211        papi
svc-ica                 tcp        1494
svc-natt                udp        4500
sys-svc-openflow-tcp    tcp        6633                System (not editable)
svc-lpd                 tcp        515
svc-microsoft-ds        tcp        445
svc-syslog              udp        514
svc-msrpc-tcp           tcp        135-139
svc-msrpc-udp           udp        135-139
svc-smtp                tcp        25
svc-http-proxy2         tcp        8080
svc-cfgm-tcp            tcp        8211
sys-svc-telnet          tcp        23                  System (not editable)
vnc                     tcp        5900-5905
```

sys-svc-cfgm-tcp	tcp	8211		System (not editable)
sys-svc-papi	udp	8211		System (not editable)
svc-web	tcp	80 443		
svc-h323-udp	udp	1718-1719		
svc-sccp	tcp	2000	sccp	
svc-bootp	udp	67-69		
svc-telnet	tcp	23		
svc-http	tcp	80		
sys-svc-dhcp	udp	67-68		System (not editable)
svc-vmware-rdp	tcp	3389		
svc-ipp-udp	udp	631		
sys-svc-ntp	udp	123		System (not editable)
sys-svc-adp	udp	8200		System (not editable)
svc-noe-oxo	udp	5000	noe	
svc-vocera	udp	5002	vocera	
svc-esp	esp	0		
svc-http-proxy1	tcp	3128		
svc-sec-papi	udp	8209	sec-papi	
svc-l2tp	udp	1701		
svc-rtsp	tcp	554	rtsp	
svc-gre	gre	0		
sys-svc-tftp	udp	69		System (not editable)
svc-sip-tcp	tcp	5060		
svc-pptp	tcp	1723		
svc-snmp	udp	161		
svc-svp	119	0	svp	
sys-svc-http	tcp	80		System (not editable)
any	0	0		
svc-icmp	icmp	0		
svc-smb-tcp	tcp	445		
sys-svc-snmp-trap	udp	162		System (not editable)
sys-svc-syslog	udp	514		System (not editable)
any-v6	255	0		
svc-pcoip2-tcp	tcp	4172		
svc-v6-icmp	icmpv6	0		
svc-ssh	tcp	22		
sys-svc-kerberos-tcp	tcp	88		System (not editable)
sys-svc-ftp	tcp	21		System (not editable)
sys-svc-icmp	icmp	0		System (not editable)
svc-h323-tcp	tcp	1720		
svc-ntp	udp	123		
svc-pop3	tcp	110		
sys-svc-kerberos-udp	udp	88		System (not editable)
svc-netbios-ns	udp	137		
svc-adp	udp	8200		
sys-svc-snmp	udp	161		System (not editable)
svc-v6-dhcp	udp	546-547		
svc-dns	udp	53	dns	
svc-netbios-dgm	udp	138		
svc-http-proxy3	tcp	8888		

```
svc-sip-udp              udp    5060
svc-kerberos             udp    88
sys-svc-msrpc-udp        udp    135-139       System (not editable)
sys-svc-dns              udp    53            System (not editable)
svc-sips                 tcp    5061    sips
sys-svc-bootpc           udp    68            System (not editable)
svc-pcoip2-udp           udp    4172
svc-pcoip-tcp            tcp    50002
svc-noe                  udp    32512   noe
svc-nterm                tcp    1026-1028
svc-ike                  udp    500
svc-snmp-trap            udp    162
sys-svc-gre              gre    0             System (not editable)
sys-svc-sec-papi         udp    8209          System (not editable)
svc-smb-udp              udp    445
svc-ftp                  tcp    21      ftp
svc-https                tcp    443
```

In addition to the list of predefined aliases, you may want to create your own service alias to simplify firewall rules that handle certain types of traffic.

Creating a Service Alias

Creating a service is a straightforward process. The following is the general format for the command. The alg parameter is optional.

```
netservice  name  ports/protocols  [alg]
```

A service can also be created to represent multiple ports or a range of ports. The following shows the inclusion of the TCP/UDP protocols, and list or range of ports or protocols.

```
netservice  name  tcp/udp list/range ports/protocols  [alg]
```

The previous section shows an extensive list of services. The following are a few examples with explanations to hopefully help you understand the command:

```
netservice svc-gre 47
```

The previous command defines the service alias of svc-gre as protocol 47. If there is just a single numerical value after the service name, then the alias is for a protocol.

```
netservice svc-pptp tcp 1723
```

This command defines the service alias of svc-pptp for a single TCP port, 1723.

```
netservice svc-dhcp udp list "67 68" alg dhcp
```

If you need to define a list or range of ports, you need to first specify the protocol, TCP or UDP. Then you need to specify that you are defining a list or range, and the list of ports needs to be enclosed within double quotes. If you are defining a range, the first number is the starting port of the range and the second number is the ending port of the range. These values should not be separated by a dash (-).

The previous command defines a netservice for UDP ports 67 and 68. If you want to limit the service alias to a specific application, the `alg` parameter (Application Level Gateway) can be entered, followed by the application.

Configuration ➤ ADVANCED SERVICES ➤ Stateful Firewall ➤ Network Services will bring you to the menu where you can create or modify a network service. Figure 8.2 displays the creation of a network service for the gopher protocol.

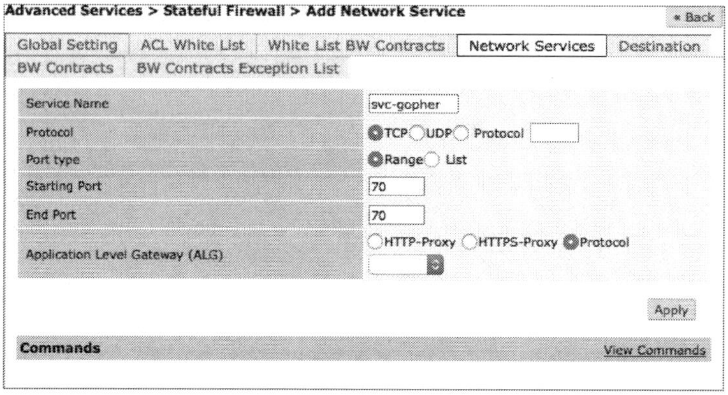

FIGURE 8.2
Network service

An optional parameter when defining a service is *application layer gateway (ALG)*. As the name implies, ALG is a gateway to an application. Even though an application such as SIP or DNS uses standard ports to communicate on the application server side, the client side may use nonstandard or even dynamic ports to communicate. If this is the case, a simple port-based rule will not block the communication. The `alg` parameter allows the firewall to evaluate the data based upon characteristics other than ports, allowing the firewall to provide the proper controls even if the communication is not using the standard ports for the specified data type.

Actions

First, the source, destination, and service values of a packet are evaluated against a firewall rule. If all three items match, then an action is performed with the inbound packet. Here is the list of firewall actions that can be performed, followed by an explanation of what each action does:

- `deny`
- `dst-nat`
- `dual-nat`
- `permit`

- redirect
- route
- src-nat

deny

This action denies or blocks any packets that match the firewall rule. This is the default action when a new rule is created in the WebUI.

dst-nat

Matching packets will be forwarded and redirected to a new destination. Then, `dst-nat` readdresses the packet with the new destination IP address. This is also referred to as *forwarding* or *port forwarding*.

The packet can also be redirected to a different port. As an example, the following firewall rule will take any HTTP traffic and redirect it to the IP address 1.2.3.4 using TCP port 8080 instead of the packet's original TCP port 80:

```
user  any  svc-http  dst-nat  ip  1.2.3.4  8080
```

Note that `dst-nat` only works with virtual AP profiles (VAPs) configured for tunnel or decrypt tunnel forwarding. Both tunnel and decrypt tunnel forwarding were explained in Chapter 2, "Understanding the Aruba OS Environment."

src-nat

The packet will be forwarded, and it will be sourced with the controller IP address, specifically the IP address of the interface that resides on the same subnet as the default gateway. This often is the controller IP address, but it does not have to be.

The `src-nat` address can also be a pool of addresses. If the pool has more than one IP address, the sourced address of the outbound traffic will be spread among the pool of addresses. The following CLI output shows the creation of a pool of addresses from 10.1.70.240 through 10.1.70.250. It also shows the access list allow-with-nat with a firewall rule allowing any traffic and assigning a `src-nat` address from the pool.

```
(config) #ip nat pool "nat-pool-test" 10.1.70.240 10.1.70.250
(config) #ip access-list session "allow-with-nat"
(config-sess-allow-with-nat)#any any any src-nat pool "nat-pool-test"
```

The following CLI command will display the NAT address pools that are defined on the controller. The pool dynamic-srcnat is defined by the system.

```
#show ip nat pool

NAT Pools
---------
```

```
Name             Start IP      End IP        DNAT IP   Flags
----             --------      ------        -------   -----
nat-pool-test    10.1.70.240   10.1.70.250   0.0.0.0
dynamic-srcnat   0.0.0.0       0.0.0.0       0.0.0.0
```

Note that src-nat only works with VAP profiles configured for tunnel or decrypt tunnel forwarding. Be aware that the controller will issue proxy ARP responses for any IP address in the NAT pool.

dual-nat

This will forward the packet, and perform both source NAT and destination NAT on the packets. A NAT pool needs to be defined, specifying the start and end IP addresses of the pool, along with the destination NAT address. Note that dual-nat only works with VAP profiles configured for tunnel or decrypt tunnel forwarding.

permit

This forwards the packet without any restrictions.

redirect

This can be used to redirect packets across a GRE tunnel or to an external services interface (ESI), such as an external antivirus service. When redirecting to a GRE tunnel, this function can be used to perform such tasks as forwarding traffic between the internal network and the DMZ network.

The following firewall rule is an example of how redirect can be used to forward HTTP traffic to a GRE tunnel identified as 100:

```
user any svc-http redirect tunnel 100
```

The Aruba Airheads online community has a very good article explaining how to configure this, titled, "How Do I Redirect Guest Access across a GRE Tunnel to a DMZ Network?" Redirect can also be used to automatically forward traffic to an ESI server. The ESI server is a server or service that provides inspection of the traffic, such as antivirus or content filtering. The following command forwards all traffic from a network usernet to an ESI group defined as avchk.

```
alias usernet any any redirect esi-group avchk direction forward
```

route

The route action is used with wireless networks that are operating in bridge or split-tunnel forwarding mode. This can be used with the dst-nat or src-nat parameters. When used with dst-nat, the destination IP address is changed to the IP address that is configured in a NAT pool. The NAT pool needs to be configured on the controller. With remote APs, you use route src-nat. It changes the source IP to the IP of the external interface of the RAP, and uses an implied NAT pool.

Extended Actions

In addition to performing an action, after the firewall rule has matched the source, destination, and service, it can also perform an extended action. An *extended action* is an optional task that can be performed, or that will modify the way the rule is executed. Extended actions are optional, and multiple extended actions can be selected for a rule.

blacklist

ArubaOS has the ability to block all access from a designated client MAC address. This total blocking of access is known as *blacklisting*. When a client is blacklisted, the firewall will add the MAC address of the client device to the client blacklist. A blacklisted client is not allowed to associate to any SSID on any AP connected to that controller. The list of blacklisted clients is not synchronized to other controllers in the cluster. If the client is already connected to the network, an 802.11 deauthentication frame will be sent to disconnect the client from the network. By default, the blacklist time is 3,600 seconds, which is 60 minutes, and it is a setting that can be changed in the VAP profile.

There are multiple ways that a client device can be blacklisted. One of the methods is the result of a client packet matching a firewall rule that has the blacklist option enabled. For example, a firewall rule may blacklist a user on the guest network if they try to SSH to the default gateway.

The following CLI output shows the command to display a list of clients that have been blacklisted. The reason, session-blacklist, indicates that the client was blacklisted due to a firewall blacklist extended action.

```
#show ap blacklist-clients

Blacklisted Clients
-------------------
STA                reason              block-time(sec)   remaining time(sec)
---                ------              ---------------   -------------------
00:24:d7:6a:71:24  session-blacklist   320               3280
```

classify media

If the classify media extended action is specified, the controller will sample some of the UDP traffic to detect if the traffic is media. If it is, the controller will tag the packets so that they can be prioritized accordingly; either as video (priority 5) or voice (priority 6).

disable-scanning

Unfortunately, this book has not yet explained adaptive radio management (ARM), which will be covered in Chapter 12, "Adaptive Radio Management." Nevertheless, the `disable-scanning` extended action needs to be explained.

When ARM is enabled, APs periodically switch to other channels to perform network scans. These scans are used to collect RF information about the network environment. For most types of user traffic, the period of time that the AP is on another channel is short enough to be insignificant, and it does not affect most client communications. There may be a risk that these short periods of time could cause communications problems for specific types of data, especially voice over IP. If so, a firewall rule can be configured to identify the data type, and disable ARM scanning while that type of data traffic is present. ARM scanning is only disabled on the AP that is handling the specific traffic, and only for as long as that traffic type is present.

dot1p-priority

This extended action allows you to specify an 802.1p priority that will be assigned to the packet when the firewall forwards the packet. The 802.1p amendment defined a mechanism used for quality of service (QoS). The priority can be a value from 0 to 7, with 7 being the highest priority.

log

When processing firewall rules, you may want to document or track some of the client activity that the firewall is allowing or denying on the network. A log message will be generated for each packet that matches a firewall rule with the `log` extended action enabled. A security log entry will be generated, and can be viewed using the following command, shown in the following CLI output:

```
# show log security 10

Apr 24 22:17:38 :124006:  <WARN> |authmgr|  {6} TCP srcip=10.1.91.101
srcport=51668 dstip=204.79.197.203 dstport=80, action=deny, role=authenticated,
policy=allowall
```

mirror

A copy of each session packet that matches the firewall rule will be forwarded to a predefined destination. This destination can be a port, a file on the controller, or an IP address. The destination is defined using the `packet-capture` command or as part of a set of default values defined in the `packet-capture-defaults` command.

Prior to ArubaOS 6.3, the destination was defined as part of the firewall settings, using the command `firewall session-mirror-destination`. I am mentioning this because there are many documents on the Internet that reference this old method. Session mirroring will be explained in much more detail in Chapter 13, "Network Monitoring."

position

Since firewall rules are processed in sequence from the top down, and since only the first rule that matches will be processed, the order of the rules is very important. When defining a new rule, you can choose where the new rule will be placed in the access list. Simply use the `position` extended action and specify the numerical position of the firewall rule. You will not be allowed to place a firewall rule in position one or two, as position one is reserved for the Global Session ACL and position two is reserved for the Role Default Session ACL. These ACLs will be explained later in this chapter.

queue

ArubaOS has two queues for processing data being sent to a wired network. This parameter can be set to either low or high. Obviously, traffic placed in the high queue will be processed faster than traffic placed in the low queue.

send-deny-response

If the firewall action is configured to deny the packet, by default the packet is simply denied without sending any notification response to the client sending the packet. The send-deny-response extended action will send an ICMP notification to the source of the packet if the packet is denied. In the WebUI, a single action reject can be selected to configure the two actions of denying the packet and sending a deny response.

This is not recommended for everyday use because it will increase network traffic; however, it can be helpful for troubleshooting firewall rules.

time-range

This specifies a range of time during which the firewall rule is valid. The `time-range` extended action command needs to be followed by the name of a predefined time range. The following CLI output shows an example of the command to create a time range, along with the command to show the time ranges defined on your controller:

```
(config) #time-range lunch periodic daily 12:00 to 13:00

(config) #show time-range

Time-Range working-hours, Periodic
---------------------------------
```

```
StartDay   Start-time   EndDay   End-time   Applied
--------   ----------   ------   --------   -------
weekday    08:00                 18:00      No

Time-Range night-hours, Periodic
--------------------------------
StartDay   Start-time   EndDay   End-time   Applied
--------   ----------   ------   --------   -------
weekday    18:01                 23:59      No
weekday    00:00                 07:59      Yes

Time-Range weekend, Periodic
----------------------------
StartDay   Start-time   EndDay   End-time   Applied
--------   ----------   ------   --------   -------
weekend    00:00                 23:59      No

Time-Range lunch, Periodic
--------------------------
StartDay   Start-time   EndDay   End-time   Applied
--------   ----------   ------   --------   -------
daily      12:00                 13:00      No
```

tos

This extended action allows you to specify a Differentiated Services Code Point (DSCP) priority value that will be assigned to the packet when the firewall forwards the packet. DSCP is a way of classifying network traffic, and is used for quality of service (QoS). The tos value can be a value from 0 to 63.

Implicit Deny All

A firewall policy consists of one or more rules. As a packet is examined against the firewall policy, it is sequentially compared against each rule, starting at the top of the list with the first rule. The following shows a sample firewall policy allow-ssh that consists of six rules:

```
ip access-list session allow-ssh
  user host 10.1.50.100 svc-ssh  permit
  user host 10.1.50.101 svc-ssh  permit
  user host 10.1.50.102 svc-ssh  permit
  user host 10.1.70.100 svc-ssh  permit
  user host 10.1.80.100 svc-ssh  permit
  user host 10.1.90.100 svc-ssh  permit
```

If this policy is applied to an interface on the controller, at the end of the policy the system assigns what is known as an *implicit deny all*. The implicit deny all is effectively any any any deny, and will deny any type of traffic from any source to any destination, effectively blocking everything. Thus the effective `allow-ssh` policy is shown here:

```
ip access-list session allow-ssh
  user host 10.1.50.100 svc-ssh  permit
  user host 10.1.50.101 svc-ssh  permit
  user host 10.1.50.102 svc-ssh  permit
  user host 10.1.70.100 svc-ssh  permit
  user host 10.1.80.100 svc-ssh  permit
  user host 10.1.90.100 svc-ssh  permit
  any any any deny
```

Remember that a role is assigned to a user and consists of one or more policies. The implicit deny all is at the end of all of the policies. The following shows a user role controller-admin consisting of two policies, with the implicit `deny all` illustrated at the end of all of the rules in all of the policies. The implicit `deny all` ensures that a user is only allowed to perform the tasks that you permit.

```
user-role controller-admin
  ip access-list session allow-ssh
    user host 10.1.50.100 svc-ssh  permit
    user host 10.1.50.101 svc-ssh  permit
    user host 10.1.50.102 svc-ssh  permit
    user host 10.1.70.100 svc-ssh  permit
    user host 10.1.80.100 svc-ssh  permit
    user host 10.1.90.100 svc-ssh  permit
  ip access-list session allow-https
    user host 10.1.50.100 svc-https  permit
    user host 10.1.50.101 svc-https  permit
    user host 10.1.50.102 svc-https  permit
    user host 10.1.70.100 svc-https  permit
    user host 10.1.80.100 svc-https  permit
    user host 10.1.90.100 svc-https  permit
    any any any deny
```

AppRF

AppRF provides application classification and control. AppRF allows the administrator to place controls and limitations based upon the type of application that is being used, or based upon the category of website that the user is visiting. AppRF is a layer 7 firewall feature that provides two methods of packet inspection. It can perform on-board deep packet inspection and enforcement, and it can extract URL and hostname information from packets and use a trusted cloud-based service to classify and identify risk. These inspection methods are complementary to each other; however, they perform packet inspection using different techniques. The following section describes how AppRF deep packet inspection (DPI) can be used to provide application visibility and control. Later in the chapter, you will read about web content classification (WebCC) and how it can be used to analyze and control web browsing behavior based upon website categories and risk level.

AppRF Deep Packet Inspection

Deep packet inspection allows the controller to more aggressively inspect the user's data. DPI is a feature that is not enabled by default. It is not a global feature, which means that it must be enabled individually on each controller, including a redundant master if one exists. It is also a feature that will require you to reboot your controller. Enabling it is a simple command or a single checkbox in the WebUI. The following CLI output shows the command to enable DPI along with the warning message informing you that the controller will need to be rebooted:

```
(config) #firewall dpi

Warning: Application visibility is enabled, this change would take effect after controller reload
```

DPI can also be enabled by selecting Enable Deep Packet Inspection near the bottom of the following WebUI menu: **Configuration ➢ ADVANCED SERVICES ➢ Stateful Firewall ➢ Global Setting**.

When DPI is enabled, the controller performs real-time layer 7 inspection and analysis of client traffic. The controller uses DPI and statistical protocol identification to classify network traffic flow. It also uses signatures for more easily identified apps, along with advanced heuristics to analyze the traffic. It can also look at the header of encrypted traffic to detect applications.

DPI may need to examine multiple packets before it can complete its application or category classification. This means that a small number of packets may need to be allowed to pass through the firewall before the classification can be completed and policy can be applied. The number of round-trip packets that would be allowed through would be in the single digits.

Application and category classification can be used to block or restrict heavy bandwidth applications, limit or control specific applications or application categories, or mark specific applications or application categories with prioritization or Quality of Service (QoS) parameters.

ArubaOS defines over 2,300 applications that can be identified. If you would like to see the complete list of applications, the following CLI command will display them alphabetically. The following output displays only a small selection of some of the 2,300 applications that are defined. To make the output easier to read, the last column, Applied, was removed.

```
#show dpi application all

Applications
------------
Name              App ID   App Category        Default Ports
----              ------   ------------        -------------
abc-news          1824     web                 tcp 80,443
adobe-connect     929      streaming           tcp 80,443,1935
bittorrent        15       peer-to-peer        tcp 1024-65535 udp 1024-65535
craigslist        1848     web                 tcp 80,443
dropbox           779      cloud-file-storage  tcp 80,443
google-groups     56       collaboration       tcp 80,443
howstuffworks     1004     social-networking   tcp 80
```

Each of the applications is categorized. ArubaOS defines over 20 application categories. If you would like to see the list of application categories, the following CLI command will display them alphabetically:

```
#show dpi application category all

Application Categories
----------------------
Name                     App Category ID   Applied
----                     ---------------   -------
antivirus                1                 0
authentication           2                 0
behavioral               3                 0
cloud-file-storage       4                 0
collaboration            5                 0
encrypted                6                 0
enterprise-apps          7                 0
gaming                   8                 0
im-file-transfer         9                 0
instant-messaging        10                0
mail-protocols           11                0
mobile                   23                0
mobile-app-store         12                0
network-service          13                0
peer-to-peer             14                0
social-networking        15                0
standard                 16                0
streaming                17                0
thin-client              18                0
tunneling                19                0
unified-communications   20                0
web                      21                0
webmail                  22                0

Total application groups = 23
```

If you would like to see which applications are part of a specific application category, you can issue the show dpi application command and specify the category, as shown in the following CLI output. This example displays the list of all applications in the antivirus application category.

```
#show dpi application category antivirus

List of Applications
--------------------
Name              App ID  App Category  Default Ports  Applied
----              ------  ------------  -------------  -------
fsecure           2249    antivirus     tcp 80,443     0
ghostsurf         1107    antivirus     tcp 12200      0
mcafee            111     antivirus     tcp 80         0
peerguardian      2006    antivirus     tcp 80,443     0
sophos-update     1096    antivirus     tcp 80         0
zonealarm-update  754     antivirus     tcp 80,443     0

Total applications in this category = 6
```

Web Content Classification

Web Content Classification (WebCC) is another inspection method that is part of AppRF. As described previously in this chapter, WebCC inspects user traffic and then uses a cloud-based system to look up the reputation and category of the site being used.

Initially, WebCC was a feature that was provided with ArubaOS 6.X, but with version 6.5, it has become a licensed feature. It is enabled separately from deep packet inspection. Instead of performing deep packet inspection, when the user traffic reaches the Aruba controller, WebCC extracts the URL and hostname information from all HTTP and HTTPS packets. This information is used to identify two aspects of the packet destination. The first is the subject category of the website and the second is the risk level of the website. The subject categorization and risk classification status is provided by Webroot®, a third-party company that Aruba has partnered with. This company has classified billions of websites into over 80 different categories. These sites are also analyzed and monitored for web reputation, and this process identifies a threat and risk level for each site. The following CLI command generates a list of the WebCC categories:

```
#show web-cc categories

Web Content Classification Category Table
-----------------------------------------
Name                          Web Category Id
----                          ---------------
uncategorized                 0
real-estate                   1
```

```
computer/internet-security      2
financial-services              3
business-economy                4
computer/internet-info          5
auctions                        6
shopping                        7
cult-and-occult                 8
travel                          9
abused-drugs                   10
adult/pornography              11
home/garden                    12
military                       13
social-networking              14
dead-sites                     15
indv-stock-advice-tools        16
training-tools                 17
dating                         18
sex-education                  19
religion                       20
entertainment/arts             21
personal-sites/blogs           22
legal                          23
local-info                     24
streaming-media                25
job-search                     26
gambling                       27
translation                    28
reference/research             29
shareware/freeware             30
peer-to-peer                   31
marijuana                      32
hacking                        33
games                          34
philosophy/political-advocacy  35
weapons                        36
pay-to-surf                    37
hunting/fishing                38
society                        39
educational-institutions       40
online-greeting-cards          41
sports                         42
swimsuits/intimate-apparels    43
questionable                   44
kids                           45
hate/racism                    46
personal-storage               47
violence                       48
keyloggers/monitoring          49
search-engines                 50
internet-portals               51
web-advertisements             52
```

```
cheating                         53
gross                            54
web-based-email                  55
malware-sites                    56
phishing                         57
proxy-avoidance/anonymizers      58
spyware/adware                   59
music                            60
government                       61
nudity                           62
news/media                       63
illegal                          64
content-delivery-networks        65
internet-communications          66
bot-nets                         67
abortion                         68
health/medicine                  69
spam-urls                        71
dynamically-generated-content    74
parked-domains                   75
alcohol/tobacco                  76
private-ip-addresses             77
image/video-search               78
fashion/beauty                   79
recreation/hobbies               80
motor-vehicles                   81
web-hosting                      82
```

Web reputation evaluates each website on a scale of 1 to 100. These values represent how risky or trustworthy a website is. The 100 point scale is broken down into five 20-point ranges, as shown in Table 8.1.

TABLE 8.1: WebCC reputation

INDEX RANGE	RISK LEVEL	DESCRIPTION
1–20	High Risk	There is a high risk that a user will be exposed to malicious links or payloads.
21–40	Suspicious	There is a higher than average risk that a user will be exposed to malicious links or payloads.
41–60	Moderate Risk	These sites are generally benign, but have exhibited some characteristics that suggest there may be a security risk. There is some risk that a user will be exposed to malicious links or payloads.
61–80	Low Risk	These sites are generally benign. There is a low risk that a user will be exposed to malicious links or payloads.
81–100	Trustworthy	These are well-known sites with strong security characteristics. There is a very low risk that a user will be exposed to malicious links or payloads.

The following CLI command displays the list of the five risk levels, along with the value ranges:

```
#show web-cc reputation

Web Content Classification Reputation Table
-------------------------------------------
RiskLevel          Score
---------          -----
high-risk           1 -  20
suspicious         21 -  40
moderate-risk      41 -  60
low-risk           61 -  80
trustworthy        81 - 100
```

As with DPI, WebCC is a feature that is not enabled by default and is not a global feature, meaning that it must be enabled individually on each controller, including a redundant master if one exists. WebCC also needs to communicate with the Webroot Internet service that is providing categorization and reputation; therefore a DNS server also needs to be configured on each controller.

Enabling WebCC and DNS can be performed using CLI commands or menu selections in the WebUI. The following CLI output shows the commands to enable WebCC and configure a DNS server. After configuring the DNS server, it is likely that you will need to reboot your controller for the DNS change to become active.

```
(config) #firewall web-cc
(config) #ip name-server 192.168.240.11
```

Enabling WebCC and specifying a DNS server from the WebUI are performed from separate menus. The DNS server can also be added by going to **Configuration ➢ NETWORK ➢ IP ➢ IP Routes & DNS** in the Domain Name Servers section.

WebCC can be enabled from the following menu: **Configuration ➢ Stateful Firewall ➢ Global Settings ➢ Enable Web Content Classification**. When enabling WebCC through the WebUI, a message will display reminding you that a DNS server needs to be configured.

After WebCC is enabled, it is a good idea to check its status. This can be easily done in the CLI using the show web-cc status command, as shown in the following output:

```
(config) #show web-cc status

Web Content Classification Status
---------------------------------
Service                                   Status
-------                                   ------
Web Content Classification enabled :      Yes
DNS/Name Server configured :              Yes
URL Cloud lookup server reachable :       Yes
```

After WebCC has been initialized and a DNS server has been defined, the WebCC process contacts the Webroot server and downloads a database containing 1 million URLs. The controller will check for updates to this database every 24 hours.

When HTTP or HTTPS user traffic arrives at the controller, the controller checks to see if WebCC is enabled. If it is, the controller attempts to look up the URL in the local cache of the controller to try to identify the URL's category and reputation. If the controller previously checked for a given URL, the information is cached to provide for faster lookup.

If the URL is not in the cache, it will then look in the downloaded database. If it is not found there, the controller will then communicate with the Webroot server to download the URL's category and reputation. WebCC statistics can be viewed using the show web-cc stats command, as shown in the following output. The DB Entries line at the bottom of the output shows that the database was successfully downloaded. If this field shows 0, it is likely that the controller was not able to contact the Webroot server to download the database. This is probably caused by the controller not being able to resolve the DNS address of the Webroot server. Confirm that the IP address of the DNS server is correct. If it is, rebooting the controller should fix this problem.

```
(config) #show web-cc stats

Web Content Classification Statistics
-------------------------------------
Name                    Counter
----                    -------
URL miss from sos              1
Database hit                   0
Private IP addresses           0
Cloud lookup                   1
Cloud response                 1
RTU updates                    0
DB Entries               1000000
```

Table 8.2 provides a description of the output from the previous command, explaining what each line means.

TABLE 8.2: WebCC statistics

LINE	MEANING
URL miss from sos	Number of times that a URL was not able to be found in the internal cache
Database hit	Number of times a URL was found in the local database after not finding it in the cache

LINE	MEANING
Private IP addresses	Number of requests that were made to web servers running on private IP addresses
Cloud lookup	Number of times the controller had to subsequently send a lookup request to the Webroot server
Cloud response	Number of times the Webroot server responded to a lookup request
RTU updates	Number of times the internal cache was updated
DB Entries	Total number of entries in the local database

User Roles

Up to this point, this chapter has explained how to create a firewall policy and how to create firewall rules that make up that policy. This chapter has also described the components that make up a firewall policy, with descriptions of each of those components. The creation of a user role was briefly described and explained at the beginning of this chapter. This section will describe the different pieces in more detail.

To start off, the following CLI commands create two firewall policies. The first policy permits web browsing, and the second policy permits e-mail.

```
ip access-list session allow-web-browsing
  user any svc-http   permit
  user any svc-https  permit

ip access-list session allow-email
  user any svc-pop3  permit
  user any svc-smtp  permit
```

After the firewall policies are created, the user role can be created. The two firewall policies can then be assigned to the role, as shown in the following CLI commands:

```
user-role temp-employee
  access-list session allow-web-browsing
  access-list session allow-email
```

A list of all of the roles defined on your Aruba network can be displayed by typing the show rights command, as shown in the following CLI output. Since the output of this command is very wide, the second half of the output is displayed below the first half, and only two roles are displayed to make it easier to read.

```
(config) #show rights

RoleTable
---------
Name            ACL  Bandwidth              ACL List                          →
----            ---  ---------              --------                          →
sys-ap-role     11   Up:No Limit,Dn:No Limit sys-control/,sys-ap-acl/         →
temp-employee   91   Up:No Limit,Dn:No Limit global-sacl,apprf-temp-emplo     →

→ ACL List                                   Type
→ --------                                   ----
→                                            System (not editable)
→ yee-sacl/,allow-web-browsing/,allow-email/ User
```

The first column displays the name of each role. Although you and I may appreciate a logical role name, such as temp-employee, the computer simply identifies the role using an access control list (ACL) number, as displayed in the second column. In this example, temp-employee is ACL number 91. The third column displays whether bandwidth limitations are configured on the role. Traffic bandwidth can be limited upstream (Up) from the wireless client to the controller, or downstream (Dn) from the controller to the wireless client. The ACL List column lists all of the firewall policies that make up the role. In this example, the temp-employee role is made up of the four policies in the following list. The first two policies are created automatically by the controller and will be explained later in this chapter. The last two policies are the policies that we assigned to the role.

- global-sacl
- apprf-temp-employee-sacl
- allow-web-browsing
- allow-email

The final column, Type, specifies whether the role is a system role or a user role.

If you would like to examine even more detailed information about the role, the show rights command can be issued, followed by the name of a role. The output of this command is quite extensive, so we will look at it one section at a time. The following CLI output shows the command and the first section of output:

```
#show rights temp-employee

Valid = 'Yes'
CleanedUp = 'No'
Derived Role = 'temp-employee'

 Up BW contract = temp-employee-up (1000000 bits/sec) (per-user)   Down BW
contract = temp-employee-down (2000000 bits/sec) (per-user)

 L2TP Pool = default-l2tp-pool
```

```
PPTP Pool = default-pptp-pool
Number of users referencing it = 0
Periodic reauthentication: Disabled
DPI Classification: Enabled
Youtube education: Disabled
Web Content Classification: Enabled
IP-Classification Enforcement: Enabled
ACL Number = 91/0
Max Sessions = 65535

Check CP Profile for Accounting = TRUE
```

Some of the key items in the show rights *rolename* output are the bandwidth status, DPI and WebCC settings, the ACL number, along with the name of the captive portal profile. Note that there are upstream and downstream bandwidth contracts defined for this role. If a captive portal profile was assigned to this role, an additional line of output would display the name of the captive portal profile assigned, as shown here:

```
Captive Portal profile = guest-cp-profile
```

The next section of output from the show rights temp-employee command is displayed in the following CLI output. This is broken up into two sections: Application Exception List and Application BW-Contract List. Both of these sections are part of AppRF and have to do with bandwidth contracts or exceptions to bandwidth contracts, and are applied to specific applications or application categories. The first section, Application Exception List, specifies one or more applications or application categories that are exempt from the bandwidth contract that is assigned to the role. The second section, Application BW-Contract List, can set a bandwidth contract for a specific application or application category, and supersede the role's total bandwidth contract.

```
Application Exception List
--------------------------
Name        Type
----        ----
antivirus   appcategory

Application BW-Contract List
----------------------------
Name              Type             BW Contract    Id  Direction
----              ----             -----------    --  ---------
social-networking web-cc-category  social-media   3   upstream
social-networking web-cc-category  social-media   3   downstream
```

The next section of output from the show rights temp-employee command shows additional information that makes this one of the more valuable commands to know. This section displays the names of the policies that make up the role, along with all of the rules that make up the policies. This is one of a very few places where you can see the role, the list of policies, and the details of the rules together, and in the order in which they are processed. The list of rules and the order in which they are processed is extremely valuable for analyzing and troubleshooting the permission provided by a role.

The first section, access-list List, displays the list of firewall policies that make up the role. In this example, there are four of them. The first two policies are created automatically by the controller and will be explained later in this chapter. The last two policies are the policies that we assigned to the role.

Below this list is a section with a breakout of each policy assigned to the role. Each policy is shown in the order that the controller firewall will process it, with a listing of the rules that make up that policy. The Aruba firewall is a top-down first-match process, and it is very important to be able to visualize the effective rule implementation. For this reason, the CLI output show rights *rolename* gives a very readable list of the firewall rules applied to the user role.

Typically this output is very wide, containing a column for each of the different extended actions. In this example some of the blank or lesser important columns were removed from the output to make it easier to read. When reading through the next two sections, "Global Session ACL" and "Role Default Session ACL," you may want to refer back to this CLI output.

```
access-list List
----------------
Position  Name                       Type
--------  ----                       ----
1         global-sacl                session
2         apprf-temp-employee-sacl   session
3         allow-web-browsing         session
4         allow-email                session

global-sacl
-----------
Priority  Source  Destination  Service  Application          Action  IPv4/6
--------  ------  -----------  -------  -----------          ------  ------
1         any     any                   appcategory gaming   deny    4
2         any     any                   appcategory gaming   deny    6

apprf-temp-employee-sacl
------------------------
Priority  Source  Destination  Service  Application          Action  IPv4/6
--------  ------  -----------  -------  -----------          ------  ------
1         any     any                   app hulu             deny    4
2         any     any                   app hulu             deny    6
```

```
allow-web-browsing
------------------
Priority  Source  Destination  Service    Application  Action   IPv4/6
--------  ------  -----------  -------    -----------  ------   ------
1         user    any          svc-http                permit   4
2         user    any          svc-https               permit   4

allow-email
-----------
Priority  Source  Destination  Service    Application  Action   IPv4/6
--------  ------  -----------  -------    -----------  ------   ------
1         user    any          svc-pop3                permit   4
2         user    any          svc-smtp                permit   4

Expired Policies (due to time constraints) = 0
```

Global Session ACL

Starting with version 6.3 of ArubaOS, as an enhancement to AppRF, Aruba added the Global Session ACL. The *Global Session ACL* (global-sacl) is a global system-generated firewall policy that is automatically created and assigned in the first position of most roles. The global-sacl may not be deleted from the role, or moved from the first position. However, the global-sacl does not have to contain any firewall rules.

There are a few roles that have special uses or functions, for which the global-sacl is not assigned. Currently these roles are:

- ap-role
- default-iap-user-role
- guest-logon
- logon
- sys-ap-role

As noted earlier, the global-sacl is automatically the first policy in the role and cannot be moved. It also cannot be removed from a role. Another important thing to note is that the global-sacl can contain only application or application category rules, meaning rules based upon DPI or WebCC applications, categorization, or reputation.

The function of the global-sacl is to provide a method to globally block access to certain applications or application categories. Since the global-sacl is automatically the first policy of any user-oriented role, any firewall rules assigned to global-sacl would apply to every user on the network. Using the global-sacl, a company administrator can implement system-wide controls that effectively implement company policy across the entire organization, assigning all users the same application rules.

For example, you could block access to a DPI specified app, such as *businessweek* by issuing the following CLI commands:

```
(config) #ip access-list session global-sacl
(config-sess-global-sacl)#any any app businessweek deny
(config-sess-global-sacl)#ipv6 any any businessweek deny
```

You could also block access to a DPI specified application category such as *gaming*, by issuing the following CLI commands:

```
(config) #ip access-list session global-sacl
(config-sess-global-sacl)#any any appcategory gaming deny
(config-sess-global-sacl)#ipv6 any any appcategory gaming deny
```

If you have WebCC enabled, you can also block access to WebCC-defined categories, such as *auctions*, or any of the five reputation levels, such as *high-risk*, as shown in the following CLI commands:

```
(config) #ip access-list session global-sacl
(config-sess-global-sacl)#any any web-cc-category auctions deny
(config-sess-global-sacl)#any any web-cc-reputation high-risk deny
```

Although the configuration examples have shown CLI commands, the global-sacl can also be configured in the WebUI in the Configuration menu or from the Dashboard menu. Navigating to **Configuration ➢ SECURITY ➢ Access Control ➢ Policies** will bring you to the menu where you can edit the global-sacl policy.

You can also edit the global-sacl policy from the dashboard menu, using the following menu path: **Dashboard ➢ Traffic Analysis [AppRF on older versions of the OS] ➢ Block/Unblock ➢ Global Policies**.

Role Default Session ACL

The Role Default Session ACL is also known simply as the *role session ACL*. Similar to the global-sacl, the role session ACL is a system-generated firewall policy that is automatically created and assigned to most roles. The role session ACL is always in position 2 in the user role's policy list, and it may not be moved or deleted. Like the global-sacl ACL, the role session ACL does not have to contain any firewall rules.

The role session ACL is not assigned to the following roles:

- ap-role
- default-iap-user-role
- guest-logon
- logon
- sys-ap-role

Unlike the global-sacl, which is universal and applies to every role, a new role session ACL is automatically created for each role. The role session ACL is automatically the second policy in the role and cannot be moved. It also cannot be deleted. The role session ACL is named after the role that created it. All role session ACL names are created using the following naming scheme: apprf-*role-name*-sacl. Since it is tied directly to a role, it is automatically deleted when its corresponding role is deleted.

Similar to the global-sacl, the role session ACL can contain only application or application category rules, meaning rules based upon DPI or WebCC applications, categorization, or reputation.

The role session ACL provides the administrator with the ability to easily apply application rules directly to a role without having to make changes to firewall policies that may be assigned to other user roles.

As with configuring the global-sacl, role session ACL rules can be created from the CLI or the WebUI. **Configuration ➢ SECURITY ➢ Access Control ➢ Policies** will bring you to the menu where you can edit the role session ACL policy.

You can also edit the role session ACL policy from the dashboard menu, by going to **Dashboard ➢ Traffic Analysis [AppRF on older versions of the OS] ➢ Block/Unblock ➢ Per-role Policies**.

CHAPTER 9
Captive Portal

IN THIS CHAPTER, YOU WILL LEARN ABOUT THE FOLLOWING:

- Captive Portal Process
- Captive Portal Overview
  - Authentication Server and Server Group
  - Post Logon Role
  - Captive Portal Profile
  - Initial Role
  - AAA Profile
  - SSID Profile
  - VLAN and DHCP Server
  - Virtual AP Profile
  - AP Group
  - Captive Portal Page
- Guest-Provisioning Account
  - Guest-Provisioning Page
- Connecting to ClearPass Guest
  - Guest User Database
  - Captive Portal Profile
  - Initial Role

Providing WLAN access for guest users is a common practice for most organizations. The main goal of providing access to guests is typically to allow them to access resources on the Internet. The amount of access varies by organization, and can be controlled using roles, policies, and firewall rules—topics covered in Chapter 8, "Policy Enforcement Firewall." Guests are usually provided limited or no access to the organization's internal network.

Captive portal is one of the most commonly used technologies to control guest access. This is going to seem strange, but captive portal has nothing to do with wireless networking. Captive portal is an authentication and access control technology that can work on wired or wireless networks. If you have ever stayed at a hotel with wired network access in the guest rooms, one of the first things that happens after connecting your computer to the network cable is the appearance of the captive portal logon page. Captive portal is heavily used because it is an easy authentication method for a guest to navigate. It uses a standard web browser, and does not require any additional software or configuration for the guest to logon to the network.

ArubaOS provides basic captive portal services. The network administrator or a guest-provisioning user, such as a receptionist or security guard, can create guest accounts. A guest user can then logon to the network using that account. The captive portal can also be configured to allow anyone to logon using an e-mail address. The e-mail address is not validated; however, it is checked to ensure proper e-mail format.

The captive portal built into the controller can provide basic services for a small or medium-sized organization that does not have many visitors. The captive portal server cannot provide the ability for guests to register themselves and create their own user accounts; therefore, guest accounts are created by an administrator, or a designated person or group of people. Any organization that does not meet this profile should consider a more robust guest management solution, such as Aruba ClearPass Guest.

This chapter will explain the captive portal process, along with the components that make up the captive portal that is built into ArubaOS. The focus of this chapter will be on the ArubaOS-based captive portal; however, since many Aruba customers use ClearPass Guest as their captive portal server, there will be some explanation of the configuration differences between the two captive portal environments.

Captive Portal Process

Captive portal provides an easy authentication environment for users connecting to an untrusted network. Figure 9.1 shows a detailed list of numbered tasks performed during a WLAN captive portal logon. Before explaining these steps, let us review the process at a high level. As you will see, DNS is a key component to making this process work.

The client connects to the network and obtains an IP address. A browser is opened. The user enters a web page or URL address and a DNS lookup is performed to obtain the IP address of the URL destination. The Aruba controller intercepts the first HTTP/HTTPS session from the client and redirects the client to the captive portal logon page using HTTP 302 Moved Temporarily messages. The username and password are entered into the logon form, and submitted to the Aruba controller. The controller validates the user identity and then, using DNS and HTTP 302 Moved Temporarily messages, redirects the client to a valid URL

Now that you have a cursory view of the process, let us go through the detailed step-by-step explanation of what happens. The following numbered steps refer to what is happening in Figure 9.1.

1. The first step in the process is for the client to connect to the SSID. This process is known as an *802.11 authentication and association*. Once the client is associated to the WLAN, the client is able to begin sending and receiving data frames.

2. The WLAN is an untrusted network, which means that the client will always be assigned an initial role, and may be required to authenticate on the network. In this example, captive portal authentication is enabled. In a captive portal environment, the client is assigned an initial role that will typically allow DHCP, DNS, and limited HTTP/HTTPS. These protocols are used to facilitate logon using captive portal.

FIGURE 9.1
Captive portal process flow

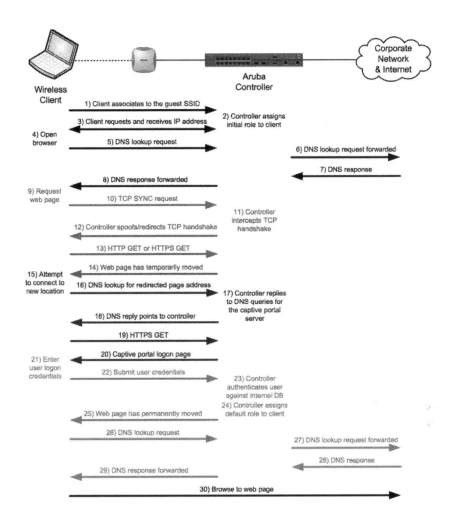

3. After the client is assigned an initial role, the client will request and receive an IP address, subnet mask, and gateway address. These parameters could be statically configured, but they are typically obtained using DHCP. In a controller-based captive portal environment, it is common for the Aruba controller to be configured as the DHCP server for the guest network, although any external DHCP server can be used.

4. After the client has an IP address, a web browser needs to be opened, and the client needs to attempt to connect to a web page. Many modern operating systems will either trigger the default browser to open or will launch a special browser, sometimes known as a *captive network assistant (CNA)*.

5. and 6. When the browser is opened, the browser is likely configured with a default or initial URL, or the user will type in a URL, such as www.westcott-consulting.com. The client OS will use DNS to translate this URL into an IP address in order to load the web page. The DNS resolver sends a DNS lookup request to the controller, which then forwards it to the corporate network or to the Internet, depending upon where the DNS server resides. Since the user's initial role allows DNS, the controller acts as a layer 2 or layer 3 switch and forwards the DNS request.

7. and 8. If the DNS server resolves www.westcott-consulting.com, then the IP address for the URL is returned to the client. This DNS response is sent to the controller, which again acts as a layer 2 or layer 3 switch and forwards the DNS response to the wireless client.

9. After the client receives the IP address of www.westcott-consulting.com, the client browser requests the web page from the web server, using the IP address instead of the hostname.

10. The client initiates TCP SYNC to the server IP address it obtained from the DNS response. The browser is an HTTP/HTTPS client and uses TCP as its layer 4 protocol to communicate with the web server. Therefore, it needs to complete a three-way TCP handshake with the web server before it can request the web page from the web server. The handshake is initiated with the TCP SYNC request.

11. and 12. When the TCP SYNC request arrives at the controller, the firewall processes the request using the rules that are part of the initial role. This role and the rules contained in it are critical to the success of the captive portal. The captive portal firewall policy is typically assigned to the initial role, which should provide the necessary rules. The captive portal policy performs a DST-NAT on the TCP SYNC request, with the controller ip and controller port 8080. Basically, if the source port is TCP 80, the destination IP address is replaced by the controller IP address, and the destination port is replaced by TCP 8080. If the source port is TCP 443, the destination IP address is still replaced by the controller IP address, but the destination port is replaced by TCP 8081 instead. In brief, the firewall policies have redirected the HTTP/HTTPS traffic to the internal web server of the controller.

13. Now that the client believes it is communicating with www.westcott-consulting.com, the browser sends an HTTP GET for www.westcott-consulting.com.

14. The controller responds to the request, redirecting the client to the captive portal page. It does this by telling the client that www.westcott-consulting.com has temporarily moved to https://securelogin.arubanetworks.com/*string that identifies client*.

15. At this point, the browser closes the connection and attempts to connect to the new web page address: `https://securelogin.arubanetworks.com/`*string that identifies client*. However, in order to do so, the client needs an IP address for this new web page.

16. The client OS will use DNS to attempt to translate this new web page address into an IP address. The DNS resolver on the client machine sends a DNS lookup request to the controller. Again, since the user's initial role allows DNS, the controller acts as a layer 2 or layer 3 switch and forwards the DNS request.

17. The controller intercepts any DNS queries for `securelogin.arubanetworks.com`, which are directed to the IP address of the controller that is serving up the captive portal page.

18. The controller sends the DNS response to the client.

19. The client browser sends an HTTPS GET to the controller IP address.

20. The controller replies by sending the captive portal logon page, which will appear in the client's browser window.

21. and 22. The client enters a username and password into the captive portal logon page, and clicks the Log In button to submit the credentials to the Aruba controller.

23. In addition to acting as the web server for the captive portal logon page, the Aruba controller is the authentication server. The controller validates the user credentials against the internal user database. The internal user database is typically used for guest accounts, although an external database can also be used instead (e.g., RADIUS or LDAP).

24. After the user credentials are validated, the controller changes the role of the client from the initial role to the default role. A server assigned role could also be assigned in lieu of the default role.

25. At this point the client is redirected to either the initial web page (`www.westcott-consulting.com`), or to a predefined page, known as a *welcome page*. In order to redirect the client to `www.westcott-consulting.com`, the controller spoofs a reply from `www.westcott-consulting.com`, telling the client that the page has permanently moved. This supersedes the temporary relocation that occurred earlier.

26. and 27. The client once again uses DNS to attempt to resolve `www.westcott-consulting.com` to an IP address. The DNS resolver sends a DNS lookup request to the controller, which then forwards it to the corporate network or to the Internet, depending upon where the DNS server resides. The post authentication user role that is now assigned to the guest allows DNS. The controller acts as a layer 2 or layer 3 switch, and forwards the DNS request.

28. and 29. If the DNS server resolves www.westcott-consulting.com, then the IP address is returned to the client. This DNS response is sent to the controller, which again acts as a layer 2 or layer 3 switch and forwards the DNS response to the wireless client.

30. At this point, the client browser can communicate with the www.westcott-consulting.com server.

Captive Portal Overview

It is important to remember that captive portal is a layer 3 authentication protocol. When connecting to a network using a layer 3 authentication protocol, the authentication occurs after you obtain an IP address. Another important fact to remember is that captive portal is not strictly a wireless technology; therefore, you do not enable captive portal on an SSID. Since captive portal can work with wired or wireless networks, it is not configured on the SSID, but rather in the initial role.

With ArubaOS, WLANs are by default untrusted connections. Any connection to an untrusted network results in an initial role being assigned to the client before authentication. Therefore, if you want to require captive portal authentication, you need to enable it as part of the initial role.

The captive portal profile hierarchy is similar to the hierarchy for an 802.1X/EAP connection; however, since 802.1X/EAP is a layer 2 authentication method and captive portal is a layer 3 authentication method, there are some differences. Figure 9.2 illustrates the different configuration profiles that are part of creating a captive portal connection, and the relationships between these profiles. This list does not attempt to show all of the profiles; rather, it shows the key profiles needed to configure a captive portal–enabled virtual AP.

Authentication Server and Server Group

The captive portal logon page simplifies the collection of the user's credentials, but it does not actually provide user authentication. Therefore, an authentication server and server group need to be configured on the Aruba controller as a means to verify the credentials. Typically, captive portal logons are authenticated against the internal database that resides on the master controller. There is a preconfigured server group, also named internal. If the internal server and server group are used, you can simply use them; no additional authentication server configuration tasks are required.

The top left of Figure 9.2 shows the relationship between the two steps, authentication server and server group. It also shows that the authentication server and server group need to be defined as part of the first steps when creating a guest WLAN. If you plan to use an external server, refer back to Chapter 5, "Profiles," for the necessary commands to define one.

CAPTIVE PORTAL OVERVIEW

FIGURE 9.2
Profile hierarchy

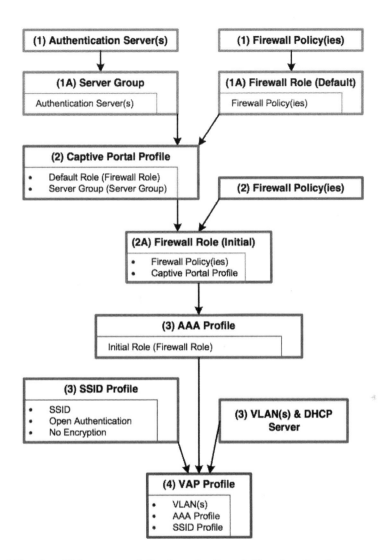

The following CLI command displays the list of all authentication servers, followed by the command to display information about the internal server.

```
#show aaa authentication-server all

Auth Server Table
-----------------
Name      Type    FQDN  IP addr       AuthPort  AcctPort  Status   Requests
----      ----    ----  -------       --------  --------  ------   --------
Internal  Local   n/a   10.1.50.100   n/a       n/a       Enabled  0
all       Radius  none  127.0.0.1     1812      1813      Enabled  0
radius01  Radius  none  10.254.1.21   1812      1813      Enabled  0
radius02  Radius  none  10.254.1.23   1812      1813      Enabled  0
ldap01    Ldap    n/a   10.254.1.51   389       n/a       Enabled  0
```

```
#show aaa  authentication-server internal

Internal Server
---------------
Host      IP addr       Retries  Timeout  Status
----      -------       -------  -------  ------
Internal  10.1.50.100   3        5        Enabled
```

The following CLI commands assign the `internal` server group to the captive portal profile.

```
aaa authentication captive-portal "guest-cp-profile"
server-group "internal"
```

In a master/local controller environment, the default behavior is to authenticate all requests from the guests on the local controllers against the internal database, which resides on the master controller. This default is to ensure that valid guests can authenticate through any controller they may attach to. This can be overridden on a controller-by-controller basis.

For example, if the master controller is in New York City, and you have a local controller in London, you can configure the London controller to use its own internal database. Guest accounts would have to be created specifically on the London controller by an administrator or a guest-provisioning account. Any guest user logging on at the London office would be authenticated against the internal database on the London controller. When the following CLI command is executed on a local controller, it will direct the local controller to use its own internal database instead of the internal database on the master controller.

```
(config) #aaa authentication-server internal use-local-switch
```

To identify which internal database is being used by a local controller, you can execute the following CLI command on the local controller. This command displays the IP address of the internal database that the local controller is referencing. This address will be either the IP address of the master controller or the local controller's own IP address.

```
(config) #show aaa authentication-server internal

Internal Server
---------------
Host      IP addr       Retries  Timeout  Status
----      -------       -------  -------  ------
Internal  10.1.80.100   3        5        Enabled
```

Post Logon Role

The goal of any authentication is to initially limit the client access to only the functionality required to collect and verify the client credentials. After the user credentials have been verified, the limited "pre-authenticated" role needs to be replaced by a role that gives the user greater access, while still controlling what they have access to. The post logon role is assigned according to the role derivation process that was explained in Chapter 7, "Role Derivation." No matter how the user is assigned the post logon role, the role and its policies need to be defined at the beginning of the creation of the guest WLAN, as illustrated in upper-right section of Figure 9.2.

The controller has a predefined role, guest, that allows DHCP, DNS, ICMP, HTTP, and HTTPS. As the administrator, you can use this role or you can create another, although it is recommended that you make a copy of this guest user role. When using the predefined guest role, you should evaluate it to ensure that it provides the proper access or restrictions for your particular network. It is recommended that you create a firewall policy that blocks all access to your organization's internal networks. Since firewall policies are processed sequentially, this policy should be placed after the DHCP policy and before the DNS policy. Chapter 8, "Policy Enforcement Firewall," explained how to create firewall rules, policies, and roles.

Captive Portal Profile

The main profile that defines the flow of the captive portal experience is the *captive portal profile*. It is this profile that defines the particular web logon page that will be used, and the server group for verifying the user credentials, as well as the post-logon role assignment.

Following the illustrations in Figure 9.2, the captive portal profile is created after the server group and the required guest roles. As with many of the profiles on the Aruba controller, it is typical to make only a few changes and allow the rest to be the default settings. The captive portal page can display two different logon windows: a user logon window and a guest logon window. The user logon window prompts the user for a username and password. If a user successfully logs on using the user login, the user would be assigned the role that is defined in the default role field, assuming that the authentication server did not specifically assign a role (this was covered in Chapter 7, "Role Derivation").

The guest login window prompts the user for an e-mail address. The format of this e-mail is validated, but the address itself is not. If a user logs on using the guest login, the user would be assigned the role that is defined in the default guest role field. Note that with this "anonymous" logon no other role assignment is possible, since there is no real authentication. The anonymous guest will be assigned to the default guest role.

Configuration ➢ SECURITY ➢ Authentication ➢ L3 Authentication ➢ Captive Portal Authentication will bring you to the menu where you can enable or disable the user and guest login windows, along with defining the default role and the guest default role. Figure 9.3 displays this menu.

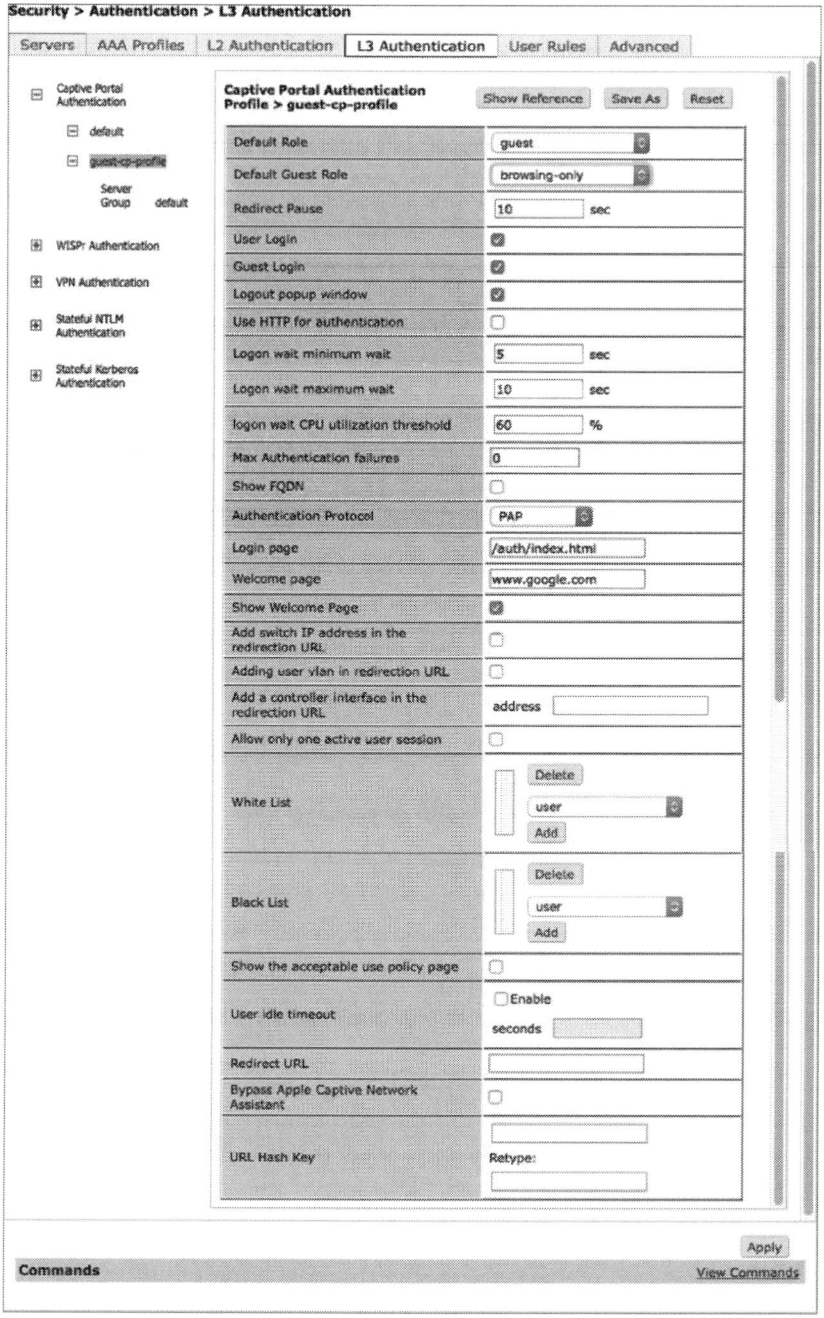

FIGURE 9.3
Captive portal profile

You can configure the captive portal profile so that after a user is successfully authenticated, the web browser is automatically redirected to a different page instead of the page the user intended to access initially. This designated page is referred to as a *redirect URL*. Most hospitality customers use this feature to get the attention of guests by directing them to their home page.

The following CLI commands perform the previous tasks. The captive portal profile is created with both user and guest login enabled. Guest is defined as the default role and browsing-only is defined as the guest default role. A redirect URL is also defined.

```
aaa authentication captive-portal "guest-cp-profile"
default-role "guest"
default-guest-role "browsing-only"
user-logon
guest-logon
redirect-url http://www.arubanetworks.com
```

Initial Role

As explained earlier, the initial role is the key trigger for the captive portal. As with any role, the initial role consists of firewall policies, which identify what access rights the user has when connected to the network. Since captive portal is a layer 3 authentication method, the user needs to connect to the wireless network and obtain an IP address before attempting to log on with the captive portal.

A guest logon role is preconfigured on the Aruba controller and is often used as a template for creating a new role for your guest network. This custom guest logon role will be used as the initial role for the newly attached guest user. It should include the following policies: ra-guard, logon-control, captiveportal, v6-logon-control, and captiveportal6. Because the typical guest network has open authentication, meaning anyone can connect, it is recommended that you limit the number of TCP sessions per user. By default, the max session setting has a value of 65,535. You can limit this to a maximum of 128 per user. The following CLI commands create a new role and assign the policies to the role:

```
(config) #user-role guest90-logon
(config-role) #access-list session ra-guard
(config-role) #access-list session logon-control
(config-role) #access-list session captiveportal
(config-role) #access-list session v6-logon-control
(config-role) #access-list session captiveportal6
(config-role) #max-sessions 128
```

In addition to assigning the necessary firewall policies to the role, the captive portal profile needs to be assigned to this role in order to trigger the connection to the captive portal, as illustrated in Figure 9.4. The following CLI commands assign the captive portal profile to the role:

```
(config) #user-role guest90-logon
(config) (config-role) #captive-portal guest-cp-profile
```

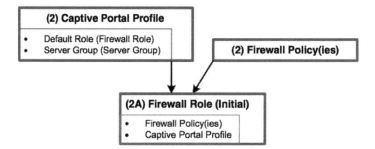

FIGURE 9.4 Initial role

This new guest logon role will be assigned as the initial role in the AAA profile for the guest network. The policies in this role provide the necessary protocols, such as DHCP, DNS, HTTP, and HTTPS. These protocols will allow the client to get an IP address and initiate the connection to the captive portal server. You can also configure these settings in the WebUI by going to **Configuration ➢ SECURITY ➢ Access Control ➢ User Roles**.

AAA Profile

Configuration of the AAA profile to allow the guest network to support captive portal authentication is extremely easy. An AAA profile needs to be created, and the newly created guest logon role needs to be selected as the initial role assigned to the AAA profile. The following CLI commands create the AAA profile and assign the initial role to it:

```
(config) #aaa profile "guest90-aaa-profile"
(AAA Profile "guest90-aaa-profile") #initial-role "guest90-logon"
```

These settings can also be configured from the WebUI interface by navigating to **Configuration ➢ SECURITY ➢ Authentication ➢ AAA Profiles ➢ AAA**.

Figure 9.5 shows the Edit Role menu where a role can be modified.

SSID Profile

Since captive portal is a layer 3 authentication profile, when it is being configured, the user simply connects to the unauthenticated and unencrypted SSID prior to going through the layer 3 captive portal authentication process. Therefore, the SSID profile simply needs to contain the SSID. The following CLI commands create an SSID profile with an SSID of guest90:

```
(config) #wlan ssid-profile "guest90-ssid-profile"
(SSID Profile "guest90-ssid-profile") #essid guest90
```

FIGURE 9.5
Edit role menu

You can create the SSID profile from the WebUI by going to **Configuration** ➢ **ADVANCED SERVICES** ➢ **All Profiles** ➢ **Wireless LAN** > **SSID**.

VLAN and DHCP Server

When you create a VAP, you will assign a VLAN to it. The user traffic on the VAP will be placed on this VLAN. The VLAN for the guest WLAN should be created solely for guest traffic. In addition to creating the VLAN, an IP address also needs to be assigned to it in order for captive portal to work properly. Remember that VLANs are created on each controller where user traffic is terminating. The following CLI commands create VLAN 93, assign the IP address 192.168.9.1 to it, and enable source NAT:

```
(config) #vlan 93
(config) #interface vlan 93 ip nat inside
(config) #interface vlan 93 ip nat outside
(config) #interface vlan 93
(config-subif) #ip address 192.168.9.1 255.255.255.0
```

The Aruba Airheads Community website has an excellent article titled, "What Is the Difference between 'ip nat inside' and 'ip nat outside'" that you should search for and read if you are not familiar with the concepts.

Configuration ➢ **NETWORK** ➢ **VLANs** ➢ **VLAN ID** in the WebUI will bring you to the menu where you can create the VLAN.

Configuration ➢ **NETWORK** ➢ **IP** ➢ **IP Interfaces** in the WebUI will bring you to the menu where you can assign the IP address to the VLAN.

The following CLI command displays the VLANs that are configured on the controller and the IP addresses that are assigned to them:

```
#show ip interface brief

Interface              IP Address / IP Netmask       Admin    Protocol
vlan 90                10.1.90.100 / 255.255.255.0   up       up
vlan 1                 unassigned / unassigned       up       down
vlan 91                10.1.91.3 / 255.255.255.0     up       up
vlan 93                192.168.9.1 / 255.255.255.0   up       down
loopback               unassigned / unassigned       up       up
```

The following command displays VLANs and IP addresses, and also includes NAT details:

```
#show vlan status

Vlan Status
-----------
VlanId  IPAddress                Adminstate  Operstate  PortCount →
------  ---------                ----------  ---------  --------- →
1       unassigned/unassigned    Enabled     Down       0         →
90      10.1.90.100/255.255.255.0  Enabled   Up         3         →
91      10.1.91.2/255.255.255.0  Enabled     Up         2         →
93      192.168.90.1/255.255.255.0  Enabled  Up         1         →


→ Nat Inside   Mode     Ports             AAA Profile   Option-82
→ ----------   ----     -----             -----------   ---------
→ Disabled     Regular  Pc0-7             N/A           Disabled
→ Disabled     Regular  GE0/0/0-0/2       N/A           Disabled
→ Disabled     Regular  GE0/0/0 GE0/0/3   N/A           Disabled
→ Disabled     Regular  GE0/0/0           N/A           Disabled
```

It is suggested that you use an external DHCP server to provide IP addresses to guest users, although for networks with a limited number of guest users, the internal DHCP server can be used. The following CLI commands will create an address pool for network 192.168.9.0. Make sure that you issue the service dhcp command. This command starts the DHCP server process on the controller.

```
(config) #ip dhcp pool guest-cp-pool
(config-dhcp)#network 192.168.9.0 255.255.255.0
(config-dhcp)#default-router 192.168.9.1
(config-dhcp)#dns-server 10.254.1.21
(config-dhcp)#exit
(config) #service dhcp
(config) #end
```

If you want to check the DHCP pool, the following CLI command will display all of the configuration settings. If you created more than one pool, all of the pools will be displayed, along with their respective settings.

```
# show ip dhcp database

DHCP enabled

# guest-cp-pool
subnet 192.168.9.0 netmask 255.255.255.0 {
    option vendor-class-identifier  "ArubaAP";
    option vendor-encapsulated-options  "10.1.90.100";
    option domain-name-servers 10.254.1.21;
    option routers 192.168.9.1;
    range 192.168.9.3 192.168.9.254;
    authoritative;
}
```

Both VLAN and DHCP server were explained in more detail in Chapter 4, "Getting Started."

Virtual AP Profile

At this point, all of the necessary components have been created to build the VAP profile; AAA profile, SSID profile, and VLAN. Figure 9.6 illustrates these components.

FIGURE 9.6
Virtual AP profile

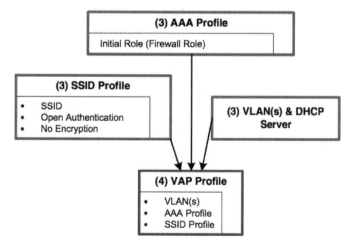

In addition to assigning the AAA profile, SSID profile, and VLAN to the VAP profile, you may want to specify the forwarding mode for the VAP. In Chapter 2, "Understanding the ArubaOS Environment," the four forwarding modes were explained: GRE/tunnel (default), bridge, decrypt-tunnel, and split-tunnel.

The following CLI commands create the VAP profile and assign the VLAN, AAA profile, and SSID profile to the VAP. Note that if the VAP is configured for bridge forwarding mode, captive portal is not supported.

```
(config) #wlan virtual-ap guest90-vap
(Virtual AP profile "guest90-vap") #vlan 93
(Virtual AP profile "guest90-vap") #aaa-profile guest90-aaa-profile
(Virtual AP profile "guest90-vap") #ssid-profile guest90-ssid-profile
```

You can create the VAP profile using the WebUI by going to **Configuration** ➢ **ADVANCED SERVICES** ➢ **All Profiles** ➢ **Wireless LAN** ➢ **Virtual AP**.

AP Group

After the configuration of the VAP profile, it needs to be assigned to an AP group in order for the VAP to be advertised. VAPs and AP groups were discussed in more detail in Chapter 5, "Profiles." These CLI commands assign the VAP profile to the AP group.

```
(config) #ap-group controller90
(AP group "controller90") #virtual-ap guest90-vap
```

Configuration ➢ **WIRELESS** ➢ **AP Configuration** ➢ **AP Group** will bring you to the menu where you can create or select the AP group using the WebUI. After selecting the AP group, from the **Wireless LAN** ➢ **Virtual AP** submenu, you can assign the VAP to the AP group.

Captive Portal Page

When you created and saved the captive portal profile, the controller created a web login page specifically for that profile. The look of the captive portal login page can be customized. A background graphic can be uploaded to the controller, text can be added, and an acceptable use policy can also be added. The page customizations are simple in scope; however, an effective logon page can be created.

Configuration ➢ **MANAGEMENT** ➢ **Captive Portal** ➢ **Customize** will bring you to the menu where you can select and customize each page. Select your captive portal profile from the pull-down menu at the top of the page. At the bottom of the Customize menu is a link, View CaptivePortal, which will allow you to see what the captive portal page looks like.

Guest-Provisioning Account

When using the internal database for guest authentication, it is necessary for someone to logon to the controller and create guest accounts. Creation of a guest account can be performed by an administrator with the root role, but it is not practical to require an administrator to create all guest accounts. It is also not safe to allow general users to have administrative privilege to the controller so that they can create guest accounts. The solution is the guest-provisioning role. To simplify this process of creating guest accounts, the network administrator can create a guest-provisioning administrative account for a receptionist, administrative assistant, or help desk support person. A guest-provisioning administrative account is a management user account that only has access to the guest-provisioning page.

The guest-provisioning account needs to have access to the controller where the accounts will be created, normally the master controller. If the internal database on a local controller is being used for guest accounts, then the guest-provisioning account would be provided access on that local controller.

A guest-provisioning account named reception can be easily created from the CLI using the commands shown in the following output:

```
(config) #mgmt-user reception guest-provisioning
Password:********
Re-Type password:********
```

A guest-provisioning account can also be easily added from the following WebUI menu: **Configuration** ➤ **MANAGEMENT** ➤ **Administration**.

The guest-provisioning account can create guest accounts and can edit or delete only those accounts created using that guest-provisioning account. An admin user can create, edit, or delete any account in the internal database.

Guest-Provisioning Page

To simplify the task of creating and managing guest users, the guest-provisioning user is directed to a simple web page solely for creating guest users. This provisioning page is the menu for the guest-provisioning user to manage guest accounts in the user database. The guest-provisioning user must enter a username and password for any account that is being created. From **Configuration** ➤ **MANAGEMENT** ➤ **Guest Provisioning** ➤ **Guest Fields**, the admin user can add more fields to the form that is used to create or edit a guest user account.

Figure 9.7 displays the menu where you can modify the form used to create or edit guest accounts. The field selected in the Details column will be added to the form. Any field selected in the Listing column will be displayed in the database list of guest users. At the top right of the guest-provisioning page is a link, Preview Current Settings, which will allow you to see what the guest-provisioning page looks like.

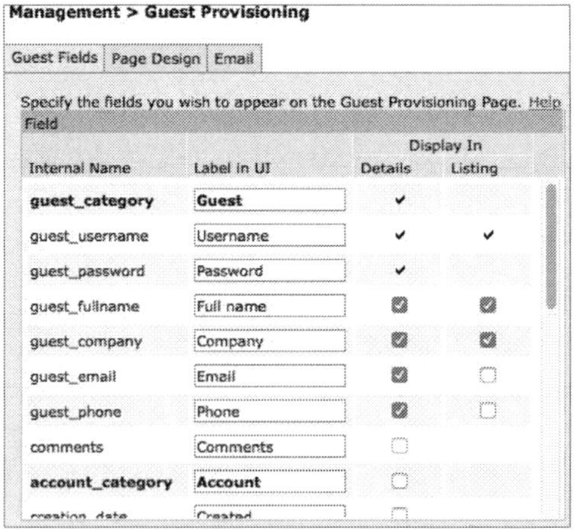

FIGURE 9.7 Guest-provisioning fields

Connecting to ClearPass Guest

ClearPass Guest is an extremely powerful guest management platform. It provides many features for managing guest users that are not supported on the Aruba controller by itself. ClearPass Guest allows for self-registration, sponsorship, social logon, and many different levels of guest operators, all of which provides many more features than the guest-provisioning account on the Aruba controller. Although ClearPass Guest is a separate product, since it is often integrated with the Aruba controller, this section will explain the tasks that need to be performed on the controller to facilitate the controller to operate with it.

Whether you are using the built-in captive portal or an external captive portal such as ClearPass Guest, the process of intercepting and redirecting the DNS request is essentially the same. The difference is that the captive portal redirection is to the external ClearPass Guest server instead of the internal server on the controller. The following is a summary of the differences when using ClearPass Guest.

- ▶ The guest database on ClearPass will be used instead of the internal database on the controller.
- ▶ The captive portal profile will redirect the login page to the ClearPass Guest page that you create.
- ▶ The initial role must have HTTP and HTTPS permission to the ClearPass server to allow access to captive portal page.

Guest User Database

In order to use the extra functionality of the ClearPass Guest database, you need to authenticate the guest users on the ClearPass server. This means you will need to configure ClearPass as an authentication server and add it to a server group. The following CLI commands define a ClearPass server as an authentication server on the Aruba controller:

```
(config) #aaa authentication-server radius clearpass1
(RADIUS Server "clearpass1") #host 10.254.1.23
(RADIUS Server "clearpass1") #key aruba123
```

Configuration ➢ SECURITY ➢ Authentication ➢ Servers ➢ RADIUS Server will bring you to the menu where you can create the RADIUS server using the WebUI.

The following CLI commands define a server group, clearpass-srv-group, which contains the ClearPass server:

```
(config) #aaa server-group clearpass-srv-group
(Server Group "clearpass-srv-group") #auth-server clearpass1 position 1
```

Configuration ➢ SECURITY ➢ Authentication ➢ Servers ➢ Server Group will bring you to the menu where you can create the server group and assign the RADIUS servers to the server group.

Captive Portal Profile

When using ClearPass Guest with captive portal authentication, a few changes need to be made to the captive portal profile. The server group specified in the captive portal profile needs to be the one pointing to the ClearPass server. Additionally, the web login page needs to redirect the user to the correct web login page hosted on the ClearPass guest server. After the ClearPass server is defined as an authentication server and added to a server group, the following CLI commands will assign the clearpass-srv-group server group to the captive portal profile:

```
aaa authentication captive-portal "clearpass-cp-profile"
server-group "clearpass-srv-group"
```

When a ClearPass Guest captive portal is being used, most of the settings in the captive portal profile are no longer needed, because the ClearPass Guest server will take over these responsibilities. There are, however, two settings that you need to make. The first is to specify the default role. Although ClearPass will typically directly assign a role using a vendor-specific attribute (VSA), specifically the Aruba-User-Role VSA, if the role derivation is not successful, the user is assigned the captive portal profile default role; therefore, you should plan and design your network accordingly.

The other change is to specify the ClearPass Guest captive portal page as the logon page. In ClearPass Guest, when the web logon is created, a page name is assigned. This page name is the logon filename that the captive portal profile will redirect the user to. The following CLI commands configure the captive portal profile to redirect to the ClearPass Guest server cp1.westcott-consulting.com with the captive portal page of arubalogon.php, and assign guest as the default role. In this example, the domain name cp1.westcott-consulting.com would have to be able to be resolved by a DNS server. An IP address could be used instead of a domain name.

```
aaa authentication captive-portal "clearpass-cp-profile"
default-role "guest"
login-page https://cp1.westcott-consulting.com/guest/arubalogon.php
```

Navigating to **Configuration** ➢ **SECURITY** ➢ **Authentication** ➢ **L3 Authentication** ➢ **Captive Portal Authentication** will bring you to the menu where you can define the default role and the location of the logon page.

Initial Role

The initial role provides the user with the necessary permissions to navigate to the captive portal page prior to authenticating onto the network. The initial role typically contains the logon-control policy, which allows essential network protocols such as DHCP and DNS. The initial role typically also contains the captiveportal policy, which allows HTTP and HTTPS to the captive portal server. Since the ClearPass captive portal server is external to the Aruba controller, firewall rules need to be added to the initial role through a policy (in this example the captiveportal policy) to allow HTTP and HTTPS to reach the external captive portal server. The CLI commands following the next paragraph will add the necessary firewall rules to the initial role, in this example through the captiveportal policy, allowing the guest user to browse to the captive portal logon page on the ClearPass Guest server (10.254.1.23).

Do not forget that in addition to defining the initial role and adding the necessary firewall rules, the captive portal profile needs to be added to the initial role, which is also included as the last command in the following CLI commands.

```
(config)# ip access-list session captiveportal
(config-sess-captiveportal)# alias user host 10.254.1.23 svc-http permit
(config-sess-captiveportal)# alias user host 10.254.1.23 svc-https permit
(config-sess-captiveportal)# user-role guest90-logon
(config-role)# captive-portal clearpass-cp-profile.
```

A newer and more efficient way of allowing the user's HTTP and HTTPS traffic to reach the captive portal server is by adding the server information to the captive portal profile's white list. This method is also more flexible, since it is easier to add, remove, or modify firewall access to the captive portal server.

The first step in using the captive portal profile white list is to define a netdestination alias for your captive portal server or servers. The following CLI commands show the creation of a netdestination alias named `MyClearPassServers`. For illustration purposes, one server is referenced using a hostname and the other an IP address.

```
netdestination MyClearPassServers
name cp1.westcott-consulting.com
name 192.168.240.77
```

After you create and define the netdestination alias, it then needs to be added to the captive portal profile white list. This can be done using the following CLI commands:

```
aaa authentication captive-portal "guest-cp-profile"
whitelist MyClearPassServers
```

The netdestination alias can also be added using the WebUI. **Configuration ➢ SECURITY ➢ Authentication ➢ L3 Authentication ➢ Captive Portal Authentication** will bring you to the menu, shown in Figure 9.8, where you can perform this task.

FIGURE 9.8 Captive portal profile white list

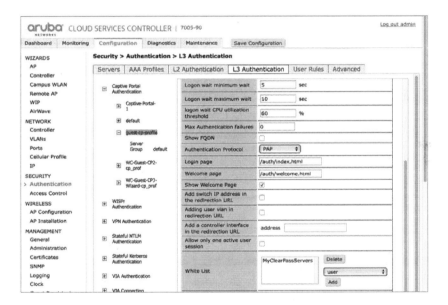

After the netdestination alias is added to the white list, the controller performs a couple of interesting tasks. It first creates a firewall policy allowing HTTP and HTTPS access to the netdestination. The name of the firewall policy is the captive portal profile name with `_list_operations` appended to it. This firewall policy is system-generated and cannot be edited. If the netdestination is removed from the white list, the firewall policy is deleted. The following CLI output shows the firewall policy created for the `guest-cp-profile`:

```
# show ip access-list guest-cp-profile_list_operations

ip access-list session guest-cp-profile_list_operations
```

```
guest-cp-profile_list_operations
--------------------------------
Priority  Source  Destination          Service    Application  Action   Queue  IPv4/6
--------  ------  -----------          -------    -----------  ------   -----  ------
1         user    MyClearPassServers   svc-http                permit   Low    4
2         user    MyClearPassServers   svc-https               permit   Low    4
```

The second interesting task that the controller performs is it assigns this newly created firewall policy to any role that is configured to use the captive portal profile. The firewall policy is automatically set as the first policy in the role, as shown in Figure 9.9. This is an extremely useful feature. Once the white list is configured, any time a captive portal profile is assigned to a role, the role is automatically configured to allow the user access to the captive portal server.

FIGURE 9.9
Initial role with white list enabled

CHAPTER 10

Network Expansion

IN THIS CHAPTER, YOU WILL LEARN ABOUT THE FOLLOWING:

- Master/local Communications
  - IKE Preshared Keys
  - IKE Certificates
  - Local Controller Settings
- Fault Tolerance
  - Virtual Router Redundancy Protocol
  - Redundancy Design
  - AP Redundancy Using VRRP
  - Backup LMS-IP
  - AP Fast Failover
  - Master Controller Redundancy
  - Redundancy Comparison
- Centralized Licensing
- Centralized Upgrade
- AP Image Preload
- AP Image Preload with Centralized Upgrade

IN 1997, 802.11 WIRELESS NETWORKING BECAME A standard. In the early days of 802.11, most installations came about because of a need to solve a specific business problem or task. The early wireless products were slow and expensive, which limited the number of installations.

Over time, the speed of 802.11 increased and the cost of wireless networks began to decrease. Companies began installing APs in conference rooms for convenience and, over time, throughout their organizations.

Nowadays, wireless networks have become the core network access method for users in most businesses. Organizations continue to add more APs to increase the coverage area of their networks along with providing denser, faster networks.

As more APs are added to existing networks and as larger networks are being deployed, additional controllers may be needed to support and manage these networks. Additional controllers are also implemented in distributed environments, such as remote or satellite offices that are closer to the APs and the users. The Aruba architecture uses a master/local platform, which was described in Chapter 2, "Understanding the Aruba OS Environment."

This chapter will explain how to expand your wireless network using local controllers, and will provide the details of the relationship between the master and local controllers. This chapter will also cover the tasks necessary to configure this environment.

As an organization becomes more dependent upon wireless networking, it is important to make sure that users have continuous access to the network by implementing a fault-tolerant environment. This chapter will also explain how to protect the network infrastructure by implementing redundancy and failover. The Aruba architecture provides multiple technologies that can be used to ensure high availability of the wireless network.

Master/Local Communications

The master controller is the core of the Aruba architecture. The first controller that is installed is configured as a master, as explained in Chapter 2. The process of initially configuring the master controller was described in Chapter 4, "Getting Started." In smaller environments, an organization can often build an Aruba network with a stand-alone master controller, with all of the APs communicating through the master. As wireless demand and the number of APs increase, it will become necessary to expand the network by adding one or more additional controllers. These additional controllers are referred to and configured as local controllers.

The primary purpose of the local controller is additional horsepower and localization of that horsepower. The most common reason to add more controllers to your wireless network is that your AP count is greater than the hardware limit of your particular controller.

Another reason to add more controllers is to support network design criteria. Remember that the APs tunnel user data back to the controller. The controller then places the user data onto the network backbone. Very often, the network design is better served by multiple points of egress provided by multiple controllers than by a single controller.

Layer 2 and layer 3 settings are configured on all controllers. The remaining settings (WLAN, firewall, WIDS/WIPS, ARM, and others) are configured on the master controller, which automatically distributes these settings to all of the local controllers. This ensures that configurations are consistent between controllers and provides a single point of configuration for the group of controllers.

The settings are distributed to the local controllers when either the Save Configuration selection is made in the WebUI interface or when a `write memory` command is performed at the CLI. The settings that are transferred from the master controller to the local controllers include AP group parameters, virtual AP profiles, firewall roles and policies, WIPS/WIDS policies, ARM parameters, along with many others.

The configuration information that is transferred from the master controller to the local controller may contain security information such as WPA or WPA2 passphrases. Therefore it is necessary for the master and local controllers to communicate using encryption. IPsec encryption is used, and is configured using either an IKE preshared key, or using a certificate.

IKE Preshared Keys

When configuring master/local communications to use a preshared key, you have a choice of configuring all of the controllers to use a single IKE global preshared key, as illustrated in Figure 10.1, or you can configure the controllers so that the master controller communicates with each local controller using individual preshared keys, as illustrated in Figure 10.2. In either instance, the key must be between 6 and 64 characters long.

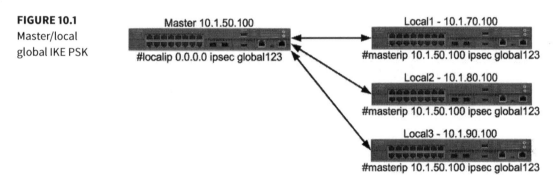

FIGURE 10.1 Master/local global IKE PSK

Figure 10.1 shows a master controller and three local controllers. All of the controllers will use the same preshared key to communicate between the master controller and each of the local controllers—in this example, global123. The master controller is configured with a global or wildcard IP address of 0.0.0.0. Each of the local controllers points to the IP address of the master controller—in this example 10.1.50.100—using the IKE preshared key of global123. Using the same key is convenient, but it is less secure. Figure 10.1 includes the CLI commands needed to configure each controller.

To configure a more secure environment, the controllers should be configured similar to the example in Figure 10.2. In this configuration, each master/local pair uses a unique preshared key. In this configuration the local controllers will each point to the master controller, but with a unique IKE preshared key. The master controller must be configured using a separate command for each local controller, setting a unique preshared key for each controller. Figure 10.2 includes the CLI commands needed to configure each controller.

FIGURE 10.2
Master/local unique IKE PSKs

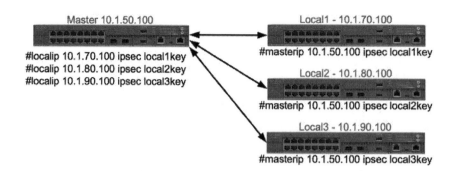

Chapter 4 explained that the best way to create a local controller was to build the controller as a master, update the OS, and then convert it to a local controller. To convert a master to a local, all you need to do is to enter the `masterip` command, as shown in the following CLI output. In this example the master controller is 10.1.50.100 and the IKE preshared key is `local70aruba123`. Since the role of the controller is changing from a master to a local, a reboot is required.

```
(config) #masterip 10.1.50.100 ipsec local70aruba123
This configuration change requires a reboot.
 PLEASE SAVE THE CONFIGURATION AND REBOOT.
```

Configuration ➢ NETWORK ➢ Controller ➢ System Settings will bring you to the menu where you can make these changes using the WebUI interface.

This menu can be confusing because there are two sections where the IKE preshared key can be entered. The top section of the menu is where you specify the settings if you are configuring a local controller, as shown in Figure 10.3. If you are changing the controller role from a master to a local, you would select Local and then enter the IP address of the master, along with the IKE preshared key. If the controller is already a local controller, you can use this menu to change the key.

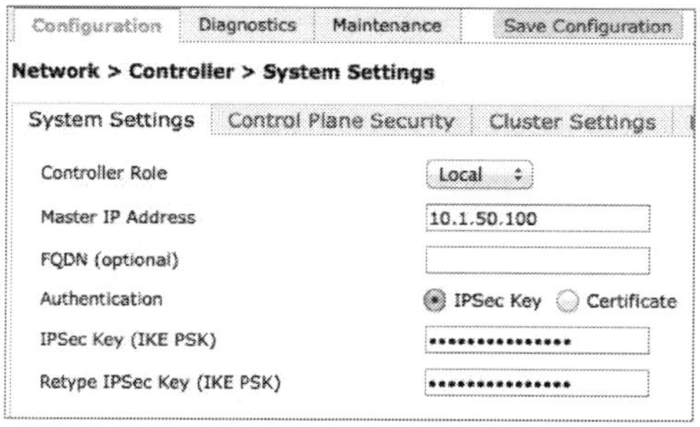

FIGURE 10.3
Local controller IKE settings

Further down on the menu is the local Controller IPsec Keys section where you configure the IKE preshared keys if you are configuring the master controller. In this section, you can configure a global key and you can configure individual keys for specific local controllers. In Figure 10.4, a global key was created and assigned to the IP address 0.0.0.0; individual keys were created for two local controllers, 10.1.70.100 and 10.1.80.100; and a third key is being created for the local controller, 10.1.90.100. Typically, you will configure a global key or you will configure individual keys, usually not both.

FIGURE 10.4
Master controller IKE settings

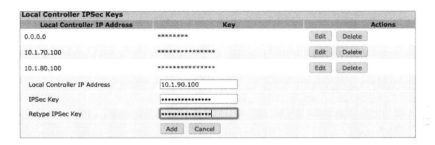

After the local controllers are configured, you can go to the master controller to see the status of the local controllers, as shown in the following CLI output. The output was too wide for this book, so it is split. Notice the Configuration State is successful and Config ID is the same for all three controllers. This indicates that the configuration is currently synchronized between the master and each local.

```
#show switches

All Switches
------------
IP Address     Name       Location         Type     Model      Version
----------     ----       --------         ----     -----      --------
10.1.50.100    7010-50a   Building1.floor1 master   Aruba7010  6.4.2.3_47524 →
10.1.70.100    7005-70    Building1.floor1 local    Aruba7005  6.4.2.3_47524 →
10.1.80.100    7005-80    Building1.floor1 local    Aruba7005  6.4.2.3_47524 →

   Status  Configuration State  Config Sync Time (sec)  Config ID
   ------  -------------------  ----------------------  ---------
→  up      UPDATE SUCCESSFUL    0                       9
→  up      UPDATE SUCCESSFUL    10                      9
→  up      UPDATE SUCCESSFUL    10                      9
```

IKE Certificates

Another method of providing secure communications between the master controller and the local controllers is by using certificates. The certificates can be either factory-installed or custom-installed. This section will explain how to configure the communications using the factory-installed certificate. To properly secure the controller, factory-installed certificates should always be replaced.

Configuring master/local communications to use certificates requires configuration on the master and the local controllers. In order to configure the controllers to use certificate-based IKE, you need to enter a command on the master controller and on the local controller. You will also need to reboot the local controller.

The first command is entered on the master controller, specifying the local controller. This specifies that the factory certificate will be used, along with the MAC address of the local controller that the master is communicating with.

You will need the MAC address of the local controller when issuing this command. You can locate the MAC address of a controller by entering the show switchinfo CLI command or by going to **Configuration** ➢ **NETWORK** ➢ **Controller** ➢ **System Settings** and selecting Loopback Interface.

After you have the MAC address of the local controller, the following CLI command will configure the master controller to use the factory certificate when communicating with the local controller whose MAC address is 00:0B:86:B8:62:80:

```
(config) #local-factory-cert local-mac 00:0B:86:B8:62:80
```

After the master controller is configured with the factory certificate, you also need to configure the local controller to use the factory certificate when communicating with the master controller. For this you will need both the IP address and the MAC address of the master controller. As stated previously in this section, you can locate the MAC address of a controller by issuing the show switchinfo CLI command or in the Loopback Interface section of the WebUI.

Although redundancy will be explained later in this chapter, if master redundancy is enabled, you also need the MAC address of the backup master controller.

The following CLI output shows two commands. The first command will configure the local controller to use the factory certificate when communicating with a master controller with the IP address of 10.1.50.100 and MAC address of 00:0B:86:9B:00:97. The second command is identical to the first command, but includes the MAC address of a backup controller. In this example there is a backup controller with a MAC address of 00:0B:86:9A:6B:57.

```
(config) #masterip 10.1.50.100 ipsec-factory-cert master-mac-1 00:0B:86:9B:00:97
This configuration change requires a reboot.
 PLEASE SAVE THE CONFIGURATION AND REBOOT.

(config) #masterip 10.1.50.100 ipsec-factory-cert master-mac-1 00:0B:86:9B:00:97
master-mac-2 00:0B:86:9A:6B:57
This configuration change requires a reboot.
 PLEASE SAVE THE CONFIGURATION AND REBOOT.
```

MASTER/LOCAL COMMUNICATIONS

The show `local-cert-mac` command can be executed on the master controller to see the certificate state, as shown in the following CLI command output. If the Switch IP of the local field is empty, the master controller has not yet communicated with the local controller using the certificate.

```
(config) #show local-cert-mac


Local Switches configured by Local Certificate
----------------------------------------------
Switch IP of the Local   MAC address of the Local Certificate   Cert-Type →
----------------------   ------------------------------------   --------- →
10.1.80.100              00:0B:86:BE:7A:40                      Factory   →

→ CA cert
→ -------
→ Factory-CA-Cert
```

The factory certificate can also be configured from **Configuration ➢ NETWORK ➢ Controller ➢ System Settings**.

Figure 10.5 shows the local Controller Certificates menu where the factory certificate is enabled on the master, and the MAC address of the local controller is entered.

FIGURE 10.5
Enabling the factory certificate on a master controller

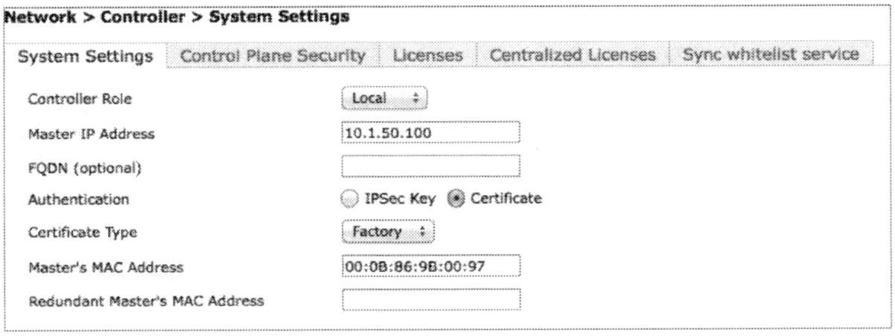

FIGURE 10.6
Enabling the factory certificate on a local controller

Figure 10.6 shows where the factory certificate is enabled and selected on a local controller, along with the field where the MAC address of the master controller is entered. If master redundancy is enabled, the MAC address of the backup controller would also need to be entered. When these changes are applied, a pop-up window will notify you that the controller needs to be rebooted.

The local controller certificates are also displayed on this menu in the local Controller Certificates section, as shown in Figure 10.7. As with the show local-cert-mac CLI command, if the Switch IP of the local field is empty, the master controller has not yet communicated with the local controller using the certificate.

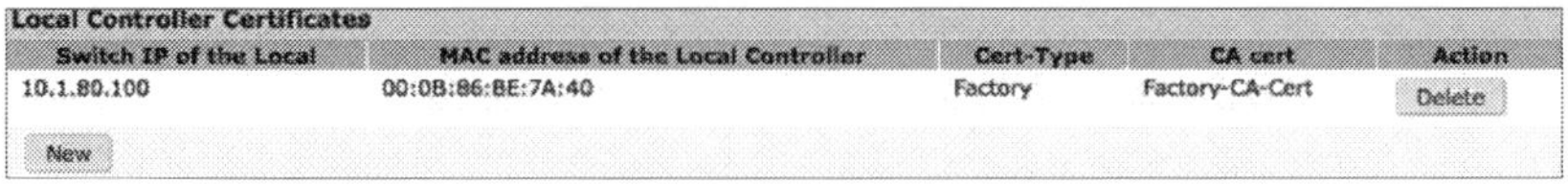

FIGURE 10.7
Local controller certificates

Local Controller Certificates				
Switch IP of the Local	MAC address of the Local Controller	Cert-Type	CA cert	Action
10.1.80.100	00:0B:86:BE:7A:40	Factory	Factory-CA-Cert	Delete
New				

Local Controller Settings

After the local controller is up, running, and communicating with the master controller, most of the changes that you will make will be on the master controller. These settings will then get pushed to the local controller using IPsec communications.

It is important to remember that there are many settings that are unique to every controller. Most of these will be configured as part of the initial setup of each controller. However, at times these changes may need to be modified if changes are made to the network infrastructure. The following is a list of some of the settings that are unique to each controller, whether master or local.

- IP address/subnet mask/default gateway
- Hostname
- DNS servers
- SMTP servers
- IP routing information
- Spanning tree configuration
- Port settings/port ACLs
- DHCP pools
- NAT pools
- Time zone and daylight savings settings
- SNMP and syslog settings
- RAP white list/VPN pools
- Local user database values
- RADIUS client details and source interfaces
- Authentication certificates
- Custom captive portal parameters

- Firewall settings
- WebCC and AppRF settings

Fault Tolerance

As wireless networks become more critical parts of your business model, network uptime becomes very important. Another aspect of network growth is the installation of additional equipment to provide fault tolerance. *Fault tolerance*, also known as *redundancy*, provides failover or backup if a device fails or becomes unavailable. The primary goal of redundancy is to keep the APs operating and providing access to the users. Another prominent reason for redundancy is to provide failover for the master controller. There are multiple ways of providing failover on an Aruba network; virtual router redundancy protocol (VRRP), backup LMS, and high availability. This chapter will explain the different methods and designs, why they are used, and how to implement them.

Virtual Router Redundancy Protocol

Virtual router redundancy protocol (VRRP) is an industry standard for providing interface redundancy. A key component of VRRP is the shared IP address known as the *virtual IP (VIP)*. Generally, the VIP is shared between two devices that periodically exchange status heartbeats. These heartbeats are periodic transmissions between the two devices. One device is designated as the active device and the other device is designated as the standby device. If the heartbeats fail, the standby device considers the active device to be unreachable and it will begin communicating using the VIP. There are multiple scenarios in the Aruba environment for configuring VRRP between two controllers, while supporting redundant designs.

VRRP can be used to provide for AP failover, or it can be used to provide redundancy for the master controller. This section will explain how to configure VRRP with its virtual IP, and then later in the chapter you will learn how to configure and verify master controller redundancy.

In order to configure VRRP, both controllers must be connected to the same layer 2 network. Since a main characteristic of VRRP is that both devices must be able to service the same virtual MAC address, both the active and standby controllers must be able to communicate in the same layer 2 network, or subnet.

When VRRP is configured on the two controllers, you determine which is the *primary* (VRRP master) controller and which is chosen to be the *standby* (VRRP backup) controller. This is specified by entering priority information, which will be explained later in this chapter. In addition to choosing the primary and standby controllers, you must define the shared or virtual IP (VIP), as illustrated in Figure 10.8.

FIGURE 10.8
VRRP VIP

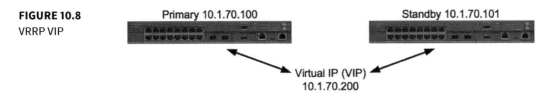

Referring to Figure 10.8, the VIP will reside on the active controller. When VRRP is first configured, assuming all participating controllers are up and operational, the VIP (10.1.70.200) will reside on the primary controller (10.1.70.100). If the primary controller goes down, then the VIP will move to the standby controller (10.1.70.101). The active controller will have two IP addresses: its assigned address and the virtual address.

Configuring VRRP Using the WebUI

Before exploring the different design and usage scenarios, let us continue with the details of configuring a VRRP pairing between two controllers. VRRP is often configured using the WebUI, so in this example I will show you the configuration using the WebUI first and then the equivalent CLI commands. You can find the VRRP configuration menu by going to **Configuration ➢ ADVANCED SERVICES ➢ Redundancy**.

You should always build VRRP on the primary controller first, and then configure the standby controller. I personally like to build the VRRP pair using the following procedure:

1. Build the primary first in the Down admin state.
2. Then, build the standby, also in the Down admin state.
3. After they are both built, go back to the primary and change it to the Up admin state.
4. Validate that the primary is up as the VRRP master.
5. Go to the standby and change it to the Up admin state.
6. Validate that the standby is up as the VRRP backup.

I admit that this procedure is extra cautious; however, it only takes a couple of extra minutes to perform these tasks. Later in this chapter, master controller redundancy will be explained in detail. You will learn that this procedure can prevent you from accidentally wiping out the configuration on your master controller when configuring redundancy.

The VRRP configuration process begins on the primary controller by clicking the Add button on the redundancy menu. The Add Virtual Router menu will appear, as displayed in Figure 10.9. The following settings should be entered:

- Virtual Router ID (VRID): The VRID is a number between 1 and 255, and needs to be unique on the layer 2 network. The VLAN number can be a good number to use if it is between 1 and 255.
- Advertisement Interval (secs): The default value is 1, although it is not displayed. Leave this field blank.
- Authentication Password: It is up to eight characters long. If multiple VRRP devices are on the same network and inadvertently configured with the same VRID, this password can prevent misconfiguration between different servers that were not intended to be paired with each other.
- Description: This is simply a name for you to identify the primary controller.
- IP Address: This is the virtual IP (VIP) address.
- Enable Router Pre-emption: Typically, do not enable.
- Priority: A value between 1 and 254. With a primary controller and a standby controller, it does not matter what the values are as long as the primary is larger than the standby. I typically use 200 for the primary controller and 100 for the standby controller.
- Admin State: Leave this as DOWN (for now).
- VLAN: This is the VLAN between the primary and standby controllers that will be used to communicate the keepalive frames.

After entering this information you will need to click the Done button. **Do not** forget to click the Apply button. The Apply button is often overlooked when configuring VRRP.

The next step is to configure the VRRP settings on the standby controller. All of the settings will be the same as the primary except for the description and the priority.

- Description: This is simply a name to help you to identify the standby controller.
- Priority: A value between 1 and 254. As stated in the previous section, the value does not matter as long as the value for the standby controller is less than the primary. I typically use 100 for the standby controller (200 for the primary controller).

After entering this information you will need to click the Done button. Do not forget to click the Apply button, as it is often overlooked when configuring VRRP.

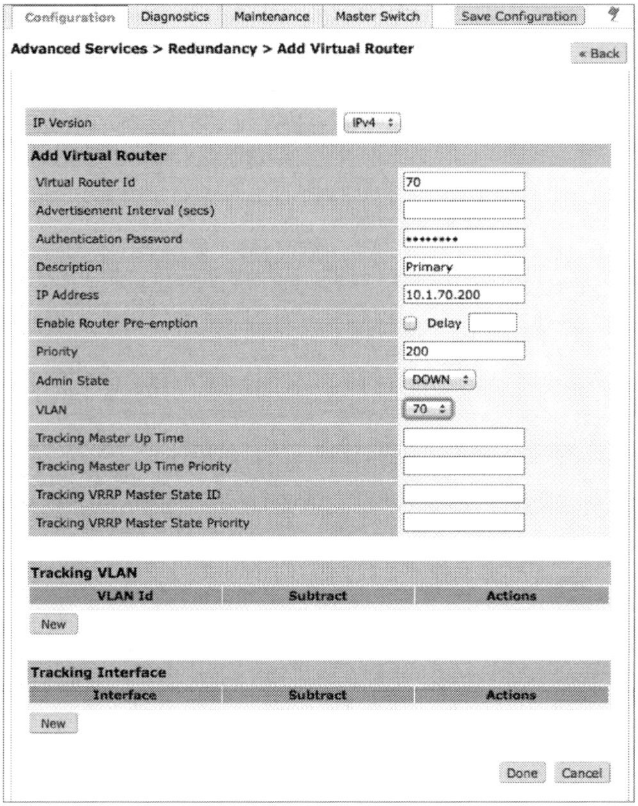

FIGURE 10.9
Adding a virtual router

At this point, both of the controllers are configured for VRRP; however, both are configured with the admin state as down. Each controller should display the VRRP admin state as down and the operational state as init. Go back to the primary controller and change the admin state to up. Again, click the Done button and do not forget to click the Apply button. The admin state of the primary controller should now be up, and the operational state should be Master. If the operational state does not display as Master, refresh your browser once or twice and the operational state should update itself and display correctly, as shown in Figure 10.10.

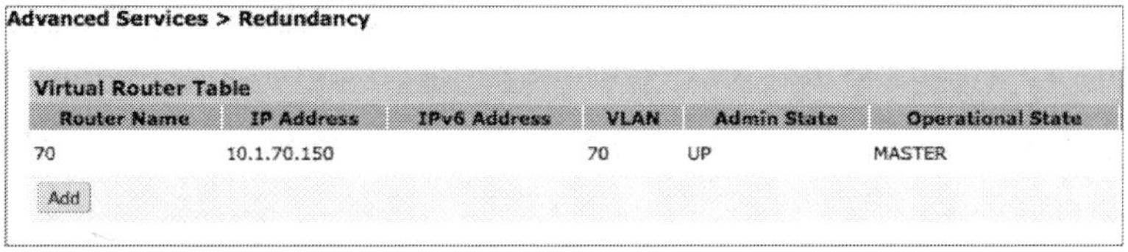

FIGURE 10.10
VRRP master operational state

After the primary controller displays Master for the VRRP state, you can now go to the standby controller and change its admin state to up. Again, do not forget to click the

Done button and then the Apply button. The admin state of the secondary controller should be up and the operational state should be Backup. You may need to refresh your browser once or twice for the correct admin state to show, as you see in Figure 10.11.

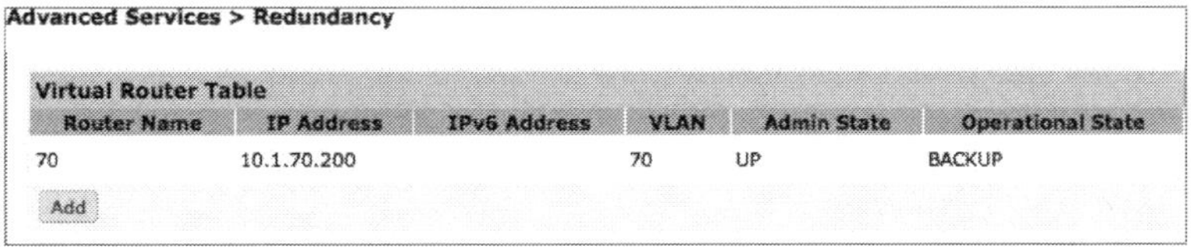

FIGURE 10.11
VRRP backup operational state

Router Name	IP Address	IPv6 Address	VLAN	Admin State	Operational State
70	10.1.70.200		70	UP	BACKUP

Advanced Services > Redundancy — Virtual Router Table

Configuring VRRP Using the CLI

The previous section explained the details and steps of configuring VRRP using the WebUI. This section will show how to perform those same steps using the CLI.

As I recommended in the WebUI section, configure VRRP on the primary controller first and then on the standby controller. Also, configure both of them in the down state. Then after both are configured, bring the primary up, verify it is running as the VRRP master, and then bring the standby up.

The tasks are listed here:

- Create the VRRP with the VRID of 70.
- Set the authentication password to aruba123.
- Identify it as the primary controller.
- Set the VIP as 10.1.70.200.
- Configure the priority as 200.
- Define VLAN 70 to be used for keepalive.

The following CLI commands will perform these tasks. Notice that when the IP address and VLAN are defined, the controller alerts you that the VRRP is currently in the shutdown state, which is what we initially desire.

```
(config) #vrrp 70
(config-vrrp) #authentication aruba123
(config-vrrp) #description "Primary"
(config-vrrp) #ip address 10.1.70.200
vrrp is in shutdown state

(config-vrrp) #priority 200
(config-vrrp) #vlan 70
vrrp is in shutdown state
```

After the primary controller is configured, the following CLI commands can be used to configure the standby controller:

```
(config) #vrrp 70
(config-vrrp)#authentication aruba123
(config-vrrp)#description "Standby"
(config-vrrp) #ip address 10.1.70.200
vrrp is in shutdown state

(config-vrrp) #priority 100
(config-vrrp) #vlan 70
vrrp is in shutdown state
```

You can check the VRRP status using the command show vrrp, as shown in the following CLI output. This command can be run on the primary or standby controller. Notice that the admin state is down. You can run the command encrypt disable before you run the show vrrp command to expose the VRRP authentication password. This will allow you to check for a password mismatch between the two controllers. These commands are useful when troubleshooting VRRP.

```
#show vrrp
Virtual Router 70:
    Description Primary
    Admin State DOWN, VR State INIT
    IP Address 10.1.70.200, MAC Address 00:00:5e:00:01:46, vlan 70
    Priority 200, Advertisement 1 sec, Preemption Disable Delay 0
    Auth type PASSWORD, Auth data: ********
    tracking is not enabled
```

After VRRP is configured on both the primary and secondary controllers, you need to enable VRRP on both of them; first the primary and then the secondary. When VRRP is created on any controller, it is automatically configured in the shutdown state. To enable VRRP, you actually disable it from being shut down by issuing the no shutdown command. After these commands are performed on the primary controller, verify that it is up and running as the VRRP master. After you confirm that the primary controller is running as the VRRP master, you will need to perform these commands on the standby controller to enable VRRP and to confirm that it is operating as the VRRP backup.

The following CLI output shows the commands to enable VRRP and then the command to show the VRRP status:

```
(config)#vrrp 70
(config-vrrp)#no shutdown

(config-vrrp)#show vrrp
Virtual Router 70:
    Description Primary
    Admin State UP, VR State MASTER
    IP Address 10.1.70.200, MAC Address 00:00:5e:00:01:46, vlan 70
```

```
Priority 200, Advertisement 1 sec, Preemption Disable Delay 0
Auth type PASSWORD, Auth data: ********
tracking is not enabled
```

Redundancy Design

The previous section of this chapter explained how to configure two controllers to use VRRP and share an IP address. This shared IP address resides on the primary controller until there is a problem, at which time the virtual IP address transitions to the standby controller, which takes over the responsibilities of the primary controller.

VRRP is one method of providing redundancy. Later in this chapter you will learn about other methods, along with some of the differences between them. However, before introducing you to the additional redundancy methods, let us take a look at some of the architectural design and functional uses for redundancy.

There are three general design models for implementing redundancy:

- Active/standby
- N:1 active/standby
- Active/active

Active/Standby

The *active/standby redundancy model* provides the most robust form of redundancy by providing each AP with a consistent and predictable secondary location to communicate with in the event of a failure. With the active/standby model, every AP will be supported if a controller fails, providing 100 percent redundancy. An illustration of the active/standby model is shown in Figure 10.12. In this model, the APs connect to the primary controller. When the primary controller fails, the APs lose connectivity with the primary controller and establish a connection with the standby controller.

In this model, the standby solely acts as a failover controller to the primary. Since the standby controller is dedicated solely to redundancy, this method is usually the most expensive.

FIGURE 10.12
Active/standby

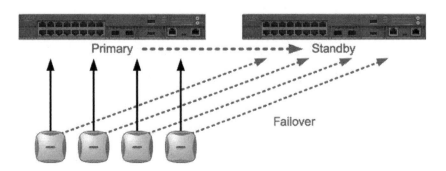

N:1 Active/Standby

Many times, the network design does not merit the expense of a fully redundant set of controllers. A decision is often made that the network is not critical enough to merit the extra cost. It may also be determined that not every AP in the environment would likely need a failover location at the same time. In these instances, an N:1 active/standby model may be a more practical and economical solution.

The *N:1 active/standby redundancy model* is also referred to as an *N+1 active/standby redundancy model*. In this model, you have a number of controllers, N, that you want to provide failover for. You install an additional unit, +1, which will act as the standby for the N number of active controllers. A graphical model of N:1 active/standby resembles a hub-and-spoke configuration.

Figure 10.13 shows three controllers. The outer two controllers are supporting APs, and are the controllers that need failover, thus N = 2. The middle controller was added to provide failover for the other controllers; this is the +1 controller.

In this scenario, you would configure the middle controller as the standby for the Primary-A controller, and you would also configure the middle controller as the standby for the Primary-B controller. The Primary-A and Primary-B controllers operate independently of each other, and each failover also operates independently.

When designing an N:1 active/standby network, you need to make sure that the standby controller can support the number of APs and users that will fail over to it. You can design it for a catastrophic failure, where both Primary-A and Primary-B fail. In this environment, that standby controller must support the total of all of the APs and users from both controllers.

You can also design it for a single controller failure, where Primary-A or Primary-B might fail due to an isolated hardware or network failure. In this scenario, the standby controller must be able to support all of the APs and users from Primary-A or Primary-B.

FIGURE 10.13
N:1 active/standby

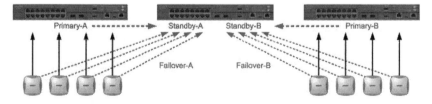

Active/Active

There is often a need to provide 100 percent failover, but the network designers do not want to dedicate a controller for the sole function of providing redundancy. By configuring an *active/active* (or *50/50*) *redundancy model*, each controller supports APs up to 50 percent of its hardware capacity, making the remaining 50 percent available for failover for another controller. The second controller would be configured in a similar fashion. This method has two distinct advantages. First, no controller is overloaded, and second, no controller is sitting idle simply waiting for another to fail.

In an active/active model, two controllers are configured with each one supporting APs and users, as illustrated in Figure 10.14. The figure shows the left controller acting as Primary-A, supporting the APs below it along with the users connected to those APs. If Primary-A fails, those APs and users would transition to the other controller, Standby-A, which is configured as its failover controller.

At the same time, the controller on the right is acting as Primary-B, supporting the APs above it along with the users connected to those APs. If Primary-B fails, those APs and users would transition to the other controller, Standby-B, which is configured as its failover controller.

In an active/active environment, it is typical to try to evenly distribute the number of APs and users between the two controllers. This is not mandatory, as long as either controller can support the total number of APs and users from both of the controllers. In the event of a controller failure, only half of the users and APs are moving to the failover controller.

FIGURE 10.14
Active/active

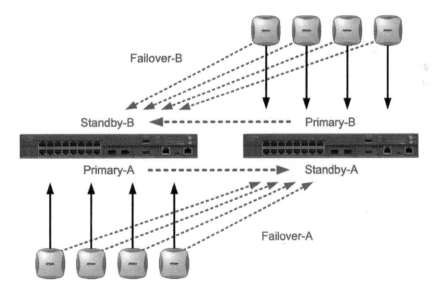

AP Redundancy Using VRRP

One of the key components of VRRP is the virtual IP (VIP) address. With VRRP, two controllers are configured to share a VIP. The VIP resides on whichever controller is functioning as the active controller. If the active controller fails, the standby controller takes over the active role, along with the VIP address.

VRRP can be used to provide AP failover. When an AP boots, it tells the controller what group the AP belongs to. The controller then takes the AP group configuration information and downloads it to the AP. One of the downloaded values, local management switch IP (LMS-IP), tells the AP the IP address of the controller with which the AP should communicate and terminate its GRE tunnel. To provide for AP redundancy, the LMS-IP address can be set to the VIP address. In this scenario, the AP will terminate its GRE tunnel to the controller operating as the active controller. If the active controller fails, the VIP will move to the other controller and the AP will establish a GRE tunnel to the VIP on the new active controller.

Backup LMS-IP

Previously I mentioned that a primary goal of redundancy is to keep APs operating and to provide access to the users. VRRP is one method of providing AP failover, which was described earlier in this chapter. In this section, you will learn about backup LMS-IP.

Unlike VRRP, whose controllers must reside on the same layer 2 network, when configuring backup LMS-IP, the controllers do not have to reside on the same layer 2 network, which can provide more flexibility for the network.

When an AP boots, it tells the controller what group the AP belongs to. The controller then takes the AP group configuration information and downloads it to the AP. One of the downloaded values, local management switch IP (LMS-IP), tells the AP the IP address of the controller with which the AP should communicate and terminate its GRE tunnel. If the AP cannot communicate with the controller, the AP will repeatedly go through a rebootstrap and reboot process, attempting to establish a GRE tunnel.

Backup LMS-IP is an additional value that the AP can be given as part of its downloaded configuration. Backup LMS-IP provides the AP with an alternate controller to establish a GRE with if it is unable to establish one with the primary controller specified by the LMS-IP, or if the AP loses connection with the LMS-IP controller.

One of the concerns or considerations when the AP connects to the backup LMS-IP is what the AP does when the LMS-IP controller is back online. There are two LMS settings that are used to determine this: lms-preemption and lms-hold-down-period. If the AP is able to reestablish communications with the LMS-IP controller, lms-preemption specifies whether you want the AP to automatically return to the LMS-IP controller or stay connected to the backup LMS-IP controller.

One issue that needs to be addressed when enabling preemption is *when* to have the AP return to the LMS-IP controller. When an AP is connected to the backup controller, you typically want it to transition back to the primary controller when it is available; however, if the primary controller comes back online temporarily, you do not want the AP transitioning back to it. You want to make sure that whatever problem occurred to cause the failover has been fixed, and that the primary controller will remain up and running before allowing the AP to reconnect to it. The lms-hold-down-period specifies how many seconds the LMS-IP controller must be available before the AP can transition back to it.

LMS-IP and backup LMS-IP are configured as parts of an AP system profile, and the AP system profile is assigned to an AP group. The following CLI commands set the LMS-IP and backup LMS-IP addresses. Preemption is enabled with a 600-second hold-down period.

```
(config) #ap-group building1
(AP group "building1") #ap system-profile "building1-ap-sys-profile"
(AP system profile "building1-ap-sys-profile") #lms-ip 10.1.50.100
(AP system profile "building1-ap-sys-profile") #bkup-lms-ip 10.1.70.100
(AP system profile "building1-ap-sys-profile") #lms-preemption
(AP system profile "building1-ap-sys-profile") #lms-hold-down-period 600
```

These settings can also be made using the WebUI. Figure 10.15 shows the menu where these settings can be made. **Configuration** ➢ **WIRELESS** ➢ **AP Configuration** will bring you to the menu where you can select the AP group. After selecting the AP group, you need to click on AP to configure the AP system profile.

FIGURE 10.15
LMS settings

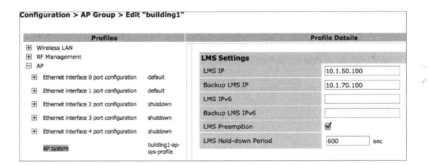

AP Fast Failover

One of the problems with using VRRP or LMS/backup LMS is that there is a delay when the APs connect to the failover controller. With either of these methods, after an AP misses eight one-second heartbeats, the AP performs a rebootstrap before connecting to the failover controller. The rebootstrap process requires the AP to disconnect clients, purge its existing configuration, establish a connection to the failover controller, and download its configuration from the failover controller. During this process, the AP radios are shut down. Individually, on an AP-by-AP basis, this slightly more than eight-second failover is not bad for general network use. However, with wireless networking being deployed as a mission-critical technology, this failover time is too long. Additionally, this process slows down when multiple APs communicate with the failover controller, while all the APs try to simultaneously establish a connection and download their configuration. On large networks, the eight-second failover can extend to several minutes while all of the APs connect with the failover controller.

In order to address the AP failover delay that was inherent with the APs performing a rebootstrap upon failover, Aruba developed a new method known as *AP Fast Failover*, also known as *High Availability (HA)*.

What AP Fast Failover does is provide a new, faster method for the APs to transition from their primary controller to their standby controller. One of the reasons this is possible is that it allows the AP to establish two GRE tunnels: one tunnel to the primary controller and a second tunnel to the standby controller. Because the AP establishes tunnels to both controllers, when the AP fails over to the second controller, it does not need to perform a rebootstrap. With AP Fast Failover, when the AP misses its eight one-second heartbeats, the AP simply activates the backup GRE to the standby controller.

AP Fast Failover also added an even faster method of AP failover, using an optional technique known as *inter-controller heartbeat*. In the past, it was the AP that maintained heartbeats with the primary controller. As I just mentioned, when an AP experienced eight lost heartbeats, the AP would initiate the transition to the failover controller. With AP Fast Failover and inter-controller heartbeat, it is the backup controller that monitors the availability status of the primary controller, not the AP. When the standby controller recognizes that the primary controller is unreachable for five heartbeats (500 milliseconds), the standby controller notifies the AP to failover. This failover should take less than one second, regardless of the number of APs involved.

Let us now take a more detailed look at the failover process using inter-controller heartbeats, as illustrated in Figure 10.16. In this scenario, realize that the roles of the primary and backup controllers are from the perspective of the AP. The AP will connect to its primary controller if it is available, and switch to its standby controller if the primary is no longer available.

In the first step of the process, the AP establishes its GRE tunnel with the primary controller defined by the LMS-IP parameter. The LMS-IP–specified controller validates the AP Fast Failover settings, and in Step 2, it notifies the AP that AP Fast Failover is enabled. The controller will also tell the AP which standby controller it is using.

The identity of the standby controller is obtained from the HA profile. In the third step, the AP then says hello to the standby controller and establishes its standby GRE tunnel. The standby controller then identifies the primary controller, along with responding hello to the AP.

Now that the AP has established GRE tunnels to both the primary and standby controllers, the standby controller begins sending heartbeats to the primary controller every 100 ms, by default. If the standby controller receives a heartbeat response, it will reset its heartbeat count back to zero. Every time a heartbeat is sent, the heartbeat count is incremented. If a response is not received, the heartbeat count is not reset to zero. This is illustrated in Steps 5 through 11 in Figure 10.16.

When the standby controller does not receive responses to five sequential heartbeats, it initiates the fast failover process. The standby controller sends an AP failover request message to the AP, as shown in Step 12. The AP then deauthenticates all clients and changes the state of the standby GRE to active. The AP also sends an AP failover response message, as shown in Step 13. At this time, the AP is active on the standby controller. The only thing left is for the clients to reauthenticate to the AP.

FIGURE 10.16
AP Fast Failover

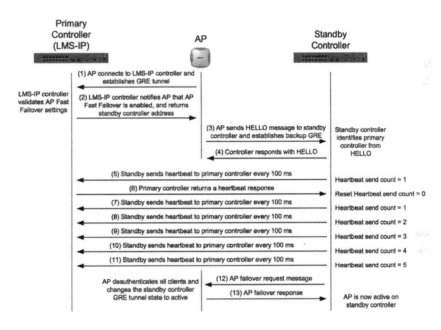

Now that you have read about how AP Fast Failover works, let us take a look at how to configure it. During its configuration you will define a high availability group profile on the master controller, and in that profile you will specify the controllers that are part of the AP Fast Failover environment. You can also enable the inter-controller heartbeat between the standby and primary controllers. The following CLI commands will create and configure the HA group profile:

```
(config) #ha group-profile ha-70-80-90
(HA group information "ha-70-80-90") #controller 10.1.70.100 role dual
(HA group information "ha-70-80-90") #controller 10.1.80.100 role dual
(HA group information "ha-70-80-90") #controller 10.1.90.100 role dual
(HA group information "ha-70-80-90") #heartbeat
```

After you have configured the HA group profile, you then need to go to each controller and add the controller to the group using the following CLI command:

```
(config) #ha group-membership ha-70-80-90
```

Client State Synchronization

AP Fast Failover does a very good job of reducing the time it takes for an AP to fail over to a backup controller. After the AP failover, any clients that were connected to the AP will need to associate and authenticate to the AP again. If 802.1X/EAP is deployed, each of these clients will need to perform a full 802.1X/EAP authentication. If a large number of APs are failing over from the primary controller to the backup controller, there will likely be a large number of clients reauthenticating, at the same time. Thus, reauthentication of these clients may be delayed, depending upon the number of clients and the ability of the authentication server to process all of the authentication requests.

Client state sync allows the clients to reconnect to the APs and reauthenticate faster using only a four-way key exchange, instead of a full reauthentication. In order to achieve this, client state sync uses IPsec to securely synchronize the client role, VLAN, and pairwise master key ID (PMKID) of each client between the active and the standby controllers.

When a client reassociates to the AP, it includes a list of PMKIDs in its reassociation request. If the standby controller has a PMK security association (PMKSA) identified by one of the PMKIDs, then the EAP authentication can be skipped.

Configuring client state sync is quite simple, requiring just two additional commands be added to the ha group-profile. The state-sync command enables client state sync, but it also requires the command pre-shared-key.

The following CLI commands will configure AP Fast Failover and client state sync on the master controller:

```
(config) #ha group-profile ha-70-80-90
(HA group information " ha-70-80-90") #controller 10.1.70.100 role dual
(HA group information " ha-70-80-90") #controller 10.1.80.100 role dual
(HA group information " ha-70-80-90") #controller 10.1.90.100 role dual
(HA group information " ha-70-80-90") #heartbeat
(HA group information " ha-70-80-90") #state-sync
Note: State-sync will not be enabled until pre-shared-key is configured

(HA group information " ha-70-80-90") #pre-shared-key aruba123
```

To enable AP Fast Failover and client state sync, the following CLI command needs to be executed on all three of the controllers (10.1.70.100, 10.1.80.100, and 10.1.90.100):

```
(config) #ha group-membership ha-70-80-90
```

Also note that some basic network design criteria must be met by both the active and standby controllers. Because the goal with client state synchronization is to facilitate the cleanest possible failover experience for the client, the controllers must support the same VLANs from the same DHCP servers. Otherwise, upon failover, the client will have to obtain a new IP address, which would disrupt its network connection.

FAULT TOLERANCE

If AP Fast Failover is enabled, the show ap database command displays not only the IP address of the controller that the AP is connected to (switch IP), but also the IP address of the standby controller (standby IP).

The following CLI output is from the 10.1.70.100 controller. This output shows that one AP is terminating its GRE tunnels to this controller as its primary controller, and three APs are terminating to this controller as their standby controller. The Flags column indicates which of the APs have standby connections.

```
(config) #show ap database

AP Database
-----------

Name          Group          AP Type    IP Address      Status          
----          -----          -------    ----------      ------          
AP115-70-1    controller70   115        10.1.90.151     Up 1h:35m:5s    
AP135-80-1    controller80   135        10.1.90.150     Up 1h:33m:2s    
AP135-80-2    controller80   135        10.1.90.153     Up 1h:33m:1s    
AP135-80-3    controller80   135        10.1.80.150     Up 1h:33m:1s    


 Flags   Switch IP      Standby IP
 -----   ---------      ----------
         10.1.70.100    10.1.80.100
 S       10.1.80.100    10.1.70.100
 S       10.1.80.100    10.1.70.100
 S       10.1.80.100    10.1.70.100

Flags: U=Unprovisioned; N=Duplicate name; G=No such group; L=Unlicensed
       I=Inactive; D=Dirty or no config; E=Regulatory Domain Mismatch
       X=Maintenance Mode; P=PPPoE AP; B=Built-in AP; s=LACP striping
       R=Remote AP; R-=Remote AP requires Auth; C=Cellular RAP;
       c=CERT-based RAP; 1=802.1x authenticated AP; 2=Using IKE version 2
       u=Custom-Cert RAP; S=Standby-mode AP; J=USB cert at AP
       i=Indoor; o=Outdoor
       M=Mesh node; Y=Mesh Recovery

Total APs:4
```

Oversubscription

Oversubscription is part of AP Fast Failover, and is a selectable option that is disabled by default. Oversubscription is not supported on some of the smaller controller hardware platforms, and the amount of oversubscription supported may differ between hardware platforms.

Oversubscription allows a controller to terminate more GRE tunnels than the controller supports, providing that the additional GRE tunnels are backup tunnels. As an example, let us make believe that you have three controllers (Controllers A, B, and C). In this example, each controller has an AP hardware limit of 64 APs, and each controller currently has 32 APs connected to it.

To support AP Fast Failover, you decide to use Controller C to provide N:1 active/standby support for Controllers A and B. This configuration requires that Controller C support 96 GRE tunnels: 32 GRE tunnels for its APs, 32 standby GRE tunnels for Controller A APs, and 32 standby GRE tunnels for Controller B APs. Oversubscription allows the controller to terminate more GRE tunnels than the hardware is able to support (or the current license limit allows), providing the additional GRE tunnels are standby tunnels. Without oversubscription this would not be possible.

In this example, if Controller A or B failed, Controller C would be able to provide failover since its hardware limit of 64 APs would not be exceeded by the additional 32 APs that failed over.

Controller C would not be able to provide failover if both Controllers A and B failed, since the additional 64 APs (on top of Controller C's own 32 APs) would exceed the controller's hardware limit.

Oversubscription can easily be enabled using the following CLI commands:

```
(config) #ha group-profile HA-70-80-90
(HA group information "HA-70-80-90") #over-subscription
```

Master Controller Redundancy

Master controller redundancy is different than the other failover methods. The primary goal of all of the other methods is to keep the APs operating and providing continuous access for the clients connected to them.

The master controller has a slightly different architecture than the local controllers. This prevents the local controllers from being able to back up the master controller, or even be promoted or converted to a master controller. If the master controller becomes unreachable, the following is a list of some of the functions that would be affected:

- Controller configuration: Since the master controller is where global configurations are made, you would not be able to make changes to the network.

- AP startup: Although APs do not have to communicate with the master controller when they boot, DHCP and DNS settings typically point APs to the master controller as their boot controller.

- WIDS/WIPS: Wireless intrusion detection and protection analysis is performed on the master controller, so rogue identification and containment could not be performed.

- Guest login: By default, the master controller maintains the internal database, which is commonly used for guest login. Guests would not be able to log in if the master controller was unreachable.
- Whitelist and blacklist functions
- Centralized license functionality

Master Redundancy Configuration

Master redundancy is provided using an active/standby design, sometimes also known as a *hot standby*. The only function of the standby master is to provide a hot replacement for the active master controller.

The standby master will periodically receive updates from the active master, and then patiently wait for the active master to someday fail so it can become the active master. I often explain to people that logically, you have one master controller, but with two physical controllers: one in active mode and one in standby mode.

Building master redundancy is a straightforward three step process. This process assumes that you already have a master controller built and are adding redundancy.

1. The first step of configuring master redundancy is to build a second master controller. master redundancy can only be performed using VRRP and between two master controllers. VRRP requires that the standby master and primary master share a VLAN. Since this new controller is going to be a backup controller, most of the configuration from the primary controller will be copied to the standby. In Chapter 4, you learned about the steps for initially configuring a controller.

2. The second step is to configure VRRP. This was explained earlier in this chapter. Once VRRP is configured and a virtual IP (VIP) address is defined, all references to the master controller will now be directed to the VIP. Both controllers will still retain their individual IP addresses; however, whichever controller is functioning as the primary master controller can also be contacted using the VIP address.

3. The final step to configure master redundancy is to configure database synchronization between the primary master and the standby master. There are databases on the master controller that do not exist on local controllers, which is one of the key reasons a local controller cannot act as a backup for a master controller, or be able to be promoted to a master controller. These databases need to be synchronized between the primary master and the standby master. By default, when master redundancy is enabled, the synchronization period is every 60 minutes, which should be acceptable for most network environments. If needed, the time can be

reduced (it is not recommended to go below 20 minutes). You can also manually synchronize the database if you want recent changes to be synchronized sooner.

Let us assume that the primary master controller and the standby master controller are not configured with VRRP yet, but are both up and running and can communicate with each other on VLAN 50. The following CLI commands will configure VRRP on the primary master controller (10.1.50.101), with the virtual router ID (VRID) of 50, a virtual IP (VIP) address of 10.1.50.100, and a priority of 200. These commands are similar to what was shown earlier in this chapter. Some of the WebUI steps that are defined earlier in this chapter are not listed in this section.

```
(config) #vrrp 50
(config-vrrp)#authentication aruba123
(config-vrrp)#description "Primary"
(config-vrrp)#ip address 10.1.50.100
vrrp is in shutdown state

(config-vrrp)#priority 200
(config-vrrp)#vlan 50
vrrp is in shutdown state
```

After configuring VRRP on the primary master controller, you also need to configure it on the standby controller. The following CLI commands will configure VRRP on the standby master controller (10.1.50.102), with the VRID of 50, virtual IP (VIP) address of 10.1.50.100, and a priority of 100:

```
(config) #vrrp 50
(config-vrrp)#authentication aruba123
(config-vrrp)#description "Standby"
(config-vrrp)#ip address 10.1.50.100
vrrp is in shutdown state

(config-vrrp)#priority 100
(config-vrrp)#vlan 50
vrrp is in shutdown state
```

Since master redundancy is being configured, in addition to the initial VRRP setup, database synchronization also need to be enabled. Before configuring the primary master controller to synchronize its database with the backup master, I like to first verify that the primary master can properly establish itself in its VRRP role. Verifying this can help prevent the new backup master from erasing the configuration on the primary master.

The no shutdown command is used to enable VRRP, as shown in the following CLI commands. The output of the show vrrp command shows that VRRP is running and that the controller is operating as the VRRP master.

```
(config)#vrrp 50
(config-vrrp)#no shutdown

#show vrrp
Virtual Router 50:
    Description Primary
    Admin State UP, VR State MASTER
    IP Address 10.1.50.100, MAC Address 00:00:5e:00:01:32, vlan 50
    Priority 200, Advertisement 1 sec, Preemption Disable Delay 0
    Auth type PASSWORD, Auth data: ********
    tracking is not enabled
```

The no shutdown command needs to be run on the standby master, too. The following CLI commands were executed on the backup master controller to enable VRRP and show its status. The output shows that VRRP is up and operating as the backup (standby), with the virtual IP address of 10.1.50.100.

```
(config)#vrrp 50
(config-vrrp)#no shutdown

#show vrrp

Virtual Router 50:
    Description Standby
    Admin State UP, VR State BACKUP
    IP Address 10.1.50.100, MAC Address 00:00:5e:00:01:32, vlan 50
    Priority 100, Advertisement 1 sec, Preemption Disable Delay 0
    Auth type PASSWORD, Auth data: ********
    tracking is not enabled
```

After you have verified that the two controllers have established VRRP with their proper roles, you can proceed with configuring database synchronization.

The following CLI commands would be configured on the primary master controller. These commands define a database synchronization period of every 60 minutes, and configures synchronization of its databases with its peer (10.1.50.102) using an IPsec key of aruba123. The master-vrrp value needs to match the VRID, which in this example is 50.

```
(config) #database synchronize period 60
(config) #master-redundancy
(config-master-redundancy)#master-vrrp 50
(config-master-redundancy)#peer-ip-address 10.1.50.102 ipsec aruba123
```

These same commands need to be configured on the standby master controller. The only difference is the standby master controller will specify the primary master controller as its peer. The following CLI commands will define a database synchronization period of every 60 minutes, and configure synchronization of its databases with its peer (10.1.50.101) using an IPsec key of aruba123, with the VRID of 50. Since this is the standby controller, it will be receiving database updates from the primary controller.

```
(config) #database synchronize period 60
(config) #master-redundancy
(config-master-redundancy)#master-vrrp 50
(config-master-redundancy)#peer-ip-address 10.1.50.101 ipsec aruba123
```

Configuration of the database synchronization and master redundancy settings can also be performed by going to **Configuration ➢ ADVANCED SERVICES ➢ Redundancy**.

Figure 10.17 shows the Database Synchronization Parameters with database synchronization enabled with a period of every 60 minutes. The Master Redundancy settings show the VRID of 50 and point to the peer IP address of the standby master controller, 10.1.50.102. These settings must also be configured on the standby master controller. The only difference is the standby master controller will point to the peer IP address of the primary master controller, 10.1.50.101.

FIGURE 10.17 Master redundancy

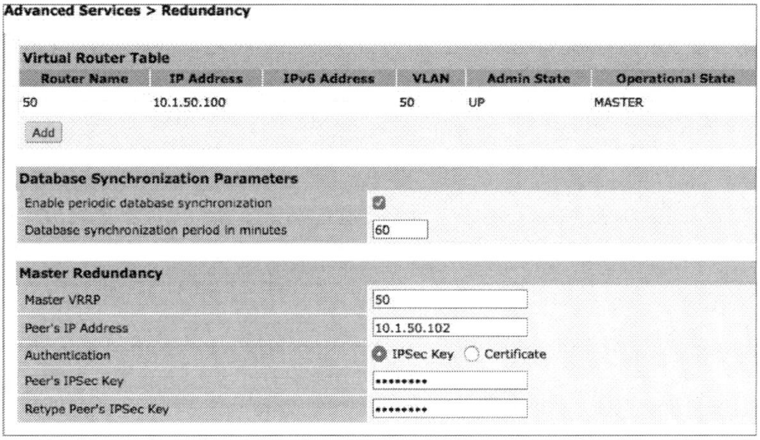

Earlier in this chapter, I recommended that you build VRRP on both controllers first, and then enable it first on the primary controller before enabling it on the standby controller. The show vrrp and show database synchronize CLI commands indicate that VRRP is configured, but not yet enabled.

```
(config) #show vrrp

Virtual Router 50:
    Description Primary
    Admin State DOWN, VR State INIT
    IP Address 10.1.50.100, MAC Address 00:00:5e:00:01:32, vlan 50
    Priority 200, Advertisement 1 sec, Preemption Disable Delay 0
```

```
        Auth type PASSWORD, Auth data: ********
        tracking is not enabled

(config) #show database synchronize

Last synchronization time: Not synchronized since last reboot

Periodic synchronization is enabled and runs every 60 minutes
Synchronization doesn't include Captive Portal Custom data
```

It is especially important to enable VRRP on the primary master before enabling it on the standby master. When VRRP is enabled, you want the configuration on the primary master pushed to the standby master. If you accidentally enable VRRP on the standby master first, it is likely that the configuration on the standby master will overwrite most of the configuration on the primary master. You will not be happy if this happens.

The `no shutdown` command is used to enable VRRP, as shown in the following CLI commands:

```
(config) #vrrp 50
(config-vrrp) #no shutdown
This configuration change requires a reboot.
 PLEASE SAVE THE CONFIGURATION AND REBOOT.

(config) #show vrrp

Virtual Router 50:
    Description Primary
    Admin State UP, VR State MASTER
    IP Address 10.1.50.100, MAC Address 00:00:5e:00:01:32, vlan 50
    Priority 200, Advertisement 1 sec, Preemption Disable Delay 0
    Auth type PASSWORD, Auth data: ********
    tracking is not enabled
```

The `show vrrp` command displays that VRRP is running. After you enable VRRP on the primary master controller and verify that VRRP is up and that the VRRP state is Master, you can then go to the standby master controller and enable VRRP on it by also issuing the `no shutdown` command.

Master Redundancy Verification

Unfortunately, I have seen multiple production networks where master redundancy was not properly configured. It is a shame, because neither the configuration nor the verification of master redundancy is very difficult. Typically, the problem has been that VRRP has been configured, but database synchronization and master redundancy have not.

Verification of master redundancy can be performed using the following five simple commands:

1. `encrypt disable`
2. `show vrrp`
3. `show master-redundancy`
4. `show database synchronize`
5. `database synchronize`

The first command is used to unhide the VRRP password in the rest of the commands. This will allow you to compare the results on each controller and ensure they match. This command only applies to your current CLI session and does not become permanently set on the controller. Therefore, the command must be executed each time you log on and want to use it. (In the CLI examples in this section, the `encrypt disable` command was not executed prior to issuing the other commands; therefore, all of the passwords and preshared keys are not displayed.)

The second command, `show vrrp`, will verify that the two master controllers are communicating with each other and are sharing a virtual IP address, and it will identify whether the controller is operating as the primary (master) or standby (backup) master controller. The following CLI command was executed on the primary master controller. The output shows that VRRP is up and operating as the master (primary), with the virtual IP address of 10.1.50.100.

```
#show vrrp

Virtual Router 50:
    Description Primary
    Admin State UP, VR State MASTER
    IP Address 10.1.50.100, MAC Address 00:00:5e:00:01:32, vlan 50
    Priority 200, Advertisement 1 sec, Preemption Disable Delay 0
    Auth type PASSWORD, Auth data: ********
    tracking is not enabled
```

The following CLI command was executed on the standby master controller. The output shows that VRRP is up and operating as the backup (standby), with the virtual IP address of 10.1.50.100.

```
#show vrrp

Virtual Router 50:
    Description Standby
    Admin State UP, VR State BACKUP
    IP Address 10.1.50.100, MAC Address 00:00:5e:00:01:32, vlan 50
    Priority 100, Advertisement 1 sec, Preemption Disable Delay 0
    Auth type PASSWORD, Auth data: ********
    tracking is not enabled
```

The third command, show master-redundancy, is like the show vrrp command, displaying the configuration and status of the master redundancy.

The following CLI command was executed on the primary master controller. The output shows the controller is operating as the primary master, and the IP address of the backup controller is 10.1.50.102.

```
#show master-redundancy
Master redundancy configuration:
    VRRP Id 50 current state is MASTER
    Peer's IP Address is 10.1.50.102
    Peer's IPSEC Key is ********
```

The fourth verification command, show database synchronize, will show if the databases have been synchronized from the primary master controller to the standby master controller. The following CLI command was performed on the primary master controller. It displays when it was last synchronized and that this database was synchronized to the other controller, 10.1.50.102, and was successful. It displays the sizes of the different databases, how long it took to synchronize, how many synchronization attempts have been made, and how many have failed.

```
#show database synchronize

Last synchronization time: Mon Aug 31 22:25:40 2015
To Master Switch at 10.1.50.102:  succeeded
WMS Database backup file size: 29828 bytes
Local User Database backup file size: 14051 bytes
CPSec Database backup file size: 3248 bytes
Synchronization took 1 second

6 synchronization attempted
0 synchronization have failed

Periodic synchronization is enabled and runs every 60 minutes
Synchronization doesn't include Captive Portal Custom data
```

The following CLI command was performed on the standby master controller. This shows that the database on this controller was synchronized from the primary master, 10.1.50.101.

```
#show database synchronize

Last synchronization time: Mon Aug 31 22:25:40 2015
From Master Switch at 10.1.50.101:  succeeded
WMS Database backup file size: 29828 bytes
Local User Database backup file size: 14051 bytes
CPSec Database backup file size: 3248 bytes
Synchronization took 1 second
```

```
6 synchronization attempted
0 synchronization have failed

Periodic synchronization is enabled and runs every 60 minutes
Synchronization doesn't include Captive Portal Custom data
```

The final verification command does not actually do any verification, but is helpful with the master controller redundancy process. The command `database synchronize` will manually perform a database synchronization. This command must be run from the primary master controller. If you have made many changes to the primary master controller, this command is useful to force database synchronization instead of waiting for scheduled synchronization to occur. It is useful to run this command after configuring and enabling master redundancy; otherwise, you would need to wait for the scheduled synchronization to occur.

This `database synchronize` command does not generate any output on the screen; it simply starts the database synchronization process. After executing this command, you should run the `show database synchronize` command to verify that the synchronization occurred along with the time that it occurred. The following CLI output indicates that the `show database synchronize` command was run along with the status of the command. If you receive this message, simply wait a short period of time and run the command again.

```
#show database synchronize

Tue Sep 01 09:57:44.742 2015


Synchronizing database now... Please wait.
Current state is: "SENDING LOCAL USER DATABASE BACKUP TO STANDBY".
```

Redundancy Comparison

With so many different redundancy models and methods, a summary or comparison is in order.

To begin, let us first look at master controller redundancy. master redundancy is very straightforward. Build two master controllers, connect them to the same layer 2 network, use VRRP to provide redundancy between the primary master and the backup master, and point local controllers to the VIP address. The primary and backup masters share a virtual IP (VIP) address and you need to make sure that database synchronization is also configured. APs will boot and be able to connect to either controller, depending upon which controller was assigned the VIP.

If an AP was connected to the primary master and the primary master failed, the VIP of the VRRP would shift to the backup controller, and the AP would connect to the backup master after eight lost GRE heartbeats. Note that the AP would still be connecting to the same LMS-IP but would have to reestablish its GRE tunnels to the new controller.

Since both the primary and backup controllers are on the same layer 2 network, client devices should be able to retain their IP addresses, although firewall states will be dropped.

VRRP can be configured between two local controllers to provide primary and backup support for APs. The two controllers would be connected to the same layer 2 network and use VRRP to share a VIP. APs would boot and connect to the controller that was assigned the VIP, and failover would be the same as described above for master/standby master. If the primary controller failed, the VIP address shifts to the backup controller and the APs rebootstrap, connecting once again to the VIP after the heartbeats timeout. Since both controllers are on the same layer 2 network, client devices should be able to retain their IP addresses, although firewall states will be dropped.

If configured, LMS-IP and backup LMS-IP allows the AP to initially connect to its primary controller (LMS-IP), and if the primary controller is unavailable, the AP can then connect to its backup controller (backup LMS-IP). Also, if an AP is already connected to the primary controller (LMS-IP), and that controller goes down, the AP can switch to the backup controller (backup LMS-IP) after it incurs eight lost GRE heartbeats. LMS-IP and backup LMS-IP addresses are often on different networks. This means that the client would wind up with a new IP address and its firewall states will also be dropped.

AP Fast Failover (HA) is not used by the AP to establish its initial connection to a controller. HA is solely used to provide fast failover for the AP from one controller to another in the event that the AP's primary controller failed. HA should be used to failover an AP between controllers on the same layer 2 network. This provides the client with the ability to quickly transition between controllers while maintaining its IP address, although transition between two controllers means that the client's firewall states would be dropped.

Multiple redundancy methods can be deployed together to provide better network access. As an example, LMS-IP and backup LMS-IP can be used to ensure that an AP can discover and connect to a controller upon bootup, while HA can allow the AP to quickly transition to a standby controller in the event of a controller failure. Combining these two methods allows APs to failover within the datacenter (HA group) and fail between datacenters (backup LMS-IP).

Currently, if an AP boots and attempts to communicate with the LMS-IP controller and the LMS-IP controller is unavailable, the AP will attempt to communicate with the backup LMS-IP controller. If the AP successfully connects to the backup LMS-IP controller, HA will not be enabled. HA will only be enabled when the AP connects to the LMS-IP controller.

Centralized Licensing

It was a wonderful day when centralized licensing was added to ArubaOS. Centralized licensing makes it much easier to support multicontroller networks. If centralized licensing is enabled, the master controller operates as the licensing server. If master redundancy is enabled and the primary controller fails, the backup controller will take over as the primary controller and as the licensing server.

Each license must be activated for a specific controller's serial number. When you purchase a license, you receive a certificate ID. You then need to log on to the licensing server (which is a server that is reachable on the Internet) to activate that certificate. After you log on to the licensing server, you need to activate the certificate ID by linking it to a controller's serial number. After you do this, you will receive a license key, which you will add to the controller to enable the license.

The license add CLI command, followed by the license key, will enable the license on the controller that it is activated with.

Prior to centralized licensing, licenses had to be added to each controller. With centralized licensing, licenses can be added to any controller, consolidated on the license master, and then distributed and made available to all controllers. Except for adding the license to a controller, the rest of the process is performed automatically by centralized licensing.

Centralized licensing can distribute the following licenses:

- AP: total access points supported
- PEF-NG: policy enforcement firewall
- RFProtect: wireless intrusion detection/protection
- xSEC: advanced security
- ACR: Suite B encryption

If any of these licenses, such as PEF-NG, are used anywhere on the network, it is necessary to install at least one license for that feature directly on the master controller. In this example, at least one PEF-NG license would need to be activated for the master controller and then installed on it. Adding licenses directly to the master controller adds the necessary features and commands to the master controller to configure the network. If you are installing a new network, you should simply activate all of the license certificates with the serial number of the master controller.

Enabling centralized licensing is extremely easy on a master/local network. From the master controller, simply go into the license profile and then enable centralized licensing. The following CLI output shows the commands needed to enable centralized licensing:

```
(config) #license profile
(License provisioning profile) #centralized-licensing-enable
```

This task could also be performed by navigating to **Configuration ➢ NETWORK ➢ Controller ➢ Centralized Licenses ➢ Configuration.**

When centralized licensing is enabled, licenses that are installed on any of the controllers are sent to the licensing server. The licensing server adds these licenses to the server's licensing table. The licensing server then shares this central pool of available licenses with each of the controllers. Whenever an AP connects to a controller, the controller will use a license from the available pool and update the licensing master that it has done so. If an AP license is issued, PEF and RFP licenses will also be taken from the pool.

The following CLI command can only be executed on the centralized license server. It shows the quantity of licenses that each controller contributed, followed by an aggregate list of the licenses in the central pool.

```
#show license aggregate
Aggregate License Table
-----------------------
Hostname   IP Address   AP  PEF RF Protect xSec Module ACR WebCC Last update
--------   ----------   --- --- ---------- ----------- --- ----- -----------
7010-50a   10.1.50.101  16  16  16         0           0   32    10
7005-70    10.1.70.100  16  16  16         0           0   0     26
7010-50b   10.1.50.102  16  16  16         0           0   0     10
7005-80    10.1.80.100  0   0   0          0           0   0     28

Total AP License Count           :48
Total PEF License Count          :48
Total RF Protect License Count   :48
Total XSEC License Count         :0
Total ACR License Count          :0
Total WebCC License Count        :32
```

Each controller has a maximum supported device count, based on the hardware performance of the controller. A controller cannot exceed its hardware license limit, even if additional licenses are available.

The following CLI command displays the hardware limits of a controller—in this example, a 7005 controller.

```
#show license platform-limits

License Platform Limits
-----------------------
Limit  Value
-----  -----
16     Access Points
16     Remote Access Points
16     Ortronics Access Points
32     Outdoor Mesh Access Points
16     Wireless Intrusion Protection Module
4096   VPN Service Module
```

```
4096    xSec Users
32      Indoor Mesh Access Points
16      120abg Upgrade
16      121abg Upgrade
16      124abg Upgrade
16      125abg Upgrade
16      Policy Enforcement Firewall Module
4096    Advanced Cryptography
0       SAP
16      WebCC
16      Beta AP
```

If the master controller fails, and you do not have a backup master controller, the local controllers will retain the shared license information for up to 30 days without communicating with the centralized license server. There are different scenarios as to what happens with the licenses after 30 days; however the proper scenario is to fix the master controller problem before the 30 days has occurred.

Centralized licensing information could also be displayed from the following WebUI menu: **Configuration ➢ NETWORK ➢ Controller ➢ Centralized Licenses ➢ Information**.

Centralized Upgrade

Centralized upgrade was added with ArubaOS 6.3, and allows you to upgrade the master controller. Through the master controller, it also allows you to centrally coordinate upgrading the operating system on the local controllers and the standby master controller (if you have master redundancy configured). The following are the logical steps needed to perform a centralized upgrade. All of the controller-oriented tasks are performed solely on the master controller. A more detailed explanation of the tasks and commands used to accomplish the centralized upgrade will be provided after this list.

1. Configure a TFTP, FTP, or SCP server.
2. Download the new OS file from the Aruba support website, and copy it to the server. The filename must not be changed.
3. Manually upgrade and reboot the master controller with the new OS.
4. Set the upgrade configuration parameters. These will define the download server (your TFTP, FTP, or SCP server), communications settings, and the file parameters to be used as the centralized upgrade source for all of the controllers.
5. Select the controllers that you want to upgrade.
6. Verify the image files. This will verify that the download server contains valid copies of the OS files needed to upgrade the different models of controllers that you will be upgrading

The first step to performing a centralized upgrade is to configure a TFTP, FTP, or SCP server. This task will not be covered in this book, but be aware that there are many options for each of these server types, depending on the operating system platform you plan to run it on. Every controller in your master/local group must also be able to communicate with this server.

Once the server is built, your second task is to place the ArubaOS files on the server. The filename needs to be similar to the following name format: ArubaOS_70xx_6.4.3.3_50954. This is typically the name format of the files in the ArubaOS download area of the support.arubanetworks.com website. The filename needs to match this naming convention, or the upgrade will not work, so do not rename the file.

You will need ArubaOS files for each of the hardware platforms you will be upgrading. So, if you will be upgrading multiple platforms, such as 7000 series controllers and 7200 series controllers, you need to place both files on the server.

The third step is to manually upgrade the master controller. The copy command was described in Chapter 3, "Aruba Controller and Software Overview," so I will skip the explanation and just stick to describing the task. The file can be copied using the copy command, which can be seen in the following CLI output. In this output, the command extends onto the second line since it was too long to fit on one line.

```
#copy ftp: 192.168.240.31 david /ftp-files/ArubaOS_70xx_6.4.2.7_50063 system:
partition 0
Password:********
Copying file:................................................................
........................
File copied successfully.
Saving file to flash:
................................................................
..................................
The system will boot from partition 0 during the next reboot.
```

This task could also be performed from **Maintenance ➢ CONTROLLER ➢ Image Management ➢ Master Configuration**.

Figure 10.18 shows the details to upgrade partition 0 using an FTP transfer. The file resides on the FTP server, 192.168.240.31, in the ftp-files folder. The FTP user account is david, and after the file is copied, the current controller configuration will be saved and the controller will automatically reboot. Remember to copy the upgrade files for all hardware platforms that you will be upgrading, and make sure that the versions and subversions of these files are the same. After the master controller is upgraded and reboots, confirm that the upgrade was successful by using the show switchinfo CLI command and verify that the controller is running the new version of ArubaOS.

FIGURE 10.18
ArubaOS upgrade

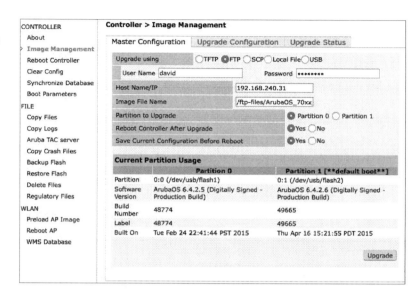

The fourth step is where the actual centralized upgrade configuration and procedure begins. The first task is to configure the upgrade profile. The following CLI output shows the commands to define the upgrade profile and then you use the show command to display the current settings. The upgrade profile defines the following parameters:

- Protocol used to download the ArubaOS file
- IP address of the download server
- Username and password used to communicate with the download server (if one is needed for the protocol being used)
- Relative path where the ArubaOS file resides on the download server
- Maximum number of controllers that can download from the server simultaneously
- Whether each controller will automatically reboot after the ArubaOS file is copied
- Whether the upgrade process is enabled or not. You can define the profile, but wait to enable it.

```
(config) #upgrade-profile
(Upgrade Profile) #protocol ftp
(Upgrade Profile) #serverip 192.168.240.31
(Upgrade Profile) #username david
(Upgrade Profile) #password aruba123
(Upgrade Profile) #filepath /ftp-files/
(Upgrade Profile) #max-downloads 2
(Upgrade Profile) #no auto-reboot
(Upgrade Profile) #upgrade-enable
(Upgrade Profile) #write mem
```

```
Saving Configuration...
Configuration Saved.

(Upgrade Profile) #show upgrade-profile
Upgrade Profile
---------------
Parameter                 Value
---------                 -----
Enable software upgrade   true
Max downloads             2
Reboot automatically      false
Protocol                  ftp
Server IP address         192.168.240.31
Username                  david
Password                  ********
File path                 /ftp-files/
```

As with most commands in a master/local controller environment, the upgrade profile is configured on the master controller. When the `write mem` command is used to save the changes on the master controller, the upgrade profile is copied to all of the local controllers along with the backup master controller (if one is configured).

The upgrade profile can also be configured from **Maintenance ➢ CONTROLLER ➢ Image Management ➢ Upgrade Configuration**, which is displayed in Figure 10.19.

FIGURE 10.19 Upgrade configuration

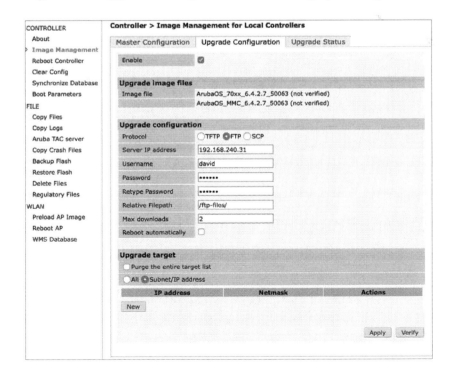

It is important to realize that with centralized upgrade, the master controller is not distributing the OS upgrade to the other controllers. The master controller is directing the other controllers to perform the OS upgrade, and directing the controllers where to download the upgrade file from. All of this information is defined in the upgrade profile.

After the upgrade profile is configured, you can type the show upgrade configuration command to check the configuration, as shown in the following CLI output. This command will also show a list of all of the image files that will be needed. In this example, there are two necessary image files: the first file will upgrade the 7000 series controllers, and the second file will upgrade the 3000 series controllers.

```
(config) #show upgrade configuration
Upgrade configuration
---------------------
Parameter              Value
---------              -----
Protocol               ftp
Server IP address      192.168.240.31
Username               david
Password               ******
File path              /ftp-files/
Max downloads          2
Reboot automatically   false
Image file             ArubaOS_70xx_6.4.2.7_50063 (not verified)
                       ArubaOS_MMC_6.4.2.7_50063 (not verified)

Upgrade target is not configured.
```

The fifth step in the process is to define the controllers that you want to upgrade. This may be all of your controllers, or it could be controllers on a specific subnet or individually defined by their IP addresses. The last line of the show upgrade configuration command, as displayed in the previous paragraph, shows a list of the target controllers that are configured. As displayed in the CLI output, no targets are currently configured.

To add a controller to the upgrade list, enter the upgrade target command, as shown in the following CLI output. Using this command, you can add networks, hosts, or all controllers. Note that this command is entered in exec mode, but not in config mode, since this is not actually making changes to the configuration file.

```
#upgrade target add net 10.1.90.0 255.255.255.0
#upgrade target add host 10.1.80.100
#upgrade target add all
```

After adding upgrade targets, make sure you use the show upgrade configuration command to verify your target controllers are correct. The upgrade target del command can be used to remove any target that you previously added. Also, the upgrade target purge command can remove all targets from the list. The following is the CLI output of the show upgrade configuration command after adding the upgrade targets discussed in the previous paragraph. These targets are actually redundant, since the add all statement includes all controllers. These three targets were added as examples, and would not be entered like this in a production network.

```
#show upgrade configuration
Upgrade configuration
---------------------
Parameter             Value
---------             -----
Protocol              ftp
Server IP address     192.168.240.31
Username              david
Password              ******
File path             /ftp-files/
Max downloads         2
Reboot automatically  false
Image file            ArubaOS_70xx_6.4.2.7_50063 (not verified)
                      ArubaOS_MMC_6.4.2.7_50063 (not verified)

Upgrade target
--------------
IP address    Netmask
----------    -------
10.1.90.0     255.255.255.0
10.1.80.100   255.255.255.255
0.0.0.0       0.0.0.0
```

It is now time to perform the sixth step of the centralized upgrade process, which is to verify that the upgrade files are available on the download server and notify the target controllers to begin upgrading. The show upgrade status command, shown in the following CLI output, displays a list of the controllers, along with their hostnames, types, model, version, and upgrade status. Notice that the upgrade images have not been verified yet.

```
#show upgrade status
All Controllers
---------------
IP Address    Hostname   Type     Model      Version         Upgrade Status
----------    --------   ----     -----      -------         --------------
10.1.50.101   7010-50a   master   Aruba7010  6.4.2.7_50063   N/A
10.1.40.100   3600-40    local    Aruba3600  6.4.2.6_49665   Waiting, image not
verified
10.1.50.102   7010-50b   standby  Aruba7010  6.4.2.6_49665   Waiting, image not
verified
10.1.70.100   7005-70    local    Aruba7005  6.4.2.6_49665   Waiting, image not
verified
```

```
10.1.80.100    7005-80    local    Aruba7005   6.4.2.6_49665   Waiting, image not
verified
10.1.90.100    7005-90    local    Aruba7005   6.4.2.6_49665   Waiting, image not
verified
```

To verify the image files and to begin the upgrade process, simply enter the upgrade verify command from the CLI interface, as shown in the following CLI output. Notice in this example that the ArubaOS file for the 7000 controllers was verified, but the ArubaOS file for the 3000 controllers could not be found.

```
#upgrade verify
WARNING: Members specified in upgrade target list will be upgraded
 and rebooted (if enabled in the upgrade profile). Do you want to proceed?
[y/n]: y
Verifying ArubaOS_70xx_6.4.2.7_50063 ...

Copying file:.......................................
File copied successfully.
Image verification (ArubaOS_70xx_6.4.2.7_50063) completed successfully

Verifying ArubaOS_MMC_6.4.2.7_50063 ...

Copying file:....
Error upgrading image: ncftpget /ftp-files//ArubaOS_MMC_6.4.2.7_50063: server
said: /ftp-files//ArubaOS_MMC_6.4.2.7_50063: No such file or directory.

Skipping.
```

This was done intentionally so you could see what happens. At this point, all of the 7000 controllers began upgrading, two at a time, since that was what was configured in the profile. The following CLI output shows the status during the upgrade process:

```
#show upgrade status

All Controllers
---------------
IP Address     Hostname   Type     Model       Version         Upgrade Status
----------     --------   ----     -----       -------         --------------
10.1.50.101    7010-50a   master   Aruba7010   6.4.2.7_50063   N/A
10.1.40.100    3600-40    local    Aruba3600   6.4.2.6_49665   Waiting, image not
verified
10.1.50.102    7010-50b   standby  Aruba7010   6.4.2.6_49665   Waiting
10.1.70.100    7005-70    local    Aruba7005   6.4.2.6_49665   Upgrade in progress
10.1.80.100    7005-80    local    Aruba7005   6.4.2.6_49665   Upgrade in progress
10.1.90.100    7005-90    local    Aruba7005   6.4.2.6_49665   Waiting
```

In order to have the 3600 controller upgrade its OS, the proper file was copied to the FTP download server and the upgrade verify command was issued again. The file was verified, and the 3600 controller was automatically instructed to perform its upgrade. At this point, all of the controllers have been upgraded and need to be rebooted, as shown in the following CLI output:

```
#show upgrade status

All Controllers
---------------
IP Address    Hostname   Type     Model      Version         Upgrade Status
----------    --------   ----     -----      -------         --------------
10.1.50.101   7010-50a   master   Aruba7010  6.4.2.7_50063   N/A
10.1.40.100   3600-40    local    Aruba3600  6.4.2.6_49665   Upgraded, reboot
required
10.1.50.102   7010-50b   standby  Aruba7010  6.4.2.6_49665   Upgraded, reboot
required
10.1.70.100   7005-70    local    Aruba7005  6.4.2.6_49665   Upgraded, reboot
required
10.1.80.100   7005-80    local    Aruba7005  6.4.2.6_49665   Upgraded, reboot
required
10.1.90.100   7005-90    local    Aruba7005  6.4.2.6_49665   Upgraded, reboot
required
```

The upgrade status can also be viewed by going to **Maintenance ➢ CONTROLLER ➢ Image Management ➢ Upgrade Status**, which is displayed in Figure 10.20.

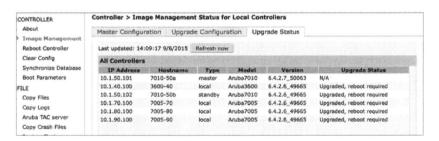

FIGURE 10.20 Upgrade configuration

The last step is to reboot the controllers. You can perform this manually or automatically. You can log on to each controller and manually perform a reboot, either through the CLI or the WebUI. You can also simply enable the auto-reboot parameter in the upgrade-profile. As soon as you do, all of the target controllers will immediately reboot.

There is a concern that you need to be aware of if you perform an automatic reboot from the upgrade server. If a global change is made on the master controller, when the configuration is saved, the changes are pushed out and saved to the local controllers. However, some settings, such as IP parameters and VLAN parameters, are configured locally on each controller. If the configuration is not saved when a change is made on a local controller, when the upgrade server triggers the automatic reboot of the local controller, any local changes that have not been saved will be lost.

If you plan to preload the new image on the APs prior to rebooting, you should wait to reboot the controllers. The next section of this chapter will explain AP image preload, along with the steps to perform this task.

When you are ready to centrally reboot the target controllers with the newly installed OS, you can do this by simply enabling auto-reboot in the upgrade profile. The following CLI output shows the commands to enable it. The show upgrade status command shows that all of the controllers are rebooting immediately after the auto-reboot is enabled.

```
(config) #upgrade-profile
(Upgrade Profile) #auto-reboot
(Upgrade Profile) #exit

(config) #show upgrade status

All Controllers
---------------
IP Address    Hostname   Type     Model       Version          Upgrade Status
----------    --------   ----     -----       -------          --------------
10.1.50.101   7010-50a   master   Aruba7010   6.4.2.7_50063    N/A
10.1.40.100   3600-40    local    Aruba3600   6.4.2.6_49665    Rebooting
10.1.50.102   7010-50b   standby  Aruba7010   6.4.2.6_49665    Rebooting
10.1.70.100   7005-70    local    Aruba7005   6.4.2.6_49665    Rebooting
10.1.80.100   7005-80    local    Aruba7005   6.4.2.6_49665    Rebooting
10.1.90.100   7005-90    local    Aruba7005   6.4.2.6_49665    Rebooting
```

AP Image Preload

When an AP boots, one of the first tasks that it performs is to compare the OS version on the AP with the OS version on the controller that the AP is initially communicating with. If the OS versions do not match, the AP will use FTP to download the OS from the controller and then reboot. The FTP download typically takes about four minutes.

If the OS on a controller is upgraded, the controller must reboot to enable the new OS. When the controller is rebooted, all of the APs that are connected to that controller will lose connection with the controller. If redundancy is enabled, these APs may connect to another controller while their original controller is rebooting. Ultimately, these APs are going to attempt to reconnect to the original controller, and when they do, they will need to upgrade their OS to match the upgraded controller.

This potentially means that multiple APs will need to perform an FTP download from the controller to upgrade their OS. These APs will be down for at least four minutes; however, if many APs are attempting to download a new OS, all simultaneously using FTP, it is likely that it will take longer.

AP image preload allows groups of APs to download the new OS software prior to rebooting the controller. The OS download can be performed over a period of time, and the number of simultaneous FTP downloads can be limited, preventing overloading of the controller. When the selected APs have all downloaded the new version of the OS, the controller can be rebooted. Once the controller is up and running again, the APs will already have downloaded the new OS file, and will simply need to reboot and reconnect to the controller. The APs will be down for only the time necessary to reboot the controller. Good redundancy planning can further limit the amount of time the APs will be down.

The AP image preload process is simple and straightforward. Following is an overview of the steps, followed by some detailed steps:

- Copy the new OS to the controller's non-boot partition.
- Specify the APs to be preloaded (if you are not preloading all of them).
- Preload the OS onto the APs.
- Reboot the controller using the new OS partition.

The first step is to determine which system partition on the controller is currently functioning as the default boot partition. Once you have identified the default boot partition, copy the new Aruba OS onto the controller's other partition. After the image is copied to this partition, **do not** reboot the controller.

The following CLI command and output show the two system partitions on the controller. Notice that system partition 0 is currently the default boot partition, so the new Aruba OS should be copied to system partition 1.

```
# show image version
-----------------------------------
Partition            : 0:0 (/dev/usb/flash1) **Default boot**
Software Version     : ArubaOS 6.4.2.10 (Digitally Signed - Production Build)
Build number         : 50952
Label                : 50952
Built on             : Wed Jul 22 13:21:13 PDT 2015
-----------------------------------
Partition            : 0:1 (/dev/usb/flash2)
Software Version     : ArubaOS 6.4.2.10 (Digitally Signed - Production Build)
Build number         : 50952
Label                : 50952
Built on             : Wed Jul 22 13:21:13 PDT 2015
```

The Aruba OS can be updated using the copy command, which can be seen in the following CLI output. The AP image preload is performed from the controller that the AP is terminated to. If you have multiple local controllers with APs terminating to them, then this process will need to be performed on each of the local controllers.

In this output, the copy command extends onto the second line since it was too long to fit on one line.

```
#copy ftp: 192.168.240.31 david /ftp-files/ArubaOS_70xx_6.4.2.11_51218 system:
partition 1
Password:********
Copying file:...................................
File copied successfully.
Saving file to flash:
.................................................................................
..........................................
The system will boot from partition 1 during the next reboot.
```

The next step is to copy the OS to the APs. If you are selecting specific APs or AP groups to be preloaded, you need to select them first, as shown in the following CLI output. If you will be preloading all of the APs, you do not need to perform either of these commands.

```
#ap image-preload add ap-name 9c:1c:12:c0:85:e2
#ap image-preload add ap-group building1-ap-group
```

The next step is to preload the OS onto the APs. As part of this command, you can also specify how many APs will be allowed to simultaneously download the OS.

At this stage, you will issue the command to begin the AP image preload process. The following CLI commands show first how to preload only the APs that you have selected, followed by the command to preload all of the APs terminating to this controller. You can also specify how many simultaneous downloads will be allowed (the default value is 10).

```
#ap image-preload activate specific-aps partition 0 max-downloads 5

#ap image-preload activate all-aps partition 0 max-downloads 5
```

The last task you need to do is reboot the controller using the new OS that you just copied to the system partition. This can easily be performed using the reload command.

AP image preload can also be performed from the WebUI interface at **Maintenance ➢ WLAN ➢ Preload AP Image**.

AP Image Preload with Centralized Upgrade

There is nothing special or unique about performing both AP image preloading and centralized upgrade together. I have demonstrated this dozens of times to classes and it works very well. Previously in this chapter, you learned the steps to do each of them individually; however, I thought it would be worthwhile to document how to do them together. This section provides the step-by-step process.

1. On the master controller, identify the partition to copy the new OS to. In this example, it would be partition 1.

   ```
   # show image version
   ----------------------------------
   Partition          : 0:0 (/dev/usb/flash1) **Default boot**
   Software Version   : ArubaOS 6.4.2.11 (Digitally Signed - Production Build)
   Build number       : 51218
   Label              : 51218
   Built on           : Wed Aug 12 06:58:23 PDT 2015
   ----------------------------------
   Partition          : 0:1 (/dev/usb/flash2)
   Software Version   : ArubaOS 6.4.2.10 (Digitally Signed - Production Build)
   Build number       : 50952
   Label              : 50952
   Built on           : Wed Jul 22 13:21:13 PDT 2015
   ```

2. Copy the new OS to the partition on the master controller. Note that the copy command was too long to fit on one line. After copying the file, you will need to reboot the master controller.

   ```
   #copy ftp: 192.168.240.31 david /ftp-files/ArubaOS_70xx_6.4.2.12_51328
   system: partition 1
   Password:********
   Copying file:................................................................
   ..............................
   File copied successfully.
   Saving file to flash:
   ................................................................................
   ..................................................
   The system will boot from partition 1 during the next reboot.

   (Upgrade Profile) #reload
   Do you really want to restart the system(y/n): y
   System will now restart!
   ```

3. On the master controller, configure the centralized upgrade profile settings and then verify that they are set correctly. Make sure that auto-reboot is disabled, and do not forget to write mem.

   ```
   (config) #upgrade-profile
   (Upgrade Profile) #protocol ftp
   (Upgrade Profile) #serverip 192.168.240.31
   (Upgrade Profile) #username david
   (Upgrade Profile) #password aruba123
   (Upgrade Profile) #filepath /ftp-files/
   (Upgrade Profile) #max-downloads 2
   (Upgrade Profile) #no auto-reboot
   (Upgrade Profile) #upgrade-enable
   ```

```
(Upgrade Profile) #write mem
Saving Configuration...

Configuration Saved.

(Upgrade Profile) #show upgrade-profile

Upgrade Profile
---------------
Parameter                  Value
---------                  -----
Enable software upgrade    true
Max downloads              2
Reboot automatically       false
Protocol                   ftp
Server IP address          192.168.240.31
Username                   david
Password                   ********
File path                  /ftp-files/
```

4. You now need to specify the controllers that you want to upgrade. The following CLI output shows three examples for defining target controllers. After the target controllers are defined, perform an upgrade verify on the master controller. This will first verify the necessary upgrade files are available. This command will then automatically notify each of the target controllers to download the upgrade file to the partition that is not the current default boot partition.

```
#upgrade target add net 10.1.90.0 255.255.255.0
#upgrade target add host 10.1.80.100
#upgrade target add all

#upgrade verify
WARNING: Members specified in upgrade target list will be upgraded
 and rebooted (if enabled in the upgrade profile). Do you want to proceed?
[y/n]: y
Verifying ArubaOS_70xx_6.4.2.12_51328 ...

Copying file:....................................
File copied successfully.
Image verification (ArubaOS_70xx_6.4.2.12_51328) completed successfully

Verifying ArubaOS_MMC_6.4.2.12_51328 ...

Copying file:..........................
File copied successfully.
Image verification (ArubaOS_MMC_6.4.2.12_51328) completed successfully
```

5. On the master controller, verify that all of the local controllers have downloaded the latest OS file. This may take some time. The upgrade status of each controller should be Upgraded, reboot required. At this point **do not** reboot any of the controllers. It is now time to perform the AP image preload.

```
#show upgrade status

All Controllers
---------------
IP Address    Hostname   Type     Model      Version           Upgrade Status
----------    --------   ----     -----      -------           --------------
10.1.50.101   7010-50a   master   Aruba7010  6.4.2.12_51328    N/A
10.1.40.100   3600-40    local    Aruba3600  6.4.2.11_51218    Upgraded, reboot
required
10.1.50.102   7010-50b   standby  Aruba7010  6.4.2.11_51218    Upgraded, reboot
required
10.1.70.100   7005-70    local    Aruba7005  6.4.2.11_51218    Upgraded, reboot
required
10.1.80.100   7005-80    local    Aruba7005  6.4.2.11_51218    Upgraded, reboot
required
10.1.90.100   7005-90    local    Aruba7005  6.4.2.11_51218    Upgraded, reboot
required
```

6. The AP image preload task is performed on a controller-by-controller basis, and is performed on any controller that has an AP terminating to it. The show ap database command displays a list of all of the APs, along with the controller (switch IP) that each of the APs is terminating to. As a network administrator, you should already know this information. In this example, AP image preload needs to be performed on the following controllers: 10.1.70.100, 10.1.80.100, and 10.1.90.100. In order to make the screen output easier to read, I removed the following three columns of information that were not necessary for this example: Flags, Switch IP, and Standby IP:

```
#show ap database

AP Database
-----------
Name                Group    IP Address    Status          Switch IP
----                -----    ----------    ------          ---------
18:64:72:c4:78:70   default  10.1.90.151   Up 10h:15m:49s  10.1.90.100
9c:1c:12:c0:85:7a   default  10.1.90.152   Up 10h:15m:18s  10.1.90.100
9c:1c:12:c0:85:e2   default  10.1.70.151   Up 10h:16m:2s   10.1.70.100
d8:c7:c8:c0:97:28   default  10.1.90.150   Up 10h:15m:30s  10.1.90.100
d8:c7:c8:c0:98:24   default  10.1.90.153   Up 10h:15m:22s  10.1.90.100
d8:c7:c8:c0:cc:e0   default  10.1.80.150   Up 10h:15m:25s  10.1.80.100
```

```
Flags: U = Unprovisioned; N = Duplicate name; G = No such group; L = Unlicensed
       I = Inactive; D = Dirty or no config; E = Regulatory Domain Mismatch
       X = Maintenance Mode; P = PPPoE AP; B = Built-in AP; s = LACP striping
       R = Remote AP; R- = Remote AP requires Auth; C = Cellular RAP;
       c = CERT-based RAP; 1 = 802.1x authenticated AP; 2 = Using IKE version 2
       u = Custom-Cert RAP; S = Standby-mode AP; J = USB cert at AP
       M = Mesh node; Y = Mesh Recovery

Total APs:6
```

7. Log on to a controller on which you want to perform the AP image preload. You do not need to copy the upgraded OS to this controller because this was performed automatically using the centralized OS upgrade. You will need to identify which partition has the new OS software, which you can do using show image version.

```
#show image version
----------------------------------
Partition            : 0:0 (/dev/usb/flash1)
Software Version     : ArubaOS 6.4.2.11 (Digitally Signed - Production Build)
Build number         : 51218
Label                : 51218
Built on             : Wed Aug 12 06:58:23 PDT 2015
----------------------------------
Partition            : 0:1 (/dev/usb/flash2) **Default boot**
Software Version     : ArubaOS 6.4.2.12 (Digitally Signed - Production Build)
Build number         : 51328
Label                : 51328
Built on             : Wed Aug 19 14:37:13 PDT 2015
```

8. At this point, you can specify individual APs or AP groups that you want to preload, and then activate that image preload for the specific APs, or you can activate the image preload for all of the APs. Examples of both are displayed in the following CLI output. Remember, this is only performing the AP image preload for the APs connected to this controller. You will need to perform Steps 7 and 8 for each controller that has APs terminated to it.

```
#ap image-preload add ap-name 9c:1c:12:c0:85:e2
#ap image-preload add ap-group building1-ap-group
#ap image-preload activate specific-aps partition 1 max-downloads 5

Or

#ap image-preload activate all-aps partition 1 max-downloads 5
```

9. After you begin the AP image preload, you can monitor the status using the following CLI command. The Preload State column shows that all of the APs have

completed the preload of the new OS. (In order to make the screen output easier to read, I removed the last four columns, of information: Start Time, End Time, Failure Count, and Failure Reason.) The command show ap image version will show detailed information for each AP, including the running image version and the flash image version. I did not include output for this command since each line contains over 330 characters.

```
(7005-90) #show ap image-preload status all

AP Image Preload Parameters
---------------------------
Item                        Value
----                        -----
Status                      Active
Mode                        All APs
Partition                   1
Build                       51328
Max Simultaneous Downloads  5
Start Time                  2015-09-11 13:34:46

AP Image Preload AP Status Summary
----------------------------------
AP Image Preload State  Count
----------------------  -----
Preloaded               4
TOTAL                   4

AP Image Preload AP Status
--------------------------
AP Name            AP Group   AP IP         AP Type  Preload State
-------            --------   -----         -------  -------------
d8:c7:c8:c0:97:28  default    10.1.90.150   135      Preloaded
d8:c7:c8:c0:98:24  default    10.1.90.153   135      Preloaded
18:64:72:c4:78:70  default    10.1.90.151   115      Preloaded
9c:1c:12:c0:85:7a  default    10.1.90.152   225      Preloaded
```

10. After you have verified that the APs have been preloaded with the new OS, you can go back to the master controller and complete the centralized image upgrade. If you enable auto-reboot in the upgrade-profile on the master controller, all of the target controllers will automatically reboot, completing the upgrade process. Check the upgrade status using the show upgrade status command.

```
(config) #upgrade-profile
(Upgrade Profile) #auto-reboot
(Upgrade Profile) #exit

(config) #show upgrade status
```

```
All Controllers
---------------
IP Address    Hostname   Type     Model      Version         Upgrade Status
----------    --------   ----     -----      -------         --------------
10.1.50.101   7010-50a   master   Aruba7010  6.4.2.7_50063   N/A
10.1.40.100   3600-40    local    Aruba3600  6.4.2.6_49665   Rebooting
10.1.50.102   7010-50b   standby  Aruba7010  6.4.2.6_49665   Rebooting
10.1.70.100   7005-70    local    Aruba7005  6.4.2.6_49665   Rebooting
10.1.80.100   7005-80    local    Aruba7005  6.4.2.6_49665   Rebooting
10.1.90.100   7005-90    local    Aruba7005  6.4.2.6_49665   Rebooting
```

CHAPTER 11

Access Points

IN THIS CHAPTER, YOU WILL LEARN ABOUT THE FOLLOWING:

- AP Types
  - Campus AP
  - Remote AP
  - Instant AP
  - Unified AP
- Aruba Activate
  - Activate Folders
  - Adding an AP to Activate
  - Individually Assigning an AP to a Folder
  - Assigning APs to Folders Using Rules
- Campus AP
  - Control Plane Security
  - Converting IAPs to CAPs
- Remote AP
  - VPN Server Configuration
  - Creating an AP Group
  - Configuring a RAP
  - VAP Data Forwarding Modes
  - VAP Remote AP Operation Modes
  - Forwarding Modes and Operation Modes
- Air Monitor
- Spectrum Monitor
- Mesh AP
- Secure Jack

THIS CHAPTER WILL EXPLAIN THE DIFFERENT MODES that an AP can operate in and the functionality that it can provide. You will see how to configure these different modes as well as how they operate and behave. Some of the configuration procedures will be explained in depth, whereas others will be briefly explained because they are covered extensively in other chapters.

Aruba APs falls into one of four different hardware types, each of which can be configured to operate with an Aruba controller and ArubaOS:

- AP (Campus AP, or CAP)
- Remote AP (RAP)
- Instant AP (IAP)
- Unified AP (UAP)

An Aruba AP (or radio) can operate in one of the following five functional modes:

- Campus AP
- Remote AP
- Air monitor
- Spectrum monitor
- Mesh AP

AP Types

Aruba sells many different models of APs, offering a variety of capabilities. Ignoring the individual models for now, there are four different hardware families or types of APs that you can purchase: AP, remote AP, instant AP, and unified AP.

Campus AP

The Aruba AP, also referred to as a campus AP, is the AP family that is typically used with an Aruba controller. All campus APs have a model number that begins with the letters "AP" followed by a specific number, such as AP-335. Campus APs can be physically connected to PoE-enabled ports on an Ethernet switch. When the ports are powered on, the APs will automatically attempt to connect to the controller, as described in Chapter 2, "Understanding the Aruba OS Environment." Campus APs cannot function as autonomous APs.

Remote AP

An AP with RAP as part of its model number is sometimes referred to as a hardware RAP. Any Aruba AP can operate as a remote AP, but a hardware RAP is specifically designed for this purpose, providing an easier installation and configuration process. Any AP operating as a remote AP builds an L2TP/IPsec connection back to an Aruba controller across an Internet connection. Through this VPN connection the RAP communicates with the Aruba controller, providing WLAN or wired Ethernet services to users and forwarding user traffic back to the enterprise network.

The VPN settings required by a remote AP must be initially configured on the controller and are pushed to the RAP during provisioning. The configuration and operation of remote APs will be explained in depth later in this chapter.

Instant AP

Aruba has another product family known as Instant APs (IAPs). Instant APs build a cooperative network without the use of a central controller. With an instant network, the IAPs build a cluster within a layer 2 network environment, with one of the IAPs taking over the responsibility of a central manager. This central manager is referred to as a virtual controller (VC).

A cluster of IAPs will function in a similar way that an AP group functions on a controller. An Aruba instant network has many features and functions that are comparable to the controller-based network; however, it is a different and separate environment, designed for smaller network environments. The IAPs were also designed to allow an instant network to grow and migrate to a controller-based network. This migration path is provided by allowing IAPs to operate as campus APs or remote APs. This conversion is reversible, allowing the IAP to be reset to factory default settings, which forces the IAP to function as an IAP again.

Some organizations operate both Aruba controller-based networks and Aruba instant networks at different locations within their organization. In this type of environment, when organizations purchase new APs, it is common for them to purchase solely IAPs, since they can be provisioned to operate on either an Aruba instant network or an Aruba controller network. There are a few ways of converting an IAP to operate on a campus network. None of these methods are difficult; however, the conversion is an extra step that is not needed with a standard campus AP.

An additional feature of an IAP is that it can easily be configured as a remote AP. In fact, an IAP and a hardware RAP both ship with the IAP firmware preloaded on them. The IAP software gives these APs their easy installation and configuration process.

When a factory-default IAP or RAP boots, similar to a campus AP, it has a predefined boot sequence that it uses to identify its function mode and to download its configuration. This sequence is shown in the following list.

1. Obtain an IP address using DHCP. If no DHCP server, then assign IP address from 169.254.x.x/16 (APIPA).
2. Search for VC. If VC exists, join the cluster, obtain slave role, apply the config from VC.
3. If VC does not exist, declare itself as the VC.
4. If DHCP option 43 returned IP address of an AirWave server, obtain configuration from the AirWave server.
5. Connect to Activate.
6. Check if Activate provisioning rule exists.
7. If rule exists, then direct to AirWave, or Aruba Central, or controller (as CAP/RAP).
8. If no provisioning rule is configured, then load the default instant config and advertise "instant" SSID.

NOTE *Every 5 minutes, an unconfigured IAP will attempt to connect to Activate to check if any provisioning rule is configured. It will take action accordingly if one is found.*

Most Aruba partners and resellers purchase IAPs for internal testing and demonstrations because of the IAP's flexibility to operate as an instant AP, a campus AP, or a RAP.

Unified AP

Aruba recently announced the unified AP (UAP) software. The UAP software is a consolidation of the features of the three other AP types (campus AP, remote AP, and instant AP) into a single OS. The UAP software replaces the need for Aruba to sell three different types of APs. All new Aruba APs, beginning with ArubaOS 6.5.2, will ship as UAP-enabled APs.

Since a UAP will be capable of taking on one of many different roles, the boot process is much more extensive, combining the discovery process from all three AP types into a single logic flow.

The following is a sequential list of the boot sequence that the UAP uses to identify its function mode and download its configuration. Steps 1–4 and 9 can be used to connect to a controller running ArubaOS. Notice that the first four steps are the same ones used by a campus AP when discovering its initial controller. These steps were described in detail in Chapter 2. Step 9 uses Aruba Activate to configure the UAP to function as a campus AP or as a remote AP. Using Activate to configure an AP will be explained in the section "Aruba Activate," later in this chapter. If any step in the process is successful, the boot sequence process stops processing any additional steps.

1. Connect to controller—Statically set master address.
2. Connect to controller—DHCP option 43/60.
3. Connect to controller—ADP (multicast 239.0.82.11 and broadcast).
4. Connect to controller—DNS (aruba-master.domain).
5. Search for VC. Join IAP cluster if VC exists.
6. If DHCP option 43 returned IP address of an AirWave server, obtain configuration from the AirWave server.
7. Activate—Direct to AirWave server.
8. Activate—Direct to Aruba Central server.
9. Activate—Direct to controller (CAP/RAP config).
10. Broadcast provisioning SSID.

The boot sequence of a UAP is an amalgamation of all the current methods into one AP operating system. Therefore, understanding the AP configuration methods in this chapter should provide you with most of the knowledge needed for the UAP as they become available.

Aruba Activate

Aruba Activate is a free Aruba Networks cloud-based service that allows automatic initialization of Aruba's cloud-based products to support zero-touch provisioning (ZTP). This includes the 70xx cloud-based controllers, Mobility Access Switches, UAPs, and any

AP with the IAP firmware on it (IAPs and RAPs). This section will focus on the interaction of Activate and the APs.

When an IAP, RAP, or UAP boots up in a factory-default state, it contains no configuration or provisioning settings. The previous two sections of this chapter described the boot sequence for IAP firmware APs and UAPs. This section of the chapter describes what occurs if the AP reaches a step when it attempts to configure itself using Activate. With Activate, a new (or factory-reset) IAP, RAP, or UAP can automatically configure itself using ZTP. The tasks needed to automate this process will be explained shortly.

> **NOTE** *Activate can perform more tasks than automatically configuring an IAP, RAP, or UAP to communicate with an ArubaOS controller; however, that is all this book will be focusing on.*

After reading this section, if you would like to learn more about Activate, go to the Aruba support website and download the *Aruba Activate User Guide*.

Every active Aruba Networks customer has an Activate account. Activate is linked to Aruba's supply-chain and ERP system. The moment Aruba ships a cloud-based device such as an IAP, RAP, or UAP, the MAC address and serial number of the device is automatically added to the customer's activate account. From within the account, the customer can specify rules that will begin the AP configuration process. Let us take a look at the process.

When a new or factory-default IAP, RAP, or UAP is connected to the network and is powered on, after the device receives an IP address, at some point in the boot process it may attempt to communicate with the Activate server. If it does, the AP includes its certificate and MAC address in this communication to identify itself to the Activate server. This process is illustrated as Step 1 in Figure 11.1.

FIGURE 11.1 Configuring RAP Using Activate

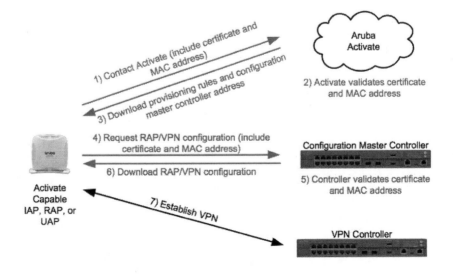

The Activate server checks the certificate and MAC address that the AP presents, as illustrated in Step 2. If the AP is authenticated and a provisioning rule exists for the AP, Activate will return provisioning information along with the address of the configuration master controller that is specified with the rule. This is illustrated in Step 3.

In the example illustrated in Figure 11.1, the AP is being configured to function as a RAP. Therefore, in Step 4 the AP sends a request to the configuration master for RAP/VPN configuration. This request includes the certificate and MAC address. The AP is using this information to identify itself to the configuration master controller. In Step 5, the identity of the AP is confirmed, and the corresponding RAP/VPN configuration is downloaded to the AP.

After the AP receives the new RAP/VPN configuration (Step 6), it must reboot itself to implement the new configuration. Step 7 illustrates the AP operating as a RAP, establishing a VPN connection with a different controller that is operating as a VPN server. In a smaller network environment, the configuration master controller may also operate as the VPN controller; however, in a larger environment it is common for them to be separate controllers.

To summarize the process, the AP boots and steps through the boot sequence to attempt to configure itself. If it reaches the Activate step, it sends its certificate and MAC address to the Activate server. Activate looks up the AP in its database, validates the credentials of the AP, and points the AP to its configuration master controller.

The AP then sends its certificate and MAC address to the configuration master controller. The controller validates the certificate and looks up the MAC address in the RAP whitelist. If the AP is validated, then the RAP/VPN configuration is sent to the AP.

You may be wondering what certificate the AP sends to Activate. Every AP from Aruba has a Trusted Platform Module (TPM) chip, which carries the certificate. The certificate is signed by the corporate Aruba CA. Activate verifies the certificate and thereby validates this as an Aruba AP.

The AP will reboot and load the RAP/VPN software and configuration. The AP will send its certificate and MAC address to the VPN controller, and try to establish the RAP/VPN connection. The VPN controller will validate the AP in the RAP whitelist and establish a VPN tunnel with the VPN controller.

The controller that the AP is configured to establish its Generic Routing Encapsulation (GRE) tunnel does not have to be the same controller that the AP communicates with to establish its RAP/VPN tunnel, as illustrated in Figure 11.2. The RAP must first establish its VPN connection. Then through the VPN, the RAP can be configured with an LMS-IP address pointing to a different controller.

FIGURE 11.2
Configuring RAP GRE tunnels

The example in this section explained the process of configuring a RAP using Activate. Activate can also be used to configure an IAP or UAP to operate as a campus AP. When configuring a campus AP, the process starts the same as it does for configuring an IAP or UAP as a RAP. The AP communicates with Activate, which instructs the AP to convert itself to a campus AP and reboot. The AP will boot, obtain its six pieces of information, and connect to the controller as an unprovisioned AP.

At this point the administrator will need to provision the AP, assigning it an AP name and group, as described in Chapter 2. At the time this book was written, there was no automated way to completely convert and provision a campus AP from Activate. It appears that may change in the future.

Activate Folders

Let us take a look at how to set up Activate to support zero-touch provisioning. When you first log in to Activate, you should create one or more folders. Folders are logical groupings of tasks typically based on initialization function for the devices you place in the folder.

Activate allows you to create seven different types of provisioning tasks, as displayed in the following list. Only one IAP task can be assigned to a folder. Therefore, if one group of APs needs to be provisioned as RAPs and some as CAPs, you will need to create two folders, each with its own rule. You can create folders and subfolders to organize your devices, such as by location if you wish. The top folder would hold the subfolders but would contain no rules or devices. The subfolders would hold the devices and the rules for those devices.

The following is a list of the folder configuration options:

- IAP to AirWave
- IAP to RAP
- IAP to CAP
- IAP to Aruba Central
- Switch to AirWave
- Controller to AirWave
- Branch to master controller

The Setup menu, as shown in Figure 11.3, displays a folder named Concord, with two subfolders. One was named `Concord IAP-CAP` and the other `Concord IAP-RAP`. Each folder will have a rule in it that performs the provisioning task specified. The figure currently displays the rule to provision an IAP to a CAP.

FIGURE 11.3
Activate folders and rules

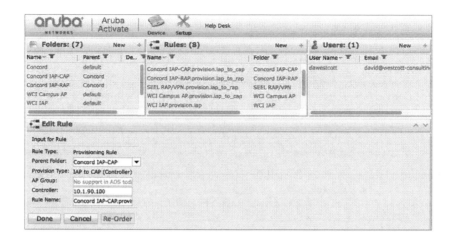

After creating the necessary folders and the rules that you want, you then will assign one or more APs to the appropriate folder. When the IAP, RAP, or UAP that is assigned to the folder is powered on for the first time (or after being reset to factory default), it will initially communicate with Activate, which will identify the folder the AP is assigned to and provide the AP with its provisioning information.

Adding an AP to Activate

If for some reason your IAP, RAP, or UAP is not listed in your list of devices on Activate, you can add it manually. From the upper-right corner of Activate, click Add Devices. The Manually Add Devices window will appear, along with directions, as shown in Figure 11.4.

To manually add an IAP, RAP, or UAP to Activate, you will need its MAC address along with a cloud activation key. The MAC address can be found on a tag that is affixed to the AP or packaging. You can also log in to the WebUI of the AP, and then under the Access Points header in the main dashboard, you can click on the AP name. The MAC address will be displayed in the Info section in the lower left.

FIGURE 11.4:
Manually Add Devices

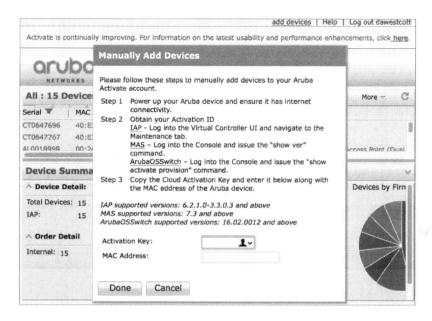

The cloud activation key needs to be obtained through the WebUI of the AP. In order for the key to be displayed in the WebUI, the AP must be connected to the Internet and able to communicate with device.arubanetworks.com. After logging in to the WebUI, click on the Maintenance link in the upper-right corner. The cloud activation key should be displayed, as shown in the following output. If the key is not displayed, it is likely that the AP is not able to communicate with the server device.arubanetworks.com.

```
Name:                    Aruba Operating System Software
Type:                    105
Build Time:              2015-02-11 08:33:34 PST
Version:                 6.3.1.8-4.0.0.10_48549
Website:                 http://www.arubanetworks.com
Legal:                   Copyright (c) 2002-2015, Aruba Networks, Inc.
Cloud Activation Key:    FXGH654K
```

Once you have the MAC address and the activation key, you will need to enter it in the Manually Add Device window of your Activate account. After the device is added to Activate, you will be able to assign it to a folder, which will allow it to be configured.

Individually Assigning an AP to a Folder

If you are using Activate to provision a small number of APs, it may be easy enough to individually assign each AP to an Activate folder. An IAP, RAP, or UAP can be easily added to Activate from the Device menu. Once added from the list of devices, select the device that you want to configure. In the Device Detail window, click the Edit button and then choose the folder you want to assign to the AP, as shown in Figure 11.5.

After the AP has been assigned to a new folder, when a new or factory-default AP is rebooted, it will use the provisioning rule from the folder to receive its provisioning information, informing the AP where to proceed to download its boot configuration.

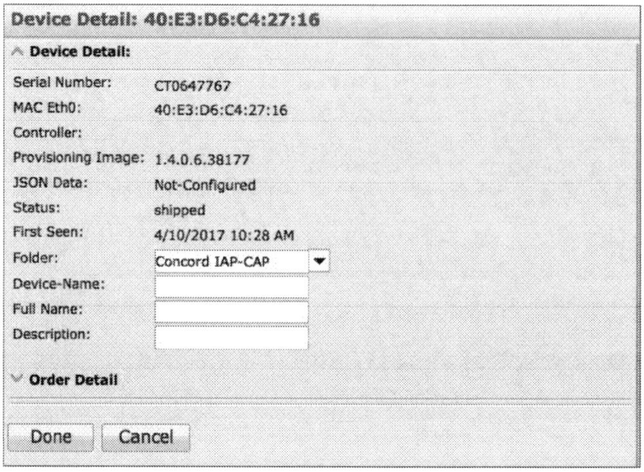

FIGURE 11.5
Assigning an AP to a folder

Device Detail: 40:E3:D6:C4:27:16	
Device Detail:	
Serial Number:	CT0647767
MAC Eth0:	40:E3:D6:C4:27:16
Controller:	
Provisioning Image:	1.4.0.6.38177
JSON Data:	Not-Configured
Status:	shipped
First Seen:	4/10/2017 10:28 AM
Folder:	Concord IAP-CAP
Device-Name:	
Full Name:	
Description:	
Order Detail	
Done Cancel	

This method is very effective when sending RAPs, IAPs, or UAPs to remote users or sites. The new, factory-default AP can be shipped directly to the remote location. Since the AP has no configuration, there is no security risk if it is lost or stolen during shipment. When the AP is shipped, it is placed in the default folder of your Activate account, which should be configured with no rules. After you confirm that the AP was received, you can move the AP to another folder, which will allow the AP to be configured. At this point the process is done.

Assigning APs to Folders Using Rules

Let us imagine that you are deploying a wireless network in a new building and you have ordered 50 IAPs for the installation. You are planning for the IAPs to be configured to operate as campus APs, and you want Activate to stage the new APs when they are booted for the first time. As in Figure 11.3, you have created a Concord folder with the Concord IAP-CAP subfolder. You have assigned the IAP-CAP rule to the folder and specified the IP address of your controller.

You do not want to individually move each of the new IAPs from the "default" folder to the Concord IAP-CAP folder. Activate provides the ability to automate this with a Move To Folder rule that will allow you to move a group of APs to a different folder. The criterion for this rule can be one of the following five pieces of information matching a value that you specify:

- Device Category
- Part Number

- PO Number
- Billing Info
- External IP Address Range

In the example shown in Figure 11.6, if the PO Number contains 20170402, then any of the APs that are affiliated with that PO will be moved to the folder `Concord IAP-CAP`. When any of these APs are powered on, they will receive the provision profile associated with this folder.

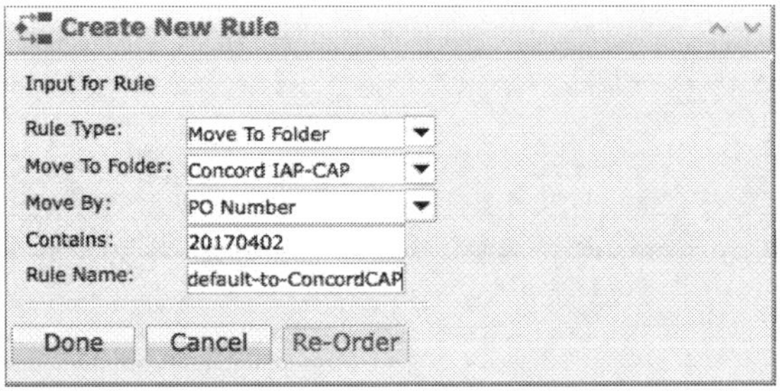

FIGURE 11.6 Move To Folder rule

Campus AP

Up to this chapter in the book, all references and explanations regarding APs have been about campus APs. This chapter has introduced instant APs, remote APs, and unified APs. Additionally, it has assumed that the AP is operating in the traditional role of an AP connected to a controller, advertising WLANs and providing wireless networking to client devices. This is the most common mode for controller base APs to operate.

Chapter 2 described the boot process of a campus AP, and this section will provide a brief review of that process. Chapter 2 explained that the AP needs six pieces of information to initially boot:

- AP Name
- Group
- IP Address
- Subnet Mask
- Default Gateway
- IP Address of Initial Controller

After obtaining the needed information, the AP would proceed to communicate with the initial controller to update its OS (if needed), download its LMS-IP, download its configuration, and build its GRE tunnels to the AP's terminating controller (typically defined by the LMS-IP address).

When an AP communicates with the controller regarding any of its settings or configuration, it uses a control protocol called *Process Application Programming Interface (PAPI)*. PAPI uses UDP port 8211 to perform these communications. PAPI uses a light form of encryption mainly to obscure the data. Since early wireless implementations were designed with dedicated networks deployed to carry just the AP traffic, the wireless control and data traffic were isolated from other network users, and this presented very little security risk. Nowadays, AP-to-controller traffic typically travels across the same network as the rest of the enterprise traffic, giving you a very good reason to secure PAPI traffic by implementing control plane security.

Control Plane Security

The primary function of control plane security (CPsec) is to protect the PAPI communication between the controller and the APs. CPsec has been enabled on the Aruba controller by default for many years. However, it has become common practice to disable CPsec, which is not recommended. CPsec is easy to manage and should be kept enabled.

The concept of CPsec is quite simple: encapsulate PAPI frames as a payload inside IPsec frames. Since PAPI is considered payload, it is not altered and is still used to communicate control traffic; it is simply made more secure. The key function of CPsec is to secure the control plane communications so that it cannot be viewed, manipulated, or impersonated.

The Aruba controller and APs have X.509 certificates installed on them during the manufacturing process, with the private keys protected by tamper-resistant hardware known as a Trusted Platform Module (TPM). Older AP models do not have the factory certificate installed on them and will not be discussed in this book—they are all end of sale and many are end of support. If you have one of the old APs and are now implementing CPsec, the ArubaOS User Guide provides information about them.

Configuring CPsec is a fairly straightforward process. The first step is to enable it. It is enabled by default, but in the past it was common to disable it. Figure 11.7 shows the window where it can be enabled. The window can be reached through the following menu path; **Configuration ➢ NETWORK ➢ Controller ➢ Control Plane Security**. CPsec can also be enabled from the CLI using the following commands:

```
(config) #control-plane-security
(Control Plane Security Profile) #cpsec-enable
```

If you are enabling CPsec on an already installed network, you need to plan the implementation since the APs have to reestablish the connection with the controller as the APs enable CPsec.

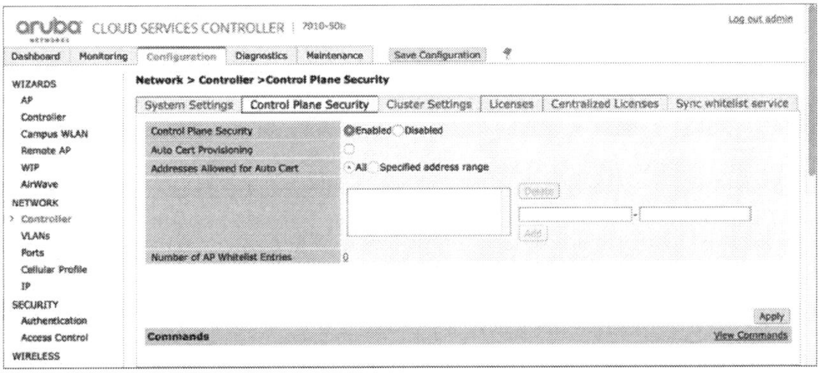

FIGURE 11.7
Enabling CPsec

After CPsec is enabled, you need to add the APs to the campus AP whitelist. One way of adding APs to the whitelist is to manually add each AP, one by one. This is definitely not an ideal way of adding them because this will take the most time; however, you should be familiar with this procedure in case you need to use it. You can reach the whitelist window using the following menu path: **Configuration ➢ WIRELESS ➢ AP Installation ➢ Whitelist ➢ Campus AP ➢ Entries**. Note that the Entries button is near the top at the far right, as seen in Figure 11.8. This button is often not displayed due to scrolling of a smaller browser window.

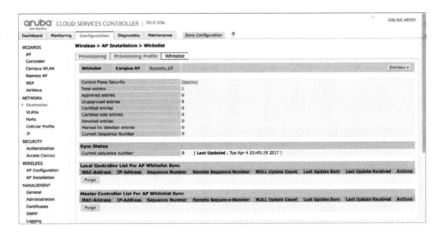

FIGURE 11.8
CPsec AP whitelist

Once you are in the whitelist entries window, you can click the New button to add an AP to the whitelist. You will need the MAC address of the AP to perform this task. You can also add the AP to the whitelist from the CLI using the following command:

```
#whitelist-db cpsec add mac-address 04:bd:88:ca:8d:c0
```

Obviously, if you have a large number of APs that need to be added to the whitelist, adding them individually one by one will take a great deal of time. Another way of adding APs is by using Auto Cert Provisioning. This feature allows you to automatically add a group of APs to the whitelist. This group can be all the access points currently connected to your controller, or it can be any AP within a range of IP addresses.

Auto Cert Provisioning is configured from the same window where CPsec is enabled, as shown in Figure 11.9. The Auto Cert Provisioning check box specifies that you want to automatically add the APs to the whitelist. The line below the check box allows you to define the grouping of APs that will be added to the whitelist—all or a specified IP address range. This can also be performed from the CLI using the following commands. This example is allowing all APs to be added to the whitelist:

```
(config) #control-plane-security
(Control Plane Security Profile) #auto-cert-prov
(Control Plane Security Profile) #auto-cert-allow-all
```

FIGURE 11.9
Auto Cert Provisioning

You can see the AP whitelist from the Entries window or from the CLI prompt using the following command:

```
#show whitelist-db cpsec
```

You can also manage the whitelist database using the whitelist-db command. The following CLI output shows a whitelist entry being deleted from the database, followed by a display of all of the whitelist editing capabilities using the whitelist-db cpsec command:

```
#whitelist-db cpsec del mac-address 04:bd:88:ca:8d:c0

#whitelist-db cpsec ?
add                 Add a whitelist DB entry
del                 Delete a whitelist DB entry
modify              Modify a whitelist DB entry attributes
purge               Purge the list
revoke              Revoke a Whitelist DB entry
```

Converting IAPs to Campus APs

As you learned earlier in this chapter, instant APs are very flexible because they can operate as an IAP, RAP, or campus AP. Converting an IAP to a campus AP can be performed in two different ways. If an IAP is already operating as an instant AP, the individual AP or the entire instant cluster can be manually converted to campus APs. If the IAP is a new IAP and has not been installed or configured yet, it can be connected to the network and converted to a campus AP using Activate. The following two sections will explain both of these methods.

Converting Using Virtual Controller

An IAP can be converted to a campus AP either individually or as part of a group if the IAP is part of an instant cluster. The process is the same for both scenarios. The difference is in the selection.

Converting an individual IAP to operate as a campus AP is a simple process. If you do not have any other IAPs on your network, when you connect the IAP to the network and power it on, since it is the first IAP on the network it will automatically advertise an SSID with the name "instant." From a computer, connect to this SSID and then browse to instant.arubanetworks.com. This will bring you to the Virtual Controller management interface of the IAP. When prompted, log in to the IAP using the user name "admin" and the password "admin."

After you have logged in, choose the Maintenance menu (upper-right corner) and then click the Convert tab. From the dropdown field Convert One Or More Access Points to, choose Campus APs Managed By A Mobility Controller, and in the Hostname Or IP Address Of Mobility Controller field, enter the IP address of the controller, as shown in Figure 11.10. Click the Convert Now button to initiate the conversion. Remember, this process will allow you to convert one IAP or a whole cluster.

FIGURE 11.10
Converting an IAP

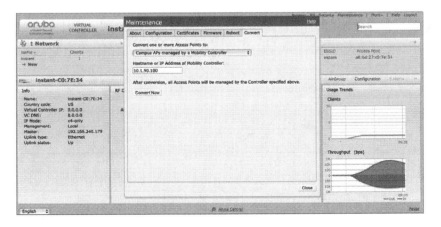

If you have an instant cluster, you can convert all of the IAPs in the cluster to campus APs using the same process. This can be useful if you have a group of new IAPs that you want to convert. Simply connect all of them to the same layer 2 network and let them connect and form an instant cluster. After all of the IAPs are running and connected to the cluster, simply log in to the virtual controller and perform the same conversion process that was explained in the previous paragraph.

This is also the same process you would use if you were converting an existing instant network to a controller-based network. Beware that the conversion process will delete any existing configuration on the VC, so you may want to perform a backup on the VC first. After the APs are converted to campus APs, you will still have to provision them by providing an AP name and group to each AP.

Converting Using Activate

A more efficient method of converting a group of new (or factory reset) IAPs, RAPs, or UAPs to operate as a campus AP is to use Activate. Activate will automatically convert the APs when they initially boot. This is done by creating an Activate provisioning rule for a folder and assigning the AP to that folder. You need to make sure that the VLAN that you first connect the APs to allows the APs to communicate to the Internet in order to connect to the Activate server. The Activate process and all of the necessary components were explained earlier in this chapter in the "Aruba Activate" section.

Remote AP

This section describes the functional mode of remote access points. As mentioned previously in this chapter, any AP can be provisioned to function as a remote AP. Remote APs are commonly used to support small branch offices where only one or two APs are needed, or to support remote employees working from home. Remote APs can also be used to provide access to the enterprise network for users who travel and are typically forced to use unsecured public networks. Remote APs are especially useful for remote meetings or offsite conferences, providing access to many employees.

One of the advantages of a remote AP is that it is simply another AP connected to the Aruba controller. It is managed, configured, and controlled by the Aruba controller and is able to extend the enterprise network to remote users. The wireless user experience can be identical remotely as it is at the corporate offices. In addition to making management easier, since the user experience is the same anywhere on the network, user training and support is simpler.

A remote AP connects to the Aruba controller using an L2TP/IPsec VPN connection. This VPN connection allows the remote AP to securely connect to your enterprise network through an Internet accessible network connection. Through the VPN connection, the remote AP can communicate with a controller on your enterprise network, download its AP configuration, and advertise WLANs. The remote AP is configured and managed from the master controller and behaves like any other AP on the network, except rather than communicating with the controller across the enterprise's route/switch Ethernet network, it communicates with the controller through its L2TP/IPsec VPN connection.

Any Aruba AP (campus AP, IAP, UAP, or hardware RAP) is capable of operating as a remote AP. AP models that are specifically identified as RAPs, such as the RAP-3 and RAP-109, are designed with the intent of them operating as a more portable device. Hardware RAPs may have additional features to support a traveling user or a remote office environment, such as multiple Ethernet ports, PoE output for devices such as VoIP phones, security slots for physically locking them down, or USB ports that can provide cellular wireless backhaul.

VPN Server Configuration

No matter how the remote AP is being configured, or what type of AP will be functioning as a remote AP, a controller must be configured as a VPN server for the RAP to connect to. Although the RAP is using standard L2TP/IPsec protocols, due to the other ArubaOS features and WLAN capabilities that it is providing, the VPN server must be an Aruba controller. Configuring VPN services to support remote APs does not require the PEF-VPN license.

The VPN server is easily configured from the WebUI. The following menu path will bring you to the configuration window: **Configuration ➢ ADVANCED SERVICES ➢ VPN Services ➢ IPSEC**. The following is a list of the key settings needed along with information about each setting.

- Enable L2TP: This needs to be enabled (it is by default).
- Enable XAuth: If the remote AP will be using certificate authentication, this must be enabled.
- Authentication Protocols: Enable PAP.
- DNS and WINS Servers: Enter the appropriate server addresses for your network environment.
- Address Pools: This is the pool of IP addresses that the VPN server will use to assign an IP address to the remote AP. This will be the AP's inner IP address that it uses after the VPN is established. This address does not need to be a routable address on the network. However, having a valid layer 3 network defined for the address pools allows for basic troubleshooting from anywhere on the enterprise network.

▶ IKE Shared Secrets: If the remote AP will be configured for user name and password authentication, an IKE shared secret is also needed. Click the Add button and simply enter the IKE shared secret and then verify it. This method of authentication requires a great deal of administrative overhead since each remote AP has to be configured individually with user credentials. It is possible to configure the remote APs to all use the same credentials, but that would provide a much less secure environment. If an AP does not have a TPM, such as an AP-103H, you will have to use this method; otherwise, it will be much easier and more secure to use certificate based authentication (XAuth).

The following CLI output shows a basic set of commands to configure a VPN server. This configuration will allow both certificate authenticated clients and clients authenticating using a user name, password, and IKE preshared key.

```
(config) #vpdn group l2tp
(config-vpdn-l2tp)#enable
(config-vpdn-l2tp)#ppp authentication PAP
(config-vpdn-l2tp)#client configuration dns 10.254.1.21
(config-vpdn-l2tp)#client configuration wins 10.254.1.21
(config-vpdn-l2tp)#ip local pool rap-pool-90 10.1.90.220 10.1.90.230
(config) #crypto-local isakmp xauth
(config) #crypto isakmp key aruba123 address 0.0.0.0 netmask 0.0.0.0
```

Creating an AP Group

The first step in configuring an Aruba controller to support remote APs is to create an AP group for the remote APs. This AP group functions just like any other AP group, assigning virtual AP (VAP) profiles, the LMS-IP address, and any other configuration parameters that you will download to the remote AP during provisioning.

Configuring a RAP

After configuring the controller to function as a VPN server, the next step is to configure your APs as VPN clients. When Aruba first introduced the ability for an AP to function as a remote AP, the AP had to be physically connected to the network where the Aruba controller was running to provision it. After the RAP was configured, it could then be shipped to where it would be deployed.

This process could present a security risk, exposing the configured remote AP to the possibility of getting lost or stolen in its configured state. This process was also less convenient and more costly, required the AP to be shipped twice—first to the person who would be configuring it, and then after it was configured, to the person who would be using it. It also required a skilled person from the wireless networking team to have to manually touch and configure every remote AP.

To help make the process of configuring a remote AP more efficient, Aruba introduced a process known as zero-touch provisioning (ZTP), with the RAP-2 and RAP-5 supporting this process. This new method of configuration allowed the RAP to be shipped directly to the end user in its factory-default state. The end user would connect the RAP's Ethernet 0 port to an Internet connection, and the RAP's Ethernet 1 port would be connected directly to a computer's wired Ethernet port. After a few minutes, the RAP would provide the computer with an IP address, and the user would open a web browser. The RAP would display a simple web page in the browser window. The end user would enter an IP address or URL that would direct the RAP to an Aruba controller. From the controller, the RAP would download the current version of Aruba code and the VPN client configuration. The RAP would automatically reboot and establish its VPN connection.

This process worked well but was limited to the two RAP models only, and it required interaction from an end user. Although the required task was secure, due to the limited hardware support and end user involvement it was not ideal. This method has been replaced with a newer, better method, and is no longer used with newer remote APs

With the addition of Activate and the instant AP image on the IAPs, RAPs, and UAPs, Aruba introduced an improved version of ZTP. Two key advantages of the new ZTP process is that it supports a broader set of APs and it only requires the end user to plug in the AP and connect it to their Ethernet network that has Internet access.

Like the RAP-2 and RAP-5, the new APs can be shipped in the factory-default state directly to the end user. The only action required by the end user is to connect the Ethernet port of the AP to an Internet connection and power it on. Within a few minutes, the AP will communicate with the Aruba Activate server, which provides the AP with directions on where to go to download its VPN client configuration. After the configuration is downloaded, the AP will automatically reboot and establish its VPN connection.

The following sections of this chapter will describe how to manually configure a username-authenticated remote AP and a certificate-authenticated remote AP, followed by the tasks necessary to automatically configure any instant image AP (or UAP) as a remote AP using Aruba Activate.

Manual Provisioning

The oldest and still valid method of provisioning an AP to function as a remote AP is to manually provision it. Although any version of AP may be provisioned manually, manual provisioning is required when you want to configure a campus AP to function as a remote AP. Unlike IAPs, UAPs, and RAPs, the OS on campus APs does not communicate with Aruba Activate, so they cannot be automatically configured and thus require manual provisioning.

When manually provisioning an AP as a remote AP, you have the option of configuring the AP to use a user name/password/IKE preshared key for VPN authentication, or the AP can authenticate using a certificate and its MAC address. The following sections will explain both methods.

> **NOTE** *As mentioned previously in this chapter, the only time you should consider configuring a remote AP to use a user name, password, and IKE shared secret is when the AP does not support TPM.*

Whichever method is used, the AP must first be staged on the master controller. This means that the AP is connected to an Ethernet port that provides connectivity to the controller. After the AP boots, performs master controller discovery, and connects to the controller, it will be in the controller's AP database and can be provisioned.

User Name Authenticated RAP

If you have ever configured a VPN client on a computer so that it could connect back to the enterprise network, you most likely entered the following four pieces of information into the VPN software: user name, password, IKE preshared key, and the IP address or DNS hostname of the VPN server. This is the same information you need to enter when provisioning a campus AP to function as a remote AP using a user name, password, and IKE shared secret.

The AP provisioning menu can be reached using the following menu path: **Configuration ➢ WIRELESS ➢ AP Installation**. The window will display a list of APs; select the AP you want to configure and then click the Provision button.

The provisioning window will now be displayed, as shown in Figure 11.11 (to save space, some sections of the window were omitted from the figure). The first task is to select the remote AP group in the AP Parameters section. Then in the Authentication Method section, next to Remote AP select Yes, to indicate that you are provisioning the AP as a remote AP. In the Remote AP Authentication Method section, select Pre-shared Key and then enter and confirm the IKE PSK that you will be using. This key needs to match the key that you entered when you configured the controller as the VPN server.

Below the IKE PSK fields, is where you will enter the user credentials that the AP will use to authenticate to the VPN server. If you select Use Automatic Generation, you will need to click the two Generate buttons by the User Name and Password fields. These buttons will automatically generate a user name and password for the AP. The remote AP will be provisioned with the system-generated user name and password, and the username and password will also be automatically added to the internal user database on the controller. In Figure 11.11, Use Automatic Generation was not selected, and therefore the two Generate buttons could not be selected and the user name and password were entered manually.

FIGURE 11.11 Manually provisioning the RAP

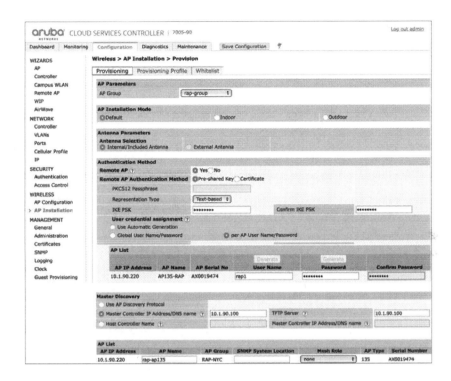

It is important to document which AP is provisioned with which user credential so that if the need arises, you can disable the correct account, blocking the AP's ability to establish its VPN connection.

If you are provisioning multiple APs at the same time (which you can do if all the APs are the same model), it may be tempting to use the Global User Name/Password button that allows you to assign a single user name and password to all the selected APs. This is not recommended, since you will have no way to block access to a single remote AP. Instead, you should select Per AP User Name/Password either with Use Automatic Generation or without it. If you do not use it, you will need to manually enter the user name, password, and password confirmation.

At this point the only two steps left are to specify the IP address or DNS hostname of the VPN server and to name the AP. The server address is entered in the Master Controller IP Address/DNS Name field of the Master Discovery section. The TFTP Server field will automatically be filled in with the same value. Do not change this.

Finally, at the bottom of the provisioning menu is the AP List section. Below the AP Name header you will need to enter the name of the remote AP. You should include RAP as part of the name, because it makes it easier to quickly identify or separate the remote APs when looking at an AP list. RAP-jsmith or RAP-johnsmith are good naming conventions.

After entering all these settings, click the Apply And Reboot button. The settings will be written to the remote AP and it will reboot.

When you configured the RAP, if you did not automatically generate a username and password, you will need to go to the internal database and create an account. If you do not, the RAP will attempt to authenticate but will be unsuccessful.

The Internal database can be accessed using the following menu path: **Configuration ➢ SECURITY ➢ Authentication ➢ Servers ➢ Internal DB**. In the Internal Database window, click the Add User button to begin. Only three pieces of information are needed: user name, password, and the role. For role, choose "ap-role," as shown in Figure 11.12, from the Role list.

FIGURE 11.12 Adding a RAP user

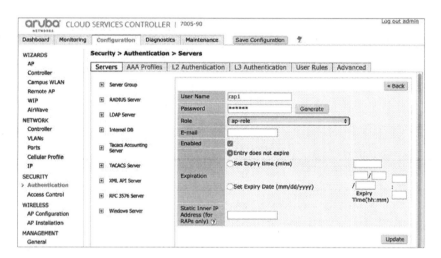

When any client authenticates to the Aruba controller, the client is assigned a role. This is true even for the RAP authenticating as a VPN client. After the RAP establishes its VPN tunnel, it is through this tunnel that the RAP communicates to the controller, performing the typical tasks of an AP. The "ap-role" role allows all of the common AP protocols, such as PAPI, CPsec, FTP, and GRE. If you would like to see all of the protocols allowed, you can use the CLI command `show rights ap-role` to see the role, policies, and all the firewall rules.

The RAP user account can also be added from the CLI prompt, as shown next. User accounts are added to a database on the controller, not as part of the `running-` or `start-up-config` files. Therefore, the command is executed from the # prompt and not from the `configure terminal` prompt. If redundant controllers are used for terminating RAPs, each controller will need to have the user accounts created in the local database since the user database is not replicated between controllers.

```
#local-userdb add username rap3 password aruba123 role ap-role
```

Certificate-Authenticated RAP

As mentioned in the previous section, certificate-authenticated remote APs are the preferred choice. Certificate-based remote APs are easier to deploy and manage. If a remote AP is lost or stolen, they are also easier to restrict since each remote AP has a unique set of credentials. All that is needed is the AP name or MAC address of the AP, which can be easily looked up in the whitelist and removed from the list.

Manually provisioning a remote AP to use certificate authentication is even easier than provisioning one for user name authentication. The process begins at the AP provisioning menu, which can be reached using the following menu path: **Configuration ➢ WIRELESS ➢ AP Installation**. The window will display a list of APs. Select the AP you want to provision and then click the Provision button.

The provisioning window will now be displayed. You can refer back to Figure 11.11 if you would like to see what the menu looks like. The first task is to select the remote AP group in the AP Parameters section. Then in the Authentication Method section, next to Remote AP select Yes. This will indicate that you are configuring the AP as a remote AP. In the Remote AP Authentication Method section, select Certificate. Because the AP was staged as a certificate-based remote AP, the AP will automatically be added to the remote AP whitelist. This precludes the need to manually add the remote AP to the whitelist.

At this point the only two steps left are to specify the IP address or DNS hostname of the VPN server and to name the AP. The server address is entered in the Master Controller IP Address/DNS Name field of the Master Discovery section. The TFTP Server field will automatically be filled in with the same value. Do not change this.

Finally, at the bottom of the provisioning menu is the Remote AP List section. Below the AP Name header enter the name of the RAP. You should include RAP as part of the name, because it makes it easier to quickly identify or separate remote APs when looking at an AP list. RAP-jsmith or RAP-johnsmith are good naming conventions.

After entering all these settings, click the Apply And Reboot button. The settings will be written to the remote AP and it will reboot. ArubaOS will also automatically add the MAC address of the remote AP into the remote AP whitelist database. With the MAC address in the whitelist, the remote AP is now approved to authenticate its VPN connection to the Aruba controller.

If you need to add, delete, or modify the remote AP entries in the whitelist, you can reach the whitelist window using the following menu path: **Configuration ➢ WIRELESS ➢ AP Installation ➢ Whitelist ➢ Remote AP ➢ Entries**. Note that the Entries button is near the top at the far right. This button is often not displayed due to scrolling of a smaller browser window.

You can see the Remote AP whitelist from the Entries window where you manually added the APs or from the CLI prompt using the following command:

```
#show whitelist-db rap
```

You can also manage the Remote AP whitelist database from the CLI by using the `whitelist-db` command. The following CLI output shows a whitelist entry being deleted from the database, followed by a display of all the whitelist editing capabilities using the `whitelist-db rap` command. The whitelist database synchronizes with all of the controllers in a master/local configuration, so there is no need to add the MAC addresses to all the controllers.

```
#whitelist-db rap del mac-address d8:c7:c8:c0:98:24

#whitelist-db rap ?
add                 Add a RAP Whitelist Entry
del                 Delete a RAP Whitelist Entry
modify              Modify a RAP Whitelist Entry
purge               Purge the list
revoke              Revoke a RAP Whitelist Entry
```

Aruba Activate

Zero-touch provisioning utilizes the instant or UAP software to contact the Activate server, which directs the AP to the correct controller for provisioning. This automatic configuration occurs when the AP boots for the first time, or when the AP is booted again after it is reset to factory default. The "IAP to RAP" redirection for automatic provisioning is done in Activate by creating a remote AP provisioning rule for a folder and assigning the AP to that folder. The process and all of the components were explained earlier in this chapter in the "Aruba Activate" section.

Activate itself does not provision the AP. It merely directs the AP to a controller where the provisioning information is preloaded. The AP will then communicate with the controller and download the provisioning information. The AP is only allowed to download the configuration if the AP is in the Remote AP whitelist.

Activate has an option that lets you export a list of APs as a whitelist script. The column headers of Activate provide the ability to filter and sort the list of APs that are displayed. Clicking the Whitelist CLI button at the top right of the AP list will export the list to a text file. The contents of the text file include directions, along with CLI commands that can be executed on the controller.

VAP Data Forwarding Modes

Up to this point, this section has focused on how to configure and provision the remote AP and how it establishes a connection to the VPN server. The secure VPN tunnel that is established between the remote AP and the controller allows these two devices to securely communicate configuration settings (in other words, control traffic). Since client traffic is typically already encrypted by the client device and decrypted by the controller, it is not necessary for the VPN connection to encrypt it again. Therefore, to optimize performance, client data is only encapsulated in the IPsec tunnel. If for any reason you need to have the VPN connection encrypt the client data, the AP System profile has a Double Encrypt option that will provide IPsec encryption for all data.

It is important to remember that a remote AP is typically configured to advertise a WLAN (SSID) at a remote location. To do this, you need to assign a VAP profile (WLAN) to the AP group that the remote AP has been provisioned to. The VAP profile can be configured with one of four forwarding modes. Each forwarding mode provides a different method to process the user traffic and place it on the wired network. The four forwarding methods are Tunnel, Bridge, Split-Tunnel, and Decrypt-Tunnel. Each VAP can be assigned its own forwarding mode, depending on the needs of the VAP.

If a remote AP has one or more additional wired ports, each port can be individually configured with one of the four forwarding modes. This setting is made in the Wired AP profile. These forwarding modes will be explained in the following four sections.

Tunnel

When a VAP is configured for Tunnel mode, all WLAN traffic is encapsulated in a GRE tunnel and forwarded to the controller, as illustrated in Figure 11.13. Tunnel mode assumes that the client and controller will be handling encryption. The AP does not encrypt the client data.

FIGURE 11.13 Tunnel mode

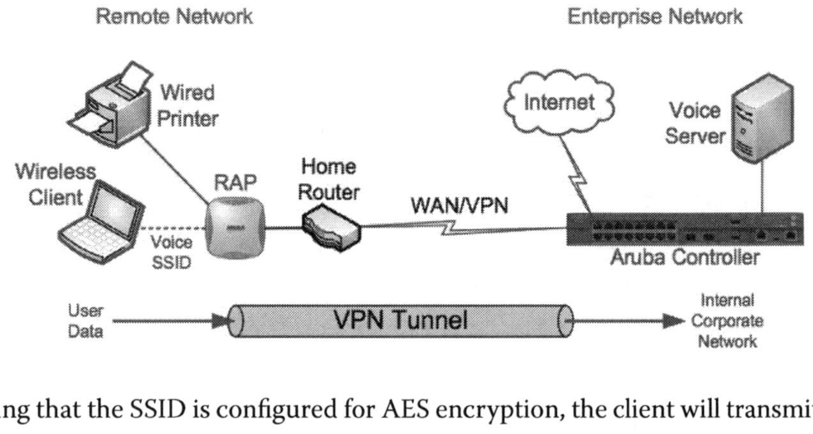

Assuming that the SSID is configured for AES encryption, the client will transmit the encrypted data to the remote AP. The AP will encapsulate the encrypted data packets in a GRE tunnel and forward it to the controller through the VPN tunnel. The VPN will not encrypt the data; it will only tunnel it back to the controller. When the controller receives the data, it will remove it from the VPN tunnel, and then from the GRE tunnel. The AES encrypted data will then be decrypted and forwarded onto the enterprise network.

All wireless client traffic will be sent to the controller. The controller will process and forward the traffic. Even traffic destined for the Internet must first be forwarded to the enterprise network before it can be routed to the Internet. If the traffic is destined for a device on the remote network where the remote AP is located, the controller would then have to send the data back to the network where it originated.

The previous explanation referred to the client using AES encryption. Although other encryption methods such as WEP or TKIP could be used, both of these methods were deprecated in 2012 by both the IEEE and the Wi-Fi Alliance. These methods are still supported by ArubaOS for compatibility with older client devices. However, if either method is applied to a WLAN, that WLAN will only support legacy 802.11a/b/g data rates. Because of this limitation, the examples in this chapter will refer to AES as the only encryption method that will be used.

Figure 11.13 displays the remote network on the left and the enterprise network on the right. The remote network consists of a remote AP with a client connected to it wirelessly and a printer connected to it using an Ethernet cable. The remote AP is physically connected to a home router and is building a VPN connection back to an Aruba controller that resides on the enterprise network. The controller could be in a demilitarized zone (DMZ) or could be on the internal network. Since there are numerous options, the enterprise firewall architecture is not illustrated.

If the controller is behind a firewall, the remote AP will use Network Address Translation-Traversal (NAT-T) on UDP port 4500 to negotiate the firewall. On the firewall, UDP port 4500 will need to be opened and forwarded to the controller for the remote AP to be able to communicate with the controller. The enterprise network shows a voice server and a connection for user traffic to reach the Internet.

Below the network diagram is a logical diagram illustrating that all user data from the devices connected to the remote AP, whether wireless or wired, is sent to the controller inside the VPN tunnel. When the data arrives at the enterprise network, the controller will strip the data from the tunneled frames, apply the firewall rules from the user's role, and forward it as permitted.

When Tunnel mode is deployed, all data is forwarded to the VPN server (Aruba controller) from the remote AP. The devices connected to the remote AP do not have direct access to any resources on the remote network. Any access to the remote network must be tunneled to the enterprise network and then routed back to the remote network.

> **NOTE** *Tunnel mode works well in environments where the client traffic must inherently communicate back to the enterprise network, such as in an environment where voice clients must communicate with a voice server.*

If any of the wired ports on the remote AP are configured for Tunnel mode, the wired traffic is always encrypted by the remote AP using IPsec, prior to the traffic being tunneled back to the VPN controller. Tunnel mode allows wired or wireless VLANs to be changed using VSA, as described in Chapter 7, "Role Derivation."

Bridge

When a VAP is configured for Bridge mode, all WLAN traffic is bridged locally at the Remote AP and placed onto the remote LAN, as illustrated in Figure 11.14.

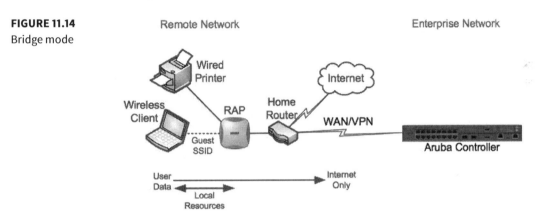

FIGURE 11.14
Bridge mode

Assuming that the SSID is configured for AES encryption, the client will transmit the encrypted data to the remote AP. The remote AP will decrypt the client data, apply any firewall rules from the user role, and route or NAT the client data onto the uplink Ethernet interface of the remote AP, thus bridging the data onto the remote network. None of the client data will have access to the enterprise network. Since the client traffic is being placed on the remote LAN, the client will be able to communicate directly with any local resources, such as printers and servers that are also connected to the remote network. Internet traffic will be forwarded through the remote or home router.

Figure 11.14 displays the remote network on the left and the enterprise network on the right. The remote network consists of a remote AP with a client connected to it wirelessly and a printer connected to it using an Ethernet cable. The remote AP is physically connected to a home router and is building a VPN connection back to an Aruba controller for communication and PAPI traffic. The controller could be installed in a DMZ, or it could be connected to the internal network. Since there are numerous options, the enterprise firewall architecture is not illustrated in the figure. If the controller is behind a firewall, UDP port 4500 would need to be opened and forwarded to the controller for the RAP to be able to communicate with the controller.

Below the network diagram is a logical diagram illustrating that all user data from the devices connected to the remote AP, whether wireless or wired, is placed directly onto the remote network. All of the devices have access to the remote network's local resources. The user's data is never forwarded to the enterprise network. If the user data is bound for the Internet, then the local home router will forward the data directly to the Internet.

Bridge mode works well in a guest environment. As an example, the CEO wants to have a remote AP at home to be able to easily connect to the corporate network while working from home. His wife and children obviously want wireless Internet access and the CEO does not want to have to install a second AP, or provide his family with his wireless credentials. A guest or family WLAN can be created and advertised from the remote AP. This WLAN would typically be configured with a WPA2/AES-PSK, and the traffic would be bridged onto the local network and then routed to the Internet as needed.

The remote AP's IPsec tunnel will securely forward any necessary control traffic and any 802.1X/EAP exchanges if the WLAN is configured to use 802.1X/EAP authentication. Firewall enforcement of the role assigned to the client is performed by the remote AP. With Bridge mode, captive portal authentication is not supported.

If any of the wired ports on the remote AP are configured for Bridge mode, the wired traffic is bridged locally at the remote AP and placed on the LAN. The wired traffic can only communicate with devices on the remote network or out to the Internet through the remote or home router.

Configuring Tunnel mode on a remote AP's VAP was performed by simply choosing Tunnel from the Forward Mode dropdown menu. Configuring a RAP VAP for Bridge mode initially requires selecting Bridge from the Forward Mode dropdown menu; however, there are some other settings that may need to be set or verified.

Bridge mode clients will need to obtain an IP address from the remote network. An IP address can be obtained from the local home router that the remote AP is connected to, or you can configure the remote AP to act as a DHCP server. The remote AP DHCP settings are configured from the AP System profile, as shown in Figure 11.15. In order for the RAP DHCP server to function, the VLAN specified in Remote-AP DHCP Server VLAN must be the same VLAN that is specified in the VAP profile. If the two VLANs match, then the RAP DHCP server will be used. If they are different, DHCP will come from the local network.

These settings can also be made from the CLI prompt, using the following commands:

```
(config) #ap system-profile rap-dhcp
(AP system profile "rap-dhcp") #rap-dhcp-server-id 192.168.11.1
(AP system profile "rap-dhcp") #rap-dhcp-default-router 192.168.11.1
(AP system profile "rap-dhcp") #rap-dhcp-pool-start 192.168.11.2
(AP system profile "rap-dhcp") #rap-dhcp-pool-end 192.168.11.254
(AP system profile "rap-dhcp") #rap-dhcp-pool-netmask 255.255.255.0
```

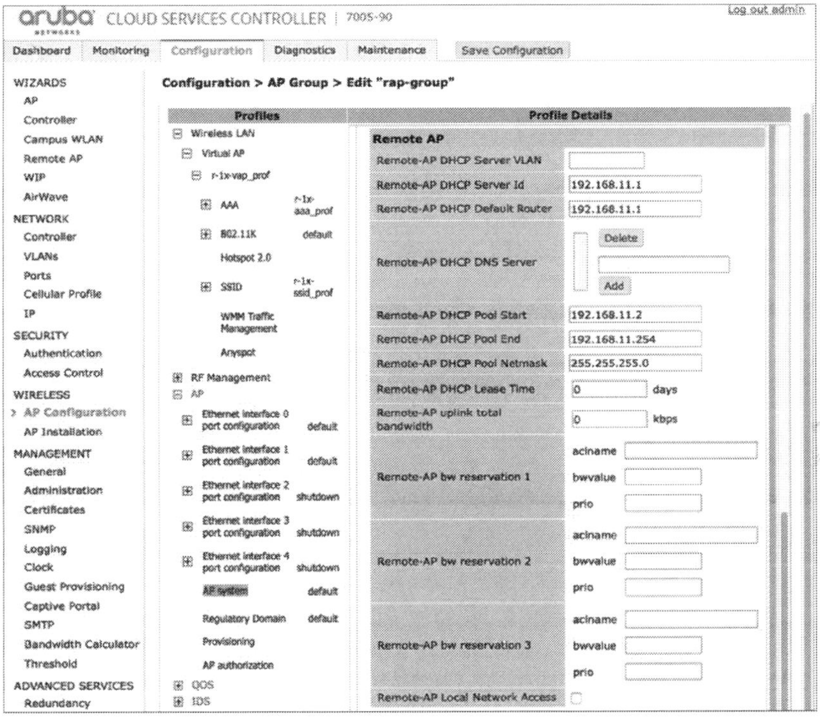

FIGURE 11.15
Configuring DHCP for Bridge mode

Split-Tunnel

Tunnel mode and Bridge mode each have desired strong points. Split-Tunnel leverages the strengths of both of these on the same WLAN. Split-Tunnel provides full tunneled access to the corporate enterprise network and bridge traffic onto the remote LAN, based on the destination of the packet.

When a VAP is configured for Split-Tunnel mode, the traffic is intelligently tunneled to the enterprise network or bridged onto the remote LAN. This path selection is based on firewall rules that are downloaded to the RAP.

Figure 11.16 displays the remote network on the left and the enterprise (corporate) network on the right. The remote network consists of a remote AP with a client connected to it wirelessly and a printer connected to it using an Ethernet cable. The remote AP is physically connected to a home router, and the remote AP is building a VPN connection back to an Aruba controller that resides on the enterprise network. The home router also provides an egress out to the Internet.

FIGURE 11.16
Split-Tunnel mode

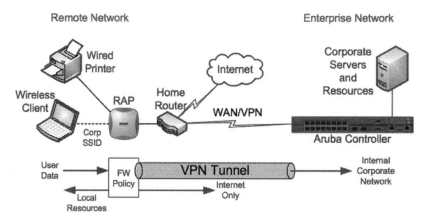

The controller could be in a DMZ or it could be on the internal network. Since there are numerous options, the enterprise firewall architecture is not illustrated. If the controller is behind a firewall, the remote AP will use NAT-T on UDP port 4500 to negotiate the firewall. On the firewall, UDP port 4500 will need to be opened and forwarded to the controller for the remote AP to be able to communicate with the controller.

If a VAP is assigned to the AP group that the remote AP belongs to, when an 802.1X/EAP client authenticates to the WLAN, the role assigned to the client is downloaded and applied on the remote AP. This means that the firewall processing of the client traffic is now performed at the remote AP instead of the controller. This is necessary since the split-tunnel decision making needs to be performed at the RAP in order to determine where the traffic will be forwarded.

Below the network diagram is a logical diagram illustrating the user data from the devices connected to the remote AP, whether wireless or wired, forwarded to the corporate network or NAT'd onto the home network to be sent to the local printer or to the Internet through the home router.

When the 802.1X/EAP client data is transmitted to the remote AP, the remote AP decrypts the data so that it can inspect the destination and contents of the frame. The remote AP then checks the frame against the client's firewall rules. If the traffic is destined for the enterprise network, the remote AP re-encrypts the data using IPsec and sends it to the enterprise network through the VPN tunnel.

If upon inspection the client data is not destined for the enterprise network, the remote AP will NAT the traffic onto the local network. Client traffic on the local network can communicate with any of the local resources at the remote location, or it can be sent to the Internet through the home router.

Split-Tunnel works well in an 802.1X/EAP corporate environment. If an employee has a remote AP at home, their local or Internet traffic will be expedited onto the local network or forwarded to the Internet. This limits only corporate traffic to be sent back to the enterprise network.

Split-Tunnel also works well if a remote AP is installed at a satellite or remote office environment. In this environment, Split-Tunnel could be used for both the employee 802.1X/EAP VAP and for a captive portal–enabled guest network VAP.

If any of the wired ports on the remote AP are configured for Split-Tunnel, like the wireless client, the wired traffic is checked against the client's firewall rules. If the traffic is destined for the enterprise network, the remote AP encrypts the data using IPsec and sends it to the enterprise network through the VPN tunnel.

If the wired traffic is not destined for the enterprise network, the remote AP traffic will be bridged onto the local network. The wired traffic can communicate with any of the local resources at the remote location, or it can be sent to the Internet through the home router.

Split-Tunnel requires the following tasks to be performed for it to work:

- Create netdestination defining corporate network
- Create split-tunnel firewall policy
- Create a user role and assign split-tunnel policy to the user role
- Define role derivation process for assigning user role
- Set VAP forward mode to Split-Tunnel

The first task is to create a destination alias for the corporate network. This can be easily performed using the following CLI commands. Make sure all the corporate network ranges are part of this destination alias. In this example, the corporate network consists of networks 192.168.240.0/24 and 10.0.0.0/8.

```
(config)#netdestination corpnet
(config-dest)#network 192.168.240.0 255.255.255.0
(config-dest)#network 10.0.0.0 255.0.0.0
```

After the destination alias is created, the split-tunnel firewall policy can be created. This policy should first allow DHCP. Next, be sure to include any "deny access" rules required to limit and control access to any resources that the remote user should not have access to. Then the policy will check if the traffic should be forwarded to the corporate network. And finally, any other traffic will be placed on the local network using the route src-nat command. This command will use the IP address of the remote AP as the source of the traffic. The following CLI commands will define the policy and rules:

```
(config)#ip access-list session split-tunnel-policy
(config-sess-split-tunnel-policy)#any any svc-dhcp permit
(config-sess-split-tunnel-policy)#alias corpnet alias corpnet any permit
(config-sess-split-tunnel-policy)#alias user any any route src-nat
```

The following CLI example of the split-tunnel policy is more restrictive. You do not have to use these examples; you can define whatever firewall rules you want.

```
(config) #ip access-list session split-tunnel-policy
(config-sess-split-tunnel-policy)#any any svc-dhcp permit
(config-sess-split-tunnel-policy)#user alias corpnet any permit
(config-sess-split-tunnel-policy)#alias user any any route src-nat
```

Since clients are assigned user roles, not policies, a user role needs to be created and the policy should be assigned to the role, as defined in the following CLI commands:

```
(config) #user-role corp-split-role
(config-role) #session-acl split-tunnel-policy
```

Next you need to specify how the authenticating client will be assigned the user role. The client can receive a role through a VSA, a server-derived role, or a default role. This process was explained in Chapter 7.

Finally, in the VAP profile, the forwarding mode needs to be set to Split-Tunnel. When operating in Split-Tunnel mode, VLANs cannot be changed with a VSA, server derivation rule, or user derivation rule. The VLAN assigned to the VAP will be the VLAN the user receives.

Decrypt-Tunnel

When a VAP is configured for Decrypt-Tunnel mode, all WLAN traffic is encapsulated and forwarded to the controller, similar to Tunnel mode. The difference is that when the client sends the data to the remote AP, the remote AP decrypts the data first before forwarding it to the controller. Although enabling Decrypt-Tunnel on a VAP that is operating on a remote AP is technically a valid configuration, it is typically not a wise decision. Since by default the remote APs VPN tunnel does not provide any encryption for the client traffic, decrypting the client traffic and then tunneling it across the Internet to the Aruba controller is not a wise security choice. Therefore, this configuration will not be explained any further.

VAP Remote-AP Operation Modes

The previous section "VAP Data Forwarding Modes" described the four possible forwarding modes. In addition to selecting the forwarding mode that will be used, when assigning a WLAN to a remote AP, you must specify the Remote-AP Operation mode. The VAP profile can be configured with one of four operation modes. The Remote-AP Operation mode defines how the VAP is advertised and its availability when there is a connectivity issue between the remote AP and the VPN server.

The four Remote-AP Operation modes are Standard, Always, Backup, and Persistent. Each VAP can be assigned its own operation mode, depending on the needs of the VAP. These operation modes will be explained in the following sections.

Standard

When a remote AP boots and establishes its VPN connection to the controller, at that time the remote AP will download the configuration of any VAP configured with Standard operation mode. Any VAPs configured with Standard operation mode will be up and running. Simply stated, if the VPN tunnel is up, the WLAN is up. Standard mode can be used with any of the forwarding methods (Tunnel, Bridge, Split-Tunnel, and Decrypt-Tunnel).

Standard operation mode is commonly used with Tunnel and Split-Tunnel forwarding modes, since these operating modes require a tunnel to the controller and tunnel modes are useless if the tunnel is down.

The remaining three operation modes are applicable only to Bridge mode VAPs.

Always

When a VAP is configured with the Always operation mode, if the remote AP has power and a connection to an Ethernet network, then the VAP is up and running. Always mode can only be used with Bridge mode data forwarding. The VAP configuration is stored in the flash of the remote AP, so obviously the remote AP must connect to the VPN server at least once so that the VAP profile can be downloaded to the remote AP. The VAP can only be configured with an open or PSK-enabled SSID.

Always operation mode works well with the home guest network that was described in the "Bridge" section of this chapter. As long as the AP has power and a link, the VAP is operational.

Backup

Backup operation mode is typically not the first choice for a VAP; however, it can be very useful as part of the WLAN capabilities provided by a remote AP. With Backup mode, the VAP is only up when the remote AP cannot establish a VPN connection with the controller. When the VPN is reestablished, the Backup mode VAP is disabled. The VAP can only be configured with an open or PSK-enabled SSID.

The first example of Backup operation mode is often referred to as "hotel mode." If a remote AP is plugged into an Ethernet network at a hotel, or any Ethernet network that has a captive portal, the captive portal will prevent the remote AP from establishing a VPN tunnel to the Aruba controller. If the remote AP is unable to build its VPN tunnel, the Backup mode (hotel mode) VAP will be advertised. This WLAN will allow the wireless user to connect to the SSID, and the remote AP will NAT the user traffic to the captive portal server, as illustrated in Figure 11.17. The wireless user will be prompted with the captive portal logon page and be allowed to log on to the hotel network. If the user authentication is successful, since the user traffic is being NAT'd through the remote

AP, it is the MAC address of the remote AP that is allowed to access the Internet by the hotel firewall.

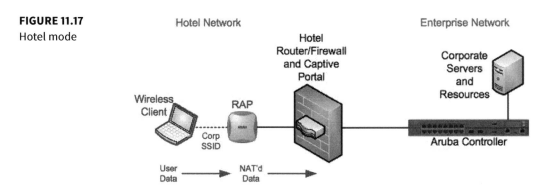

FIGURE 11.17
Hotel mode

After the remote AP is allowed to communicate to the Internet and it successfully builds its VPN tunnel to the controller, the Backup mode VAP will be shut down.

Another good use of a Backup operation mode configured VAP is to provide backup access to the Internet for employees who usually connect using an 802.1X/EAP split-tunnel connection. If the VPN tunnel disconnects, the split-tunnel-enabled VAP, which is operating in Standard operation mode, will also disconnect. This will prevent the wireless client from accessing either the corporate network or the Internet. In this situation, it can be useful to have a Backup operation mode VAP enabled to provide temporary Internet access for the employee, until the VPN tunnel and the 802.1X/EAP split-tunnel VAP is working again.

Persistent

With Persistent operation mode, the VPN tunnel must first be established for the VAP to be enabled. Once the VPN tunnel is up, if it goes down the VAP will continue to operate. The Aruba manual states that Persistent mode was designed for 802.1X/EAP-based VAPs. Unfortunately, Persistent mode works only with VAPs using Bridge forwarding mode, whereas most 802.1X/EAP-based VAPs are configured for Split-Tunnel forwarding mode. Therefore, you have little reason to use Persistent operation mode. One instance where Persistent mode can be used is if you are using Bridge forwarding mode and you want initial authentication to go to the controller. Once authenticated, user traffic is locally bridged to the Internet. If the VPN tunnel is down, then already authenticated users continue to work, whereas the new users cannot authenticate.

Forwarding Modes with Operation Modes

The previous few sections described the four forwarding modes and the four operation modes. Table 11.1 provides a cross-reference of the usage of the forwarding modes with the operation modes. Decrypt-Tunnel mode is not included in the chart since it is not recommended for use in a remote AP.

In this chapter, examples were provided of instances for using the different forwarding modes. These uses are listed in the chart enclosed in parentheses.

TABLE 11.1: Forwarding modes with operation modes

OPERATION MODES	FORWARDING MODES		
	TUNNEL	BRIDGE	SPLIT-TUNNEL
Standard	<ul><li>VAP enabled when VPN tunnel is up</li><li>(Voice VAP)</li></ul>	<ul><li>VAP enabled when VPN tunnel is up</li></ul>	<ul><li>VAP enabled when VPN tunnel is up</li><li>(Employee 802.1X/EAP VAP)</li><li>(Guest captive portal VAP)</li></ul>
Always	Not supported	<ul><li>VAP is always enabled</li><li>Open or PSK enabled SSID</li><li>VAP profile stored on remote AP</li><li>(Home guest VAP)</li></ul>	Not supported
Backup	Not supported	<ul><li>VAP enabled when VPN tunnel is down</li><li>Open or PSK-enabled SSID</li><li>VAP profile stored on remote AP</li><li>(Hotel temporary VAP)</li></ul>	Not supported
Persistent	Not supported	<ul><li>VAP enabled when VPN tunnel is established</li><li>VAP stays enabled if VPN tunnel goes down</li></ul>	Not supported

Air Monitor

The Air Monitor (AM) function can be configured on any radio on any IAP, UAP, campus AP, or RAP. AM is a radio mode that does not provide support for any VAPs, and it is dedicated to scanning the 802.11 channels for layer 2 information. Although APs will also scan channels other than the channel the AP is operating on, AMs perform faster scanning, providing the controller with more information and quicker access to the information. The more time an AP or AM spends sampling the RF environment, the more accurate and timely the wireless intrusion prevention (WIP) calculations.

AMs can also be used by the controller to provide wireless and/or wired rogue AP containment. This means that if you have deployed AMs in your network, the APs will not be called on to perform this task, making them more available to support wireless users.

The additional scanning performed by AMs will provide more statistical information to the controller or to an external monitoring server if you are using one, such as an AirWave server. There are conditions when an AP cannot perform scans, such as when the AP is hosting high-priority traffic from voice or video clients. During these times, the amount of data that the AP contributes will be greatly reduced. Implementing AMs should always be considered when designing a wireless network that will operate with large amounts of high-priority traffic.

RF statistical information such as number of devices, retry rates, received signal strength indicator (RSSI) level, frame types/size distribution, and interference levels can greatly help with WLAN troubleshooting.

AMs can also be easily used for performing remote packet captures. Since an AM is not providing wireless support for any client devices, an AM can be temporarily set to a specific channel to monitor and capture packets. When the packet analysis is complete, the AM will return to scanning all the specified channels. Remote packet capture is explained extensively in Chapter 13, "Network Monitoring."

AMs are also useful if you want to perform spectrum analysis. When performing spectrum analysis, it is best to dedicate the AP as a spectrum monitor (SM), which is often done by converting an existing AP or AM temporarily to be an SM. If you temporarily convert an AP to be an SM, the AP can no longer advertise WLANs, forcing wireless clients to connect to another AP (which is typically not as big an issue as you may think). However, it will provide less RF coverage and possibly even a coverage hole (which is a big issue). Because an AM does not provide any wireless services to clients, temporarily converting an AM to an SM will not disrupt any wireless network services.

Much of the information that an AM is looking at when it is scanning is management and control frames. Since these frames are transmitted at the lowest data rates, the cell coverage of an AM is typically larger than the high-capacity AP deployments that are typically being installed. This means that you may need to install one AM for every three, four, or even five APs.

Now that you have a better understanding of the uses and benefits of installing AMs, let us look at how to set them up and their configuration and scanning settings. The first task is to create a group dedicated to AMs. You should name it something logical like "am-group." From the Configuration menu for the AP group, create an AM radio profile for each band (such as 11a-am and 11g-am) and set the Mode to "am-mode," as shown in Figure 11.18.

FIGURE 11.18
Selecting the AM mode

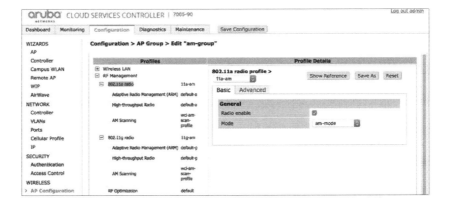

After setting the mode to "am-mode," you then need to create an AM Scanning profile, as shown in Figure 11.19. This profile does not have many options. Go to the Advanced menu to see the settings. Aruba recommends not changing any of the dwell time settings under any circumstance (unless advised by Aruba's Technical Assistance Center [TAC] team).

FIGURE 11.19
AM Scanning profile

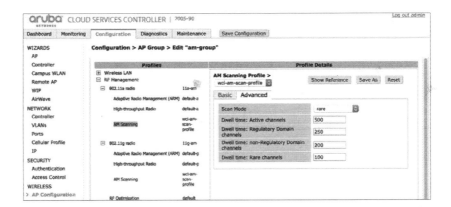

The only setting you should change is the scan mode, and Rare is the recommended setting. This setting will scan the entire 2.4 GHz range, 5 GHz range, and the 4.9 GHz range (used for public safety in most regulatory domains).

Spectrum Monitor

When an AP is configured as a spectrum monitor (SM), it operates only as a layer 1 sensing device. Spectrum monitoring can be configured individually on a radio-by-radio basis. An AP or AM can be part of an AP group that is configured to operate as an SM, or an AP or AM can be temporarily overridden to operate as an SM; providing an easy method for returning the AP or AM back to its original status.

Spectrum monitoring will not be explained further in this chapter as it is covered extensively in Chapter 13.

Mesh AP

A last functional mode is mesh AP. A mesh AP operates in the same way as a campus AP, with the exception that a campus AP uses Ethernet to forward its traffic to the controller whereas a mesh AP uses a wireless connection to forward its traffic. Wireless mesh will not be explained further in this chapter since there is an entire chapter, Chapter 14, "Wireless Mesh," devoted to the topic.

Secure Jack

Aruba uses the term Secure Jack to refer to a wired port that is enabled, untrusted, and configured with an authentication method such as 802.1X/EAP or captive portal. Some APs and all RAPs have additional ports that can be used to connect wired devices. The default behavior of these ports differs, depending on which port it is. Ethernet 0 and 1 are configured with the default profile, which enables them as trusted ports. The rest of the Ethernet ports are configured in shutdown mode by default.

Ports in the Trusted state behave as simple switch ports and will allow anybody to connect with no authentication and no user role. If the extra port is not being used on the AP, it is a good idea to shut it down or add authentication by making it untrusted. The normal default mode is set up so that regardless of which port you plug in as an uplink the AP can connect to the network and function. However, the convenience of having two ports enabled and trusted needs to be weighed against the potential risk of a rogue user plugging in to the second port and receiving uncontrolled access to the network.

You configure whether the wired ports on an AP are enabled and/or trusted in the Wired AP profile, as shown in Figure 11.20. From this menu you can create one or more profiles, depending on your needs. This menu also allows you to select the forwarding mode for the wired client traffic.

On a remote AP, Ethernet 0 should always be connected as the uplink port. Campus APs may use other options for redundancy or backup.

FIGURE 11.20
Secure Jack

If the port is configured as untrusted, then an AAA profile can be assigned to the port, as shown in Figure 11.21. The AAA profile can be selected from this menu but can only be modified from the Authentication menu or the All Profiles menu. Configuring an AAA profile was explained in Chapter 6, "Authentication and Encryption."

FIGURE 11.21
Wired AAA profile

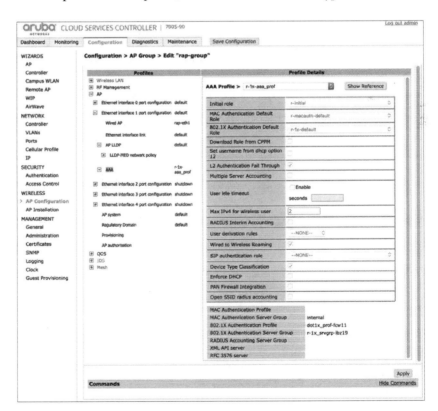

CHAPTER 12

Adaptive Radio Management

IN THIS CHAPTER, YOU WILL
LEARN ABOUT THE FOLLOWING:

- ARM History
- ARM Radio Configuration
  - ARM Scanning
  - AP Channel and Power Selection
  - Dynamic Frequency Selection Channels
- Client Match
  - Client Match Data Collection
  - Sticky Clients
  - Band Steering/Band Balancing
  - Load Balancing
  - Move Client Process
  - Client Match Process Review
- ARM Profile Settings

ADAPTIVE RADIO MANAGEMENT (ARM) IS AN ARUBA-PATENTED technology that is designed to make the wireless network more reliable and self-tuning, and to provide a better-connected experience for the wireless user. This chapter begins by examining the history of ARM followed by an in-depth explanation of the current version of ARM and how it operates.

ARM History

The first version of the Aruba operating system was known as Aruba AirOS version 2.2. This first release required an initial manual radio calibration. Then after initialization of the radios, there was an automatic process known as Auto Radio Resource Allocation, or Auto-RRA. Auto-RRA allowed the APs to automatically change channel, and if an AP failed, nearby APs could increase their power to help provide coverage for the missing AP.

Adaptive Radio Management (ARM) was introduced in version 2.3. With ARM, the initial calibration was available but no longer required; however, the manual initialization was optional. These early versions of ARM were focused on monitoring the network environment and automatically setting the channel and power on the APs. This greatly reduced the complexity of installing a wireless system.

Aruba changed the name of the operating system from Aruba AirOS to ArubaOS when version 3 was introduced. Version 3 retained the same version of ARM as 2.4 had. Later, with the release of version 3.4 a major upgrade to ARM was made with the introduction of ARM 2.0.

ARM 2.0 was a significant upgrade from the earlier version. In addition to automatically monitoring and adjusting the AP's channel and power settings, ARM 2.0 monitored client activity and was able to interact with clients, moving them to a better band or channel.

ARM 2.0 introduced the following key features and capabilities to enhance the client experience:

Band Steering   This helped to decrease the number of clients connecting to the 2.4 GHz radios and make them connect to the 5 GHz radios instead. If a client sent a 2.4 GHz probe request to an AP, the AP would check to see if the client was on the list of 5 GHz–capable devices. If so, the AP would then take into consideration the client RSSI signal level and the load of the AP. If the signal level was strong enough, the AP decided to steer the client to the 5 GHz radio. The AP would do this by only responding to the 5 GHz probe request. The client would think that only 5 GHz APs existed, defaulting the client to connect to the network using a 5 GHz connection. Band steering was only performed when the client initially attempted to connect to an AP.

Spectrum Load Balancing   This was developed to distribute clients between APs in denser deployment environments. When a client attempted to connect to an AP, if the AP's client load was at or above a predefined threshold value, the AP would deny the client access. This would force the client to attempt to connect to another AP. If the client was denied by two APs in a row, it would be allowed to connect to the third AP it tried. Spectrum load balancing was only performed on new clients, not clients already associated to the AP.

Co-channel Interference Mitigation   This feature helped reduce co-channel interference (CCI). When greater numbers of APs are deployed in close proximity, it is likely that two or more APs will end up on the same channel, and more likely to interfere with each other. CCI interference mitigation is also known as Mode Aware ARM. If ARM detected higher coverage levels than necessary, it would turn an AP into an air monitor (AM). This would help avoid higher levels of interference on the channel. Later, if gaps in coverage are detected, then ARM would turn the AM back into an AP.

Airtime Fairness   This helped to more evenly distribute transmissions to the client, dividing the transmissions by time as opposed to packets. WLAN devices use CSMA/CA to obtain access to the medium. CSMA/CA provides each device with equal access to transmit a frame. Unfortunately, slower transmissions will take longer, unfairly hindering the throughput of faster devices. Using the airtime fairness "fair-access" option, each transmission from the AP to the client is provided with the same amount of airtime, not media access. By providing access based on airtime, each transmission is affected equally with the addition of any new devices on the network. Airtime fairness only affects downstream traffic from the AP to the client, since Aruba does not have the ability to change the 802.11 behavior of client devices.

The current iteration of ARM, known as ARM 3.0, was introduced with ArubaOS 6.3. In addition to automatically monitoring and adjusting the AP's channel and power settings, a new client management technology called Client Match was introduced. Client Match incorporates a set of client optimization tools and enhanced algorithms that continuously collects session performance metrics from client devices, and then uses this data to intelligently steer a client to a better AP or radio. This chapter will include an explanation of Client Match and how it operates.

With the transition of ARM from one version to the next, AP support for ARM has also changed. As newer features were added, more hardware capabilities were needed, making some of the older devices incapable of supporting some of the newer features. Historically, at the point when these older devices did not support the new features, the wireless technology had advanced enough that organizations were considering upgrading the devices anyway.

Older APs do not support some of the newer features, and some newer APs only support the features that have been released in the newest versions of ArubaOS. The following is a general summary of the features supported by the different families of APs, followed by Table 12.1, which visually shows the compatibility.

Legacy 802.11 a/b/g APs These APs worked with the original version of ARM and with ARM 2.0. These APs do not work with ARM 3.0.

802.11n APs All of these APs supported ARM, ARM 2.0, and ARM 3.0 with Client Match.

802.11ac These APs support only ARM 3.0 with Client Match.

TABLE 12.1: ARM support by AP family

AP FAMILY	ARM	ARM 2.0	ARM 3.0/CLIENT MATCH
802.11 a/b/g	Yes	Yes	No
802.11 n	Yes	Yes	Yes
802.11 ac	No	No	Yes

As with ARM 2.0, ARM 3.0 continued to provide the capability of the controller to dynamically adjust the channel and power of each AP based on the information it received while scanning the frequencies. Additionally, ARM 3.0 included a major enhancement to previous versions of ARM with the introduction of Client Match.

When Client Match is enabled on a controller with 802.11n APs, the Client Match features override any of the ARM 2.0 features (legacy band steering, load balancing, or station handoff assist). If you have any 802.11ac APs deployed, these APs are not even capable of supporting any of the ARM 2.0 features; therefore, Client Match should be enabled.

In order for ARM to perform its tasks, it requires that information about the RF environment is gathered by the controller. This chapter will explain how ARM scanning is performed for gathering the RF information needed to configure AP channel and power settings along with how Client Match functions.

ARM Radio Configuration

If ARM scanning is enabled, each AP continually scans all the RF channels in the regulatory domain that the AP is operating within. The AP monitors the activity on each channel. The information that ARM collects on all the channels is used to determine the best channel and power settings for each AP.

ARM settings are assigned to an AP group and are configured separately for each band: 2.4 GHz and 5 GHz. ARM is calculated individually for each radio.

The following sections explain the scanning process that ARM uses, the AP channel and power selection process, and dynamic frequency selection channels and avoidance. Figure 12.1 displays the ARM Profile Advanced menu. Many of the settings in this menu will be referenced in this chapter.

ARM Scanning

The ARM scanning process begins with the AP operating on an assigned channel. The AP operates on this channel for 10 seconds (`arm scan-interval`), advertising its assigned SSIDs and communicating with client devices. After the 10 seconds of serving SSIDs to its clients, the AP switches to another valid channel in its 802.11d-defined regulatory domain. The AP will stay on this channel for an interval of time less than the beacon interval (beacon interval by default is about 100 milliseconds). This interval of time is no longer user configurable.

When the AP is scanning the other channel, it will collect RF information from that channel. Because the default AP beacon interval is approximately 100 milliseconds, by listening to a channel for a period less than the beacon interval, the controller ensures that the AP will not miss an opportunity to transmit its beacons. The period of time is less than the beacon interval by a large enough value such that it can ensure that the AP has enough time to transmit all its beacons (if the AP is advertising multiple SSIDs). After the scanning interval is over, the AP returns to its assigned channel, where it will stay again for 10 seconds and serve SSIDs and support clients. The AP then repeats the scanning process by moving to another valid channel and monitoring that channel. The AP continues this process of operating on its assigned channel for 10 seconds and then monitoring another regulatory domain channel.

FIGURE 12.1
ARM Profile Advanced menu

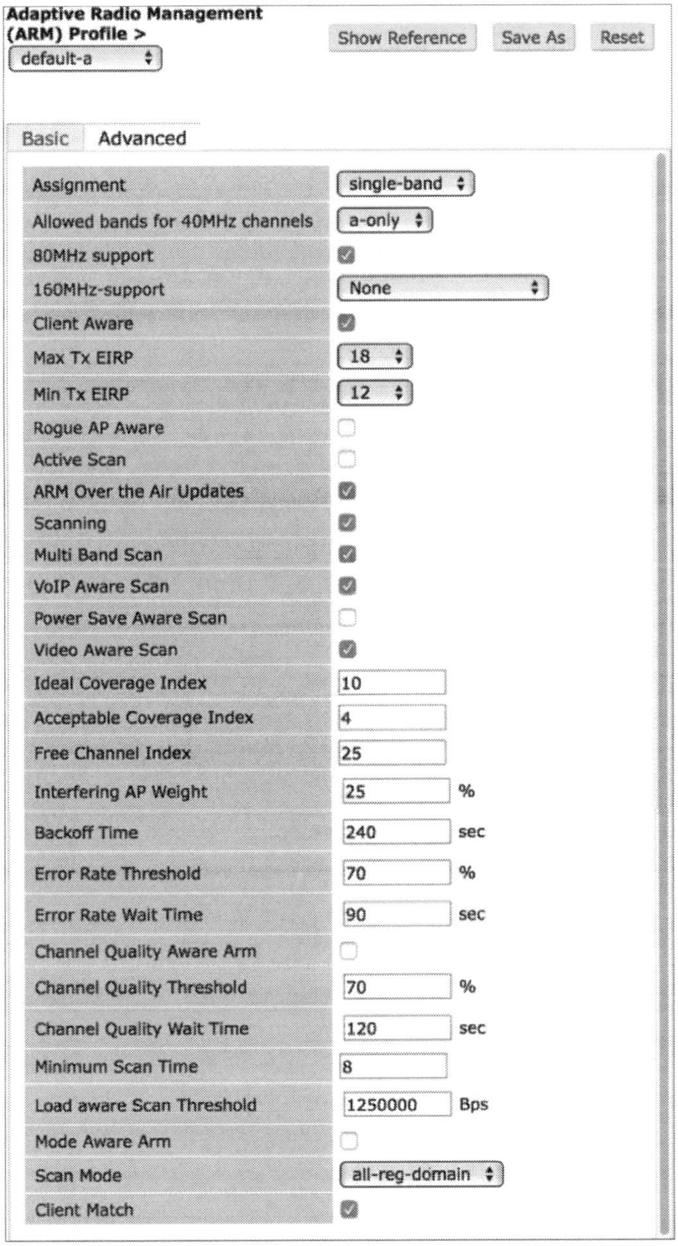

Adaptive Radio Management (ARM) Profile > default-a	
Basic **Advanced**	
Assignment	single-band
Allowed bands for 40MHz channels	a-only
80MHz support	☑
160MHz-support	None
Client Aware	☑
Max Tx EIRP	18
Min Tx EIRP	12
Rogue AP Aware	☐
Active Scan	☐
ARM Over the Air Updates	☑
Scanning	☑
Multi Band Scan	☑
VoIP Aware Scan	☑
Power Save Aware Scan	☐
Video Aware Scan	☑
Ideal Coverage Index	10
Acceptable Coverage Index	4
Free Channel Index	25
Interfering AP Weight	25 %
Backoff Time	240 sec
Error Rate Threshold	70 %
Error Rate Wait Time	90 sec
Channel Quality Aware Arm	☐
Channel Quality Threshold	70 %
Channel Quality Wait Time	120 sec
Minimum Scan Time	8
Load aware Scan Threshold	1250000 Bps
Mode Aware Arm	☐
Scan Mode	all-reg-domain
Client Match	☑

By default the ARM scanning interval is 10 seconds. The following CLI command can be used to enable a more aggressive scanning process that automatically adjusts according to client activity on the AP. If aggressive scanning is enabled, three scanning modes will be used: default, moderate, and aggressive.

```
(config) #rf arm-profile default-g aggressive-scan
```

The default scanning mode continues to scan at 10-second intervals. If more than 80 percent of the clients are idle, a moderate scanning mode will be enabled and scanning will occur every 5 seconds. If there are no clients connected to the AP, then the aggressive mode will be enabled and scanning will occur every second. If client activity on the AP increases, the scanning mode will automatically change back to moderate mode or default mode.

Any RF signals that the scanning AP hears are reported back to the controller. While scanning channels, the AP also gathers information about the following: PHY and MAC errors, noise floor, retry frames, low-speed frames, non-unicast frames, fragmented frames, and bandwidth. Remember, the AP is scanning the channel and looking at what is happening with any RF on the channel, from any devices, not just your devices.

There are conditions when the AP may need to pause its ARM scanning. At times an AP will not scan on a different channel in order to avoid possibly causing connection issues with one or more clients that are connected to the AP. Any pausing of scanning is performed on an AP-by-AP basis and is intended to minimize the disruption of communication by clients caused by the AP leaving its designated channel to scan another.

Table 12.2 lists four conditions that can cause the AP to pause scanning, along with an explanation of each setting. The CLI parameters can be set from the `rf arm-profile` command, and the WebUI settings can be reached using the following menu path: **Configuration ➢ WIRELESS ➢ AP Configuration ➢ RF Management ➢ 802.11a radio (or 802.11g radio) ➢ Adaptive Radio Management (ARM)**.

TABLE 12.2: Settings that can pause ARM scanning

WEBUI SETTING	CLI SETTING	EXPLANATION
Power Save Aware Scan	`ps-aware-scan`	An AP will pause scanning if this is enabled and a client is in power save mode.
VoIP Aware Scan	`voip-aware-scan`	An AP will pause scanning if this is enabled and a client has an active VoIP session.
Video Aware Scan	`video-aware-scan`	An AP will pause scanning if this is enabled and there is at least one video frame every 100 milliseconds.
Load Aware Scan Threshold	`load-aware-scan-threshold`	An AP will pause scanning if this is enabled and the APs traffic load is higher than the specified threshold.

ARM also adds a buffer to the scanning process to make sure that the controller has enough samples before it will consider changing the channel or power settings of an AP. By default the minimum scan time is 8, which means that a channel must be scanned at least 8 times before a channel or power setting change can be made to an AP.

AP Channel and Power Selection

When the AP is scanning the other channels and collecting RF information, the AP will create two indexes: a coverage index and an interference index. The coverage index is a metric used by an AP to measure RF coverage. It is calculated by the controller for all the Aruba APs on a specific channel. The interference index is a metric used by an AP to measure co-channel interference (CCI) and adjacent channel interference (ACI). The interference index is calculated for all APs, including any neighbor APs on a specific channel along with adjacent channels.

The details of these two indexes are beyond the level of complexity that this book is focusing on. What is important to know is that these indexes are used in choosing the best channel for an AP and the best transmit power setting for an AP.

When deciding the best channel for an AP, ARM uses the interference index. This index contains the following information:

- The AP's co-channel interference it sees on the channel
- The AP's adjacent channel interference it sees on the channel
- The AP's neighbors' view of co-channel interference on the channel
- The AP's neighbors' view of adjacent channel interference on the channel

If the controller finds a channel that has less interference than the current channel the AP is operating on, the controller will move the AP to the new channel. After the AP has been moved to the new channel, it will begin scanning and collect a new set of data for the new channel. Any time an AP is moved to a new channel, it will not change channels again for at least four minutes.

Some conditions will prevent the AP from moving to a new channel. The move will not happen if ARM is disabled or set to maintain its current settings. The move also may not happen if the Client Aware setting is enabled. If Client Aware is enabled and clients are associated to an AP, that AP will not change its channel until all clients on the AP are not active or communicating with the AP.

The controller will use the coverage index to determine if the transmit power of the AP should be changed. The coverage index uses the APs weighted calculation of the SNR of all valid Aruba APs on a specific channel, along with the neighbor APs' weighted calculation of the SNR of the valid Aruba APs on a specific channel. If the controller determines that the AP transmit power should be changed, the power can only be set as low as the Min Tx EIRP or as high as the Max Tx EIRP value. These two values can be set by the

WLAN administrator to make sure that the signal of any AP cannot go below a certain level or above a certain level.

As with the channel setting, the power setting will not be changed if ARM is disabled or set to maintain its current settings. After the AP power has been changed, it will begin scanning and collect a new set of data. It also will not change power levels again for at least four minutes.

Dynamic Frequency Selection Channels

Some of the frequencies allocated to 802.11 radios are also used by other technologies. The U-NII-2 and U-NII-2 Extended bands fall into this category. The channel ranges affected are 52 through 64, and 100 through 140. In both of these bands, the 802.11 devices are the secondary users of the band. Therefore, in order for an AP to operate on either of these bands, it is required to incorporate a technology known as dynamic frequency selection (DFS).

A DFS-compliant wireless device must listen for the presence of a signal by primary-use/mission-critical devices. These devices are primarily weather radar, satellite radar, and military radar.

If an AP detects radar on its current channel, it will move off the channel within 260 milliseconds and choose the channel that has the lowest interference index. After the AP moves to a new channel, it will restart its scanning process. If it detects radar on its new channel, it will again change channels; otherwise, it will stay on the new channel and wait at least four minutes before a channel change can occur again. After an AP moves to a new channel, it will not return to the original channel for at least 30 minutes.

DFS rules are collectively mandated by the regulatory domains; therefore, they cannot be modified. They also supersede any other ARM rules or limitations regarding channel changes.

Client Match

The goal of this section is to provide you with an understanding of how Client Match works, and to provide you with a solid foundation of Client Match should you want to delve deeper into how it functions.

Client Match was first introduced as part of ArubaOS 6.3 and was created to be an enhancement to ARM 2.0. It was designed to consistently and continuously monitor clients, and use the information collected from monitoring to manage three different client/AP mismatch conditions:

- Sticky Client
- Band Steering/Band Balancing
- Load Balancing

The Sticky Client feature addresses clients that do not easily roam between APs. When and why a client chooses to roam from one AP to another is a decision that is made solely by the client. This is how the 802.11 standard is designed. Some clients roam easily between APs whereas others tend to "stick" to an AP, remaining connected to an AP even after the signal quality has declined.

Roaming behavior of each client model or type is different. Due to the variety of client devices, along with lack of ability to individually manage them, it is not possible to modify the behavior on a client-by-client basis. Therefore, Client Match is not designed to be a roaming tool or provide enhancement to the roaming process.

Unfortunately there is no standard for when or why a client roams. This varies from vendor to vendor. As a result, in an enterprise environment with many APs, the client may not choose the best AP to connect to, or the client may not choose to roam, even when a better AP is available. It is in these situations that Client Match can provide assistance in helping move a client to a better AP.

Prior to the development of Client Match, ARM 2.0 implemented a technology known specifically as band steering. This technology is still implemented on the controller for support of older AP hardware. The difference between the earlier implementation of band steering versus Client Match is that the earlier technology steered the client to a different band only at the time of initial client association, whereas Client Match continuously monitors the client and can steer the client to a better radio band whenever one is identified.

Client Match automatically implements the new band steering technology. If Client Match is enabled, then its band steering logic is implemented, and the earlier version, even if enabled, will be ignored.

Load balancing monitors the clients connected to the WLAN and attempts to move clients from overloaded APs and channels to APs and channels that have less activity. The controller monitors the channels and clients to identify which APs are overloaded and which are underloaded. The controller then identifies whether it can move a client from an overloaded AP to an underloaded one, while making sure that the quality of the client connection is maintained.

When a client attaches to an AP, Client Match will monitor the client for at least four minutes. Client Match is designed to move a client to a better AP if it decides that a better AP exists. This decision is based on a series of decision-making algorithms that are described and explained in this chapter. The following section will explain how Client Match collects the client data that is used in the decision-making process and is followed by sections about each of the algorithms.

Be aware that in a high-density client environment you may want to customize the Client Match settings. You should not make any changes to any of the Client Match settings without consulting the Aruba Support Team, since even a small change in Client Match settings can cause a great impact on client behavior.

Client Match Data Collection

When Client Match is enabled, an Aruba AP will send probe request data to the controller that the AP receives from any client. The controller collects these probe requests from the clients and combines them into a virtual beacon report (VBR) for each client. These VBRs describe how the client looks to the network, how strong each AP hears the client, and whether the client is connected to the best AP.

When a client attempts to connect to a wireless LAN, the client typically begins the process by broadcasting probe request frames. These frames are sent by all of the client's radios sequentially across every channel of the regulatory domain that the client is operating in. Each radio within RF range of the client that receives the probe request will reply with a probe response frame. The information received from the probe response is used by the client to select the radio it will associate with.

After the client selects an AP and connects to it, the client still continues to periodically send probe requests and receive probe responses on the other channels. This process keeps the client up to date, allowing it to monitor other APs that are available for it to connect to, should it decide to roam.

When the AP receives probe requests from a client, the AP collects the client MAC address, signal level, and timestamp and sends it to the controller. It is possible that the AP will receive probe requests from clients that are connected to other networks, such as a neighbor's network. The controller will only keep data for clients that it can perform Client Match on. This means it only keeps data for clients that are associated to an AP that is connected to your controller. The data collection process is illustrated in Figure 12.2. The figure illustrates a probe request being sent to each AP on both the 2.4 channels (illustrated by the dotted lines) and 5 GHz channels (illustrate by the solid lines).

FIGURE 12.2 Client Match data collection

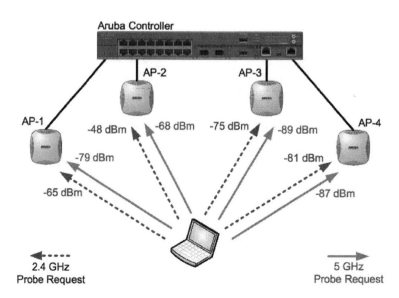

In addition to the AP collecting information from probe requests, ArubaOS 6.4.2.3 (and higher) adds the ability for the AP to collect client signal data from the following frame types: block ACKs, management frames, control frames, null data packets, and data frames <= 36 Mbps. The AP sends the client RF information to the controller every 30 seconds. The AP sends information about each client that has been connected for the past two minutes.

The controller builds a VBR for each client from the signals that are received from all the APs. To limit the amount of data collected for each client, the VBR includes a list of the best 16 or 32 radios (depending on the controller model) that hear the client. This includes data from both 2.4 GHz radios and 5 GHz radios. The following CLI command and output shows the data collected for a specific client, showing all the radios that have heard this client:

```
#show ap virtual-beacon-report client-mac a4:31:35:17:97:a1


Client MAC :a4:31:35:17:97:a1
Current association :AP-2 (04:bd:88:3b:d9:b0)
Steer attempts/Success :2/2
Consecutive (Fails/BTM Rej/BTM Timeouts) :0/0/0
Bandsteer window (Steers/Start time/Expiry time) :1/May 10 16:52:52/May 10 17:22:52
Client Device Type :AppleTV
Current state :Steerable
Active media sessions :No
Client Supported Channels :{36,4}{52,4}{100,11}{149,4}{165,1}
Current Time :May 11 13:07:02 2017


STA Beacon Report
-----------------
AP     IP address       Radio              ESSID    Signal (dBm) →
--     ----------       -----              -----    ------------ →
AP-1   192.168.240.192  04:bd:88:28:de:70  WC-emp   -79          →
AP-1   192.168.240.192  04:bd:88:28:de:60  WC-emp   -65          →
AP-2   192.168.240.189  04:bd:88:3b:d9:b0  WC-emp   -68          →
AP-2   192.168.240.189  04:bd:88:3b:d9:a0  WC-emp   -48          →
AP-3   192.168.240.199  04:bd:88:3c:8d:70  WC-emp   -89          →
AP-3   192.168.240.199  04:bd:88:3c:8d:60  WC-emp   -75          →
AP-4   192.168.240.188  04:bd:88:3b:d8:50  WC-emp   -87          →
AP-4   192.168.240.188  04:bd:88:3b:d8:40  WC-emp   -81          →


→ Last update        Add time        Channel/EIRP/Clients  Flag
→ -----------        --------        --------------------  ----
→ May 11 13:06:58    May 3 10:12:12  60/18/1
→ May 10 20:15:16    May 3 10:12:12  11/9/1                S
```

```
→ May 11 13:06:43    May  3 10:12:13   100/18/5              *
→ May 10 20:14:58    May  3 10:12:13   6/9/0                 S
→ May 11 13:06:48    May  3 10:12:52   60/18/1
→ May 10 20:15:00    May  3 05:42:51   11/9/0                S
→ May 10 20:14:56    May  3 05:42:53   52/18/2               S
→ May 10 20:14:56    May  3 05:42:53   11/9/0                S
→ VBR Flags *-Associated S-Stale U-Unsupported Channel
```

After the data is collected and the VBR is created, the controller will send a table to each of the APs. Each AP will only receive the VBR for clients that are associated to it. The following CLI command and output shows the data sent to a specific AP. This command displays the data sent to the AP for all clients connected to the AP. The output was truncated to only include information for one specific client (prior to truncating the output, information for four clients was originally displayed).

```
#show ap arm virtual-beacon-report ap-name AP-2 | begin a4:31:35:17:97:a1
Client MAC:a4:31:35:17:97:a1
Dual band:Yes
Active Voice:No
11v BTM capable:No
Steerable:Yes
Dual network capable:No
VHT Capable:No
Current Association:04:bd:88:3b:d9:b0

Virtual Beacon Report
---------------------
AP                  Channel  Signal (dBm)  EIRP  Assoc  VHT
--                  -------  ------------  ----  -----  ---
04:bd:88:28:de:70   60       -77           18           Y
04:bd:88:3b:d9:b0   100      -68           18    Y      Y
04:bd:88:3c:8d:70   60       -86           18           Y

Interface:wifi1
Rx VBR Reports:27725

Total Clients:4
```

As a wireless network administrator, you always want to have as many clients associated to the 5 GHz band as possible. This is especially true with 802.11ac clients. To check the statistics of clients on each band, the show ap association command will display this information at the end of the command output. The following shows the last five lines of the show ap association command, displaying the total number of clients along with the breakdown of the band capabilities of the clients.

```
Num Clients:2487
Total num of dual-band capable clients:2407
Total num of dual-band capable clients in 2.4G band:29
```

CLIENT MATCH   385

```
Total num of dual-band capable clients in 5G band:2378
Total num of single-band only clients:56
```

Sticky Clients

This section explains the step-by-step logic that is used by the Sticky Client algorithm, as shown in Figure 12.3. Each step is explained in detail.

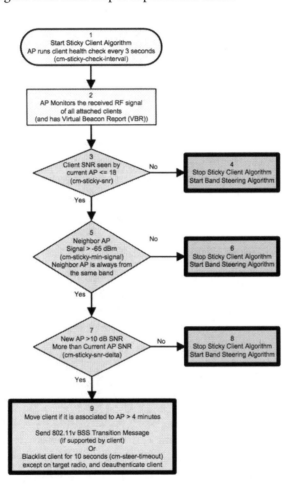

FIGURE 12.3 Sticky Client algorithm flowchart

The Sticky Client algorithm begins at Task 1 and is performed on the AP. The algorithm checks the health of the clients every three seconds. This three-second interval is a configurable setting, `cm-sticky-check-interval`.

As part of its normal function, in Task 2 the AP monitors the received RF signal of all the clients that are connected to it. The AP also receives its VBR every 30 seconds from the controller. The VBR tells the AP about the neighbor APs and how strongly they are receiving signals from the AP's clients.

In Task 3, the AP checks to see if the client signal-to-noise ratio (SNR) is less than or equal to 18 dB. If the signal is greater than 18, the client is not considered sticky, and the client does not need to be moved to another AP due to stickiness, as described in Task 4. The client may still be moved by band steering or load balancing.

If the client SNR is less than or equal to 18 dB, then the algorithm proceeds with Task 5 and checks to see if a neighbor AP has a signal greater than −65 dBm, which is a configurable setting, `cm-sticky-min-signal`. The algorithm only evaluates neighbor APs operating on the same band. If the signal is not greater than −65 dBm, the algorithm will proceed to Task 6 and the client will not be moved.

Finally, if the SNR is less than or equal to 18 dB, and a neighbor AP has a signal greater than −65 dBm, the algorithm will proceed to Task 7 and check if the SNR of the new AP is 10 dB more than the current AP. If this is false, the algorithm will proceed to Task 8 and the client will not be moved. If these three conditions are true, the algorithm will proceed to Task 9 and attempt to move the client to the new AP, providing the client has been associated to the current AP for at least four minutes.

The process that is used to move a client from one AP to another will be explained later in this chapter in the section "Move Client Process."

Band Steering/Band Balancing

This section explains the step-by-step logic that is used by the Band Steering algorithm, as shown in Figure 12.4. Each step is explained in detail.

The Band Steering algorithm begins at Task 1 and is performed on the AP. As part of its normal function, in Task 2 the AP monitors the received RF signal of all the clients that are connected to it. The AP also receives its VBR every 30 seconds from the controller. The VBR tells the AP about the neighbor APs and how strongly they are receiving signals from the AP's clients.

In Task 3, the AP checks to see if the client is dual band capable. The AP does this by looking at the VBR and seeing if the client has two entries for the same MAC address. Band steering will also only occur between two radios within a single AP. Therefore, if the AP is not dual band capable, band steering cannot be performed and the algorithm stops processing as described in Task 4.

The Band Steering algorithm will only steer a client from the 2.4 GHz radio to the 5 GHz radio. So, if the client is dual band capable and associated to the 2.4 GHz radio, the process can continue. If not, band steering cannot be performed and the algorithm stops processing as described in Task 6.

In Task 7, the algorithm proceeds to check if the client SNR is greater than 18 dB, which is a configurable setting, `cm-sticky-snr`. It also checks if the 2.4 GHz signal is less than −45 dBm, which is a configurable setting, `cm-band-g-max-signal`. If both conditions are true, the algorithm proceeds to process. If not, band steering cannot be performed and the algorithm stops processing as described in Task 8.

FIGURE 12.4
Band Steering algorithm flowchart

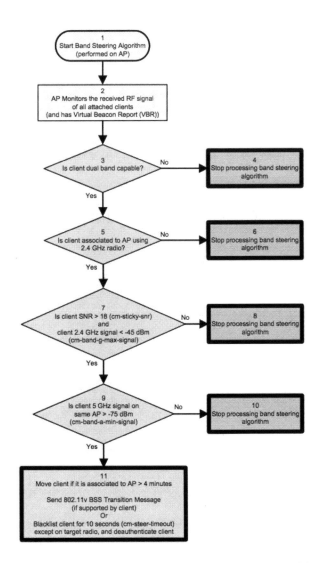

The final check in Task 9 is to see if the client's 5 GHz signal (on the same AP) is greater than −75 dBm, which is a configurable setting, cm-band-a-min-signal. If this is false, the algorithm will proceed to Task 10 and the client will not be moved. If these conditions are true, the algorithm will proceed to Task 11 and attempt to move the client to the new AP, providing the client has been associated to the current AP for at least four minutes.

The process that is used to move a client from one AP to another will be explained later in this chapter in the section "Move Client Process."

Load Balancing

This section explains the step-by-step logic that is used by the Load Balancing algorithm, as shown in Figure 12.5. Each step is explained in detail.

FIGURE 12.5
Load Balancing algorithm flowchart

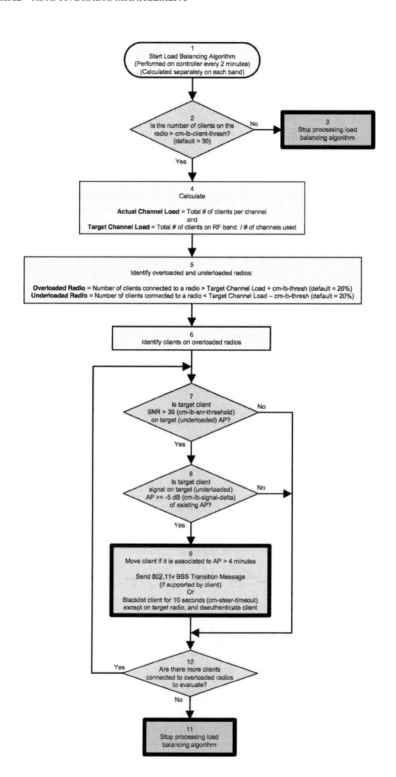

The Load Balancing algorithm begins at Task 1, and unlike the other two algorithms, the load balancing calculations are performed on the controller. Each band is calculated separately, and load balancing is evaluated every two minutes. The objective of load balancing is to steer clients from overloaded radios to underloaded radios.

The first evaluation in the load balancing process, shown in Task 2, is to check to see if the number of clients connected to a radio is greater than 30. The client count is a configurable setting, cm-lb-client-thresh. If the number of clients is at or below the threshold, then load balancing does not need to be performed. If it is above the threshold, the process continues. Remember, load balancing is evaluated individually for each radio on each AP.

If the number of clients is above the threshold, Task 4 begins the process by calculating the actual channel load. Actual channel load is the total number of clients per RF channel. Remember, an RF channel is a subgroup of the RF band, either a subgroup of the 2.4 GHz band or a subgroup of the 5 GHz band.

After the actual channel load is calculated, the controller calculates the target channel load, which is the total number of clients on the RF band divided by the number of channels used. This calculates how many clients would be on each channel, if the clients were evenly distributed across all the used channels on that band.

Task 5 uses the target channel load as the basis to define thresholds to determine which radios are over- or underloaded. By default, the overloaded threshold is 20 percent greater than the target channel load. So any radio with more clients than this value is considered overloaded. The underloaded threshold is 20 percent less than the target channel load. So any radio with fewer clients than this value is considered underloaded. The 20 percent value is a default value and is a configurable setting, cm-lb-thresh.

After the algorithm identifies the over- and underloaded radios, in Task 6 the controller identifies the clients that are connected to overloaded radios. From this list, the controller will evaluate each client to determine which clients can be moved to an underloaded radio.

In Task 7, once the clients on overloaded radios have been identified, the controller will try to identify the potential candidates to be moved. Potential move clients are defined as the target clients. To determine if a target client can be moved, the controller will evaluate the SNR of each client relative to a target (underloaded) radio. If the client's SNR on the target radio is less than 30, then the target client's signal is not considered strong enough to make a move, and the client will not be moved. The SNR value of 30 is a default value and is a configurable setting, cm-lb-snr-threshold.

The target client will also not be moved if its signal is not at least 5 dB better than on the client's existing connected (overloaded) AP, as shown in Task 8. The goal is to move weaker clients to improve the user's client experience. This 5 dB value is a default value and is a configurable setting, cm-lb-signal-delta.

If the signal strength conditions for the target client are true, the algorithm will proceed to Task 9 and attempt to move the client to the new radio, providing the client has been associated to the current radio for at least four minutes. The process that is used to move a client from one AP to another will be explained in the upcoming section "Move Client Process."

Each client connected to an overloaded radio is evaluated to see if it can be moved to an underloaded radio. Task 10 checks if there are additional clients connected to overloaded radios that have not yet been evaluated. If so, the flowchart loops back to Task 7 and evaluates another client.

Move Client Process

The ultimate goal of Client Match is to make sure that each client device does not have a bad or subpar connection on the WLAN. The status of the client connection and whether the client should move to a different AP is determined using the three algorithms: Sticky Client, Band Steering, and Load Balancing. If any of the algorithms decide that a client should be moved to a new AP, the process of moving a client is the same, regardless of the reason. This section describes that process.

After one of the algorithms determines that a client needs to be moved from one radio to another, it is the controller that is responsible for coordinating the move process. This process is performed using one of two methods. One method deauthenticates the client, disconnecting the client from the wireless network and steering it to the target AP. The other method uses 802.11v BSS Transition Management (BTM) to request that the client move to a different BSSID. The method used is determined by the capabilities of the client. All clients can be moved using the deauthentication method, but not all clients support 802.11v.

The logic for how a client is moved from one AP to another is shown in Figure 12.6 and will be explained step-by-step in this section.

The move client process is also referred to as a directed steer of a client. The process to steer a client begins with one of the three algorithms determining that a client is a candidate to be moved along with identifying the target AP for the client to move to. As part of the algorithm, the controller is notified to start a directed steer of the client, as specified in Task 1.

As part of the move process, the controller must identify the APs that are involved in the move process, as shown in Task 2. The source radio is the radio that the client is currently connected to and is being moved from. The target radio is the radio that has been identified as being able to provide a better connection for the client. Finally, the neighbor radios are all the other radios that have seen the client and are in the VBR.

Once a target radio has been identified for a client, the MAC address of the client will be added to the client restriction table of each neighbor radio. This table blacklists the client on a radio-by-radio basis. Clients remain in the client restriction table and are temporarily blacklisted from the neighbor radios and from the source radio for a short period of time, specified by the `cm-steer-timeout` parameter.

FIGURE 12.6
Client Match: Move client process

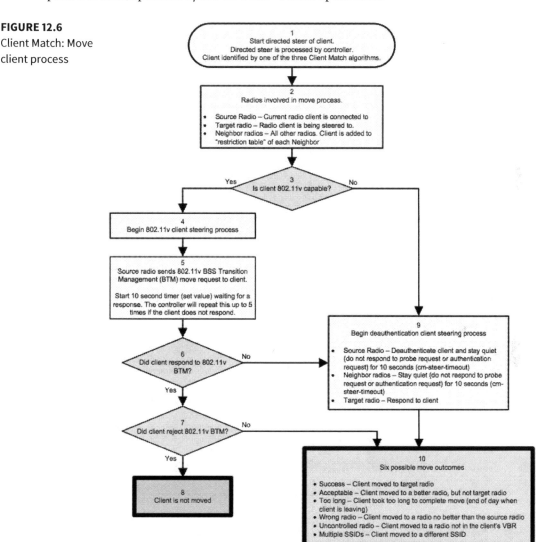

The next step is Task 3, which identifies whether the client supports 802.11v. These clients can be directly told which BSSID the controller would like the client to move to. Since this method directly specifies the target radio, it should provide a smoother steer than the deauthentication method; however, as previously mentioned, not all clients support 802.11v.

When a client associates to the network, if it is 802.11v capable it will advertise its capabilities. The controller identifies this when the client associates to the network. As part of the association request frame, there is a BSS transition bit that identifies whether

802.11v is supported by the client. The controller records the status of this bit for the client and simply needs to look up the status for the client.

If the client supports 802.11v, the controller will begin the 802.11v client steer process, as indicated in Task 4.

To steer the client using 802.11v, the source radio sends an 802.11v BTM frame, which requests that the client move from the source AP to the target AP, as described in Task 5. When the AP sends this request, it waits 10 seconds for a response. The 10-second timer is a set value that cannot be changed. If the client does not respond, the AP will resend the BTM frame and wait again. The AP will transmit the frame up to five times.

If the client responded to the BTM (Task 6) and the response was a Reject frame (Task 7), the AP and controller will honor this response and the client will not be moved, as illustrated in Task 8.

If in Task 6 the client did not respond to the 802.11v request, the controller will try to move the client using the deauthentication client steering method that begins with Task 9. The deauthentication method will also be used if the client does not support 802.11v.

In the deauthentication process, the source radio sends a deauthentication frame to the client, disconnecting the client from the source radio. When the client attempts to reconnect, the only radio that should respond will be the target. This is achieved by the controller adding the MAC address of the client to the client restriction table of each neighbor radio, preventing the AP from replying to probe requests or authentication requests.

After the controller attempts to move the client to the target AP, there are six possible outcomes that may have occurred, as seen in Task 10. Table 12.3 displays the six possible outcomes along with an explanation of each.

TABLE 12.3: Client move possible outcomes

OUTCOME	DESCRIPTION
Success	The client was successfully moved to the target radio.
Acceptable	The client did not move to the target radio but moved to a better radio than its source radio.
Too Long	The client took too long to complete the move. It is likely that the client left or was leaving the building.
Wrong Radio	The client did not move to the target radio but moved to a radio that was no better than its source radio.
Uncontrolled Radio	The client did not move to the target radio but moved to a radio that was not in the client's VBR. If this occurs, it typically will happen in a high-density deployment of APs.
Multiple SSIDs	The client did not move to the target radio but moved to a different SSID. This can occur if the client has credentials for multiple SSIDs.

Client Match Process Review

Up to this point many different components of the Client Match process have been explained. This section will briefly review the process, tying together the pieces and logic, as shown in Figure 12.7.

FIGURE 12.7
Client Match overview

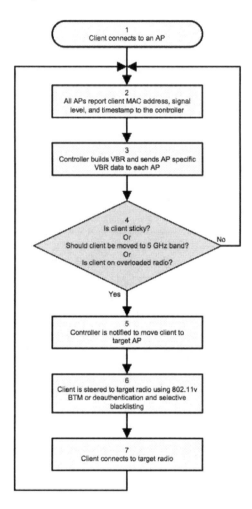

The process begins with Task 1, with the client connecting to an AP. After the client connects, the APs collect the client MAC address, signal level, and timestamp, and then periodically sends the data to the controller, as shown in Task 2. The controller uses this information to build a VBR for each client, in Task 3. The controller then sends only part of the VBR to the AP for the clients that are associated to it.

In Task 4 the AP checks to see if the client is sticky. If the client is not, the AP checks to see if the client is connected to a 2.4 GHz radio and should be moved to a 5 GHz radio. Then the controller checks to see if the client is connected to a radio that is overloaded. If any of these conditions are true, the AP notifies the controller that the client needs to be moved to a better radio, as seen in Task 5. The move will only be triggered if the client is connected to the AP for more than four minutes. If none of the three conditions are true or the client has been connected to the AP for less than four minutes, then the controller continues to collect data and update the VBR and the APs. The controller will continue to monitor the client to determine if the client status changes.

In Task 6, the controller attempts to move the client to a new target AP. The controller uses 802.11v BTM or deauthentication and selective blacklisting to steer the client to the target AP. If deauthentication is used, after the client is disconnected from its source AP, the only AP that will respond to the client is the target AP that the client is being steered to.

Finally in Task 7, the client has been moved to a new radio and the process begins again. The Client Match process is performed for each client connected to the wireless network.

ARM Profile Settings

The ARM profile is part of the RF Management settings in the AP Group. ARM settings are configured on a per-radio basis, since the RF requirements for the 2.4 GHz devices may differ from the requirements for the 5 GHz devices. Many of the ARM settings can be made from the WebUI, as seen earlier in this chapter in Figure 12.1.

Because of the complexity of ARM, some of the settings can only be changed from the CLI. This is especially true of the Client Match settings, where Client Match is the only setting that is available from the WebUI.

This section of the chapter provides the ARM and Client Match profile settings so that you can interpret and understand the processes better. The ARM channel and power settings should be modified with caution, and it is recommended that you do not change Client Match settings on your own.

The following CLI command can be used to display all the ARM parameters and values for a specific ARM profile—in this example, the default-a profile.

```
#show rf arm-profile default-a

Adaptive Radio Management (ARM) profile "default-a" (Predefined (editable))
------------------------------------------------------------------
Parameter                                               Value
---------                                               -----
Assignment                                              single-band
Allowed bands for 40MHz channels                        a-only
80MHz support                                           Enabled
160MHz-support                                          None
Client Aware                                            Enabled
Max Tx EIRP                                             18 dBm
```

Min Tx EIRP	12 dBm
Rogue AP Aware	Disabled
Scan Interval	10 sec
Aggressive scanning	true
Active Scan	Disabled
ARM Over the Air Updates	Enabled
Scanning	Enabled
Multi Band Scan	Enabled
VoIP Aware Scan	Enabled
Power Save Aware Scan	Disabled
Video Aware Scan	Enabled
Ideal Coverage Index	10
Acceptable Coverage Index	4
Free Channel Index	25
Interfering AP Weight	25 %
Backoff Time	240 sec
Error Rate Threshold	70 %
Error Rate Wait Time	90 sec
Channel Quality Aware Arm	Disabled
Channel Quality Threshold	70 %
Channel Quality Wait Time	120 sec
Minimum Scan Time	8
Load aware Scan Threshold	1250000 Bps
Mode Aware Arm	Disabled
Scan Mode	all-reg-domain
Client Match	Enabled
Client Match Report Interval (sec)	30
Allows Client Match to Automatically Clear Unsteerable Clients after Ageout	Enabled
Client Match Unsteerable Client Ageout Interval	2 Days 0 Hours
Client Match Band Steering G Max Signal (-dBm)	45
Client Match Band Steering A Min Signal (-dBm)	75
Client Match Sticky Client Check Interval (sec)	3
Client Match Sticky Client SNR (dB)	18
Client Match SNR Delta Bound(dB)	10
Client Match Sticky Min Signal	65
Client Match Steering Timeout (sec)	10
Client Match Load Balancing Threshold (%)	20
Client Match IOS Steering Backoff Interval (sec)	300
Client Match VBR Stale Entry Age (sec)	120
Client Match Max Steering Failures	2
Client Match Load Balancing Client Threshold	30
Client Match Load Balancing SNR Threshold (dB)	30
Client Match Load Balancing Signal Delta Bound (dB)	5
Client Match 802.11v BSS Transition Management	Enabled
Dynamic Bandwidth Switch	Disabled
Dynamic Bandwidth Switch Wait Time (sec)	30
Dynamic Bandwidth Switch Triggering Indicator CCA ibss Threshold (%)	10
Dynamic Bandwidth Switch Triggering Indicator Beacon Failed Threshold	30

```
Dynamic Bandwidth Switch Triggering Indicator CCA
        intf Threshold (%)                              30
Dynamic Bandwidth Switch Clear Time (min)               30
Client Match MU Client threshold                        15
Client Match MU SNR threshold (dB)                      30
```

The following series of tables display the Client Match functions, parameters, and default values at the time that this book was written. Each table is grouped by similar function. As mentioned previously in this chapter, you should not make any changes to any of the Client Match settings without consulting the Aruba Support Team.

BAND STEERING FUNCTION	CLI PARAMETER	DEFAULT VALUE
Client Match Band Steer G Band Max Signal (-dBm)	cm-band-g-max-signal	45
Client Match Band Steer A Band Min Signal (-dBm)	cm-band-a-min-signal	75

LOAD BALANCING FUNCTION	CLI PARAMETER	DEFAULT VALUE
Client Match Load Balancing threshold (%)	cm-lb-thresh	20
Client Match Load Balancing client threshold	cm-lb-client-thresh	30
Client Match Load Balancing SNR threshold (dB)	cm-lb-snr-thresh	30
Client Match Load Balancing signal delta bound (dB)	cm-lb-signal-delta	5

CLIENT STEERING FUNCTION	CLI PARAMETER	DEFAULT VALUE
Allow Client Match to automatically clear unsteerable clients after ageout	cm-unst-ageout	Enabled
Client Match Unsteerable Client Ageout Interval	cm-unst-ageout-interval	2 Days 0 Hours
Client Match Restriction timeout (sec)	cm-steer-timeout	10
Client Match Max steer failures	cm-max-steer-fails	2 Days 0 Hours
Client Match 11v BSS Transition Management	cm-dot11v	Enabled

DATA COLLECTION FUNCTION	CLI PARAMETER	DEFAULT VALUE
Client Match report interval (sec)	cm-report-interval	30
Client Match VBR Stale Entry Age (sec)	cm-stale-age	120

IOS STEER FUNCTION	CLI PARAMETER	DEFAULT VALUE
Client Match IOS Steer Backoff interval (sec)	`cm-steer-backoff`	300

MU-MIMO FUNCTION	CLI PARAMETER	DEFAULT VALUE
Client Match MU Client threshold	`cm-mu-client-thresh`	15
Client Match MU SNR threshold (dB)	`cm-mu-snr-thresh`	30

CHAPTER 13

Network Monitoring

IN THIS CHAPTER, YOU WILL LEARN ABOUT THE FOLLOWING:

- **Logging**
  - Logging Configuration
  - Configuring Syslog Server
- **Packet Analysis**
  - Port Monitoring
  - Packet Capture Command
  - Firewall Mirroring
  - AP/AM Capture
  - Packet Capture Synopsis
- **Spectrum Analysis**
  - Configuring a Spectrum Monitor
  - Spectrum Monitoring Using the WebUI
  - Chart Types
  - Spectrum Analysis CLI Command

When you are managing an Aruba WLAN, it is important to be familiar with the tools that can help you troubleshoot problems that arise on your network. This chapter will begin by explaining how to configure and access logging information. From there it will describe the four methods of capturing packets on an Aruba controller, followed by an overview of how to perform spectrum analysis using ArubaOS.

Unfortunately this chapter is not going to teach you how to troubleshoot, as the knowledge from that topic could encompass multiple books. This chapter will focus on the tools that ArubaOS provides to help troubleshoot wireless issues. The commands and resources will be described to provide you with information that you will need when troubleshooting network problems.

Troubleshooting and problem solving always begins with understanding the basics of the systems being analyzed. I suggest reading *CWNA: Certified Wireless Network Administrator Official Study Guide: Exam CWNA-106* (Sybex, 2014) and *CWAP: Certified Wireless Analysis Professional Official Study Guide: Exam PW0-270* (Sybex, 2011) to help you understand the information that the tools in this chapter provide.

Logging

Sometimes the best place to get a deeper view of what is going on is to let the system tell you itself. ArubaOS has the ability to generate logs for events that occur on the controller. This insight can be helpful in determining what did or did not happen related to the different tasks or processes. Logs can show information about security, network, user, or authentication events.

In ArubaOS, logging is configurable, allowing you to specify the level of detail you wish to see. There are eight levels of activity logging. Generating debugging logs will write many more log entries and require more CPU resources and file space. The controller has a limited amount of storage, which restricts the amount of logging information that can be retained. When a log reaches its capacity, the newest log message overwrites the oldest log message; this is sometimes referred to as a *rolling* log.

Logging is also grouped into six categories: arm, network, security, system, user, and wireless, as shown in the following CLI output:

```
#show  logging level

LOGGING LEVELS
--------------
Facility  Level
--------  -----
arm       warnings
network   warnings
security  warnings
system    warnings
user      warnings
wireless  warnings
```

The logging level of each of these categories can be set separately from each other. ArubaOS provide eight levels of logging. Each level has a numerical value, with 0 being the most critical and 7 being the least critical, as can be seen in Table 13.1.

TABLE 13.1: Logging levels

SEVERITY LEVEL	VALUE	DESCRIPTION
Emergencies	0	Panic condition, system is unusable
Alerts	1	Condition requires immediate attention and correction
Critical	2	Any critical conditions
Errors	3	Error conditions
Warnings	4	Warning messages
Notifications	5	Significant events of a normal nature
Informational	6	Messages of general interest to system users
Debugging	7	Messages containing information useful for debugging

Whichever logging level is set, logs will be generated for that level and all lower levels. As an example, the default logging level is warnings, which means that logs will be generated for level 4 and below: warnings, errors, critical, alerts, and emergencies.

If you are trying to log a specific event, the necessary logging level must be configured prior to the event occurring. Before increasing the logging level, remember that the higher the logging level, the more levels will be included, and the more logs will be generated. This means that the log files will populate faster and roll over faster.

If you need to retain logs for a longer duration of time, you should configure the controller to send the log messages to a syslog server. Syslog is an industry-standard message logging method. A syslog server can collect log messages from one or more network devices, store these messages, and provide an environment from which you can review the log messages at a later time. Configuring syslog servers will be covered later in this chapter.

Logging consists of two parts. The first is the configuration of the logging level. This defines what information will be logged and the severity level of the information. This log information is generated locally on the controller, and over time will be replaced by newer log entries. The second part of logging is defining a syslog server. As log messages are generated, this information can be sent to an external server for offline storage and access. One or more syslog servers can be defined, along with filters that can refine what log messages get sent to which syslog server.

Logging Configuration

The default logging level of each of the logging categories is set to warnings, as shown in the following CLI output:

```
(config) #show logging level

LOGGING LEVELS
--------------
Facility  Level
--------  -----
arm       warnings
network   warnings
security  warnings
system    warnings
user      warnings
wireless  warnings
```

When setting a logging level, two parameters are required: the category for which the logging level is being set and the severity level of the messages being logged. Table 13.2 shows the syntax options for the most basic configuration of the logging level.

TABLE 13.2: logging level command

COMMAND	SEVERITY LEVEL	CATEGORY
logging level	emergencies	ap-debug
	alerts	arm
	critical	arm-user-debug
	errors	network
	warnings	security
	notifications	system
	informational	user
	debugging	user-debug
		wireless

After defining the category and security level, you may define a subcategory if you want to be more specific. Selecting a subcategory is optional, and not all categories have subcategories. Table 13.3 lists the categories along with the current possible subcategories for each. You can generate the subcategory list using the following command:

    logging level emergencies <category> subcat ?

TABLE 13.3: logging level subcategories

CATEGORY	SUBCATEGORY	DESCRIPTION
ap-debug	all	Enable logging of all subcategories
	ap-config	AP configuration logging
	ha	HA logging
	sdn	SDN logging for AP (ofald)
network	all	Enable logging of all subcategories
	dhcp	Logging for DHCP
	gp	PaloAlto Networks Global Protect Network logging
	mobility	Mobility logging
	packet-dump	Protocol packet dumps
	sdn	SDN logging for AP (ofald)
security	HA	HA logging

CATEGORY	SUBCATEGORY	DESCRIPTION
	AAA	AAA logging
	all	Enable logging of all subcategories
	auth-amon	Auth AMON logging
	certmgr	Certificate manager logging
	cpsec	CPsec logging
	db	Local database logging
	dot1x	Dot1X logging
	firewall	Firewall logging
	ids	IDS logging (correlated logs)
	ids-ap	IDS logging on AP
	ike	IKE logging
	kerberos	Kerberos logging
	mobility	Mobility logging
	ntlm	NTLM logging
	packet-trace	Packet trace logging
	vpn	VPN logging
	webserver	Web server logging
	wl-sync	Whitelist sync logging
system	all	Enable logging of all subcategories
	amon	AMON-related logging
	amon-ale	AMON-ALE related logging
	amon-amp	AMON-AMP related logging
	ap	AP (SAPD, AP-STM, APIFMGR, MESHD) logging
	ap-config	AP configuration logging
	ap-license	AP license logging
	configuration	Configuration logging
	gp	PaloAlto Networks Global Protect Network logging
	ha	HA logging

CATEGORY	SUBCATEGORY	DESCRIPTION
	mapc	IF-MAP client logging
	messages	Messages logging
	pan	PaloAlto Networks Interface logging
	reg-tbl	Regulatory table logging
	snmp	SNMP logging
	webserver	Web server logging
user	all	Enable logging of all subcategories
	captive-portal	Captive portal user logging
	client-match	ARM Client Match user logging
	dot1x	Dot1X logging
	mapc	IF-MAP client logging
	pan	PaloAlto Networks Interface logging
	radius	RADIUS user logging
	voice	Voice user logging
	vpn	VPN logging
user-debug	all	Enable logging of all subcategories
	configuration	Dot1X user logging
wireless	all	Enable logging of all subcategories

The final customization of the logging level is the selection of a process. Selecting a process is optional, with a choice of over 60 processes to choose from. The following CLI output lists all the available processes along with a brief description:

```
(config) #logging level emergencies wireless process ?
aaa                 AAA logging
activate            Logging for Activate
anti_virus          Logging for Anti Virus
approc              Logging for AP processes
armd                Logging for ARM Process
aruba-central       Logging for Aruba Central
authmgr             Logging for user authentication
ble_relay           Logging for BLE Relay
bocmgr              Logging for BOC Manager
cert_dwnld          Logging for Cert Download Process
```

certmgr	Certifcate Manager logging
cfgm	Logging for Configuration Manager
cpsec	CPSec logging
crypto	Logging for VPN (IKE/IPSEC)
cts	Logging for transport service
dbsync	Logging for Database Synchronization
dds	Logging for DDS Process
dhcpd	Logging for DHCP packets
esi	Logging for External Services Interface
extifmgr	Logging for External Interface Manager
fpapps	Logging for Layer 2,3 control
fw_visibility	Logging for FW Visibility Process
gsmmgr	Logging for GSM Manager
ha_mgr	Logging for HA_MGR
hcm	Logging for Health Check Process
httpd	Logging for Apache
hwmon	Logging for hwMon task
iapmgr	Logging for IAP manager process
ip_flow_export	Logging for IP Flow Export Process
ipstm	Logging for IPSTM Process
l2tp	Logging for L2TP
licensemgr	Logging for license manager
lldp	Logging for LLDP Process
localdb	Logging for local database
mdns	Logging for MDNS Proxy
mobileip	Logging for Mobile IP
msghh	Logging for msg handler helper
npppd	Logging for NPPPD
ofa	Logging for OpenFlow Agent Process
ospf	Logging for OSPF
packetfilter	Logging for packet filtering of messaging and control frames
phonehome	Logging for Phone Home
pim	Logging for Protocol Independent Multicast
pppd	Logging for PPP
pppoed	Logging for PPPoE
pptp	Logging for PPTP
processes	Logging for run-time processes
profmgr	Logging for Profile Manager
publisher	Logging for publish subscribe service
radvd	Logging for Router Advertisement daemon
resolvwrap	Logging for Resolvwrap Process
rfm	Logging for RF Troubleshooting Manager
rsync	Logging for Rsync
snmp	SNMP logging
spectrum	Logging for Spectrum process
stm	Logging for Station Management
survival	Logging for Auth Survival Server
syslogdwrap	Logging for Syslogd Wrap
traffic	Logging for traffic

```
ucm                     Logging for UCM Process
util-proc               Logging for Util Proc
web_cc                  Logging for Web Content classification
wms                     Logging for Wireless Management (Master switch only)
```

Logging levels are defined as part of the running-config file. When an Aruba controller is initially configured, there are only two logging levels that are specifically defined in running-config, as shown in the following CLI output:

```
#show running-config | include logging
Building Configuration...
logging level warnings security subcat ids
logging level warnings security subcat ids-ap
```

All logging level parameters can also be configured using the WebUI, except for specifying the logging process, which can only be set through the CLI. The Logging Level menu is shown in Figure 13.1. The following menu path will bring you to this menu: **Configuration ➢ MANAGEMENT ➢ Logging ➢ Levels**. On the screen you can select one or more categories or subcategories. Then at the bottom of the list you can choose the logging level for the grouping that you selected.

FIGURE 13.1
Logging levels

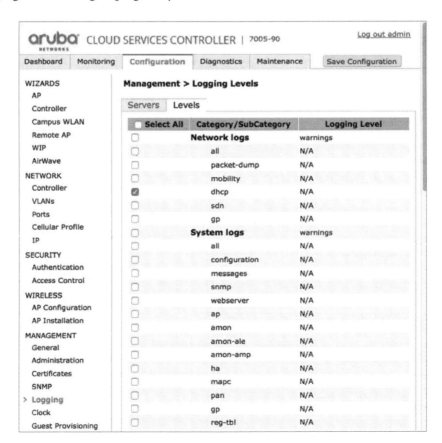

Configuring the Syslog Server

The `logging level` command defines what logs are generated locally by ArubaOS. As mentioned earlier in this chapter, you can configure one or more syslog servers to automatically move logs off the Aruba controller onto another server. When configuring syslog, you have the option to use the controller's local log settings or configure settings specific to the given syslog server. For example, the local logging level on the controller may be set to use the default values, whereas the syslog server settings can be more aggressive for the user logs, such as enabling debugging for all subcategories. This way, local logs can contain fewer log entries, whereas the syslog server can contain a more extensive set of log entries.

Specifying a syslog server on an Aruba controller is a straightforward process, requiring a maximum of four pieces of information:

- IP address of the syslog server
- Type
- Severity
- Facility

Think of the syslog server settings as a filtering and forwarding process for the logs that are being generated. The `logging level` command defines what logs are generated by the controller. The syslog process then takes the generated logs, and whichever logs match the syslog settings, the syslog process forwards these logs to the syslog server. The four parameters of the syslog server, specified as part of the `logging` command, are explained in this section.

IP Address of the Syslog Server The IP address of the syslog server simply tells the controller where to send the log messages, and it is the minimum required parameter when specifying a syslog server. The Aruba controller can be configured with more than one syslog server if you desire. The following CLI command defines 192.168.240.31 as the external syslog server:

    (config) #logging 192.168.240.31

Type (Default = all) Instead of sending every log message to the syslog server, `type` can specify which type of messages to be sent. If `type` is not specified, the default value is `all`. You can specify nine different types as shown in the following list:

- `ap-debug`: AP debug logs
- `arm`: ARM logs
- `arm-user-debug`: ARM user debug logs
- `network`: Network logs
- `security`: Security logs

- `system`: System logs
- `user`: User logs
- `user-debug`: User debug logs
- `wireless`: Wireless logs

It is possible to specify different IP addresses with different types; which would allow one type of log message to be sent to one syslog server and a different type of log message to be sent to another syslog server. The following CLI output shows two log servers being defined, with network logs sent to one and security logs sent to the other. The third command displays the logging server configuration.

```
(config) #logging 192.168.240.41 type network
(config) #logging 192.168.240.42 type security
(config) #show logging server

Remote Server: 192.168.240.41

FACILITY MAPPING TABLE
----------------------
local-facility  severity  remote-facility
--------------  --------  ---------------
network         All       local1


Remote Server: 192.168.240.42

FACILITY MAPPING TABLE
----------------------
local-facility  severity  remote-facility
--------------  --------  ---------------
security        All       local1
```

Severity (Default = `all`) The output of the log messages being sent to the syslog server can be further refined by specifying the severity level of the log messages that you want sent. severity is defined as one of the eight levels, ranging from emergencies to debugging. If severity is not specified, the default value is all. severity can be specified along with the IP address, allowing only a certain level of logging to be sent to a syslog server.

The following CLI output shows two log servers being defined. Network logs with a severity of errors are being sent to one syslog server and security logs with a severity of errors are being sent to the other syslog server. The third command displays the logging server configuration.

```
(config) #logging 192.168.240.41 type network severity errors
(config) #logging 192.168.240.42 type security severity errors
(config) #show logging server
```

```
Remote Server: 192.168.240.41

FACILITY MAPPING TABLE
----------------------
local-facility   severity   remote-facility
--------------   --------   ---------------
network          errors     local1


Remote Server: 192.168.240.42

FACILITY MAPPING TABLE
----------------------
local-facility   severity   remote-facility
--------------   --------   ---------------
security         errors     local1
```

Facility (Default = local1)   When the controller forwards a log message to the syslog server, it marks or tags each message with a facility value. facility can be a value local0 through local7. If a facility value is not specified, the default value is local1. The facility value is simply a tag that is used by the syslog server to identify different log streams. Each value has no intrinsic meaning. The syslog server can use these different facility values to separate log messages from different sources and store them in separate log files.

ArubaOS allows you to specify a different facility value for all log messages sent to a syslog server. The following CLI command changes the syslog facility from the default value of local1 to local5. Once this command is executed, every log message will be sent to a syslog server tagged with the facility value of local5.

```
(config) #logging 192.168.240.41 type network severity errors facility local5
```

The following CLI output shows two log servers being defined. Network logs are being sent to one syslog server tagged with a facility value of local6 and security logs are being sent to the other syslog server tagged with a facility value of local7. The third command displays the logging server configuration.

```
(config)#logging 192.168.240.41 type network severity errors facility local6
(config)#logging 192.168.240.42 type security severity errors facility local7
(config)#show logging server

Remote Server: 192.168.240.41

FACILITY MAPPING TABLE
----------------------
local-facility   severity   remote-facility
--------------   --------   ---------------
network          errors     local6
```

```
Remote Server: 192.168.240.42

FACILITY MAPPING TABLE
----------------------
local-facility   severity   remote-facility
--------------   --------   ---------------
security         errors     local7
```

It is also possible to send more than one log to the same syslog server. To accomplish this, you simply need to issue two logging commands pointing to the same server with different logging parameters, as shown in the following CLI output:

```
(config) #logging 192.168.240.41 type network facility local6
(config) #logging 192.168.240.41 type security facility local7
(config) #show logging server

Remote Server: 192.168.240.41

FACILITY MAPPING TABLE
----------------------
local-facility   severity   remote-facility
--------------   --------   ---------------
network          All        local6
security         All        local7
```

As you have seen, the logging command provides you with an assortment of options to customize logging to one or more syslog servers. The syslog server can also be configured using the WebUI, as shown in Figure 13.2. This menu path will bring you to the menu where you can define syslog servers: **Configuration ➢ MANAGEMENT ➢ Logging ➢ Servers**.

FIGURE 13.2
Syslog server configuration

Packet Analysis

Packet analysis can be useful when you are monitoring or troubleshooting a network. ArubaOS provides four ways to perform packet analysis. These methods use different techniques and capture data at different physical and logical points on the network. This section will describe how to perform each of these methods along with examining the data that is collected.

Packet analysis allows you to watch the communications that are occurring so that you can monitor each of the steps. This can be useful when troubleshooting complex processes.

These are the four packet analysis methods:

- Port monitoring
- `packet capture` command
- Firewall mirroring
- AP capture

While the details of how to use the packet analysis software such as Savvius Omnipeek and Wireshark are beyond the scope of this book, it is important to understand how the packet analyzers interface with the controller. There are two ways to view packets using a packet analyzer. The first way is to generate a packet analyzer–compatible file, save it to your computer's local file system, and then open it with your packet analysis software. The second way is to configure your packet analysis software to monitor network traffic, and listen for specific packets on an IP address and port. You can configure the ArubaOS, controller, or APs to redirect or mirror data directly to the address of the computer performing the analysis.

The objective of this section is to provide the knowledge and resources to capture the packets and integrate the ArubaOS, controller, and APs with the packet analysis software. Understanding the packets and data is too complex a topic to address. There are many books, articles, and blogs that specifically discuss the details about the packets, fields, and the many different types of packet exchanges that occur on the network. If you decide you want to learn more about packet analysis, be prepared because this is a topic that can take years to master.

Port Monitoring

To capture packets on a switched Ethernet port, it is necessary to copy the packets to another port where a packet analyzer can receive and monitor the packets. All inbound and outbound packets will be copied.

Port monitoring is easy to configure. On the monitoring port where the packet analyzer is connected, you specify the number of the port that you want to monitor. For example, Figure 13.3 illustrates a laptop computer running packet analysis software connected to

Gigabit Ethernet (GE) port 0/0/6. This port would be configured to monitor Gigabit port 0/0/14, which in this example is where a DHCP server is connected to the controller.

FIGURE 13.3
Port monitoring

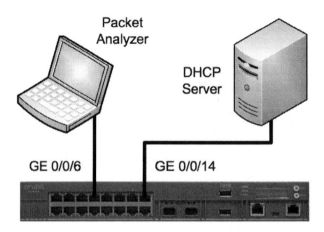

To configure port mirroring for the example configuration, you will tell GE 0/0/6 to monitor GE 0/0/14. After the configuration is made, all of the data flowing in and out of GE 0/0/14 will be duplicated on GE 0/0/6. The following CLI output shows the commands needed to implement this configuration. The first command selects port GE 0/0/6, and the second command instructs it to monitor port GE 0/0/14. The third command displays the current port monitoring status.

```
(config) #interface gigabitethernet 0/0/6
(config-if)#port monitor gigabitethernet 0/0/14
(config-if)#show port monitor

Monitor Port   Port being Monitored
------------   --------------------
GE 0/0/6       GE 0/0/14
```

After port monitoring is configured, you need to run packet analysis software, such as Omnipeek or Wireshark, and configure the software to capture packets using the Ethernet interface that is connected to GE 0/0/6. The packet analysis computer should be the only device connected to GE 0/0/6.

When you are done capturing packets, you should disable port monitoring on the controller. The following CLI output shows the commands needed to disable this feature. The first two commands disable port monitoring, and the third command displays the current port monitoring status. If port monitoring is disabled, the show port monitor command should not generate any output.

```
(config) #interface gigabitethernet 0/0/6
(config-if)#no port monitor gigabitethernet 0/0/14
(config-if)#show port monitor
```

packet-capture Command

The packet-capture command provides the ability to define packet capture settings for data path traffic and control path traffic. These settings are configured from the controller CLI prompt and are not available from the WebUI interface. In addition to defining the settings, the packet-capture command can be used to initiate the packet capture. This command allows you to perform a packet capture without needing additional hardware or software. The packet stream that is captured is taken directly from the data path or the control path of the controller. The previous sentence is important to remember, since ArubaOS has multiple ways of capturing packets. With the packet-capture command, the controller is taking the frames that have already arrived at the controller, and then sends them off to where they can be analyzed.

The packet-capture command is not part of the running-config file, which means that the settings are not saved when the controller is rebooted. Also note that the packet-capture command is local to each controller. If you want to save the configuration settings, you can use the packet-capture-defaults command to define the settings in the running-config file. The packet-capture-defaults command will be explained later in this section.

Let us begin by looking at the packet-capture settings. You can do this using the show packet-capture command as shown in the following CLI output. The output of this command is divided into three sections. The first section shows the capture destination settings, the second section shows the control path settings, and the last section shows the data path settings. Let us take a look at what each section is used for; we will save the capture destination for last.

```
#show packet-capture

Active Capture Destination
--------------------------
Destination     Disabled


Active Capture (Controlpath)
----------------------------
Interprocess    Disabled
Sysmsg          Disabled
TCP             Disabled
UDP             Disabled
Other           Disabled


Active Capture (Datapath)
-------------------------
Wifi-Client     Disabled
Ipsec           Disabled
```

controlpath

The controlpath option of the packet-capture command allows you to capture packets that are destined for the controller. Capturing control path traffic is not done often, but it can be used to investigate network or RADIUS issues. The previous CLI output shows the five different control path categories that can be configured. For example, to troubleshoot a problem you may want to capture control path traffic using UDP ports 1812 and 1645, as shown in the first command of the following CLI output. You may also want to capture all TCP traffic, as defined in the second command. The third command displays the packet-capture settings, and the final command shows how to disable those settings.

Always disable the packet-capture settings when you are done troubleshooting because it adds unnecessary CPU processing to the controller. This step is often overlooked.

```
#packet-capture controlpath udp 1812,1645
#packet-capture controlpath tcp all
#show packet-capture

Active Capture Destination
--------------------------
Destination    Disabled


Active Capture (Controlpath)
----------------------------
Interprocess   Disabled
Sysmsg         Disabled
TCP            Enabled    Ports: All
UDP            Enabled    Ports: 1812 1645
Other          Disabled


Active Capture (Datapath)
-------------------------
Wifi-Client    Disabled
Ipsec          Disabled

#no packet-capture controlpath udp
#no packet-capture controlpath tcp
```

When capturing interprocess, SYSMSG, TCP, or UDP control path traffic, you can either specify all ports, or you can individually specify up to 10 individual ports of each type. If you specify multiple ports, each port number must be separated by a comma with no spaces between them.

datapath

The datapath option of the `packet-capture` command allows you to capture packets from an IPsec peer or from a Wi-Fi client. Because of the way that the Aruba APs tunnel encrypted data back to the controller, it is difficult to monitor the user data at the AP. The `packet-capture datapath` command allows you to monitor the user data after the controller has decrypted it.

When enabling a data path capture of an IPsec peer, you will need to know the inner IP address of the peer. To enable data path capture of a Wi-Fi client, you will need to know the MAC address of the client's Wi-Fi adapter.

The following CLI output shows configuration for capturing IPsec traffic from an IPsec peer. The first command defines the output destination for the data path capture. This is necessary because when you are performing an IPsec capture, the data cannot be sent to the controller's internal file system. The second command of the following CLI output enables packet capture of the data path traffic with the IPsec peer of 10.1.80.100.

```
#packet-capture destination ip-address 192.168.240.176
#packet-capture datapath ipsec 10.1.80.100
```

The next CLI output shows the command to capture traffic from the wireless client with the MAC address of 00:24:D7:6A:71:24. A question mark was entered after the MAC address of the client to show you the capture options. As you can see, you can choose to capture decrypted packets only, encrypted packets only, or both. Let me explain the differences between capturing decrypted packets and encrypted packets.

```
#packet-capture datapath wifi-client 00:24:d7:6a:71:24 ?
all                 Capture both decrypted and encrypted packets
decrypted           Capture decrypted packets only
encrypted           Capture encrypted packets only
#Packet-capture datapath wifi-client 00:24:d7:6a:71:24 all
```

When the controller sends packets to be transmitted to clients, the controller takes the plain-text data, runs it through an encryption process, and then forwards the encrypted data to the AP to be transmitted. When a client sends data to the controller, the AP receives the client's encrypted data; the AP forwards it to the controller using a GRE tunnel, where it is decrypted by the decryption process; and then the plain text is processed by the controller. If you choose to capture decrypted packets, the `packet-capture` command will capture the plain-text packets from the data stream on the inside of the encrypt/decrypt engine. If you choose to capture encrypted packets, the `packet-capture` command will capture the encrypted packets from the data stream on the outside of the encrypt/decrypt engine. If you choose all, both encrypted and decrypted packets will be captured, which does not provide much benefit over one or the other. If you are troubleshooting higher layers of the communication, then choosing decrypted will reveal all the layers in the client packet. If you only want or need to look at the 802.11 headers, then you can choose encrypted. In the second CLI command of the previous output, you can see that all packets are being captured.

The show packet-capture command displays the current configuration. Note that both IPsec and Wi-Fi traffic is being captured in our example. In a real troubleshooting situation, you would probably not want to capture both of these at the same time.

```
#show packet-capture

Active Capture Destination
-------------------------
Destination    IP         192.168.240.176


Active Capture (Controlpath)
----------------------------
Interprocess   Disabled
Sysmsg         Disabled
TCP            Disabled
UDP            Disabled
Other          Disabled


Active Capture (Datapath)
-------------------------
Wifi-Client    Enabled    Mac: 00:24:d7:6a:71:24    Filter: All
Ipsec          Enabled    Peer: 10.1.80.100
```

The final three commands disable the settings that were explained in this section. *Always* disable the packet-capture settings when you are done troubleshooting because it adds unnecessary CPU processing to the controller. This step is often overlooked.

```
#no packet-capture datapath ipsec
#no packet-capture datapath wifi-client
#no packet-capture destination
```

Destination

The packet-capture command allows you to define a destination that specifies where any data path captures will be sent or stored. This destination is used not only by the packet-capture command when it is configured to capture packets, but is also used when firewall mirroring (session mirroring) is configured. Firewall mirroring will be explained later in this chapter.

A packet capture can be sent to an interface on the controller, the IP address of a remote device, or the local file system of the controller. The packet-capture command followed by a question mark displays the parameters used to define the different options. The packet capture destination is one of these parameters:

```
#packet-capture ?
controlpath      Enable controlpath capture. Captured packets are
                 stored in /var/log/oslog/filter.pcap. Only capture
                 to local-filesystem is supported.
copy-to-flash    Copy captured packets to flash.
datapath         Enable datapath capture. Captured packets are stored
                 in /var/log/oslog/datapath.pcap or mirrored out of
                 the controller.
destination      Configure capture destination.
reset-pcap       Delete old pcap files and restart active capture.
```

Control path traffic is always automatically output to a log file, filter.pcap. This file resides on the controller's local file system and is not affected by the specified destination.

The following CLI output shows examples of how to use the packet-capture command to define each of the three output destinations available for data path captures. Only one destination can be defined at a time:

```
#packet-capture destination interface 0/0/6
#packet-capture destination ip-address 1.2.3.4
#packet-capture destination local-filesystem
```

Capture to an Interface

When the packet capture destination is set to an interface, the captured data path traffic will be sent to a physical port on the controller, typically a Gigabit Ethernet port. You will need to physically connect a computer running packet analysis software to the interface. After the computer is connected, run packet analysis software, such as Omnipeek or Wireshark. Configure the packet analysis software to capture packets using the Ethernet adapter that you are using to connect to the interface.

Capture to an IP Address

If the packet capture destination is set to an IP address, the packets will be transmitted across the network directly to the address of the specified device. Make sure that the IP address corresponds to a computer that is configured with packet analysis software. The controller can be configured to forward data path traffic or IPsec to the computer with that IP address. It is highly recommended that the destination be a wired computer. If the destination computer is a wireless machine, it is possible for you to capture both the desired packets along with capturing the data again as it is being sent to your computer for analysis.

To transport this data across the network, the captured traffic must be placed in a separate package so that it can be redirected to the packet analysis computer. The controller does this by wrapping the traffic in a GRE tunnel. Each frame is encapsulated in a GRE frame and transported across the network to the computer that is performing the analysis. A GRE frame is defined as IP protocol 47.

When the computer with the analysis software receives the GRE frames, the software needs to be configured to interpret the frame as a GRE frame, displaying the tunneled data. Fortunately, many of the packet capture programs, such as Wireshark and Omnipeek, recognize GRE frames. These programs understand that the GRE frames encapsulate and forward other frames. They take the encapsulated data and display it decoded it as if it were the actual data stream, which it essentially is.

Remember, when data is transmitted, a header is added to the frame that identifies where it is coming from and going to. When that frame is being encapsulated, GRE is simply adding an additional header to the frame. This would be similar to writing a letter to send to someone. When the letter is written, you place the letter in an envelope and address that envelope. Encapsulation would simply put that letter and envelope inside another envelope. Just as the recipient of your letter recognizes that there are two envelopes and that the content is the letter, the packet analysis programs are able to recognize that the actual payload is the contents of the inner frame.

Capture to the Local File System

When a packet capture is sent to the local file system, it is stored on the controller in one of two log files: `filter.pcap` or `datapath.pcap`. Capturing to the controller's file system has the advantage of being able to capture data when you do not have a packet analyzer available. The file can be exported and viewed at a later time, or from another system. This can be very helpful for collecting troubleshooting data from a remote site or when working with the Technical Assistance Center (TAC). A potential problem of capturing to the controller's file system is that the capture file may exceed the available storage space.

As specified previously, if control path traffic is being captured, it is output only to the file system, and it is stored in the file `/var/log/oslog/filter.pcap`. If the data path traffic is being captured, and if its output is being sent to the file system, it is stored in the file `/var/log/oslog/datapath.pcap`.

These filenames cannot be viewed on the controller, but access to both of these files is available using multiple options. The first method is to display the file contents directly from the CLI prompt. This can be performed for either of the files. The following CLI output shows sample captures from the control path file and the data path file:

```
#show packet-capture controlpath-pcap

15:39:00.748600 IP 127.0.0.1.8210 > 127.0.0.1.8210: UDP, length 85
```

```
15:39:00.816879 IP 127.0.0.1.8210 > 127.0.0.1.8210: UDP, length 84
15:39:00.816998 IP 127.0.0.1.8210 > 127.0.0.1.8210: UDP, length 88
15:39:02.819748 IP 127.0.0.1.8210 > 127.0.0.1.8210: UDP, length 84
15:39:02.819826 IP 127.0.0.1.8210 > 127.0.0.1.8210: UDP, length 88
15:39:04.823459 IP 127.0.0.1.8210 > 127.0.0.1.8210: UDP, length 84
15:39:04.823575 IP 127.0.0.1.8210 > 127.0.0.1.8210: UDP, length 88

#show packet-capture datapath-pcap
16:17:08.838489 ARP, Request who-has 10.1.90.153 tell 10.1.90.100, length 42
16:17:08.838536 IP 10.1.90.100 > 10.1.90.152: GREv0, length 98: gre-proto-0x8280
16:17:08.840229 IP 10.1.90.152 > 10.1.90.100: GREv0, length 84: gre-proto-0x8280
16:17:08.840275 ARP, Reply 10.1.90.153 is-at 00:24:d7:6a:71:24, length 28
16:17:41.346013 IP 10.1.90.152 > 10.1.90.100: GREv0, length 96: gre-proto-0x8280
16:17:41.346109 IP 10.1.90.153.60431 > 52.170.24.150.443: Flags [F.], seq 2879408985, ack 2059848798, win 59, length 0
16:17:41.420225 IP 52.170.24.150.443 > 10.1.90.153.60431: Flags [.], ack 1, win 507, length 0
16:17:41.420283 IP 10.1.90.100 > 10.1.90.152: GREv0, length 102: gre-proto-0x8280
```

The packet-capture command also provides a method of copying either the control path capture file or the data path capture file to the flash partition where you can see and copy the file. The resulting filenames are controlpath-pcap.tar.gz or datapath-pcap.tar.gz. Once the file is in the flash partition, it can be easily copied to your computer using FTP or TFTP. The following CLI output shows the commands to copy the control path and data path files to the flash partition of the controller. The dir command and its output are also shown, displaying the file information for both files.

```
#packet-capture copy-to-flash controlpath-pcap
#packet-capture copy-to-flash datapath-pcap

#dir
-rw-r--r--    1 root   root    117275 Mar  9 23:22 controlpath-pcap.tar.gz
-rw-r--r--    1 root   root    325902 Mar  9 23:22 datapath-pcap.tar.gz
```

The following CLI commands will copy each of the files from the flash partition to an FTP server at the IP address 192.168.240.31. The FTP user account is david and the files will be copied to the folder /ftp-files. The files will also be renamed to include the date of the files (controlpath-2017-03-09.tar.gz and datapath-2017-03-09.tar.gz).

```
#copy flash: controlpath-pcap.tar.gz ftp: 192.168.240.31 david /ftp-files controlpath-2017-03-09.tar.gz
Password:********
```

```
#copy flash: datapath-pcap.tar.gz ftp: 192.168.240.31 david /ftp-files
datapath-2017-03-09.tar.gz
Password:********
```

The final method of copying the control path and data path files can be performed through the log files. The `logs.tar` file should be generated, and it should include the tech-support information. The resulting file, `logs.tar`, must then be copied to your computer using FTP or TFTP.

To view the captured data with a packet analyzer, you must uncompress the file after it is on your computer and then extract it. The pcap capture file can then be opened using packet analysis software. The following CLI output shows the command to create the log file, followed by a copy command to transfer the files to an FTP server. In this example, the log file was renamed to include the date as part of the name.

```
#tar logs tech-support
This operation may take a while, Please do not power cycle the box
#copy flash: logs.tar ftp: 192.168.240.31 david /ftp-files logs-march-9.tar
Password:********
```

After the log file is copied to a local disk, the contents will need to be extracted using compression software, which should be available on your local computer. At this point, the file containing the control path capture is `/var/log/oslog/filter.pcap` and the file containing the data path capture is `/var/log/oslog/datapath.pcap`. After you locate the files, you can open them using packet analysis software such as Omnipeek or Wireshark.

At some point, you may want to erase the contents of either of these two capture files from the controller's file system. The following two CLI commands erase the contents of these files:

```
#packet-capture reset-pcap controlpath-pcap
#packet-capture reset-pcap datapath-pcap
```

packet-capture-defaults

Previously in this chapter you learned that the `packet-capture` configuration settings are not stored as part of the running configuration on the controller. Although this is true, with the `packet-capture-defaults` command it is possible to retain `packet-capture` settings when the controller is rebooted. These default settings are local to each controller and are not shared between a master controller and its local controllers. At any time the default settings can be overridden by using the `packet-capture` command.

The `packet-capture-defaults` command allows the configuration of both the control path and data path capture parameters, along with the ability to specify the capture destination. The `packet-capture-defaults` command functions the same as the `packet-capture` command, with the addition of preserving the settings during a reboot.

The following set of `packet-capture-default` commands are equivalent to the `packet-capture` commands earlier in this chapter. The first command defines the output destination for the data path capture. This is necessary because when performing an IPsec capture, the data cannot be sent to the controller's internal file system. The second command of the following CLI output enables packet capture of the data path traffic with the IPsec peer of 10.1.80.100. The third command enables capture of decrypted traffic from the wireless client with the MAC address of 00:24:D7:6A:71:24. The `show packet-capture` command displays the current configuration. The final two commands disable these settings.

```
#configure terminal
Enter Configuration commands, one per line. End with CNTL/Z

(config) #packet-capture-defaults destination ip-address 192.168.240.176
(config) #packet-capture-defaults datapath ipsec 10.1.80.100
(config) #packet-capture-defaults datapath wifi-client 00:24:d7:6a:71:24 decrypted

(config) #show packet-capture-defaults

Default Capture Destination
---------------------------
Destination    IP       192.168.240.176


Default Capture (Controlpath)
-----------------------------
Interprocess    Disabled
Sysmsg          Disabled
TCP             Disabled
UDP             Disabled
Other           Disabled


Default Capture (Datapath)
--------------------------
Wifi-Client    Enabled    Mac: 00:24:d7:6a:71:24    Filter: Decrypted
Ipsec          Enabled    Peer: 10.1.80.100

(config) #no packet-capture-defaults datapath ipsec
(config) #no packet-capture-defaults datapath wifi-client
```

Firewall Mirroring

So far in this chapter you have learned about packet capture using port monitoring and capturing packets internally on the controller using the `packet-capture` command. The next packet capture method uses the controller's firewall to specify what data will be captured. The mechanism uses firewall rules to mirror the data of interest, thus the term *firewall mirroring*. This data is mirrored to an IP address.

Capturing user data is generally not possible because the data is encrypted. When a wireless client sends a frame, the client first encrypts the data to be sent, and then adds an 802.11 header to the encrypted data. The client then transmits this frame to the AP. The AP encapsulates the frame inside an 802.3 frame and forwards it to the controller.

When the controller receives this frame, it first strips off the 802.3 header and discards it. The controller then takes the 802.11 header and extracts the layer 2 source and destination addresses. At this point, what is left is the encrypted data (assuming encryption is enabled). The controller decrypts this data and is left with the original plain-text content. The controller proceeds to take the layer 2 source address, as well as the layer 2 destination address, along with the data, and proceeds to forward it to the firewall process to be evaluated against the firewall rules. The firewall rules determine what action will be performed on the frame.

In Chapter 8, "Policy Enforcement Firewall," you learned that firewall rules perform an action on every frame (typically permitting or denying the frame from continuing to be transported across the network). In addition to performing an action on each frame, firewall rules can be configured to perform an optional extended action—an additional function or task. One of these extended actions is firewall mirroring.

If the extracted frame matches a firewall rule that has mirroring enabled, then not only will the firewall action be performed, but a copy of the frame (layer 2 source address, layer 2 destination address, and decrypted data) will be forwarded (mirrored) to the destination defined by the `packet-capture` command, `packet-capture destination ip-address 1.2.3.4`. When firewall mirroring is enabled, the packet capture destination must be set to an IP address.

Note that in earlier versions of ArubaOS (prior to ArubaOS 6.3), the firewall mirror destination was defined as part of the firewall command. This is no longer the case. The firewall mirror destination is now specified using the `packet-capture` command.

The mirrored firewall frame will be wrapped in a GRE tunnel and sent to the destination IP address. Each frame will be encapsulated in a GRE frame and transported across the network to the computer that is performing the analysis. Most packet analysis software is able to recognize the GRE header as the transport method, and simply strip it off and discard it, allowing the analysis to focus on the payload.

A very nice feature of firewall mirroring is that it allows you to target the data that is being captured. Firewall policies are applied through user roles, allowing rules to be granular, capturing a specific set of frames.

AP/AM Capture

The final capture method that will be explained is how to perform a capture using an AP or air monitor (AM) as the RF listening device. This method allows you to choose an AP or AM on your network, configure it to listen to the wireless transmissions, and send the information that it hears to a computer configured for packet analysis. This is different than using the `packet-capture` command; you will learn the differences shortly.

If you have ever performed a packet capture on an 802.3/Ethernet network, you know that in order to properly capture all of the data, you need to place the adapter in promiscuous mode. By default, an Ethernet adapter only listens to broadcast, multicast, and unicast frames addressed directly to the address of the adapter. Promiscuous mode allows the Ethernet adapter to capture any frames that it sees, whether or not they are addressed to the device.

When performing a wireless capture from a laptop computer, a wireless adapter is typically connected to an SSID on a specific channel, and similar to an Ethernet adapter, it only listens to broadcast, multicast, and unicast frames addressed directly to it. A wireless adapter needs to be placed into what is known as RF monitor mode (comparable to promiscuous mode) in order to be able to capture all wireless frames that it hears. This method of packet capture allows you to capture the 802.11 management and control frames, including beacons, ACKs, probe requests and responses, and RTS/CTS, to name a few.

A limitation of RF monitor mode is that many client adapters and operating system drivers do not support it. Therefore, if you want to perform a packet capture on many laptop computers, it is necessary to buy a special wireless adapter that has drivers that can make it operate in RF monitor mode. An alternative to this is to use an Aruba AP or AM to perform the capture, since they can inherently operate in RF monitor mode.

This section describes how to configure APs and AMs to perform wireless packet captures. Packet capture and analysis is too complex a topic to try to address the different options and details. There are good articles and blogs on the Internet that specifically discuss the different capture types, along with details about the packet header and data field and contents presented in those fields.

Capture Procedures

Performing a packet capture from an AP is a straightforward process. Using the `ap packet-capture` command, an AP or AM is configured to send a copy of the wireless traffic to the IP address of a computer running packet analysis software. Prior to ArubaOS 6.2, the command was known as `pcap`. The `pcap` command has been deprecated from the OS and replaced with `ap packet-capture`.

Since the AP is transporting wireless frames across the wired network, the frames need to be encapsulated. The AP does not use GRE for this; it uses a specified UDP header address. Typically UDP 5000 or 5555 are used.

On the computer running the packet analysis software, the software is configured to listen to traffic being received on the network interface. In addition to the captured traffic, other traffic is likely being received on this interface. To isolate just the traffic captured by the AP, the analysis software needs to be configured with a filter to only listen for frames with a specific destination port, such as UDP 5000.

ap packet-capture Command

To configure packet capture from an AP or AM, you can use the CLI or the WebUI. The WebUI can be a little confusing, so the CLI commands will be explained first. Configuring packet capture from the CLI is more powerful and flexible, so it is recommended that you use the CLI.

When AP packet capture is enabled, you are instructing the AP or AM to send a stream of frames directly from the AP or AM to your packet analyzing computer. If the AP is a RAP, it is configured to use L2TP/IPsec to transport control traffic. If it is a campus AP or AM with CPsec enabled, then it is configured to use IPsec to transport control traffic. To perform an AP packet capture in either of these scenarios, you must enable the AP to directly transport the frames using a separate UDP port, outside of the L2TP/IPsec or IPsec communication stream. This is easily enabled and disabled using the following CLI commands:

```
#ap packet-capture open-port 5000
#ap packet-capture close-port 5000
```

After the UDP port has been opened, if needed, the `ap packet-capture` command can be used to begin the capture. The following is a list of some of the parameters used with the command, along with a description of each. When issuing the command, the AP can be specified by ap-name, ip-addr, or ip6-addr.

`raw-start`   Stream the packets from the AP driver to the specified client. Raw captures will send anything received by the AP or AM to the analyzing computer.

`ap-name <ap-name>`   The name of the AP streaming the packets.

`ip-addr <ipv4-addr>`   The IPv4 address of the AP streaming the packets.

`ip6-addr <ipv6-addr>`   The IPv6 address of the AP streaming the packets.

`<target-ip>`   The IP address of the analyzing computer.

`<target-port>`   The UDP port number—typically 5000 for Omnipeek or 5555 for Wireshark.

\<format\> This specifies the capture format. The format options are 0-pcap, 1-peek, 2-airmagnet, 3-pcap+radio header, 4-ppi, 5-peek with 11n/11ac header.

radio \<0-1\> The ID of the radio performing the capture. 0 = 5 GHz, 1 = 2.4 GHz.

channel \<channel\> The radio channel to capture (used with AM only and is optional). You should instead use the am scan command, explained later in this section.

The following CLI output shows a packet capture being enabled using an AP. A raw capture is being started, using AP AP225-90-1, sending the packets to the analyzer at 192.168.240.169, using UDP 5000 for Omnipeek (the frames will be in peek format), and capturing the 5 GHz radio 0.

```
#ap packet-capture raw-start ap-name AP225-90-1 192.168.240.169 5000 1 radio 0
Packet capture has started for pcap-id:3
```

When the capture is started, it is important to note the pcap-id that is displayed at the end of the output. This ID is needed when you want to stop the capture process. Using the previous example, when you are done performing the capture, the following CLI command shows how to stop the capture. To do this, you need to know the AP name, the pcap-id, and which radio you are capturing from.

```
#ap packet-capture stop ap-name AP225-90-1 3 radio 0
Packet capture has stopped for pcap-id:3
```

If you do not remember the ID, or if you simply want to see the configuration of the capture settings, the following CLI output displays the command to show the status of the AP packet capture for a specific AP or AM:

```
#show ap packet-capture status ap-name AP225-90-1

Packet Capture Sessions at AP225-90-1, IP 10.1.90.152
----------------------------------------------------
pcap-id  filter  type  intf              channel  max-pkt-size
-------  ------  ----  ----              -------  ------------
14               raw   9c:1c:12:88:57:b0  149      0


   num-pkts  status       url  target                Radio ID
   --------  ------       ---  ------                --------
   2374      in-progress       192.168.240.169/5000  0



   Wired Packet Capture
   --------------------
   Target-IP  Target-Port  Packet-Cnt  Duration (sec)
   ---------  -----------  ----------  --------------
```

Packet Capture from Air Monitors

Let us take a look at the advantages of performing a packet capture using an air monitor instead of an AP.

In the previous example, you configured an AP to perform the packet capture. When an AP is chosen, it captures packets on its home channel—the channel(s) that it is operating on. During the capture, the AP will forward any packets that it hears. Unfortunately, 802.11 is a half-duplex environment, which means that the radio can either be transmitting or receiving, but not doing both at the same time. Because of this, when an AP is transmitting packets, the receiver circuits are shut down; thus, an AP cannot monitor at the same time that it is transmitting. However, it wants to make sure that the computer doing analysis receives both sides of the conversation. Therefore, the AP will forward a copy of what it is transmitting to the analysis computer, as if the AP heard the traffic.

If you want to capture a complete view of what is transmitted in the air, then you can perform that packet capture from an AM, providing the AM is within range to hear the transmissions from both the client and the AP. To begin a capture from an AM, you first want to specify the channel(s) that you want the AM to listen to. This can be done using the `am scan` CLI command. The following CLI examples show how to configure an AM with an IP address of 10.1.90.155 to scan using channel 36 as a 20 MHz channel, a 40 MHz channel (+), or an 80 MHz channel (E). If the channel is set to (0), all channels will be scanned, as shown in the last example.

```
#am scan 10.1.90.155 36
#am scan 10.1.90.155 36+
#am scan 10.1.90.155 36E
#am scan 10.1.90.155 0
```

Once the channel is selected, the commands to capture packets using an AM are the same as in the previous section that described how to capture packets using an AP.

Disable AP/AM Packet Capture

When you configure an AP or AM to perform a packet capture, you are actually sending a command to the AP or AM and configuring settings on it. The commands are not being performed on the controller, but passed through to the AP or AM. Because of this, there are no commands available on the controller that can display a list of APs that are currently performing packet captures. This means that if you configured an AP or AM to capture packets and did not stop the process, you will continue to have a stream of frames sent across the network. When you are performing packet analysis on a controller, it is important to document the troubleshooting process.

Although not an ideal solution, rebooting the controller will stop any AP or AM from capturing packets, since the commands are sent directly to the AP or AM and no lines are written to the startup-configuration file. The show ap packet-capture status ap-name <apname> command will display the capture status of a specific AP. You would need to repeat this command for any AP that you suspect was still capturing packets.

One suggestion is to use the show audit-trail | include "ap packet-capture" command. This command will show any entries in the command history that contains the text ap packet-capture. This will list any commands that were used to start or stop the packet capture process on an AP or AM. Any commands in the history will also include the name or IP address of the AP or AM that the command was issued against. At that point, the show ap packet-capture status ap-name <apname> command can be used to identify the status of the AP or AM.

WebUI Packet Capture

To configure packet capture from an AP or AM, you can also use the WebUI. The process begins at the **Monitoring ➢ CONTROLLER ➢ Access Points** menu (or Air Monitors menu); select an AP and then click the Packet Capture button, as shown in Figure 13.4. If you are presented with an ESSID/BSSID list, choose one of the BSSIDs. It does not matter which one because you will be undoing this selection in the next window.

FIGURE 13.4
WebUI packet capture

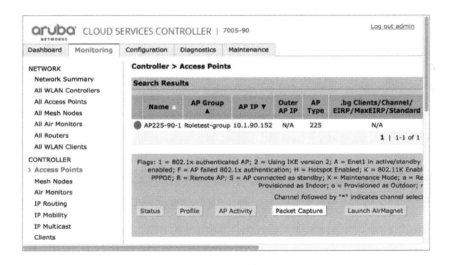

At the next window that appears, click the New Raw Packet Capture button. In the Raw Packet Capture section, you will enter the target IP address of the analyzing computer, enter the UDP port (5000), select the capture format of peek, and select the radio (802.11a), as shown in Figure 13.5. If this was an AM, you would also enter the channel. After you enter this information, click the Start button to begin the capture.

FIGURE 13.5
New raw packet capture

This window will continue to display the configuration and status of the packet capture, as shown in Figure 13.6. The pcap-id is also displayed at the beginning of the line. When you are done with the packet capture, you can select the capture session by clicking the select box at the beginning of the line and then clicking the Stop button.

FIGURE 13.6
WebUI packet capture status

Configuring Omnipeek

In addition to configuring the Aruba AP or AM to capture and send the data, a computer needs to be configured with software to receive the data. This section will explain the tasks necessary to process the data using Omnipeek, which is a very powerful product for performing packet analysis.

On the controller side you should have entered the AP packet-capture command similar to the CLI output shown here. Note that UDP port 5000 is being used, and capture format 1 (peek) has been chosen.

```
#ap packet-capture raw-start ap-name AP225-90-1 192.168.240.169 5000 1 radio 0
```

After loading Omnipeek, click the New Capture icon or select New Capture from the File menu. In the Capture Options window, select Adapter along the left, expand the Module: Access Point Capture Adapter by clicking the > character to its left, and then double-click on New Adapter. Enter a name for the adapter and either enter an IP address for a specific AP or AM, or leave the IP field blank to support any AP or AM. In this example, the adapter was named Aruba_AP_Capture, as shown in Figure 13.7.

FIGURE 13.7 Configuring Omnipeek

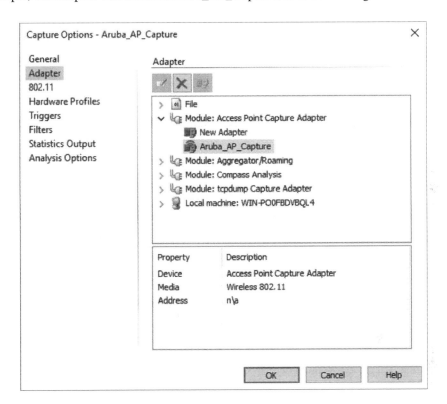

With the new adapter highlighted, click OK at the bottom of the window. The Omnipeek capture window will appear. Click the bright green Start AP Capture button in the upper-right corner of the capture window. At this point, you should see 802.11 frames displayed in the Omnipeek capture window.

Configuring Wireshark

Another popular option for analyzing packets is Wireshark. Wireshark is a free packet analysis software program that runs on many OS platforms. This section will explain the tasks necessary to process the capture data using Wireshark.

On the controller side, you should have entered the AP packet-capture command similar to the CLI output shown here. Note that UDP port 5555 is being used and capture format 0 (pcap) has been chosen.

```
#ap packet-capture raw-start ap-name AP225-90-1 192.168.240.169 5555 0 radio 0
```

After loading Wireshark, select the network interface that the computer is using to connect to the corporate network. The Wireshark window is displayed in Figure 13.8.

Above the list of interfaces is the section Capture with a field labeled "…using this filter." Since the AP or AM is sending the data with a destination port of UDP 5555, enter **udp port 5555** into the field and press the Enter key. This will instruct Wireshark to begin the capture and only capture UDP 5555 packets. These settings can also be configured from the **Capture ➢ Options** menu.

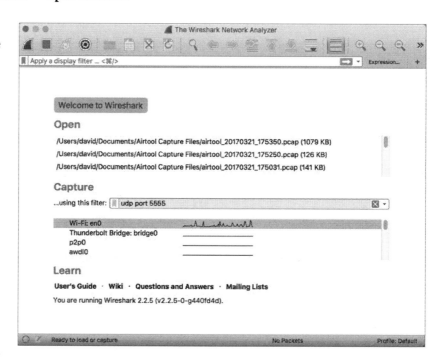

FIGURE 13.8
Wireshark capture

It is important to understand that the display filter and capture filter in Wireshark are two different things, performing two different functions. The display filter displays the packets of interest after the packets are captured. Different options and combinations can be made to look at the packets in different ways. The capture filter is used to filter or restrict the packets that Wireshark receives and retains. Anything that does not match the capture filter is discarded and is not part of the capture file.

When the capture begins, the Info column will most likely display all the packets as ARUBA_ERM. In order for Wireshark to translate these packets, you need to enable a decode filter. From the Analyze drop-down menu, select Decode As and a new decode window will appear. In the bottom-left corner, click the plus sign to add a decode rule. Enter the following values in the rule, as shown in Figure 13.9:

    Field: Aruba ERM Type

    Value: 0

    Type: Integer, base 10

Default: Use default value—none or ZVT

Current: ARUBA ERM PCAP (Type 0)

FIGURE 13.9
Wireshark decode settings

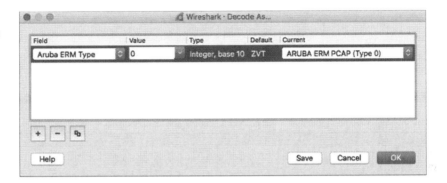

After entering these settings, click the Save button. The Decode window will appear and Wireshark will begin to decode any packets that have already been captured and any new packets that are captured.

Packet Capture Synopsis

Four different packet capture methods were explained in this chapter. These methods capture different types of data from different physical and logical places on the network. This section will provide a brief recap of these methods along with a description of the types of data captured.

Port monitoring allows you to connect an analysis computer directly to an Ethernet port on the controller and monitor all traffic from another port. As the packets travel in or out of the monitored port, a copy is forwarded to the monitoring port, where the analysis computer is connected. The traffic is not modified in any way. As an example, if the traffic is GRE frames between an AP and the controller, that is what you will see in your analysis software.

The *packet-capture command* captures the control path or data path traffic from the internal pathways of the controller. A port interface, IP address, or the local file system can be specified as the capture destination, although there are some specific limitations. Control path traffic can only be captured to /var/log/oslog/filter.pcap on the local file system. Data path traffic should be redirected to an external IP address. When the packet-capture command forwards any captures to an IP address, the traffic is encapsulated as a GRE frame.

Firewall mirroring takes a copy of any packet that matches a firewall rule that has mirror specified as an extended action and forwards it to an IP address. This capture is performed at the controller and will gather the data after it has been decrypted. Firewall mirroring uses GRE frames to forward the captured frames to the IP address of the analyzing computer.

The `ap packet-capture` command allows the radio of an AP or AM to capture frames from the RF environment near the AP or AM, and forward those frames to the IP address of an analysis computer. The data is forwarded to the computer with a destination port of UDP 5000 or UDP 5555 headers. The packet analysis software must be configured to receive this specific data stream and to filter it. This capture method will capture any 802.11 management, control, or data frames that the AP or AM can hear. The location of the monitoring AP or AM needs to be considered in relation to the location of any clients and the APs that the clients are communicating with. Because the commands are run on the AP or AM and the controller decrypts the traffic, all encrypted traffic will be displayed as encrypted packets and the plain-text data will not be shown. This type is used more when the interest is to analyze the 802.11 frames and headers.

Spectrum Analysis

If you have the RFProtect license installed on the Aruba controller, then ArubaOS allows you to configure an AP as a spectrum monitor (SM) and use it to perform layer 1 spectrum analysis. Spectrum analysis allows you to monitor the RF signals that are present around the AP.

Spectrum analysis can help monitor and identify the different types of RF signals in your environment, and it can assist you in understanding if and how those signals are detrimentally affecting your network. This knowledge can help you improve the design and performance of your network, or troubleshoot issues related to connectivity speed and reliability.

The goal of this section is to help you understand how to use ArubaOS to perform spectrum analysis. This section also explains the many charts that are available. Due to the size of the charts, it may be difficult to read the details in the figures in this chapter. Use this chapter and the figures as guidance when performing spectrum analysis on your own network, where you will be able to monitor live data. The figures and descriptions are designed to help you understand the information that the charts are providing and how the information is presented.

Remember, the focus is on understanding how ArubaOS is presenting the data, not the data itself. For understanding the data, you will need to understand RF, and that is not the objective of this book.

To perform spectrum analysis using ArubaOS, three configuration items are required. The first task is to configure an AP as a spectrum monitor. Second, you will need a computer with a browser, which will allow you to visually display spectrum data.

And finally, you need to select the spectrum monitor, telling it to direct the monitored data to the spectrum analyzer program running in the browser.

Configuring a Spectrum Monitor

ArubaOS provides three ways of configuring an AP to be a spectrum monitor. Each method performs the task in a slightly different way, and will be explained in the following sections of this chapter. When an AP is configured as a spectrum monitor (SM), spectrum information is collected and sent to the controller. Numerous CLI commands can be used to display this data.

The SMs can also be configured to forward the information to a computer where you can view and analyze the data visually through charts. This data can also be captured or recorded to be analyzed at a future time.

All of these capabilities will be explained in this chapter.

Spectrum Monitor Group

The first method of configuring an AP as a spectrum monitor is to create an AP group dedicated for spectrum monitoring and then assign one or more APs to that group. Figure 13.10 shows an AP group named "Spectrum-group." After the group is created, you need to create 2.4 GHz and 5 GHz radio profiles and select spectrum-mode for each. In this figure the profiles are named 11a-sm and 11g-sm, with the profile mode for each set to spectrum-mode. The following CLI output shows the commands to perform these tasks. The first command creates a radio profile named "11a-sm." The second command sets the radio mode to spectrum. The last two commands create an AP group named Spectrum-group and assign the 11a-sm radio profile to the group. This sequence would need to be repeated for the 11g radio profile.

```
(config) #rf dot11a-radio-profile 11a-sm
(802.11a radio profile "11a-sm") #mode spectrum-mode
Warning: If there is an entry for a radio in 'ap spectrum local-override'
profile on the local controller that terminates the AP, that entry will override
the mode selection in the radio profile.

(802.11a radio profile "11a-sm") #ap-group Spectrum-group
(AP group "Spectrum-group") #dot11a-radio-profile 11a-sm
```

Make sure that you create a new profile and do not modify the default radio profile. I know of two instances when the administrator forgot, changed the default radio profile to spectrum monitor mode or air monitor mode, and with the click of the Apply button, hundreds of APs were converted to monitoring mode, effectively shutting down the entire network.

It is also good practice to create radio profiles for access point mode and air monitor mode as well. You should choose logical names and be consistent, such as 11g-ap, 11a-ap, 11g-am, and 11a-am.

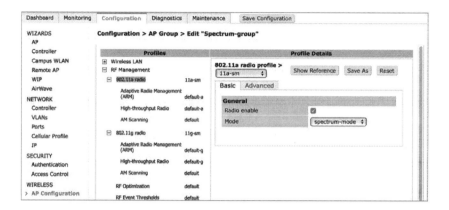

FIGURE 13.10
Spectrum mode AP group

A dedicated spectrum monitor group can be handy to have, but most people do not permanently deploy spectrum analyzers. In some instances, people have some spare APs configured permanently as SMs, to be temporarily deployed on location as needed.

Spectrum Local Override

It is more common to temporarily convert an AP or AM to be an SM, and then convert it back when you are done using it. If this is how you intend to perform spectrum analysis, you may be tempted to temporarily provision an AP or AM to the spectrum group. Do not do this. Provisioning an AP or AM forces a reboot of the AP or AM. Also, when you return it back to its original AP group, you need to remember the name of the original group. There is a much better way, spectrum local override, which is explained here.

Spectrum local override allows you to temporarily convert an AP or AM radio to spectrum mode. When you are done, you can simply delete the radio from the override list. The override happens immediately upon clicking the Apply button, and does not require the AP or AM to reboot.

The spectrum local override menu is found in the All Profiles menu, using the following menu path: **Configuration ➢ ADVANCED SERVICES ➢ All Profiles ➢ AP ➢ Spectrum Local Override**.

In this menu, as shown in Figure 13.11, you select the radio band that you want to override, enter the AP name, and click the Add button (make sure you know the name of the AP, or have copied it before you begin the override process). In this example, the 2.4 GHz radio for AP115-AM has already been added to the override list, and the 5 GHz radio is about to be added. The radios are not overridden until the Apply button is clicked.

FIGURE 13.11
Spectrum local override

The radios can also be overridden from the CLI. Overriding an AP is a configuration change that is made to the running-configuration. This means that if the controller is rebooted without saving the running-configuration to the startup-configuration, the AP will return to its original AP group provisioned state upon reboot. The following CLI output will override AP115-AM and add it to the list for both 2.4 GHz and 5 GHz:

```
(config) #ap spectrum local-override
(Spectrum Local Override Profile) #override ap-name AP115-AM spectrum-band 2ghz
(Spectrum Local Override Profile) #override ap-name AP115-AM spectrum-band 5ghz
```

When you are done using the overridden SM, you should delete it from the spectrum override list so that it can function again as either an AP or an AM.

To perform this task from the WebUI, use the same menu where you initially performed the override. The Spectrum Local Override menu is found in the All Profiles menu, using the following menu path: **Configuration ➢ ADVANCED SERVICES ➢ All Profiles ➢ AP ➢ Spectrum Local Override**. In this menu, as shown in Figure 13.11, you select the override entry that you want to remove and click the Delete button. The radio is not removed from the override list until the Apply button is clicked.

To remove an SM from the override list using the CLI, you first need to know the name of the SM. You can use the show ap active command to display all of the operating APs (this list includes APs, AMs, and SMs). Any AP with Spectrum^ in either of the radio columns is currently overridden and operating as an SM. The following CLI output removes AP115-AM from the override list for both the 2.4 GHz radio and the 5 GHz radio:

```
(config) # ap spectrum local-override
(Spectrum Local Override Profile) #no override ap-name AP115-AM spectrum-band 2ghz
(Spectrum Local Override Profile) #no override ap-name AP115-AM spectrum-band 5ghz
```

Hybrid Mode

The final method of configuring an AP to perform spectrum analysis is to configure it to operate in what is known as hybrid mode (Figure 13.12). When in hybrid mode, an AP can perform the duties of an access point (advertising SSIDs and supporting clients), while also acting as a spectrum analyzer. A key caveat to this is that the AP can only function as a spectrum analyzer on the channel or channel range that the AP is operating on. Hybrid mode does consume additional CPU cycles, so in a high-density client environment, or an environment where latency-sensitive applications are being used (such as VoIP), you may be better off using a dedicated SM.

To enable hybrid mode, navigate to the AP Group menu, and from the RF Management menu modify the radio profile. From the radio profile Advanced menu, you need to enable the Spectrum Monitoring checkbox. Many-first time users of this feature forget to go to the Advanced menu and tend to change the mode to spectrum-mode instead of selecting the checkbox. Be very careful not to do this. If you do, upon applying the changes, all of the APs in that group will immediately become spectrum monitors, and you will very quickly receive phone calls that the network is down since you have just changed all of the APs in that group to spectrum monitors.

Remember that you are changing this setting for the AP group, so all APs in this AP group will now be operating in hybrid mode.

FIGURE 13.12
AP hybrid mode

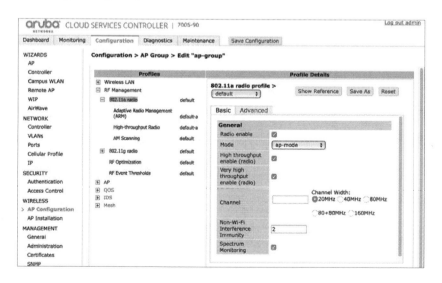

Hybrid mode can easily be configured from the CLI. The following CLI output shows the process. The hybrid setting is made to the radio profile. The first command will display the running configuration beginning with the ap-group section. In this output you need to identify the AP group that you want to make the change to—in this case, warehouse. The radio profiles listed below the AP group name are the radio profiles that need to be modified. If the profiles are not listed, then the default radio profile is assigned to the AP group. After identifying the radio profile, you need to select the profile and then enable spectrum monitoring by entering the command:

```
(config) #show running-config | begin ap-group
ap-group "warehouse"
   dot11a-radio-profile "11a-ap"
   dot11g-radio-profile "11g-ap"
(config) #rf dot11a-radio-profile 11a-ap
(802.11a radio profile "11a-ap") #spectrum-monitoring
```

If the client density per AP is high or if the application is sensitive to latency (such as VoIP), then do not use hybrid mode. There are also many exceptions to what is being monitored or displayed when using hybrid mode, so it is better to have a dedicated spectrum monitor or perform spectrum analysis using spectrum local override.

Spectrum Monitoring Using the WebUI

After one or more APs are configured as spectrum monitors, you can now begin performing spectrum analysis. This is begun from the following WebUI menu: **Monitoring ➢ SPECTRUM ➢ Spectrum Analysis**. This will open another browser window. You may be prompted to install Adobe Flash Player and to allow Flash Player to use your local storage to store information. You will need to do both to continue.

At this point you are in the Spectrum Analysis window, as shown in Figure 13.13. However, before you continue, you need to select the spectrum monitor radios that you want to use for monitoring. You can choose up to four radios. To select the radios, you can either click on the Spectrum Monitors tab at the top of the window, or you can click the "here" link in the text below the menus. Either selection will bring you to the Spectrum Monitors menu.

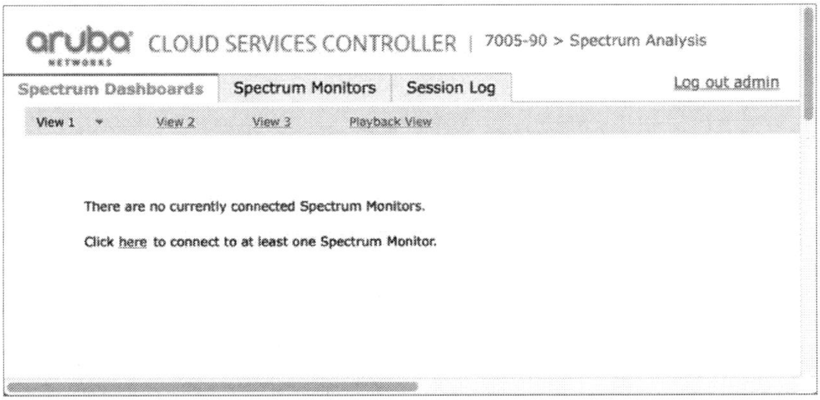

FIGURE 13.13
Spectrum Analysis initial window

When you click the Add button in the Spectrum Monitors window, the list of available spectrum monitors will be displayed, as shown in Figure 13.14. Notice that AP225-90-1 is actually an AP with hybrid mode enabled. This AP happens to be an 802.11ac AP using an 80 MHz channel, as indicated by the text 149E. If you were to choose this AP, you would see spectrum data only on the APs operating channels 149, 153, 157, and 161. A spectrum analyzer can be selected by only one person at a time. Therefore, when you are done doing your analysis it is important to disconnect from the spectrum monitors.

FIGURE 13.14
Adding a spectrum monitor

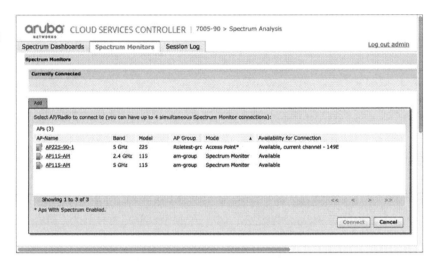

Figure 13.15 shows three spectrum monitors connected. At any time you can disconnect from a spectrum monitor or choose another.

FIGURE 13.15
Selected spectrum monitors

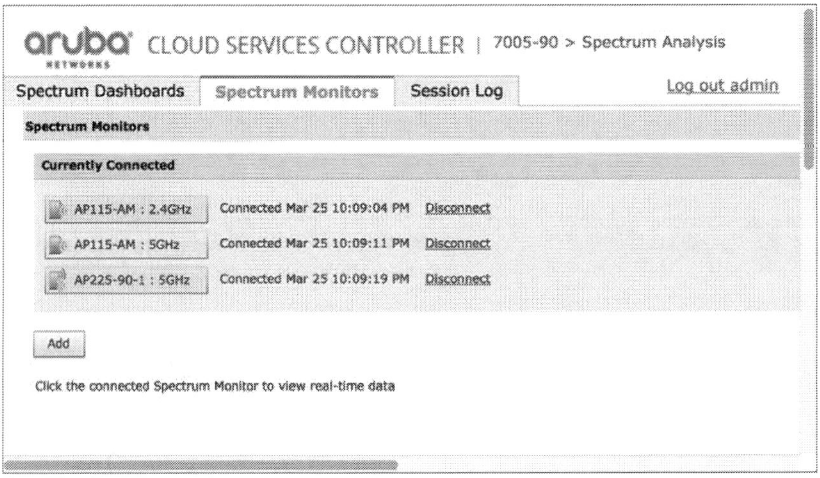

You are now ready to go to the spectrum dashboards by selecting the tab at the top of the window. When you do, a dashboard will appear as shown in Figure 13.16. The program provides four views: View 1, View 2, View 3, and Playback View (used when playing back a recorded capture). Initially you are placed in View 1. Each view has four charts, with each chart window able to be customized. You can switch between views by choosing the specific view from a menu above the top-left chart. You can rename the view you are currently using by clicking the down arrow just to the right of the view name and selecting Rename.

FIGURE 13.16
Spectrum Analysis view window

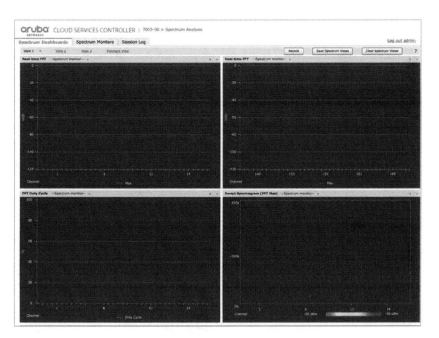

If you lose the connection while doing spectrum analysis using the WebUI, the spectrum monitors will be disconnected from your computer and you will have to reselect them.

RF Options

When an SM is scanning the selected frequency, it uses what is known as a 312 KHz resolution bandwidth (RBW). This essentially means that it is sampling in 312 KHz chunks or groupings. The data collected is then displayed across the selected frequency range.

When scanning the 2.4 GHz band, the entire band can be scanned at the same time. It is different for the 5 GHz channels, as there are multiple bands or ranges of channels. Therefore, it is necessary to tell the SM which band to scan.

The options menu of many of the charts allows you to choose the band that the chart is scanning. If the selected SM is a 2.4 GHz radio, there is no band selection option. If the selected SM is a 5 GHz radio, you have a choice of three ranges of frequencies, or bands.

The three bands are 5 GHz lower, 5 GHz middle, and 5 GHz upper. To properly analyze the data that is displayed, it is important to know which channels or bands are to be scanned.

Table 13.4 shows the four bands (2.4 GHz and 5 GHz) along with the beginning and ending channels of each band. The table also displays the number of channels scanned in each band, as well as a list of each channel number.

TABLE 13.4: Spectrum channel ranges

BAND	STARTING CHANNEL #	ENDING CHANNEL #	NUMBER OF CHANNELS	CHANNEL LIST
2.4	1	14	14	1 through 14
5 GHz lower	36	64	8	36, 40, 44, 48, 52, 56, 60, 64
5 GHz middle	100	140	11	100, 104, 108, 112, 116, 120, 124, 128, 132, 136, 140
5 GHz upper	149	165	5	149, 153, 157, 161, 165

Table 13.5 shows the four bands along with the beginning and ending frequency of each band. The frequency range is defined by the center frequency and a frequency span. Half of the span is below the center frequency and half is above.

TABLE 13.5: Spectrum frequency ranges

BAND	BEGINNING FREQUENCY (MHZ)	ENDING FREQUENCY (MHZ)	CENTER FREQUENCY (MHZ)	FREQUENCY SPAN (MHZ)
2.4	2402	2494	2448	92 (-/+ 46)
5 GHz lower	5170	5330	5250	160 (-/+ 80)
5 GHz middle	5490	5710	5600	220 (-/+110)
5 GHz upper	5735	5835	5785	100 (-/+ 50)

Types of Detected Devices

Many of the charts can automatically display Wi-Fi and non-Wi-Fi devices. Others can be explicitly configured to monitor and display specific types of devices. The following is a list of the types of devices that an SM can detect and identify:

- Wi-Fi APs (2.4 GHz or 5 GHz)
- Microwave (2.4 GHz only)—Common residential microwave ovens (with single magnetron). Other industrial, healthcare, or manufacturing equipment may also be placed in this category.

- Bluetooth (2.4 GHz only)—Any Bluetooth device. Bluetooth uses frequency hopping spread spectrum.
- Fixed Frequency (Others)—All other fixed-frequency devices. Many fixed-frequency devices, such as fixed-frequency audio, video, and cordless phones, have similar RF signatures. It is possible that these devices could be classified in this category.
- Fixed Frequency (Cordless Phones)
- Fixed Frequency (Video)—Video devices that continuously transmit on a single frequency. Often used for surveillance or video distribution. Typically operating at close to 100 percent duty cycle.
- Fixed Frequency (Audio)—Continuously transmitting wireless audio devices, such as speakers or microphones.
- Frequency Hopper (Other)—Frequency hopper signal that is not classified in one of the other categories.
- Frequency Hopper (Cordless Network)—Cordless phone handset being used as part of a phone call. Some cordless phones use both 2.4 GHz and 5 GHz simultaneously (one band for upstream communications and the other for downstream communications). In this situation, the device would be classified on both bands.
- Frequency Hopper (Cordless Base)—The base station for cordless phones. When phones are not transmitting, the base station will periodically verify that it can communicate with the handsets.
- Frequency Hopper Xbox (2.4 GHz only)
- Microwave Inverter (2.4 GHz only)—Some newer microwave ovens. Duty cycle may be close to 100 percent. Some dual-magnetron ovens may also be classified in this category. Other industrial, healthcare, or manufacturing equipment may also be placed in this category.
- Generic Interferer—Any device that is detected that cannot be classified in one of the other categories.

Chart Types

The spectrum analyzer offers 14 different charts, with each chart providing some level of customization. In the Spectrum Dashboard, each view displays four charts that can be monitored simultaneously. Each chart can be switched to full-screen mode, and while in full-screen mode you can customize the information that is displayed in the chart. Each chart can be customized individually with settings relevant to that chart.

Though it is not part of the customization menu, choosing which spectrum monitor radio for a chart is the first customization choice, as shown in Figure 13.17.

FIGURE 13.17
Selecting the spectrum monitor

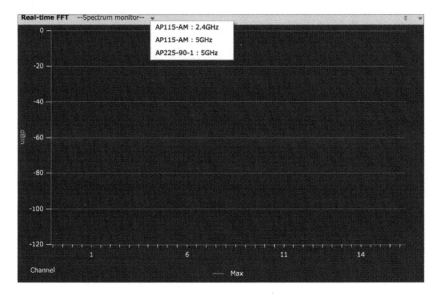

The next step would be to replace the current chart with one of the 13 other charts. The down arrow in the upper-right corner of the chart allows you to do this, as shown in Figure 13.18. Depending on the current chart, the down arrow may also have some additional chart-specific options.

FIGURE 13.18
Selecting a different chart

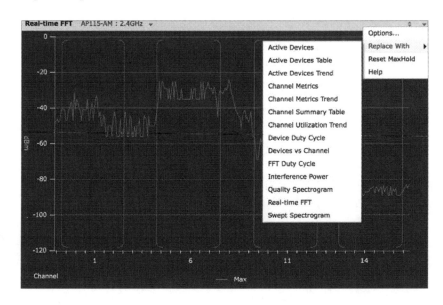

To switch a chart to full-screen mode, to the left of the down arrow is a double arrow, which is the resizing option. Clicking on it will maximize the current chart, making it take up the space that the original four charts occupied, as shown in Figure 13.19. The other charts are still part of your current view; they are just hidden in the background, allowing you to focus solely on the current chart.

When the chart is resized, an options menu will likely appear along the right side of the chart, allowing you to customize the chart that you are currently viewing. A small number of charts do not have this in the options menu.

Any option changes you make will immediately take effect in the chart you are viewing. It is nice to be able to focus on a single chart, and to be able to see the details in full-screen mode. If you click the OK button, the changes will be retained and the chart will be minimized, returning you to the initial four-chart view. If you click the Cancel button, or the resize button, the chart will return to its normal size, and all option changes will be lost.

FIGURE 13.19
Resizing a chart

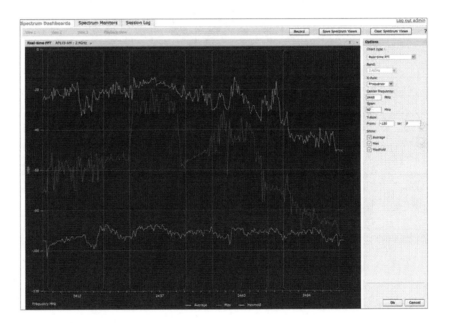

Now that the basic menu functions have been explained, each of the following subsections will describe one of the charts. The explanation will highlight the key component of the specific chart and how to read the data that is displayed. The focus will be on how to read the data, not how to interpret the data.

The first four charts that are described (Real-Time FFT, FFT Duty Cycle, Swept Spectrogram, and Quality Spectrogram) are key charts that are used when performing spectrum analysis.

Real-Time FFT

The Real-Time Fast Fourier Transform (FFT) chart, shown in Figure 13.20, is a line chart that displays the RF power levels detected across the selected band. This chart is updated every second. The X-axis at the bottom of the chart shows the channels or frequency range that is being displayed. The options menu on the right allows you to change between channel or frequency view. The Y-axis shows the power level scale, ranging from −120 dBm (decibels relative to a milliwatt) to 0 dBm; the bigger the number, the stronger the signal. Note that the range is in negative values, so −20 dBm is stronger than −50 dBm.

FIGURE 13.20
Real-Time FFT

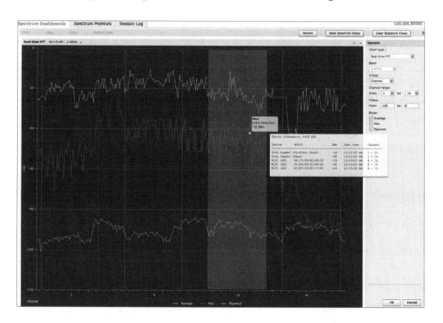

In the options menu, the average, max, and maxhold data is selected, so all three sets of data are being charted. At the center below the chart is the legend for the chart. The following list describes what each set of data is displaying:

Average   The average power level of all the samples that were recorded during the last 10 sweeps of the band.

Max   The highest power level recorded during the last 10 sweeps of the band.

Maxhold   The highest maximum power level recorded since the chart was reset. The maxhold data can be reset from a menu that appears when you click the down arrow at the top-right corner of the chart.

In the middle of Figure 13.20 are two boxes of text, with a small dot at the bottom-left corner of the small box. These boxes appear by moving the mouse pointer over the chart.

If the pointer lingers over one of the data lines, the small box appears, indicating which data set you are looking at, the frequency at that point, and the signal level.

On the chart are sets of vertical lines that indicate the general areas where channels 1, 6, 11, and 14 operate. If you move the mouse pointer into one of these areas, the larger box appears, listing the types of devices that are seen on the channel where the mouse pointer is currently positioned. The box also displays RF information about these devices.

The Real-Time FFT chart provides important information for analyzing the RF spectrum; however, this chart only provides half of the necessary information for properly understanding the environment. As mentioned at the beginning of this section, the Real-Time FFT chart is a power chart, displaying how strong a signal is being detected by the receiver within a specific frequency range. The strength of the signal is important, but you also need to know what percentage of time the signal was at that power level. A strong signal generated at a high percentage of the time is something that may affect the performance on your network. However, the same strong signal generated at a low percentage of the time is not likely going to cause problems.

Therefore, when viewing the Real-Time FFT chart, you should also be viewing the chart discussed in the following section: the FFT Duty Cycle.

FFT Duty Cycle

The FFT Duty Cycle chart is a line chart that shows the duty cycle, or percentage of usage, across the selected band, as shown in Figure 13.21. This chart is updated every second. The X-axis at the bottom of the chart shows the channels or frequency range being displayed. The options menu on the right allows you to change between channel or frequency view. The Y-axis shows the percentage of time the signal is at least 20 dB higher than the noise floor, at the indicated frequency.

In the options menu, the duty cycle, max hold, and max hold of last x sweeps data can be selected. At the center below the chart is the legend for the chart. The following list describes what information the three data sets display:

Duty Cycle The duty cycle over the last second

Max Hold The maximum duty cycle value recorded since the chart was last reset

Max Hold of Last x Sweeps The maximum duty cycle value recorded over the last x scans of the band

As with the Real-Time FFT chart, moving the mouse pointer over the chart will display additional information about the devices operating where the mouse pointer is currently positioned.

FIGURE 13.21
FFT Duty Cycle

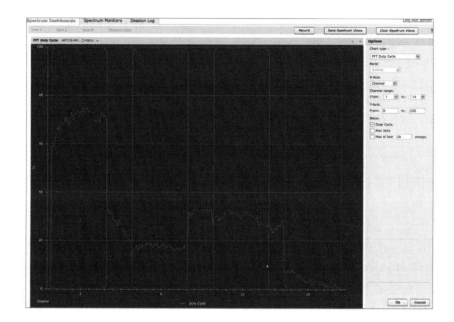

Swept Spectrogram

The Swept Spectrogram chart, shown in Figure 13.22, is known as a waterfall chart because the RF pattern flows across the chart. It shows the density of the power or duty cycle across the selected band. This chart is updated every second. Each update presents a new narrow bar of color along the bottom, pushing the previous bar upward. Over time you can see the history and trends of the monitored data.

The X-axis at the bottom shows the channels for the frequency range that is being displayed. The options menu on the right allows you to change between channel or frequency view. The legend at the bottom shows the color map range.

The way the Swept Spectrogram chart works is it takes one second of FFT data from either the Real-Time FFT or the FFT Duty Cycle chart, converts the data to a color value (based on the legend at the bottom of the chart), and then displays a line of colored dots across the bottom of the chart. A second later, the previously recorded data is moved up and a new line of data is displayed based on the current data that was collected. Therefore, the Y-axis is time measured in seconds. If this chart is full, then the top of the Y-axis is 300 seconds ago, and the bottom is the most recent sample.

FIGURE 13.22
Swept Spectrogram

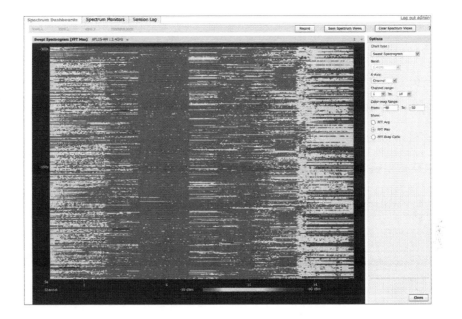

In the options menu, you can change the chart to display the Real-Time FFT average, Real-Time FFT max, or FFT duty cycle data. The color-map range also allows you to change the range of values, indicated by the color range in the legend. The FFT charts display the data as it is happening, whereas the Swept Spectrogram chart presents the data over a long period of time.

Quality Spectrogram

The Quality Spectrogram chart is also a waterfall chart, but it uses data from RF noise, non-Wi-Fi utilization and duty cycles, and retries to calculate a weighted metric. The goal of the weighted metric is to represent the quality of the frequency range being monitored.

A color representation of this is calculated based on the color range displayed in the legend at the bottom of the chart. The X-axis at the bottom shows the channels or frequency range that is being displayed, as shown in Figure 13.23. The options menu on the right allows you to change the chart data based on channel quality or channel availability. The chart is updated every five seconds; therefore, the Y-axis is time measured in five-second increments.

FIGURE 13.23
Quality Spectrogram

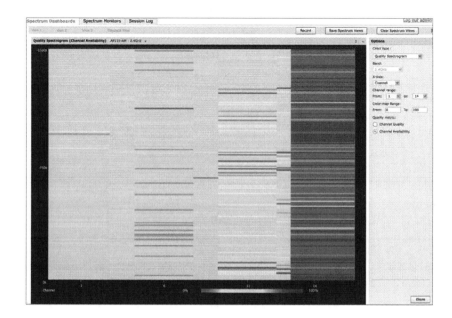

Active Devices

The Active Devices chart displays a pie-chart breakdown of the types of devices visible by the SM, as shown in Figure 13.24. Although an objective of an SM is to monitor layer 1 signals, it is able to identify Wi-Fi signals by the BSSID of the WLAN, and tracks each BSSID as a separate device. If an AP is advertising multiple SSIDs, the SM treats this as RF signals from multiple APs; therefore, the number is not necessarily accurate relative to the physical radios, but it does accurately reflect the individual device broadcasts. This chart does not have a set update interval; it is automatically updated as the number of devices changes.

As stated previously in this chapter, SMs monitor layer 1, RF signals. So, theoretically, an SM would not be able to identify a quantity of physical APs since it would have to be able to identify the radio's MAC address, which is part of the layer 2 information. While operating as an SM and monitoring layer 1 RF signals, the chipset of the AP is designed to be able to extract some layer 2 information from the RF signals and report that information to the controller. This feature allows the spectrum analyzer to include some layer 2 information about the network, such as AP BSSID addresses and SSID values.

FIGURE 13.24
Active Devices

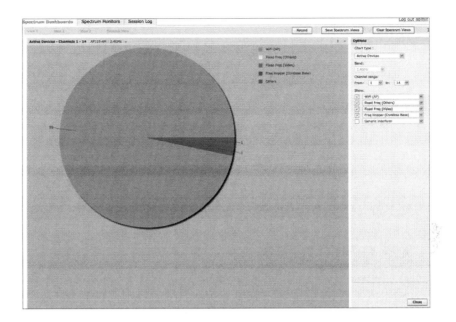

The options menu allows you to specify the channel range and to choose the device categories that you want tallied up.

Active Devices Table

The Active Devices Table displays a list of all devices identified by the SM, as shown in Figure 13.25. Once again, the SM identifies the BSSID addresses, not the physical address of the radio. This means that a single radio may show up multiple times if it is advertising multiple WLANs.

This chart does not have an options menu, but the chart can be sorted, filtered, or searched. Clicking on any column will sort the list by the contents of that column. Clicking the column again will sort the list in reverse order. By clicking the icon below a column header, you can filter the device list. When filtering, you will be prompted to enter information specific to the selected column. Each column has different filtering parameters. The down arrow at the top-right corner of the chart will bring up a menu that will allow you to export the list of devices.

The Active Devices Table includes a BSSID column and an SSID column. Note that both of these columns actually contain layer 2 information.

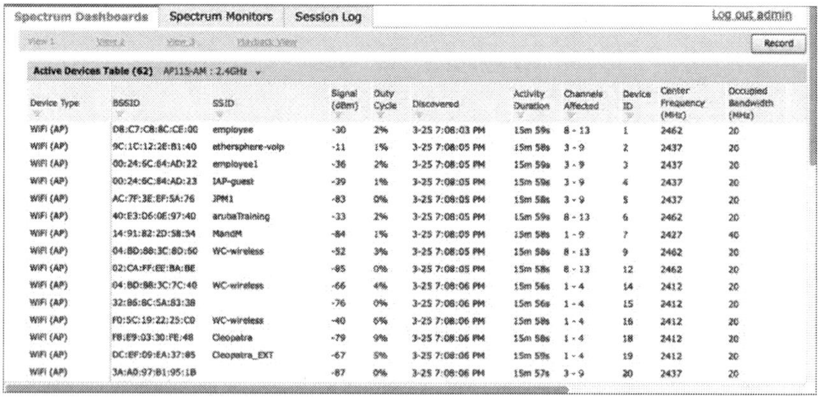

FIGURE 13.25
Active Devices Table

Active Devices Trend

The Actives Device Trend is a line chart that displays the number of devices on the network over a period of time, as shown in Figure 13.26. The X-axis at the bottom displays the time range and the Y-axis indicates the number of devices. The Options menu on the right allows you to select a time period of 10, 30, or 60 minutes. The chart is updated every five seconds. You can also select up to five device type categories to track. Below the chart is a legend identifying which line represents which category.

FIGURE 13.26
Active Devices Trend

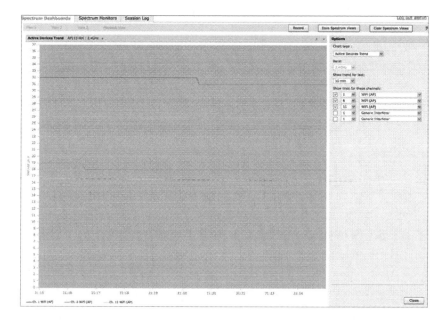

Channel Metrics

Channel Metrics is a bar chart that can display one of three different sets of data. The X-axis at the bottom shows the channels for the frequency range that is being displayed, and the Y-axis displays a percentage value. The chart is updated every five seconds. The options menu allows you to choose a channel range along with selecting one of the three data sets: channel utilization (default), channel availability, or channel quality.

The channel utilization chart displays a stacked bar chart. The data bar above each channel, as shown in Figure 13.27, indicates the percentage of the channel that is being used by "WiFi Utilization" and "Non-WiFi + WiFi ACI Utilization."

FIGURE 13.27
Channel metrics

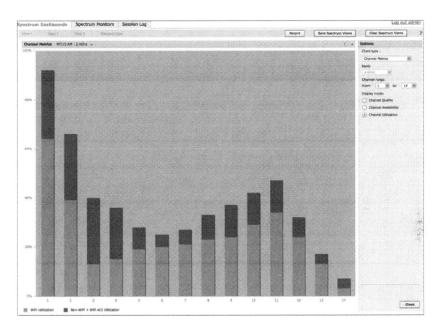

Adjacent channel interference (ACI) is interference on the current channel caused by Wi-Fi devices on adjacent channels. It generally does not exist in 5 GHz networks since the channels are separated from one another. However, ACI is prominent in 2.4 GHz networks due to channel overlap.

Figure 13.28 shows a graphical representation of the 2.4 GHz channels. The figure shows that channels 2 through 5 overlap with both channels 1 and 6. It also shows that channels 7 through 10 overlap with channels 6 and 11. This means that an AP operating on channel 1 will most likely cause ACI on channels 2 through 5, depending on the proximity of the APs to one another. An AP operating on channel 11 will most likely cause ACI on channels 7 through 10, and an AP operating on channel 6 will most likely cause ACI on channels 2 through 5, and 7 through 10.

The channel availability chart and the channel quality charts each display only one data value per channel. The channel availability chart displays the percentage of each channel that is available for use. The channel quality chart displays a weighted metric value per channel. This value is derived from different RF data, including noise, non-Wi-Fi utilization and duty cycles, and certain types of retries. Channel quality is not directly related to Wi-Fi channel utilization.

FIGURE 13.28
2.4 GHz channel overlap

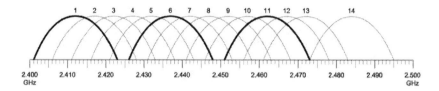

Channel Metrics Trend

By default the Channel Metrics Trend chart is a line chart that displays the relative quality of the chosen channels over a period of time, as shown in Figure 13.29. The chart is updated every five seconds. The X-axis at the bottom displays the time range, and the Y-axis indicates a quality value from 0 through 100. The options menu allows you to select a time period of 10, 30, or 60 minutes. You can also select up to five channels to monitor. Below the chart is a legend identifying which line represents which channel.

FIGURE 13.29
Channel Metrics Trend

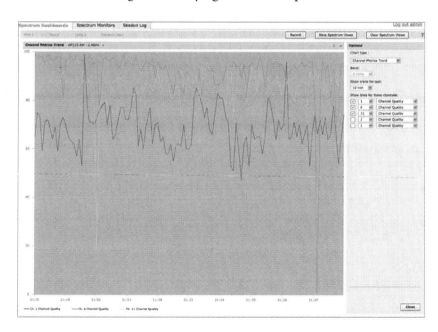

SPECTRUM ANALYSIS

The options menu also allows you to select channel availability instead of channel quality. This change can be made for each monitored channel on a channel-by-channel basis.

Channel Summary Table

The Channel Summary Table displays a list of the channels monitored by the selected SM, as shown in Figure 13.30. This chart displays a summarized list of device info, utilization, and signal info for each channel. The chart is updated every five seconds. This chart does not have an options menu; however, you can sort by clicking on any column header. The down arrow at the top-right corner of the chart will bring up a menu that will allow you to export the table.

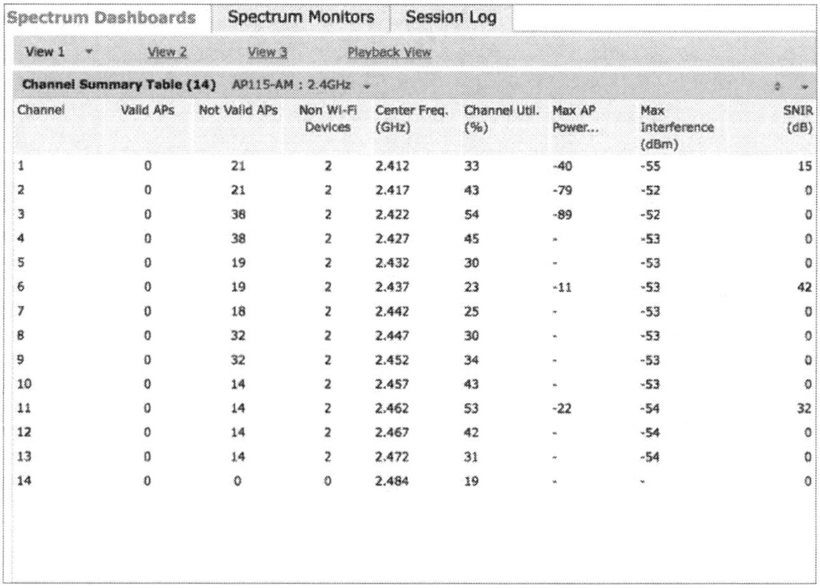

FIGURE 13.30
Channel Summary Table

Channel	Valid APs	Not Valid APs	Non Wi-Fi Devices	Center Freq. (GHz)	Channel Util. (%)	Max AP Power...	Max Interference (dBm)	SNIR (dB)
1	0	21	2	2.412	33	-40	-55	15
2	0	21	2	2.417	43	-79	-52	0
3	0	38	2	2.422	54	-89	-52	0
4	0	38	2	2.427	45	-	-53	0
5	0	19	2	2.432	30	-	-53	0
6	0	19	2	2.437	23	-11	-53	42
7	0	18	2	2.442	25	-	-53	0
8	0	32	2	2.447	30	-	-53	0
9	0	32	2	2.452	34	-	-53	0
10	0	14	2	2.457	43	-	-53	0
11	0	14	2	2.462	53	-22	-54	32
12	0	14	2	2.467	42	-	-54	0
13	0	14	2	2.472	31	-	-54	0
14	0	0	0	2.484	19	-	-	0

Channel Utilization Trend

The Channel Utilization Trend chart is a line chart that displays the percentage of total utilization of up to five selected channels over a period of time, as shown in Figure 13.31. The chart is updated every five seconds. The X-axis at the bottom displays the time range, and the Y-axis displays a percentage value. The indicated value represents utilization due to Wi-Fi devices, non-Wi-Fi interferers, and adjacent channel interference (ACI).

FIGURE 13.31
Channel Utilization Trend

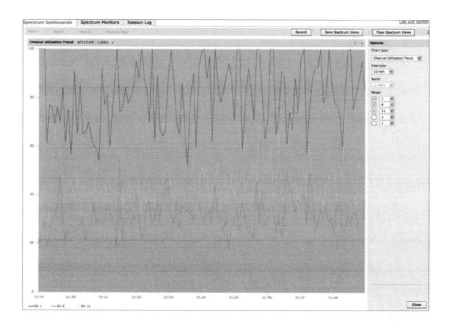

Device Duty Cycle

The Device Duty Cycle chart is a stacked bar chart that shows the duty cycle of the selected device types on each channel, as shown in Figure 13.32. The chart is updated every five seconds. The X-axis at the bottom displays the time range, and the Y-axis displays a percentage value. Each bar represents the percentage of time that the indicated device type is operating or transmitting on the channel.

FIGURE 13.32
Device Duty Cycle

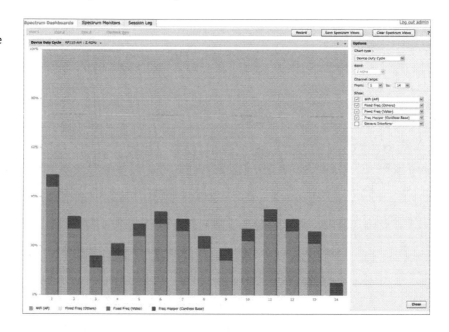

Wi-Fi devices cooperate and share the channel, taking turns to transmit. Other devices, such as video equipment, can operate at up to 100 percent utilization. This chart calculates the utilization of each category separately; therefore, it is possible for the total duty cycle of all of the devices to be more than 100 percent.

Devices vs. Channel

The Devices vs Channel chart is a stacked bar chart that shows the number of devices operating on each channel, as shown in Figure 13.33. The chart is updated every five seconds. The X-axis at the bottom shows the channels for the frequency range that is being displayed, and the Y-axis displays the number of devices. In the options menu, you can specify up to five device types to track.

The devices for each tracked device type on each channel is totaled and displayed in the stacked bar chart. When displaying 2.4 GHz Wi-Fi devices, since Wi-Fi devices overlap into multiple neighboring channels, each Wi-Fi device is potentially counted on all of these channels. This interference between neighboring channels is known as adjacent channel interference (ACI).

As an example, in Figure 13.33 the chart displays 32 Wi-Fi devices on channel 1 and 18 Wi-Fi devices on channel 6. Since channel 1 overlaps with channels 2 through 5, and since channel 6 also overlaps with channels 2 through 5, devices from channels 1 and 6 are likely counted as devices on the channels in between (2 through 5). This is especially obvious when looking at channels 3 and 4 in the figure, with both channels indicating 47 Wi-Fi devices. This total is just slightly less than the total of the channel 1 devices (32) and the channel 6 devices (18).

The signal of a 2.4 GHz AP overlaps with its four neighboring channels, so an AP operating on channel 1 overlaps with channels 2 through 5. However, the signal is weaker with each channel farther away from the channel the AP is operating on, and the amount of channel overlap is also less. So an AP operating on channel 1 will cause more ACI on channel 2 and less on channel 5. Due to the location of the SM relative to the APs that it is hearing, the SM may be able to hear an AP on a channel, but not be able to hear the ACI caused by an AP on the adjacent channels. Thus, the AP may be counted on some channels but not others.

This scenario does not apply to the 5 GHz channels since those channels do not overlap.

Interference Power

The Interference Power chart is a stacked pinpoint chart that displays a point indicating the power level of individual devices relative to the channel that the device is operating on, as shown in Figure 13.34.

FIGURE 13.33
Devices vs Channel

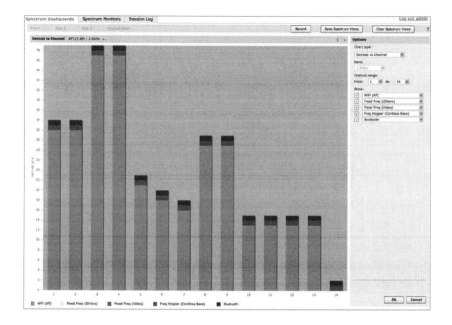

FIGURE 13.34
Interference Power

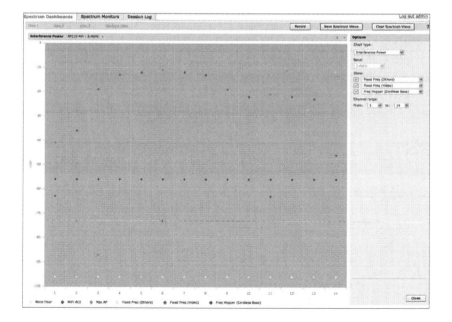

The chart is updated every five seconds. The X-axis at the bottom of the chart shows the channels or frequency range that is being displayed. The Y-axis shows the power level scale, ranging from −100 dBm (decibels relative to a milliwatt) to 0 dBm at the top of the chart. Note that the range is in negative values, so −20 dBm is stronger than −50 dBm. This chart simply displays power level, without taking into consideration duty cycle.

By default the chart displays the noise floor, Wi-Fi ACI, and Max AP. Three other device type categories can also be selected. The Max AP indicates the strongest powered AP on the specific channel. The Wi-Fi ACI displays the Wi-Fi power on adjacent channels. The chart is displaying detected power levels only.

Remember that the power level of a signal should always be evaluated with duty cycle levels for that signal. Focusing solely on power level can be deceptive. If the duty cycle is low, the effect of interference on other devices may be minimal even with a high power level.

The noise floor indicator is an extremely important value and can be found only on this chart. All of the other charts, including this chart, display the maximum or current power level of monitored devices. However, many devices are not always transmitting. Knowing the noise floor is very important. One of the key determinants to Wi-Fi performance and transmission speed is how strong the RF signal is relative to the noise floor: signal-to-noise ratio (SNR).

If you move the mouse pointer over one of the indicators, information about that device will be displayed.

Spectrum Analysis CLI Command

Although spectrum analysis is primarily graphically based, ArubaOS CLI provides a set of commands that are very useful for providing information obtained from an SM. The following CLI output shows the show ap spectrum command, along with the list of available options:

```
#show ap spectrum ?
ap-list               Show list of APs being monitored
channel-metrics       Shows channel quality, availability and utilization
channel-summary       Shows channel summary information
client-list           Show list of WiFi clients being monitored
debug                 Show Spectrum Monitor debugging information
device-duty-cycle     Shows duty cycle by device type
device-history        Show history of non-WiFi devices
device-list           Show list of non-WiFi devices being monitored
device-log            Show time log of non-WiFi devices
device-summary        Shows devices vs channel information
interference-power    Shows list of interference power
local-override        Spectrum Override Profile (local to this controller)
monitors              Show all Spectrum Monitors registered on this
                      controller
tech-support          Display all information for an AP
```

CHAPTER 14

Wireless Mesh

IN THIS CHAPTER, YOU WILL LEARN ABOUT THE FOLLOWING:

- Mesh Architecture
  - Mesh Point Portal
  - Mesh Point
  - Mesh Link
  - Mesh Cluster
- Configuring a Mesh Network
  - Mesh Cluster Profile
  - Mesh Radio Profile
  - WLAN Profile
  - 802.11 Radio Profile
  - Mesh High-Throughput SSID profile
  - AP Wired Port Profile
  - Recovery Profile
- Mesh AP Provisioning
- Mesh Status

SOMETIMES IT CAN BE INCONVENIENT OR EVEN impossible to run data cables to an AP, or it may be too much effort to do so for a temporary installation. In these instances, enterprise mesh-connected APs may be an alternate solution to provide connectivity. Mesh can provide a temporary way to extend the network to point-of-sale machines at an event. It can provide access to green spaces such as parks, fields, or community spaces between buildings. These are just a few of the many environments where wireless mesh can be used to extend the enterprise network.

In a previous chapter you learned about campus and remote APs. This chapter will explain the components of a wireless mesh network, how wireless mesh networks behave, and how to configure them. Defining a mesh network using ArubaOS is a quick and easy task. If needed, many options are available to customize and fine-tune it. ArubaOS mesh networks are used to provide point-to-point or point-to-multipoint connections and do not require extensive customization.

Mesh Architecture

An ArubaOS mesh network is a network in which one or more access points are forwarding or transporting the user data using a wireless network instead of an Ethernet network. There are numerous reasons for deploying mesh networks. In some instances, installing Ethernet cables is either unfeasible or impractical, possibly when connecting outdoor surveillance cameras. A mesh network can be used to create a wireless bridge between two wired networks, such as connecting together the networks in two separate buildings, or providing a wireless connection between a guard shack and the main office building. Additionally, a mesh network can be set up to extend the wireless range out from a building into more remote areas, such as parking lots and recreational areas, along with numerous other types of outdoor areas that may not have wired access back to the main building. A mesh network can be used to quickly create a temporary or short-term network, saving the time and expense of installing cabling. Whatever the reason, a mesh network may provide the solution you need when installing physical cable is not possible or impractical.

When configuring and working with a mesh network, remind yourself that the only difference is that the Ethernet backhaul has been replaced with an RF radio mesh backhaul. That is it. All of the other features and capabilities of the network and the access point are essentially the same.

Any AP that is functioning as part of a mesh network is generically known as a mesh node. There are two types of mesh nodes: mesh portals and mesh points. In the following sections, you will learn about the role and functionality of these devices.

To begin learning about mesh, let us look at an illustration of a mesh network and learn about the components, their roles, and how they work with each other. Figure 14.1 is an illustration of a basic two-node mesh network. Refer to this figure as you read about the components in the following sections.

Mesh Point Portal

The mesh point portal (MPP) is commonly referred to simply as a mesh portal. This is the AP that connects to the enterprise wired network. It provides the access layer connection back into the wired network for the mesh points. Without at least one functioning MPP, the mesh network would not be able to forward the user traffic back to the enterprise network.

When a mesh network is installed, the MPP will advertise a Mesh SSID (MSSID). The MSSID is defined by the network administrator as part of the mesh cluster profile and is used to identify the mesh network. This is important because multiple mesh networks can exist in the same physical area, and the MSSID is used to direct the mesh nodes to the correct mesh network in the same way that an SSID on an AP is used to direct wireless clients to the correct wireless network.

FIGURE 14.1
Basic two-node mesh network

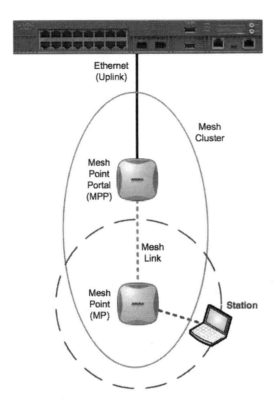

By default, mesh RF channels are auto configured. When the MPP boots, it will use ARM to choose a channel, or you can manually configure it for a specific channel. If the network is a temporary solution, you may want to let ARM choose the channel for you. If the network is permanent, consider manually configuring the channel.

Radio settings are made in the radio profile and will be covered later in this chapter. Whether the channel is set dynamically or manually, all of the mesh nodes will transmit and receive using the same channel. Since 802.11 is a shared medium using carrier sense multiple access with collision avoidance (CSMA/CA) for media access, when any mesh node is transmitting, the others must wait before they can transmit. Therefore, it is important to try to limit the number of mesh nodes in a mesh cluster. Figure 14.2 illustrates a mesh cluster with an MPP and three mesh points operating on channel 149. If any node is transmitting data, the other nodes cannot since they are sharing the same channel.

FIGURE 14.2
Multiple-node mesh cluster

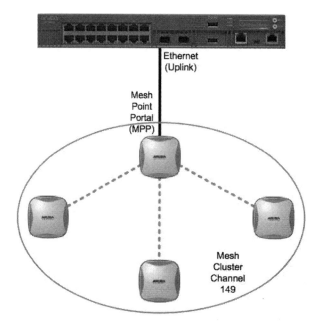

When an AP is initially configured as an MPP, it needs to be rebooted so it can apply its new configuration. After an MPP boots, it loads the environment variables during the boot process and identifies that it is configured to operate as an MPP. Next, it loads its Ethernet networking settings, communicates with the controller over the Ethernet connection, and enables its mesh radio to advertise the MSSID. The other radio can be configured for access mode, operating like a typical Aruba AP, advertising VAPs and handling user traffic. If you do not want the other radio to advertise a WLAN, it can also be configured as an air monitor or spectrum monitor, or you could simply disable it.

The mesh radio can also be configured to advertise VAPs; however, I recommend that it be configured solely for mesh backhaul, rather than sharing its wireless access between mesh activities and client activities. This is accomplished by disabling client access on the radio that is used for the mesh backhaul, typically the 5 GHz radio.

A mesh network can have multiple mesh portals to provide failover/redundancy; however, if you have multiple mesh points, it is possible that they could choose the same portal, leaving one portal overloaded and the other underutilized. An alternative may be to create two clusters, as illustrated in Figure 14.3. In this scenario, the mesh points would be configured to be able to connect to both clusters. They would use a priority value to connect to one cluster, and would connect to the other cluster only if its primary cluster was unavailable.

FIGURE 14.3
Multiple mesh clusters

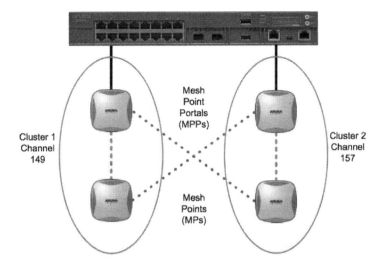

Mesh Point

When a mesh point connects to the mesh network, it connects in a similar way that a wireless client connects to an AP. The mesh point (MP) is configured with one or more MSSIDs to scan for when it is powered up (multiple MSSIDs are prioritized to provide cluster failover capability, which will be explained later in this chapter in the "Mesh Cluster" section). The MPP will advertise the mesh SSID, the MP will scan for the MSSID from its list, and once the MSSID is found, the MP will associate and connect to the MPP using the matching MSSID. Once an MP connects to the portal, it too will advertise the MSSID. When an additional MP is powered on, it will search for the MSSID from its list, and it will choose to connect to one of the existing mesh nodes—which could be the MPP, or if the link algorithm prefers, the MP could connect to the existing MP instead, creating a "multihop" network. There are different selection methods, which are typically based on link quality and hop count. Figure 14.4 illustrates a multihop mesh cluster. In a latency-sensitive or bandwidth-heavy-use environment, multihop mesh clusters should be avoided or at least minimized if possible. In addition to sharing the medium, each additional hop generally decreases the data throughput by 50 percent. Note that in Figure 14.4 multiple upstream paths are illustrated, but each node can maintain only one upstream path at a time.

To provision an MP, it must first be connected to the Ethernet network and be able to communicate with the Aruba controller. After it is configured and rebooted, it no longer needs an Ethernet connection. In fact, you need to be careful to make sure you disconnect the MP from the wired network, because it could create a network loop if both the wired and wireless connections are running at the same time.

FIGURE 14.4
Multihop mesh cluster

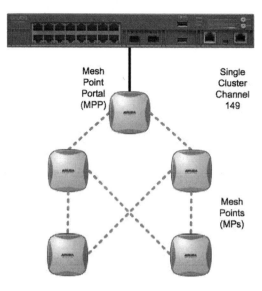

When an MP boots, it performs an RF scan looking for the MSSID being advertised by neighboring mesh nodes. A neighboring node could be the MPP or another MP. After the MP establishes a wireless connection with its neighbor, it will use DHCP to obtain an IP address and its settings via the MPP's wired interface and proceed to behave like any other Aruba AP—with the difference being that it is communicating over the mesh network instead of the Ethernet connection.

It is important to remember that when the MP boots, it receives its DHCP address from a DHCP server located on the Ethernet network that the MPP is connected to, even if the Ethernet port on the MP is connected to a different Ethernet network. You should know that all of the Ethernet MAC addresses from the MPs will be presented onto the network on the MPP's wired interface. So in the case of Figure 14.4, the wired uplink from the MPP would show five MAC addresses on its wired interface (one for the MPP, and one for each of the MPs).

Mesh Link

A mesh link is the connection between any two mesh nodes. The upstream node toward the controller is referred to as the parent and the downstream node away from the controller is referred to as the child. Every link between a parent and a child is referred to as a hop. Figure 14.4 illustrates some of the possible links in a multihop mesh cluster.

A mesh node will attempt to connect using the highest transmission rate when establishing a mesh link. If it cannot, it will successively step down to the next highest rate until it is able to establish a connection. By default, all data rates are available in the mesh radio profile. It is possible to enable or disable certain data rates; however, it is probably best to keep all of the rates selected.

Mesh Cluster

The mesh cluster is the logical group of nodes that form the mesh network. The MPP initially advertises the cluster name (MSSID) and its capabilities. When an MP is powered on, it will attempt to connect to another mesh node with the same cluster configuration (MSSID). Mesh clusters are configured as part of the AP Group settings. An MP can connect to only one cluster at a time; however, it can be programmed with multiple clusters for redundancy.

When a mesh cluster is assigned to an AP group, a priority value is also assigned. The value is a number between 1 and 16, with the lowest number being the highest priority. If an MP cannot connect to the cluster with the highest priority, it will then attempt to connect to the mesh cluster with the next highest priority value. If no configured cluster is found, the MP will attempt to connect using the recovery profile cluster. The recovery profile will be explained in more detail later in this chapter in the section "Recovery Profile."

Let us imagine that an MP is configured to connect to Cluster1 with priority of 1, and Cluster2 with priority of 2. For some reason the MP is able to communicate with the MPP for Cluster1 and the MPP for Cluster2, but cannot connect to either due to a misconfiguration. If the MP cannot connect, it would be referred to as an orphan node. Having an orphan node is not good because there is no way to wirelessly communicate with the MP to correct the problem. This could mean that it would be necessary to physically connect a cable to the MP to reprovision it. This can be especially problematic if the MP is in a difficult-to-reach location, such as at the top of a light pole.

If an MP cannot establish a connection with any of the mesh clusters defined for its AP group, ArubaOS has a system-generated recovery profile as a mesh network of last resort. The recovery profile is generated by the master controller, it cannot be edited, and it has a priority value of 16. The recovery profile will be explained in more detail later in this chapter.

Configuring a Mesh Network

A mesh network consists of two or more APs forwarding network traffic using wireless communications instead of Ethernet. An AP group should be configured for each mesh cluster that you are configuring, and I recommend that each AP group should only contain the APs that will be part of the mesh network. Profiles that affect the mesh network consist of the following:

- Mesh cluster profile
- Mesh radio profile
- WLAN profile

- 802.11 radio profiles (both 2.4 GHz and 5 GHz radios)
- High-throughput SSID profile
- Adaptive Radio Management (ARM) profile
- AP wired port profile
- Recovery profile (read-only)

The following sections of this chapter will describe these profiles along with some of the key settings of the mesh network. Many advanced options are available when configuring a mesh network, that will not be covered in this chapter. Unless you are configuring an elaborate mesh environment, you will likely be able to configure a viable and functional mesh network without having to make many changes.

Mesh Cluster Profile

The mesh cluster profile provides the identity of the mesh network. The mesh cluster profile is easily configured and consists of three basic settings:

- Cluster name (the MSSID)
- RF band
- WPA2-AES passphrase

The mesh cluster profile name describes the mesh cluster and is used as part of the configuration to assign a mesh cluster to an AP group. Within the mesh cluster config the cluster name is the Mesh SSID (MSSID) for the cluster. Since it is an SSID, it can be up to 32 characters long and it is case sensitive. The MSSID is used by the mesh nodes so that they can discover and identify the mesh network that they are configured for. The MSSID should be a simple and logical name, and it must be unique between the different clusters. There is no reason to be fancy or creative. The only devices that will see it will be the mesh nodes. You should not include any spaces in the cluster name. Including a space in the cluster name can cause problems if you also enable encryption on the mesh cluster, which you should always do. You should always change the cluster name to something other than the default value of "aruba-mesh."

The RF band defines which band (2.4 GHz or 5 GHz) will be used by the mesh nodes to establish the mesh network and to transport traffic between the mesh nodes. The RF Band value in the cluster profile simply defines the band. The channel can be dynamically selected by Aruba's Adaptive Radio Management (ARM), or it can be manually selected in the 802.11 Radio profile, which will be explained later in this chapter. It is generally recommended that you not use the 2.4 GHz band because it is more susceptible to interference and is slower than the 5 GHz band.

The final step in configuring the mesh cluster is to enable encryption. By default, encryption is not enabled since this would require a default WPA2-AES passphrase, which would not be a good security practice. Therefore, WPA2-AES needs to be enabled, and either a WPA2-AES Hexkey or a WPA2-AES passphrase needs to be entered. It is easier to enter a passphrase—an alphanumeric value from 8 to 63 characters long. You should use a long, complicated passphrase, since you will have to type this passphrase in only once, when you initially configure the mesh cluster. The passphrase will be automatically and securely downloaded to each mesh node when it is added to the mesh AP group.

The mesh cluster profile can be easily created either from the WebUI or from the CLI. If you want to create and configure the mesh cluster profile from the WebUI, you should first create an AP group using the following WebUI menu path: **Configuration ➢ WIRELESS ➢ AP Configuration ➢ AP Group ➢ New**.

After creating the AP group, select it so that you can configure the mesh profile for it. After selecting the AP group, go to Mesh profile and select the Mesh Cluster profile. From here, you can create or add an existing mesh cluster profile. When adding the mesh cluster profile, choose a priority value in the range of 1 to 15 (priority 16 is by default the recovery profile). Figure 14.5 shows adding a profile named mesh1-cluster with a priority of 1. Do not modify the default profile; it is better in most cases to leave any default profiles untouched and to create new profiles. This allows you to revert back to the default profile if you have problems with the profile you created, and it provides a template that can be used if you need to create other profiles.

FIGURE 14.5
Creating a mesh cluster

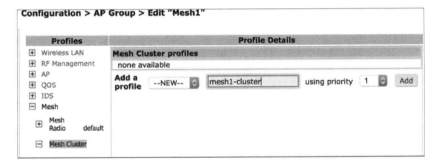

You can assign more than one mesh cluster profile to an AP group. Each cluster profile would be assigned a priority value from 1 to 15, with 1 being the highest priority. The cluster profile with the lowest priority number is the primary mesh cluster, with any others functioning as backup clusters, and it is the only cluster that the MPP will use (MPPs will only use the highest priority mesh cluster that is configured in the AP group). You should also never make a mesh cluster the primary in more than one AP group.

After creating and assigning the mesh cluster profile and its priority value to the AP group, select it so that you can configure its cluster name, RF band, and WPA2-AES Hexkey or Passphrase. As Figure 14.6 shows, you enter the cluster name (MSSID) and select either the a band (5 GHz) or the g band (2.4 GHz). The band that you choose will be used for mesh backhaul. Below the RF band, you will need to change the encryption type from the default value of opensystem to wpa2-psk-aes. When you change the encryption type, you will then be able to enter the WPA2 Hexkey or Passphrase (I recommend using the WPA2 passphrase since it is easier to enter).

FIGURE 14.6
Mesh cluster settings

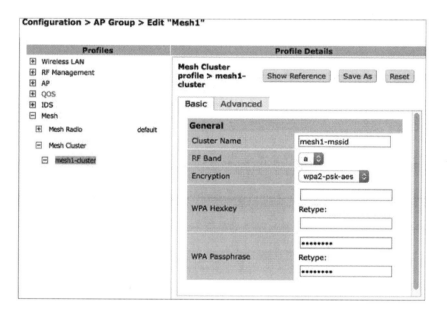

On a mesh network that is already configured and functioning, if you need to modify mesh cluster settings you should instead create and assign a new mesh cluster profile, and then delete the current profile once it has been applied to all the APs that were part of the original mesh cluster. The mesh APs will also need to be reprovisioned to implement the new settings, which will be explained later in this chapter in the "Mesh AP Provisioning" section. The new profiles should be provisioned on the furthest MPs first, working your way back to the MPPs after all the MPs have been reprovisioned. This will help prevent mesh nodes from losing contact with the cluster, which could occur if changes were not properly distributed to all the mesh nodes. All the mesh cluster profile settings can also be configured using the CLI. The following CLI commands create a mesh cluster profile mesh1-cluster, set the cluster name to mesh1-mssid, specify that the a band (5 GHz) will be used for mesh traffic, set the encryption passphrase to aruba123, and enable WPA2-AES encryption.

```
(config) #ap mesh-cluster-profile mesh1-cluster
(Mesh Cluster profile "mesh1-cluster") #cluster mesh1-mssid
(Mesh Cluster profile "mesh1-cluster") #rf-band a
(Mesh Cluster profile "mesh1-cluster") #wpa-passphrase aruba123
(Mesh Cluster profile "mesh1-cluster") #opmode wpa2-psk-aes
```

The mesh cluster profile can now be assigned to an AP group. The following CLI commands create an AP group mesh1, and then assign the profile to the AP group with a priority of 1:

```
(config) #ap-group mesh1
(AP group "mesh1") #mesh-cluster-profile mesh1-cluster priority 1
```

Mesh Radio Profile

The Mesh Radio profile allows you to change allowed data rates and hop and link values, along with mesh path and link selection algorithms. You should create a mesh radio profile and assign it to the mesh section of the AP group, as shown in the following CLI output. However, in most cases, the Mesh Radio profile should be left at the default settings.

```
(config) #ap mesh-radio-profile "mesh1-mesh-radio"
(Mesh Radio profile "mesh1-mesh-radio") #ap-group "mesh1"
(AP group "mesh1") #  mesh-radio-profile "mesh1-mesh-radio"
```

WLAN Profile

Like any other AP connected to the controller, a mesh AP is capable of advertising one or more WLANs from either or both radios. This is done by assigning virtual AP (VAP) profiles to the mesh AP group. In order to provide better performance, a mesh AP is typically configured to use one radio to establish and maintain the mesh connection, and the other radio is configured to advertise WLANs and handle client traffic. The VAP profile allows you to choose the RF band that the WLAN will operate on, as shown in Figure 14.7. If you limit the RF band in the WLAN profile, such as setting it to g, you are stating that this WLAN profile will never operate on the a band, no matter where it is deployed or whatever AP group it is assigned to. If you are deploying a WLAN throughout your organization for voice devices, and the devices only operate on the g band, then this would be fine. However, if your intent is to only restrict the band that the WLAN operates on when configured on a mesh AP, then you will need to disable the radio in the 802.11 radio profile instead, which you will see in the section "802.11 Radio Profile."

FIGURE 14.7
Virtual AP profile

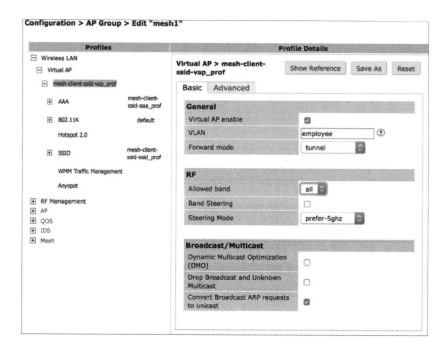

The following CLI commands can also be used to assign a VAP profile to a mesh AP group. Note that technically there is no such thing as a "mesh" AP group. An AP group is simply a group of APs, regardless of how you configure them. Therefore, the following commands are simply assigning a VAP to an AP group. In this instance, the AP happens to be using mesh to backhaul the traffic.

```
(config) #ap-group mesh1
(AP group "mesh1") #virtual-ap mesh-client-ssid-vap_prof

(config) #wlan virtual-ap mesh-client-ssid-vap_prof
(Virtual AP profile "mesh-client-ssid-vap_prof") #allowed-band all
```

A mesh network may also be created to bridge two wired networks together. In this configuration, you may not need to assign any WLANs to the mesh AP group.

802.11 Radio Profile

The 802.11a or 802.11g radio profiles are used to specify the operating mode and settings for the 5 GHz or 2.4 GHz radios. These profiles are very important when configuring a mesh network. As mentioned earlier in this chapter, it is often prudent to prevent the mesh backhaul radio from advertising WLANs and supporting client traffic. Figure 14.8

shows an 802.11a radio profile 11a-mesh1 with the radio disabled. The radio will still function as a mesh radio but will not advertise any WLANs, even if they are assigned to the AP group.

FIGURE 14.8
802.11a radio profile

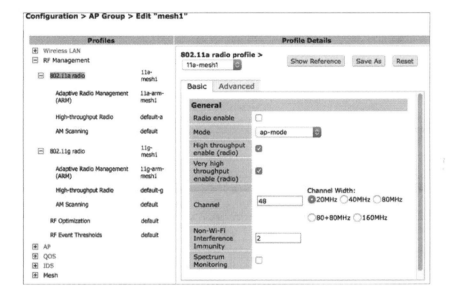

The radio can also be disabled using the following CLI commands:

```
(config) #rf dot11a-radio-profile "11a-mesh1"
(802.11a radio profile "11a-mesh1") #no radio-enable
```

Another important function of the radio profile is to manually configure the radio settings, such as the AP channel, channel width, radio features, and power settings. To manually configure these settings on the AP, disable the ARM assignment in the Adaptive Radio Management (ARM) profile, as shown in Figure 14.9. If ARM is enabled, it will take precedence over the manual settings.

ARM can also be disabled using the following CLI commands. These commands create an ARM profile 11a-arm-mesh1, disable ARM in that profile, and then assign the ARM profile to the mesh profile 11a-mesh1.

```
(config) #rf arm-profile "11a-arm-mesh1"
(Adaptive Radio Management (ARM) profile "11a-arm-mesh1") #assignment "disable"
(Adaptive Radio Management (ARM) profile "11a-arm-mesh1") #rf dot11a-radio-profile "11a-mesh1"
(802.11a radio profile "11a-mesh1") #arm-profile "11a-arm-mesh1"
```

FIGURE 14.9
Adaptive Radio Management (ARM) Profile

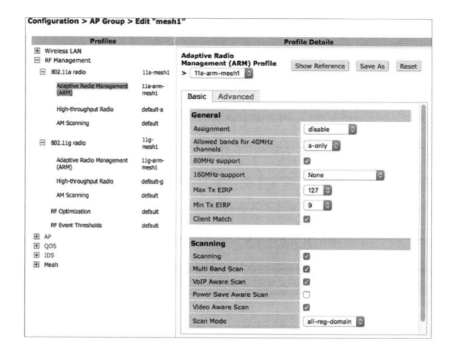

Mesh High-Throughput SSID Profile

The Mesh High-Throughput SSID profile allows you to make extremely advanced and specific changes to the 802.11n high throughput (HT) or 802.11ac very high throughput (VHT) radios. Any changes in this profile should be made cautiously.

AP Wired Port Profile

One of the more common uses of a mesh network is to connect an isolated remote Ethernet device or a remote Ethernet network to the corporate network. Examples are using a mesh network to connect to a surveillance camera, a computerized sign, or possibly a guard shack at the entrance to your campus, as illustrated in Figure 14.10. To make this happen, you must enable the Ethernet port in use on the MP. After enabling the port, you can configure it as either a trusted or an untrusted port. If it is a trusted port, any Ethernet device could be plugged into the MP and would be able to communicate back to the controller without any restrictions, based on the configuration of the Ethernet port on the MP. In this scenario, an Ethernet switch could also be connected to the MP, providing the ability for many devices to communicate back to the controller through the mesh network. The trusted port would need to be configured for Bridge Forwarding mode, as well as an access or trunk port, since a mesh link is capable of backhauling multiple VLANs.

FIGURE 14.10
Wired backhaul using mesh

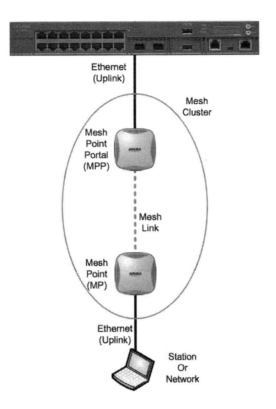

The Ethernet port on the MP could also be configured as an untrusted port. With the Ethernet port configured as untrusted, any device that connects to that port would be assigned an initial role and may be required to log on to the network. When configured as an untrusted port, the port would need to be configured for Tunnel forwarding mode. Split-Tunnel and Decrypt-Tunnel forwarding modes are not supported on the Ethernet ports of a mesh node.

Figure 14.11 shows the wired AP profile settings for Ethernet port 1, which is assigned to the mesh1 AP group. In the profile, the Ethernet port is enabled, trusted, and using Bridge forwarding mode. In this figure, the port is configured as an access port; however, it can also be configured as a trunk port if needed.

Of course, this configuration can also be performed through the CLI. In the upcoming CLI output, the mesh1-ap-profile wired AP profile is created and configured first. The mesh1-bridge wired port profile is created, and the AP profile is assigned to it. Finally, the mesh1-bridge is defined as the Ethernet 1 profile and assigned to the AP group.

To try to simplify the process to make it easier to understand, you first create a set of configuration parameters, kind of like a recipe of settings. In this example, this is the wired-ap-profile named mesh1-ap-profile.

FIGURE 14.11
Wired AP Profile

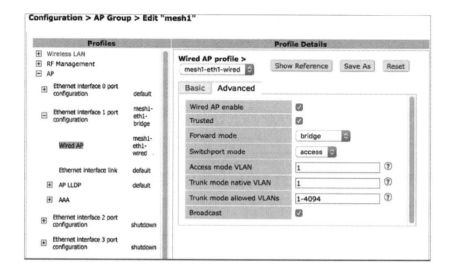

You then add this recipe of settings to a port profile. The port profile does not specify what port (enet1 or enet2) but simply that it is a profile for a port. In this instance, it is being added to a wired port profile named mesh1-bridge.

Now that you have a wired port profile, you can select an AP group and assign the profile to any of the ports—enet1, enet2, enet3, or enet4, depending on your needs. In the example, the mesh1 AP group has been selected and the profile is being assigned to enet1.

```
(config) #ap wired-ap-profile "mesh1-ap-profile "
(Wired AP profile "mesh1-ap-profile") #wired-ap-enable
(Wired AP profile "mesh1-ap-profile") #trusted
(Wired AP profile "mesh1-ap-profile") #forward-mode "bridge"
Warning: 802.1x and Captive portal authentication is not supported in wired
Bridge mode

(Wired AP profile "mesh1-ap-profile") #ap wired-port-profile "mesh1-bridge"
(AP wired port profile "mesh1-bridge") #wired-ap-profile "mesh1-ap-profile"

(AP wired port profile "mesh1-bridge") #ap-group "mesh1"
(AP group "mesh1") #enet1-port-profile "mesh1-bridge"
```

Recovery Profile

When an MP is created, it is assigned one or more mesh clusters. Each mesh cluster has a priority value from 1 to 15, with 1 being the highest priority. When the MP boots, it will attempt to connect to the cluster with the lowest priority number. If it is unable to, it will attempt to connect to the cluster with the next lowest priority number, if more than one cluster is assigned to the MP.

If a network administrator makes a change to the mesh cluster and is not careful, there is a possibility (albeit small) that the MP will not receive those changes from the controller since an MP relies on the mesh network to communicate with the controller. This could mean that the cluster configuration on the MP does not match that of the MPP. This would prevent the MP from joining the mesh network. If the MP is unsuccessful connecting to the cluster with the lowest priority, and then each subsequent cluster that is assigned to its mesh profile, then the MP could end up in what is referred to as an orphan state. To prevent this from happening, a recovery profile is automatically created and assigned to every mesh node when it is initially provisioned.

The recovery profile is dynamically created by the master controller and cannot be modified. A cluster name and encryption key is assigned as part of this profile, and the profile is assigned a priority of 16, making it the lowest priority cluster. The recovery profile MSSID is advertised by the mesh nodes just like the cluster MSSID; however, it is advertised as a hidden MSSID. An MP will attempt to connect to the other clusters for 5 minutes. If it is unable to connect to any of the clusters assigned to that MP, the recovery profile will be used. The following CLI output displays a recovery profile:

```
#show ap mesh-recovery-profile

AP Mesh Recovery Profile
------------------------
Item             Value
----             -----
Cluster Name     Recoveryqi90J45oqG9LPJRW
RF Band          a
Encryption       wpa2-psk-aes
WPA Hexkey       ********
WPA Passphrase   N/A
```

An MPP will always use the first cluster profile. Since it is simply responsible for advertising the MSSID, it is up to the MP to establish a connection to the MPP. If the MP does connect using the recovery profile, the connection will not forward user data. Its purpose is to provide the MP with the ability to communicate back to the controller so that it can be reconfigured via its wireless connection. If this were not possible, you would have to physically reconnect the MP to the Ethernet network to reprogram it. This could be a costly and time-consuming task if the MP is mounted in a difficult-to-access location, such as a light pole or the eaves of a building. The following CLI output shows mesh-point1 is operating using the recovery profile. The flags UMY identify the recovery state of the MP. This occurred because a change to the mesh cluster was made while the MP was rebooting. This caused the MPPs to advertise a new MSSID that the MP was not aware of. Note that when an MP is in recovery, the MP will not broadcast any MSSIDs, and no wired bridging will function until the MP is reprovisioned and brought back online normally.

```
#show ap database

AP Database
-----------
Name           Group  AP Type  IP Address    Status     Flags  Switch IP    Standby IP
----           -----  -------  ----------    ------     -----  ---------    ----------
mesh-point1    mesh1  225      10.1.50.150   Up 14m:29s UMY    10.1.50.101  0.0.0.0
mesh1-portal1  mesh1  225      10.1.50.153   Up 14m:9s  M      10.1.50.101  0.0.0.0
mesh1-portal2  mesh1  225      10.1.50.154   Up 14m:8s  M      10.1.50.101  0.0.0.0

Flags: U = Unprovisioned; N = Duplicate name; G = No such group; L = Unlicensed
       I = Inactive; D = Dirty or no config; E = Regulatory Domain Mismatch
       X = Maintenance Mode; P = PPPoE AP; B = Built-in AP; s = LACP striping
       R = Remote AP; R- = Remote AP requires Auth; C = Cellular RAP;
       c = CERT-based RAP; 1 = 802.1x authenticated AP; 2 = Using IKE version 2
       u = Custom-Cert RAP; S = Standby-mode AP; J = USB cert at AP
       i = Indoor; o = Outdoor
       M = Mesh node; Y = Mesh Recovery

Total APs:3
```

Because the MP was using the recovery profile, it was able to communicate with the controller using a wireless connection. The cluster profile was able to be modified, and the new set of changes were able to be sent to all the mesh nodes, allowing all the mesh nodes to be rebooted and able to see each other again, as shown in the following CLI output:

```
#show ap mesh active

Mesh Cluster Name: mesh1-mssid-update
-------------------------------------
Name           Group  IP Address    BSSID              Band/Ch/EIRP/MaxEIRP →
----           -----  ----------    -----              -------------------- →
mesh-point1    mesh1  10.1.50.150   9c:1c:12:88:5e:31  802.11a/36/15/22.5   →
mesh1-portal1  mesh1  10.1.50.153   04:bd:88:28:87:51  802.11a/36/15/22.5   →
mesh1-portal2  mesh1  10.1.50.154   04:bd:88:28:dc:11  802.11a/36/15/22.5   →


→ MTU   Enet Ports  Mesh Role  Parent         #Children  AP Type  Uptime
→ ---   ----------  ---------  ------         ---------  -------  ------
→       Off/Tunnel  Point      mesh1-portal2  0          225      2m:53s
→ 1500  -/Tunnel    Portal     -              0          225      2m:49s
→ 1500  -/Tunnel    Portal     -              1          225      2m:49s
```

To prevent orphan nodes from occurring, try to limit changes to the mesh configuration. If you must make changes to any of the mesh profiles, determine the topology of the mesh network and always reprovision/reboot the most distant (highest hop count) mesh nodes first, and work your way back to the portal. The following CLI command can be used to display the topology of the mesh network along with the hop count of each of the mesh nodes:

```
#show ap mesh topology

Mesh Cluster Name: mesh1-mssid-update
------------------------------------
Name              Mesh Role  Parent         Path Cost  Node Cost  Link Cost →
----              ---------  ------         ---------  ---------  --------- →
mesh-point1       Point      mesh1-portal2  1          0          0         →
mesh1-portal1     Portal     -              0          0          0         →
mesh1-portal2     Portal     -              0          1          0         →


→ Hop Count  RSSI  Rate Tx/Rx  Last Update  Uplink Age  #Children
→ ---------  ----  ----------  -----------  ----------  ---------
→ 1          48    6/6         5m:27s       15m:33s     0
→ 0          0     -           5m:13s       25m:6s      0
→ 0          0     -           5m:33s       25m:7s      1
```

As stated earlier in this section, the master controller automatically generated the recovery profile and it is dynamically created by each master controller. This means that you should never move an MP or MPP from one Aruba master controller to another, because the recovery profile will be different, unless the AP that is being moved is brought up on the wire and reprovisioned from the new master controller. The cluster profiles may be identical, allowing the MP to connect to the other mesh nodes. However, if the MP lost its connection and attempted to resort to the recovery profile, it would not be able to.

Mesh AP Provisioning

The provisioning process for a mesh AP starts just like the process for a campus AP. To provision a mesh AP, whether it is an MP or a MPP, it must initially be connected to the Ethernet network and it must communicate with either the master controller or one of the local controllers. As with any campus AP, a mesh AP needs six pieces of information to boot:

- IP address
- Subnet mask
- Default gateway
- AP name

- AP group
- IP address of the controller the AP will initially communicate with

In Chapter 4, "Getting Started," you learned that the AP name and group are usually configured statically and the rest of the settings are typically configured dynamically. A mesh AP requires one additional setting, which is the mesh role.

You should configure the AP through the ArubaOS WebUI, and not through the CLI. You will need to first go to the Configuration menu, using the following menu path: **Configuration ➢ WIRELESS ➢ AP Installation ➢ Provisioning**. From this menu, select the AP and then click the Provision button at the bottom of the list. At the top of the Provisioning menu select the AP group that you configured for the mesh network. Then at the bottom of the Provisioning menu, name your AP. To the right of the name select the mesh role—either mesh point or mesh portal, as displayed in Figure 14.12. You then need to apply and reboot.

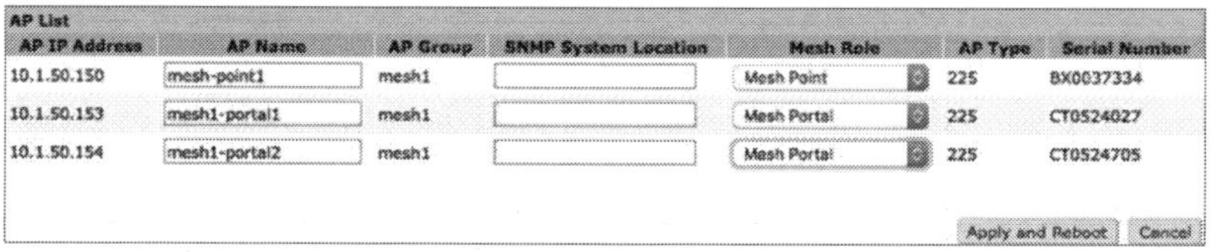

FIGURE 14.12 Configuring a mesh AP

AP IP Address	AP Name	AP Group	SNMP System Location	Mesh Role	AP Type	Serial Number
10.1.50.150	mesh-point1	mesh1		Mesh Point	225	BX0037334
10.1.50.153	mesh1-portal1	mesh1		Mesh Portal	225	CT0524027
10.1.50.154	mesh1-portal2	mesh1		Mesh Portal	225	CT0524705

The AP must be allowed to fully reboot before you can remove it from the Ethernet network and deploy it as a mesh node. If the mesh node is an MPP, it can be allowed to remain connected to the Ethernet network. Leaving the AP connected to the Ethernet network is necessary because the mesh configuration needs to be downloaded to the AP along with the mesh recovery profile. The downloading of the configuration occurs on the Ethernet network after the AP reboots. After the MP is rebooted and has received its configuration, it can be removed from the Ethernet network and deployed.

Mesh Status

This section introduces you to some of the CLI commands and WebUI screens that will help you check the status of the mesh network and the mesh nodes. We will start off by looking at some of the WebUI menus. The Monitoring menu has a Mesh submenu from which you can see the topology of your mesh network or get details about any of the nodes. You can get to this menu using the following path: **Monitoring ➢ CONTROLLER ➢ Mesh Nodes**.

From the Mesh Nodes menu click the Topology button to see which nodes are connected to which. Once the topology is displayed, you can click on any of the nodes to get detailed information about the node, as shown in Figure 14.13.

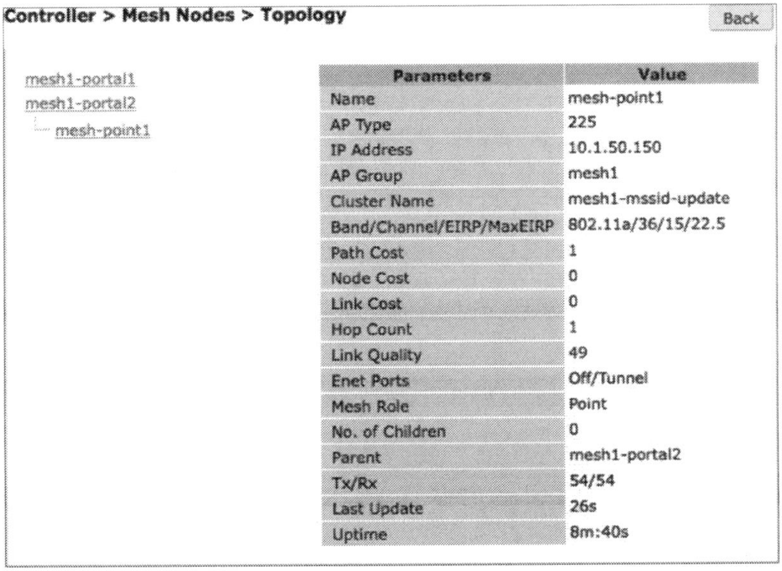

FIGURE 14.13
Mesh topology

Parameters	Value
Name	mesh-point1
AP Type	225
IP Address	10.1.50.150
AP Group	mesh1
Cluster Name	mesh1-mssid-update
Band/Channel/EIRP/MaxEIRP	802.11a/36/15/22.5
Path Cost	1
Node Cost	0
Link Cost	0
Hop Count	1
Link Quality	49
Enet Ports	Off/Tunnel
Mesh Role	Point
No. of Children	0
Parent	mesh1-portal2
Tx/Rx	54/54
Last Update	26s
Uptime	8m:40s

Controller > Mesh Nodes > Topology

- mesh1-portal1
- mesh1-portal2
  - mesh-point1

Also from the Mesh Nodes menu, if you select a mesh node and then click the Profile button, you will see general information about the mesh AP and then detailed information about each of the radios. If you select a mesh node and then click the AP Activity button, this will allow you to see the WLANs that the mesh node is advertising. From this menu, you can click on the BSSID to display a screenful of statistics and charts regarding the selected network.

You can use an assortment of CLI commands to see the status of the mesh network and to troubleshoot it. The following CLI command displays a list of the active mesh APs that are currently registered on the controller where the command is executed. This is a good command to get an overview of the mesh nodes.

```
#show ap mesh active

Mesh Cluster Name: mesh1-mssid-update
-------------------------------------
Name           Group  IP Address    BSSID              Band/Ch/EIRP/MaxEIRP →
----           -----  ----------    -----              -------------------- →
mesh-point1    mesh1  10.1.50.150   9c:1c:12:88:5e:31  802.11a/36/15/22.5   →
mesh1-portal1  mesh1  10.1.50.153   04:bd:88:28:87:51  802.11a/36/15/22.5   →
mesh1-portal2  mesh1  10.1.50.154   04:bd:88:28:dc:11  802.11a/36/15/22.5   →


→ MTU   Enet Ports Mesh Role Parent         #Children AP Type Uptime
→ ---   ---------- --------- ------         --------- ------- ------
→       Off/Tunnel Point     mesh1-portal2  0         225     3d:5h:40m:43s
→ 1500  -/Tunnel   Portal    -              0         225     3d:20h:20m:7s
→ 1500  -/Tunnel   Portal    -              1         225     3d:20h:20m:7s

Total APs :3
```

Just as you can display the mesh topology from the WebUI, you can also display it from the CLI, as shown in the following output. This command lists the clusters and all the mesh nodes. The parent and children columns help identify the mesh hierarchy.

```
#show ap mesh topology

Mesh Cluster Name: mesh1-mssid-update
-----------------------------------
Name           Mesh Role  Parent         Path Cost  Node Cost  Link Cost →
----           ---------  ------         ---------  ---------  --------- →
mesh-point1    Point      mesh1-portal2  1          0          0         →
mesh1-portal1  Portal     -              0          0          0         →
mesh1-portal2  Portal     -              0          1          0         →


→ Hop Count  RSSI  Rate Tx/Rx  Last Update  Uplink Age      #Children
→ ---------  ----  ----------  -----------  ----------      ---------
→ 1          43    6/6         4m:20s       3d:5h:32m:9s    0
→ 0          0     -           3m:51s       3d:20h:20m:53s  0
→ 0          0     -           4m:9s        3d:20h:20m:53s  1

Total APs :3
(R): Recovery AP. (N): 11N Enabled. (AC): 11AC Enabled. For Portals 'Uplink Age'
equals uptime.
```

The following CLI command displays the clusters that are provisioned on a specific AP. This command is also helpful to identify the recovery profile settings, and can be used to help you identify an MP that has the same recovery profile as the other MPs or MPPs in its cluster.

```
#show ap mesh debug provisioned-clusters ap-name mesh-point1

Mesh Cluster Profile: Recovery Cluster Profile
-----------------------------------------
Item            Value
----            -----
Cluster Name    Recoveryqi90J45oqG9LPJRW
RF Band         a
Encryption      wpa2-psk-aes
WPA Hexkey      56F6ECDC21BA93102CEFDEB97632CB2B7A8471FBA85CA6CCAAFE2A......
WPA Passphrase
Priority        16

Mesh Cluster Profile: mesh1-cluster
-----------------------------------
```

MESH STATUS

```
Item              Value
----              -----
Cluster Name      mesh1-mssid-update
RF Band           a
Encryption        wpa2-psk-aes
WPA Hexkey
WPA Passphrase    D750EAC71F2980B2568EEB44CE98EC497299C5AA7B2CD146D158E86272BCAC41
Priority          1
```

CHAPTER 15

Wireless Intrusion Prevention

IN THIS CHAPTER, YOU WILL LEARN ABOUT THE FOLLOWING:

- Channel Scanning
- WIP Device Classification
  - AP Classification
  - Client Classification
- Using the WIP Wizard
  - Rogue Classification
  - WIP Policy
  - Infrastructure
  - Intrusion Detection
  - Protection
- Detection methods
  - Ad Hoc and Wireless Bridge identification
  - MAC Address Match Methods
  - AP Traffic Inspection
- Security Summary Dashboard
- IDS Commands

WIRELESS INTRUSION PREVENTION (WIP) IS AN IMPORTANT component of many wireless networks. WIP is used to help protect the network from unknown or untrusted APs or client devices, or attacks against the network.

The threat to your network could be from a client or AP that is intentionally trying to compromise your network, in the same way that a thief might try to pick the lock on a door, or counterfeit an identity badge to sneak past a security guard. The threat could also be from a client or AP that is unintentionally misconfigured and inadvertently providing access to your network—similar to the security risk that is present when someone forgets to close or lock a door or window.

WIP reports do nothing to secure your network unless some form of action is taken based on those reports. Consider, if your goal is to secure a building, monitoring and periodically checking all the doors and windows can help you identify security risks and provide status updates on the condition of your property. However, these status updates do nothing to actually secure your building. Unless you monitor the building, and act on the information, you have really done nothing. Network monitoring needs to be treated similarly. Monitoring and auditing, combined with actions, define a proper security plan.

The WIP system is made up of a few components. WIP running on a local controller uses the Aruba APs and AMs to listen to the wireless network and collect information about clients and APs. This information is ultimately forwarded to the master controller, which is where WIP processing and decision making is performed.

WIP has many interrelated components and is easier to configure using the WIP wizard than using the CLI. The WIP wizard is shown later in this chapter.

Channel Scanning

The key to WIP is to monitor the RF spectrum for Wi-Fi signals. By scanning the 2.4 GHz and 5 GHz bands, the WIP system can find and identify clients and APs that may be a threat to your network. Every Wi-Fi device that is seen by an Aruba AP or AM is considered a monitored device and will be categorized as valid, interfering, neighbor, or rogue.

Access points use ARM scans to also gather WIP information. Your Aruba APs will of course monitor the channels that they are operating on. If ARM is enabled, as part of the ARM scanning process the APs will periodically scan the other regulatory channels, as explained in Chapter 12, "Adaptive Radio Management." In addition to ARM scanning, or if ARM scanning is disabled, air monitors (AMs) can be deployed to provide WIP scanning.

AMs provide extra visibility. If ARM scanning is disabled, air monitors must be deployed to provide WIP scanning. If ARM scanning is enabled, AMs can be deployed along with APs to provide more WIP information, along with faster gathering of that information. As an AP scans the Wi-Fi bands, it must still service its assigned channel and clients. At times, there are conditions that will cause an AP to pause ARM scanning. Both of these conditions slow down the gathering of WIP data.

AMs, on the other hand, just perform scanning. They do not have to service clients; therefore, they can gather information much quicker than APs.

Both ARM and AM scanning are configured in the RF Management profile assigned to the AP group. Both profiles are defined separately and are assigned to AP groups.

ArubaOS defines three sets of channels that can be scanned by ARM and AMs. The following list defines these three channel sets:

Regulatory Domain Channels   All channels that belong to the regulatory domain of the country that the AP is configured for.

All Regulatory Domain Channels   All channels that belong to any regulatory domain of any country that the AP is able to be configured for. The regulatory domain channels set is a subset of this. Table 15.1 lists the frequencies and channels in this group.

TABLE 15.1: All regulatory domain channels

FREQUENCY RANGE	CHANNELS
2412 MHz to 2472 MHz (5 MHz increments)	1 to 13
5100 MHz to 5895 MHz (5 MHz increments)	20 to 179

Rare Channels   These are channels that are outside of the regulatory domain. Table 15.2 lists the frequencies and channels in this group.

TABLE 15.2: Rare channels

FREQUENCY RANGE	CHANNELS
2484 MHz	14
4900 MHz to 4995 MHz (5 MHz increments)	180 to 199
5000 MHz to 5100 MHz (5 MHz increments)	200 to 219

To modify either the Adaptive Radio Management profile or the AM Scanning profile, you must navigate to **Configuration ➣ WIRELESS ➣ AP Configuration**, select an AP group, and then proceed to RF Management and choose the radio you want to configure, as shown in Figure 15.1. This figure highlights the four profiles where you can specify Scan Mode.

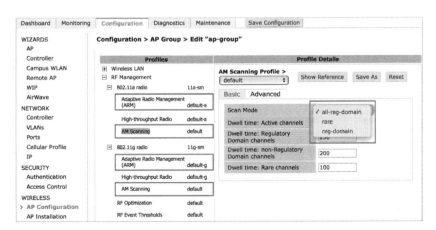

FIGURE 15.1 Setting Scan Mode

When configuring the scan mode for an AM, any of the three scan sets can be selected: regulatory domain channels, all regulatory domain channels, or rare channels. When configuring the scan mode for ARM, only regulatory domain channels or all regulatory domain channels can be selected.

The scan mode can also be set through the CLI, as shown in the following CLI commands. Scanning must be enabled in the ARM profile and is enabled by default.

```
rf am-scan-profile "default"
  scan-mode "rare"
rf arm-profile "default-a"
  scan-mode "reg-domain"
```

WIP Device Classification

A key goal of WIP is to identify APs and clients that are not part of your network but whose RF signal is seen by your network. These devices need to be monitored to identify the level of threat that they pose. As part of the identification process, each AP is placed into one of six different categories, and clients are placed into one of three different categories.

This categorization is performed automatically by the controller and can be manually overridden by an administrator of the controller. The following two sections list the AP and client classification categories along with a brief description of each. Some of the categorization processes will be explained later in this chapter.

AP Classification

The following is a list of AP classification categories along with brief descriptions of each:

Interfering   An AP that has been detected wirelessly but no additional information is available yet to further classify the AP.

Valid   An Aruba AP known and managed by your controller, or an AP that has been manually marked as valid by a controller administrator.

Rogue   An AP that has been detected wirelessly and on the wired network.

Suspected Rogue   An AP that has been detected wirelessly. It has not been detected on the wired network. The controller believes it may be connected to the wired network due to other indicators, but it is not certain. To avoid accidentally mislabeling it as a rogue and causing a false positive, it is marked as a suspected rogue.

Neighbor   A neighbor is essentially a known interfering AP, although any AP can be marked as a neighbor. A neighbor AP is manually marked by a network administrator or by a WIP rule.

Manually Contained AP   An AP that is being contained by manually configuring denial-of-service (DoS).

Client Classification

The following is the list of client classification categories along with brief descriptions of each:

Valid Client   Any client that has successfully authenticated to one of your SSIDs and is listed in the client database on your controller.

Manually Contained Client   A client that is being contained by manually configuring DoS.

Interfering Client   A client that has been detected wirelessly that has not been categorized as a valid client.

Using the WIP Wizard

The WIP Wizard is a key component for configuration of WIP settings and can be easily started from the following WebUI menu path: **Configuration ➢ WIZARDS ➢ WIP**. The WIP menu option is only available if the RFProtect license is installed. If the license is not installed, the option is not even displayed in the wizard's menu. The wizard allows you to configure five categories of settings:

- Rogue Classification
- WIP Policy
- Infrastructure
- Intrusion Detection
- Protection

The WIP menu will move you through each of these configuration menus when you click Next at the bottom-right corner of each menu. The following sections of this chapter will explain each of these menus along with the available settings. The current menu is highlighted along the left side of the window.

Rogue Classification

Rogue classification is done on the master controller and spans information gathered by all APs and AMs known to the master controller. As information is gathered, it is passed back to the master controller, and regardless of which AP group the AP or AM is provisioned for, the information is combined into a single view. This allows information gathered by one local controller to be shared with other local controllers in the same master/local structure.

This menu allows you to create your own classification rules that are processed against the discovered APs to determine if any should be reclassified. The processing of classification rules is performed on the master controller. Each rogue classification rule is made up of up to seven pieces:

- Rule name
- # of Discovering APs
- SNR(dB)
- SSID
- Classification
- Confidence
- Enabled

The rule name is simply an ASCII name up to 32 characters long that is used to logically identify a rule. Up to 32 rules can be defined, but a maximum of 16 can be enabled at one time. Figure 15.2 shows the rogue classification menu where rules can be created.

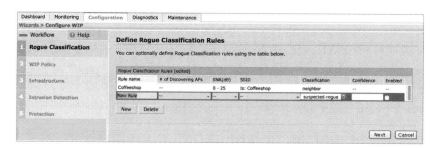

FIGURE 15.2 Rogue classification rule

Each rule can consist of up to three conditions: discovered AP count, SSID, and SNR. The discovered AP count is a single value that specifies a minimum or maximum number of Aruba APs that must see the discovered AP. The SSID specification allows you to specify a maximum of six SSIDs. This list can be checked to see if the SSID of a discovered AP matches any of the SSIDs in the list. The list can also be checked to see if the SSID of the discovered AP does not match one of the SSIDs on the list. The final condition checks the SNR level of the discovered AP. The SNR setting can check the signal level of the discovered AP, and compare it against a defined minimum and/or maximum value.

If the rule is enabled and the conditions in the rule match, the discovered AP can be classified as either a suspected rogue or a neighbor. A confidence level value can be entered in the rule, which can help gauge the risk level of different APs.

When the master controller processes the rules, it processes them from the top down. Each rule is evaluated for a match, and then the system moves to the next rule in the list. The list of rules is evaluated until one of two conditions is met. First, if a true rule classifies the target AP as a neighbor, rule processing is stopped. Second, if the target AP breaks enough suspected-rogue rules, such that the confidence level reaches 100 percent, rule processing stops for that AP and it is categorized as a suspected rogue. For efficiency, and to prevent false positives, it is recommended that you organize the neighbor classification rules at the top of the list.

WIP Policy

WIP policy focuses on client activity, and evaluates for client or infrastructure based threats. Although the list of possible threats is large, not every threat is applicable to your network setup. For example, the WIP policy can be set to guard against TKIP authentication replay attacks; however, if your network does not support TKIP, then it is a waste of processor time to try to protect against that type of threat.

Rogue classification rules apply to all wireless networks associated to the master controller, but the WIP policies are applied to individual AP groups. Multiple WIP policies can be created and a policy can be applied to one or more AP groups. Figure15.3 shows the creation of a policy named wips-policy-1. Once you create the policy, select it and assign it to one or more AP groups. When moving between the steps in the wizard, you must select the policy before clicking the Next button.

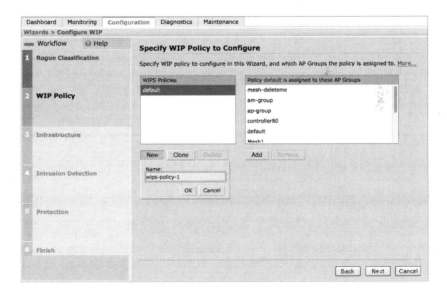

FIGURE 15.3
WIP policy

The following CLI commands will create the IDS profile and assign it to the AP group:

```
(config) #ids profile wips-policy-1
(IDS Profile "wips-policy-1") #ap-group ap-group
(AP group "ap-group") #ids-profile wips-policy-1
```

Infrastructure

To properly apply the WIP policy, the controller must evaluate the Wi-Fi infrastructure it sees running and decide which devices to apply the policy to.

WIP works best when it is running on the same controllers that are controlling your APs and AMs. If the wireless environment in your organization consists solely of Aruba APs connected to your controllers, WIP knows which APs are yours, as well as the configuration of your wireless environment, including valid SSIDs and authentication methods. This means that WIP can easily identify devices that do not match your configuration.

WIP can be deployed as part of your Wi-Fi network or as an overlay. At times organizations have multiple wireless networks operating. This could be because they are replacing one network with another, or numerous other reasons. In this environment, you can configure WIP to identify your valid wireless network by providing configuration characteristics, such as what authentication and encryption methods are used, which SSIDs are deployed, and which channels are valid, as shown in Figure 15.4. Although the controller running WIP may not have firsthand knowledge of valid APs and clients, this descriptive information is used to categorize valid and nonvalid APs and clients.

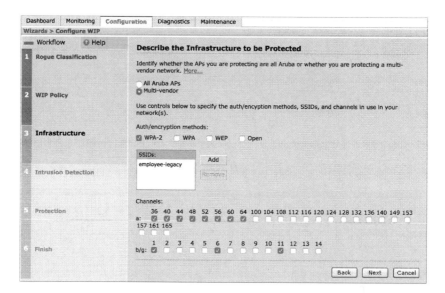

FIGURE 15.4 Infrastructure settings

Intrusion Detection

The main configuration of the WIP policy is performed in the Intrusion Detection section of the wizard. The Intrusion Detection menu is divided into two sections. The top half is for configuring intrusion detection for infrastructure devices, and the lower half is for configuring intrusion detection for client devices.

This menu allows you to set specific detection features. Both the infrastructure and client settings are configured using similar methods. Each has five levels of configuration:

- High
- Medium
- Low
- Off
- Custom

When choosing high, medium, or low, a default set of detection mechanisms are enabled. Table 15.3 displays the list of all infrastructure detection mechanisms. This table indicates which mechanisms are enabled by default for each intrusion levels. Table 15.4 displays the list of all client detection mechanisms, and indicates which mechanisms are enabled by default for each intrusion level. The default settings are simply the initial configurations. You will need to evaluate your environment and determine the settings that are best for your needs.

In addition to choosing high, medium, or low, you can also turn off intrusion detection or you can customize the list of mechanisms, individually selecting or deselecting each mechanism. To customize the list, click the text Allow Custom Settings above the list on the right. After you select Custom, each intrusion mechanism can be enabled or disabled individually, as shown in Figure 15.5.

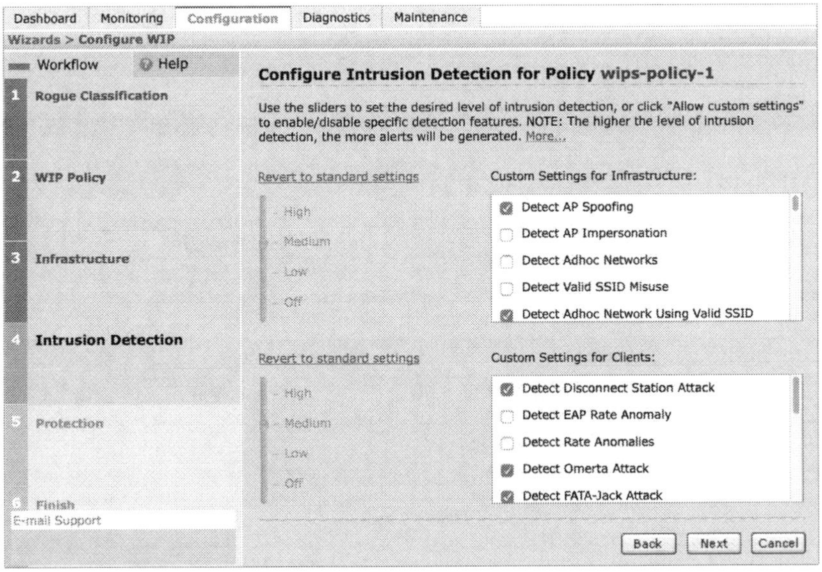

FIGURE 15.5 Custom settings

Before enabling custom settings, choose one of the four levels from the list on the left (high, medium, low, or off). The custom settings will start with whichever level is selected when you choose customize.

> **NOTE** *A description of each of the intrusion mechanisms appears in the ArubaOS Users Guide. Since the list of mechanisms is fairly long, and since they are already well documented, they will not be listed and defined in this book.*

TABLE 15.3: Intrusion detection for infrastructure (default settings)

INFRASTRUCTURE DETECTION MECHANISM	HIGH	MEDIUM	LOW
Detect AP Spoofing	Yes	Yes	Yes
Detect AP Impersonation	Yes	—	—
Detect Adhoc Networks	Yes	—	—
Detect Valid SSID Misuse	Yes	—	—
Detect Adhoc Network Using Valid SSID	Yes	Yes	—
Detect Windows Bridge	Yes	Yes	Yes
Detect Wireless Bridge	Yes	—	—
Detect 802.11n 40MHz Intolerance Setting	Yes	—	—
Detect Active 802.11n Greenfield Mode	Yes	—	—
Detect AP Flood Attack	Yes	—	—
Detect Client Flood Attack	Yes	—	—
Detect Bad WEP	Yes	—	—
IDS Signature:Deauth-Broadcast	Yes	—	—
IDS Signature:Disassoc-Broadcast	Yes	—	—
IDS Signature:Deauth-Broadcast-From-Valid-AP	Yes	Yes	Yes
IDS Signature:Disassoc-Broadcast-From-Valid-AP	Yes	Yes	Yes
IDS Signature:Netstumbler Generic	—	—	—
IDS Signature:Netstumbler Version 3.3.0.x	—	—	—
IDS Signature:Wellenreiter	—	—	—
Detect Misconfigured AP	Yes	Yes	—

INFRASTRUCTURE DETECTION MECHANISM	HIGH	MEDIUM	LOW
Privacy	Yes	Yes	—
Require WPA	Yes	Yes	—
Detect CTS Rate Anomaly	Yes	—	—
Detect RTS Rate Anomaly	Yes	—	—
Detect Invalid Address Combination	Yes	—	—
Detect Malformed Frame - HT IE	Yes	—	—
Detect Malformed Frame - Assoc Request	Yes	—	—
Detect Malformed Frame - Auth	Yes	—	—
Detect Malformed Frame - Large Duration	Yes	—	—
Detect Overflow IE	Yes	—	—
Detect Overflow EAPOL Key	Yes	—	—
Detect Beacon Wrong Channel	Yes	—	—
Detect Devices with an Invalid MAC OUI	Yes	—	—
Detect Wireless Hosted Network	Yes	—	—

TABLE 15.4: Intrusion detection for clients (default settings)

CLIENT DETECTION MECHANISM	HIGH	MEDIUM	LOW
Detect Disconnect Station Attack	Yes	Yes	—
Detect EAP Rate Anomaly	Yes	—	—
Detect Rate Anomalies	Yes	—	—
Detect Omerta Attack	Yes	Yes	—
Detect FATA-Jack Attack	Yes	Yes	—
Detect Block ACK DoS	Yes	—	—
Detect ChopChop Attack	Yes	—	—
Detect TKIP Replay Attack	Yes	—	—
Detect Hotspotter Attack	Yes	Yes	—
Detect Valid Client Misassociation	Yes	Yes	Yes

CHAPTER 15 WIRELESS INTRUSION PREVENTION

CLIENT DETECTION MECHANISM	HIGH	MEDIUM	LOW
Detect Unencrypted Valid Clients	Yes	Yes	—
IDS Signature:AirJack	Yes	—	—
IDS Signature:ASLEAP	Yes	—	—
IDS Signature: Null Probe Response	—	—	—
Detect Power Save DoS Attack	Yes	Yes	—

Protection

The Protection menu is the final menu of the WIP wizard. In this menu, you can choose the protection levels and mechanisms that will be used for APs and clients. You can select what you will be containing, such as rogues, suspected rogues, or misconfigured APs, as shown in Figure 15.6.

FIGURE 15.6
Protection

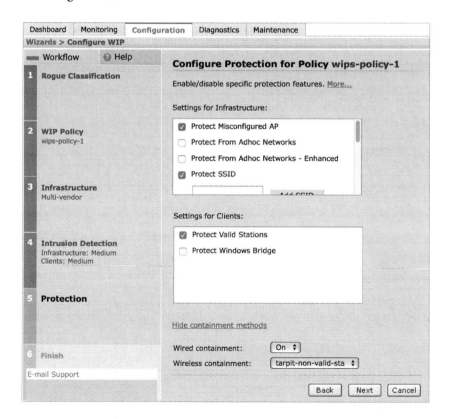

Tables 15.5 and 15.6 display the protection policy setting options for both infrastructure devices and clients. These tables also indicate which settings are enabled by default. The default settings are simply the initial configurations. You will need to evaluate your environment and determine the settings that are best for you.

TABLE 15.5: Infrastructure protection policy (default settings)

SETTINGS FOR INFRASTRUCTURE	ENABLED
Protect Misconfigured AP	Yes
Protect From Adhoc Networks	—
Protect From Adhoc Networks - Enhanced	—
Protect SSID	Yes
Protect 802.11n High Throughput Devices	—
Protect 40MHz 802.11n High Throughput Devices	—
Protect From AP Impersonation	—
Protect From Wireless Hosted Networks	—
Rogue Containment	Yes
Suspected Rogue Containment	Yes
Suspected Rogue Confidence level > 90	Yes
Suspected Rogue Confidence level > 80	—

TABLE 15.6: Client protection policy (default settings)

SETTINGS FOR CLIENTS	ENABLED
Protect Valid Station	Yes
Protect Windows Bridge	—

WIP allows both wired and wireless containment methods to prevent unauthorized devices from connecting to your network. Although wireless containment is allowed by ArubaOS, its use may not be legal in your regulatory domain. When rogue containment is enabled on a controller operating in the United States, the wizard displays a warning, as shown in Figure 15.7. Since some organizations have been fined large sums of money, and the laws regarding wireless containment are vague, you should consult your legal counsel before using any wireless containment methods.

FIGURE 15.7 Containment warning

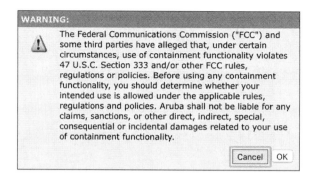

If you choose to use wireless containment, I highly recommend that you deploy air monitors and that you keep its use short lived. Use it long enough to protect the infrastructure until the threat can be removed. Wireless containment requires the Aruba AP or AM to transmit frames directed to the rogue AP or client. When wireless containment is active, valid clients will be impacted. If the rogue device is operating on a channel other than the Aruba AP, the AP cannot perform the containment unless it changes to the channel that the rogue device is operating on. Aruba APs are capable of doing this; however, there are numerous restrictions on doing so. Since an Aruba AM does not support client devices, it can freely change to any channel to provide rogue containment.

ArubaOS offers five containment methods:

- Deauth-only (wireless)
- None
- Tarpit-all-sta (wireless)
- Tarpit-non-valid-sta (wireless)
- ARP cache poisoning (wired)

Wireless containment will only be effective against rogues that operate in the same regulatory domain that has been configured on the controller. APs and AMs cannot transmit outside of the regulatory domain they are operating in, even when containing rogues.

Deauth-Only (Wireless)

If a client is connected to a rogue AP, deauth-only will trigger an Aruba AM or AP to impersonate the rogue AP and send 802.11 deauthentication frames to the client, disconnecting the client from the rogue AP. The Aruba AM or AP will also impersonate the client and send 802.11 deauthentication frames to the rogue AP, telling the rogue AP that the client is disconnecting from it. Since the Aruba AM or AP sends a continuous stream of deauthentication frames, this is disruptive to all devices operating on the same channel, because the Aruba AM or AP is using up valuable transmission time.

This method is also most effective if AMs are installed, or if the rogue AP happens to be on the same channel as a nearby Aruba AP. If the rogue is on a different channel and AMs are not installed, an Aruba AP can do rogue containment if Rogue AP aware ARM scanning is enabled in the ARM profile. If this is enabled, an Aruba AP may change to the same RF channel as the rogue in order to be able to send deauthentication frames. This is typically not good for the valid clients connected to the Aruba AP since the rogue may be operating on an RF channel that is not ideal for the clients, and the valid clients also have to contend with the flood of deauthentication frames.

Tarpitting (Wireless)

Tarpitting is a process in which an Aruba AP or AM impersonates a rogue AP, encouraging the rogue clients to connect to the Aruba AP or AM on its own, and then the Aruba AP or AM does not respond to the clients. The client will indicate that it is connected to the wireless network, which it is, but the client will not obtain an IP address, nor will it be able to pass any traffic.

In order to perform tarpitting, when the Aruba AP or AM sees the rogue AP and client, the Aruba AP or AM sends spoofed deauthentication frames to each of them. The Aruba AP or AM tells the rogue AP that the client is disconnecting and tells the client that the rogue AP is disconnecting.

The Aruba AP or AM advertises the same SSID that the rogue AP is advertising. After the client is deauthenticated, it will attempt to reconnect to the SSID that the rogue AP was advertising. When the client attempts to reconnect to the SSID, the Aruba AP or AM will respond, and hopefully the client will connect to the Aruba AP or AM.

After the client connects to the Aruba AP or AM, physically the client is communicating and connected to the AP. However, the client will not receive an IP address, and the Aruba AP or AM will ignore any communications made by the client. The client will be connected without the ability to communicate. If the client reconnects to the rogue AP, the Aruba AP or AM will tarpit the client again.

Tarpitting performs containment more efficiently than the deauthentication process because fewer deauthentication frames need to be sent, and once the client has been contained, the controller simply needs to monitor the rogue AP and clients.

Tarpitting can be enabled using one of two methods: disable all clients (tarpit-all-sta) or disable nonvalid clients (tarpit-non-valid-sta). ArubaOS has the ability to automatically classify clients based on their behavior. Based on this classification, tarpitting can be configured to contain all clients or just those that are not valid.

ARP Cache Poisoning (Wired)

The controller identifies the IP address of each rogue AP or client. The Aruba AP or AM will send an ARP request on the Ethernet network every second. An ARP request is sent by the Aruba AP or AM for the default gateway of the rogue device, using a spoofed IP address of the device that is being contained. The Aruba AP or AM also sends an ARP response, using a spoofed IP address of the default gateway. All spoofed MAC addresses are locally administered so that the traffic is dropped. This exchange of frames attempts to fool the device being contained and the default gateway.

If the Aruba AP, AM, or controller is on a trunked Ethernet port, it is able to transmit on multiple VLANs. If the rogue AP or client is connected to a different VLAN than the Aruba AP or AM, the rogue device can still be contained.

Detection Methods

In the "Intrusion Detection" section of this chapter, the infrastructure and client detection methods were listed as part of the WIP wizard configuration process. As mentioned previously in this section, all of the intrusion mechanisms are listed and defined in the ArubaOS Users Guide, so they will not be listed in this book.

This section, however, will provide some additional information about how ArubaOS is able to identify ad hoc devices, along with how rogue APs can be detected either by using the monitored APs' MAC addresses or by using traffic inspection.

Ad Hoc and Wireless Bridge Identification

The identification of an ad hoc device or a wireless bridge is a fairly simple process. When any wireless device transmits a data frame, the frame has a field known as the Frame Control field. Within the Frame Control field there are two subfields: ToDS and FromDS. Each of these fields is one bit in size. A simple explanation of these fields is that they identify if the frame is being sent to an AP or from an AP. So looking at Table 15.7, when the ToDS field is 1 and the FromDS field is 0 a client is sending a frame to an AP.

When an Aruba AP or AM receives a frame, the master controller can easily identify an ad hoc node because both fields are 0. If the master controller processes a frame with both fields set to 1, it knows that this is a wireless bridge or a mesh AP.

TABLE 15.7: ToDS/FromDS overview

WIRELESS TRANSMISSION	TODS	FROMDS
Ad hoc client sending a data frame	0	0
Client sends a data frame to an AP	1	0
AP sends a data frame to a client	0	1
A wireless bridge or mesh AP forwarding a data frame to another bridge or mesh AP	1	1

MAC Address Match Methods

The "Channel Scanning" section of this chapter explains how the Aruba APs and AMs perform scanning so that the master controller can identify APs and clients that are connected to your network, or operating within or near your wireless network. An Aruba AP, AM, or controller (if learn-system-wired-macs is enabled) builds a list of all wired MAC addresses from all of the VLANs defined. If the AP is trunked to multiple networks, the AP will build its list from all of the networks that it is connected to. This setting is disabled by default and can be modified from the following WebUI menu: **Configuration ➢ All Profiles ➢ IDS ➢ IDS WMS General**. It can also be enabled using the following CLI commands:

```
ids wms-general-profile
  learn-system-wired-macs
```

When an Aruba AP or AM hears another AP, the BSSID address of the AP is captured and the controller compares it to the list of wired MAC addresses. The controller will classify the monitored AP as a rogue if any of the following are true:

Equal   The BSSID matches an Ethernet address.

Plus One   The BSSID matches an Ethernet address, except the last bit is one digit greater.

Minus One   The BSSID matches an Ethernet address, except the last bit is one digit less.

AP Traffic Inspection

Another method that ArubaOS uses to classify rogue APs is by inspecting the frames that are being transmitted. When a wireless device transmits data, there are four logical addresses that are part of the frame:

- Layer 2 source
- Layer 2 destination
- Transmitter
- Receiver

> **NOTE** *An 802.11 wireless frame technically consists of four address fields; address1, address2, address3, and address4. These four fields represent five identities; layer 2 source, layer 2 destination, transmitter, receiver, and BSSID address. For the traffic inspection explanation, the four logical addresses in the previous list are all we need.*

As part of the traffic monitoring process, in addition to monitoring the Ethernet MAC addresses of client devices connected to the wired network, the Aruba AP, AM, and Aruba controller will build a list of the MAC addresses of any wired gateways that they see on their Ethernet connections.

At times, the gateway transmits frames that need to be forwarded by the Aruba controller and AP. As an example, the gateway may need to send a broadcast frame. In the following sections, this information is used to illustrate how the controller can identify that a rogue is connected to the network.

Layer 2: Transmission from Valid AP

In this example, you will learn how traffic inspection processes a frame being transmitted from a valid AP on a layer 2 network. In Figure 15.8, since all of the devices are connected to the same layer 2 network (VLAN 10), the Ethernet MAC address of the gateway (router) will be tracked by the Aruba AP, AM, or controller.

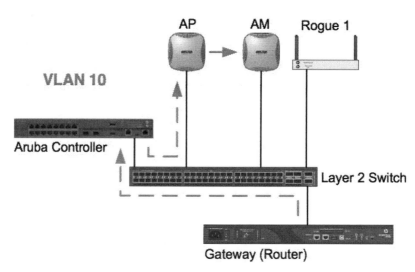

FIGURE 15.8
Layer 2: Aruba AP broadcast frame

The figure illustrates the transmission of a broadcast frame by the dashed line being sent from the gateway to the Aruba controller, which will then use GRE to encapsulate the frame and forward it to the AP, which will transmit it out into the air. Table 15.8 shows the addressing that is assigned to this frame.

TABLE 15.8: Layer 2: Aruba AP broadcast frame addressing

LAYER 2 SOURCE	LAYER 2 DESTINATION	TRANSMITTER	RECEIVER
Gateway	Layer 2 broadcast	Aruba AP	Layer 2 broadcast

When the AP transmits the frame, the Aruba AM receives the frame. The traffic inspection process knows that the gateway is the source of the frame, and from Ethernet monitoring by the Aruba AP, AM, and controller, it knows that the gateway is connected to the wired layer 2 network. From the header of the wireless frame, traffic inspection also sees that the device transmitting the frame is the Aruba AP, which the Aruba AP, AM, and controller know is a valid AP.

In this scenario, it is able to determine that a valid AP on your wireless network is transmitting a frame from a device on your wired network.

Layer 2: Transmission from Rogue AP

In this example, you will learn how traffic inspection processes a frame being transmitted from a rogue AP on a layer 2 network. In Figure 15.9, since all of the devices are connected to the same layer 2 network (VLAN 10), the Ethernet MAC address of the gateway (router) will be tracked by the Aruba AP, AM, or controller.

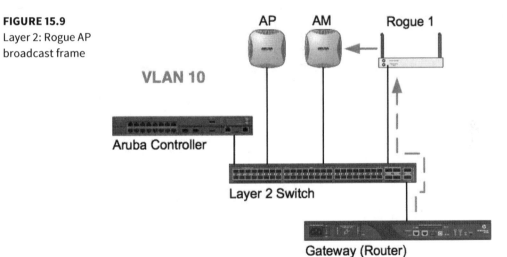

FIGURE 15.9
Layer 2: Rogue AP broadcast frame

The figure illustrates the transmission of a broadcast frame by the dashed line being sent to the rogue AP, which will transmit it out into the air. Table 15.9 shows the addressing that is assigned to this frame.

TABLE 15.9: Layer 2: rogue AP broadcast frame addressing

LAYER 2 SOURCE	LAYER 2 DESTINATION	TRANSMITTER	RECEIVER
Gateway	Layer 2 broadcast	Rogue AP	Layer 2 broadcast

When the rogue AP transmits the frame, the Aruba AM receives the frame. The traffic inspection process knows that the gateway is the source of the frame, and from Ethernet monitoring by the Aruba AP, AM, and controller, it knows that the gateway is connected to the wired layer 2 network. From the header of the wireless frame, traffic inspection sees that the device transmitting the frame is the rogue AP, which the Aruba AP, AM, and controller do not identify as a valid AP.

In this scenario, it is able to determine that a rogue AP is physically connected to your wired network, and is transmitting a frame from a device on your wired network. It is this affiliation that identifies this AP as a rogue.

Layer 3: Transmission from Rogue AP

In this example, you will learn how traffic inspection processes a frame being transmitted from a rogue AP on a different layer 3 network. In Figure 15.10, the Aruba equipment is connected to VLAN 10, and the rogue AP is connected to VLAN 20. Since the devices are not connected to the same layer 2 network, the Ethernet MAC address of the gateway (router) on VLAN 20 will be not be tracked by the Aruba AP, AM, or controller.

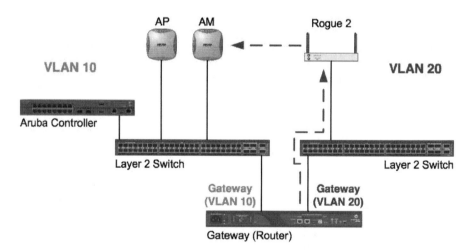

FIGURE 15.10 Layer 3: rogue AP broadcast frame

The figure illustrates the transmission of a broadcast frame by the gateway on VLAN 20. The dashed line indicates the broadcast sent to the rogue AP, which is connected to a different layer 2 switch. The rogue AP will transmit it out into the air. Table 15.10 shows the addressing that is assigned to this frame.

TABLE 15.10: Layer 2: rogue AP broadcast frame addressing

LAYER 2 SOURCE	LAYER 2 DESTINATION	TRANSMITTER	RECEIVER
Gateway (VLAN 20)	Layer 2 broadcast	Rogue AP	Layer 2 broadcast

When the rogue AP transmits the frame, the Aruba AM receives the frame. The traffic inspection process does not know the MAC address of the gateway's VLAN 20 Ethernet interface. From the header of the wireless frame, traffic inspection sees that the device transmitting the frame is the rogue AP, which the Aruba AP, AM, and controller do not identify as a valid AP.

In this scenario, since an unknown AP is transmitting from an unknown source Ethernet address, the rogue AP is classified as an interfering AP.

To configure the network so that the rogue AP is properly identified as a rogue, it is necessary for an Aruba controller, AP, or AM to be connected to VLAN 20. One of these devices can either be physically connected to VLAN 20, or it can be trunked to VLAN 20. By physically connecting, or trunking a device to VLAN 20, the MAC address of the VLAN 20 gateway will be tracked by ArubaOS. Once it is tracked, it can then be referenced and used by the traffic inspection processes as part of rogue detection.

Security Summary Dashboard

If you want to quickly see a summary of the discovered APs and clients on your network, the Security dashboard is a good place to begin. This menu also displays containment and detection events. The menu can be reached from the WebUI using the following menu path: **Dashboard ≻ Security**.

The dashboard is broken up into three sections. The upper-left section lists the discovered APs and clients. This section can provide a summary or detail view. When the detail view is displayed, the suspected rogue classification can be expanded to display four different levels of confidence.

The upper-right section displays containment and detection events. These events are broken out and display events from the last 4 hours, 24 hours, and all events.

Both sections at the top of the window display the number of devices that match each of the different categories. Clicking on any of the numbers will automatically configure a filter to display all of the matching APs, clients, or events in the lower section of the window, as shown in Figure 15.11.

FIGURE 15.11 Security summary dashboard

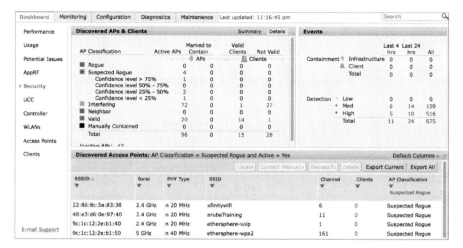

IDS Commands

After IDS profiles are created, they are deployed by assigning them to an AP group. The IDS menu is a profile section in the AP group menu and can be reached from the following menu path: **Configuration ➢ WIRELESS ➢ AP Configuration**, select an AP group, and then select the IDS menu. From this menu, you can choose different IDS profiles or make changes to any of the profiles.

Because there are so many IDS settings, the CLI commands can be complex and overwhelming. However, the CLI commands are a good resource for reviewing the IDS settings and fine-tuning them. The following CLI command displays a list of IDS commands that can be used to display the IDS profiles and parameters:

```
#show ids ?
ap-classification-rule        IDS AP Classification Rule profile
ap-rule-matching              Show the IDS Active AP Rules Profile
dos-profile                   Show an IDS Denial Of Service Profile
general-profile               Show an IDS General Profile
impersonation-profile         Show an IDS Impersonation Profile
management-profile            Show the IDS WMS Management Profile
profile                       Show an IDS Profile
rap-wml-server-profile        Show an IDS RAP WML Server Profile
rap-wml-table-profile         Show an IDS RAP WML Table Profile
rate-thresholds-profile       Show an IDS Rate Thresholds Profile
signature-matching-profile    Show an IDS Signature Matching Profile
signature-profile             Show an IDS Signature Profile
unauthorized-device-profile   Show an IDS Unauthorized Device Profile
wms-general-profile           Show the IDS WMS General Profile
wms-local-system-profile      Show the IDS WMS Local System Profile
```

The following CLI commands display a list of the AP classification rules, followed by the detailed configuration of each rule:

```
#show ids ap-classification-rule

IDS AP Classification Rule Profile List
---------------------------------------
Name             References  Profile Status
----             ----------  --------------
Rogue-rule-1     0
Rogue-rule-2     0

Total:2

#show ids ap-classification-rule Rogue-rule-1

IDS AP Classification Rule Profile "Rogue-rule-1"
-------------------------------------------------
Parameter                      Value
---------                      -----
SSID                           rule1-ssid1
Match SSIDs                    true
Min SNR value                  0
Max SNR value                  25
Discovered APs count           2
Check for Min Discovered APs   true
Classify To AP Type            suspected-rogue
Confidence level increase      10

#show ids ap-classification-rule Rogue-rule-2

IDS AP Classification Rule Profile "Rogue-rule-2"
-------------------------------------------------
Parameter                      Value
---------                      -----
SSID                           rule2-ssid1
SSID                           rule2-ssid2
Match SSIDs                    false
Min SNR value                  1
Max SNR value                  26
Discovered APs count           3
Check for Min Discovered APs   true
Classify To AP Type            neighbor
Confidence level increase      5
```

The CLI can be used to display the unauthorized device profile settings, as shown in the following output. In the output you can see many of the unauthorized device settings that were configured in the wizard for wips-policy-1:

```
#show ids unauthorized-device-profile wips-policy-1

IDS Unauthorized Device Profile "wips-policy-1"
-----------------------------------------------
Parameter                                          Value
---------                                          -----
Protect 802.11n High Throughput Devices            false
Protect 40MHz 802.11n High Throughput Devices      false
Detect Active 802.11n Greenfield Mode              true
Detect Adhoc Networks                              true
Protect from Adhoc Networks                        false
Protect from Adhoc Networks - Enhanced             false
Detect Adhoc Network Using Valid SSID              true
Adhoc Network Using Valid SSID Quiet Time          900 sec
Allow Well Known MAC                               N/A
Detect Devices with an Invalid MAC OUI             true
MAC OUI detection Quiet Time                       900 sec
Detect Misconfigured AP                            true
Protect Misconfigured AP                           true
Detect Bad WEP                                     true
Privacy                                            true
Require WPA                                        true
Valid 802.11g channel for policy enforcement       1
Valid 802.11g channel for policy enforcement       6
Valid 802.11g channel for policy enforcement       11
Valid 802.11a channel for policy enforcement       36
Valid 802.11a channel for policy enforcement       40
Valid 802.11a channel for policy enforcement       44
Valid 802.11a channel for policy enforcement       48
Valid 802.11a channel for policy enforcement       52
Valid 802.11a channel for policy enforcement       56
Valid 802.11a channel for policy enforcement       60
Valid 802.11a channel for policy enforcement       64
Valid 802.11a channel for policy enforcement       149
Valid 802.11a channel for policy enforcement       153
Valid 802.11a channel for policy enforcement       157
Valid 802.11a channel for policy enforcement       161
Valid and Protected SSIDs                          employee-legacy
Valid MAC OUIs                                     N/A
Rogue AP Classification                            true
Overlay Rogue AP Classification                    true
OUI-based Rogue AP Classification                  true
Propagated Wired MAC based Rogue AP Classification true
Rogue Containment                                  true
Suspected Rogue Containment                        true
```

Suspected Rogue Containment Confidence Level	90
Detect Station Association To Rogue AP	true
Detect Unencrypted Valid Clients	true
Unencrypted Valid Client Detection Quiet Time	900 sec
Detect Valid Client Misassociation	true
Detect Valid SSID Misuse	true
Protect SSID	true
Protect Valid Stations	true
Valid Wired MACs	N/A
Detect Windows Bridge	true
Protect Windows Bridge	false
Detect Wireless Bridge	true
Wireless Bridge detection Quiet Time	900 sec
Detect Wireless Hosted Network	true
Wireless Hosted Network Quiet Time	900 sec
Protect From Wireless Hosted Networks	false

Index

Symbols

| (pipe) operator, 42–45
~# (tilde-pound) prompt, AP configuration, 90–91

Numbers

8P8C (eight-position, eight-contact) console port, 40
802.1X authentication profile, preshared key authentication, 178
802.1X/EAP network, 113–115, 151–152
    and AAA (Authentication, Authorization, Accounting), 146
    AAA profile, 151, 162–163
    access control, 119–120
    authentication profile, 121–122
    authentication server, 151
    certificate, 190–191
    configuration completion, 129
    connection components, 147
    dynamic server selection, 156
    fall-through authentication, 155
    firewall policy, 161–162
    firewall role, 162
    internal database, 151–152
    LDAP server, 153–154
    named VLANs, 165–166
    profile, 161
    RADIUS server, 152–153
    role derivation, 208–210, 212–213
    server group, 154–155
    server-derivation rules, 156–161
    SSID profile, 163–164
    VAPs (virtual access points), 150
    virtual AP profile, 166–167
    VLAN pools, 164–165
    VLAN(s), 164
802.11 authentication and association, 260
802.11 frame, GRE tunnel, 26
802.11 radio profile, mesh network, 470–471
802.11 standard
    basics, 9
    BSA (basic service area), 9
    BSS (basic service set), 9
    BSSID (basic service set identifier), 9, 11–12
    common references, 13–14
    DS (distribution system), 9
    ESS (extended service set), 9–11
    ESSID (extended service set identifier), 9–10
    evolution, 2–3
    origin, 281
    SSID (service set identifier), 9
    STA (station), 9–10
    terminology, 9
    WDS (wireless distribution system), 9
802.11 wireless frame, address fields, 499
802.11g band, 13
802.3
    Ethernet frame, 24
    GRE tunnel, 26
802.3 Ethernet frame, vs. 802.11 frame, 24

INDEX

A

AAA (Authentication, Authorization, Accounting) framework, 145–148
AAA profile
    802.1X/EAP authentication, 151, 162–163
    captive portal authentication, 176, 270
    MAC authentication, 171–172
    overview, 122–124
    preshared key authentication, 179
access control, 119–120, 144
access ports, configuring, 79–80
ACI (adjacent channel interference), 379, 451
ACLs (access control lists), 49, 145, 220–221. *See also* global-sacl (Global Session ACL); role session ACL
ACMA (Australian Communications and Media Authority), 7
Activate. *See* Aruba Activate service
Active Devices chart, 448–449
Active Devices Table chart, 449–450
Active Devices Trend chart, 450
active/active, redundancy design, 296–297
active/standby, redundancy design, 295
AD (Active Directory), 145
admin, setting, 67
ADP (Aruba Discovery Protocol), ArubaOS, 22–23
advanced customer, 108
AES encryption, 163–164, 181
air monitors, packet capture from, 426
airtime fairness, ARM 2.0, 374–375
Alerts logging level, 400
aliases, 224–227
Always operation mode, 365
AM (Air Monitor) function, 367–369
any destination alias, firewall policy structure, 222
AP (access point)
    CLI interface, 89–90
    console CLI, 90
    provisioning, 89, 96–98
AP boot process, 20, 29–32
AP configuration
    ~# (tilde-pound) prompt, 90–91
    apboot>, 91–96
    console CLI, 90
    overview, 89–90
AP Fast Failover
    HA (High Availability), 313
    redundancy design, 299–301
AP forwarding modes
    ArubaOS, 32–38
    bridge mode, 34–35
    decrypt-tunnel, 35–37
    GRE/tunnel, 33–34
    overview, 32–33
    split-tunnel, 37–38
    table, 38
AP group, 129, 132–133, 274
AP image preload, 324–332
ap packet-capture command, network monitoring, 424–425
AP provisioning, mesh network, 477–478
AP redundancy, VRRP (virtual router redundancy protocol), 297–298
AP system profile, 130–132
AP traffic inspection, detection methods, 499–500
AP types, 334–336
AP using VRRP, redundancy design, 297–298
AP wired port profile, mesh network, 472–474
AP wizard, 48
AP/AM capture, network monitoring, 423
AP/AM packet capture, disabling, 426–427
apboot>, AP configuration, 91–96
ap-debug category of logging level, 402
AppRF
    deep packet inspection, 244–246
    overview, 243–244
    WebCC (Web Content Classification), 246–251
APs (access points), 2. *See also* Client Match; thin AP; VAPs (virtual access points)
    adding to Activate, 340–341
    adding to folders, 341–343
    AM (Air Monitor) function, 367–369
    ARM (adaptive radio management), 375
    Aruba Activate service, 336–343
    backup LMS-IP, 298
    controller-based, 13–14
    converting, 347–348
    deploying, 7–8
    forwarding modes with operation modes, 366–367
    guests and employees, 111
    master controller, 19
    mesh AP, 370
    Secure Jack, 370–371
    SM (spectrum monitor), 369–370
ARC4 encryption algorithm, 180
ARM (adaptive radio management). *See also* Client Match
    ACI (adjacent channel interference), 379
    AP channel and power selection, 379–380

AP support, 375
band steering/band balancing, 396
CCI (co-channel interference mitigation), 379
Client Match, 375–376
client steering, 396
data collection, 396
DFS (dynamic frequency selection) channels, 380
disable-scanning, 240
history, 373–376
IOS steer function, 397
load balancing, 381, 396
MU-MIMO function, 397
Profile Advanced menu, 377
profile settings, 394–397
scanning process, 376–379
scanning RF channels, 376
Sticky Clients, 381
ARM 2.0
airtime fairness, 374–375
Band Steering, 374
CCI (co-channel interference mitigation), 374
Spectrum Load Balancing, 374
ARM 3.0, 375
ARP cache poisoning (wired), WIP Wizard, 497–498
Aruba Activate service
adding APs, 340–341
assigning APs to folders, 341–343
converting APs, 347–348
features, 336–339
folder activation, 339–340
ZTP (zero-touch provisioning), 336–337
Aruba Mobility Controller, 7
Aruba Networks, founding, 3–4
ArubaOS. *See also* OS (operating system)
ADP (Aruba Discovery Protocol), 22–23
AP boot process, 20
AP forwarding modes, 32–38
architecture, 17–18
configuration download, 23
configuring, 109
DHCP options 43 and 60, 22
DNS lookup, 23
GRE (Generic Routing Encapsulation) tunnel, 24–27
layer 2 addressing, 24
local controller, 27–29
master controller, 18–19
multi-controller AP boot process, 29–32
OS update, 23
static, 21–22

ArubaOS channels, 8
attributes, 204
AUDITTRAIL-HISTORY.log, 53
authentication. *See also* machine authentication; WPA2 authentication
explained, 144
layer 2 vs. layer 3, 148–149
process, 146–148
supplicant, 146
authentication methods, 149
authentication profile, 120–122
authentication server
802.1X/EAP authentication, 151
CLI (command line interface), 265
authentication server and server group, 115–119
authenticator, 147
autonomous AP, 2
Auto-RRA, 373

B

backup LMS-IP, 298–299. *See also* LMS-IP (local management switch IP address)
Backup operation mode, 365–366
band steering/band balancing
ARM (adaptive radio management), 396
ARM 2.0, 374
Client Match, 386–387
Sticky Clients, 386–387
basic customer, 108
b/g band, 13
BKUP-LMS-IP parameter, 130
blacklisting, 239
boot command, 95–96
boot partition, 52
Bridge identification, detection methods, 498
Bridge mode, 34–35, 38, 359–361
BSA (basic service area), 9
BSS (basic service set), 9
BSSID (basic service set identifier), 9, 11–12
BYOD (bring your own device), 145–146, 158
bypass, enabling, 83

C

CA (certificate authority), 182
CAP (campus AP)
Auto Cert Provisioning, 346
converting IAPs to, 347–348
CPsec (control plane security), 38, 344–346

explained, 33–34
features, 334
overview, 343–344
PAPI (Proprietary Access Protocol Interface), 344
virtual controller, 347–348
captive portal authentication
    802.11 authentication and association, 260
    AAA profile, 176, 270
    AP group, 274
    certificate, 189–190
    ClearPass Guest, 276–280
    CNA (captive network assistant), 261
    components, 174–175
    firewall policy, 175
    firewall role, 175
    guest login window, 267
    guest-provisioning account, 274–275
    guest-provisioning page, 275–276
    initial role, 269–270
    layer 3, 148
    logon page, 264
    master/local controller, 266
    overview, 259–260
    page, 274
    post logon role, 267
    process, 260–264
    profile, 267–269
    profile hierarchy, 264–265
    profile white list, 279–280
    role derivation, 216–218
    server and server group, 264–266
    SSID profile, 176, 270–271
    VAP profile, 176, 273–274
    VLAN and DHCP server, 271–273
    VLAN(s), 176
capture
    destinations, 416–417
    to interface, 417
    to IP address, 417–418
    to local file system, 418–420
capture destinations, packet analysis, 417–420
capture procedures, network monitoring, 423–431
capturing user data, 422
CCI (co-channel interference mitigation), ARM 2.0, 374
centralized licensing, 314–316. *See also* licenses
centralized upgrade, 316–324
certificates. *See* IKE certificates
Channel Metrics chart, 451–452
Channel Metrics Trend chart, 452–453

channel ranges, spectrum analysis, 440
channel scanning, WIP (wireless intrusion prevention), 484–486
Channel Summary Table chart, 453
Channel Utilization Trend chart, 453–454
channels, ArubaOS, 8
charts for spectrum analyzer
    Active Devices, 448–449
    Active Devices Table, 449–450
    Active Devices Trend, 450
    Channel Metrics, 451–452
    Channel Metrics Trend, 452–453
    Channel Summary Table, 453
    Channel Utilization Trend, 453–454
    Device Duty Cycle, 454–455
    Devices vs Channel, 455–456
    FFT Duty Cycle, 445–446
    Interference Power, 455–457
    Quality Spectrogram, 447–448
    Real-Time FFT (Fast Fourier Transform), 444–445
    resizing, 443
    Swept Spectrogram, 446–447
ClearPass Guest, captive portal authentication, 276–280
CLI (command line interface). *See also* commands
    802.1X/EAP authentication profile, 178
    802.11a radio profile, 471
    AAA profile, 171, 176, 179, 270
    AES encryption, 164
    AP Fast Failover, 301
    AP group, 274
    AP image preload, 325–332
    ap packet-capture, 424–425
    AP wired port profile, 474
    ARM profile settings, 394–396
    ARM scanning, 377–378
    authentication server, 152–154, 265
    Bridge mode, 360
    campus AP and CPsec, 346
    captive portal profile, 269
    capture to destinations, 416–420
    centralized licensing, 314–316
    centralized upgrade, 317, 320–324
    certificate-authenticated RAP, 356
    channel scanning, 486
    channels for ArubaOS, 8
    ClearPass Guest, 277–280
    Client Match data collection, 383–385
    client state synchronization, 302
    controller configuration, 109

controlpath, 414
CPsec (control plane security), 344
datapath, 415–416
destination aliases, 225–227
DHCP leases, 173
guest-provisioning page, 274–276
Hybrid mode (spectrum analysis), 436–437
IDS, 504–507
IKE certificates, 286–287
IKE preshared keys, 284–285
initial role, 199–200, 269
invert option, 227
listing servers, 154
LMS-IP, 299
logging configuration, 401, 404–406
logging levels, 400
MAC address match methods, 499
master redundancy configuration, 306–309
master redundancy verification, 309–312
mesh cluster profile, 468–469
mesh status, 479–481
Omnipeek, 428
packet capture from air monitors, 426
packet-capture, 413, 420–421
port monitoring, 412
RADIUS server, 152–153
RAP VPN server configuration, 350
recovery profile, 475–477
regulatory domain, 7
role conditions, 202
server groups, 155, 158
server rules, 206
set role command, 157
spectrum analysis, 457
spectrum local override, 435
Split-Tunnel mode, 363–364
SSID profile, 164, 171, 176, 179, 270
syslog server configuration, 407–410
untrusting wired ports, 197–198
user accounts, 169–170
user roles for firewall policies, 251–255
VAP profile, 166–167, 174, 176, 179, 273–274
VLAN and DHCP server, 271–273
VLAN(s), 179
VLANs, 176
VPN server configuration, 350
VRRP (virtual router redundancy protocol), 293–295
VSAs (vendor specific attributes), 158–161
WebCC (Web Content Classification), 246–248
WIP policy, 489
Wireshark, 429
WPA2 authentication, 164
CLI command environment, 42
CLI configuration
　networking, 77
　VRRP (virtual router redundancy protocol), 293–295
CLI setup wizard, initial setup, 63–68
Client Match. *See also* APs (access points); ARM (adaptive radio management)
　ARM (adaptive radio management), 375–376
　band steering/band balancing, 386–387
　data collection, 382–385
　load balancing, 387–390
　move client process, 390–392
　overview, 380–381
　process overview, 393–394
　Sticky Clients, 385–386
　VBR (virtual beacon report), 382–385
client state synchronization, 302–303
client steering, ARM (adaptive radio management), 396
clients
　intrusion detection, 493–494
　protection policy, 495
CNA (captive network assistant), 261
commands, viewing and hiding, 57–58. *See also* CLI (command line interface)
community string, 83
configuration wizards, 47–48, 109
console CLI, AP configuration, 90
console connection, 62
console port, 40–41
control traffic, 34
controller destination alias, 223
controller IP
　networking, 82
　WebUI configuration, 87
Controller setup window, 68
Controller WebUI
　AP installation, 96–98
　AP Wizard, 98–102
controller6 destination alias, firewall policy structure, 223
controllers. *See also* inter-controller heartbeat; Local controller; Master controller
　AP boot process, 29–32
　Aruba Mobility Controller, 7
　configuring settings, 18

CPBoot, 55–56
deployment mode, 69
failover, 300
firewall, 49
flash NVRAM, 50–51
flash partition, 53–55
licenses, 69
operating hardware, 50–55
overview, 48–49
partition structure, 50–51
resetting to factory defaults, 58–59
RFProtect WIPS, 50
RoW (Rest of World) controllers, 7
saving changes, 56–57
system partitions, 51–53
viewing and hiding commands, 57–58
VPN (virtual private network) server, 49–50
WebUI-AP installation, 96–98
WebUI-AP Wizard, 98–102
controlpath option, packet analysis, 414
country codes, listing, 66
CPBoot, 55–56
CPsec (control plane security). *See also* security basics
AP whitelist, 345
campus AP, 344–346
explained, 34
networking, 77–78
WebUI configuration, 85
Critical logging level, 400
crossover cable, 40–41
CSR (certificate signing request), 181–186
Ctrl+P, 67
customers, 108
CWNA (Certified Wireless Network Administrator), 1
CWNP (Certified Wireless Network Professional), 1, 6

D

data collection, ARM (adaptive radio management), 396
data integrity, 144
database synchronize command, 312
datapath option, packet analysis, 414–415
DB-9 to RJ-45 adapter, 41
deauth-only (wireless), WIP Wizard, 496–497
Debugging logging level, 400
decrypt-tunnel, 35–38, 364
deep packet inspection, 244–246
default gateway, 80, 87
default role, 207

default.bak, 54
default.cfg file, 54
destination aliases, 224–227
detection methods
AP traffic inspection, 499–500
Bridge identification, 498
layer 2, 500–502
layer 3, 502–503
MAC address match methods, 499
ToDS/From DS, 498
Device Duty Cycle chart, 454–455
Devices vs. Channel chart, 455–456
DHCP leases, displaying, 173
DHCP options 43 and 60, 22, 30
DHCP server
configuring, 86–87
networking, 81–82
WebUI configuration, 86–87
digital certificates
802.1X/EAP, 190–191
applying, 188–189
captive portal, 189–190
CSR (certificate signing request), 183–186
obtaining, 182–183
overview, 181–182
self-signed certificate, 186–188
WebUI management, 188–189
disabling spanning-tree, networking, 82
disabling VLAN 1
networking, 84
WebUI configuration, 87
DNS lookup, ArubaOS, 23
DS (distribution system), 9
DSAs (device-specific attributes), 197
DSCP (Differentiated Services Code Point), 242
DSSS (direct sequence spread spectrum), 2, 12
dynamic server selection, 802.1X/EAP authentication, 156

E

EAP termination, 151–152
Emergencies logging level, 400
enabling bypass, networking, 83
encrypting wireless transmissions, 36
encryption
explained, 144
WEP (Wired Equivalent Privacy), 180
WPA2/AES, 181
WPA/TKIP, 180

environment variables, 89
Errors logging level, 400
ESI (External Services Interface), role derivation, 211–212
ESS (extended service set), 9–11
ESSID (extended service set identifier), 9–10
Ethernet cable, 41
extended actions
    blacklist, 239
    classify media, 239–240
    disable-scanning, 240
    dot1p-priority, 240
    firewall policy structure, 239–242
    log, 240
    mirror, 240–241
    position, 241
    queue, 241
    send-deny-response, 241
    time-range, 241–242
    tos, 242

F

factory certificate, 287–288
factory defaults, resetting controller, 58–59
failover controller, 300
fall-through authentication, 155
fault tolerance, 289–295. *See also* networking
FCC (Federal Communications Commission), 7
FFT Duty Cycle chart, 445–446
FHSS (frequency hopping spread spectrum), 2, 12
fieldCerts directory, 54
filter-id IETF attribute, 158–159
firewall, 49
firewall actions
    deny, 237
    dst-nat, 237
    dual-nat, 238
    forwarding, 237
    permit, 238
    port forwarding, 237
    redirect, 238
    route, 238–239
    src-nat, 237–238
firewall mirroring
    network monitoring, 421–422
    packet capture, 431–432
firewall policy
    802.1X/EAP authentication, 161–162
    captive portal authentication, 175
    creating, 251
    MAC authentication, 171
    overview, 219–220
    preshared key authentication, 178
firewall policy structure. *See also* PEF (Policy Enforcement Firewall)
    vs. ACLs, 220–221
    actions, 236–239
    any destination alias, 222
    controller destination alias, 223
    controller6 destination alias, 223
    destination aliases, 224–227
    extended actions, 239–242
    firewall service, 228–233
    global-sacl (Global Session ACL), 255–256
    implicit deny all, 242–244
    invert option, 227–228
    ipv6-reserved-range destination alias, 223–224
    localip destination alias, 224
    mswitch destination alias, 223
    overview, 221
    role session ACL, 256–257
    service aliases, 235–236
    services, 233–235
    source, destination, aliases, 222–224
    user destination alias, 222–223
    user roles, 251–257
    vrrp_ip destination alias, 224
firewall role
    802.1X/EAP authentication, 162
    captive portal authentication, 175
    MAC authentication, 171
    preshared key authentication, 178
firewall service, 228–233
flash NVRAM, 50–51
flash partition, 50–51, 53–55
flashbackup.tar.gz, 54
folders
    activating, 339–340
    adding APs, 341–343
forwarding modes, 33, 366–367
frequency ranges, spectrum analysis, 440
FTP (file transfer protocol), 23

G

gateway, default, 80, 87
Gbps (gigabits per second), 3
global-sacl (Global Session ACL), 255–256. *See also* ACLs (access control lists)

INDEX

GMT (Greenwich Mean Time), 67
GRE (Generic Routing Encapsulation) tunnel, 24–27, 33–34, 38
guest login window, captive portal authentication, 267
guest-provisioning account, captive portal authentication, 274–275
guest-provisioning page, captive portal authentication, 275–276

H

HA (High Availability), 300, 313
help command, 92
hot standby, 305
Hotel mode operation mode, 366
HR-DSSS (High-Rate DSSS), 2, 12
HT (high throughput), 3, 13

I

IAP (Instant APs), converting to campus APs, 334–335, 347–348
IDS commands, WIP (wireless intrusion prevention), 504–507
IEEE (Institute of Electrical and Electronics Engineers), 2
IEEE 802.11
    basics, 9
    BSA (basic service area), 9
    BSS (basic service set), 9
    BSSID (basic service set identifier), 9, 11–12
    common references, 13–14
    DS (distribution system), 9
    ESS (extended service set), 9–11
    ESSID (extended service set identifier), 9–10
    evolution, 2–3
    origin, 281
    SSID (service set identifier), 9
    STA (station), 9–10
    terminology, 9
    WDS (wireless distribution system), 9
IEEE standards, optional elements, 5
IETF (Internet Engineering Task Force), 205
IETF attribute filter-id, 158–159
IKE certificates, 285–286
IKE preshared keys, 283–285. *See also* PSK (preshared key) authentication
implicit deny all, firewall policy structure, 242–244
Informational logging level, 400
infrastructure
    detection mechanism, 492–493
    protection policy, 495
    WIP Wizard, 490
initial role
    assigning, 175
    captive portal authentication, 269–270
    role derivation, 199–201
initial setup
    CLI setup wizard, 63–68
    menu, 62
    objectives, 62–63
    WebUI setup wizard, 68–74
inter-controller heartbeat, 300. *See also* controllers
Interference Power chart, 455–457
intermediate customer, 108
internal server group, 170
intrusion detection, , 490–494
invert option, firewall policy structure, 227–228
IOS steer function, ARM (adaptive radio management), 397
IP addresses
    assigning, 86
    capture to, 417–418
    controllers, 87
    layer 2 authentication, 148–149
    syslog server, 407
    WebUI configuration, 86
ipconfig, 90–91
ipv6-reserved-range destination alias, firewall policy structure, 223–224
ISM (Industrial Scientific and Medical) frequency band, 2
ISO 3166 standard, 7

K

keywords, managing with pipe (|) operator, 42–43

L

layer 2
    addressing, 24
    detection methods, 500–502
    vs. layer 3 authentication, 148–149
    and layer 3 devices, 66
layer 3
    authentication, 210–211
    detection methods, 502–503
LDAP (Lightweight Directory Access Protocol) server, 802.1X/EAP authentication, 153–154
licenses. *See also* centralized licensing
    adding, 69–70, 75–77

displaying, 75
installing, 84, 89
saving and rebooting, 84, 89
license.txt file, 54
licensing, activation key, 74–75
LMS-IP (local management switch IP address), 130, 299–300, 313. *See also* backup LMS-IP
load balancing
    ARM (adaptive radio management), 381, 396
    Client Match, 387–390
    Sticky Clients, 387–390
Local controller. *See also* controllers; master controller
    ArubaOS, 27–29
    explained, 18
    factory certificate, 287–288
    network expansion, 324–332
    settings, 288–289
local file system, capture to, 418–420
localip destination alias, firewall policy structure, 224
logging. *See also* network monitoring
    configuration, 401–406
    levels, 400–401, 406
    overview, 399–401
    syslog server configuration, 407–410
logging level command, 402, 407
logon role, role derivation, 198–199
logs.tar archive, 54

M

MAC (media access control) sublayer, 2
MAC addresses
    802.11 Ethernet frame, 24
    802.3 Ethernet frame, 24
    assigning, 11
    match methods, 499
MAC authentication
    AAA profile, 171–172
    firewall policy, 171
    firewall role, 171
    internal database, 168–170
    internal server group, 170
    profile, 170–171
    role derivation, 207–208
    SSID profile, 172
    VAP (virtual access point), 167–168
    VAP profile, 174
    VLANs, 172–173
machine authentication, 209. *See also* authentication
master controller. *See also* controllers; local controller
    AP updates, 20–21
    and APs, 18–19
    configuration, 19
    configuring, 64
    configuring APs, 19
    discovery by AP, 21
    factory certificate, 287
    global settings, 19
    local and global settings, 19
    redundancy design, 304–312
    regulatory domain, 18–19
    WebUI, 21
master/local communications
    IKE certificates, 285–286
    IKE preshared keys, 283–285
    overview, 282–283
master/local controller, captive portal authentication, 266
Mbps (megabits per second), 2
mesh AP, 370. *See also* wireless mesh
mesh AP provisioning, 477–478
mesh cluster profile, 465–469
mesh clusters, 462–465, 467
Mesh High-Throughput SSID profile, 472
mesh link, 464
mesh network. *See also* wireless mesh
    802.11 radio profile, 470–471
    AP provisioning, 477–478
    AP wired port profile, 472–474
    configuring, 465–466
    MPP (mesh point portal), 475
    nodes, 461–462
    recovery profile, 474–477
    VHT (very high throughput), 472
    wired AP profile, 474
    wired backhaul, 473
    WLAN profile, 469–470
mesh portals, 462
mesh radio, 462
Mesh Radio profile, 469
mesh status, 478–481
mesh topology, 478–479
MIMO (multiple-input multiple-output), 3
mini USB console connection, 41
monitoring. *See* network monitoring
move client process, Client Match, 390–392
MP (mesh point), 463–464
MPP (mesh point portal), 460–463, 475
MSSID (Mesh SSID), 460, 463, 465–466
mswitch destination alias, firewall policy structure, 223

multi-controller AP boot process, ArubaOS, 29–32
MU-MIMO (multi-user MIMO) function, 3, 397

N

N:1 active/standby, redundancy design, 296
NAC (network access control), 144–145
NAD (network access device), 147
named VLANs, 165–166
netservice, defined, 228
network category of logging level, 402
network expansion, 324–332. *See also* fault tolerance
    AP image preload, 324–332
    centralized licensing, 314–316
    centralized upgrade, 316–324
    HA (High Availability), 300
    inter-controller heartbeat, 300
    Local controller, 324–332
    Master/Local communications, 282–289
network monitoring. *See also* logging; SM (spectrum monitor)
    ap packet-capture command, 424–425
    AP/AM capture, 423
    capture procedures, 423–431
    firewall mirroring, 421–422
    Omnipeek configuration, 428–429
Network Summary screen, 96
networking. *See also* fault tolerance; packet analysis
    access ports, 79–80
    CLI configuration, 77
    controller IP, 82
    CPSec, 77–78
    default gateway, 80
    DHCP server, 81–82
    disabling spanning-tree, 82
    disabling VLAN 1, 84
    enabling bypass, 83
    licenses, saving, and rebooting, 84
    NTP (Network Time Protocol), 83
    SNMP (Simple Network Management Protocol), 83
    syslog, 84
    time zone, 83
    trunk port, 79
    VLANs, 78
    Wireshark configuration, 429–431
networks, multicontrollers, 166
no shutdown command, 307–308
nodes, mesh network, 461–462
noise floor indicator, spectrum analysis, 457

Notifications logging level, 400
NPS (Network Policy Server), 147
NTP (Network Time Protocol)
    networking, 83
    WebUI configuration, 87–88
NV (non-volatile) RAM, 50–51

O

OFDM (orthogonal frequency division multiplexing), 2, 12–13
Omnipeek, configuring, 428–429
OpenSSL command, private key and self-signed certificate, 187–188
operation modes, forwarding modes with, 366–367
original.cfg, 54
OS (operating system), upgrading via USB flash drive, 52. *See also* ArubaOS
OS Image Management menu, 52–53
OS update, ArubaOS, 23
OSI model, 2
OSPF (open shortest path first), 19
oversubscription, 303–304

P

packet analysis. *See also* networking
    capture destinations, 417–420
    controlpath option, 414
    datapath option, 414–415
    destination, 416–421
    overview, 411
    packet-capture command, 413
    packet-capture-defaults command, 420–421
    port monitoring, 411–412
packet capture
    from air monitors, 426
    disabling AP/AM, 426–427
    firewall mirroring, 431–432
    packet-capture command, 431–432
    port monitoring, 431
    WebUI, 427–428
packet-capture command
    destination, 416–420
    packet analysis, 413
    packet capture, 431–432
packet-capture-defaults command, packet analysis, 420–421
PAPI (Proprietary Access Protocol Interface), 22–23, 34
    campus AP, 344
partition structure, 50–51

passwords, enabling, 67
PEF (Policy Enforcement Firewall), 18, 193. *See also*
firewall policy structure
  ACLs (access control lists), 220–221
  overview, 219
PEF-NG (Policy Enforcement Firewall Next Generation), 49
Persistent operation mode, 366
PHY (physical) technology, 12, 197
ping, 90
pipe (|) operator, 42–45
PoE (Power over Ethernet) settings, 18
port monitoring
  packet analysis, 411–412
  packet capture, 431
post logon role, captive portal authentication, 267
private certificates, 182
profile-hierarchy command, 140–142
profiles
  802.1X/EAP authentication, 161
  AAA (Authentication, Authorization, Accounting), 122–124
  access control, 119–120
  AP group, 132–133
  AP system, 130–132
  authentication, 120–122
  authentication server, 115–119
  captive portal authentication, 267–269
  cloning, 138–140
  customers, 108
  hierarchy, 110–111
  MAC authentication, 170–171
  managing, 136–142
  server group, 115–119
  show references command, 137–138
  SSID (service set identifier), 124–127
  virtual AP, 127–129
  virtual APs, 110–115
  VLAN, 127
  WebUI configuration menus, 133–136
provision-ap controller CLI command, 102–105
provisioning menu, 96–98
PSK (preshared key) authentication, 179, 214. *See also*
IKE preshared keys
  802.1X authentication profile, 178
  AAA profile, 179
  components, 177
  firewall policy, 178
  firewall role, 178
  SSID profile, 179
  VAP profile, 179
  VLAN(s), 179
public certificates, 181–182

Q

Quality Spectrogram chart, 447–448

R

radio terminology, 12–14
RADIUS (Remote Authentication Dial-In User Services), 145
RADIUS server, 117, 152–153
RAP (remote RAP)
  advantage, 348
  AP group, 350
  captive portal, 148
  certificate-authenticated, 355–356
  configuring, 350–351
  configuring using Activate, 337–338
  features, 334
  GRE/Tunnel, 33–34
  manual provisioning, 351–352
  overview, 348–349
  user name authenticated, 352–354
  VPN server configuration, 349–350
  ZTP (zero-touch provisioning), 356
RBAC (role-based access control), 144–145, 193
RBW (resolution bandwidth), spectrum analysis, 439
Real-Time FFT (Fast Fourier Transform) chart, 444–445
recovery profile, mesh network, 474–477
redundancy design
  active/active, 296–297
  active/standby, 295
  AP Fast Failover, 299–301
  AP using VRRP, 297–298
  backup LMS-IP, 298–299
  client state synchronization, 302–303
  comparison, 312–313
  Master controller, 304–312
  N:1 active/standby, 296
  oversubscription, 303–304
regulatory domain, 7–8, 18–19
remote AP, 38
reset command, 95
RF (radio frequency), 2
RF channels, scanning, 376
RFProtect WIPS, 18, 50
RJ-45 console port, 40

rogue AP, transmission from, 501–503
rogue classification, WIP Wizard, 487–489
role assignment, 194–196
role conditions, 3
role derivation
    802.1X/EAP authentication, 208–210, 212–213
    AAA profile and initial role, 200
    AAA profile and user role, 204
    captive portal authentication, 216–218
    default role, 207
    defined, 193
    DSAs (device-specific attributes), 197
    ESI (External Services Interface), 211–212
    initial connection, 196
    initial role, 199–201
    layer 2 authentication, 198, 210
    layer 3 authentication, 210–211
    logon role, 198–199
    MAC authentication, 207–208
    machine authentication, 209
    physical connection, 196–198
    with server authentication, 204–207
    server authentication, 209–210
    server rules, 206
    server-assigned-role, 205–206
    SSID base role, 214
    user rules, 201–204
    vendor-specific attribute-assigned role, 205
    VLAN derivation, 214–216
    WPA2 passphrase role, 214–216
role session ACL, 256–257. *See also* ACLs (access control lists)
role/VLAN derivation flowchart, 195–196
rollover cable, 41
root certificate store, 182
RoW (Rest of World) controllers, 7, 66
RSTP (Rapid Spanning Tree Protocol), 82

S

Secure Jack, 370–371. *See also* wired ports
security basics, 144–145. *See also* CPsec (control plane security)
security category of logging level, 402–403
security summary dashboard, WIP (wireless intrusion prevention), 503–504
self-signed certificates, 186–188
server and server group, captive portal authentication, 264–266
server authentication, 204–207, 209–210

server groups
    802.1X/EAP authentication, 154–155
    creating, 155
    defined, 117
    listing, 158
server rules, creating, 206
server-assigned-role, 205–206
server-derivation rules, 156–161
servers, listing, 154
service, defined, 228
service alias
    creating, 235–236
    defined, 228
service aliases, firewall policy structure, 235–236
session ACL, 49
set role command, 157
show database synchronize command, 308, 311
show rights command, 251
SM (spectrum monitor). *See also* network monitoring
    chart selection, 442
    configuring, 433
    features, 432–433
    overview, 369–370
    resizing charts, 443
    selecting, 442
    switching chart modes, 443
    WebUI, 437–439
SNMP (Simple Network Management Protocol)
    networking, 83
    WebUI configuration, 88
SNR (signal-to-noise ratio), spectrum analysis, 457
spanning tree, 68, 82
spectrum analysis
    ACI (adjacent channel interference), 451
    Active Devices chart, 448–449
    Active Devices Table, 449–450
    Active Devices Trend chart, 449–450
    AP group, 433–434
    Channel Metrics chart, 451–452
    Channel Metrics Trend chart, 452–453
    channel ranges, 440
    Channel Summary Table, 453
    Channel Utilization Trend chart, 453–454
    chart types, 441–443
    CLI command, 457
    configuring, 433
    detected devices, 440–441
    Device Duty Cycle Chart, 454–455
    Devices vs. Channel chart, 455–456

FFT Duty Cycle, 445–446
frequency ranges, 440
hybrid mode, 436–437
Interference Power chart, 455–457
local override, 434–435
noise floor indicator, 457
Quality Spectrogram, 447–448
RBW (resolution bandwidth), 439
Real-Time FFT (Fast Fourier Transform), 444–445
RF options, 439–440
SNR (signal-to-noise ratio), 457
Swept Spectrogram, 446–447
view window, 439
Spectrum Load Balancing, ARM 2.0, 374
split-tunnel, 37–38, 361–364
SSH and telnet, 42
SSID (service set identifier), 9
SSID base role, 214
SSID profile
    802.1X/EAP authentication, 163–164
    captive portal authentication, 176, 270–271
    MAC authentication, 172
    overview, 124–127
    preshared key authentication, 179
SSL (Secure Sockets Layer) protocol, 186
STA (station), 9–10
Standard operation mode, 365
static, ArubaOS, 21–22
Sticky Clients
    ARM (adaptive radio management), 381
    band steering/band balancing, 386–387
    Client Match, 385–386
    load balancing, 387–390
    overview, 385–386
supplicant, 146–147
Swept Spectrogram chart, 446–447
switch role, setting, 65–66
switches, 66
syslog
    networking, 84
    WebUI configuration, 88
syslog server
    configuring, 407–410
    Facility() parameter, 409
    IP addresses, 407
    parameters, 407–409
    Severity() parameter, 408
system category of logging level, 403–404
system partitions, 51–53

T

TAC (Technical Assistance Center), 55
tarpitting (wireless), WIP Wizard, 497
telnet and SSH, 42
terminal access, 39–40
terminal software, configuring, 41
thin AP, 14–15. *See also* APs (access points)
tilde-pound (~#) prompt, 90–91
time zone
    networking, 83
    WebUI configuration, 87–88
TKIP (Temporal Key Integrity Protocol), 180
TLS (Transport Layer Security) protocol, 186
ToDS/From DS, detection methods, 498
tpm directory, 54
trunk port, configuring, 79
Tunnel mode, 357–359

U

UAP (Unified AP), 336
Upgrade, 316–324
USB console connection, 41
user accounts, listing, 169–170
user category of logging level, 404
user data, capturing, 422
user destination alias, firewall policy structure, 222–223
user identification, 115–119
user interface
    CLI command environment, 42
    console port, 40–41
    pipe (|) operator, 42–45
    SSH and telnet, 42
    terminal access, 39–40
    WebUI (web user interface), 45–47
    wizards, 47–48
user roles
    defined, 194
    firewall policy structure, 251–257
user rule derivation, 204
user rules, role derivation, 201–204
user-debug category of logging level, 404
UTC (Coordinated Universal Time), 67

V

VAP (virtual access point), transmission from, 500
VAP data forwarding modes
    Bridge, 359–361

Decrypt-Tunnel, 364
overview, 356–357
Split-Tunnel, 361–364
Tunnel, 357–359
VAP profile
    captive portal authentication, 176, 273–274
    explained, 164
    MAC authentication, 174
    overview, 127–129
    preshared key authentication, 179
VAP remote-AP operation modes
    Always, 365
    Backup, 365–366
    Hotel mode, 366
    overview, 364–365
    Persistent, 366
    Standard, 365
VAPs (virtual access points), 111–115, 150. *See also* APs (access points)
VBR (virtual beacon report), Client Match, 382–385
vendor-specific attribute-assigned role, 205
VHT (very high throughput), 13, 472
VIP (virtual IP), VRRP, 290
virtual AP, 32–33, 35
virtual controller, campus AP, 347–348
VLAN 1, disabling, 84, 87
VLAN and DHCP server, captive portal authentication, 271–273
VLAN derivation, role derivation, 214–216
VLAN derivation flowchart, 195, 213, 215, 217
VLAN pools, explained, 164–165
VLAN(s)
    802.1X/EAP authentication, 164
    captive portal authentication, 176
    creating and configuring, 78, 85
    features, 127
    MAC authentication, 172–173
    networking, 78
    preshared key authentication, 179
    WebUI configuration, 85
VPN (virtual private network) server, 49–50
VPN layer 3 authentication, 148
VRRP (virtual router redundancy protocol)
    AP redundancy, 297–298
    vs. backup LMS-IP, 298
    CLI configuration, 293–295
    overview, 289–290
    problems, 299–300
    WebUI configuration, 290–293

vrrp_ip destination alias, firewall policy structure, 224
VSA (vendor specific attribute), 157–161

W

Warnings logging level, 400
WDS (wireless distribution system), 9
WebCC (Web Content Classification), 246–251
websites
    CWNP (Certified Wireless Network Professional), 6
    Wi-Fi Alliance, 4–5
WebUI (web user interface)
    All Profiles menu, 134–135
    AP Configuration menu, 136
    Authentication menu, 135–136
    configuration, 109, 133–136
    controller IP, 87
    CPsec (control plane security), 85
    default gateway, 87
    DHCP server, 86–87
    disabling VLAN 1, 87
    IP addresses, 86
    licenses, saving, and rebooting, 89
    management certificate, 188–189
    menu hierarchy, 45–47
    NTP (Network Time Protocol), 87–88
    overview, 84–85
    packet capture, 427–428
    settings pausing RAM scanning, 378
    SNMP (Simple Network Management Protocol), 88
    static method, 21
    syslog, 88
    time zone, 87–88
    VLANs, 85
    VRRP (virtual router redundancy protocol), 290–293
WebUI setup wizard, 68–74
WEP (Wired Equivalent Privacy), 180
Wi-Fi Alliance, 4–6
Wi-Fi CERTIFIED program, 5–6
Wi-Fi Interoperability Certificate, 4–5
WIP (wireless intrusion prevention)
    AP classification, 486
    channel scanning, 484–486
    client classification, 487
    containment warning, 495–496
    detection methods, 498–503

device classification, 486–487
IDS commands, 504–507
overview, 483–484
regulatory domain channels, 485
Scan Mode, 485
security summary dashboard, 503–504
wired methods, 495
WIP policy, WIP Wizard, 489
WIP Wizard
ARP cache poisoning (wired), 497–498
deauth-only (wireless), 496–497
infrastructure, 490
intrusion detection, 490–494
Protection menu, 494–496
rogue classification, 487–489
tarpitting (wireless), 497
WIP policy, 489
WIPS (wireless intrusion prevention system), 18
wired ports. *See also* Secure Jack
making untrusted, 197–198
securing, 194
wireless controllers, 66
wireless mesh. *See also* mesh network
architecture, 460
ARM profile, 472
VAP profile, 470
wireless switch, 3–4, 66
wireless transmissions, encrypting, 36
Wireshark, configuring, 429–431
Wizards, 47–48, 109
WLAN (wireless local area network), 3–4
WLAN access, providing, 259
WLAN profile, mesh network, 469–470
WPA2 authentication, 163. *See also* authentication
WPA2 passphrase role, role derivation, 214–216
WPA2/AES encryption, 181
WPA/TKIP encryption, 180
write erase all command, 58–59

Y

yes and no answers, changing, 67

Z

ZTP (zero-touch provisioning), 336–337, 356
Zulu time, 67

Made in the USA
Middletown, DE
21 December 2017